ASCENT®
CENTER FOR TECHNICAL KNOWLEDGE

Autodesk® Inventor® 2024 Advanced Part Modeling

Learning Guide

Mixed Units - 1st Edition

ASCENT - Center for Technical Knowledge®
Autodesk® Inventor® 2024
Advanced Part Modeling
Mixed Units - 1st Edition

Prepared and produced by:

ASCENT Center for Technical Knowledge
630 Peter Jefferson Parkway, Suite 175
Charlottesville, VA 22911

866-527-2368
www.ASCENTed.com

Lead Contributor: Jennifer MacMillan

ASCENT - Center for Technical Knowledge (a division of Rand Worldwide Inc.) is a leading developer of professional learning materials and knowledge products for engineering software applications. ASCENT specializes in designing targeted content that facilitates application-based learning with hands-on software experience. For over 25 years, ASCENT has helped users become more productive through tailored custom learning solutions.

We welcome any comments you may have regarding this guide, or any of our products. To contact us please email: feedback@ASCENTed.com.

AS-INV2401-APM1MU-SG // IS-INV2401-APM1MU-SG

Contents

Preface ix

In This Guide xi

Practice Files xiii

Chapter 1: Model Appearance 1-1

1.1 Model Appearance: Visual Display 1-2
- Visual Style 1-2
- Ray Tracing 1-3
- Ground Plane 1-4
- Shadows 1-5
- Reflections 1-6
- Perspective and Orthographic Views 1-6

1.2 Model Appearance: Lighting 1-7

1.3 Model Appearance: Color and Texture 1-10
- In-Canvas Appearance Tools 1-11
- Appearance Browser 1-12

Practice 1a: Create a Lighting Style 1-18

Practice 1b: Working with Appearances 1-21

Chapter Review Questions 1-29

Command Summary 1-31

Chapter 2: Advanced Sketching and Modeling Tools 2-1

2.1 Splines 2-2
- Editing a Spline 2-4

2.2 3D Sketch Creation Tools 2-8
- 3D Sketch Tools 2-9
- Modifying 3D Sketch Entities 2-17
- Dimensioning and Constraining 2-18

2.3 Bending a Part 2-20

2.4 Unwrapping a Part 2-23

Practice 2a: Create a Swept Cut Using a 3D Sketch 2-26

Practice 2b: Imported Point Data 2-31

Practice 2c: Bending Model Geometry 2-39

Practice 2d: Unwrapping Model Geometry **2-43**

Chapter Review Questions **2-48**

Command Summary **2-51**

Chapter 3: Multi-Body Part Modeling 3-1

3.1 Multi-Body Part Modeling **3-2**
Creating the First Solid Body 3-3
Creating Additional Solid Bodies 3-3
Assigning Features to Solid Bodies 3-3
Manipulating Solid Bodies 3-4
Solid Body Display 3-8
Solid Body Properties 3-9

Practice 3a: Complex Part Design **3-10**

Practice 3b: Multi-Body Part Design **3-20**

Chapter Review Questions **3-30**

Command Summary **3-32**

Chapter 4: Advanced Work Features 4-1

4.1 Grounded Work Points **4-2**

4.2 User Coordinate Systems **4-4**

Practice 4a: Creating Geometry Using a UCS **4-8**

Chapter Review Questions **4-16**

Command Summary **4-18**

Chapter 5: Advanced Lofts, Sweeps, and Coils 5-1

5.1 Area Lofts **5-2**

5.2 Advanced Sweeps **5-5**
Guide Sweep with Rail 5-5
Guide Sweep Using a Surface 5-7

5.3 Coils **5-8**

Practice 5a: Area Loft **5-13**

Practice 5b: Sweeps **5-18**

Practice 5c: Creating a Coil **5-25**

Chapter Review Questions **5-27**

Command Summary **5-29**

Chapter 6: Generative Shape Design 6-1

6.1 **Shape Generator** **6-2**
Preparing a Model for Shape Generator 6-3
Opening Shape Generator 6-3
Material Assignment 6-4
Applying Constraints 6-5
Applying Loads 6-6
Shape Generator Settings 6-7
Preserving Regions 6-8
Assigning Symmetry 6-10
Run the Shape Generator 6-11
Promote the 3D Mesh Model 6-12

Practice 6a: Generating a Design Using Shape Generator 6-14

Chapter Review Questions 6-25

Command Summary 6-27

Chapter 7: Introduction to Surfacing 7-1

7.1 **Introduction to Surfaces 7-2**

7.2 **Basic Surfaces 7-3**

7.3 **Patch Surfaces 7-5**

7.4 **Ruled Surfaces 7-6**

7.5 **Stitch Surfaces 7-8**

7.6 **Sculpting with Surfaces 7-10**

7.7 **Thickening Solids and Offsetting Surfaces 7-12**

7.8 **Surfaces in Drawing Views 7-15**

Practice 7a: Creating a Surface I 7-18

Practice 7b: Creating a Surface II 7-21

Practice 7c: Sculpting a Surface 7-24

Practice 7d: Ruled Surface Creation 7-28

Chapter Review Questions 7-34

Command Summary 7-36

Chapter 8: Additional Surfacing Options 8-1

8.1 **Extend and Trim Surfaces 8-2**
Trim Surface 8-2
Extend Surface 8-3

8.2 **Replace Face with a Surface 8-5**

8.3 **Delete Faces 8-6**

8.4 Copy Surfaces **8-7**
Practice 8a: Extending Surfaces **8-9**
Practice 8b: Copying Surfaces **8-12**
Practice 8c: Deleting a Surface **8-16**
Practice 8d: Creating a Solid from Surfaces **8-21**
Practice 8e: Modifying Geometry with Surface Tools **8-27**
Chapter Review Questions **8-32**
Command Summary **8-34**

Chapter 9: Part Model States 9-1

9.1 Part Model States **9-2**
9.2 Opening Parts Using Model States **9-6**
9.3 Using Model States in Drawings **9-8**
Drawing Views 9-8
General Tables 9-8
Practice 9a: Part Model States **9-10**
Chapter Review Questions **9-17**
Command Summary **9-19**

Chapter 10: Copying Between Parts (iFeatures) 10-1

10.1 Creating iFeatures **10-2**
10.2 Inserting iFeatures **10-6**
10.3 iFeatures vs. Copy Feature **10-10**
10.4 Table-Driven iFeatures **10-11**
10.5 Editing iFeatures **10-15**
Editing the Inserted iFeature 10-15
Editing the source iFeature File 10-15
Practice 10a: Create and Insert an iFeature **10-18**
Practice 10b: Table-Driven iFeature **10-27**
Practice 10c: (Optional) Slotted Hole iFeature **10-33**
Chapter Review Questions **10-38**
Command Summary **10-40**

Chapter 11: iParts 11-1

11.1 iPart Creation 11-2

11.2 iPart Placement 11-12
Placing a Standard iPart 11-13
Placing a Custom iPart 11-14
Replacing an iPart 11-15

11.3 Editing an iPart Factory 11-16
Edit Table 11-16
Adding Features to an iPart 11-16

11.4 Creating iFeatures from Table-Driven iParts 11-17

11.5 Tables for Factory Members 11-18

Practice 11a: Bolt iPart Factory 11-20

Practice 11b: Create an iPart Factory 11-27

Practice 11c: iParts in Assemblies 11-37

Practice 11d: iPart Member Tables 11-39

Chapter Review Questions 11-43

Command Summary 11-46

Chapter 12: Introduction to Freeform Modeling 12-1

12.1 Creating Freeform Geometry 12-2
Creating Standard Freeform Shapes 12-2
Creating a Face Freeform 12-6
Converting Geometry to a Freeform 12-7
Deactivating and Activating Freeform Mode 12-9

12.2 Editing Freeform Geometry 12-10
Edit Form 12-10
Working with Edges 12-15
Working with Faces 12-21
Working with Points 12-24
Thickening Freeform Geometry 12-26
Controlling Symmetry 12-27
Mirroring Freeform Geometry 12-28
Deleting Entities 12-29

Practice 12a: Box Freeform Modeling 12-31

Practice 12b: Cylinder Freeform Modeling 12-43

Practice 12c: (Optional) Bridging Freeform Geometry 12-53

Chapter Review Questions 12-56

Command Summary 12-59

Chapter 13: Importing and Editing CAD Data 13-1

13.1 Importing CAD Data (AnyCAD) ... 13-2

13.2 Exporting Geometry ... 13-6

13.3 Editing the Base Solid ... 13-8

13.4 Direct Edit ... 13-12
Move ... 13-12
Size ... 13-15
Scale ... 13-16
Rotate ... 13-18
Delete ... 13-20

13.5 Attaching Point Cloud Data ... 13-22

Practice 13a: Opening a CATIA Assembly ... 13-26

Practice 13b: Opening STEP Files ... 13-30

Practice 13c: Direct Edit ... 13-35

Chapter Review Questions ... 13-46

Command Summary ... 13-50

Chapter 14: Working with AutoCAD Data 14-1

14.1 Opening AutoCAD Files ... 14-2
Opening DWG Files ... 14-2
Importing DWG Files ... 14-3

14.2 DWG File Underlays ... 14-9

Practice 14a: Import an AutoCAD DWG File into Autodesk Inventor ... 14-15

Practice 14b: Open AutoCAD DWG Data to Create a Solid ... 14-20

Practice 14c: Import Associative DWG Data into a Part File ... 14-26

Practice 14d: Associative DWG Layout ... 14-37

Chapter Review Questions ... 14-45

Command Summary ... 14-47

Chapter 15: Analyzing a Model 15-1

15.1 Analysis Types ... 15-2
Zebra Analysis ... 15-2
Draft Analysis ... 15-2
Curvature Analysis ... 15-3
Surface Analysis ... 15-4
Cross Section Analysis ... 15-5

15.2 Analysis Procedures ... 15-7

Practice 15a: Analyzing Continuity **15-13**
Practice 15b: Draft Analysis **15-21**
Practice 15c: Section Analysis **15-24**
Chapter Review Questions **15-30**
Command Summary **15-33**

Appendix A: Creating Emboss and Decal Features **A-1**

A.1 Emboss Features **A-2**
A.2 Decal Features **A-5**
Practice A1: Emboss and Decals **A-7**
Chapter Review Questions **A-12**
Command Summary **A-14**

Appendix B: Custom Sketched Symbols **B-1**

B.1 Create Sketched Symbols **B-2**
Editing Sketched Symbols B-4
Saving Symbols B-4
B.2 Place Sketched Symbols **B-6**
B.3 AutoCAD Blocks **B-9**
Practice B1: Custom Sketched Symbols I **B-11**
Practice B2: Custom Sketched Symbols II **B-17**
Chapter Review Questions **B-22**
Command Summary **B-24**

Appendix C: Drawing and Style Management **C-1**

C.1 Title Block and Border Customization **C-2**
Use Existing Title Blocks and Borders C-2
Create a New Title Block and Border C-3
C.2 Style Library Manager **C-5**
Style C-5
Style Library C-5
Style Library Manager C-5
Copy Styles Between Style Libraries C-8
Rename or Delete Styles C-8
Create a New Style Library C-8
Practice C1: Customizing the Title Block **C-10**

Practice C2: Managing Styles C-15
Chapter Review Questions C-21
Command Summary C-23

Appendix D: Working with Imported Surfaces D-1

D.1 Importing Surfaces D-2
D.2 Repairing Imported Surfaces D-4
Practice D1: Repairing Imported Data D-13
Practice D2: Manipulating Imported Surfaces D-26
Chapter Review Questions D-30
Command Summary D-32

Index **Index-1**

Preface

The *Autodesk® Inventor® 2024: Advanced Part Modeling* guide has been designed to build on the basic skills acquired from the *Autodesk Inventor: Introduction to Solid Modeling* guide. The goal of this guide is to help users achieve a higher level of productivity when designing part models using Inventor.

In this guide, various approaches to part design are covered to expand your basic skills. Specific advanced part modeling techniques covered include bending and unwrapping model geometry, multi-body design, advanced lofts, advanced sweeps, coils, generative shape design, surface modeling, and freeform modeling. The guide explains how to work efficiently with imported data as well as contains other material aimed at increasing efficiency such as Features for frequently used design elements, and model states and iParts for similar designs. Additionally, the guide covers some miscellaneous drawing tools—custom sketched symbols, working with title blocks and borders, and documenting iParts.

Topics Covered

- Advanced model appearance options
- 2D and 3D sketching techniques
- Multi-body part modeling
- Advanced geometry creation tools (bend part, unwrap, work features, area lofts, sweeps, and coils)
- Generative shape design using Shape Generator
- Creating and editing basic surfaces
- Model States
- iFeatures and iParts
- Freeform modeling
- Importing data from other CAD systems and making edits
- Working with AutoCAD DWG files
- Analysis tools
- Emboss and Decal features
- Advanced Drawing tools (iPart tables, surfaces in drawing views, and custom sketched symbols)

- Surface Repair Environment
- Creating parts and features in assemblies
- Creating and editing an assembly bill of materials
- Working with projects
- Creating and annotating drawings and views
- Customizing the Autodesk Inventor environment

Prerequisites

- Access to the 2024.0 version of the software, to ensure compatibility with this guide. Future software updates that are released by Autodesk may include changes that are not reflected in this guide. The practices and files included with this guide are not compatible with prior versions (e.g., 2023).
- The material assumes a mastery of Autodesk Inventor basics, as taught in Autodesk Inventor: Introduction to Solid Modeling. Users should know how to create and edit parts, use work features, create and annotate drawing views, etc. The use of Microsoft Excel is required for this guide.

Note on Software Setup

This guide assumes a standard installation of the software using the default preferences during installation. Lectures and practices use the standard software templates and default options for the Content Libraries.

Lead Contributor: Jennifer MacMillan

With a dedication for engineering and education, Jennifer has spent over 25 years at ASCENT managing courseware development for various CAD products. Trained in Instructional Design, Jennifer uses her skills to develop instructor-led and web-based training products as well as knowledge profiling tools.

Jennifer has achieved the Autodesk Certified Professional certification for Inventor and is also recognized as an Autodesk Certified Instructor (ACI). She enjoys teaching the training courses that she authors and is also very skilled in providing technical support to end-users.

Jennifer holds a Bachelor of Engineering Degree as well as a Bachelor of Science in Mathematics from Dalhousie University, Nova Scotia, Canada.

Jennifer MacMillan has been the Lead Contributor for *Autodesk Inventor: Advanced Part Modeling* since 2007.

In This Guide

The following highlights the key features of this guide.

Feature	Description
Practice Files	The Practice Files page includes a link to the practice files and instructions on how to download and install them. The practice files are required to complete the practices in this guide.
Chapters	A chapter consists of the following: Learning Objectives, Instructional Content, Practices, Chapter Review Questions, and Command Summary. • **Learning Objectives** define the skills you can acquire by learning the content provided in the chapter. • **Instructional Content**, which begins right after Learning Objectives, refers to the descriptive and procedural information related to various topics. Each main topic introduces a product feature, discusses various aspects of that feature, and provides step-by-step procedures on how to use that feature. Where relevant, examples, figures, helpful hints, and notes are provided. • **Practice** for a topic follows the instructional content. Practices enable you to use the software to perform a hands-on review of a topic. It is required that you download the practice files (using the link found on the Practice Files page) prior to starting the first practice. • **Chapter Review Questions**, located close to the end of a chapter, enable you to test your knowledge of the key concepts discussed in the chapter. • **Command Summary** concludes a chapter. It contains a list of the software commands that are used throughout the chapter and provides information on where the command can be found in the software.
Appendices	Appendices provide additional information to the main course content. It could be in the form of instructional content, practices, tables, projects, or skills assessment.

Practice Files

1. Type the URL *exactly as shown below* into the address bar of your Internet browser to access the Course File Download page.

   Note: If you are using the ebook, you do not have to type the URL. Instead, you can access the page by clicking the URL below.

   https://www.ascented.com/getfile/id/pistaciaPF

2. On the Course File Download page, click the **DOWNLOAD NOW** button, as shown below, to download the .ZIP file that contains the practice files.

3. Once the download is complete, unzip the file and extract its contents.

   The recommended practice files folder location is:
   C:\Autodesk Inventor 2024 Adv Part Practice Files

   Note: It is recommended that you do not change the location of the practice files folder. Doing so may cause errors when completing the practices.

Stay Informed!

To receive information about upcoming events, promotional offers, and complimentary webcasts, visit:

www.ASCENTed.com/updates

Chapter 1

Model Appearance

Modifying the display options or assigning visual appearances can help enhance the model's display for editing or presenting.

Learning Objectives

- Enhance the appearance of the surfaces and edges of a model by assigning visual styles, ray tracing, reflections, shadows, and a ground plane to the model.
- Customize and assign lighting styles to control the number, color, and intensity of light sources in a model.
- Manipulate the visual appearance of a material using the in-canvas appearance and texture tools.
- Create, assign, and edit existing appearances in the model using the Appearance Browser.

1.1 Model Appearance: Visual Display

There are a number of options that can be used to improve a model's visual display. These options are included on the *View* tab>Appearance panel, as shown in Figure 1–1.

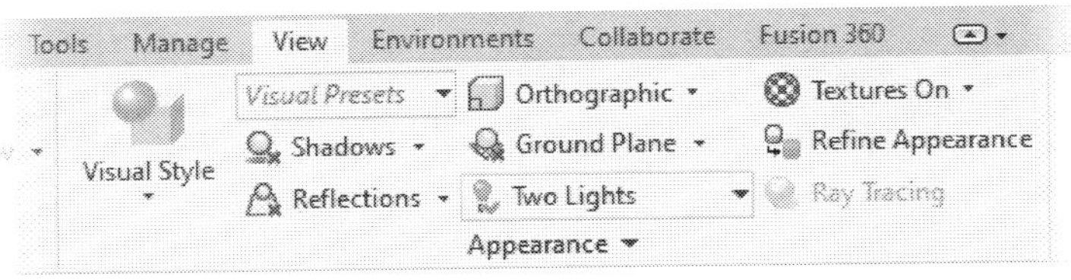

Figure 1–1

Visual Style

The Visual Style drop-down list contains options that can be assigned to provide enhanced appearance. The choice of option depends on whether you are creating or presenting the model's design. The available visual styles are shown in Figure 1–2.

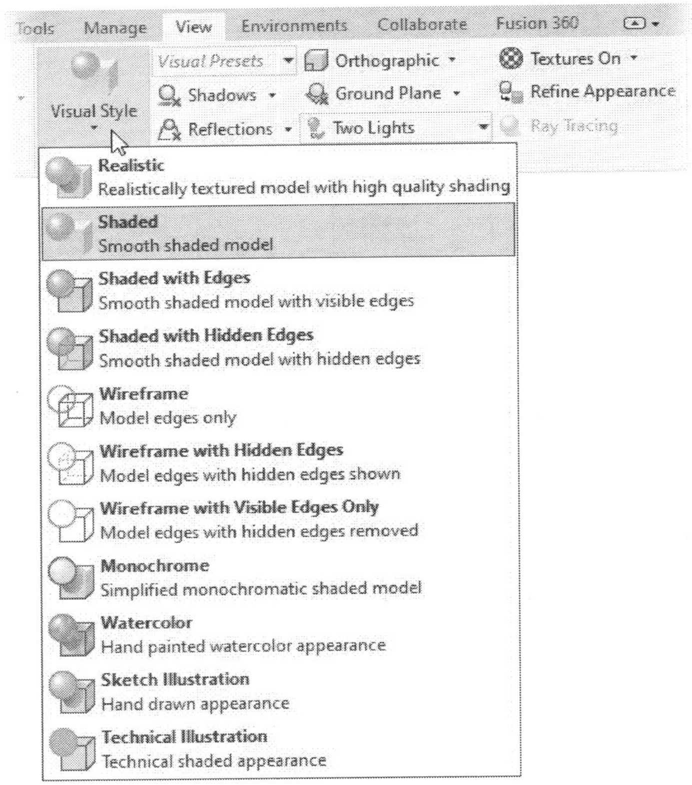

Figure 1–2

Figure 1–3 shows a few of the available visual styles.

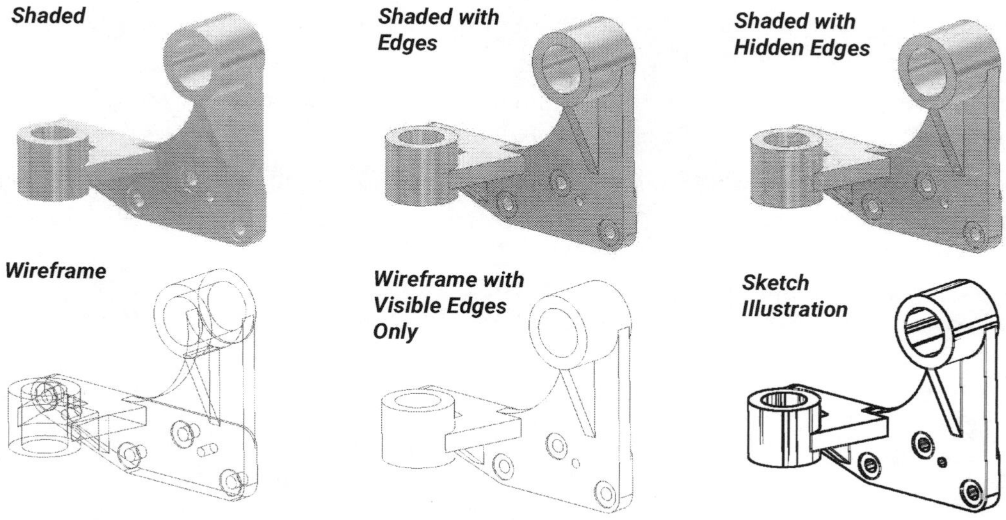

Figure 1–3

Incorporating any of the visual styles with the remaining options on the Appearance panel (e.g., Shadows, Reflections, etc.) can substantially improve the visual appearance of your models.

Ray Tracing

The **Ray Tracing** option enables you to enhance a model's visualization results when using either the **Realistic** or **Monochrome** visual styles. Ray tracing generates images by tracing the path of light through pixels in an image to simulate the effect. This technique produces an image that is highly realistic, without having to render the model in another environment.

To enable Ray tracing, in the *View* tab>Appearance panel, click  (Ray Tracing). The Ray Tracing Quality window (shown in Figure 1–4) opens when Ray Tracing is enabled. The render sample rates are **Low** (4 samples/pixel), **Draft** (16 samples/pixel), and **High** (64 samples/pixel).

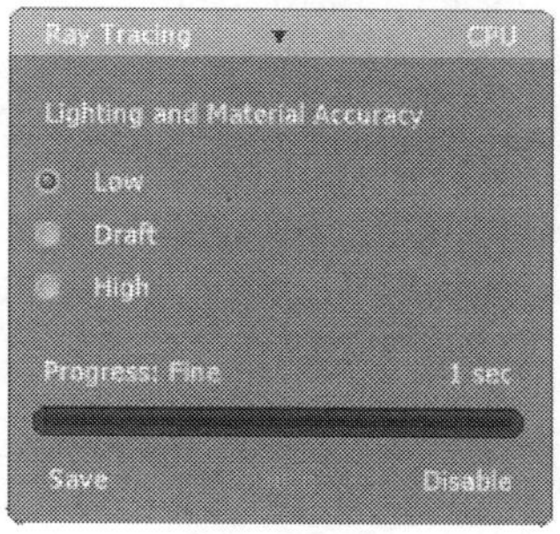

Figure 1–4

- The Progress bar indicates the rendering percentage and time display.
- Hover the cursor over the title bar of the window to expand it to set the quality (Low, Draft, or High) of the image generation.
- Click **Save**, **Pause**, or **Disable** at the bottom of the window, as required. You can also disable the render by selecting **Ray Tracing** on the ribbon.
- While **Ray Tracing** is enabled, the Ray Tracing Quality window remains open. To optimize visual space in the graphics window, it might fade from the display. Hover the cursor over the lower right-hand corner of the graphics window to display it again.

In the examples shown in Figure 1–5, a model has been assigned the **Metal-AL-6061 (Polished)** color, and the visual styles settings have been manipulated to vary the displayed image.

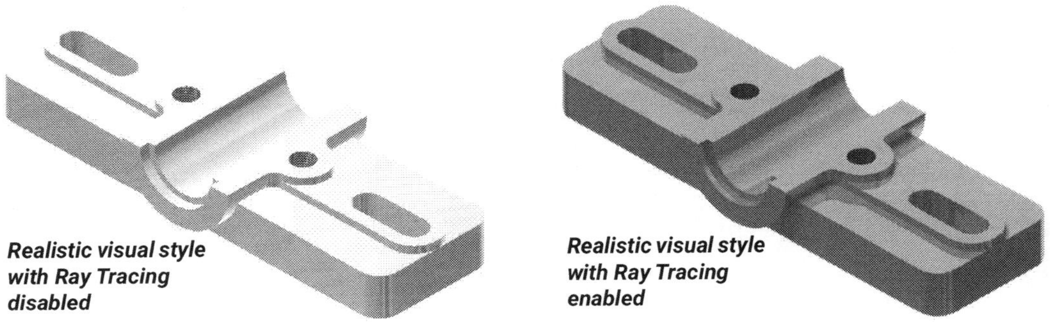

Figure 1–5

Ground Plane

In the Appearance panel, the (Ground Plane) option enables you to toggle the display of a plane that represents the ground. The ground plane can be included to help represent the up direction of the model. It is also used in conjunction with shadows and reflection to set realistic visual display settings. Consider the following about the ground plane:

- The ground plane is parallel with the Origin's XZ plane.
- The ground plane is tied to the model. If you rotate the model, the ground plane rotates with it.
- When viewing the ground plane from the top, a plane with a grid is displayed. When viewing the model from beneath the plane, only the exterior outline of the plane is displayed.
- To customize the ground plane, in the *View* tab>Appearance panel, in the Ground Plane drop-down list, select **Settings**. This option enables you to relocate the X, Y, and Z locations, its appearance, grid display, and reflection settings.
- All settings for the ground plane are stored with the document only, and do not affect other models in the current session.

An example of a model with its ground plane displayed is shown in Figure 1–6.

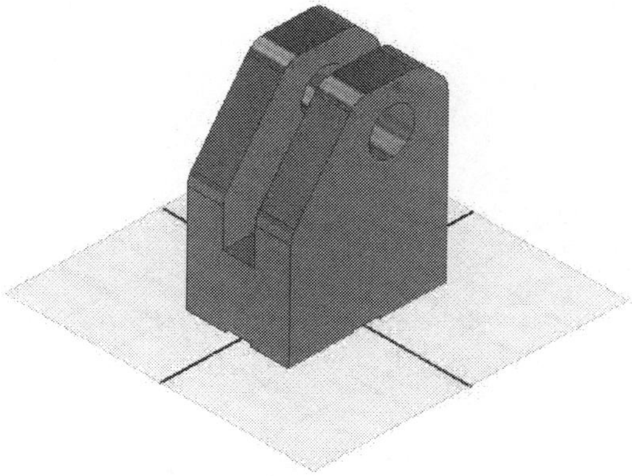

Figure 1–6

Shadows

The Shadows drop-down list () enables you to control the shadows that are assigned in a model for enhanced model visualization. Shadows can be enabled so they display on the ground, on the object, or so that ambient shadows are used. Shadows can be enabled individually or in any combination of the three shadow types. Figure 1–7 displays a model with the various shadowing effects.

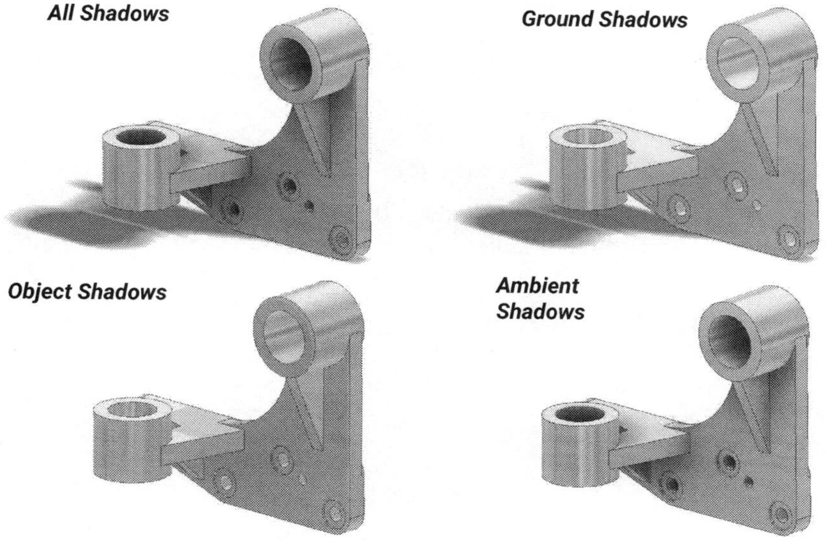

Figure 1–7

Note: *The ground plane does not need to be displayed for ground shadows to be used.*

To customize shadow settings, in the Shadows drop-down list, select **Settings** to access the active Lighting Style. Customize the shadow values in the *Shadows* tab for the active Lighting Style.

Reflections

Reflections can be cast on the ground plane by enabling (Reflections) in the Appearance panel on the *View* tab. Shadows reflect the visual style that is set in the model. By changing the Z location of the ground plane, the resulting reflection is varied. The **Settings** option in the Reflection drop-down list enables you to customize the Ground Plane which affects reflections.

> ***Note:*** *The ground plane does not need to be displayed for ground reflections to be used.*

Perspective and Orthographic Views

Traditional mechanical drawings show parts in orthographic (parallel) views, where parallel edges on the part display parallel in the drawing. Perspective views display the way that the eye sees, where parallel edges seem to converge at a vanishing point, as shown in Figure 1–8. To change to a perspective view, select the *View* tab. In the Appearance panel, expand (Orthographic) and click (Perspective).

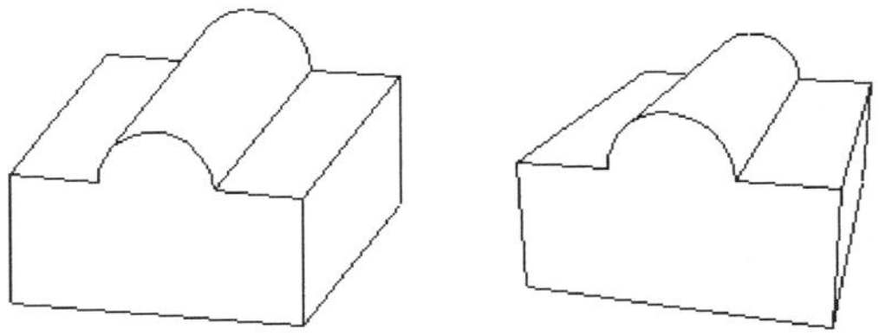

Orthographic View ***Perspective View***

Figure 1–8

The (Perspective with Ortho Faces) option enables you to view the model in perspective view while the model is in a 3D orientation and in orthographic view when in a 2D view.

> ***Note:*** *While in a perspective view, you can zoom, pan, and rotate, but the results may differ slightly than that in an Orthographic view. Refer to the "About Perspective Views" Help topic for more information on view manipulation for Perspective views.*

1.2 Model Appearance: Lighting

The appearance of parts can be changed by adjusting the lighting style. Lighting styles can be set in a part, assembly, or presentation. In a lighting style, you can control the number, color, and intensity of light sources for a file, as well as assign image-based lighting and shadows. Use the Lighting Style drop-down list (shown in Figure 1–9) to quickly assign a lighting style as an alternative to the Style and Standard Editor.

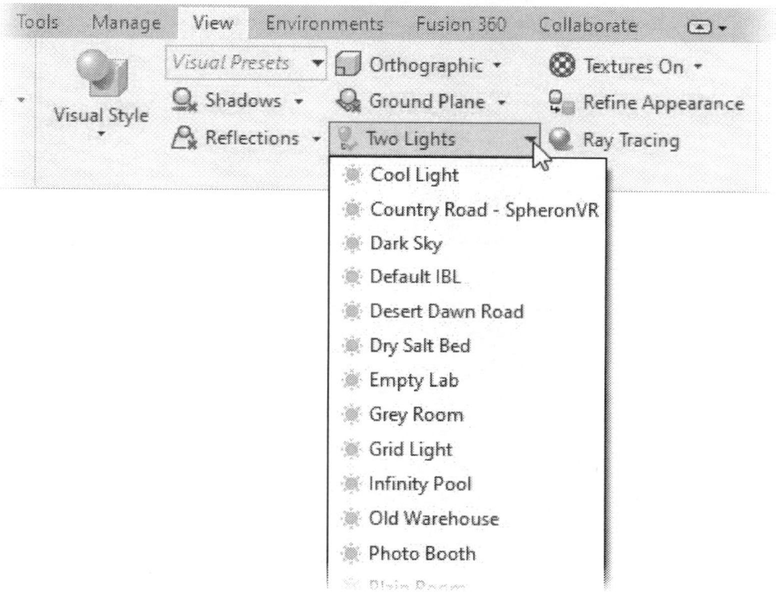

Figure 1–9

Many styles assign an image, as shown in the **Old Warehouse** and **Empty Lab** styles shown in Figure 1–10. Models can be positioned relative to the image to enhance model realism.

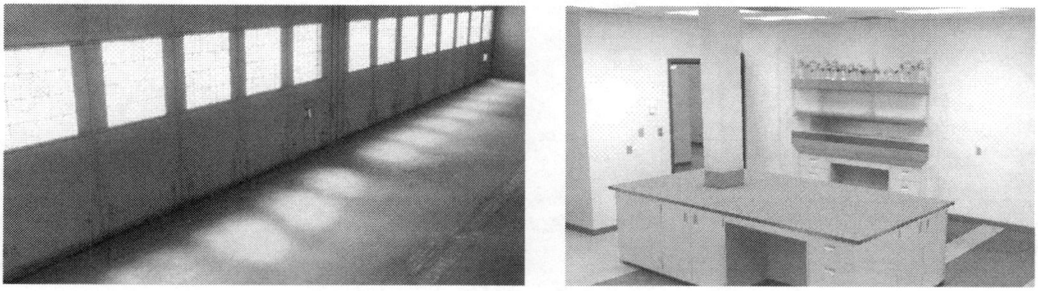

Figure 1–10

Note: *For image-based lighting styles, use the Perspective orientation to improve realism.*

If a new lighting style is required, you can use either of the following techniques to access the Style and Standard Editor:

- In the *View* tab>Appearance panel, in the Lighting drop-down list, select **Settings**.
- In the *Manage* tab>Styles and Standards panel, click (Styles Editor).

The Style and Standard Editor opens as shown in Figure 1–11.

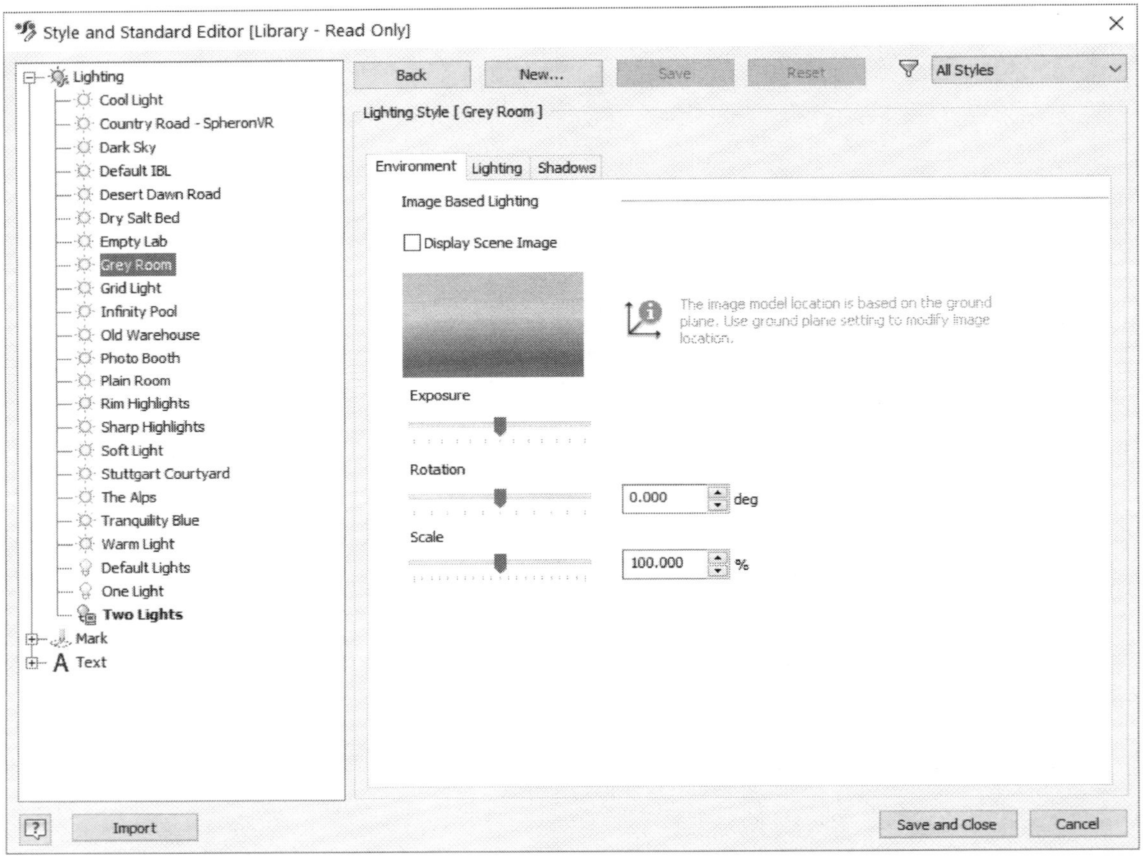

Figure 1–11

Select a lighting style to edit or create a new style. To create a new style, right-click on an existing style and select **New Style**. The selected style is copied and can be used as a starting point for the creation of the new style.

The table below describes the lighting style settings.

Tabs		Description
Environment **tab**		
	Image Based Lighting	Set the image-based lighting effects for the active light style. This tab is only available if an image has been assigned to the lighting style. To display the image in the actual scene, select **Display Scene Image**. Without this option enabled, the image is not displayed; however, by toggling this option on and off, you can control the image-based lighting effect without losing all of the specified settings. You can also adjust its exposure, rotation, and scale.
Lighting **tab**		
	Light# tabs	Select a light number tab to activate it for editing. Click  on each tab to toggle the specific light source on or off.
	Standard Light Settings	Control the horizontal/vertical position of the active light source using the sliders that surround the image of the light. You can also select the color and control the brightness of the light source. Using the two Relative movement options, you can specify that the light is fixed to the view's camera () or that the light maintains a fixed direction relative to the Viewcube ().
	All Lights	Control the brightness and ambience of the light sources for all standard lights. Use the *Brightness* slider to control the light intensity and use the *Ambience* slider to set the contrast between lit and unlit areas in the scene.
Shadows **tab**		
	Shadow Settings	Set the lighting style's shadow setting by selecting from a predefined list of shadow directions. You can also specify the shadow's density, softness, and ambient shadow intensity.

Edits you make in the dialog box are dynamically displayed on the part. You must save the edits to preserve them. Edits are saved to the active lighting style in the file.

1.3 Model Appearance: Color and Texture

Colors and textures can be added to a model to further enhance its visualization. Color and texture are combined within the appearance definition of a material. When a material is assigned, the visual appearance specified for that material is assigned to the model. The Materials and Appearance Override drop-down lists in the Quick Access Toolbar display the current material and its appearance, as shown in Figure 1–12.

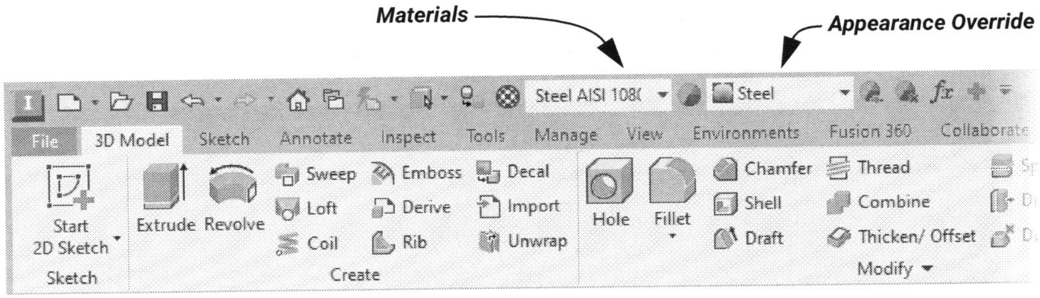

Figure 1–12

To assign a different appearance to the model while maintaining the material setting and therefore its iProperty data, select an alternate material in the Appearance Override drop-down list, as shown in Figure 1–13.

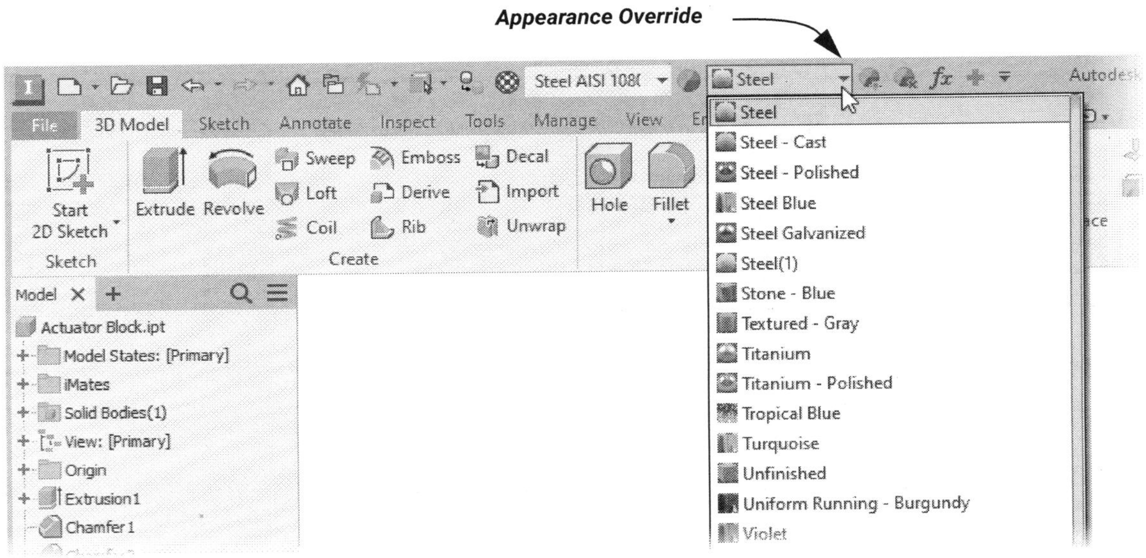

Figure 1–13

Note: *To display the model so that any of the image's texturing settings are consistently displayed, set the Visual Style to* ***Realistic****. If not, only the color of the appearance might display on the model.*

The predefined list of appearances provided in the Appearance Override drop-down list are provided from Inventor libraries. By default, the Inventor Material Library is set as the active library. To switch between libraries in the drop-down list, select an alternate library name, as shown in Figure 1–14. The default library can be set in the Project File.

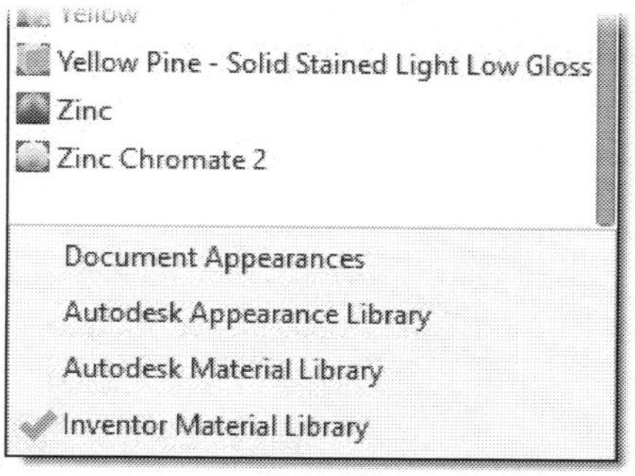

Figure 1–14

To quickly manipulate the assigned appearance, you can use the in-canvas tools.

In-Canvas Appearance Tools

The in-canvas appearance and texture tools provide you with a convenient way to change the color of an appearance or the texture mapping on the model. The tools are provided in a mini-toolbar and the icons can be used directly on the model.

How To: Edit the Existing Appearance Using the In-Canvas Tools

1. In the *Tools* tab>Material and Appearance panel, click (Adjust). The Appearance mini-toolbar opens as shown in Figure 1–15.

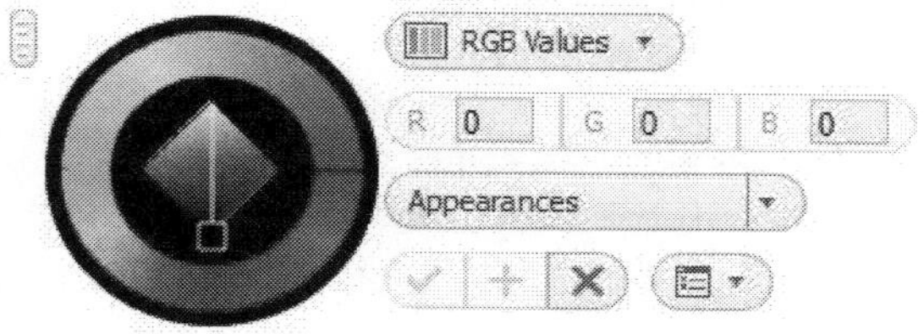

Figure 1–15

2. Using the model, select the appearance that is to be edited. You can select directly on the model when the cursor displays as the eyedropper ( ), or you can select the appearance from the Appearances drop-down list in the mini-toolbar.
   - When using the cursor, if you want to edit the color of the entire model, ensure that you select the entire model.

- To change only selected faces, surfaces, bodies, or features, select them individually. Use the Select Other drop-down list to select the required option.
- Selecting the appearance in the Appearances drop-down list enables you to first apply it to the model and then edit the Appearance. If you selected the appearance from the drop-down list, you are required to assign it to the model. Using the cursor, now displayed as a paint can ( ), select the model or individual faces, surfaces, bodies, or features to assign the edited appearance.

3. Select the method for defining the color.
   - Defining the color as a red, green, and blue value (**RGB Values**) is the default option.
   - Select the RGB Values drop-down list and select **HSL Values** to define the color with a hue, saturation, and lightness value.
4. For either the **RGB** or **HSL Values** options, enter values in the mini-toolbar or use the color wheel to define its values as follows:
   - Drag the line around its perimeter to change the value.
   - To refine the color, activate and drag the square node on the internal diamond shape at the center of the color wheel.
5. If the Appearance has a texture assigned to it, you can also do the following:
   - Scale, rotate, and translate the texture using the , , and icons that display once the model or individual faces, surfaces, bodies, or features are selected. Hover the cursor over the icons until they are active (yellow) and then press and hold the mouse button to scale, rotate, and translate, as needed.
   - Modify how the texture is mapped to the entire model. Expand the drop-down list and select a mapping option. By default, **Automatic** is used and generally provides a good representation of the texture on the model. Hovering the cursor over the other mapping options displays them in the model. This is not available if modifying individual faces.
6. Click to complete the edit and close the mini-toolbar.

Once an appearance is adjusted using the in-canvas tools, a new appearance is created that has (1) appended to the end of the name. For example, if you were adjusting the Red appearance, the adjusted appearance would be called Red(1).

Appearance Browser

The Appearance Browser (shown in Figure 1–16) can be used to create new appearances.

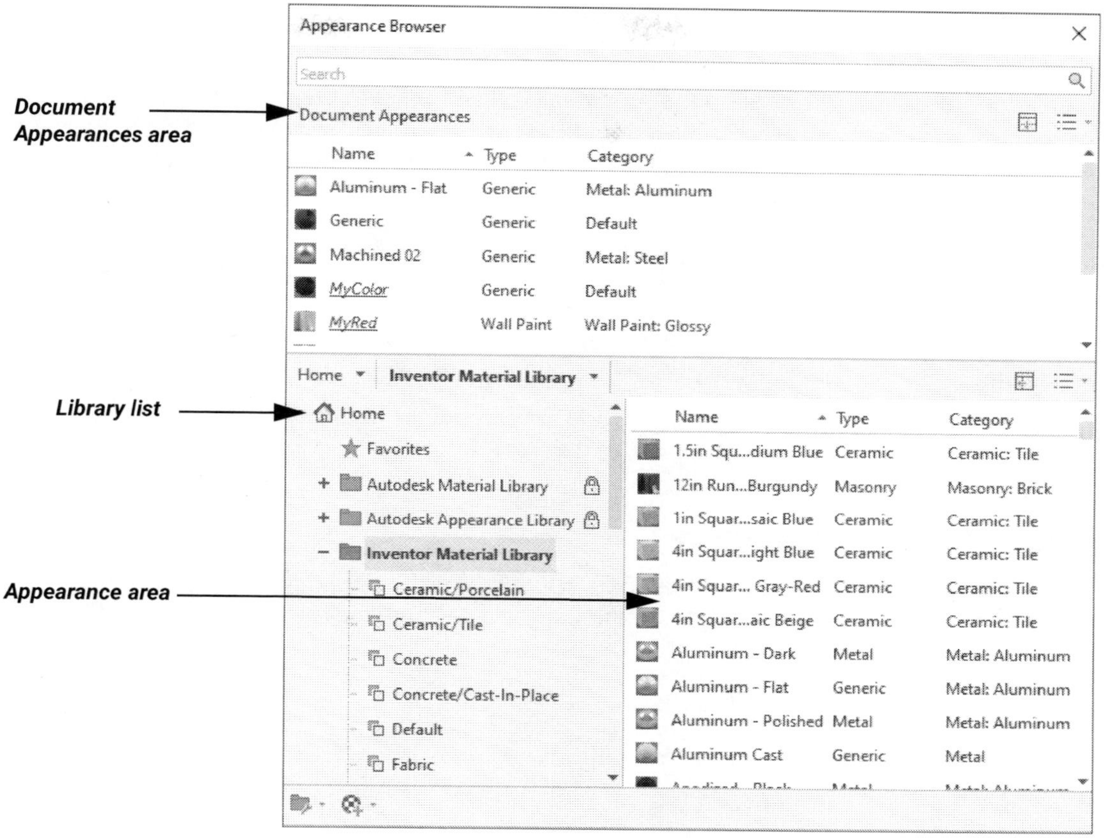

Figure 1–16

The Appearance Browser is divided into the following areas:

- *Document Appearances* area - This area includes all appearances that have been assigned to the model.
- *Library* list - The library list enables you to select the libraries where you want to look for different appearances. The Favorites node enables you to quickly access any of the appearances from the three libraries that you have marked as Favorites.
- *Appearance* area - Once a library is expanded and a group type selected, its appearances are displayed in the *Appearance* area. Using this area, appearances can be added to the *Document Appearances* area for use.

Note: *The (Shows/Hides library) panel and (Change your view) drop-down list can be used to customize the display of the Appearance Browser areas. For example, it can show whether the appearances display as detailed lists or as thumbnail images or if the list of libraries is displayed.*

Adding Appearances to the Document

In order to use a material from a library, it must be added to the Document Appearances list. Once added, it can be assigned to the model or it can be used to create a new appearance.

How To: Add a Material from a Library to the Document Appearances Area

1. In the *Tools* tab>Material and Appearance panel, click (Appearance).
2. Expand the appropriate library in the Library list.
3. Select an appearance type. The list of appearances associated with the selected type display in the *Appearance* area on the right side of the Appearance Browser.
4. Right-click an appearance and select **Add To>Document Materials** to add it to the *Document Appearances* area for use in the model.

Creating New Appearances

New Appearances can be added to a model either by reusing and modifying an existing appearance, or by using appearance templates that are available for various material types.

How To: Use the Appearance Browser to Create a New Appearance

1. In the *Tools* tab>Material and Appearance panel, click (Appearance). The Appearance Browser opens as shown in Figure 1–17. The current file only has one appearance that was assigned to it (Default), as shown in the *Document Appearances* area, and the **Inventor Material Library** is selected. If an appearance override was assigned, it would also be displayed here.

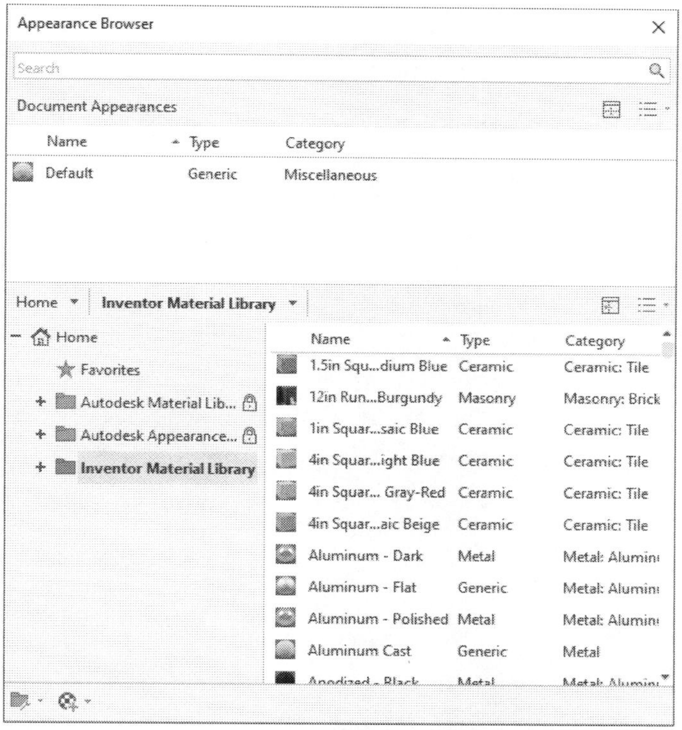

Figure 1–17

2. Right-click on an existing appearance in the *Document Appearances* area and select **Duplicate** to create its copy. The selected appearance should be one that closely resembles the settings that you want as a new appearance. Alternatively, click at the bottom of the Appearance Browser and select a type to start a new appearance.
3. Select the default name, right-click on it, and select **Rename**. Enter a new name for the appearance.

4. Right-click on the new appearance and select **Edit** to open the Appearance Editor, similar to that shown in Figure 1–18. Depending on the material type, the options and settings vary.

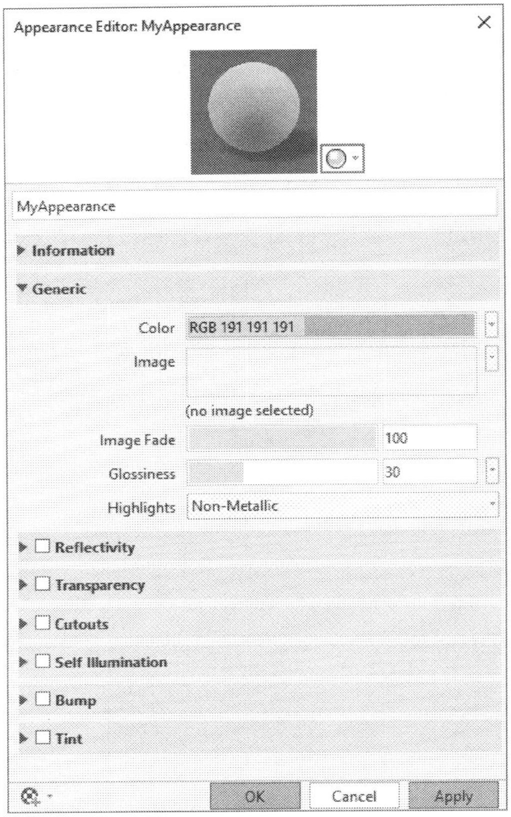

Figure 1–18

5. Define the appearance, as required.
   - Select in the *Color* field to access the Color dialog box to select or customize a new color.
   - Select in the *Image* field to import a texture for the appearance.
   - Change the settings of the *Image Fade*, *Glossiness*, and *Highlights* to customize the appearance of the texture.
   - Use other options in the Appearance Editor to further customize the new appearance by adding reflectivity, transparency, bump maps, self illumination, etc.
6. Click **OK** to complete the creation of the new appearance. The thumbnail image in the *Document Appearances* area updates to reflect the changes that were made in the Appearance Editor.

To edit an existing appearance, right-click on the appearance name in the *Document Appearances* area of the Appearance Browser and select **Edit**. Edit the options, as required, to reflect the required change.

Hint: Textures

Textures are files that can be added to any appearance. Bump maps enable you to further control the display of an image by assigning a bumpiness value. Texture images are assigned in the Generic node while bump maps are assigned in the Bump node. Similarly, maps can be assigned to other nodes.

- To assign an image, select in the *Image* field for the node and use the Material Editor Open File to browse to and select an image.
- To modify the placement of the image, right-click on the *Image* field and select **Edit Image**. The Texture Editor opens and you can refine the image's position, rotation, scale, and repeat and (in the case of a bump map) vary the amount of bumpiness.

Assigning Appearances using the Appearance Browser

The Appearance Browser can also be used as an alternative to the Appearance Override drop-down list to assign appearances to the entire model or to individual faces.

How To: Use the Appearance Browser to Assign an Appearance to the Model

1. In the *Tools* tab>Material and Appearance panel, click (Appearance). Alternatively, you can assign the new appearance using the Material Override drop-down list in the Quick Access Toolbar. Once assigned, the appearance is automatically added to the Document Appearances area.
2. To assign a new appearance, select the entire model or individual surfaces on the model, right-click on the appearance thumbnail in the *Document Appearances* area, and select **Assign to Selection**.
   - To help identify what is being selected in the model, before selecting, hover the cursor over the model so that the preview displays the entire model (dashed lines) or individual surfaces (solid lines).
3. Click × to close the Appearance Browser.

Practice 1a
Create a Lighting Style

Practice Objectives

- Create a new lighting style based on an existing style.
- Edit a lighting style to change its ambiance setting and include multiple colored lights.
- Change the lighting style that is applied to the model using the Styles and Standards Editor and the options in the Appearance panel.

In this practice, you will create a new lighting style and assign it for use with a part file. The part is shown in Figure 1–19.

Figure 1–19

Task 1: Open a part file and create a new lighting style.

1. On the Home page, select (Projects and Settings) > **Settings** to open the Projects dialog box. Project files identify folders that contain the required models.
2. Click **Browse**. In the practice files folder, select **Advanced Part.ipj**. Click **Open**. The Projects dialog box updates and a checkmark displays next to the new project name, indicating that it is the active project. The project file tells Autodesk Inventor where your files are stored. Click **Done**.This project file is used for the entire learning guide.
3. Open **handle.ipt**.
4. In the *Manage* tab>Styles and Standards panel, click (Styles Editor). The Style and Standard Editor dialog box opens.
5. Expand the **Lighting** branch and select **Two Lights**.
6. Click **New**. The New Local Style dialog box opens.

7. Enter **handle** in the *Name* field and click **OK**. The handle style is now listed in the Lighting branch.
8. Double-click on **handle** in the list to activate it. The active style is bold in the list and is applied to the model.
9. Move the *Ambience* slider to increase the amount of ambient light on the screen for all lights. Note how the model updates as you move the slider.
10. Return the *Ambience* slider to approximately the middle of the scale.
11. In the *Standard Lights* area of the *Lighting* tab, ensure that the *Light 1* tab is selected and that the (yellow light bulb) icon is active. This represents the first direct light.
12. Move the vertical slider on the right side of the image to the top and the slider on the bottom to the left side to place the light.
13. Click the **Color** icon located above the *Brightness* slider. Select one of the blue colors from the color palette. Click **OK**. Note the effect on the part.
14. Select the *Light 2* tab to activate it. Ensure that the icon is enabled (yellow). Select it, if not. The blue light you created in the last step will now have less influence on the part. Change the color of the second light to red, and move the sliders to the bottom and right positions to place this light.
15. Click **Save and Close**. Note the effect on the part.
16. Rotate the part. You will see different shades and colors on the part, depending on where you placed the lights.

Task 2: Manipulate the appearance of the model.

1. Select the *View* tab.
2. In the Appearance panel, note that the **handle** light style is currently active. In the Lighting Style drop-down list, select **Two Lights**. Note how the model updates to reflect the settings in this style.
3. Select some of the various options in the Visual Style drop-down list to manipulate the model's appearance. Leave the style set to **Shaded with Edges.**
4. In the Lighting Style drop-down list, select **Empty Lab**.
5. The default scale of the model relative to the image is incorrect. In the Lighting Style drop-down list, select **Settings**. In the *Image Based Lighting* area in the *Environment* tab, reduce the *Scale* to approximately **15%**. Click **Save and Close**.
6. In the Orthographic drop-down list, select **Perspective** to obtain a more realistic image.
7. Zoom in and orient the model. The **Shaded with Edges** visual style is not very realistic for product presentation. Change the visual style to **Realistic**.

8. Select a darker color in the Appearance Override drop-down list in the Quick Access Toolbar, shown in Figure 1–20.

Figure 1–20

9. The model should display similar to that shown in Figure 1–21.

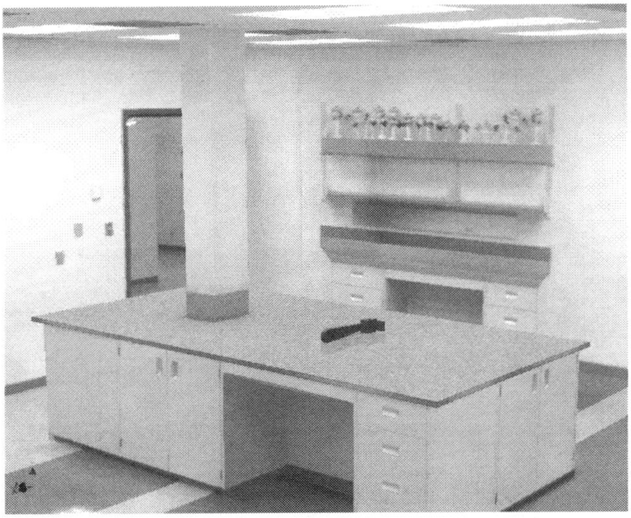

Figure 1–21

10. Save the part and close the window.

End of practice

Practice 1b
Working with Appearances

Practice Objectives

- Override the visual appearance of a material.
- Create, edit, and assign appearances to a model using the Appearance Browser and the Appearance Override drop-down list.

In this practice, you will assign a material to a model and then override its visual appearance. You will apply appearances to the entire model as well as individual surfaces. The final model is shown in Figure 1–22.

Figure 1–22

Task 1: Open a model and assign a material.

1. Open **bearing_journal.ipt**. The part is currently assigned the Generic material and visual appearance, as shown in the Material and Appearance Override drop-down lists in the Quick Access Toolbar in Figure 1–23.

Figure 1–23

2. In the Quick Access Toolbar, in the Material drop-down list, set the material to **Stainless Steel**. The visual appearance is set as Semi-Polished which is the default setting for the Stainless Steel material. The model displays as shown in Figure 1–24.

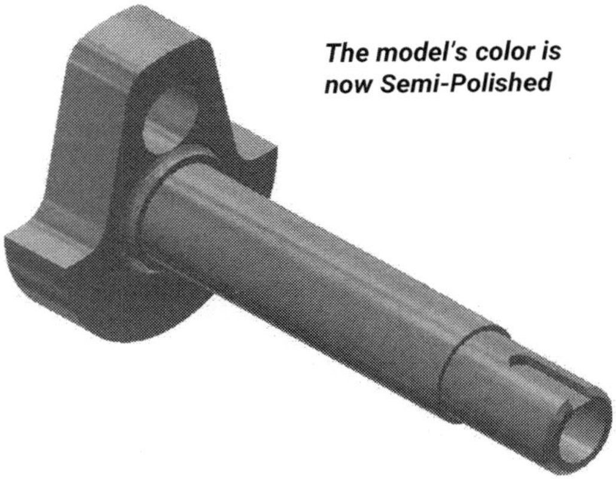

Figure 1–24

Task 2: Assign and new visual appearance and edit it.

1. In the Quick Access Toolbar, in the Appearance Override drop-down list, set the color to **Yellow**. The visual appearance of the model changes to yellow, as shown in Figure 1–25, but the material remains Stainless Steel.

Figure 1–25

2. In the *Tools* tab>Material and Appearance panel, click  (Adjust) to open the appearance mini-toolbar.

3. Hold <Ctrl> and select the two surfaces shown in Figure 1–26.

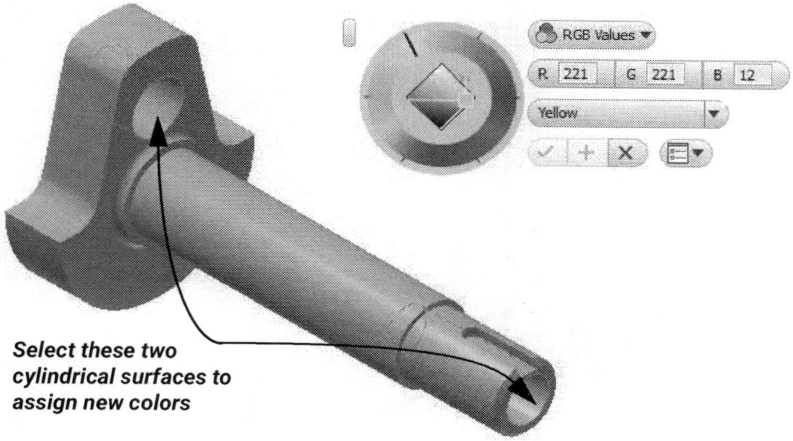

Figure 1–26

4. Maintain the RGB Values setting and use the color wheel to define the values. Drag the line around its perimeter to change the value to red. Because the surfaces were preselected, the surfaces update as you change the RGB value.

5. Click to complete the change and close the mini-toolbar. The model should display similar to that shown in Figure 1–27.

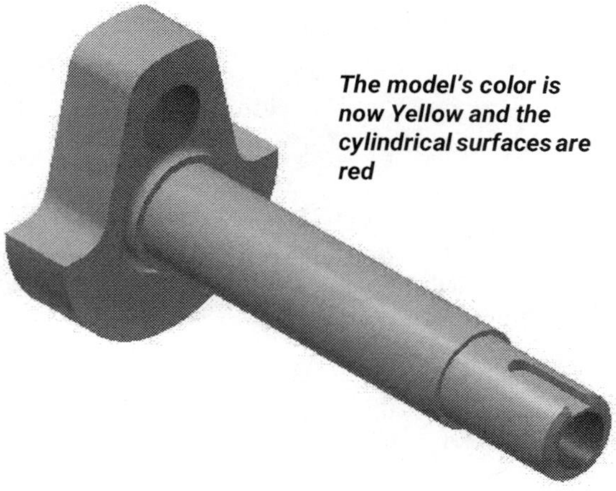

Figure 1–27

6. In the Appearance Override drop-down list, select **Rust**. The model should display similar to that shown in Figure 1–28. Note that the surface overrides on the internal surfaces that were changed to red are maintained and the Rust appearance is applied to the rest of the model. The Rust appearance was created using a texture image.

Figure 1–28

7. In the *Tools* tab>Material and Appearance panel, click (Adjust) to open the appearance mini-toolbar.
8. Hover the cursor over the model so that its entire boundary is highlighted in dashed red lines and click to select the model. If required, use the Select Other drop-down list to select the solid in order to highlight all the geometry. This enables you to edit the Rust appearance on the entire model.
9. Try and change the color of the appearance. Note how it does not change because this appearance is using a texture image.
10. Click to open the drop-down list and roll the cursor over each of the mapping options. By default, **Automatic** is used and it provides a good representation of the rust texture on the model. Depending on the surface and model shapes being assigned a textured appearance the other options might provide better representations.
11. Hover the mouse over the icon until the cursor changes to the icon. This indicates that you can now scale the texture. Drag the cursor to scale the texture.
12. Hover the cursor over the icon until the cursor changes to the icon indicating that you can now rotate the texture. Drag the cursor to rotate the texture.
13. Click to cancel the edit and close the mini-toolbar. The original texture scale and rotation is maintained.

Task 3: Create a new appearance and assign it to the model.

1. In the *Tools* tab>Material and Appearance panel, click (Appearance) to open the Appearance Browser. Alternatively, you can also click in the Quick Access Toolbar. The Appearance Browser displays as shown in Figure 1–29.

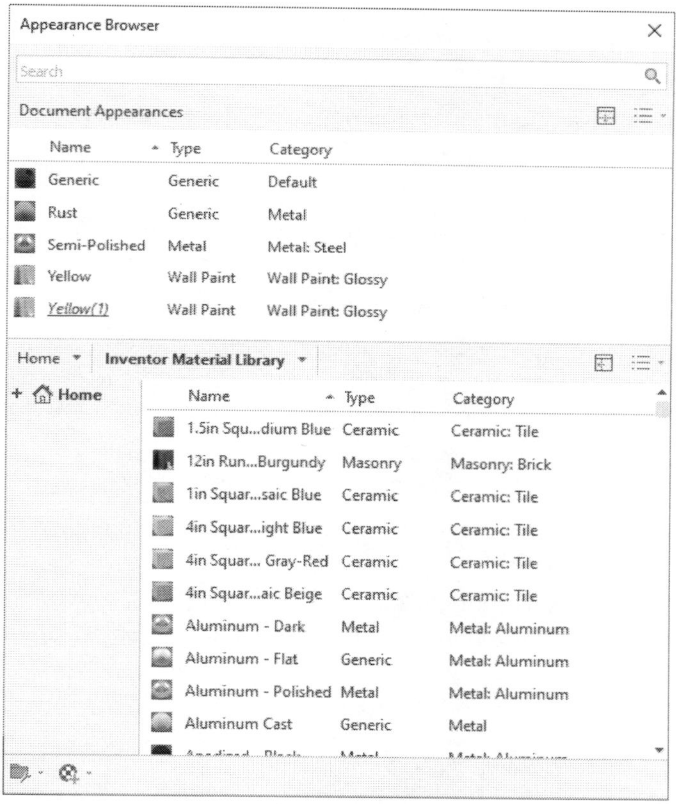

Figure 1–29

Note: *The (Change Your View) drop-down list can be used to customize the display of the Appearance Browser. For example, it can show whether the appearances display as a detailed list or as thumbnail images.*

2. Review the *Document Appearances* area. Note that there are currently five appearances listed. These correspond to all of the appearances that you have assigned to the model.
    - **Generic** was the appearance that was set when the file was opened.
    - **Semi-Polished** was used when the material was set to Stainless Steel.
    - **Yellow** was used to override the visual appearance of the Stainless Steel Material.
    - **Yellow(1)** represents the edits that were made using the mini-toolbar to create the red color.
    - **Rust** was the final override material that was used. Only appearances that have been used in the model are shown here.
3. Right-click on **Yellow(1)** and select **Rename**. Enter **MyRed** as the new name.
4. Right-click on **Generic** and select **Duplicate**. This creates a copy of the Generic appearance that you can use it as the base for a new appearance.
5. Right-click on **Generic(1)** and select **Rename**. Enter **MyColor** as the new name for the duplicated appearance.
6. Double-click on **MyColor** to open the Appearance Editor.
7. Select in the *Color* field and assign a new color to the appearance using the Color dialog box. Increase the *Glossiness* value and change the *Highlights* to **Metallic**. Additional settings can be made using other nodes in the Appearance Editor to further customize the appearance.
8. Click **OK** to complete the edit and close the Appearance Editor.
9. Hover the cursor over the model so that its entire boundary is highlighted in dashed lines and click to select the model.
10. In the Appearance Browser, right-click on **MyColor** and select **Assign to Selection** to assign the new appearance to the model. Note that the red surface overrides are still maintained.
11. Click × to close the Appearance Browser.

Task 4: Clear appearance overrides.

1. In the *Tools* tab>Material and Appearance panel, click (Clear) to open the mini-toolbar.
2. Press and hold <Ctrl> and select the two surfaces that were assigned the **MyRed** appearance.
3. Click to clear the appearance override on these surfaces. Note that the entire model now has the **MyColor** appearance assigned.
4. In the *Tools* tab>Material and Appearance panel, click (Clear) to open the mini-toolbar again.

5. Click **Select All** in mini-toolbar and click ✓ to clear all overrides in the model. This returns the visual appearance back to Semi-Polished, which was assigned with the Stainless Steel material.

Task 5: Add an appearance from the Inventor Material Library to the model.

1. In the *Tools* tab>Material and Appearance panel, click (Appearance) to open the Appearance Browser.

2. In the lower portion of the Appearance Browser, select the Home (Home) drop-down list and select **Inventor Material Library** to display a list of materials in this library. You can also expand the **Home** node and select **Inventor Material Library**.

3. Further expand the **Inventor Material Library** folder, as shown in Figure 1–30.

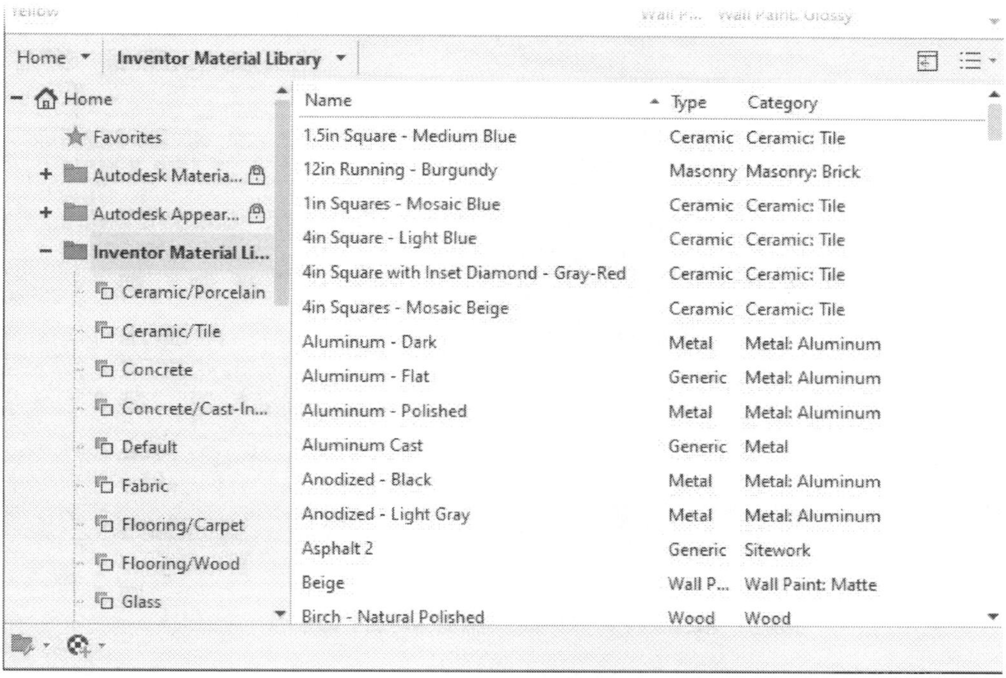

Figure 1–30

4. Select **Metal/Steel** to display the list of appearances in the Metal/Steel category.
5. Right-click the **Machined 02** appearance and select **Add to>Document Materials**.

6. Select the model in the Model browser or the graphics window and assign the **Machined 02** appearance to the selection. The model updates as shown in Figure 1–31.

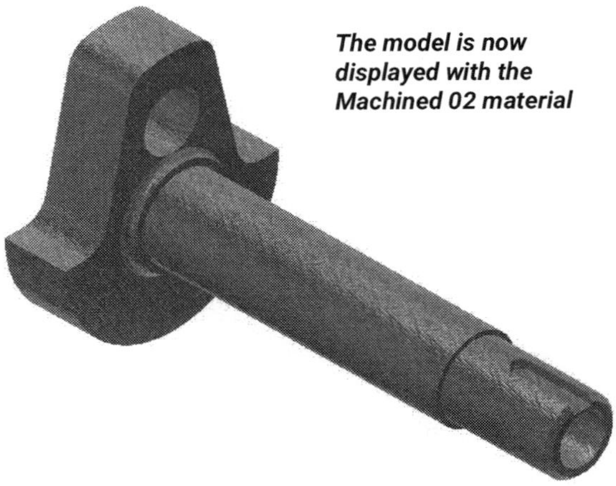

Figure 1–31

7. Close the Appearance Browser.

   The appearance could also have been assigned by selecting it and using the Appearance Override drop-down list to select the **Machined 02** appearance. In this case, once selected it would have been assigned and added to the *Document Appearances* area. This is an alternative method to adding materials using the Appearance Browser. The benefit of the Appearance Browser is that you can review the thumbnail images and copy existing materials to use as a base for new appearances.

   Note: *The additional material libraries can also be expanded and used to access other appearances. By default, their appearances are not listed in the appearance override drop-down list, so they must be added through the Appearance Browser.*

8. Save the part and close the window.

End of practice

Chapter Review Questions

1. Which of the following Appearance tools are available when the Visual Style for the model is set as **Shaded**? (Select all that apply.)
    a. Shadows
    b. Reflections
    c. Lights
    d. Ground Plane
    e. Ray Tracing

2. The ground plane must be enabled (displayed) for the shadows and ground reflections to be visible in the model.
    a. True
    b. False

3. Which of the following statements are true regarding lighting styles. (Select all that apply.)
    a. An Image-based lighting style enables you to use a predefined background image in the style.
    b. Multiple standard lights can be combined in a single lighting style.
    c. Multiple lighting styles can be applied at one time.
    d. Shadow settings are controlled in a lighting style.

4. The following icons display when working with the in-canvas appearance and texture tool. Which icon enables you to scale a texture in a material?
    a. 
    b. 
    c. 
    d. 

5. Which of the following statements are true regarding the Appearance Browser dialog box shown in Figure 1–32? (Select all that apply.)

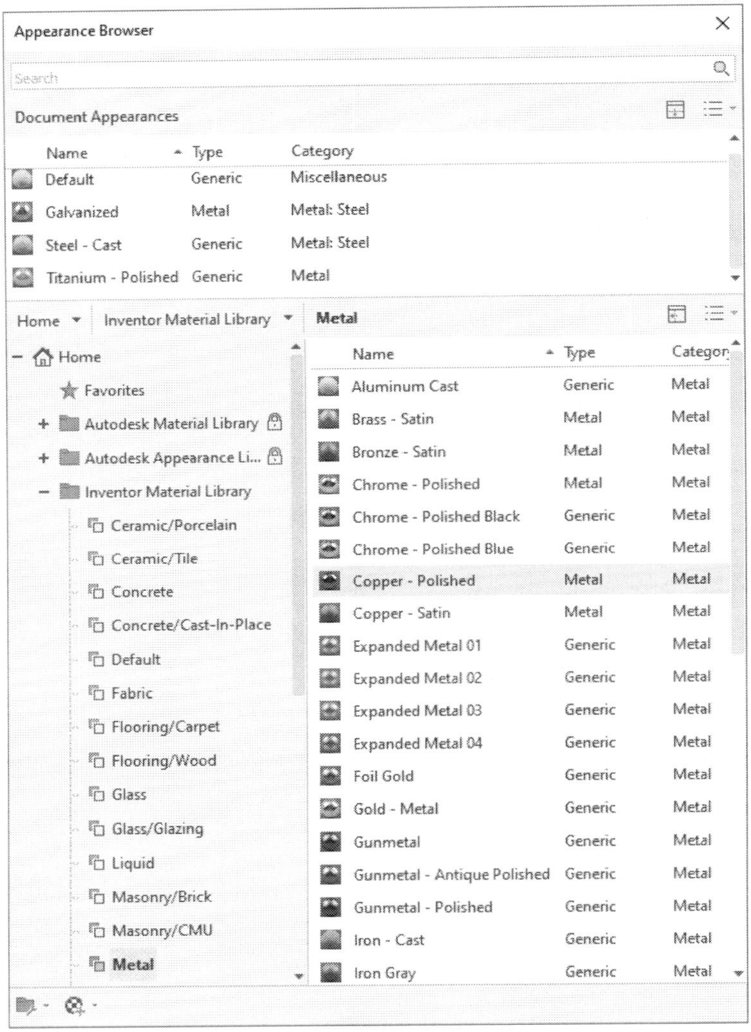

Figure 1–32

a. Four appearances have been all been previously assigned to the model.

b. The Favorites list is currently being displayed in the *Appearance* area.

c. The Metal category in the Inventor Material Library is currently displayed in the Library's Appearance area.

d. The Copper - Polished material is the currently assigned material to the model.

Command Summary

Button	Command	Location
	**Adjust (color)**	• **Ribbon:** *Tools* tab>Appearance panel
	**Appearance (Browser)**	• **Ribbon:** *Tools* tab>Appearance panel
N/A	**Appearance Override**	• **Quick Access Toolbar** • **Appearance Browser**
	**Clear (color)**	• **Ribbon:** *Tools* tab>Appearance panel
	**Ground Plane**	• **Ribbon:** *View* tab>Appearance panel
N/A	**Lighting Styles**	• **Ribbon:** *View* tab>Appearance panel
	**Orthographic**	• **Ribbon:** *View* tab>Appearance panel
	**Perspective**	• **Ribbon:** *View* tab>Appearance panel
	**Perspective with Ortho Faces**	• **Ribbon:** *View* tab>Appearance panel
	**Ray Tracing**	• **Ribbon:** *View* tab>Appearance panel
	**Reflections**	• **Ribbon:** *View* tab>Appearance panel
	**Shadows**	• **Ribbon:** *View* tab>Appearance panel
	**Styles Editor (lighting)**	• **Ribbon:** *Manage* tab>Styles and Standards panel
	**Visual Style**	• **Ribbon:** *View* tab>Appearance panel

Chapter 2

Advanced Sketching and Modeling Tools

The fundamental level sketch entities that can be created in a 2D sketch include lines, arcs, rectangles, etc. The Spline options provide additional flexibility to create smooth curved entities for creating geometry. Splines and entities such as lines and arcs can also be created in a 3D sketch. 3D sketches enable you to create entities that exist in 3D space without a sketch plane. Along with splines, lines, and arcs, there are a number of additional 3D sketch tools that can be used to create a sketch to generate complex geometry.

Learning Objectives

- Create a spline entity by placing vertices to define its control frame.
- Create a spline entity by placing points that define the exact spline shape.
- Create a 3D sketch that consists of linear, helical, arc, and bend entities.
- Create a 3D sketch by entering an equation that defines the X, Y, and Z coordinates over a specified range.
- Create 3D curves that are based on intersections of planes or the projection of geometry onto non-planar surfaces.
- Create a 3D curve that is sketched on a curved face.
- Bend 3D geometry by referencing a sketched line.
- Unwrap model geometry to create a flattened surface.

2.1 Splines

You can draw curves using Arc and Ellipse entities, but those curves can be too rigid. To create a free-form curve consider using a Spline. There are two types of splines that can be sketched: **Control Vertex** and **Interpolation**.

- For a Control Vertex Spline, the points that are placed to create the spline define the vertices of the control frame. The control frame defines the shape of the spline, as shown in Figure 2–1.

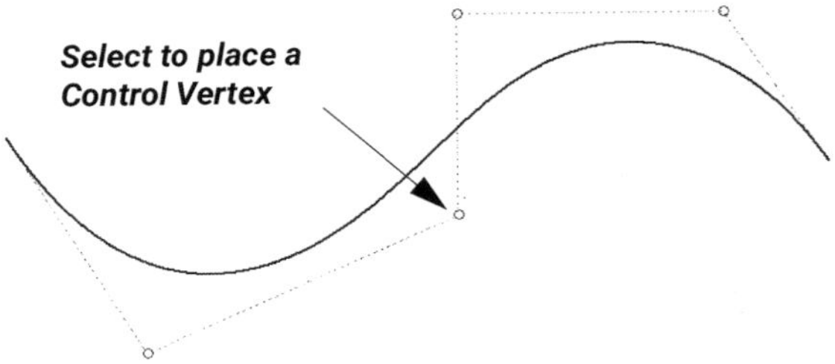

Figure 2–1

- For an Interpolation Spline, the spline is fit through the selected points, as shown in Figure 2–2.

Figure 2–2

Note: *Multiple splines can be sketched and constrained to one another using the*  *(Smooth (G2)) constraint to produce a smooth transition between entities. This constraint can also be used to constrain a spline to other sketched entities.*

You can use splines in models for many purposes, such as a base for creating surfaces, parting lines for splitting molds and drafts, or a sweep path, as shown in Figure 2–3.

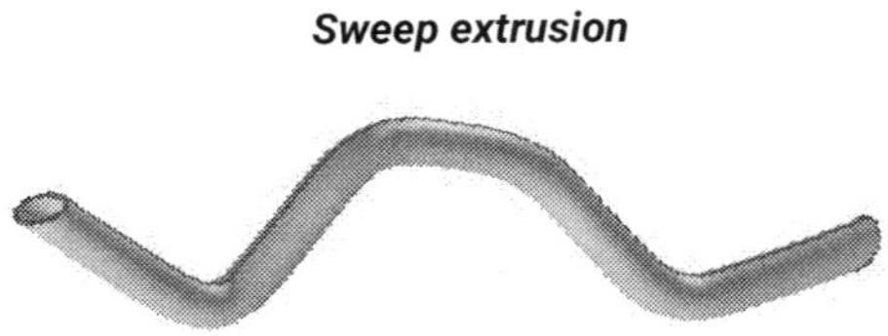

Figure 2–3

How To: Create a Spline

1. Select the type of spline that is required. The Spline options for a 2D Sketch are located with the line entities on the Create panel.
   - In the *Sketch* tab>Create panel, click (Spline Interpolation).
   - In the *Sketch* tab>Create panel, click (Spline Control Vertex).
   - If creating a spline in 3D sketch, the commands are located in the *3D Sketch* tab>Draw panel, in their own drop-down list.
2. Sketch the free-form spline by placing points or by selecting existing work points, end points, or midpoints.
   - An Interpolation spline is sketched by selecting points that will lie on the exact path of the spline.
   - A Control Vertex spline is sketched by selecting points that define the control frame.

Hint: Identifying Spline Points

To help identify splines, the end points of a Interpolation Spline display as a square shape, while the fit points along the curve display as a diamond, as shown in Figure 2–4.

Figure 2–4

3. Once all points are defined, right-click and select **Create** or click in the mini-toolbar. You can also select **Cancel [Esc]** to cancel sketching and deactivate the command, or select **Restart** to restart the spline.
4. Add dimensions and constraints to the spline's points and control vertices, similar to that shown in Figure 2–5. Interpolation Splines can be dimensioned between points.

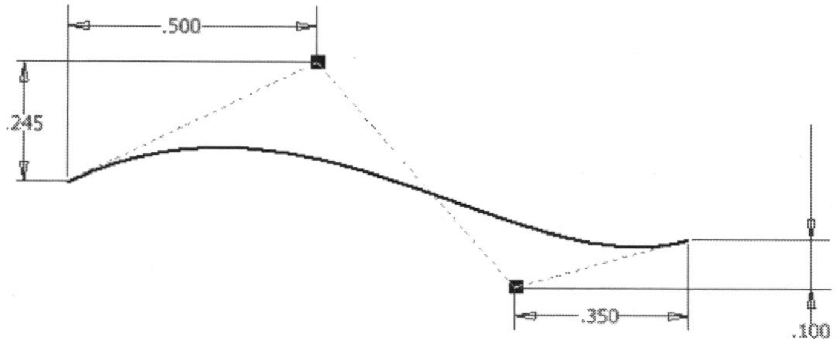

Figure 2–5

Editing a Spline

Once the spline is created, you can select the spline to edit it as follows:

- Select and drag the shape points (control vertices or interpolation points) to new locations. For Interpolation Splines, if you press and hold <Alt> while dragging, other unconstrained points also move.
- For Interpolation Splines, select and drag the tangent handles that are displayed at all shape points, as shown in Figure 2–6, to manipulate the shape of the spline. The handle must be activated to modify. To activate a handle, select the shape point, right-click, and select **Activate Handle** or select the spline to display all handles

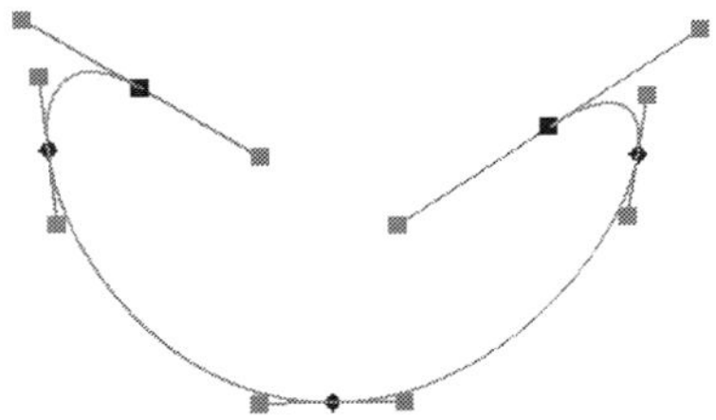

Figure 2–6

You can also edit the spline attributes using options in the shortcut menu. The spline editing options include the following:

> ***Note:*** *The options available in the shortcut menu depend on whether the spline was created as a control vertex or an interpolation spline. Additionally, where you right-click on the spline (whether the spline, point, or handles) can affect which options are displayed.*

- Select **Insert Point** in the shortcut menu to add additional internal shape points for interpolation or control vertex splines, respectively.
- Click **Display Curvature** in the marking menu to display a curvature comb that indicates the curvature along the spline, as shown in Figure 2–7. The length of each comb line is inversely proportional to the radius of the curve at that point. If the curvature comb does not display, right-click and select **Setup Curvature Display** to modify the comb's density and scale.

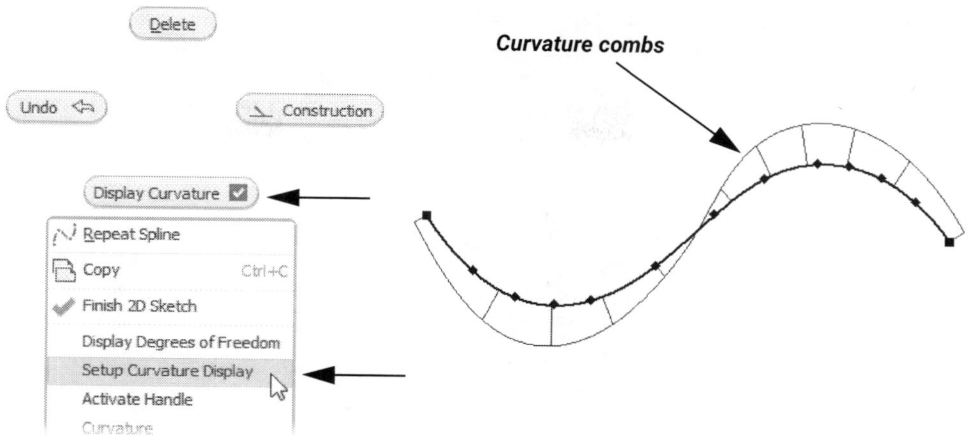

Figure 2–7

- Select **Activate Handle**, **Curvature**, or **Flat** in the shortcut menu to control the shape of the spline at the shape points. The shape point nearest to where you right-clicked is affected. The spline shown in Figure 2–8 has **Activate Handle** applied to it. This option displays a line tangent to the spline (called a handlebar) on the shape point; adjust the direction of the handlebar by dragging either end. The handlebar rotates about the shape point.

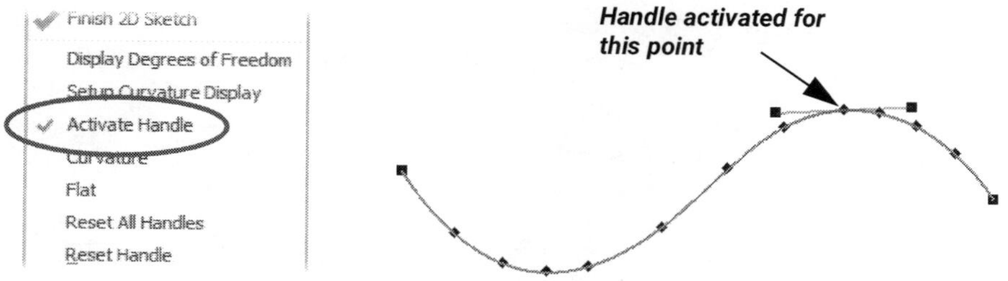

Figure 2–8

- The **Curvature** option provides an arc (called a curvature bar) on the shape point in addition to the tangent line, as shown in Figure 2–9. Drag either end of the curvature bar to change the curvature. The **Flat** option removes the curvature at the selected point.

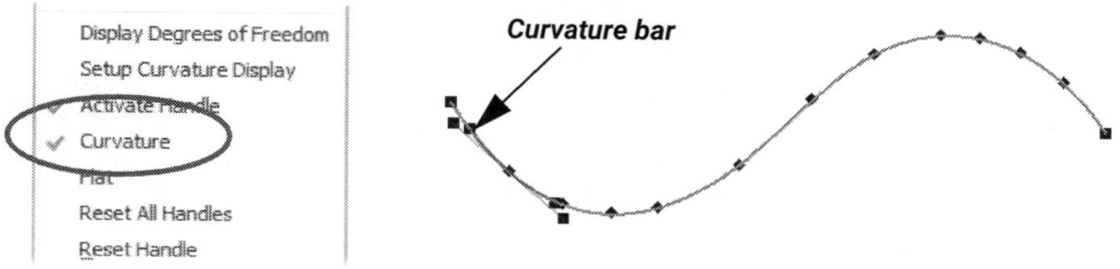

Figure 2–9

- Select **Spline Tension** in the shortcut menu to adjust how straight the spline is between shape points for an interpolation spline. Higher tensions force the spline to become straighter (and the curvature at the shape points becomes tighter). Figure 2–10 shows a spline with zero tension on the left side and maximum (100%) tension on the right side. A start point, end point, and one shape point were used to create the spline.

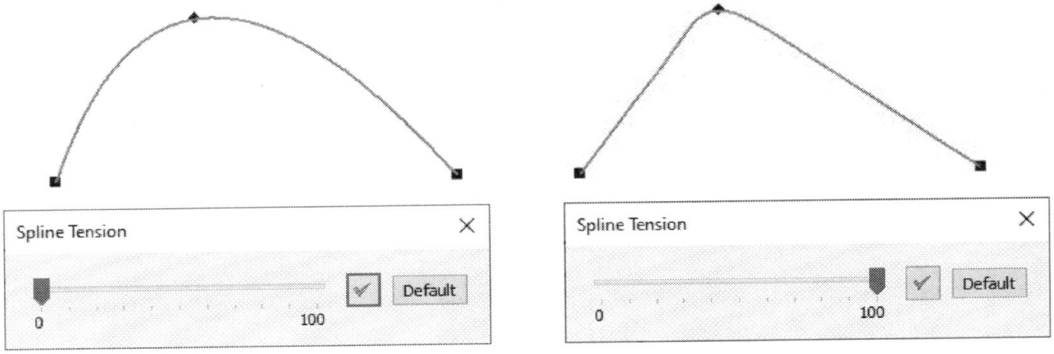

Figure 2–10

- Select **Fit Method** in the shortcut menu to edit the spline transition between shape points in an interpolation spline. The three methods available enable you to create a spline that transitions smoothly between shape points (**Standard**), a spline that uses the AutoCAD fit method (**AutoCAD**), and a spline with smoother continuity and better curvature distribution (**Minimum Energy**). The Minimum Energy method increases the file size and requires longer calculation times.

  Note: *If the spline tension is modified, the spline is automatically converted to the* ***Minimum Energy*** *Fit Method.*

- Select **Close Spline** in the shortcut menu for an interpolation spline to join the start and end points, as shown in Figure 2–11.

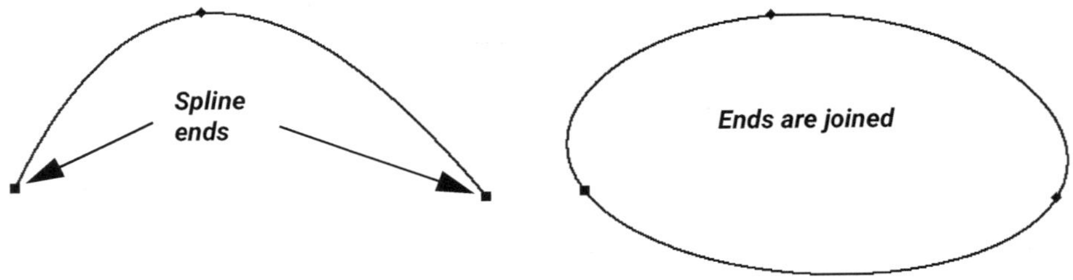

Figure 2–11

- Once spline handles have been reset for an interpolation spline, you can restore all or individual handles to their natural solve state using **Reset All Handles** or **Reset Handle**. The **Reset All Handles** option, as shown in Figure 2–12, is available on the shortcut menu when the spline is selected. The **Reset Handle** option is available on the shortcut menu when a handle is selected. Resetting a single handle restores it to a natural solve state based on the position of the other handles, not necessarily to its original solve state.

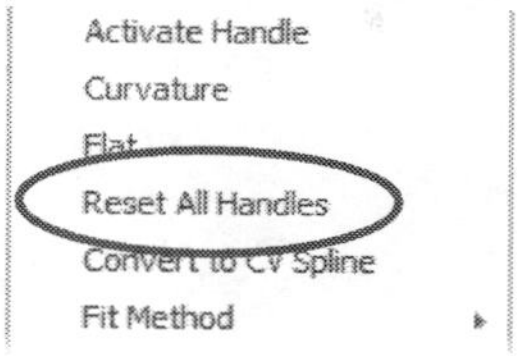

Figure 2–12

- The **Convert to CV Spline** option and **Convert to Interpolation** options enable you to switch a control vertex spline to a spline that was created using interpolation points, and vice versa. The spline shown in Figure 2–13 was originally an interpolation spline that was converted to a Control Vertex spline using **Concert to CV Spline**.

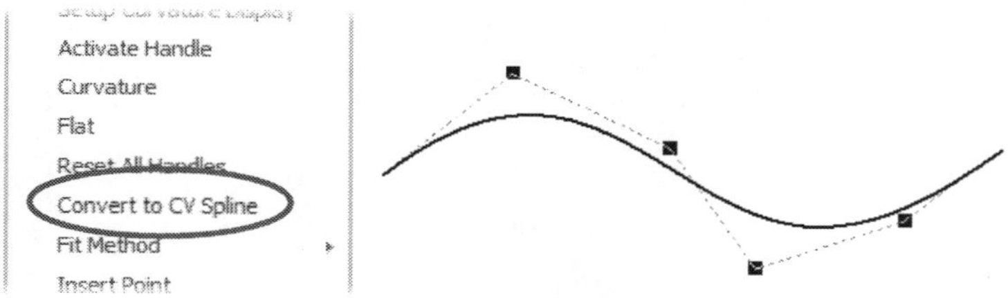

Figure 2–13

2.2 3D Sketch Creation Tools

While 2D sketching is performed in a plane, 3D sketching takes place in 3D space without a sketch plane. 3D sketches must be drawn from existing points (e.g., work points) or points on existing objects. The 3D sketch is automatically constrained to the selected vertices as it is sketched, as shown in Figure 2–14. 3D sketches can be used as profiles, rails in a loft, a path to define a 3D sweep, complex surfaces, etc.

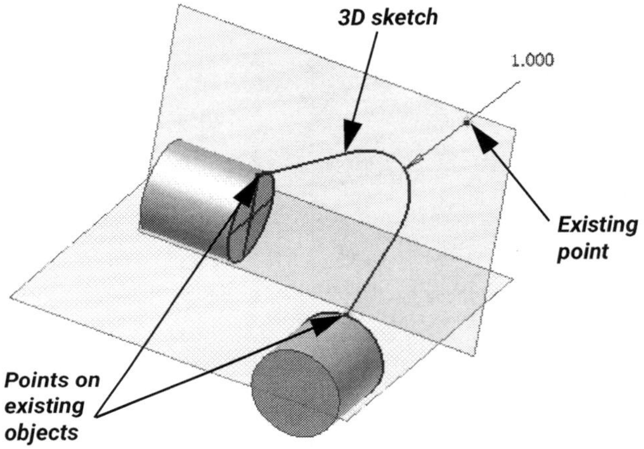

Figure 2–14

How To: Create a 3D Sketch

1. In the *3D Model* tab>Sketch panel, click  (Start 3D Sketch). The command can be found on the expanded **Start 2D Sketch** command, as shown in Figure 2–15.

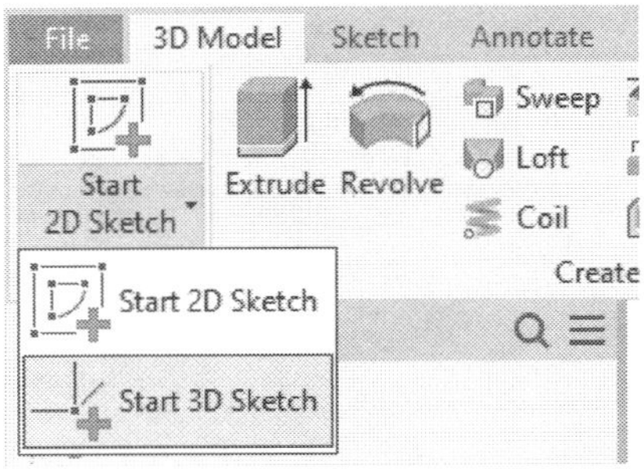

Figure 2–15

2. Use the tools on the *3D Sketch* tab (shown in Figure 2–16) to create 3D entities.

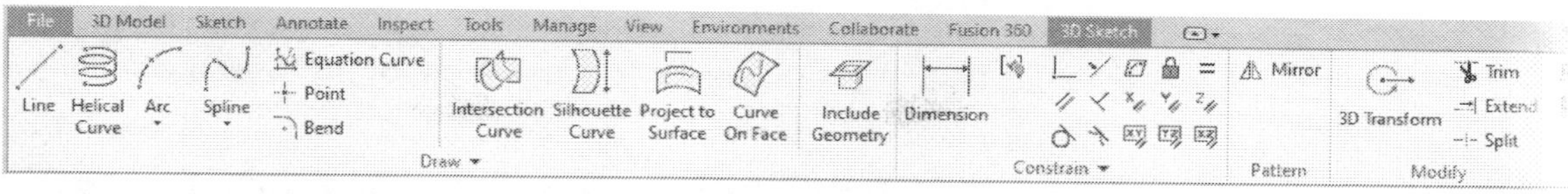

Figure 2–16

3. Modify the entities, as required, using tools on the Draw panel.
4. Using the Constrain panel, add dimensions and constraints to locate the 3D sketched entities, as required.

5. Once you finish sketching, in the Exit panel, click (Finish Sketch) or select **Finish 3D Sketch** in the context menu.

To edit a 3D sketch, right-click on its name in the Model browser and select **Edit 3D Sketch** or double-click on the 3D Sketch in the Model browser.

3D Sketch Tools

The following options in the Draw panel enable you to create entities in a 3D sketch.

Line

To sketch lines, click (Line) in the Draw panel or right-click and select **Create 3D Line**. Select points to define the line. You can also reference existing work points, sketch points, vertices, and end points. Since 3D sketches are often used to define sweeps for tubing and cabling, the sketch may need to be curved. Auto-Bend places a radius at all corners, as shown in Figure 2–17. To toggle Auto-Bend on or off, right-click and select **Auto-Bend** when creating the Line.

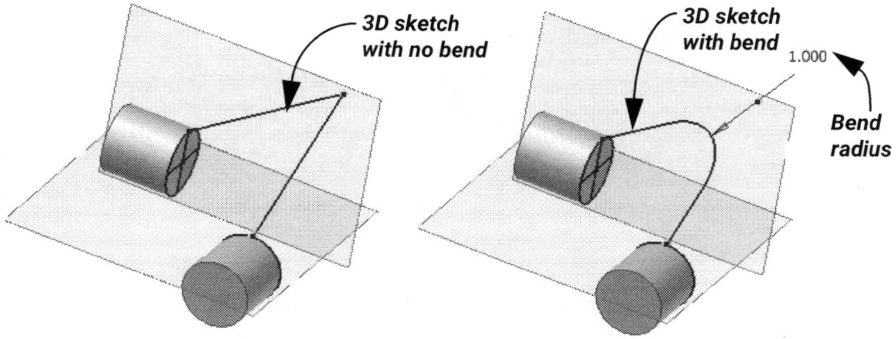

Figure 2–17

- To change the default setting for the Auto-Bend radius for the current file, click (Document Settings) (*Tools* tab> Options panel), select the *Sketch* tab and change the value in the *Auto-Bend Radius* field. If the radius value is too large for the sketch, the bend is not applied.

Hint: Improving Sketch Accuracy

Consider using the (Ortho Mode) and (Snap Object) options in the Status Bar at the bottom of the graphics window to better control how the entities are sketched. With **Ortho Mode** enabled, you can restrict sketching to the X, Y, and Z planes. With **Snap Object** enabled, you can snap to existing entities when sketching new entities.

Helical Curve

Click (Helical Curve) in the Draw panel or right-click and select **Helical Curve** to create a helical/spiral curve. The types can include a Constant Helical Curve ( ) or Variable Helical Curve ( ). For each type, you can define how the curve is created using the options in the *Definition* area. The creation types include the following:

- **Pitch and Revolution**
- **Revolution and Height**
- **Pitch and Height**
- **Spiral** (only available for Constant Helical Curves)

The values that are available to define a constant helical curves depend on the creation type that was selected. Once the sizes are entered, select the required point(s) directly on the model to define the curve. You can also set the revolution direction by clicking the and (Rotation) icons in the dialog box.

Figure 2–18 shows a Constant Helical Curve and the options used to create it.

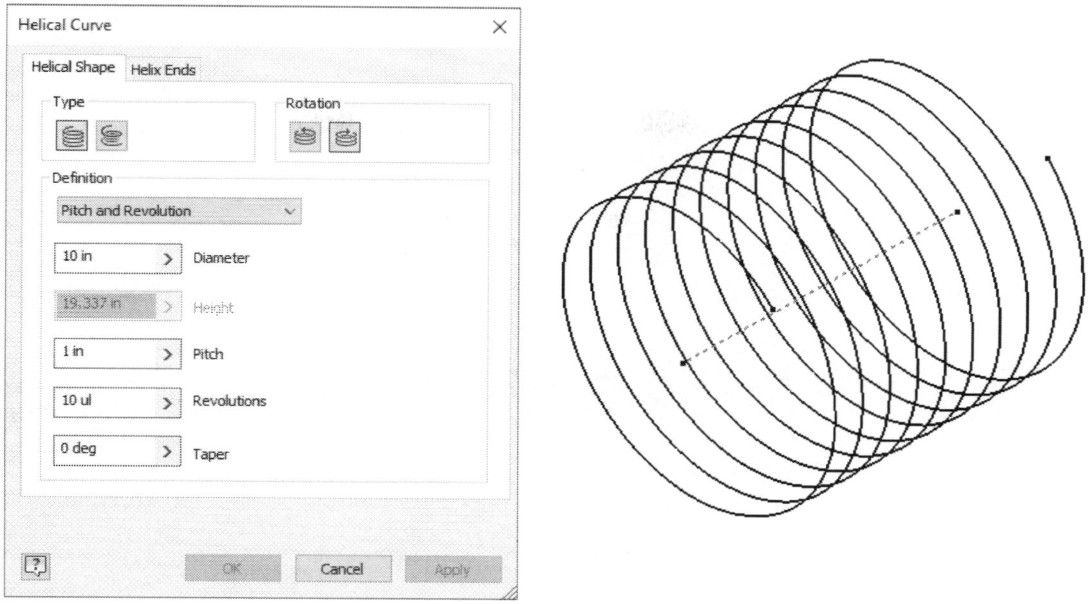

Figure 2–18

In the Helical Curve dialog box, the dimensions for variable helical curves are entered in a table format to define the varying sizes curves across its entire length, as shown in Figure 2–19.

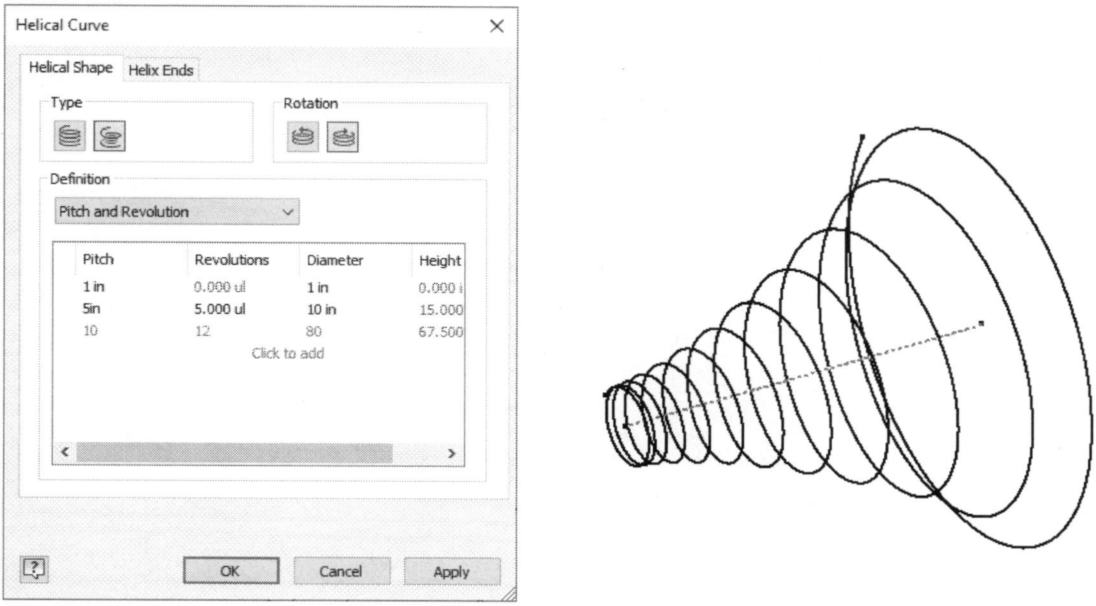

Figure 2–19

Arc

Click (Arc Three Point) or (Arc Center Point) to create an arc as you would in a 2D sketch. The Three Point arc can also be started by right-clicking and then selecting **Three Point Arc**.

Spline

Click (Spline Interpolation) or (Spline Control Vertex) to create a spline as you would in a 2D sketch.

Hint: Entering Precise Values

Consider using **Precise Input** in the expanded Draw panel to precisely define the X, Y, and Z location of the entities that are placed in the 3D sketch. This can be used for lines, helical curves, arcs, splines, and points. The Precise Input mini-toolbar enables you to enter values.

To close the mini-toolbar once active, expand and click **Close**.

Hint: Aligning and Reorienting the Sketch Triad

As you are sketching you can right-click and access commands that enable you to align and reorient the model to accurately sketch the entities. The shortcut menu options enable you to do the following:

- **Align to Plane:** Aligns the sketch triad to a plane.
- **Orient Z** and **Orient to World:** Reorients the sketching triad to a custom Z direction or to the world coordinate system. To define a custom Z direction, you can select an edge, line, axis, plane, vertex or point.
- **Snap Intersection:** Snaps an entity to the intersection of entities. This is only available when **Ortho Mode** is enabled.

Equation Curve

An Equation curve enables you to create complex entities by entering an equation that defines the entities path in the X, Y, and Z axes. To create an equation curve, in the Draw panel, click (Equation Curve). A mini-toolbar opens, as shown in Figure 2–20, providing you with the fields that you can use to define the curve and the range of values to evaluate.

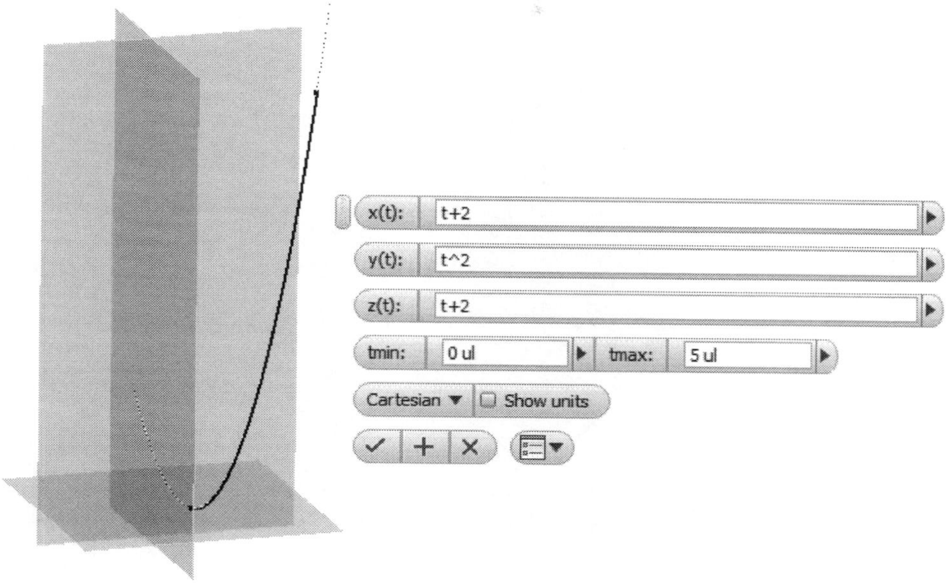

Figure 2–20

Point

Click (Point) to create sketch points or center points for use in creating your 3D sketch.

Bend

If you place lines without bends and later decide to add them, click (Bend) in the Draw panel or right-click and select **Bend**. Enter a radius in the Bend dialog box and select the two lines for the bend to join. The lines to which the bend is applied must meet at a corner.

Intersection Curve

You can create a 3D sketch curve from the intersection of two surfaces, splines, lines, work planes, or parts. The sketch automatically updates if you change either of the two objects.

Click (Intersection Curve), select the two objects to define the 3D sketch, and click **OK** to create the 3D sketch. If you are using one work plane and another object, select the work plane first. A 3D sketch created by intersecting an extruded surface and the XY Plane is shown in Figure 2–21.

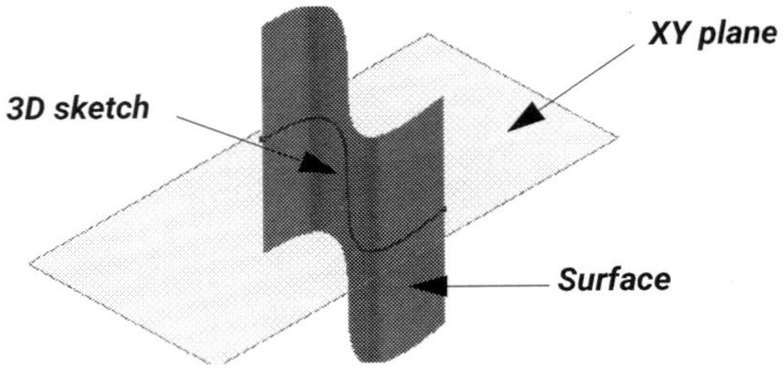

Figure 2–21

Project Curve to Surface

Click (Project to Surface) to create a sketch that is projected onto a face (2D or 3D) from a selected curve(s), as shown in Figure 2–22. The projection output can be along a selected vector, to a closest point, or wrapped to a surface that is flat, cylindrical, or conical.

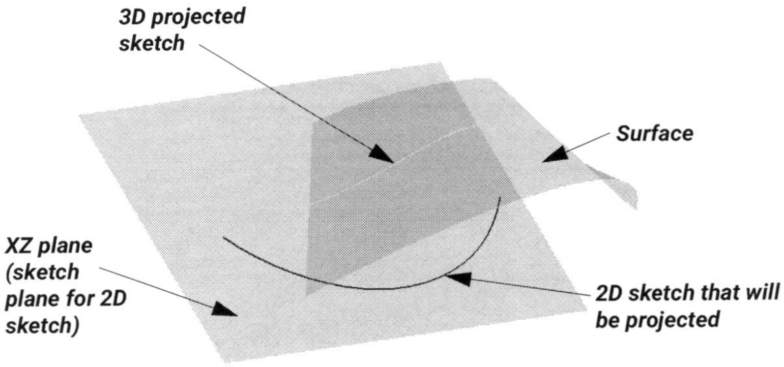

Figure 2–22

Silhouette Curve

A silhouette curve represents the contour of the model relative to a specific pull direction. The curve can include both the inner and outer design model boundaries, as shown in Figure 2–23. The curve can be best explained by imagining a light shining on the model. The curve is placed wherever there is a silhouette.

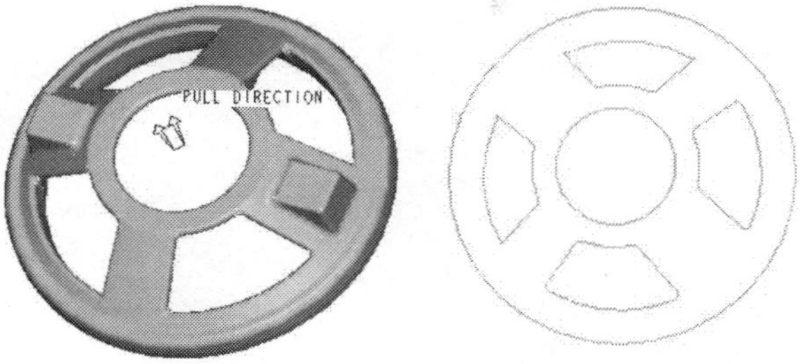

Figure 2–23

> ***Note:*** *Silhouette curves are commonly used for generating parting lines for plastic part design or for use in multi-body part design.*

Click (Silhouette Curve) and select the *Body* to use as the geometry to create the silhouette curve. In the *Exclusion* area, select whether faces, straight faces, or internal faces are to be excluded from the curve. The curve will be placed on the selected body. Define the *Direction* from which to derive the silhouette curve. The direction can be defined by a plane, face, edge, or axis.

The models shown in Figure 2–24 show two examples of silhouette curves created on similar models. In the left model, the silhouette curve feature creates two curves because the straight faces were excluded, and in the right model, it creates a single curve around the entire model because nothing was excluded.

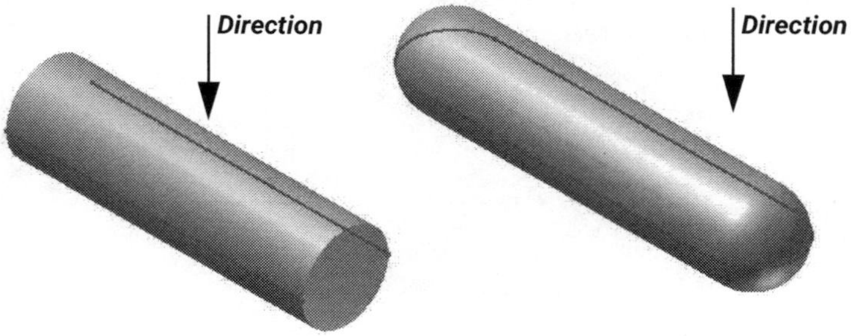

Figure 2–24

Curve on Face

A curve can be sketched directly on a face using the **Curve on Face** command. This enables you to easily locate the sketch directly on a non-planar face without having to project entities. To sketch a curve on a face, click (Curve on Face) in the Draw panel. You can select vertices, edges, or miscellaneous points to define the curve. The curve is placed on the face that is highlighted in red and is generated as a 3D interpolation spline, similar to that shown in Figure 2–25. Once sketched, you have access to the shortcut menu to close the sketch or add additional points. You can also use constraints and dimensions to fully define the curve.

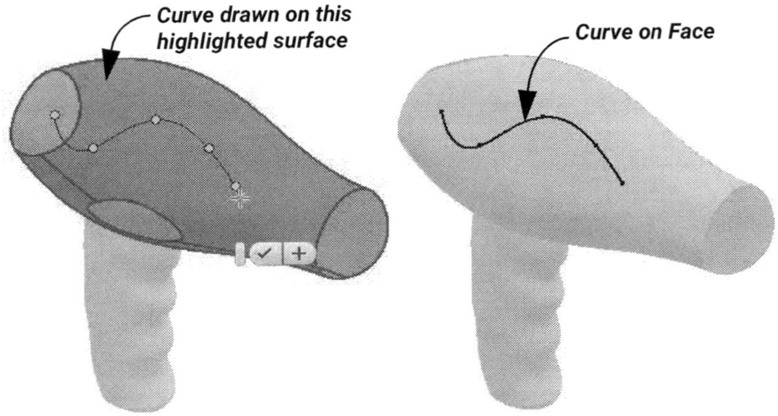

Figure 2–25

Include Geometry

To include edges from 3D objects and 2D sketches in the 3D sketch, click (Include Geometry) and select the geometry to include. Alternatively, you can select **Include Geometry** in the marking menu to initiate the command. If you change an object that was used with the option, the sketch also updates to reflect this change.

Mirror

Use the (Mirror) option in the Pattern panel to mirror 3D sketch entities. Like mirroring in a 2D sketch, the mirror plane can be a planar face, an origin plane, or a work plane.

Points

Use the (Points) option in the Insert panel to insert points from a selected Microsoft Excel file. The requirements for the spreadsheet are:

- Coordinates are on the first sheet.
- Cell A1 lists the unit of measure (a blank cell assumes the default units).
- Row 2 shows column headers (e.g., X, Y, Z).
- Row 3 and thereafter show the coordinates.
- Points reference the sketch origin.

Hint: Work Features

Use the work feature options to create work planes, axis, and points in the 3D Sketch. The Work Feature panel is not displayed by default, you must add it to the panel to use it.

Modifying 3D Sketch Entities

To activate a 3D sketch for editing, double-click on its name in the Model browser, or right-click the sketch and click (Edit 3D Sketch). You can edit using any of the following:

- Select and drag vertices, center points, or any section on a 3D entity to reposition it without entering exact coordinates.
- Double-click on the dimensions to change values.
- Right-click and select **Construction** to convert a sketched entity into a construction entity.
- Select **Delete** in the shortcut menu to delete an object in the 3D sketch. If you delete an object that was added with the **Include Geometry** option, the source object is not affected.
- Use **Extend**, **Trim**, and **Split** in the Modify panel to refine the sketch's shape. These options are also available when sketching.

- Use (3D Transform) in the Modify panel to reposition geometry in a 3D sketch. Once activated, you are provided with the transform triad and mini-toolbar. Select a manipulator handle on the triad to reposition the selected entity linearly, rotationally, or on a plane. The mini-toolbar updates as required and enables you to enter values to define the move. The mini-toolbar can also be used to control the orientation of the triad to the world, view, or local coordinate systems. In Figure 2–26, a spline entity is being moved along the X axis of the world coordinate system.

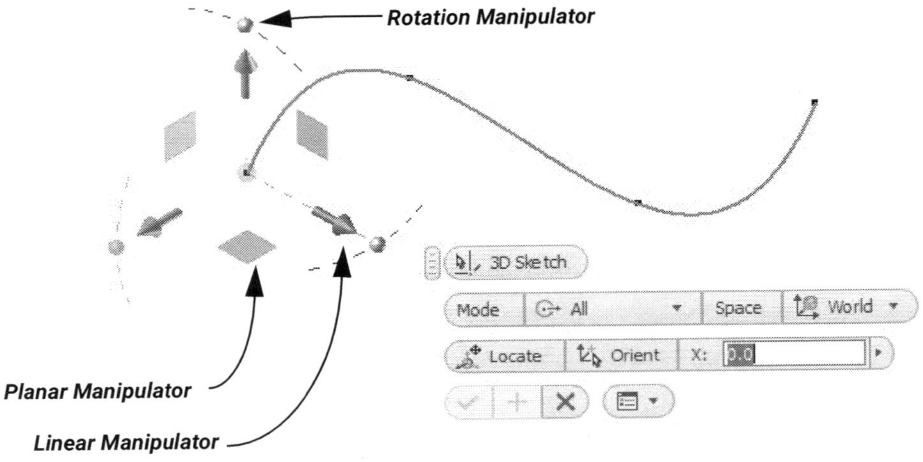

Figure 2–26

Use standard copy and paste functionality to create copies of existing sketched entities in the same sketch or in different sketches. This enables you to efficiently duplicate entities in a 3D sketch. Use the 3D Transform tool to move the pasted entities, as required. If pasted in the same sketch the new entities are pasted over the source entities and must be moved.

Dimensioning and Constraining

Using the Constrain panel, add dimensions and constraints to locate the sketched entities. The available constraint options are shown in Figure 2–27.

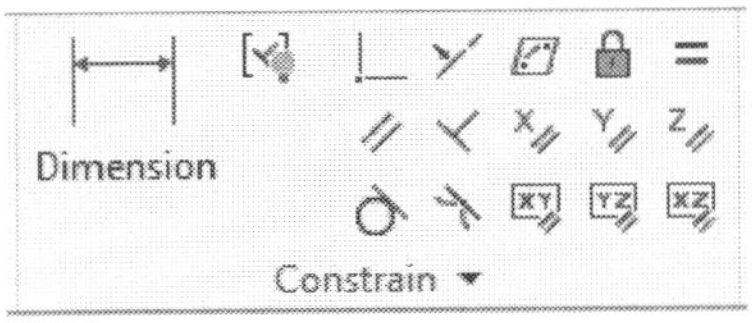

Figure 2–27

- The **Coincident**, **Parallel**, **Tangent**, **Collinear**, **Perpendicular**, **Smooth (G2)**, **Fixed**, and **Equal** constraints can be used in the same way as in a 2D sketch.

- The (On Face) constraint enables you to constrain points, lines, arc, or spline to a planar face. Optionally, you can constrain individual points to a curved face.
- The , , and constraint types can be used to constrain a line, curve, or spline handle to lie parallel with the X, Y, or Z axis, respectively.
- The , , and constraint types can be used to constrain a line, curve, or spline to lie parallel with the XY, YZ, or XZ planes, respectively.

  Note: *Assigned constraints can be deleted by right-clicking on the constraint symbol in the graphics window and selecting* ***Delete****.*

When dimensioning and constraining, you can also consider setting the **Dynamic Dimension** and **Infer Constraints** options in the Status Bar to aid in the sketching process.

- (Dynamic Dimension): Enables you to toggle whether the dynamic dimension field appears as you are sketching. This field enables you to enter exact values. When disabled, you can only select points to place the entities.
- (Infer Constraints): Enables you to control whether constraints are inferred by the Autodesk Inventor software as you are sketching or not.
- (Show/Hide Constraints): Enables you to toggle the display of constraint symbols on and off in the sketch.

Hint: 3D Sketch Properties

The Geometry Properties dialog box, shown in Figure 2–28, controls 3D sketch properties. To open the dialog box, select the entity, right-click and select **Properties**.

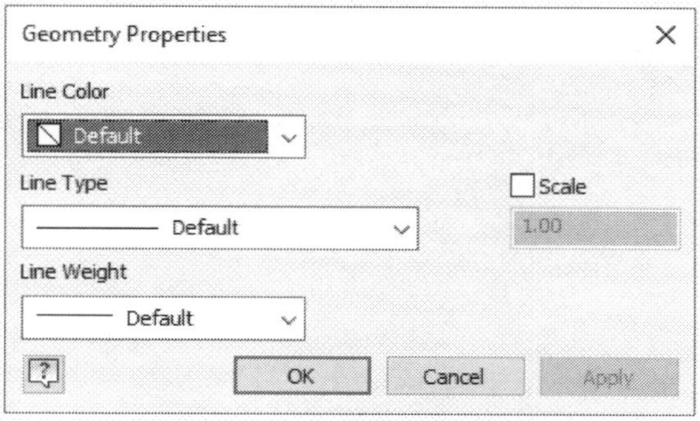

Figure 2–28

2.3 Bending a Part

The **Bend Part** option enables you to bend part geometry based on a sketch. The sketch must be a single entity and must be linear. It is not required to extend across the entire model geometry that will be bent. The Bend Part option is not intended for use with sheet metal models and is therefore located in the Part environment. Using this command enables you to create unique geometry that would be difficult to model using the standard 3D modeling tools or that might not suit the Sheet Metal environment (e.g., constant thickness). You can specify which side of the sketch is bent, the bend direction, and how the bend is calculated (i.e., the method for bending). Figure 2–29 shows two simple examples of part geometry that has been bent.

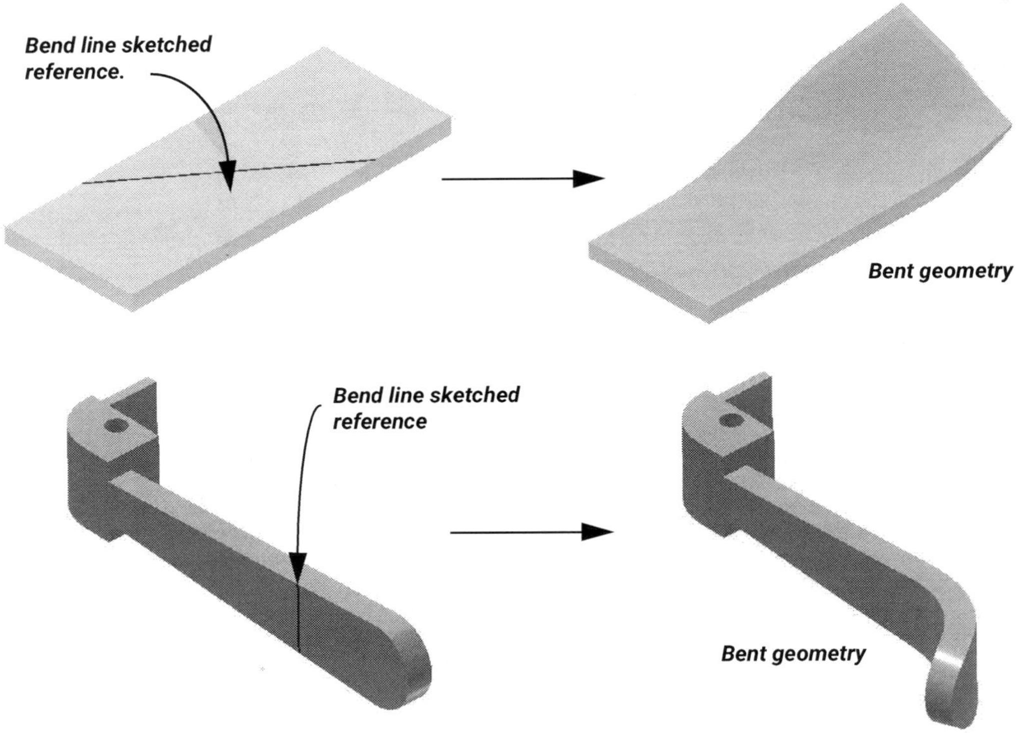

Figure 2–29

How To: Bend Part Geometry

1. Create the single linear entity sketch that will be used as the bend line.
2. In the *3D Model* tab>expanded Modify panel, click (Bend Part). The Properties panel opens, as shown in Figure 2–30.

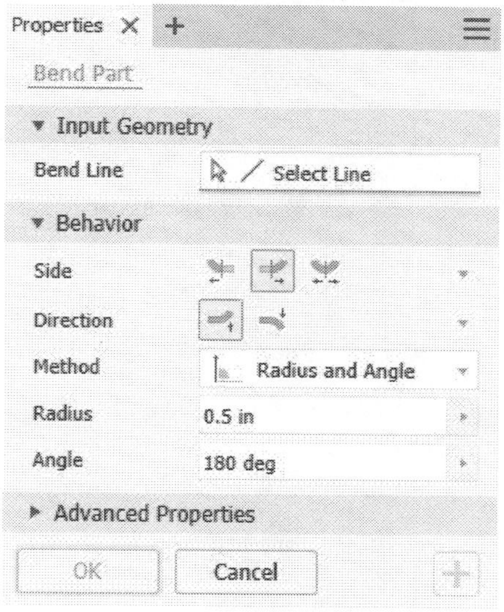

Figure 2–30

3. Select **Bend Part** (default feature name) at the top of the Properties panel to assign a new name for the feature.
4. In the *Input Geometry* area, select the *Bend Line* that will define the bend.
5. In the *Behavior* area, define the following to fully define the bend size, side, and direction.
   - Select any one of the three *Side* options to bend the geometry to side A ( ), side B ( ), or on both sides ( ).
   - Select one of the two *Direction* options to use the default bend direction ( ) or flip the direction ( ).

- Select a *Method* to define the size of the bend using the drop-down list, as shown in Figure 2–31. Depending on the method that is selected, you can enter values for *Radius*, *Angle*, and *Arc Length*, as needed.

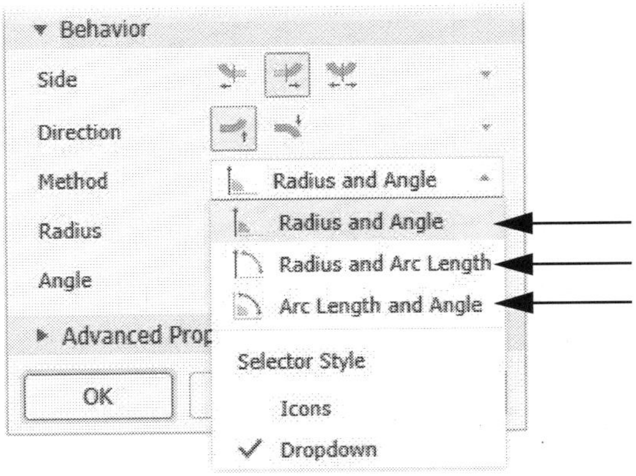

Figure 2–31

Note: *The **Selector Style** options (Icons or Dropdown) enable you to customize whether the **Method** options are provided as icons or a list. By default they are set as icons.*

6. Once the feature is defined, click **OK**. Alternatively, right-click in the graphics window and select **OK (Enter)**. To continue creating additional bends without closing the panel, click  (Apply) and define the references as needed. Once all bends have been completed, click **OK**.

2.4 Unwrapping a Part

The **Unwrap** command enables you to generate a flat surface from a selected face or faces. During creation, the surface preview displays a surface mesh and heat map, as shown in the middle in Figure 2–32. The color gradient on the preview helps identify areas of low (blue) or high (red) deformation and tension. The yellow lines identify edges. Once the unwrap feature is completed, the unwrapped geometry is displayed as a standard surface and is listed in the Surface Bodies node in the Model browser.

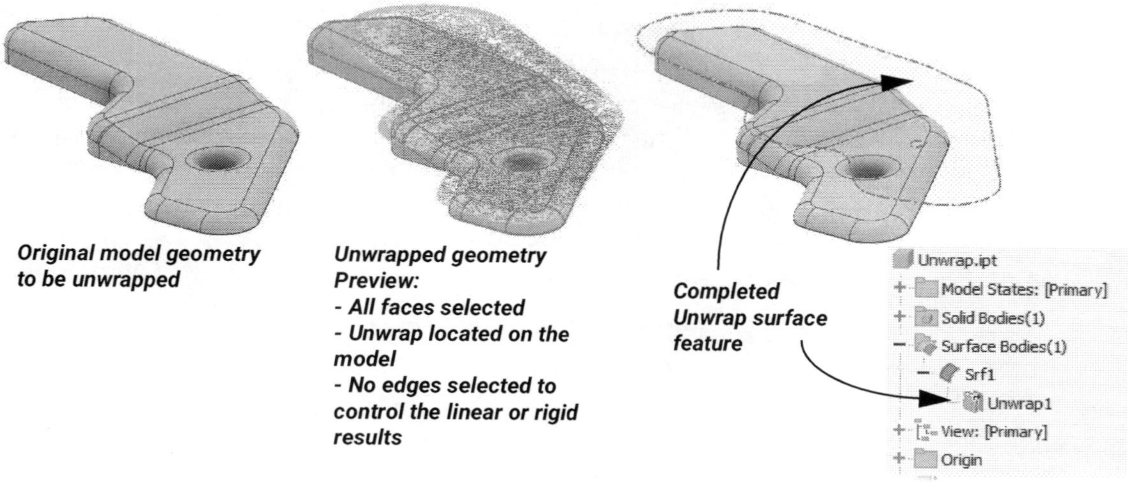

Figure 2–32

How To: Unwrap Part Faces

1. In the *3D Model* tab>Create panel, click (Unwrap). The Properties panel opens, as shown in Figure 2–33.

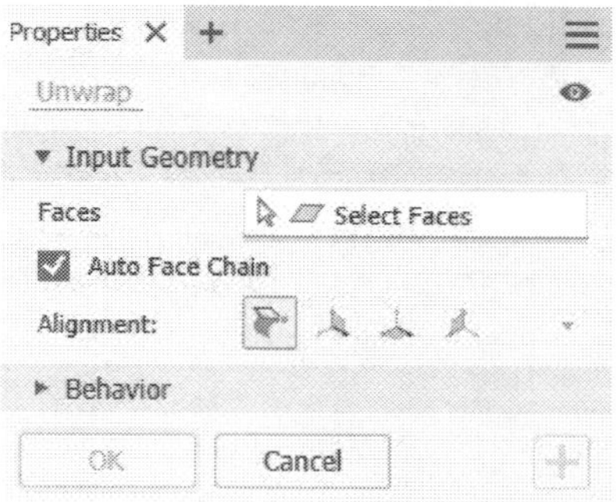

Figure 2–33

2. Select **Unwrap** (default feature name) at the top of the Properties panel to assign a new name for the feature.
3. The *Faces* field is activated by default. Select one or more faces on the model to be unwrapped.
    - Enable the **Auto Face Chain** option to automatically select all faces that are tangent to the selected face.
    - Disable the **Auto Face Chain** option to select individual faces.
4. Once a face(s) is selected, a preview of the flattened face displays on the model based on the default Alignment settings. The settings enable you to define a vertex and plane to locate the flattened face, as follows:
    - The alignment vertex is assigned by default. It selects the vertex that is nearest the location to which you selected the face that is being unwrapped. The assigned vertex is aligned with the model's center point (0,0,0). To change the vertex, activate the field, click , and select a new vertex on the model geometry that is being unwrapped.
    - Use the Alignment options to change the placement plane of the unwrapped surface. The options include aligning to the face that was selected for unwrapping on the model ( ), the XY plane ( ), the XZ plane ( ), or the YZ plane ( ). If aligning to any of the planes, you can select on the gizmo that appears on the vertex to drag or rotate the surface on the plane, as needed.

    Note: *The default alignment option is maintained from the option that was previously set the last time the command was used.*

5. In the *Behavior* area, define the following, if required. These options are not required but can be defined to refine the result. Only one of the Linear Result or Rigid Result options can be used in an unwrap operation.
    - Activate the *Linear Result* field to select edge(s) on the exterior of the face to remain straight.
    - Activate the *Rigid Result* field to select exterior edge(s) that will not unwrap.
6. Enable or disable the **Merge Result Body** option, as required. With it enabled, the resulting unwrapped surface will be generated as a single body. With it disabled, all faces that were selected for the operation will be generated as separate surface bodies that are stitched together.
7. Once the feature is defined, click **OK**. Alternatively, right-click in the graphics window and select **OK (Enter)**. To continue creating additional unwrap features without closing the panel, click (Apply) and define the references as needed. Once complete, click **OK**.

Once the unwrap surface feature is complete, it is listed in the Surface Bodies node and can be treated like any other standard surface. Consider the following:

- To edit the unwrap, right-click on the feature in the Model browser and select **Edit Feature**, or double-click on it to open the Properties panel.
- Once the surface is generated, it can be saved in different formats for review. To save the surface, right-click on it in the Model browser and select **Save Copy As**. It can be saved as a .SAT, .DWG, or .DXF file format.
- To review the surface mesh and heat map again after creation, you must edit the unwrap feature to review it. Right-click on the feature in the Model browser and select **Edit Feature**, or double-click on it to open the Properties panel and review the preview.
- With the creation of the surface, a design view called **Unwrap# Isolated** is automatically created, as shown in Figure 2–34. This design view can be activated to display only the unwrapped surface in the graphics window.

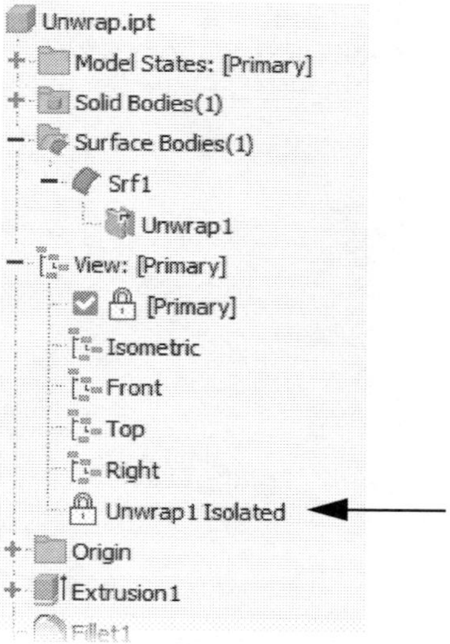

Figure 2–34

- An unwrapped surface can be displayed on its own in a drawing view by creating a new base view and selecting the **Unwrap# Isolated** design view as the representation in the Drawing View dialog box when placing the view.

Note: *In a sheet metal model, consider using this command to unwrap faces that cannot be flattened with the unfold or sheet metal flat pattern commands.*

Practice 2a
Create a Swept Cut Using a 3D Sketch

Practice Objectives

- Create a 3D sketch by placing points in the model and using those points to define the location of a 3D spline.
- Create a swept cut that references a sketched profile and a 3D sketched path.

In this practice, you create a swept cut through the model shown on the left of Figure 2–35. You use 3D sketch options to create the path for the sweep. You are provided with work planes and the order in which to create work points that are used to define the 3D sketch. Many of the menu selections are left out so that you can practice feature creation. The final model is shown on the right of Figure 2–35. The model guides a follower while rotating about the X axis.

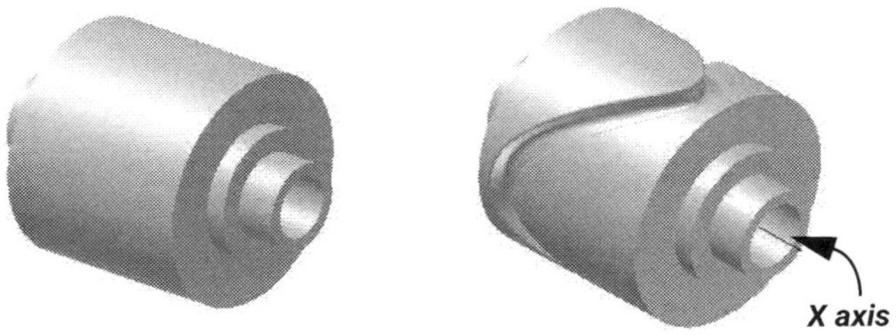

Figure 2–35

Task 1: Create work points.

In this task, you create four work points as the basis for the swept cut's 3D path.

1. Open **barrel_cam.ipt**. The work planes that have been provided will be used as references for the work points that you will create.
2. Create four work points. The planes that will be referenced to create the work points are shown in Figure 2–36.
   - Intersection of the planes 2, 6, and the XY plane.
   - Intersection of the planes 1, 3, and the XZ plane.
   - Intersection of the planes 2, 5, and the XY plane.
   - Intersection of the planes 1, 4, and the XZ plane.

   It is recommended that you select each plane directly in the Model browser to ensure that you are selecting the correct planes. If a work point does not get created after selecting three planes, then one of the planes selected might be incorrect. Most commonly it is due to selecting a plane that does not intersect with the other two.

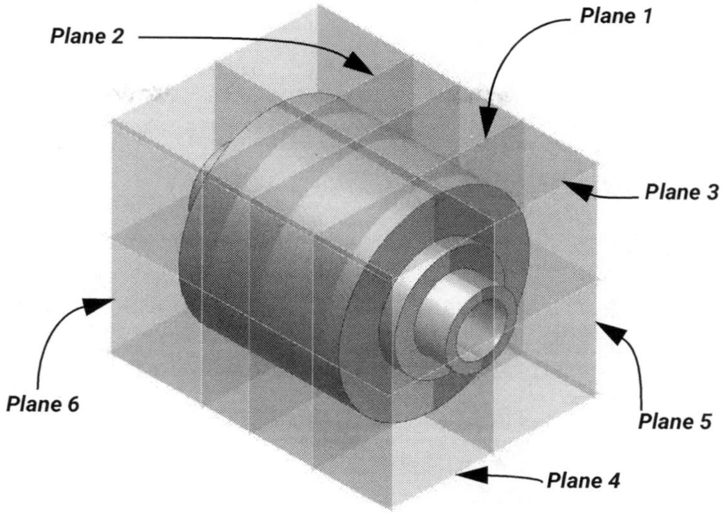

Figure 2–36

Note: *Sometimes changing the selection priority to* ***Feature Priority*** *and zooming into the model can help to select planes in a model.*

3. In the *View* tab>Visibility panel, expand **Object Visibility** and clear the **User Work Planes** and **Origin Planes** options to toggle off the visibility of all work planes and Origin planes.
4. Display the model in Wireframe (*View* tab>Appearance panel>**Visual Style**) and orient the model to the Right view. The model and work points display as shown in Figure 2–37. The model is displayed parallel to the YZ plane.

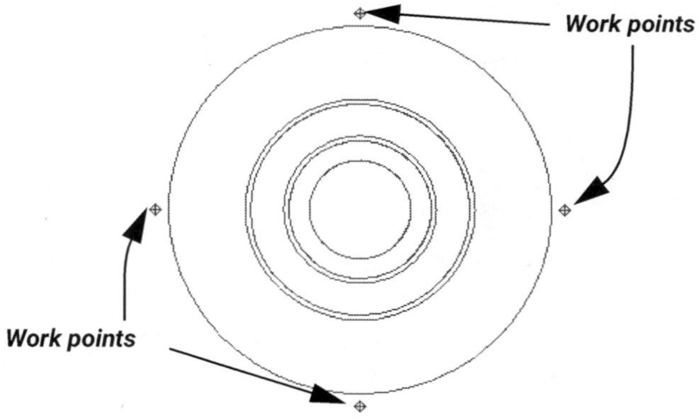

Figure 2–37

Task 2: Create a 3D sketch.

In this task, you use the 3D sketch options to create the path for the swept cut.

1. Display the model in isometric Home view.
2. Start a 3D sketch by right-clicking and selecting **New 3D Sketch**, or on the ribbon, on the *3D Model* tab, expand the Sketch panel and click (Start 3D Sketch).
3. In the Draw panel, click (Spline Interpolation) and select the existing work points in the order they were created. The model displays as shown in Figure 2–38. You must select the start point a second time to close the spline.

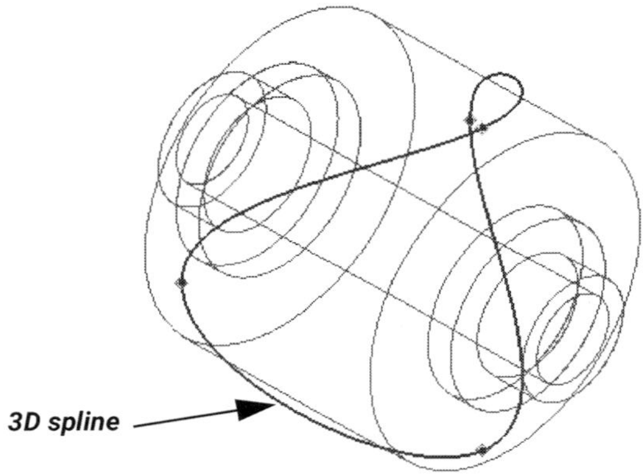

Figure 2–38

4. In the Exit panel, click (Finish Sketch).

Task 3: Create a swept cut profile.

1. Set the three default origin planes as visible.
2. Select the XZ plane in the Model browser, right-click and select **New Sketch** to activate the 2D sketch environment.
3. Project the YZ and XY work planes onto the sketch plane. You use these projected planes to locate and dimension the profile.
4. Project the work point at the intersection of 1, 3, and the XZ plane (Work Point2) onto the sketch plane. The work point location is shown in Figure 2–39. You project the work point because the sweep path must intersect the sketch plane of the profile.

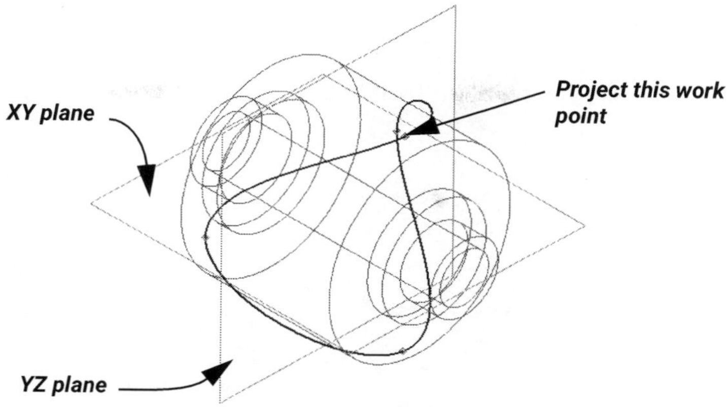

Figure 2–39

5. Sketch and dimension the profile, as shown in Figure 2–40. Constrain the sketch to the projected work point.

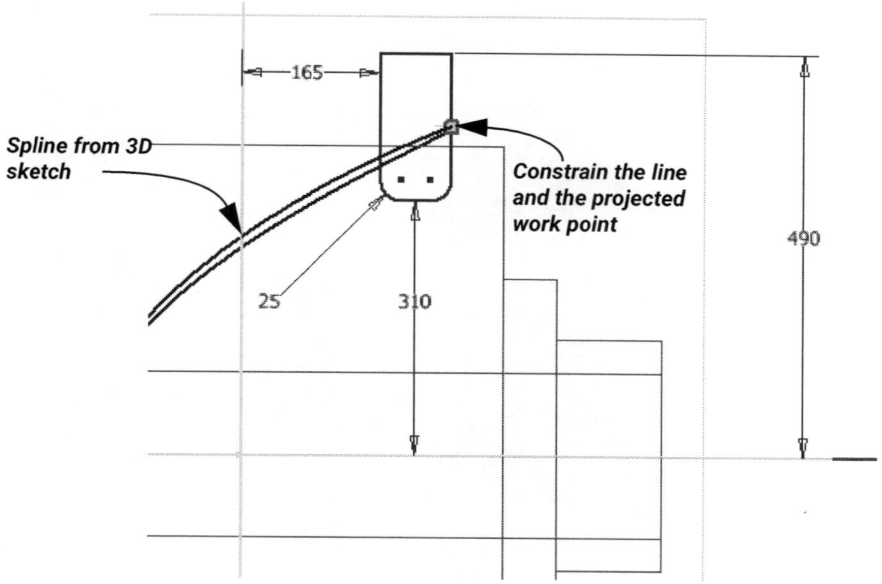

Figure 2–40

6. In the Exit panel, click ✔ (Finish Sketch).

Task 4: Create a swept cut.

1. Create a swept cut using the path and profile that have just been created. Return the model to the Shaded view display. The model displays as shown in Figure 2–41.

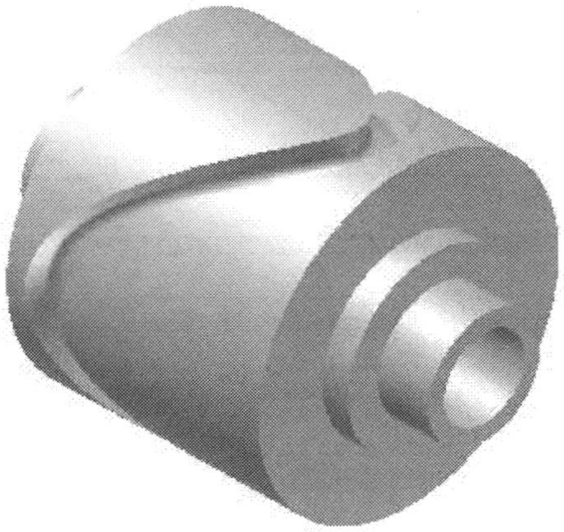

Figure 2–41

2. Add fillets of **10 mm** on the outside edges of the swept cut to remove sharp edges. Return the model to its shaded display. The model displays as shown in Figure 2–42.

Figure 2–42

3. Save and close the model.

End of practice

Practice 2b
Imported Point Data

Practice Objectives

- Create a 2D and 3D sketch that reads points from a Microsoft Excel spreadsheet file.
- Set the options for imported points in a 3D sketch to import points only, import the points with connecting lines, or import points with a connecting spline.
- Create a swept extrusion that references a sketched profile and a 3D sketched path.

In this practice, you will import point data to create both 3D and 2D sketches. Using this data, you will then create the swept geometry shown in Figure 2–43.

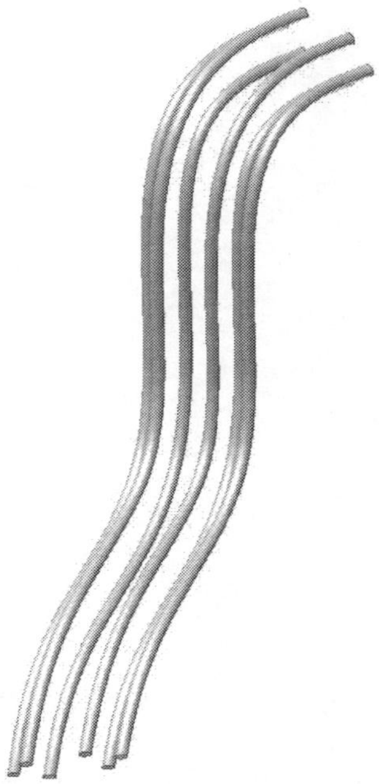

Figure 2–43

Task 1: Create a 3D sketch.

The 3D sketch can be sketched using the tools in the Draw panel, or you can import point data. In this task, you will import point data using a few different methods.

1. Create a new part file with the standard English template, **Standard (in).ipt**.

2. In the *3D Model* tab>Sketch panel, click (Start 3D Sketch). The *3D Sketch* tab is now the active tab.

3. In the Insert Panel, click (Points).

4. Select **chute_path.xls** and click **Open**. The spreadsheet was created for this practice and contains the X, Y, and Z coordinates for six points, as shown in Figure 2–44. Figure 2–44 shows the points in the default Home view.

Figure 2–44

5. In the Model browser, expand **Origin** and place the cursor over the Center Point work feature. Note that the Center Point and one of the imported points are coincident. Imported points reference the sketch origin (Center Point).

6. In the Draw panel, click (Line).

7. Right-click in the graphics window and verify that **Auto Bend** is disabled in the shortcut menu.

8. Reorient the model so that it is in the Home view, if not already. Starting from the top most point (sketch origin), select each point to draw lines between each of them, as shown in Figure 2–45. Right-click and select **OK**.

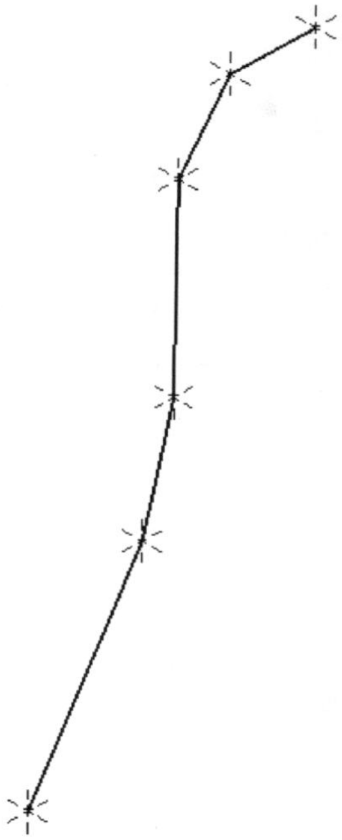

Figure 2–45

The line joining the points is not smooth. To smooth out the line, you can delete linear entities, add arcs, and assign tangency; however, doing so will change the point locations. Depending on your design intent, this might be acceptable, but for this design the points must remain as originally assigned.

9. Select all points and entities, and then delete them from the sketch.
10. In the *Tools* tab>Options panel, click (Application Options). In the Application Options dialog box, select the *Sketch* tab and enable **Auto-bend with 3D line creation** at the bottom of the window. Click **OK** to close the dialog box.
11. Select the *3D Sketch* tab.
12. In the Insert Panel, click (Points).
13. Select **chute_path.xls** and click **Options**.
14. Select **Create lines** and click **OK** in the File Open Options dialog box. This dialog box enables you to control how the points are brought into the sketch. The default option only brings in the points from the file.

15. Click **Open** to bring the points into the sketch. Note that the points have been added and lines have been drawn for you. In addition, because **Auto Blend** was enabled, the curve is smoother. The data displays as shown in Figure 2–46.

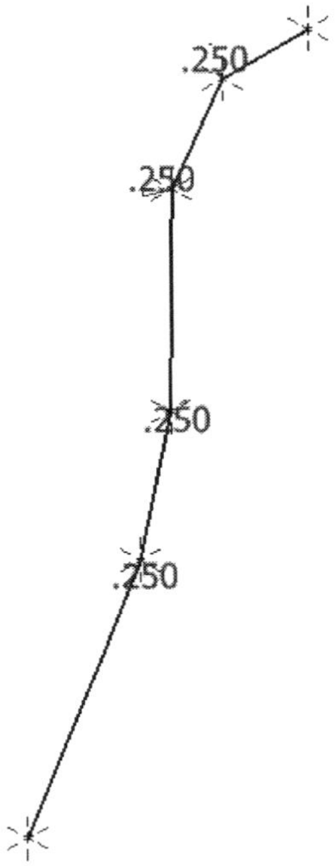

Figure 2–46

16. Select all points and entities, and then delete them from the sketch.

17. In the Insert Panel, click (Points).

18. Select **chute_path.xls** and click **Options**.

19. Select **Create spline** and click **OK** in the File Open Options dialog box.

20. Click **Open** to bring the points into the sketch as a spline. The data displays as shown in Figure 2–47.

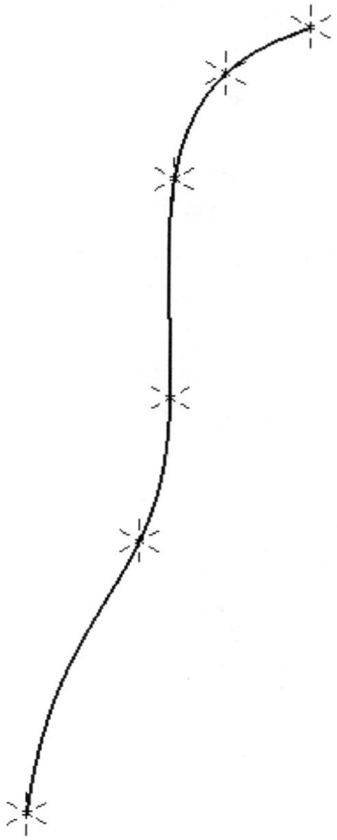

Figure 2–47

21. In the Exit panel, click ✔ (Finish Sketch).

Depending on the design intent of your model, you can consider using any one of the three methods for importing point data and using it in the 3D sketch. For the remainder of this practice, you will use the data that was brought into the 3D sketch as a spline.

Task 2: Create a 2D sketch.

1. In the *3D Model* tab>Sketch panel, click (Start 2D Sketch). Select the XY plane as the sketch plane. The *Sketch* tab is now the active tab.
2. In the Insert Panel, click (Points).
3. Select **chute_profile.xls**. Before importing the data, verify in the File Open Options dialog box that it will be brought in as points. Open the file.
4. Click **Yes** in the dialog box that opens, as shown in Figure 2–48. This message notes that although X, Y, and Z coordinates are in the file, only the X and Y coordinates will be used to import the data.

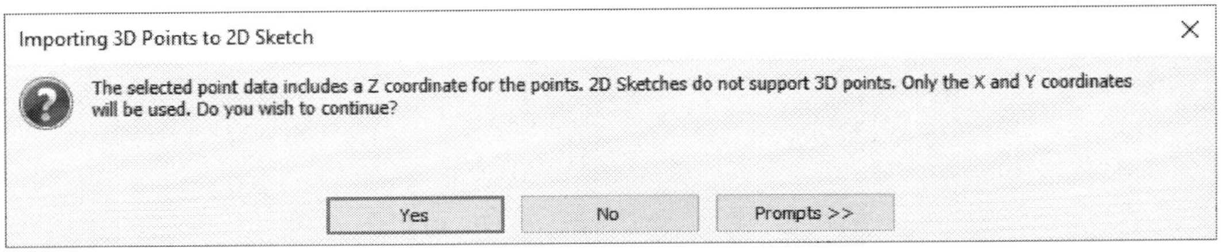

Figure 2–48

5. Reorient the model to the Front view and zoom in, as shown in Figure 2–49. Six new points have been imported.

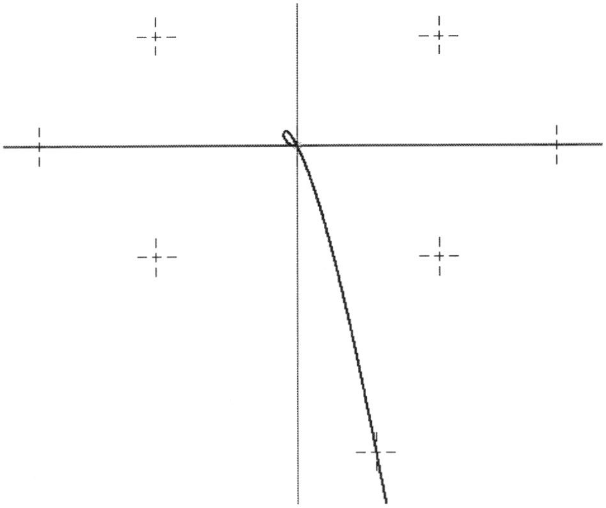

Figure 2–49

6. Sketch circular entities on all six points. Create a **.375** diameter dimension on one of the entities. Use the equal and fix constraints to locate the points where they have been imported. This ensures that all circular entities have the same diameter. The final sketch is shown in Figure 2–50.

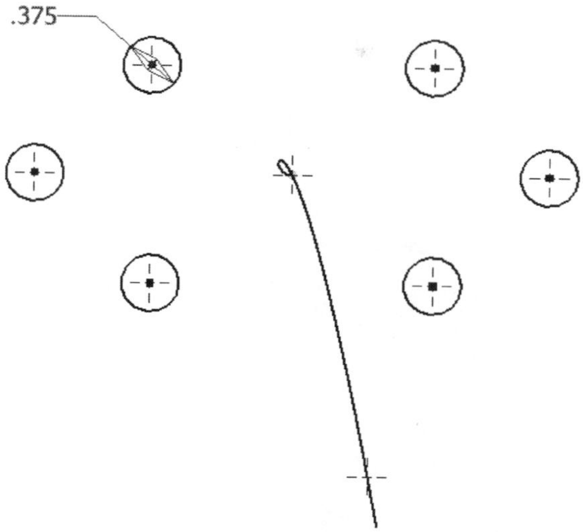

Figure 2–50

7. In the Exit panel, click (Finish Sketch).

Task 3: Create swept geometry using the 2D and 3D sketches.

1. In the *3D Model* tab>Create panel, click (Sweep).
2. Select the interior of one of the circular entities as a Profile for the sweep.
3. Disable the **Optimize for Single Selection** option, if enabled. This enables you to select multiple references. Select the remaining circular entities (six total). If the **Optimize for Single Selection** option is enabled, you must manually enable the *Profile* reference selector to select each of the six profiles.
4. Once all six circular entities are selected as profiles, activate the *Path* field and select the 3D spline curve (imported in an earlier task) as the Path reference.

5. Complete the feature. The model displays as shown in Figure 2–51.

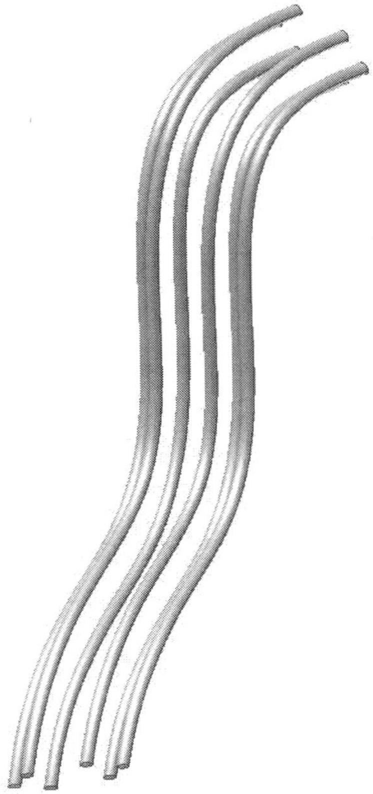

Figure 2–51

6. Save the model and close the window.

End of practice

Practice 2c
Bending Model Geometry

Practice Objective

- Create multiple bends in model geometry using the Bend Part option.

In this practice, you will open a part file that has been provided for you (shown on the left in Figure 2–52), create a sketch to define multiple bend lines, and then bend the model's geometry. The final bent part model is shown on the right in Figure 2–52.

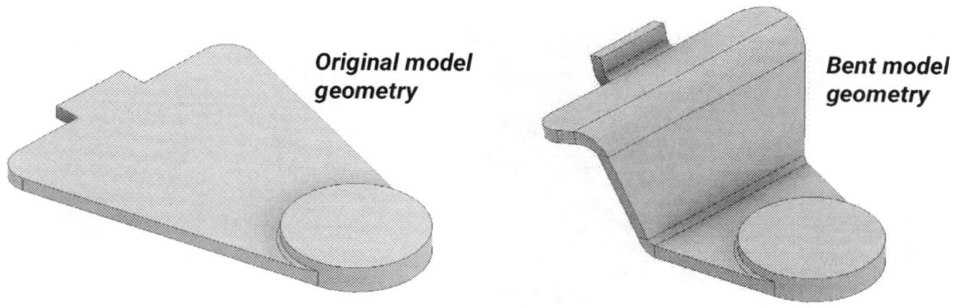

Figure 2–52

Task 1: Create a sketch to define bend lines.

1. Open **bend.ipt** and create a new sketch on the large flat top face (not the circular face).
2. Sketch and constrain the entities shown in Figure 2–53.

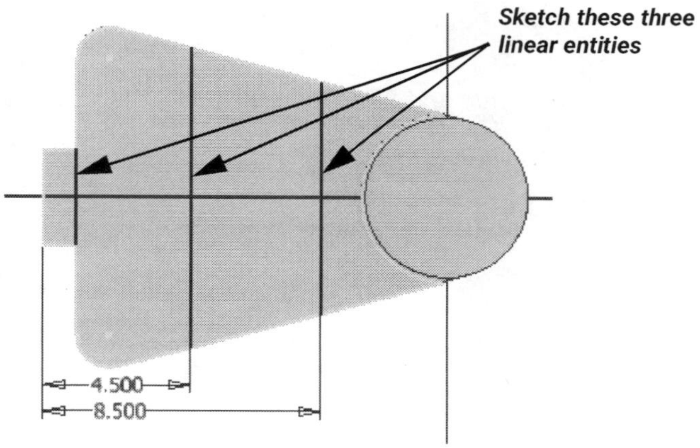

Figure 2–53

3. Finish the sketch.

4. In the Model browser, right-click on the new sketch and clear the **Dimension Visibility** option to simplify the display.

Task 2: Bend the part geometry.

1. In the *3D Model* tab>expanded Modify panel, click  (Bend Part). The Properties panel opens, as shown in Figure 2–54.

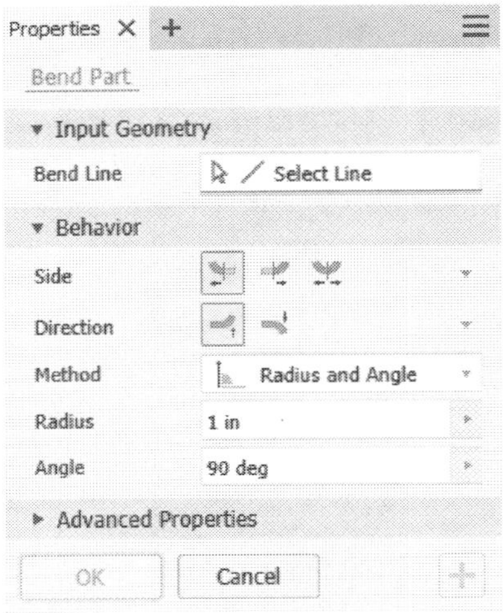

Figure 2–54

2. In the *Input Geometry* area, select the sketched line that is furthest from the cylindrical extrusion as the *Bend Line* reference. A preview of the bend displays in green.
3. In the *Behavior* area, define the following to fully define the bend size, side, and direction.
   - Ensure the **Radius and Angle** method is selected. Enter **0.25 in** and **90 deg** as the *Radius* and *Angle* values, respectively.
   - Toggle between the various *Side* and *Direction* buttons until the bend previews as shown in Figure 2–55.

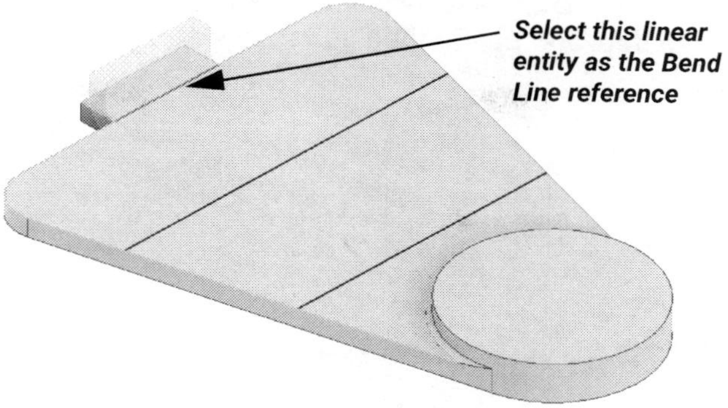

Figure 2–55

4. Click **OK**.
5. Review the Model Browser and notice that the sketch is now consumed in the Bend Part1 feature. Expand it in the Model browser, right-click the sketch name, and select **Share Sketch**. This is required in order to select the other sketched lines as bend line references.

   Note: *As an alternative to sharing the sketch, you could have created them all as separate sketches.*

6. Begin the creation of a second Bend Part feature. For this feature, select the next furthest sketched line from the cylinder. Use the **Radius and Angle** method and attempt to flip the bend downwards. Note how with the 0.25 in *Radius* value that was previously used, the bend cannot be created in this direction. Enter **1.0 in** as the new *Radius* value and maintain **90 deg** as the *Angle* value. The preview should display as shown in Figure 2–56 (FRONT view).

Figure 2–56

7. Do not click **OK**. Click (Apply) to continue creating the third Bend Part feature.

   Note: *You were unable to use (Apply) after the first bend because the sketch was immediately hidden. If the bend lines were sketched on separate sketches, it could have been used.*

8. Select the final sketched bend line and define the *Behavior* settings so that the *Radius* is **0.25 in**, the *Angle* is **75 deg**, and the final bend appears as shown in the preview in Figure 2–57.

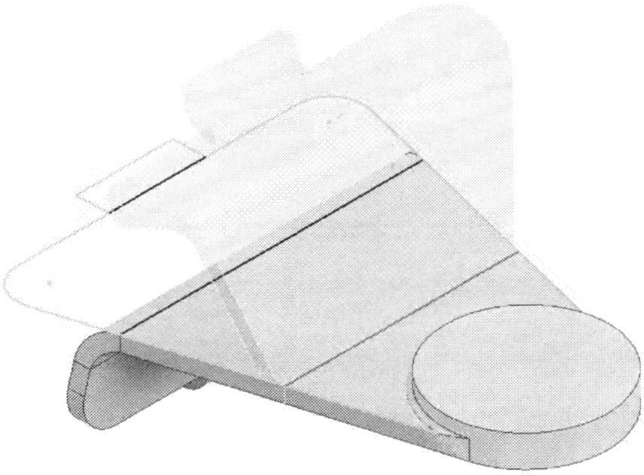

Figure 2–57

9. Prior to clicking **OK**, note how the sketch plane for the bend lines remains on what was the top face, regardless of the bends that are added. For this reason, it is important that your sketch lines are on the face that is being bent. In our example, you could not have selected the lines in the reverse order. You would have had to re-sketch on each plane after the bend.

10. Click **OK** to complete the feature. Clear the visibility of the sketch. The final bent model should appear similar to that shown in Figure 2–58.

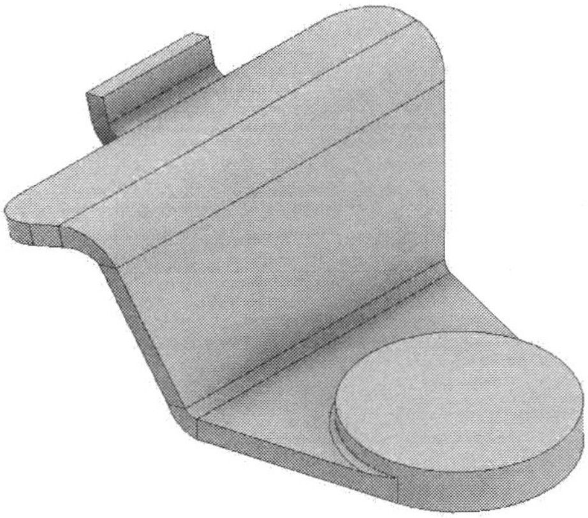

Figure 2–58

11. Save and close the file.

End of practice

Practice 2d
Unwrapping Model Geometry

Practice Objective

- Unwrap model geometry using the Unwrap option.

In this practice, you will open a part file that has been provided for you (shown on the left in Figure 2–59) and then add an Unwrap feature to it to flatten all of the model's geometry. The final flattened surface that will be generated is shown on the right in Figure 2–59.

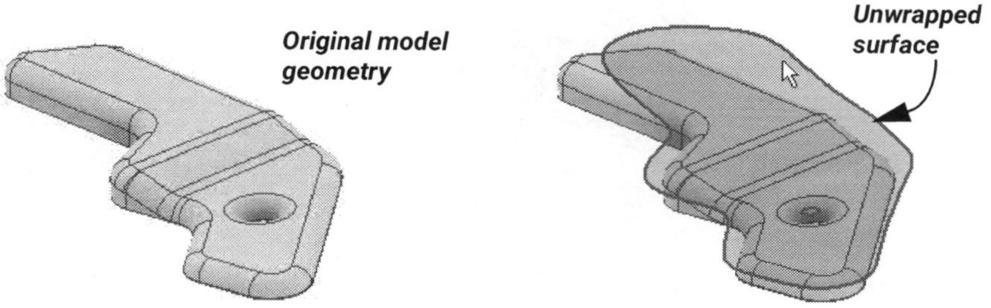

Figure 2–59

Task 1: Unwrap all geometry in the model.

1. Open **Unwrap.ipt**.

2. In the *3D Model* tab>Create panel, click  (Unwrap). The Properties panel opens, similar to that shown in Figure 2–60.

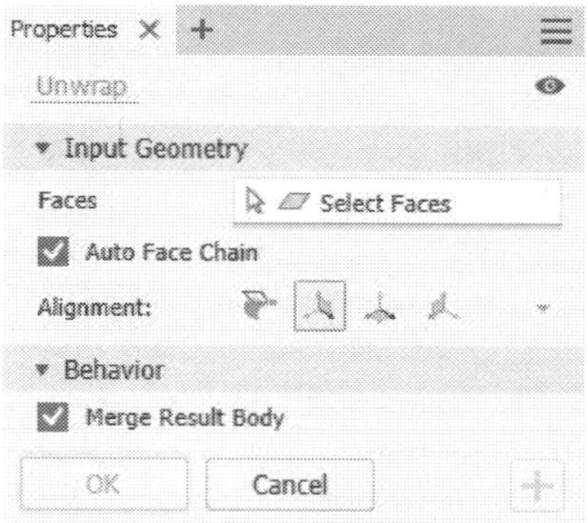

Figure 2–60

3. Ensure that the **Auto Face Chain** option is selected; if not, select it. This enables you to select a single face and all adjacent faces will automatically be selected.
4. With the *Faces* field activated, select the face shown in Figure 2–61 as the face to be unwrapped. Ensure that you select in the location shown. This selection location defines the default alignment reference.

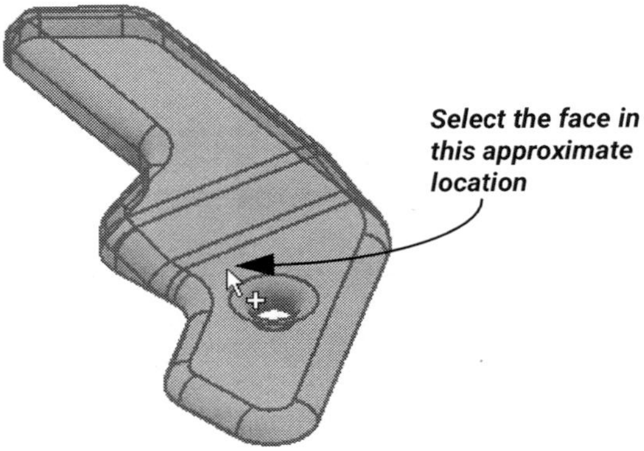

Figure 2–61

5. Once the face is selected, a preview of the flattened face displays on the model, similar to that shown in Figure 2–62. The location of the unwrapped surface is based on the default Alignment settings.

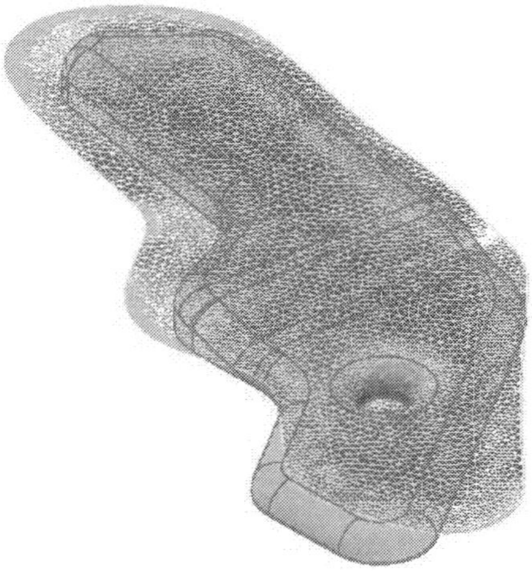

Figure 2–62

6. Select the (Align to Model) *Alignment* option, if not already set. This will place the unwrapped surface on the same face that was selected for flattening.

7. The alignment vertex is assigned by default based on the selection location you made when defining the face to unwrap. This may already be assigned properly based on your initial selection; however, to reset it, activate the field and click ⊗ to delete the default vertex. Select a new vertex on the model geometry that is being unwrapped, as shown in Figure 2–63.

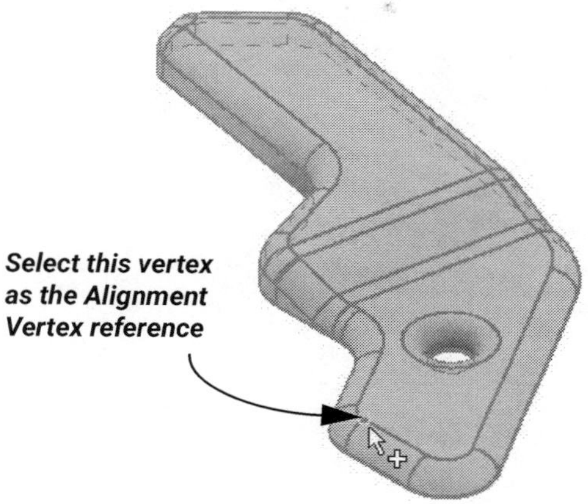

Figure 2–63

8. Enable the **Merge Result Body** option in the *Behavior* area, if not already enabled. This will generate the resulting surface as a single merged surface.
9. Review the previewed surface mesh and heat map, as shown in Figure 2–64. The color gradient on the surface defines areas of low/high deformation and tension. Blue is low and any red identifies areas of high deformation and tension. The yellow lines identify edges.

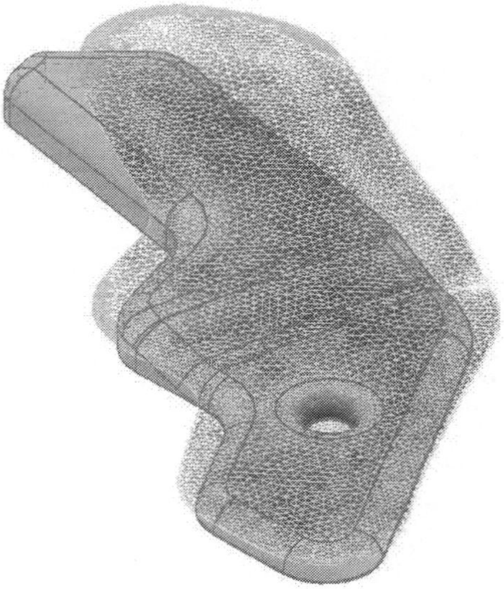

Figure 2–64

10. Click **OK** to create the surface. The model and Model browser appear as shown in Figure 2–65.

    Note: To review the deformation/heat map again, you will have to edit the surface to return to the Properties panel.

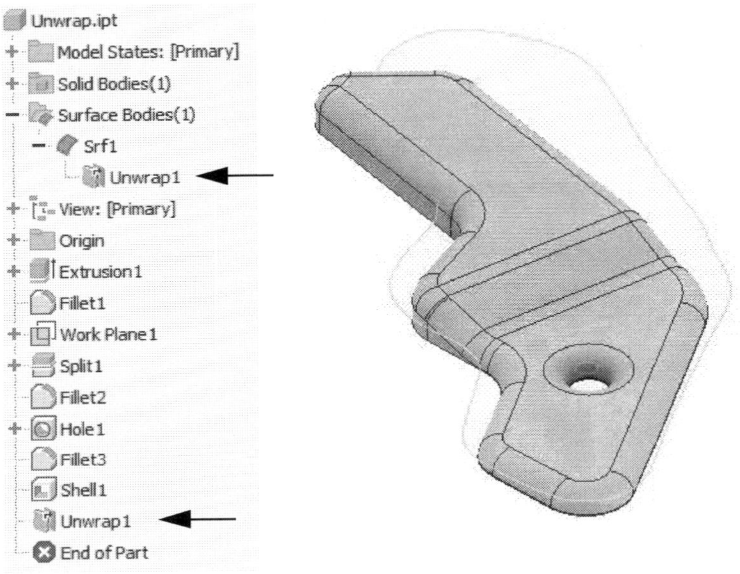

Figure 2–65

11. Expand the **View** node. A new view representation called **Unwrap1 Isolated** has been automatically created.
12. Double-click on this new design view. The unwrapped surface is displayed on its own. This can be used to create a drawing view of only the surface.
13. Activate the **Primary** view before continuing.

Task 2: Use the unwrapped surface to create geometry.

1. In the expanded Modify panel, click  (Move Bodies).
2. Select the new surface body and move it **2 in** in the *Y Offset* direction. This enables you to better view the surface and not have it interfere with the original geometry.
3. Create a new sketch on the unwrapped surface.

4. Project all of the exterior edges of the surface into the sketch. Figure 2–66 shows the sketch with the constraints displayed to help identify the edges. Complete the sketch.

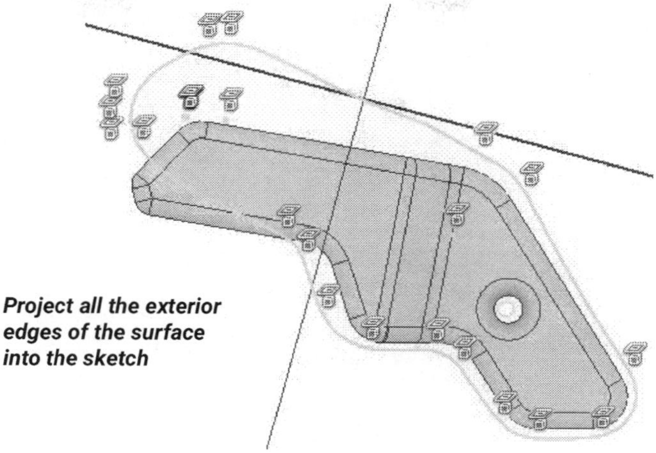

Figure 2–66

5. Begin the creation of a new Extrude feature. The new sketch profile is selected by default.

6. In the Properties panel, click  (New Solid) to create this geometry as a separate body in the model. Extrude the geometry **0.075 in** to create the original cut sheet for the geometry prior to it being bent. The model appears as shown in Figure 2–67. Additional edits can be made to the surface to extend/scale it, as needed.

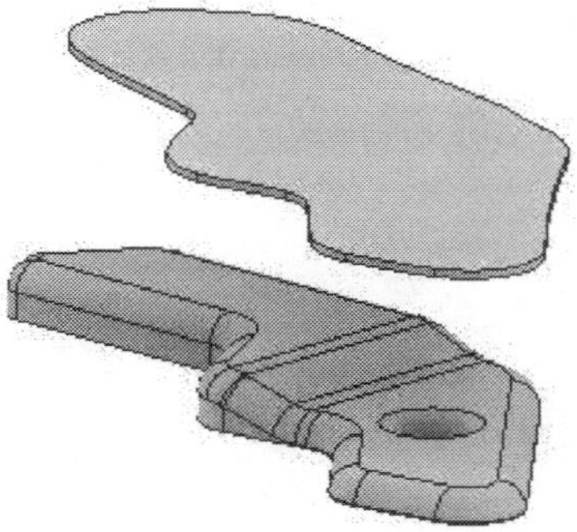

Figure 2–67

7. Save the model and close the window.

   Note: *A model state can be created to represent the cut sheet so that it can be documented on its own. Model states are discussed in the Part Model States topic and Multi-body design is discussed further in the Multi-body Design topic.*

End of practice

Chapter Review Questions

1. Which of the following correctly describes the difference between a 3D sketch and a 2D sketch? (Select all that apply.)
    a. In a 3D sketch there is no sketch plane.
    b. In a 3D sketch you use the Fillet command to add a bend between two linear entities.
    c. In a 3D sketch you have access to all of the same sketching constraints as those available in a 2D sketch.
    d. In a 3D sketch you can import points as can be done in a 2D sketch.

2. Which of the following describes how the **Include Geometry** option can be used in a 3D sketch?
    a. It enables you to copy sketched entities in a 3D sketch.
    b. It provides access to geometry creation options for creating 3D geometry using the 3D sketched entities.
    c. It enables you to reference existing entities in a model in a 3D sketch.
    d. It enables you to constrain entities in a 3D sketch.

3. Which 3D sketch tool can be used to create a curved entity that is defined by entering a formula for the X, Y, and Z axes?
    a. Interpolation Spline
    b. Control Vertex Spline
    c. Equation Curve
    d. Bend

4. You can create a 3D sketch curve from the intersection of two surfaces, work planes, or parts.
    a. True
    b. False

5. What are the three ways that imported point data can be brought into a 3D sketch? (Select all that apply.)
    a. Points only
    b. Points with arcs connecting the points
    c. Points with lines connecting the points
    d. Points with a spline connecting the points

6. Which 3D sketch tool was used to create the entity shown in Figure 2–68?

Figure 2–68

    a. Equation Curve
    b. Helical Curve
    c. Arc
    d. Control Vertex Spline
    e. Interpolation Spline

7. Only the endpoints of a spline can be dimensioned in a sketch.
    a. True
    b. False

8. If a handlebar displays on a spline point, which type of spline was created?
    a. Control Vertex Spline
    b. Interpolation Spline

9. During the creation of a Bend Part feature, you can create the sketched line that will be used to bend the model.

a. True

b. False

10. Which of the following statements are true regarding the Unwrap feature? (Select all that apply.)

a. The blue areas on the heat/tension map identify areas of high tension.

b. Once the selected face is unwrapped, you can only view the heat/tension map by editing the Unwrap feature.

c. The generated surface can be further edited using standard surfacing and modeling tools.

d. A design view must be manually created to represent the new surface in a drawing view.

Command Summary

Button	Command	Location
N/A	**3D Move/ Rotate (3D Sketch)**	• **Context menu:** In the graphics window
	**Arc Center Point (3D Sketch)**	• **Ribbon:** *3D Sketch* tab>Draw panel
	**Arc Three Point (3D Sketch)**	• **Ribbon:** *3D Sketch* tab>Draw panel • **Context menu:** In the graphics window
	**Bend (3D Sketch)**	• **Ribbon:** *3D Sketch* tab>Draw panel • **Context menu:** In the graphics window
	**Bend Part**	• **Ribbon:** *3D Model* tab>expanded Modify panel
	**Create 3D Sketch**	• **Ribbon:** *3D Model* tab>Sketch panel
N/A	**Delete (3D Sketch entity)**	• **Context menu:** In the graphics window
N/A	**Edit 3D Sketch (3D Sketch)**	• **Context menu:** In Model browser • **Context menu:** In the graphics window
	**Equation Curve (3D Sketch)**	• **Ribbon:** *3D Sketch* tab>Draw panel
	**Helical Curve (3D Sketch)**	• **Ribbon:** *3D Sketch* tab>Draw panel • **Context menu:** In the graphics window
	**Include Geometry (3D Sketch)**	• **Ribbon:** *3D Sketch* tab>Draw panel • **Context menu:** In the graphics window
	**Intersection Curve (3D Sketch)**	• **Ribbon:** *3D Sketch* tab>Draw panel
	**Line (3D Sketch)**	• **Ribbon:** *3D Sketch* tab>Draw panel • **Context menu:** In the graphics window
	**Mirror (3D Sketch)**	• **Ribbon:** *3D Sketch* tab>Pattern panel
	**Point (3D Sketch)**	• **Ribbon:** *3D Sketch* tab>Draw panel
	**Points (3D Sketch)**	• **Ribbon:** *3D Sketch* tab>Insert panel
	**Project to Surface (3D Sketch)**	• **Ribbon:** *3D Sketch* tab>Draw panel

Button	Command	Location
N/A	**Properties (3D Sketch)**	• **Ribbon:** *3D Sketch* tab>Format panel • **Context menu:** In the graphics window
	**Silhouette Curve (3D Sketch)**	• **Ribbon:** *3D Sketch* tab>Draw panel
	**Spline Control Vertex**	• **Ribbon:** *Sketch* tab>Create panel • **Ribbon:** *3D Sketch* tab>Draw panel
	**Spline Interpolation**	• **Ribbon:** *Sketch* tab>Create panel • **Ribbon:** *3D Sketch* tab>Draw panel
	**Unwrap**	• **Ribbon:** *3D Model* tab>Create panel

Chapter 3

Multi-Body Part Modeling

Top-down design is an engineering CAD methodology used in the Autodesk® Inventor® software where you create single part files in the context of an assembly model. Using the multi-body part modeling technique, the top-down design approach has been made even easier. Multi-body modeling is also used for the creation of complex plastic or cast parts that require very intricate geometry.

Learning Objectives

- Create multiple solid bodies in a single part model to ease feature creation.
- Add features to existing solid bodies instead of creating a new solid body for each feature.
- Manipulate existing solid bodies to add or remove features, move the position of bodies, split bodies, or combine multiple bodies into one body.
- Control the visibility, display settings, and properties of individual solid bodies in a model.

3.1 Multi-Body Part Modeling

Multi-body part files enable you to create your entire assembly design in the Part environment using part modeling feature commands. This technique is commonly used when creating complex plastic or cast parts that require very intricate geometry. The design is arranged into separate bodies in the single part file. Figure 3–1 shows a model that has two solid bodies (listed in the **Solid Bodies** node). **Solid2** is selected and highlighted on the model. These separate bodies can then be extracted into individual parts for a new assembly.

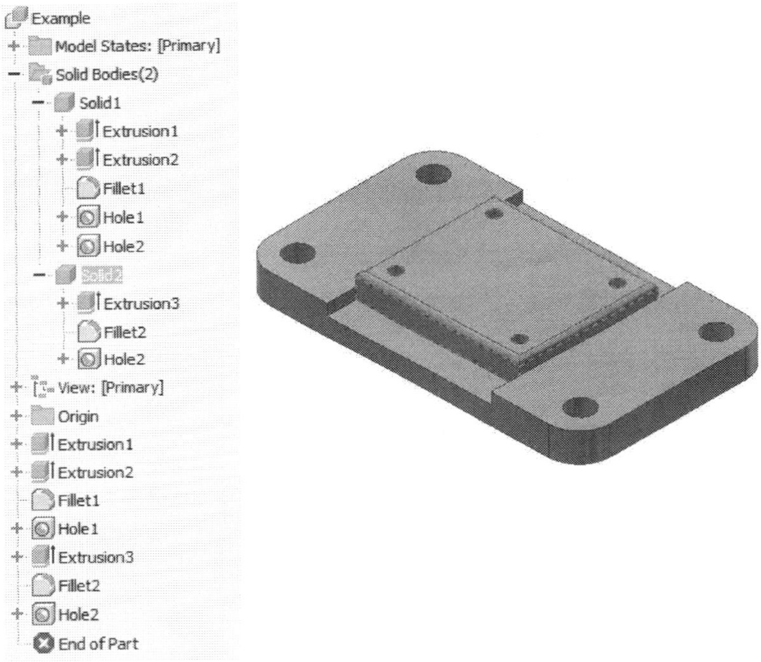

Figure 3–1

The advantages of building a part file using multi-bodies include the following:

- Top-down design is streamlined. You do not set up an initial complex file and directory structure to design in the context of a top-level assembly. The entire design resides in a single file, helping you design faster and accurately capture the model's design intent. Bodies are extracted to create parts.
- A complex part file can be better organized using separate bodies with respect to their function or position in the model.
- Relationships between bodies can be easily set up and broken.
- You can control the visibility of bodies as a group rather than at the individual feature level.

- This method is useful for plastic part design, where interior components for a predefined shape can be designed in context and then extracted.

  Note: *Multi-body assembly modeling is introduced in this learning guide to explain the modeling procedure; however, the specifics on using this technique for top-down design is taught in the Autodesk Inventor Advanced Assembly Modeling course.*

Creating the First Solid Body

With the creation of the first feature in any part file, the first solid body is automatically created. Once the base feature is created, the *Solid Bodies* folder displays in the Model browser and the first solid body is added to the folder.

Creating Additional Solid Bodies

Once the first solid body is added to the model, each additional feature is automatically applied to it, unless a new feature is explicitly set to be created as a new solid body. To create the new solid body, create its feature as you normally would; however, click (New Solid) in the feature creation dialog box or Properties panel. Once selected, a second body is added to the model.

Assigning Features to Solid Bodies

Once two or more solid bodies are in a model, the selection of the placement/sketch planes are important to correctly locate the new feature in the required solid body. Consider the following:

- When creating a sketched feature, it is by default added to the same solid body as that of the sketching plane. For features to be added to a different solid body, click in the *Solids* field of the feature dialog box or Properties panel and then select the required solid body.
- When creating a pick-and-place feature, it is by default added to the same solid body as the placement references. In the case of a fillet, for example, it is added to the same solid body as the parent feature of the placement edge. If multiple edges are selected that belong to multiple solid bodies, the feature is added to each solid body.
- When creating a sketch-based or pick-and-place feature, it is only extended through its parent solid body, even if the (Through All) distance option is selected. For features to interact with another solid body, click in the *Solids* field of the feature dialog box or Properties panel and then select additional solid bodies to be included.

Manipulating Solid Bodies

Once multiple solid bodies exist in the model, you can further manipulate them. You can redefine them as part of another solid body, move them, split them, and combine them.

> ***Note:*** *The Autodesk Inventor Advanced Assembly Modeling course discusses further manipulation options that enable you to insert additional bodies from other models, or use them to create separate parts and assemblies.*

Redefining/Removing Features in Solid Bodies

Once a feature is created and assigned to a solid body, you can re-assign it to another solid body or remove a solid body from interacting with the feature. To do so, redefine the original feature and click in the *Solids* field to activate it. You can select the new solid to apply it to or, if you want to remove a solid body from the initial selection set, hold <Ctrl> and select the solid body to remove.

Moving Bodies

You might need to move the various bodies in a multi-body part.

How To: Move a Solid Body

1. In the *3D Model* tab>expanded Modify panel, click (Move Bodies). The Move Bodies dialog box opens.
2. Select the solid bodies to move. If you need to select multiple bodies, you must click (Bodies) again after selecting the first body in order to select additional bodies.
3. Select a move operation using the drop-down list in the Move Bodies dialog box, as shown in Figure 3–2.

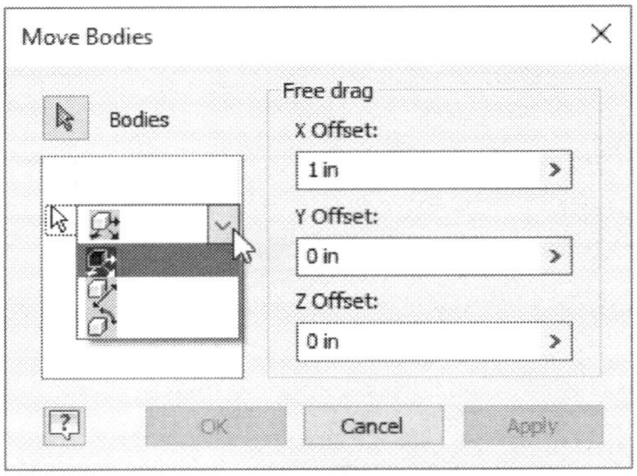

Figure 3–2

Each icon in the list enables you to move the body, as follows:

-  (Free drag): Enables you to enter a precise X, Y, or Z offset value, or drag the preview in any direction.
-  (Move along ray): Enables you to enter a precise offset value, or drag the preview offset from a selected reference.
-  (Rotate about line): Enables you to enter a precise rotational angle value, or drag the preview around a selected axis.

4. Depending on the move operation selected, enter values and select references using the right side of the dialog box to define the movement.
5. To define a second move operation, if required, select **Click to add** and select a new move operation, as shown in Figure 3–3.

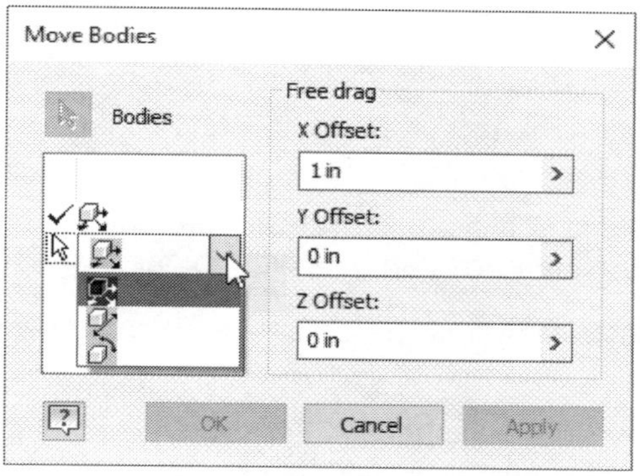

Figure 3–3

6. Continue to add move operations as required for the selected body.
7. Click **OK** to complete the feature. A Move Body feature is added to the bottom of the Model browser, as well as in each Solid Body that was moved.

Note: *To edit the Move Body feature, right-click on it, and select **Edit feature**.*

Splitting Bodies

You can split a single body so that you can manipulate the resulting bodies independently.

How To: Split a Solid Body

1. In the *3D Model* tab>Modify panel, click (Split). The Properties panel opens as shown in Figure 3–4.

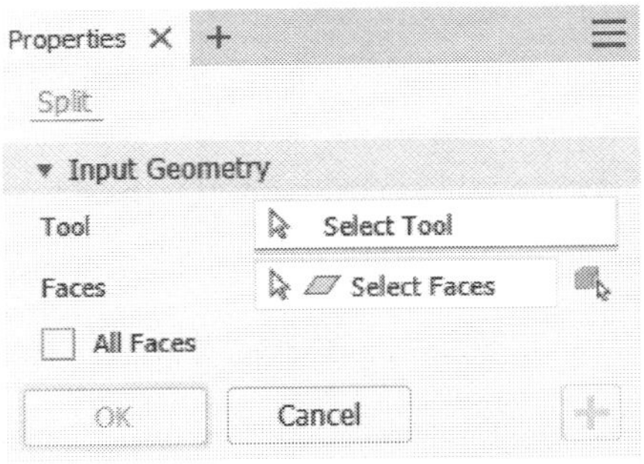

Figure 3–4

2. Select **Split** (default feature name) at the top of the Properties panel to assign a new name for the feature.
3. Ensure that the *Tool* field is active and select the reference geometry that is to define where the split is to occur. This reference can be a work plane, surface, or sketch geometry.

   Note: *The split's Tool reference must completely intersect the entire body being split.*

4. Toggle the button to enable solid selection, as shown in Figure 3–5. The faces/solid setting will persist in the Properties panel the next time the Split command is started.

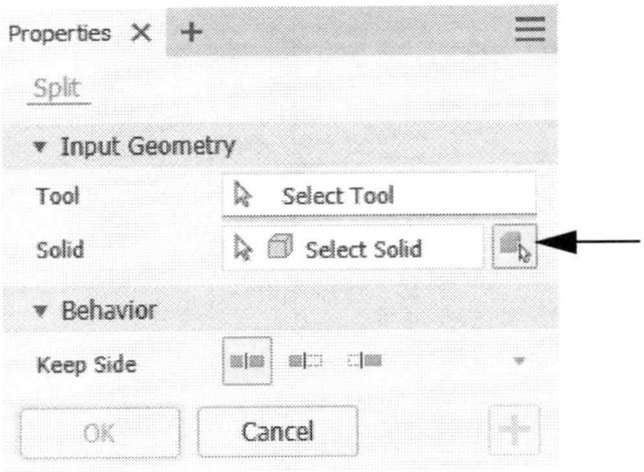

Figure 3–5

5. Ensure that the *Solid* field is active and select the solid to be split.
   - If there are multiple solids in the model, you must explicitly select the solid(s) to be split, otherwise the solid is automatically selected.

6. When splitting a solid, the Properties panel provides additional settings in the *Behavior* area. This enables you to use the split to remove geometry from the model. By default, both sides of the split are kept (); however, you can select or to remove one side of the split or the other. When one of these side options are selected, a red arrow appears on the model indicating the side that will be removed. Toggle these options as needed to remove the required side.
7. Click **OK**, right-click and select **OK (Enter)**, or press <Enter> to complete the split. To continue creating additional split features without closing the panel, click (Apply) and define the references as needed. Once all splits have been completed, click **OK**.

Hint: Splitting Using Multiple Entities in the Same Sketch

If multiple entities exist in a single sketch and each entity is to be used to create a separate split operation, consider enabling the **Keep sketch visible on (+)** option in the (Advanced Settings Menu). You can then use (Apply) to continue selecting entities without the sketch visibility being turned off, as is done when the feature is completed.

Combining Bodies

If you created two solid bodies separately during an initial design, you may decide later that they should be combined. Using the **Combine** command, you can add or remove material based on selected bodies. The **Combine** command is only available when working with solid bodies.

How To: Combine Features

1. In the *3D Model* tab>Modify panel, click (Combine). The Properties panel opens, as shown in Figure 3–6.

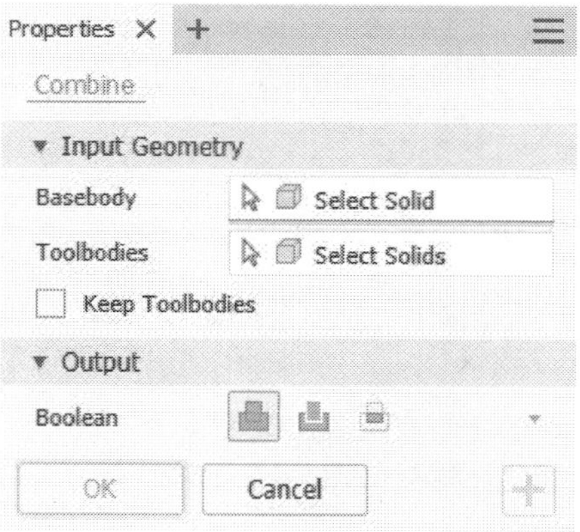

Figure 3–6

2. Select **Combine** (default feature name) at the top of the Properties panel to assign a name for the feature.
3. The *Basebody* field should be active by default. If not, select in the field to activate it and select the solid body to use as the basebody reference. The basebody is the solid body that will be kept after the operation.
4. Select in the *Toolbodies* field to activate it. Select the solid body to use as the toolbody reference. The toolbody is the solid body or bodies that will be combined with the basebody.

   Note: *You can only select one Basebody, but you can select multiple Toolbodies, if required.*

5. To maintain the toolbody as a solid body after the operation, select **Keep Toolbodies**. If you select this option, the toolbody becomes invisible. Its visibility can be enabled to manipulate or use it, as required.
6. In the *Output* area, select an operation to perform on the basebody. The available operations include joining ( ), cutting ( ), and intersecting ( ) the toolbody from the base.
7. Click **OK** to complete the feature. Completed Combine features are listed in the Model browser list and in the solid body node that was used as the basebody reference. To continue combining bodies without closing the panel, click + (Apply) and define the references as needed to create an additional feature.

Solid Body Display

Once multiple solid bodies exist in a model, you may want to individually control the visibility of various solid bodies. To control the visibility of a solid body, right-click on the solid body and enable or disable the **Visibility** option.

A representation of the model can be saved using a design view. This enables you to capture the visibility settings of the solid bodies for reuse at a later time without having to enable and disable visibility. A design view can also store other display options such as section view settings and colors. Design views can also be used to create drawing views.

How To: Save a Solid Body Display Configuration

1. Right-click on the *View* folder and select **New**. By default, the model exists as a Primary view. When a new view is created it is automatically set to be active.
2. Configure the view display.
3. Select the new view, click again (do not double-click) and enter a descriptive name for the view.

4. To lock the design view, right-click on the view name in the Model browser and select **Lock**. Locking restricts you or others from making changes to the design view representation.

To display an alternate design view, right-click on its name in the Model browser and select **Activate**. Alternatively, you can double-click on its name.

Solid Body Properties

To access the properties for a solid body, right-click on the solid body name and select **Properties**. The Body Properties dialog box opens as shown in Figure 3–7.

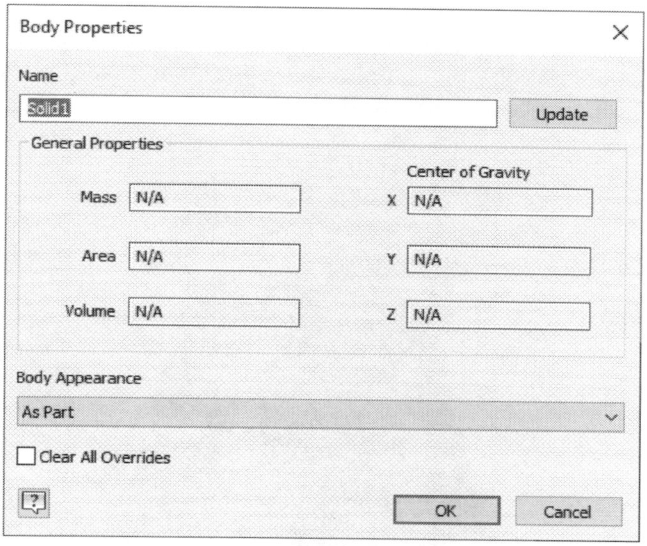

Figure 3–7

Using the Body Properties dialog box, you can do the following:

- Rename the solid body. You can also rename a solid body directly in the Model browser.
- Update and provide the general properties for the solid body.
- Set a color style for the solid body.
- Use the **Clear All Overrides** option to remove color overrides from individual faces contained in the solid body.

Practice 3a
Complex Part Design

Practice Objectives

- Create multiple solid bodies in a single part model to facilitate feature creation.
- Add features to existing solid bodies instead of creating a new solid body for each feature.
- Combine multiple solid toolbodies into the selected base body.

In this practice, you learn how using multi-body modeling to create a part can help you achieve complex results, without dealing with complex work arounds or lengthy Work Feature creation. The completed model is shown in Figure 3–8.

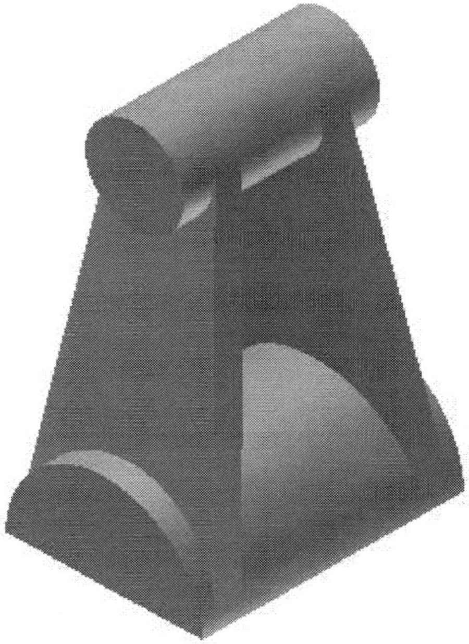

Figure 3–8

Task 1: Create an extrusion.

1. Start a new part model using the **Standard (in).ipt** template.
2. Create the sketch shown in Figure 3–9 on the XY plane. Constrain the half circle to the origin of the part file.

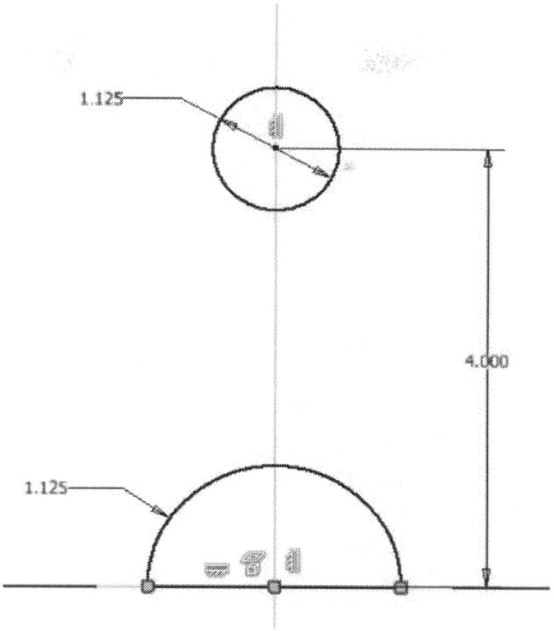

Figure 3–9

Note: *Consider renaming parameters throughout this practice to create a more dynamic and stable model that will be able to accommodate any required design changes.*

3. Extrude the half circle portion of **Sketch1** as the profile and extrude it **3 in** symmetrically, as shown in Figure 3–10. Note that because this is the first solid feature in the model, a new solid is created automatically and the Properties panel does not display Boolean options in the *Output* area.

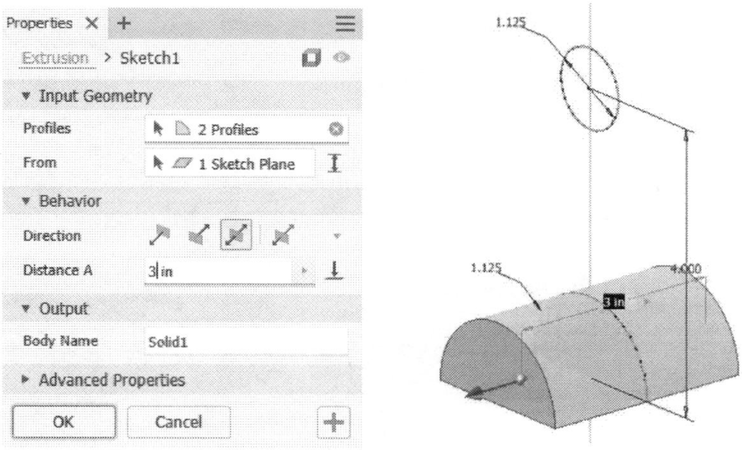

Figure 3–10

4. Review the Model browser. **Extrusion1** displays below the Origin. Expand the **Solid Bodies** node and note that currently only one solid body is in the model, called **Solid1**. Expand **Solid1** and note that **Extrusion1** displays there as well, as shown in Figure 3–11.

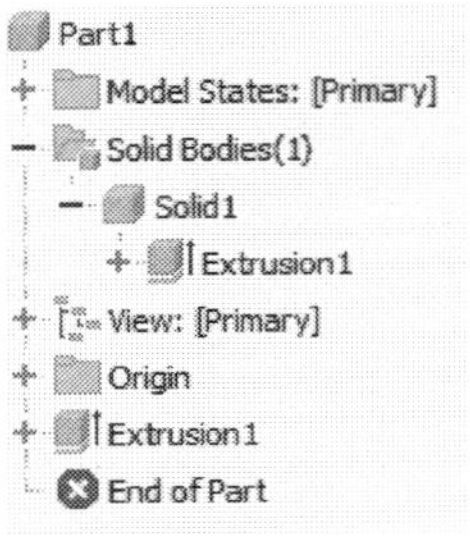

Figure 3–11

Task 2: Create a second solid body.

1. In the Model browser, expand **Extrusion1**, right-click on **Sketch1**, and select **Share Sketch**. Sketch1 is used to create the second solid body so it must be shared. Alternatively, when using the **Share Sketch** command, you can toggle on the visibility of a sketch to reuse it.
2. Extrude the circular portion of **Sketch1** as the profile and extrude it **2.25 in** symmetrically.

   Note that (Join) is selected as the Boolean option because this is the second feature in the model and it defaults as being added as a feature in the first solid body.

3. In the Properties panel, click (New Solid) (as shown in Figure 3–12) to create the feature as a separate solid body.

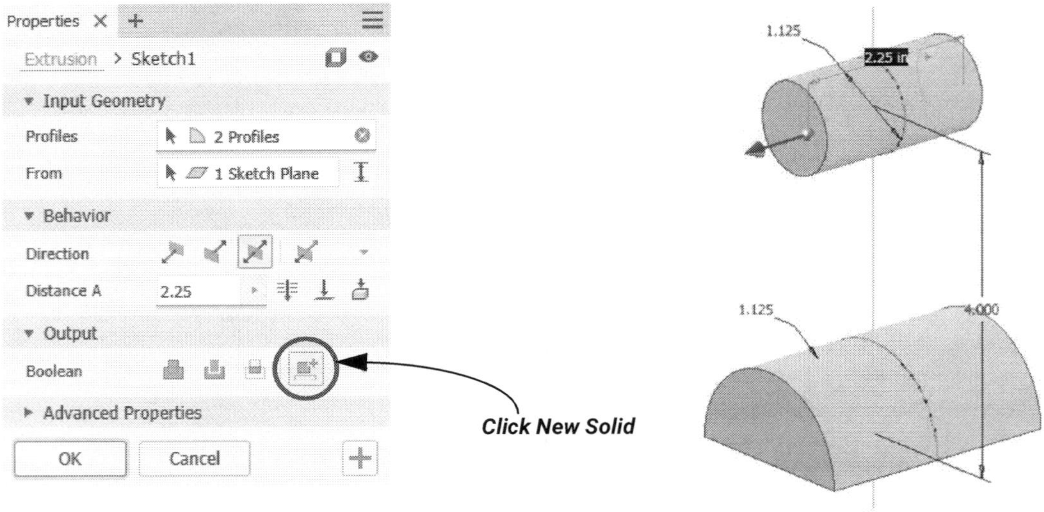

Figure 3–12

4. The *Body Name* field is added to the Properties panel indicating that the new solid will be created as **Solid2**. Maintain this default name.
5. Complete the extrude.
6. For clarity, in the Model browser, right-click on **Sketch1** and clear the **Visibility** option.
7. Review the Model browser. **Extrusion2** has been added after **Extrusion1**. Expand the **Solid Bodies** node and note that two solid bodies are now in the model. **Extrusion1** is a feature of **Solid1**, and **Extrusion2** is in **Solid2**, as shown in Figure 3–13.

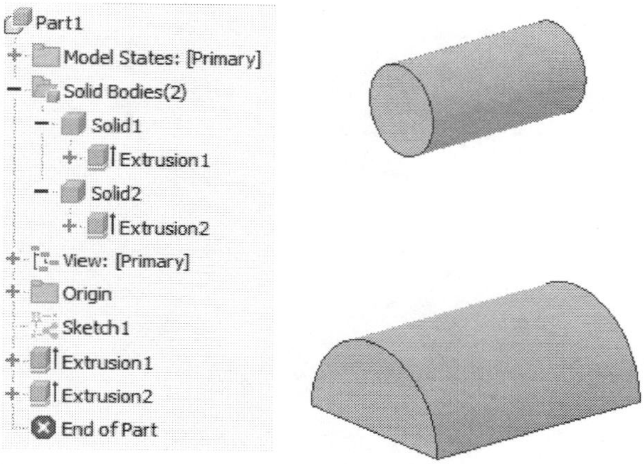

Figure 3–13

Task 3: Create a third solid body.

1. Create a new sketch using the YZ origin plane as the sketching plane.

2. Project the XY origin plane, and the edges of **Solid1** and **Solid2**, as shown in Figure 3–14. Create and constrain the entities and complete the sketch.

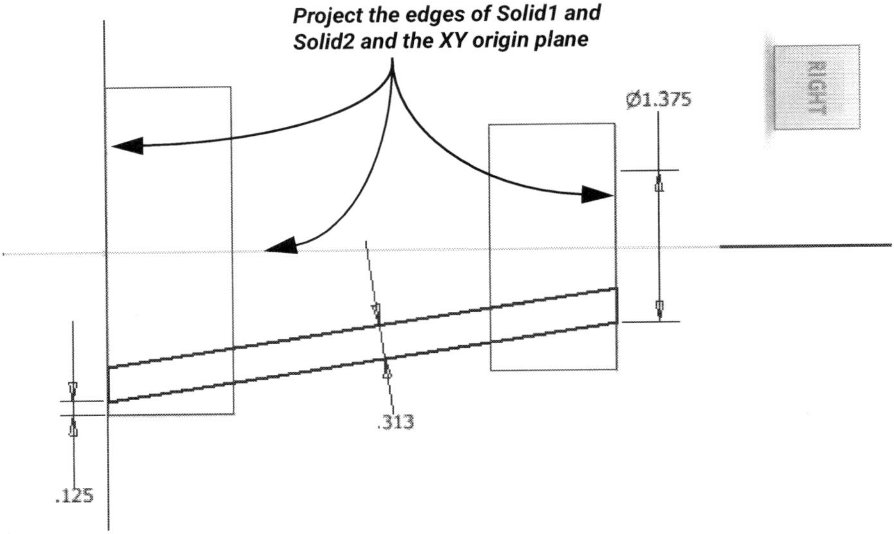

Figure 3–14

3. Extrude the sketch profile, **2.75in** symmetrically, as shown in Figure 3–15. The exact depth of the extrusion is not important as long as it extends past the limits of the other solids.

4. In the Properties panel, click (New Solid), as shown in Figure 3–15, if not already active. This creates the extrude feature as a third solid body.

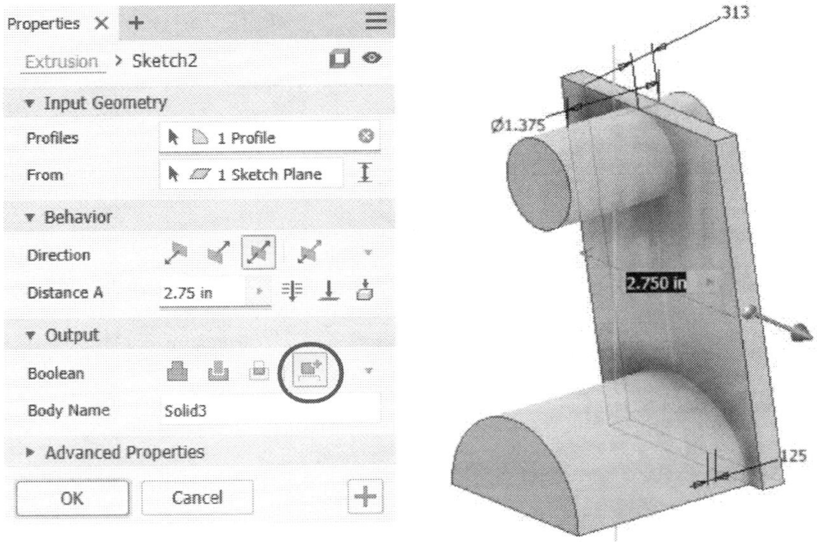

Figure 3–15

5. Complete the extrude.

Task 4: Add a new feature to an existing solid body.

1. Create a new sketch using the XY origin plane as the sketching plane.
2. Project the edge of the circle and the half circle geometry.
3. Create the sketch as shown in Figure 3–16. Use tangent constraints between the four end points of the lines and the projected curves to fully constrain the entities without dimensions.

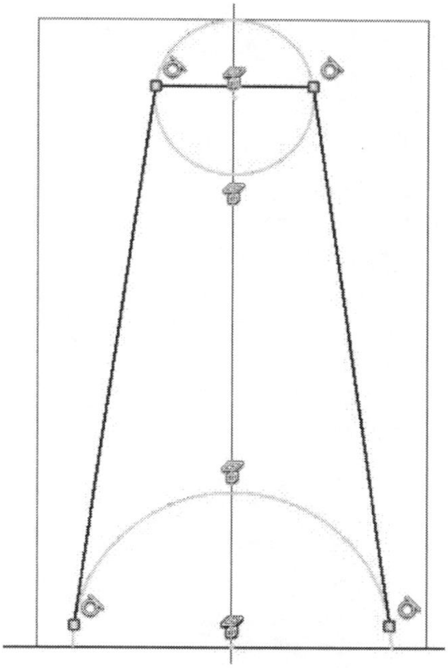

Figure 3–16

4. Extrude the new sketch profile.

5. In the Properties panel, do the following (as shown in Figure 3–17):

   - Select (Intersect) as the *Boolean* option and click in the *Solids* field to activate it. In the Model browser, select **Solid3** to include the new extrusion as part of this solid body.

   - For the *Distance A* type option, select (Through All).

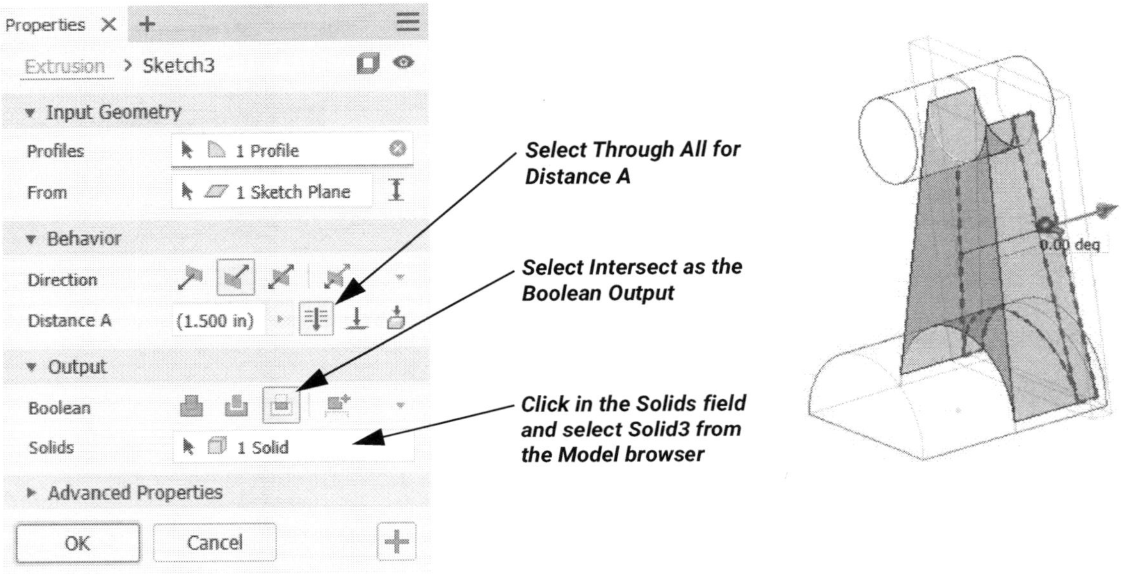

Figure 3–17

6. Complete the extrude. The model displays as shown in Figure 3–18.

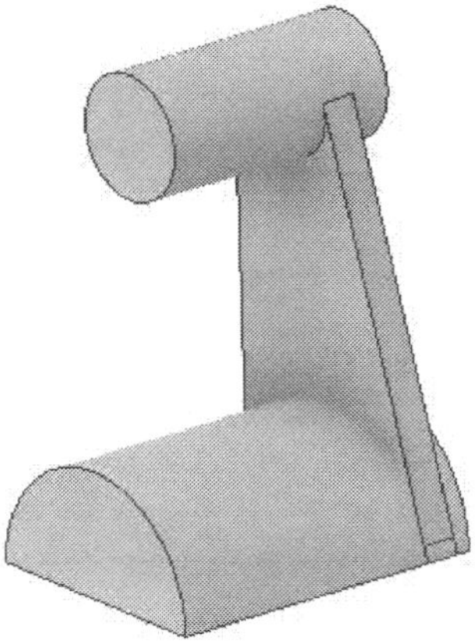

Figure 3–18

Task 5: Mirror a solid body.

1. In the Pattern panel, click (Mirror).
2. In the Mirror dialog box, click (Mirror solids).
3. In the Model browser, select **Solid3** as the solid.
4. Click (Mirror Plane) and select the XY Plane in the Model browser or its option in the dialog box.
5. Complete the mirror. The model displays as shown in Figure 3–19.

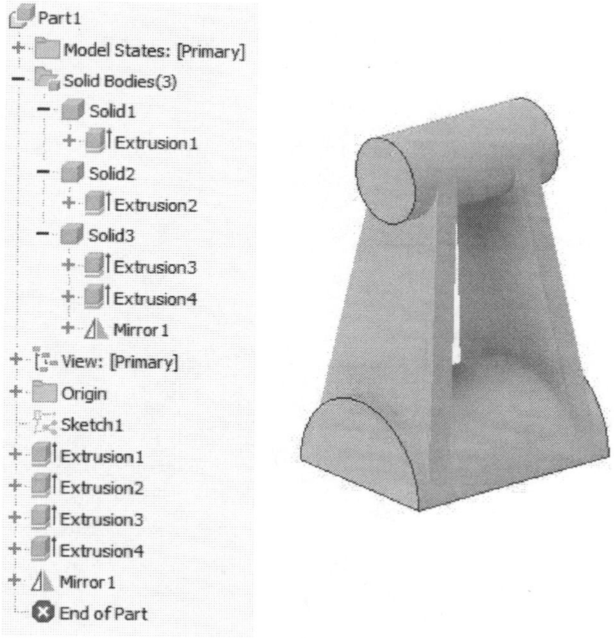

Figure 3–19

Task 6: Combine the solid bodies.

1. In the Modify panel, click (Combine).
2. In the Model browser, select **Solid1** as the Basebody reference. The solid selected as the basebody will be the solid that remains.

3. In the Model browser, select **Solid2** and **Solid3** to add as the Toolbodies references. The Properties panel displays as shown in Figure 3–20.

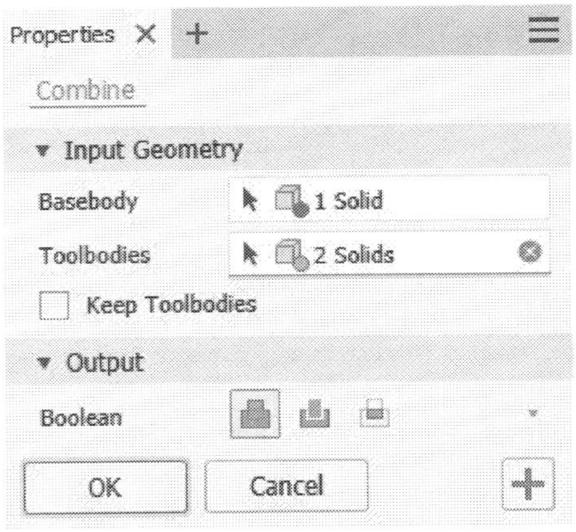

Figure 3–20

4. Click **OK** to complete the combine. The model displays as shown in Figure 3–21.

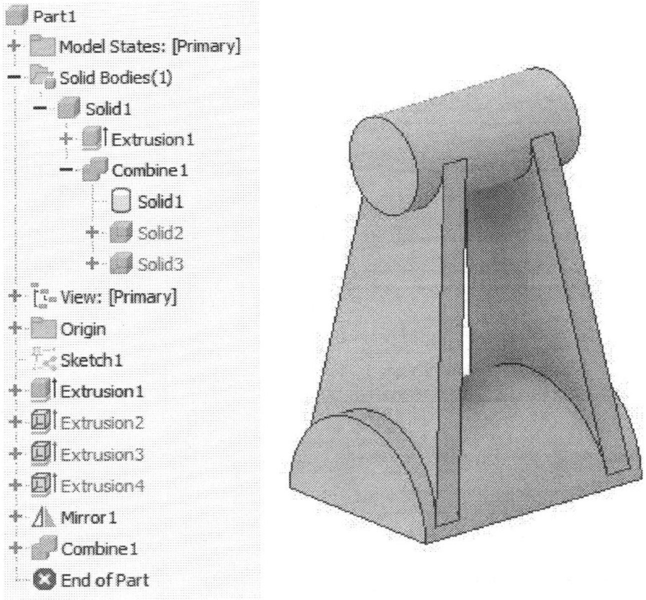

Figure 3–21

The combine tool has created a complex shape that will be easier to fillet and construct from origin planes than the alternative methods of complex plane creation and additional modeling references.

Task 7: (Optional) Complete the model.

1. Complete the model by adding the additional features shown in Figure 3–22. No additional new solids need to be created.

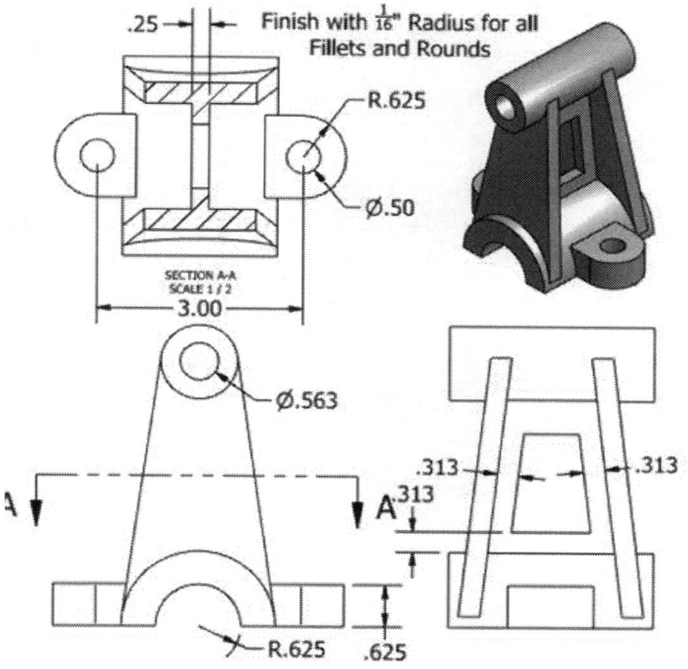

Figure 3–22

2. Save the file as **complex_part.ipt** and close the window.

End of practice

Practice 3b
Multi-Body Part Design

Practice Objectives

- Create features as multiple solid bodies in a single part model to ease feature creation.
- Add features to existing solid bodies instead of creating a new solid body for each feature.

In this practice, you will create a single part file containing two solid bodies. In creating these solid bodies, you will use the commands that are available for multi-body design. You will learn to create multiple bodies in a model, add features to the bodies, and make changes to the bodies. The completed model is shown in Figure 3–23.

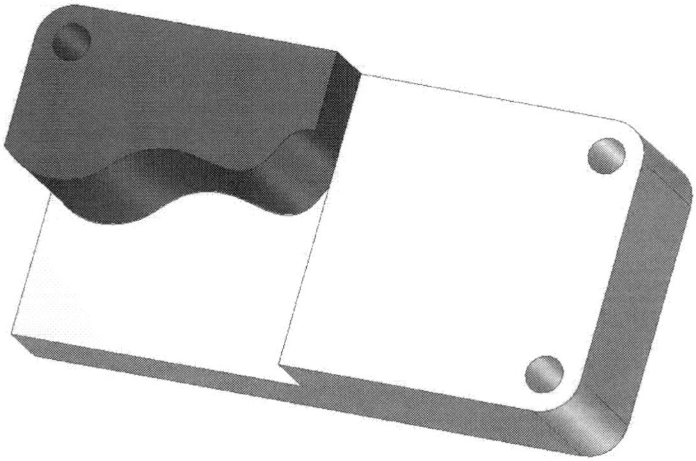

Figure 3–23

Task 1: Create a new model.

1. Start a new part model using the **Standard (in).ipt** template.
2. Create a new sketch on the XY plane.
3. Project the YZ and XZ planes.

4. Sketch a rectangular entity centered on the projected origin planes, as shown in Figure 3–24.

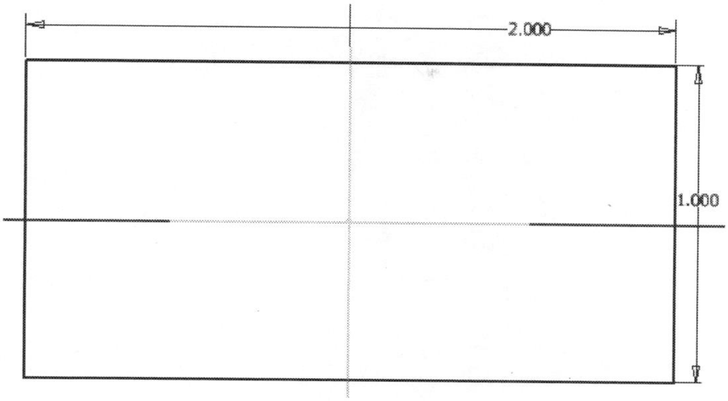

Figure 3–24

5. With the sketch still active, double-click on the 2.000 dimension and enter **width=2in**, as shown in Figure 3–25. Assigning a parameter name to a dimension directly in the Edit Dimension dialog box prevents having to do so in the Parameters dialog box.

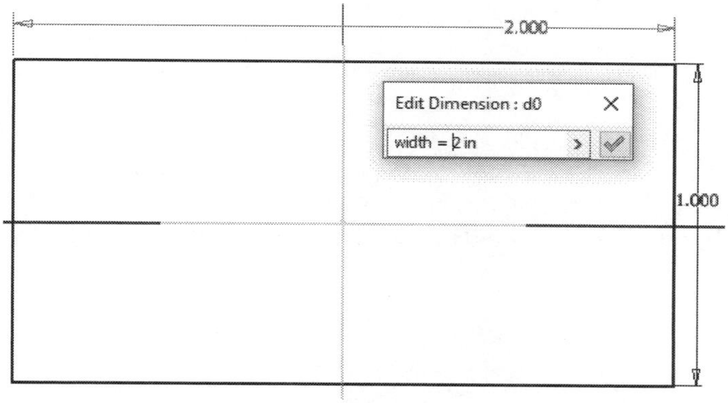

Figure 3–25

6. Double-click on the 1.000 dimension and enter **depth=1in**.
7. Finish the sketch.

8. Extrude the rectangular sketch a distance of 0.5 inches by entering **height=0.5 in** as the *Distance A* value in the Properties panel. The Properties panel displays as shown in Figure 3–26.

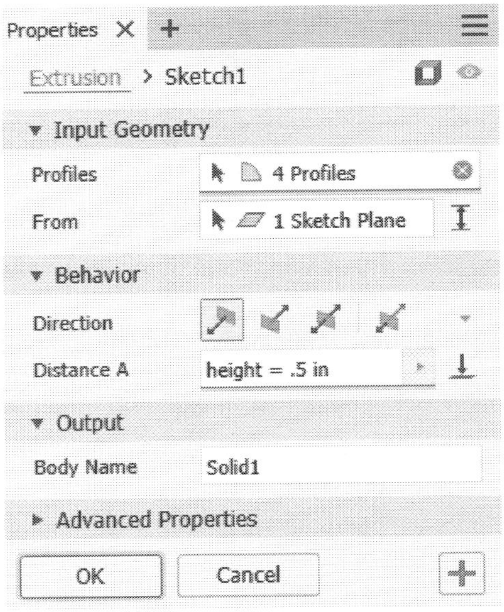

Figure 3–26

9. Complete the extrude.
10. Review the Model browser. **Extrusion1** displays below the Origin, as it is a feature of the part. Expand the **Solid Bodies** node and note that currently, only one solid body is in the model, called **Solid1**. Expand **Solid1** and **Extrusion1** displays there as well, as shown in Figure 3–27.

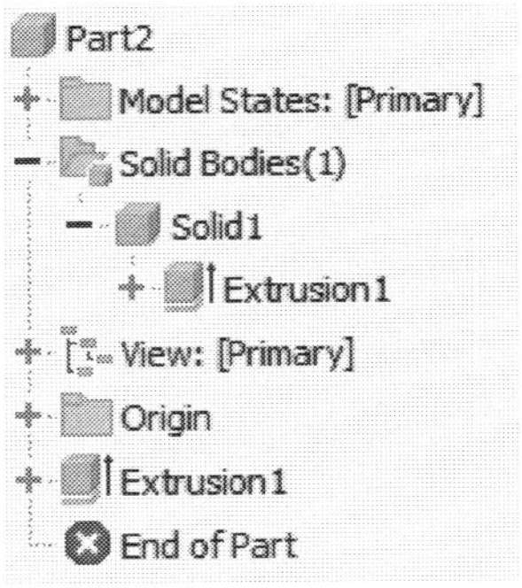

Figure 3–27

Task 2: Create additional features in the model.

1. Create a new sketch on the surface shown in Figure 3–28.
2. Project the YZ plane.
3. Sketch the linear entity shown in Figure 3–28. Align it to the YZ work plane through the center of the model. Project any additional edges to create an enclosed section on the left-hand side of the sketch plane.

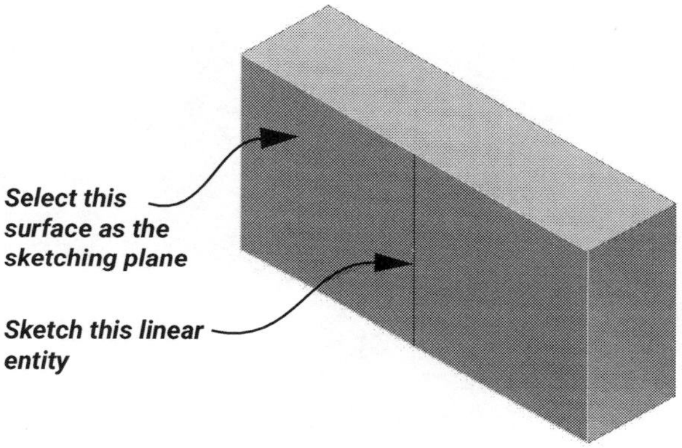

Figure 3–28

4. Finish the sketch.
5. Create an extrude. In the Properties panel, click (Cut) and select the left profile to remove. Note that (New Solid) is not selected in the panel because this is the second feature in the model and it defaults to being a feature in the first solid body.
6. Set the *Distance A* value to **cutdepth=height/2**.
7. Complete the extrude.
8. Add two **.125 in** fillets to the geometry shown in Figure 3–29.

9. Review the Model browser. **Extrusion2** and **Fillet1** have been added after **Extrusion1**. Expand the **Solid Bodies** node. Note that only one solid body, **Solid1**, is in the model, and that **Extrusion2** and **Fillet1** have been added there as well. **Extrusion1**, **Extrusion2**, and **Fillet1** are all features in **Solid1**. The model and the Model browser are shown in Figure 3–29.

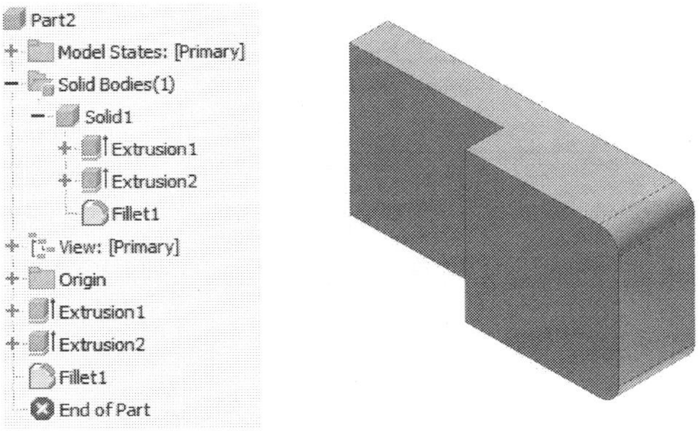

Figure 3–29

Task 3: Review the modified parameter names.

1. In the *Manage* tab>Parameters panel, click f_x (Parameters). The Parameters dialog box opens, as shown in Figure 3–30. The parameter names and equations that were entered during model creation are assigned in the dialog box.

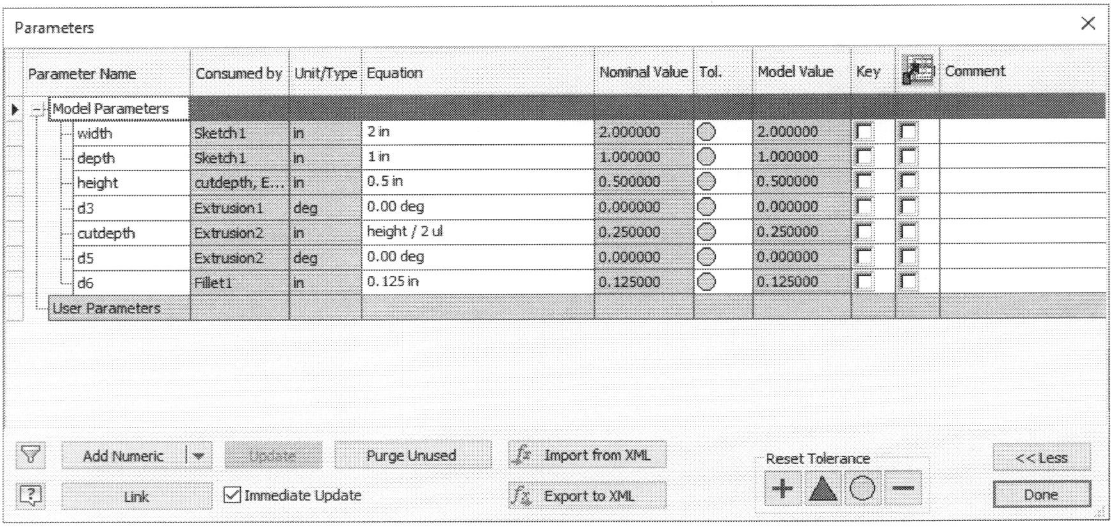

Parameter Name	Consumed by	Unit/Type	Equation	Nominal Value	Tol.	Model Value	Key		Comment
Model Parameters									
width	Sketch1	in	2 in	2.000000		2.000000			
depth	Sketch1	in	1 in	1.000000		1.000000			
height	cutdepth, E...	in	0.5 in	0.500000		0.500000			
d3	Extrusion1	deg	0.00 deg	0.000000		0.000000			
cutdepth	Extrusion2	in	height / 2 ul	0.250000		0.250000			
d5	Extrusion2	deg	0.00 deg	0.000000		0.000000			
d6	Fillet1	in	0.125 in	0.125000		0.125000			
User Parameters									

Figure 3–30

2. Close the Parameters dialog box.

Task 4: Create a second solid body in the model.

1. Create a 2D sketch on the lower surface of the model that was just cut away.
2. Sketch a spline similar to that shown in Figure 3–31. Project the required edges to create a closed sketch above the spline. Ensure that the spline and projected edges are constrained as Coincident.

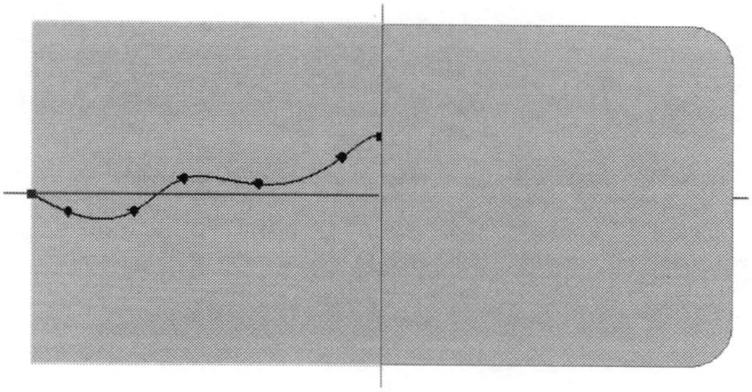

Figure 3–31

3. Once compete, click . Points display on each spline point to enable you to edit the spline in the sketch.
4. Select the points and manipulate the shape of the spline. Do not worry about dimensioning the sketch.
5. Finish the sketch.
6. Create an extrude. Select the upper section of the sketch as the section to extrude.
7. In the Properties panel, click  (New Solid) to create the extrude feature as a separate solid body.
8. Set the *Distance A* value to **height**. This creates a relationship between the two features.
9. Complete the feature.

10. Review the Model browser. **Extrusion3** has been added after **Fillet1**. Expand the **Solid Bodies** node and note that two solid bodies are now in the model. **Extrusion1**, **Extrusion2**, and **Fillet1** are all features in **Solid1**, and **Extrusion3** is in **Solid2**. A re-oriented version of the model and the Model browser display as shown in Figure 3–32.

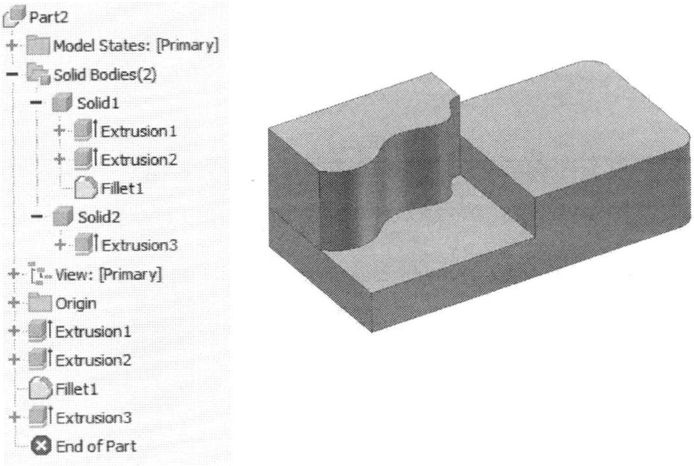

Figure 3–32

Task 5: Modify the properties of a solid body.

1. In the Model browser, right-click on **Solid2** (under the **Solid Bodies** node) and select **Properties**.
2. In the Body Appearance drop-down list, select **Blue - Wall Paint - Glossy** to change the color of **Body2**.
3. Click **Update** to update the Mass, Area, and Volume of this single body.

   Note: *You can assign a new name to the solid body in the Body Properties dialog box.*

4. Click **OK** to close the Body Properties dialog box.

Task 6: Add features to the solid bodies.

1. Create a Fillet on the two edges as shown in Figure 3–33. The two edges are from different solid bodies. Keep the default **.125 in** value as the radius for the fillets.

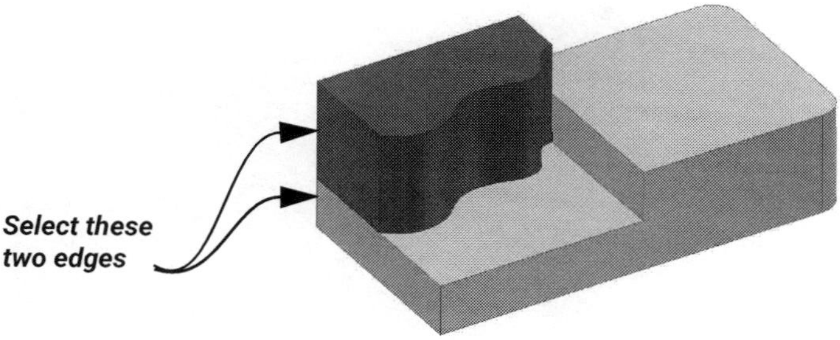

Figure 3–33

2. Complete the feature.
3. Review the Model browser. **Fillet2** has been added after **Extrusion3**, as well as to both of the solid bodies. A re-oriented version of the model and the Model browser are shown in Figure 3–34. The benefit of having them created together is that if the value changes, both update. If you want them separated, you must create them as separate features.

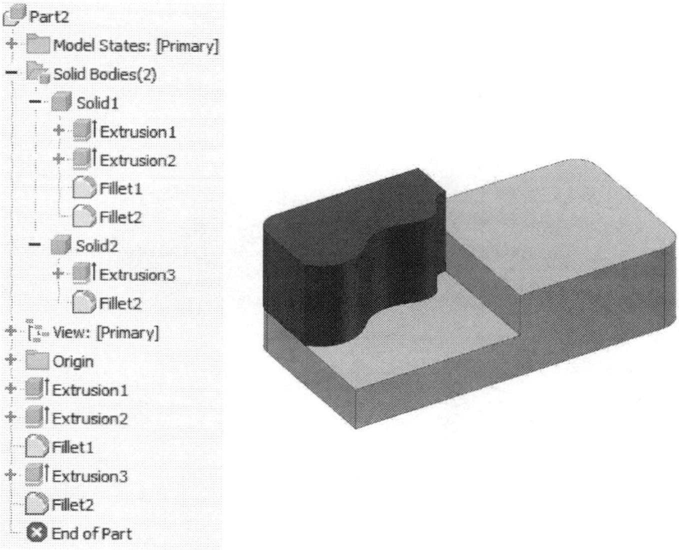

Figure 3–34

4. Re-orient the model to display the bottom of the model, as shown in Figure 3–35.

5. Create a sketch on the bottom surface and create three points at the centers of the fillets, as shown in Figure 3–35.

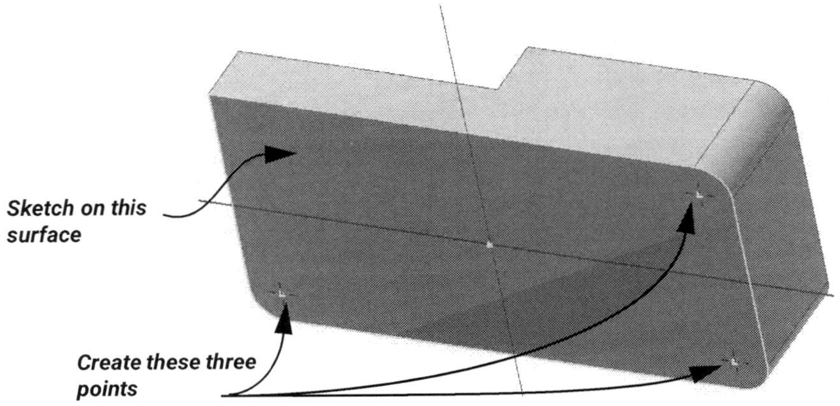

Figure 3–35

6. Complete the sketch.
7. Create holes at all three points. Set the *Termination* to **Through All** and the diameter to **.125in**.
8. Complete the feature.
9. Rotate the model, as shown in Figure 3–36, and note that the holes extrude through all of **Solid1** but not through **Solid2**. Hole1 is listed as a feature in the Model browser and a feature under the **Solid1** node. A feature is automatically added to the body from which the sketch plane is selected.

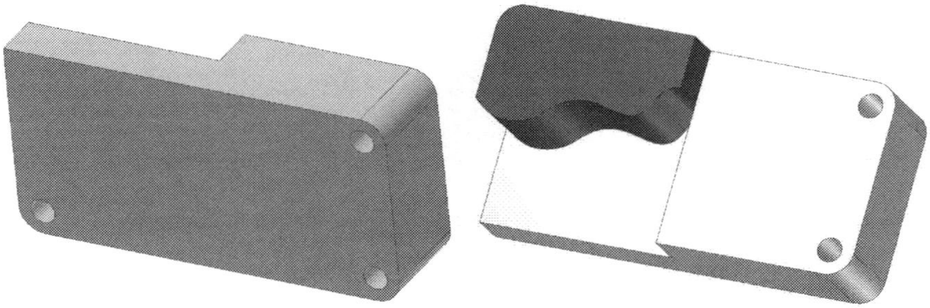

Figure 3–36

10. Double-click on **Hole1** in either location in the Model browser to edit the hole.
11. In the Properties panel, select in the *Solid* field to activate it and select **Solid2** to include the holes as part of this solid body. All sketched features enable you to assign the feature to multiple bodies.

12. Complete the feature. The holes now extrude through both solid bodies, as shown in Figure 3–37.

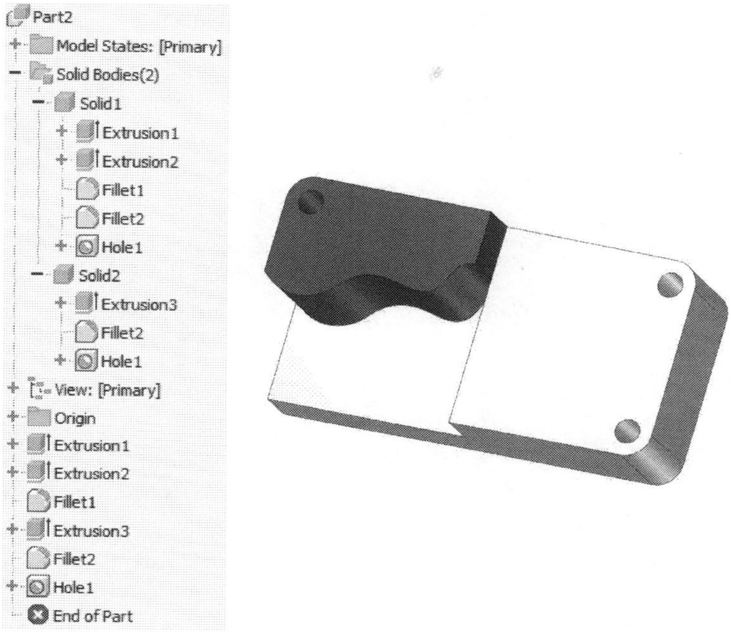

Figure 3–37

13. In the Parameters dialog box, modify the *height* parameter to **1**. You can also set it by editing the dimensions associated with **Extrusion1**.

14. In the Quick Access Toolbar, click  (Local Update) to update the model, if required. Changes to both **Solid1** and **Solid2** are due to the relationships that you set while entering the original values for the features.

15. Save the model as **solid body practice.ipt**.

End of practice

Chapter Review Questions

1. Which of the following best describes how the solid body that is created second is added to the model?
   a. The second feature is automatically applied to the first solid body, unless set otherwise.
   b. The second feature is created as its own solid body.

2. Which of the following statements are true regarding how to assign features to solid bodies? (Select all that apply.)
   a. When creating a sketched feature, it is by default added to the same solid body as that of the sketching plane.
   b. Sketched entities created as part of a feature in one solid body can reference features in a second solid body.
   c. When creating a pick-and-place feature, it is by default added to the same solid body as the placement references. If multiple references are selected that belong to multiple solid bodies, the feature fails to be created.
   d. When using a (Through All) distance option for a feature, the feature automatically extends through all solid bodies it comes in contact with.

3. Which option enables you to create a single solid body from two solid bodies?
   a. Split
   b. Combine
   c. Move Bodies
   d. Patch

4. By reviewing the list of features in the Model browser, you can determine how many solid bodies exist in the model.
   a. True
   b. False

5. Match the description of the type of Move Body operation in the left column to its icon in the right column.

Operation	Icon	Answer
a. Free Drag		
b. Move along ray		
c. Rotate about line		

Command Summary

Button	Command	Location
	**Combine**	• **Ribbon:** *3D Model* tab>Modify panel
	**Move Bodies**	• **Ribbon:** *3D Model* tab>Modify panel
N/A	**Properties (solid bodies)**	• **Context menu:** In Model browser with Solid Body node selected
	**Split**	• **Ribbon:** *3D Model* tab>Modify panel

Chapter 4

Advanced Work Features

In the *Autodesk® Inventor®: Introduction to Solid Modeling* learning guide, you learned how to use the Origin features that are provided in a new model and create basic work planes, axes, and points to help design a model. Grounded work points and user coordinate systems are additional work features that can be used to create model geometry.

Learning Objectives

- Convert an existing work point to a grounded work point.
- Create a new grounded work point relative to existing geometry.
- Create a user coordinate system that is accurately placed and oriented relative to the origin of the model.
- Create a user coordinate system that is accurately placed and oriented, in the required X and Y directions, relative to existing geometry of the model.
- Edit the translational and rotational positions and visibility of a user coordinate system.

4.1 Grounded Work Points

A grounded work point maintains its position in space, even if the reference objects in the file change. Grounded work points can be created in part or assembly files. A grounded work point can be created on its own or you can convert an existing work point.

How To: Create a Grounded Work Point

1. In the *3D Model* tab>Work Features panel, click (Grounded Point), as shown in Figure 4–1.

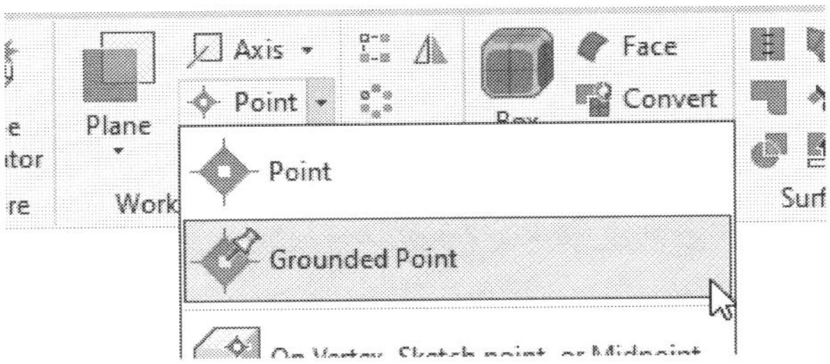

Figure 4–1

2. Select a point on the model to locate it. A triad displays on the screen at the selected location. The triad shows the positive X, Y, and Z axes and the XY, YZ, and XZ planes.
3. Using the 3D Move / Rotate mini-toolbar (shown in Figure 4–2), precisely locate the grounded work point by entering values in the entry fields.

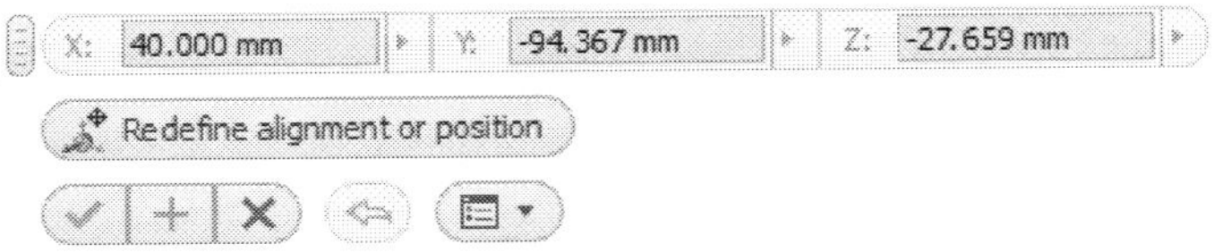

Figure 4–2

Alternatively, you can also move a grounded work point using the triad. The movement options depend on where you select the triad. The available selection areas on a triad are shown in Figure 4–3.

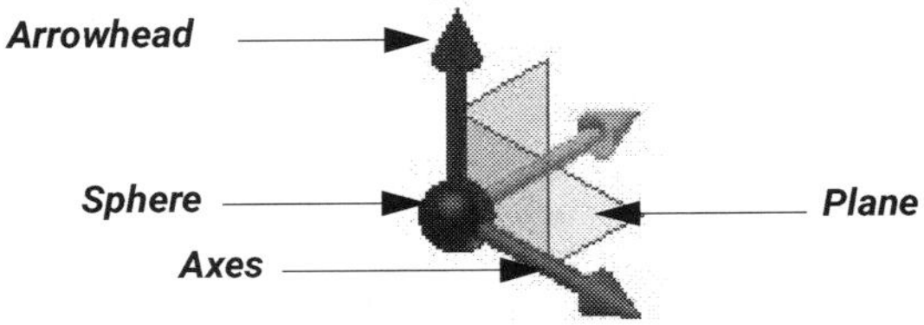

Figure 4–3

- Select the arrowhead to change its location by dragging it or by entering a value.
- Select an axis to rotate the triad by dragging it or by entering an angle. Rotating does not affect its position, but enables you to move in a particular direction.
- Select a plane to move the triad in that plane by dragging it or by entering a distance.
- Select the sphere to drag the triad freely.

4. Click or in the 3D Move / Rotate mini-toolbar to complete the creation. Clicking enables you to continue adding grounded work points.

Once created, the symbol for a grounded work point in the Model browser is a (pushpin), as opposed to the symbol for a work point.

Convert a Work Point to a Grounded Work Point

To ground an existing work point, right-click on it in the Model browser, and select **Ground**. To restore its parametric association with the part, select **Ground** again in the shortcut menu to clear its checkmark. You cannot restore associativity with the references if the grounded work point has been edited with the 3D Move/Rotate mini-toolbar.

4.2 User Coordinate Systems

A User Coordinate System (UCS) is similar to the Origin that exists in the template files in a part or assembly file. Like the Origin, a UCS consists of three planes, three axes, and a center point. The only difference is that you can have multiple UCSs in a single model that can all be oriented differently. Once created, a UCS is listed in the Model browser using a triad icon, as well as by a sequential number associated with its feature name, as shown in Figure 4–4.

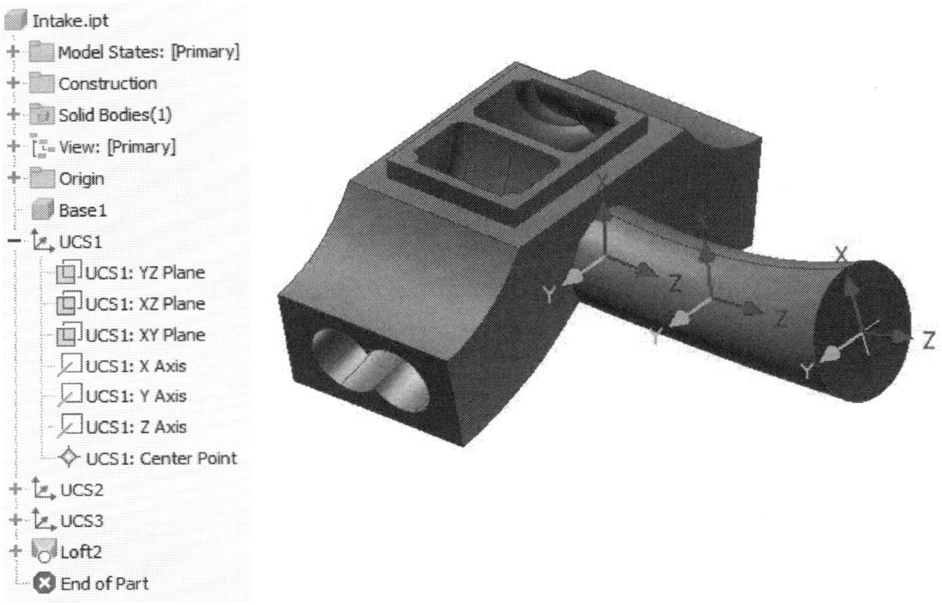

Figure 4–4

The following are practical uses for a UCS in a model:

- A UCS enables you to design models relative to any of its work features. When selecting a UCS as a 2D sketch reference, the sketch is automatically placed on its XY plane. Alternatively, you can select an alternate sketch plane in a UCS by manually selecting it in the Model browser. Additionally, sketch geometry can be aligned to any of the axes in the UCS. Changes made to plane or axis placement will reflect in any features that are children.
- A UCS can be used to provide a sketch plane for a feature that would be difficult to create using work planes alone. When a UCS or a UCS plane is used as a 2D sketch plane, the Center Point for the UCS is automatically projected into the sketch.
- A UCS can be used for measuring.
- A UCS triad can be used as a reference for orienting.
- A UCS can be used as a reference in constraining components.
- Work features in a UCS can be displayed in a drawing.

A UCS can be located in a model so that it is either located relative to the model's origin or relative to existing geometry.

Locating the UCS Relative to the Model Origin

How To: Create a UCS Relative to the Model's Origin

1. In the *3D Model* tab>Work Features panel, click (UCS).
2. Locate the UCS in the main window by dragging the cursor to the required location. The UCS displays with an attached status bar. This indicates the absolute location of the UCS relative to the model origin, as shown in Figure 4–5. Click to place the UCS or enter specific values in the entry fields.

The colors that display on each axis of the UCS triad correspond to the same colors for the model's triad. Red represents the X axis, green is the Y axis, and blue is the Z axis.

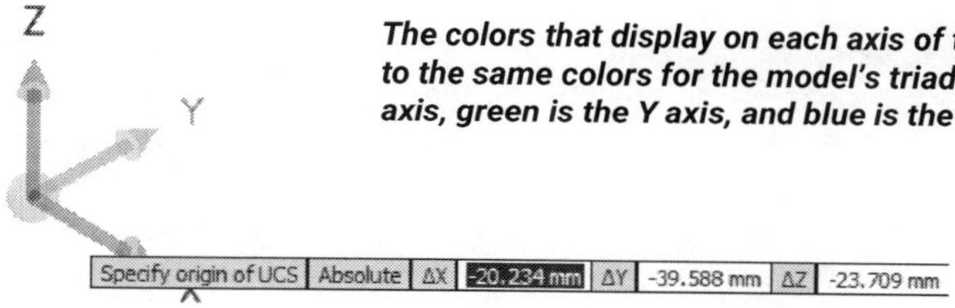

Figure 4–5

3. To refine the location of the UCS in the model, select and drag the various triad segments, as shown below. The cursor displays when the cursor is not placed on any of the triad segments. It prompts you to select a triad segment to define the type of transform.

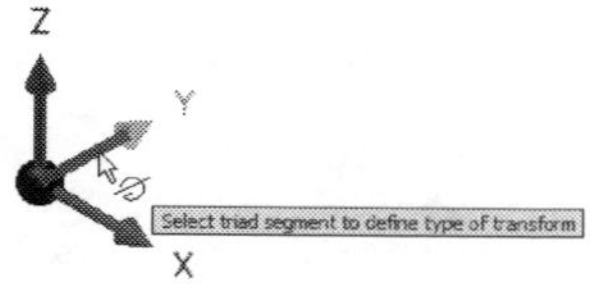	The mouse cursor displays when the cursor is placed on any of the axes. Select and drag the cursor to rotate the triad about the selected axis.
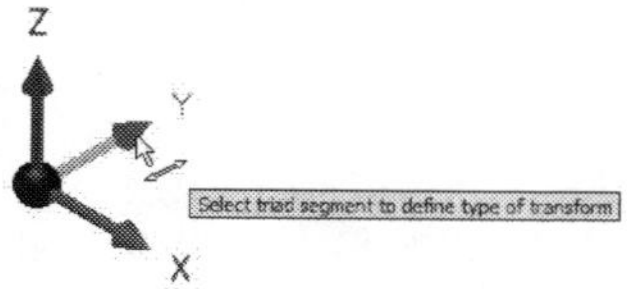	The mouse cursor displays when the cursor is placed on any of the arrowheads. Select and drag the cursor to translate the triad along the selected arrowhead's axis.
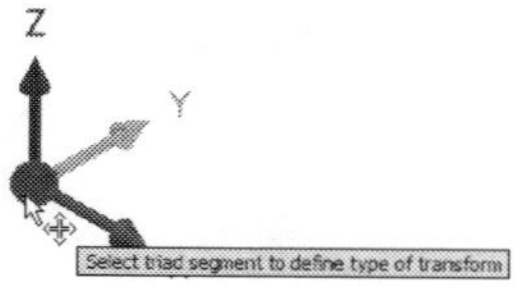	The mouse cursor displays when the cursor is placed on the UCS origin. Select and drag the cursor to translate the UCS to a new location.

- Alternatively, you can select a triad segment, enter an exact value and press <Enter> once any of the triad segments are active. To toggle through multiple fields in the Heads Up Display, press <Tab>.

4. To complete the UCS placement, right-click and select **Finish**. The additional options in the shortcut menu enable you to restart UCS placement (**Restart**), and cancel UCS placement (**Done [Esc]**).

Locating the UCS Relative to Existing Geometry

How To: Create a UCS Relative to Existing Geometry in a Part Model

1. In the *3D Model* tab>Work Features panel, click (UCS).
2. As you move the cursor over existing geometry, the triad snaps to geometry (e.g., center points, vertex, midpoints, points). Locate the UCS relative to existing geometry by selecting references. (Note that you cannot create a UCS relative to existing geometry when working in an assembly model.) The colors that display on each axis of the UCS triad correspond to the same colors for the model's triad. Red represents the X axis, green is the Y axis, and blue is the Z axis.
3. The UCS status bar prompts you to specify the direction of the X axis. Select a point on the model to define the X direction reference. The UCS reorients once selected.
4. The UCS status bar prompts you to specify the direction of the Y axis. Select a point on the model to define the Y direction reference. The UCS reorients once selected and the UCS placement is automatically completed.
5. Once the Y axis direction is defined, the UCS is automatically created. The additional options in the shortcut menu enable you to restart UCS placement (**Restart**), cancel UCS placement (**Done [Esc]**), and undo the most recent reference selection (**Back**).

Each UCS adds six parameters to the model: three positional and three angular. Each parameter is initially listed in the Parameters dialog box using its default naming convention. If these parameter values are to be used in equations, it is recommended to rename them with more descriptive names.

Redefining UCS Placement

Whether a UCS is placed relative to the model origin or relative to existing geometry, the feature's placement can be redefined.

- To redefine a UCS, right-click on the feature in the Model browser and select **Redefine Feature** or right-click on the feature in the model and select **Redefine Feature**. Select and drag the various triad segments (axis, arrowhead, or origin) to redefine its placement.Alternatively, you can double-click on a UCS name in the Model browser to redefine it.

- For UCS features that were created by referencing existing geometry, you can right-click and select **Show Inputs** to show the references that were selected as the X and Y axis references. This will help you identify the entities that were used to create the feature.
- Alternatively, you can modify the location of a UCS by editing its values in the Parameters dialog box (*Manage* tab>Parameters panel>click f_x (Parameters)). Review the **Consumed By** column to identify what feature the parameter is consumed by.

UCS Visibility and Naming

You can control the default visibility of work features in a UCS and specify an alternate prefix for UCS names using the UCS Settings dialog box. To access these options, in the *Tools* tab> Options panel, click (Document Settings). In the Document Settings dialog box, select the *Modeling* tab and click **Settings** in the *User Coordinate System* area to open the UCS Settings dialog box, as shown in Figure 4–6.

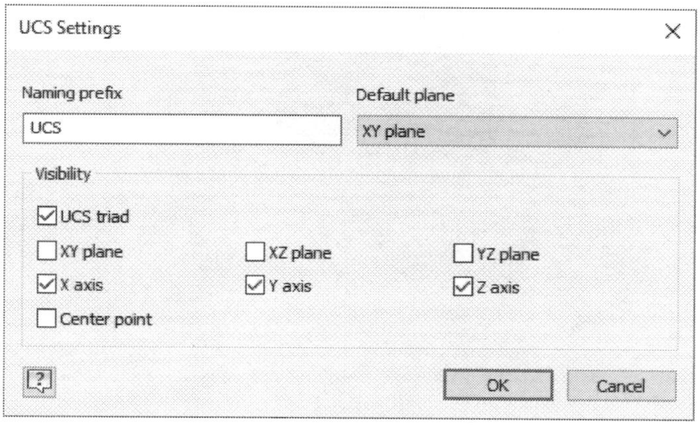

Figure 4–6

In addition to changing the naming prefix and visibility, you can specify the default plane for a UCS. The default plane is the plane that is used if the UCS is selected as a 2D sketching reference. The settings specified in the UCS Settings dialog box pertain to all UCSs in the model. Settings cannot be specified for a UCS on an individual basis.

> ***Note:*** *The naming convention used for the work features in a UCS cannot be altered. Their names are dependent on the UCS name.*

Practice 4a
Creating Geometry Using a UCS

Practice Objectives

- Create a user coordinate system that is accurately placed and oriented in the required X and Y direction.
- Edit the translational and rotational X, Y, and Z positions of existing user coordinate systems.

In this practice, you will create the lofted geometry shown in Figure 4–7. The geometry is created by sketching sections on user coordinate systems (UCS) and then creating a loft between the sections. To complete the practice, you redefine the positions and sketches on the UCS to manipulate the shape of the geometry.

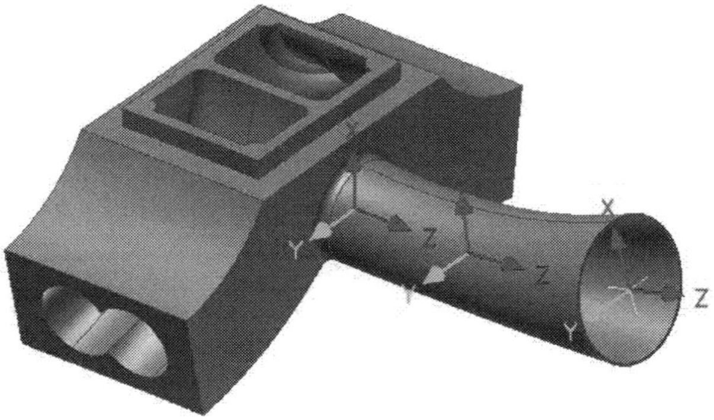

Figure 4–7

Task 1: Create a user coordinate system.

1. Open **Intake.ipt**.
2. In the Work Features panel, click  (UCS).
3. Move the cursor around the model. Note how the triad snaps to geometry.

4. Position the cursor over the circular edge shown in Figure 4–8. The triad snaps to the center of the circular edge. The status line indicates the UCS is offset 40 mm in the X direction, 0 mm in the Y direction, and -30 mm in the Z direction from the Model Origin.

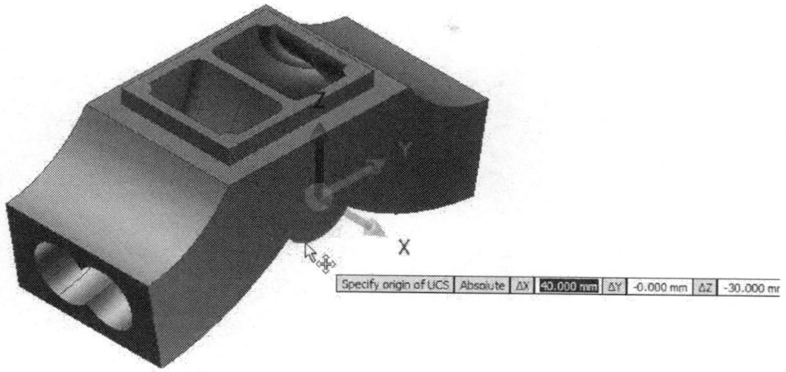

Figure 4–8

Note: *The colors that display on each axis of the UCS triad correspond to the same colors for the model's triad. Red represents the X axis, green is the Y axis, and blue is the Z axis.*

5. Select the edge.
6. The UCS status bar prompts you to specify the direction of the X axis. Hover the cursor over the midpoint vertex shown in Figure 4–9 and select this point. The UCS reorients once selected.

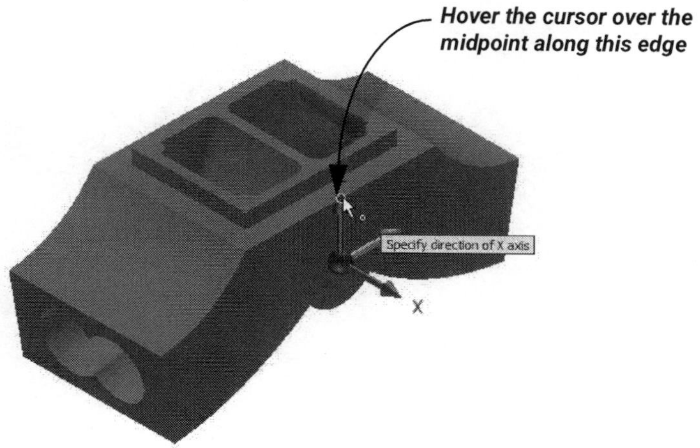

Figure 4–9

7. The UCS status bar prompts you to specify the direction of the Y axis. Select the point identified in the left image, as shown in Figure 4–10, to define the Y direction reference. The UCS reorients as shown on the right.

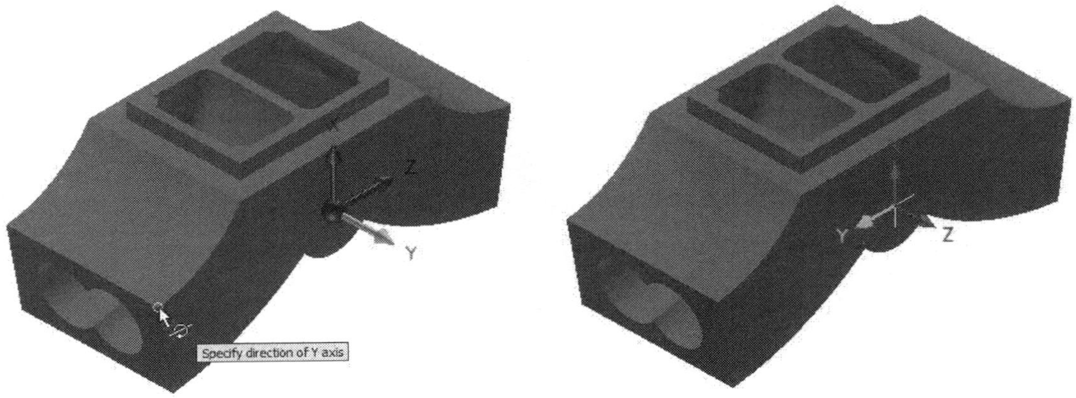

Figure 4–10

8. In the Work Features panel, click (UCS).
9. Create a second UCS using the same references.
10. Create a third UCS using the same references. The three UCS features are located directly on top of one another. The model and Model browser display as shown in Figure 4–11.

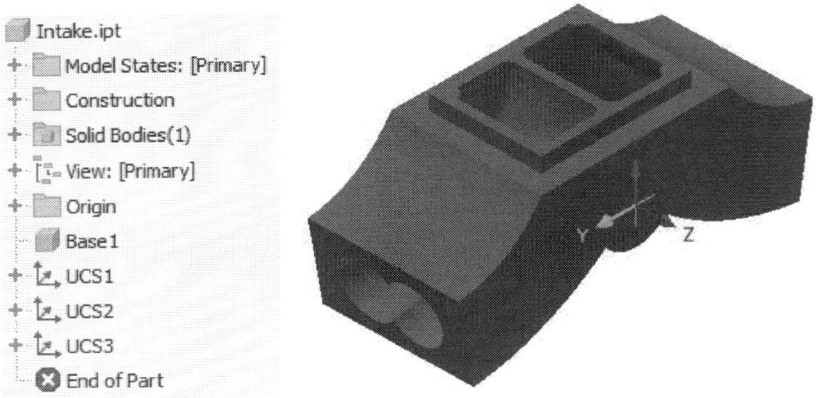

Figure 4–11

Task 2: Modify the location of the UCS.

1. In the Model browser, double-click on **UCS2** to activate the UCS for modification.

2. Click and hold the arrowhead for the Z axis, as shown in Figure 4–12.

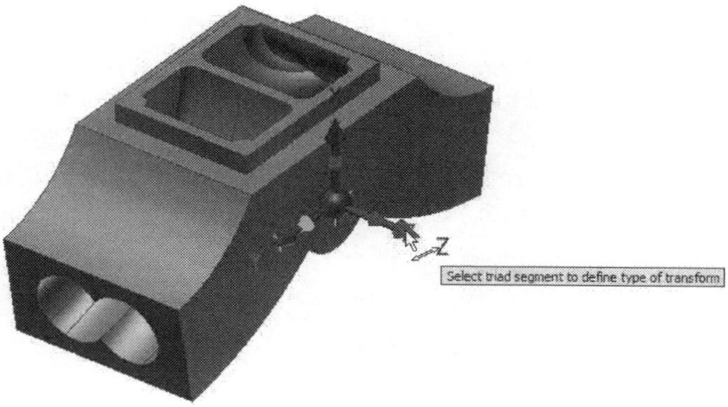

Figure 4–12

3. Drag the cursor away from the model until the status bar reads that it is offset by approximately 50mm. Release the mouse button to locate the UCS. To obtain an exact value, click and release the arrowhead for the Z axis and enter **50** while the Z field is active (highlighted in blue) and press <Enter>.
4. Click and hold the axis of the Y axis, as shown in Figure 4–13.

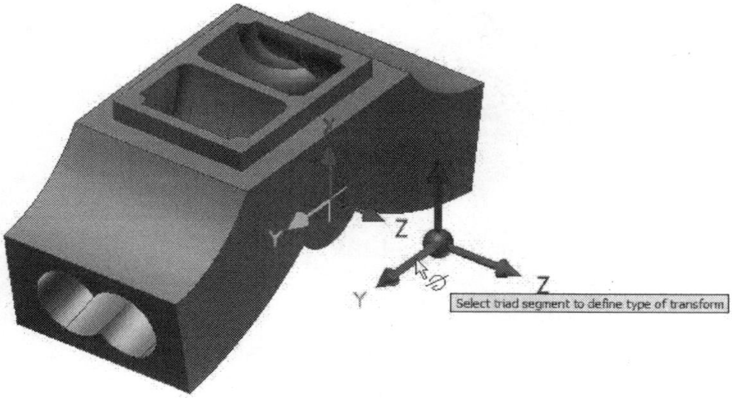

Figure 4–13

5. Drag the cursor until the status bar reads that it is approximately 5 deg (rotated towards top of model). Release the mouse button to locate the UCS. To obtain an exact value, click and release the mouse button on the axis for the Yaxis and enter **5** while the field is active (highlighted in blue) and press <Enter>. You might need to enter **-5 deg**.
6. Right-click and select **Finish** to complete the modification of UCS2.
7. Double-click on **UCS3** in the Model browser.

8. Press and hold the left mouse button on the arrowhead for the Z axis and drag it away from the model. Drag the cursor until the status bar reads that it is offset by approximately **125mm,** or enter the exact value. Release the left mouse button to locate the UCS.
9. Click and hold the axis of the Y axis. Drag the mouse until the status bar reads that it is approximately **15 deg** (rotated towards top of model) or enter the exact value. Release the mouse button to locate the UCS. You might need to enter **-15 deg**.
10. Click and hold the arrowhead for the X axis and drag it until the status bar reads that it is offset by approximately **12mm**, or enter the exact value. Release the mouse button to locate the UCS.
11. Right-click and select **Finish** to complete the modification of UCS3. The updated model displays as shown in Figure 4–14.

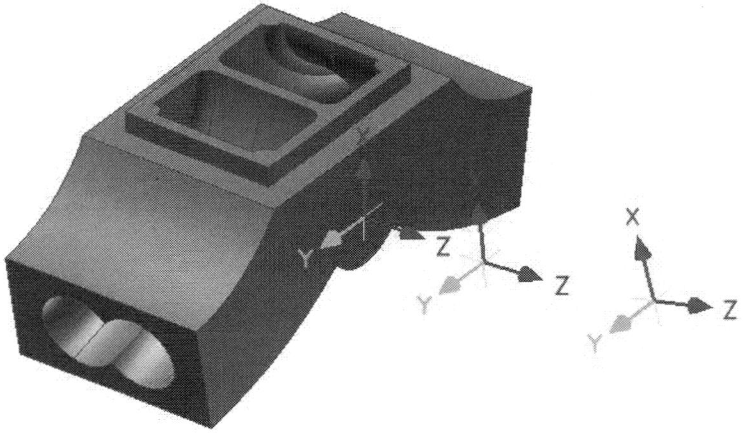

Figure 4–14

Task 3: Sketch sections on each UCS that is used to create a loft.

1. In the Sketch panel, click (Start 2D Sketch).
2. In the Model browser, select **UCS1** as the reference for the sketch. By default, if a UCS is selected as the sketch reference, the XY plane is used as the sketch plane. The Sketch tab is activated.
3. In the Create panel, click (Project Geometry) and select the circular edge that was used to place all the UCS features.
4. In the Create panel, click (Circle). Sketch the circular entity so that it is aligned with the center of the UCS and the projected edge. The sketch should be fully constrained based on these selections.
5. In the Exit panel, click (Finish Sketch).

6. In the Sketch panel, click (Start 2D Sketch) and in the Model browser, select **UCS2**.
7. In the Create panel, click (Circle). Sketch a circular entity so that it is centered on the UCS, as shown in Figure 4–15.
8. Create the **40 mm** diameter dimension as shown in Figure 4–15.

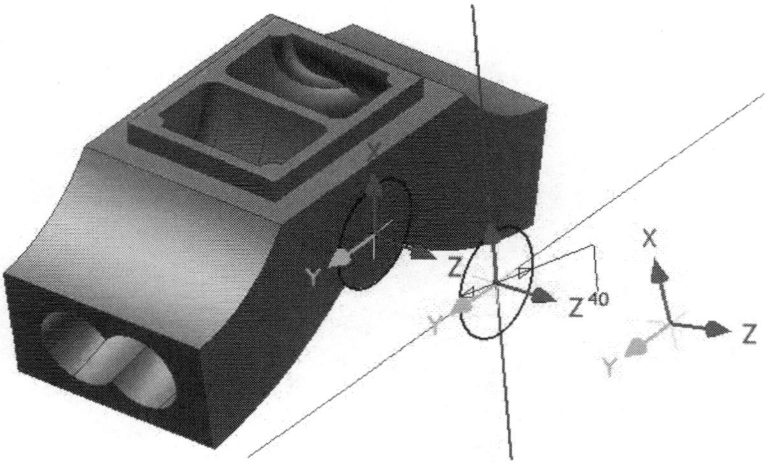

Figure 4–15

9. In the Exit panel, click .
10. Create a third circular sketch that references UCS3 and has a diameter of **55 mm**, as shown in Figure 4–16.

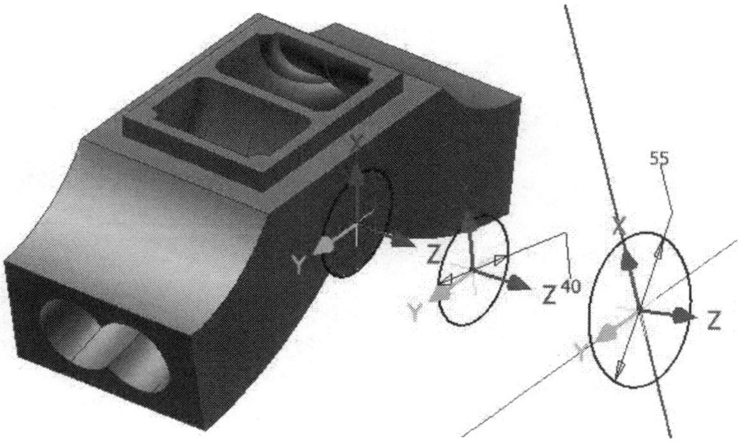

Figure 4–16

Task 4: Create a loft feature.

1. In the *3D Model* tab>Create panel, click (Loft).
2. To define the sections for the loft, first select the sketch that was created referencing UCS1 (**Sketch1**), then select the sketch that was created referencing UCS2 (**Sketch2**). To complete the loft, select the final section that was sketched referencing UCS3.
3. Click **OK** to complete the loft. The model displays similar to that shown in Figure 4–17.

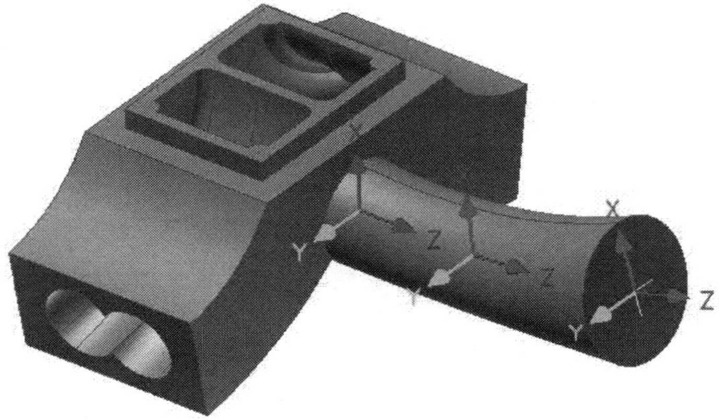

Figure 4–17

Task 5: Modify the loft's shape by modifying the UCS features.

1. In the Model browser, double-click on **UCS3** to modify it.
2. Click and hold the arrowhead for the Y axis and drag it to a new location. Release the mouse button.
3. Click and hold the axis of the Y axis. Drag the cursor to change its angular location. Release the mouse button.
4. Right-click and select **Finish** to complete the change. The model updates to reflect the change.

   As an alternative, you can modify the location of a UCS by editing its values in the Parameters dialog box (*Manage* tab>Parameters panel>click fx (Parameters)). Review the **Consumed By** column to identify which dimensions are associated with which UCS. Alternatively, you can show the references from which the UCS was created by right-clicking on the UCS name in the Model Browser and selecting **Show Inputs**.

5. Continue to modify the geometry, UCS features, and sketches to refine the shape of the loft, similar to that shown in Figure 4–18.

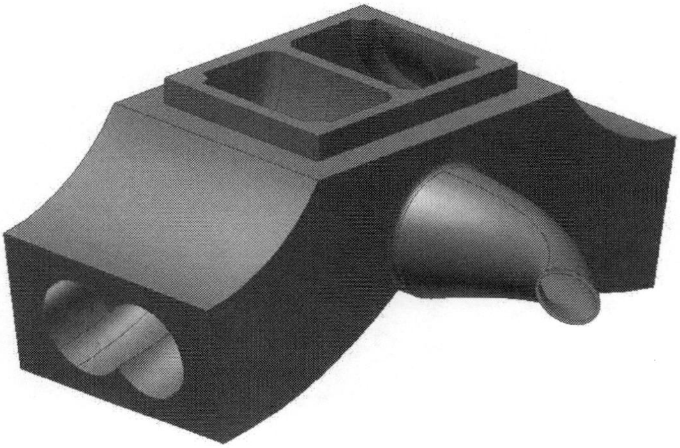

Figure 4–18

6. Save the model and close the window.

End of practice

Chapter Review Questions

1. The location of grounded work points is parametric. If there is a change made to the objects on which the points are dependent, the point location also changes.

    a. True

    b. False

2. In the Model browser, which of the following icons represents a grounded work point?

    a. 

    b. 

    c. 

3. If the mini-toolbar is being displayed as shown in Figure 4–19, which of the following features is currently being created?

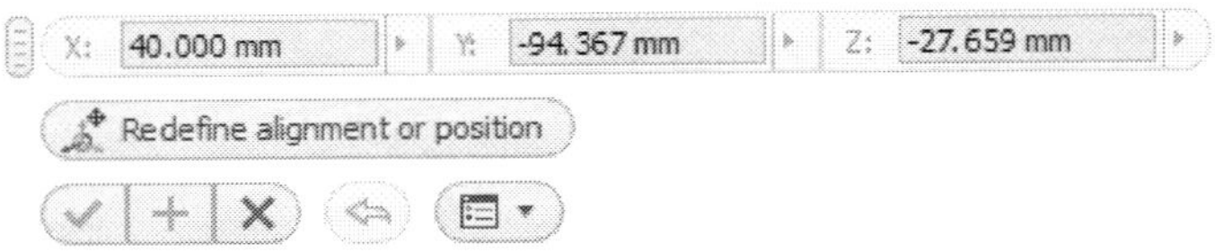

Figure 4–19

    a. Work Point

    b. Grounded Work Point

    c. Center Point

    d. UCS

4. Which of the following planes associated with a UCS, is the default sketching plane if the UCS is selected as a reference for sketching?

    a. YZ Plane

    b. XZ Plane

    c. XY Plane

5. Which area in a grounded work point's triad, as shown in Figure 4–20, enables you to freely locate the point in the model?

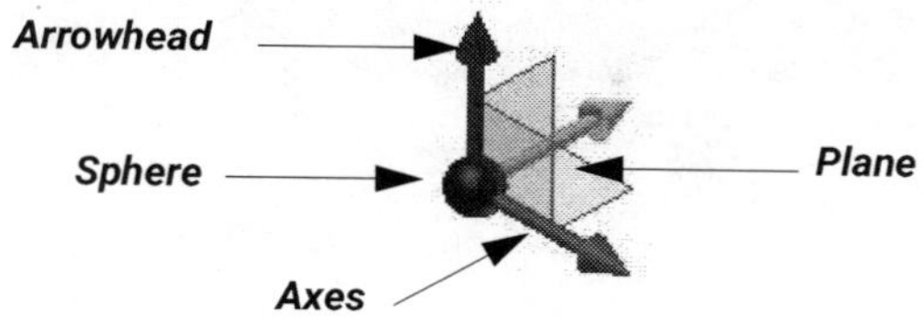

Figure 4–20

a. Arrowhead
b. Sphere
c. Axes
d. Plane

6. Which of the triad areas, as shown in Figure 4–21, is not available for use when creating a UCS?

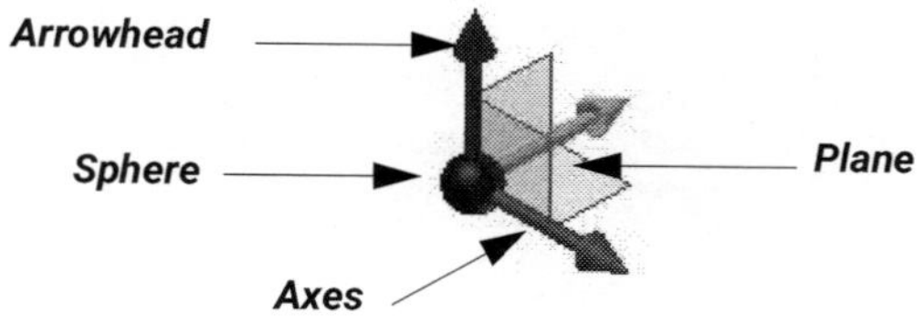

Figure 4–21

a. Arrowhead
b. Sphere
c. Axes
d. Plane

Command Summary

Button	Command	Location
	**Grounded Work Point**	• **Ribbon:** *3D model* tab>Work Features panel
	**UCS**	• **Ribbon:** *3D model* tab>Work Features panel

Chapter

5

Advanced Lofts, Sweeps, and Coils

Creating the required geometry in a model can be accomplished using many different techniques. There is no right or wrong way to create geometry. Instead, what is important is that the resulting geometry should capture your design intent and be designed in such a way that any required changes can be made easily. Understanding how to use the advanced modeling features and the advanced options for standard features will provide you with additional flexibility when you are creating geometry.

Learning Objectives

- Create an Area Loft that blends geometry between multiple profiles and intermediate points along a center line.
- Define accurate position and area dimensions for the intermediate points that are selected along the Area Loft center line.
- Create a Guide Sweep using a rail to control the scale and twist of a sweep by selecting an additional curve to use as a guiding reference for the profile.
- Create a Guide Sweep using a surface, the surface normal of which controls the twist of the profile along the path.
- Create coil-shaped geometry that adds or removes material from the model.

5.1 Area Lofts

An Area Loft feature is similar to a Rail and Center Line Loft in that it enables you to create geometry by blending between multiple profiles. Area Lofts expand on the Center Line Lofts by enabling you to define the area of sections at specified points along the path as well as define new sections along the center line and define their areas. The shape in Figure 5–1 has been blended between three selected sections. Each shows its position on the center line and its area.

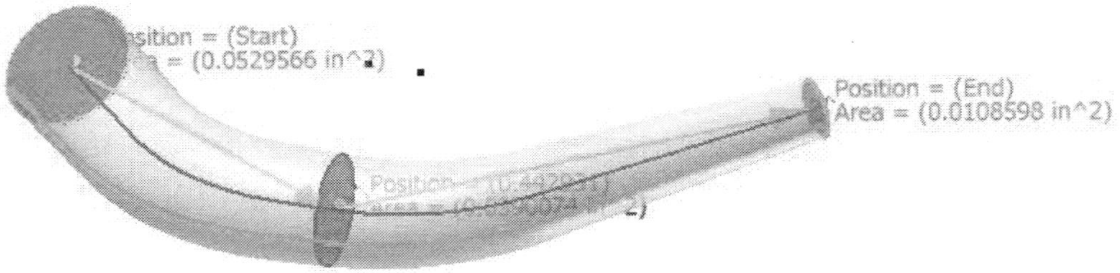

Figure 5–1

*Note: The **Area Loft** option provides support for the design of hydraulic and pneumatic components.*

How To: Create an Area Loft

1. In the *3D Model* tab>Create panel, click (Loft).
2. Click (Area Loft). The Loft dialog box refreshes as shown in Figure 5–2.

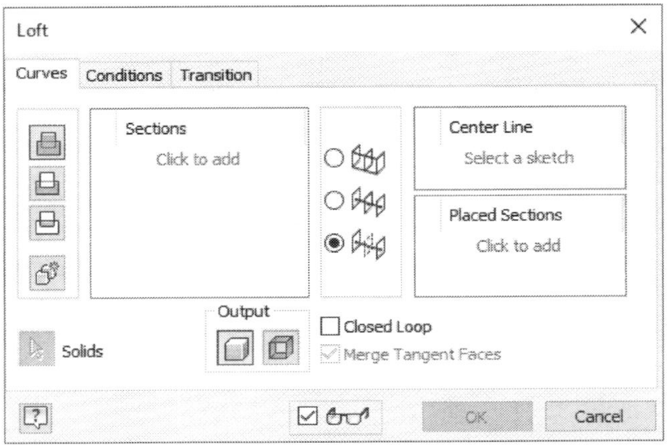

Figure 5–2

3. Select how the geometry will be added to the model. The options include adding material using a join ( ), removing material with a cut ( ), or adding material that is the result of an intersection ( ).
4. Define whether the new geometry is added as a new solid body or is combined with an existing body.
   - If the loft is the first solid feature in the model, the feature is automatically added as the first solid body.
   - If the loft is added as a secondary solid feature, you can click to add the feature as a new solid body.
   - If there are more than two solids in the model, you can select which solid to apply the loft to by clicking and selecting the body to which to apply it.
5. Select the output option as Solid ( ) or Surface ( ).
6. Select **Closed Loop** to create the loft so that the first and last section are joined.
7. Select the sections to be blended, similar to that shown in Figure 5–3. You can either select a sketched profile or an existing planar face as a profile. Existing planar faces are selected directly from the model and can only be used as the start and end sections.

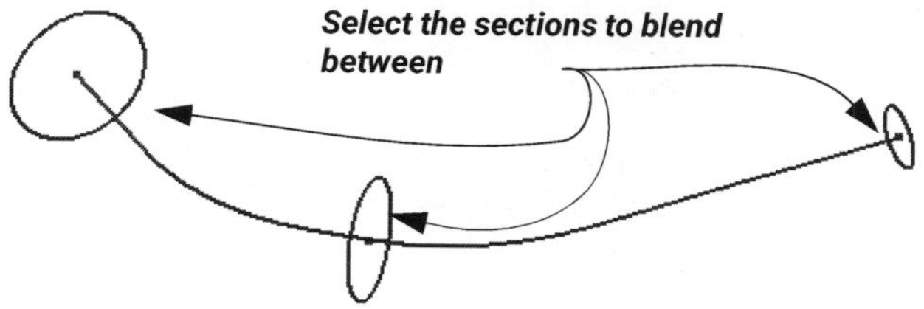

Figure 5–3

8. Activate the *Center Line* area of the dialog box and select the center line geometry to define the path that the loft will follow. The resulting geometry is previewed on the screen, similar to that shown in Figure 5–4.

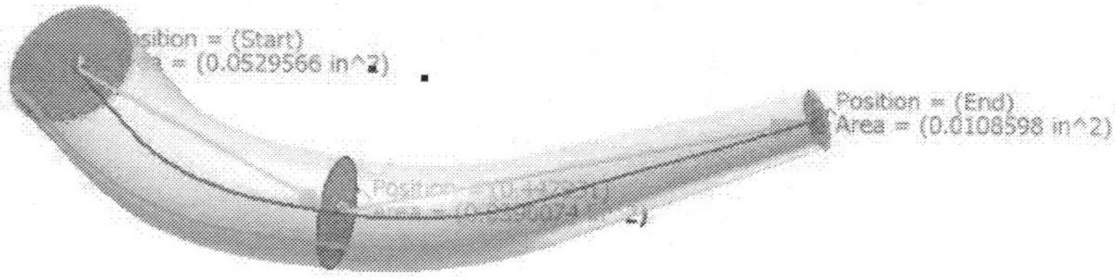

Figure 5–4

9. Activate the *Placed Section* area of the dialog box and select other points on the center line to control additional areas for the Loft. The default Position and Area dimensions are provided for each selected section or placed section.

10. In the Section Dimensions dialog box (shown in Figure 5–5), click 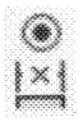 (Driving Section) to enable you to control the area of the internal sections. For placed sections you can also control their position. Edit the values, as required. Click  (Driven Section) option to disable all Section Size controls and only control the section position.

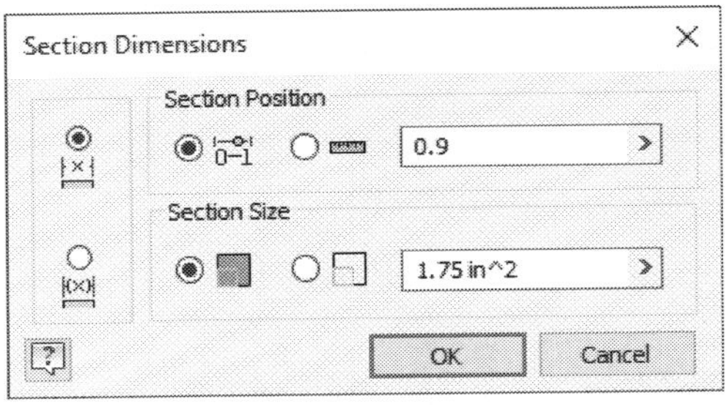

Figure 5–5

Note: *When editing the Start and End or any other selected sketched section, you cannot change the Section Position values. Only internally placed section positions can be changed.*

11. Click **OK** to close the Section Dimensions dialog box.
12. Add additional sections, as needed.
13. Click **OK** to complete the feature or right-click in the graphics window and select **OK (Enter)**. Figure 5–6 displays the completed model used in this example.

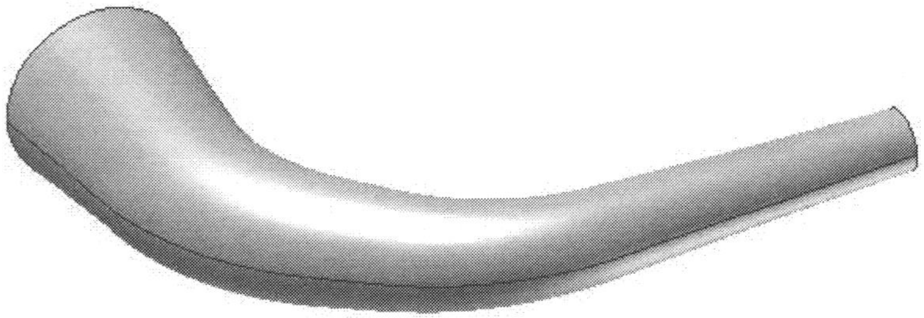

Figure 5–6

5.2 Advanced Sweeps

Path sweeps create geometry by sweeping a profile along a path. Guide Sweeps using rails and surfaces are two advanced types of path sweeps.

Guide Sweep with Rail

The Path & Guide Rail Sweep enables you to select an additional curve (Guide Rail).

How To: Create a Guide Sweep Using a Rail

1. In the *3D Model* tab>Create panel, click (Sweep).
2. Select **Sweep** (default feature name) at the top of the Properties panel to assign a new name for the feature.
3. By default, the sweep is created as a solid. To change the output to surface geometry, select at the top of the Properties panel to enable surface mode. Toggle this option off to create the geometry as a solid.
4. Select the Profile and Path references (similar to a Path sweep).
5. In the *Behavior* area, click (Guide).
6. Select a Guide Rail reference.
7. Select how the geometry will be added to the model. The options include adding material using a join ( ), removing material with a cut ( ), or adding material that is the result of an intersection ( ).
8. Define whether the new geometry is added as a new solid body or is combined with an existing body.
    - If the loft is the first solid feature in the model, the feature is automatically added as the first solid body.
    - If the loft is added as a secondary solid feature, you can click to add the feature as a new solid body.
    - If there are more than two solids in the model, activate the *Solids* field and select which solid to apply the loft to by selecting the solid in the model or Model browser.

9. Define the required *Profile Scaling* option, as shown in Figure 5–7. They enable you to control the direction(s) in which the Guide Rail should affect the profile scale along the sweep. Figure 5–8 shows an example of how the scaling affects the resulting geometry.

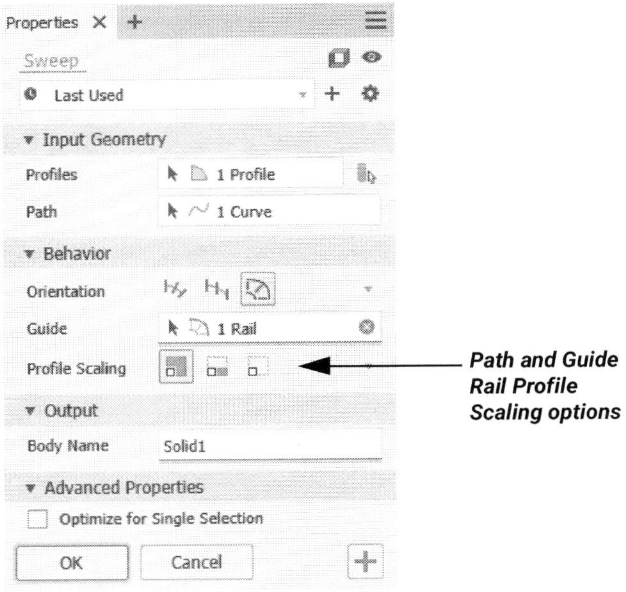

Figure 5–7

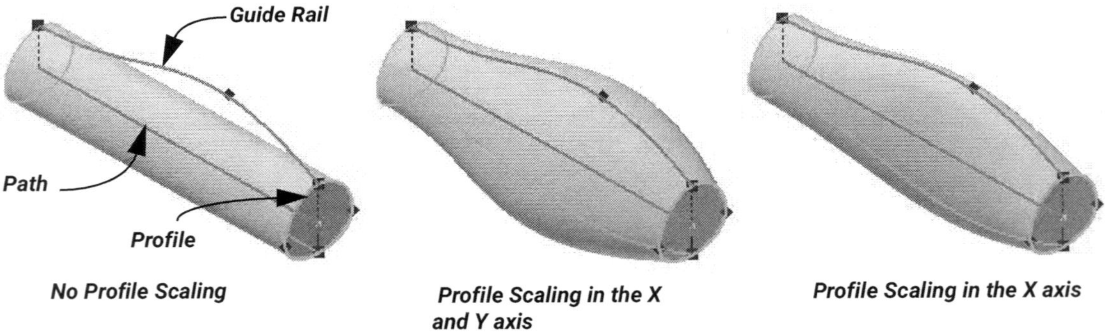

Figure 5–8

10. Once the sweep feature is defined, click **OK**. Alternatively, right-click in the graphics window and select **OK [Enter]** or press <Enter>. To continue creating additional sweep features without closing the panel, click  (Apply) and define the references as needed. Once all sweeps have been completed, click **OK**.

Guide Sweep Using a Surface

A Guide Surface using a sweep enables you to select both a surface whose normal controls the twist of the sweep and a path, as shown in Figure 5–9.

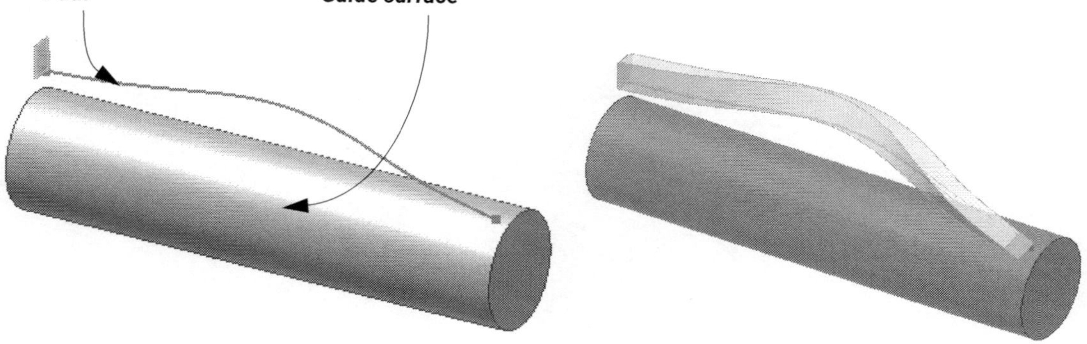

Figure 5–9

The procedure for creating this type of sweep is the same as that for a traditional Path sweep, except that the  (Guide) option is selected and a guide surface is assigned.

5.3 Coils

A helical shape is used to create springs, threads, and augers. You can create these shapes using a Coil. A coil profile is swept along a helical path or a spiral path, as shown in Figure 5–10. Similar to extrusions and revolutions, you can use a coil to add or remove material.

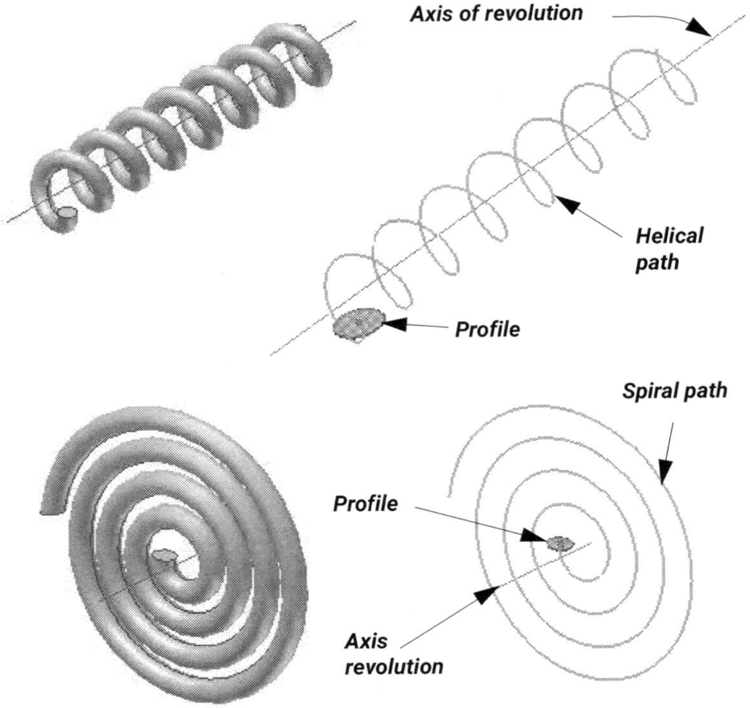

Figure 5–10

A profile and axis of revolution must exist in the model prior to creating a Coil feature.

- The profile for a coil can be defined from sketches or existing planar faces.
- The axis of revolution can be a line in a sketch or a work axis. The axis of revolution must be sketched in the same sketch as the profile, unless you are selecting a work axis or a part edge. The axis can be in any orientation, but cannot intersect the profile.

Note: *Alternatively, you can create coil type geometry using a 3D Helical Curve and sweeping a circular section along it. When using a Coil feature you have more control over the ends of the coil.*

How To: Create a Coil

1. Create the profile and axis of revolution that will be used to define the coil.
2. In the *3D Model* tab>Create panel, click (Coil). The Properties panel opens, as shown in Figure 5–11.

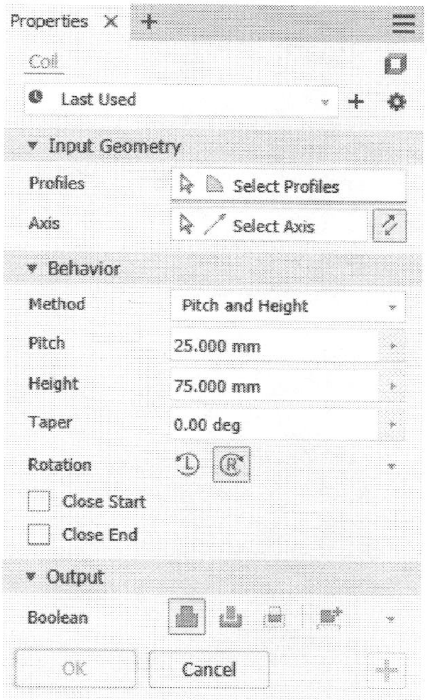

Figure 5–11

3. Select **Coil** (default feature name) at the top of the Properties panel to assign a name for the feature.
4. By default, the coil is created as a solid. To change the output to surface geometry, select at the top of the Properties panel to enable surface mode. Toggle this option off to create the geometry as a solid.
5. In the *Input Geometry* area, select the Profile(s) and Axis that will define the shape of the coil. If required, click (Reverse pitch direction along axis) to flip the direction of the coil.

6. In the *Behavior* area, define the method for coil creation using the drop-down list, as shown in Figure 5–12. Depending on the method that is selected, you can enter values for **Pitch**, **Height**, **Revolution**, and **Taper**.

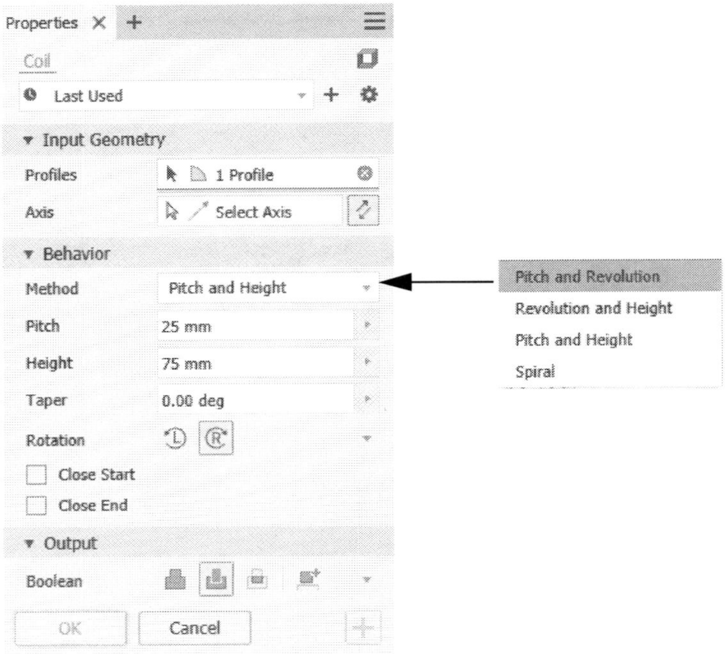

Figure 5–12

- **Pitch** sets the length per turn. For example, if the pitch is set to 0.5, there will be 0.5 units between adjacent coils.
- **Height** sets the height of the coil center line. This option is not available for a Spiral type.
- **Revolution** sets the number of revolutions of the coil.
- **Taper** enables you to determine how the radius of each turn changes over the length of the coil, so the coil is cone-shaped. A positive number increases the radius; a negative number decreases the radius. This option is not available for a Spiral type.

7. Define the direction of rotation using the  icons.

8. Select the **Close Start** and **Close End** to define the start and end shape of the coil.

   - The end of a spring might be formed so that the spring can stand upright on a flat surface. For these cases, you can enable the **Close Start** or **Close End**, as needed. Additionally, the coil can be flat or at a different angle than the rest of the spring using a Flat Angle value. When these options are cleared, the spring is uniform along its length; when enabled, the coil is deformed at the start/end to enable the spring to sit flat, as shown in Figure 5–13.

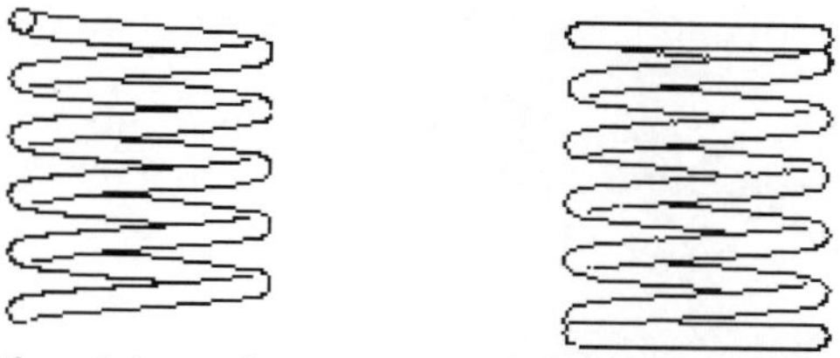

Close Start and Close End are disabled.

Close Start and Close End are enabled. Both start and end are flat.

Figure 5–13

   - When either of the **Close Start** or **Close End** options is selected, a transition angle specifies how many degrees over which the transition between the body of the spring and the flat end of the spring is achieved. For example, if set to 180 degrees, the change from the body of the spring to flat happens over one half of a rotation. The Flat Angle specifies how much of the last coil should be flat (no pitch). A Flat Angle of 360 degrees makes a complete turn at the end of the coil.

9. In the *Output* area, select how the geometry will be added to the model. The options include adding material using a join ( ), removing material with a cut ( ), or adding material that is the result of an intersection ( ).

10. Define whether the new geometry is added as a new solid body or is combined with an existing body.

   - If the coil is the first solid feature in the model, the feature is automatically added as the first solid body.
   - If the coil is added as a secondary solid feature, you can click to add the feature as a new solid body.
   - If there are more than two solids in the model, you can select which solid to apply the coil to by activating the *Solid* field and selecting the solid(s).

11. Once the coil feature is defined, click **OK**. Alternatively, right-click in the graphics window and select **OK (Enter)**. To continue creating additional coil features without closing the panel, click (Apply) and define the references as needed. Once all coils have been completed, click **OK**.

Hint: Creating Coils Using Multiple Entities in the Same Sketch

If multiple closed entities exist in a single sketch and each entity is to be used to create a separate coil operation, consider enabling the **Keep sketch visible on (+)** option in the (Advanced Settings Menu). You can then use (Apply) to continue selecting entities without the sketch visibility being turned off, as is done when the feature is completed.

Practice 5a
Area Loft

Practice Objectives

- Create an Area Loft that blends geometry between multiple profiles and intermediate points along a center line.
- Define accurate position and area dimensions for the intermediate points that are selected along the Area Loft center line.

In this practice, you will use an Area loft feature to create the bottle shown in Figure 5–14. By defining the position and area of multiple sections along the entire length of the bottle you will shape of the bottle.

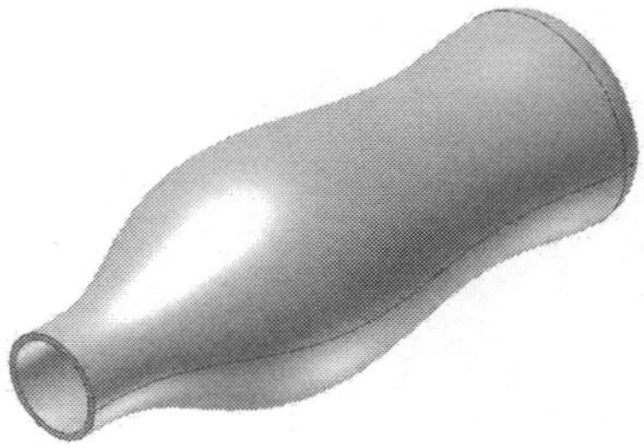

Figure 5–14

Task 1: Open a part file.

1. Open **bottle.ipt**. The part displays as shown in Figure 5–15.

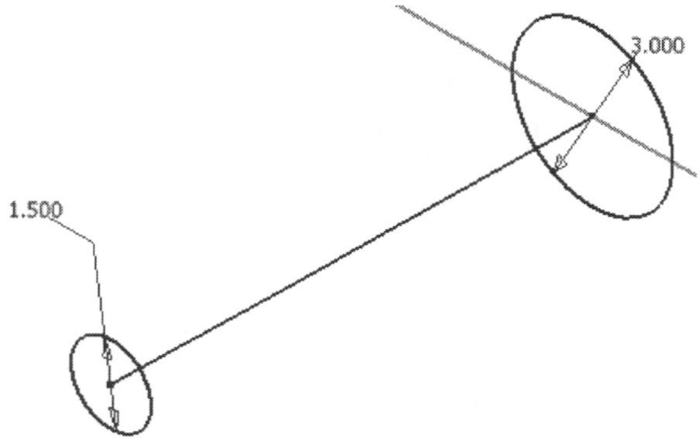

Figure 5–15

Task 2: Create a Center Line loft.

1. In the *3D Model* tab>Create panel, click (Loft).
2. In the Loft dialog box, click (Area Loft).
3. Select the two circular entities as the sections. Select the larger diameter circle for the first section (start) and the small circle for the second section (end).
4. Activate the *Center Line* area and select the linear entity that joins the two circles (Sketch 4) as the center line. The preview displays as shown in Figure 5–16. You might need to select Sketch4 directly on the model and not in the Model browser to obtain an immediate preview of the loft feature; otherwise, the preview should display when you assign additional sections.

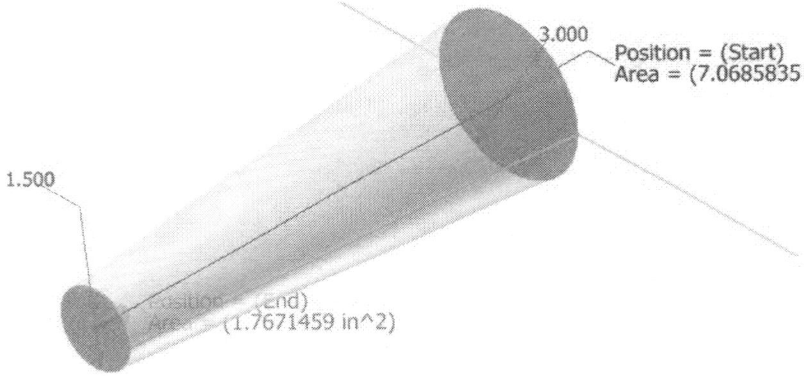

Figure 5–16

5. Orient the model similar to that shown in Figure 5–17. This is being done so you can see the dimensions of the sections and easily compare them to the graphics provided in the practice.
6. In the *Placed Sections* area, click **Click to add** and select the location, as shown in Figure 5–17, to add a section. This placement is approximate and will be modified.

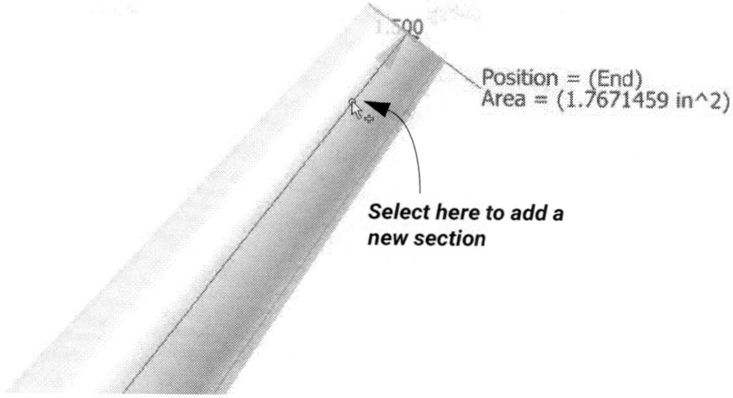

Figure 5–17

7. Ensure that  (Driving Section) is selected to enable the section area to be driven by user-defined values. Enable the *Section Size* and *Section Position* options, if required. Change the *Section Size* to **1.75 in^2** and the *Section Position* to **0.9**. Figure 5–18 shows the Section Dimensions dialog box and the model.

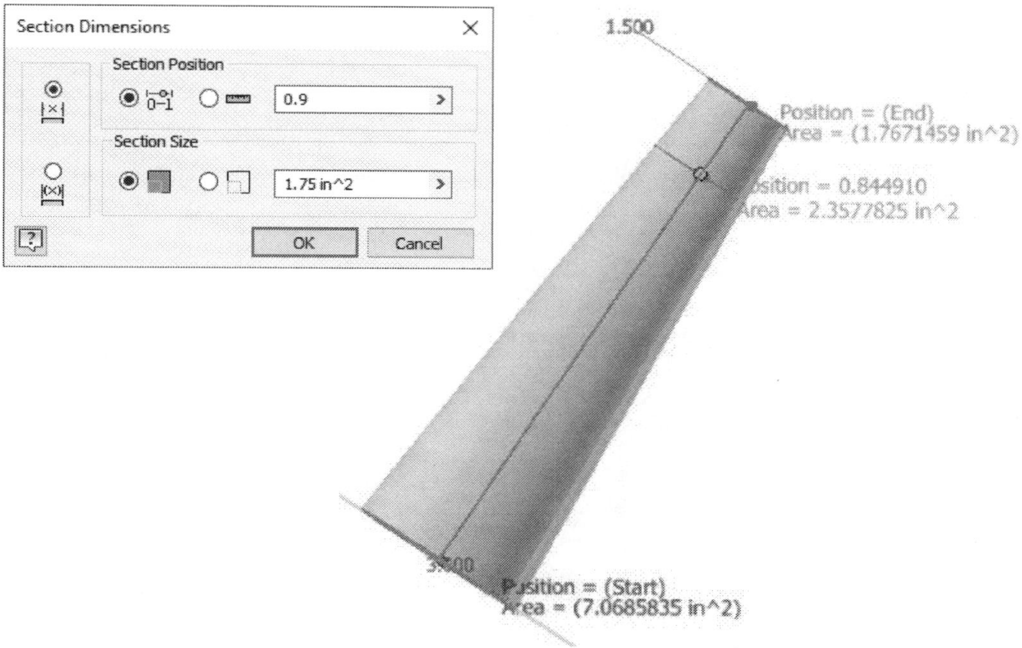

Figure 5–18

8. Click **OK** to accept the new dimensions.

9. In the *Placed Sections* area, click **Click to add**, select and dimension a second internal section, as shown in Figure 5–19.

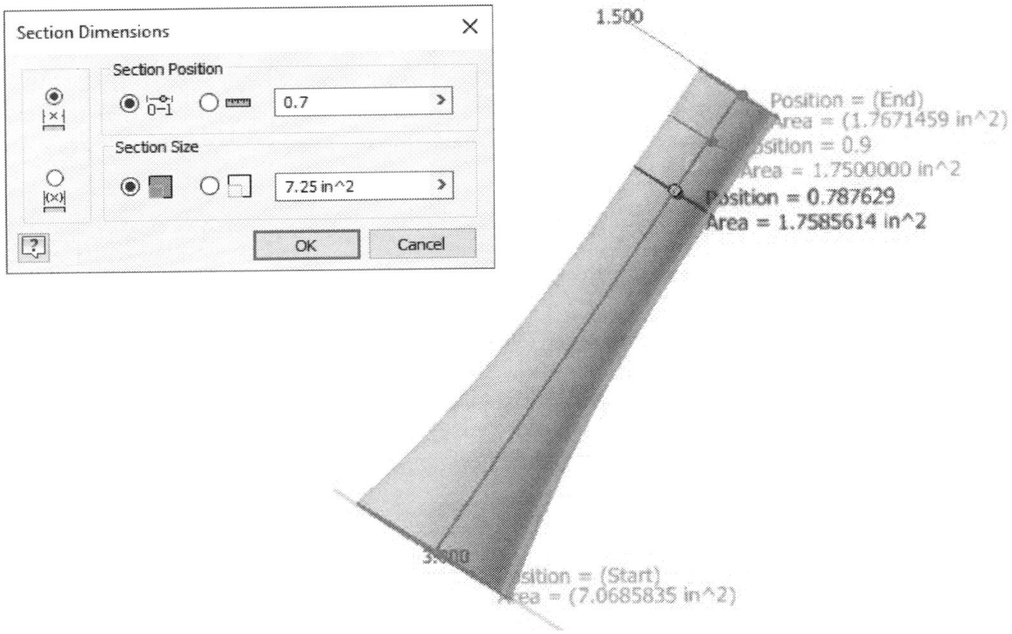

Figure 5–19

10. Continue to add sections to the loft using the Position and Area values shown in Figure 5–20.For this practice, you are not going to change the Position and Area for the Start and End sections; however, this type of modification is possible.

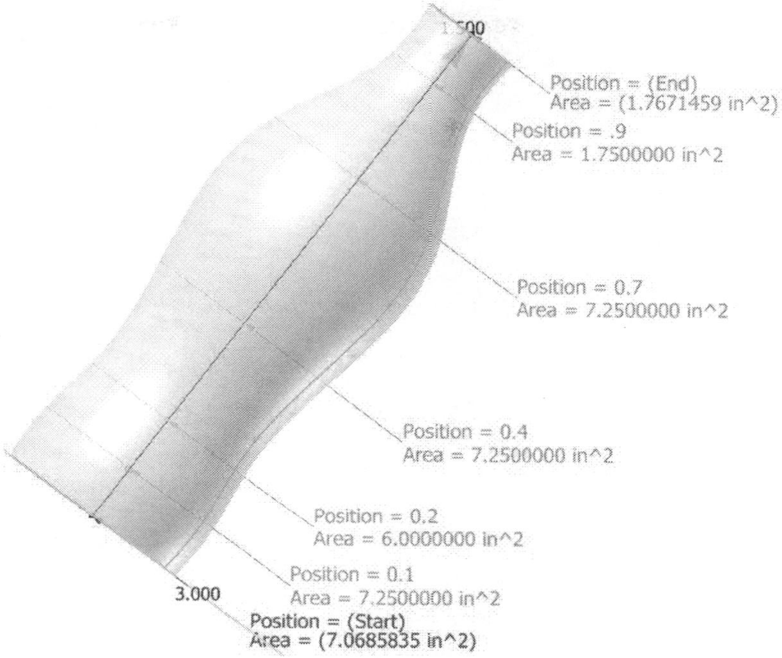

Figure 5–20

11. Click **OK** to create the loft.
12. Add a **0.5 in** fillet to the bottom of the bottle and a **0.1 in** shell. The model displays as shown in Figure 5–21.

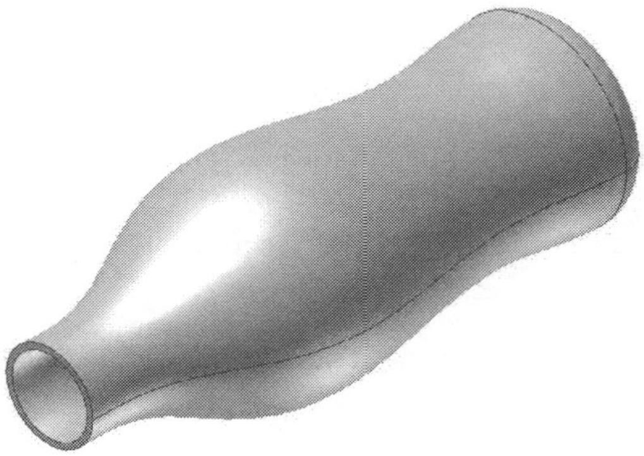

Figure 5–21

13. Save and close the model.

End of practice

Practice 5b
Sweeps

Practice Objectives

- Create a Guide sweep using a rail that incorporates the use of a profile, path, and guide rail curve to define shape of the model.
- Create a cut using the Guide sweep using a surface that keeps the profile normal to a surface along the path.

In this practice, you will create the geometry shown in Figure 5–22. All of the geometry is created using the **Path & Guide Rail** and **Path & Guide Surface** sweep options. Different options in each type are used to create the geometry.

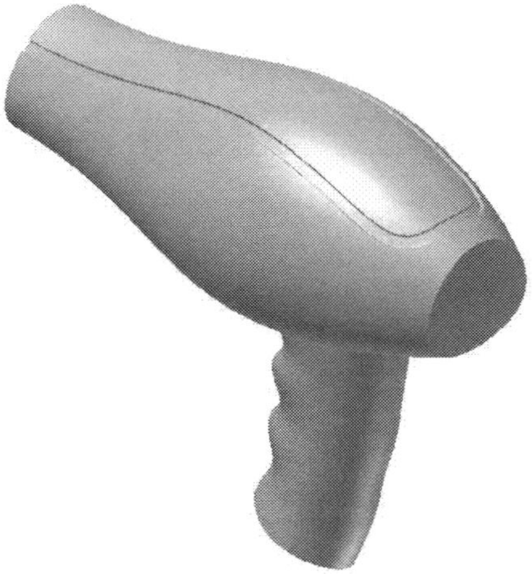

Figure 5–22

Task 1: Create a sweep to represent the body of the hairdryer.

In this task, you create a Guide Sweep to create the body of the hairdryer model. You will also manipulate the profile scaling option to see how it affects the geometry's shape.

1. Open **Hairdryer.ipt**. A number of different curves and profiles have been created for you.

2. In the *3D Model* tab>Create panel, click (Sweep). The sweep's *Orientation* option is set to (Follow Path) by default. Select the **BodyProfile** sketch as the profile for the sweep. Activate the *Path* field and select the **BodyPath** sketch as the path for the sweep. Both references and the previewed geometry are shown in Figure 5–23.

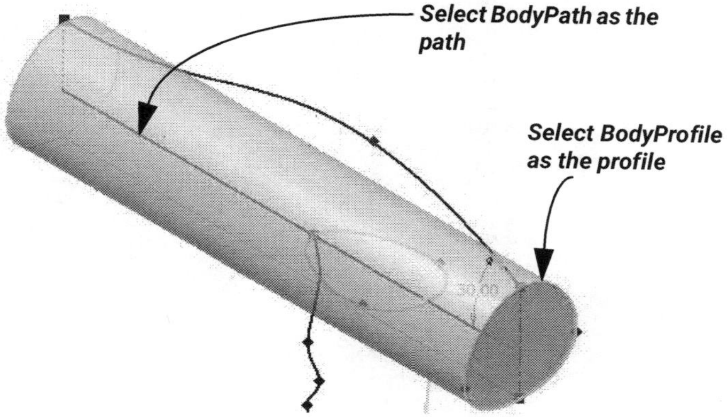

Figure 5–23

3. To enhance the shape of the body of the hairdryer, an additional curve will be included to drive the shape. In the *Behavior* area, select (Guide).
4. Click in the *Guide* field and select the **BodyGuideRail** sketch as the Guide Rail reference, as shown in Figure 5–24. The preview updates to show the enhanced shape once the additional guide curve is added.

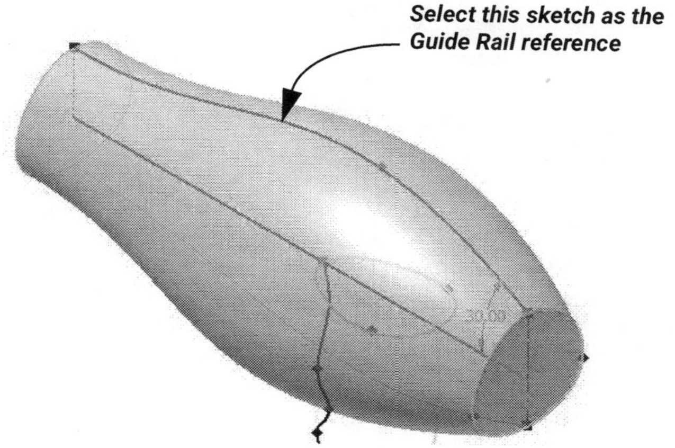

Figure 5–24

5. In the *Profile Scaling* area of the Properties panel, select (No Scaling). The preview changes to eliminate the influence of the guide curve.

6. Select (X Scaling) in the *Profile Scaling* area. The X direction is the only direction that is influenced by the Guide Curve, as shown in Figure 5–25.

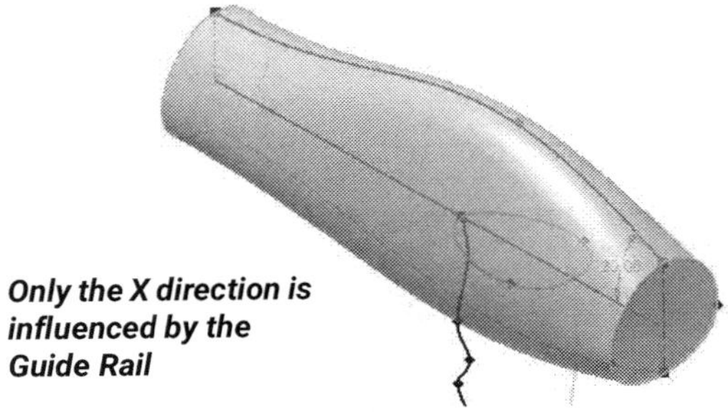

Figure 5–25

7. Change the *Profile Scaling* option back to (X & Y Scaling) to have the guide rail influence the sweep's shape in both the X and Y directions.

8. Complete the feature.

Task 2: Create a sweep for the handle of the hairdryer.

In this task, you create another Guide Sweep to create the handle of the hairdryer model.

1. Start the creation of another **Sweep** feature.

2. Select **HandleProfile** as the profile for the feature and **3D Sketch** as the path for the sweep.

3. In the *Behavior* area, select (Guide), if not already active. Note that the preview will not appear if this is already active.

4. Select **Handle_Front_Grips** as the guide rail reference. All references and the previewed geometry are shown in Figure 5–26.

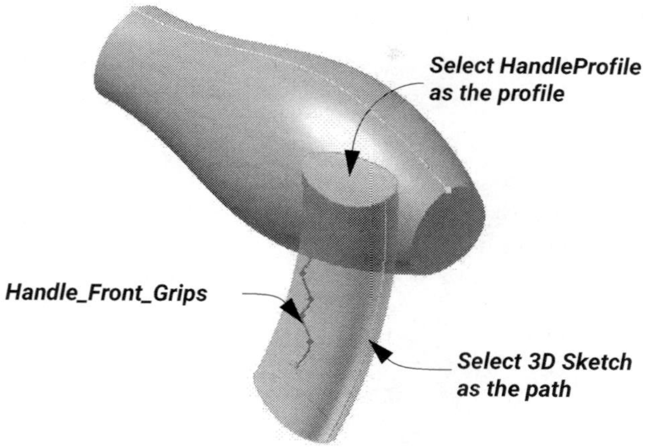

Figure 5–26

5. Under *Profile Scaling*, select  (X Scaling).
6. Complete the feature. The model updates as shown in Figure 5–27.

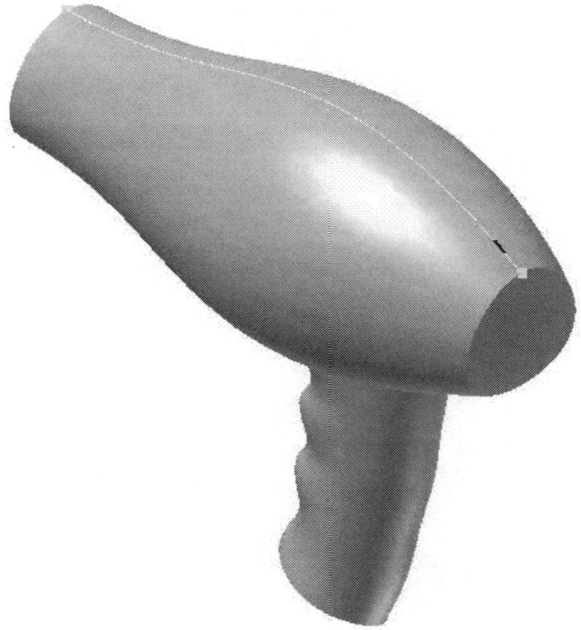

Figure 5–27

Task 3: Create a sweep that cuts away material from the top of the hairdryer.

In this task, you create a Guide Sweep using a surface to cut away material on the top of the hairdryer model.

1. Right-click **IntersectionSurface** in the Model browser and select **Visibility**.
2. Start the creation of a new 3D sketch.
3. Using the (Intersection Curve), create a new curve at the intersection of **IntersectionSurface** and the surface of the body of the hairdryer. Finish the sketch. The curve should appear as shown in Figure 5–28.

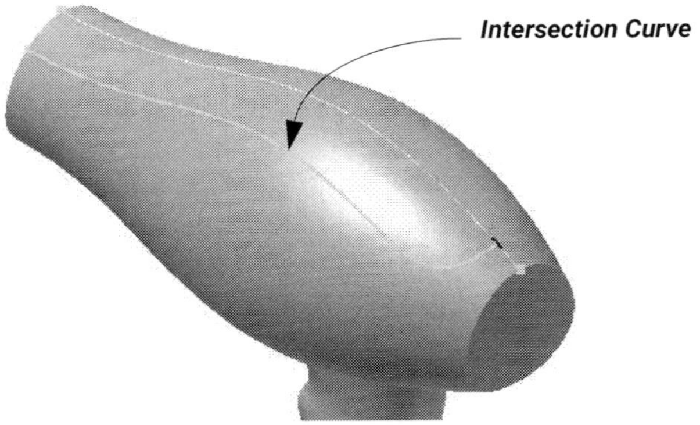

Figure 5–28

4. Start the creation of another **Sweep** feature.
5. The **Groove** sketch is preselected as the profile for the sweep because it is the only remaining section that is closed.
6. Select the curve that was just created using (Intersection Curve) as the path.
7. Set the sweep to remove material from the model and complete the feature.
8. Set the Orientation to (Follow Path).
9. Complete the feature.

10. Reorient the model to see the nozzle of the hairdryer, as shown in Figure 5–29. The cut does not remain normal to the surface of the hairdryer as it sweeps along the path.

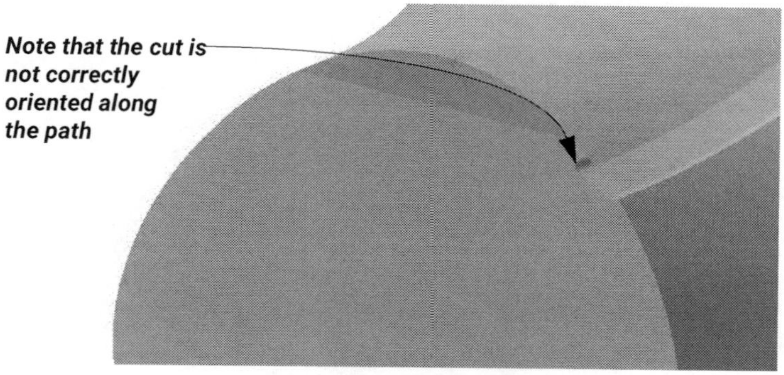

Figure 5–29

11. Edit the last Sweep feature.

12. Select  (Guide) as the sweep type.

13. Maintain the **Profiles** and **Path** options that were originally defined. Select the surface of the body of the hairdryer as the *Guide Surface* reference.

14. Complete the feature. The model updates to show that the swept cut now remains normal to the surface along the entire path, as shown in Figure 5–30.

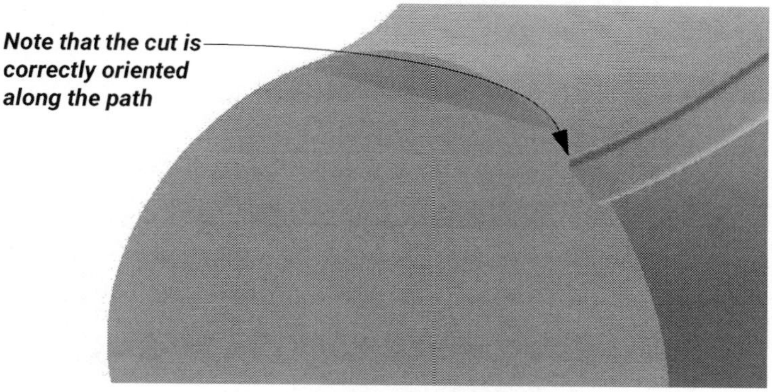

Figure 5–30

15. Mirror the cut as shown in Figure 5–31.

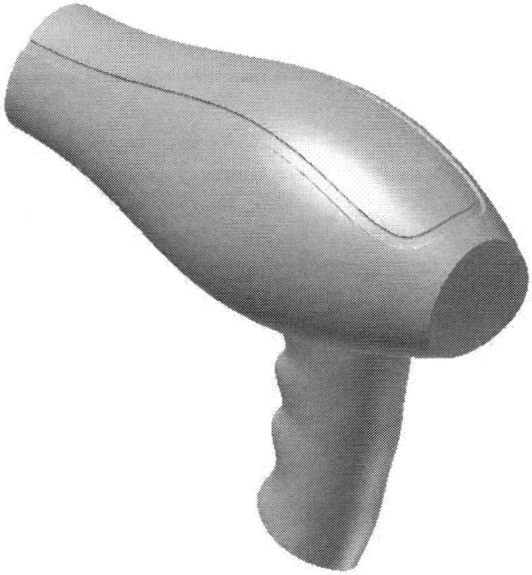

Figure 5–31

16. Save and close the model.

End of practice

Practice 5c
Creating a Coil

Practice Objectives

- Create appropriate profile and axis features to be used to create the required Coil feature.
- Create coil-shaped geometry that removes material from the model.

In this practice, you will create a coil on an existing part to create a drill bit. The completed drill bit is shown in Figure 5–32.

Figure 5–32

Task 1: Sketch the coil profiles.

1. Open **drillbit.ipt**. Review the features in the Model browser. User-defined work features will be used to place and dimension the coil profile.
2. Create a sketch on Work Plane1. Project Work Axis1 onto the sketch plane to locate and dimension the coil profiles.
3. Sketch and dimension the two circular profiles so that they are symmetric about the projected Work Axis1, as shown in Figure 5–33.

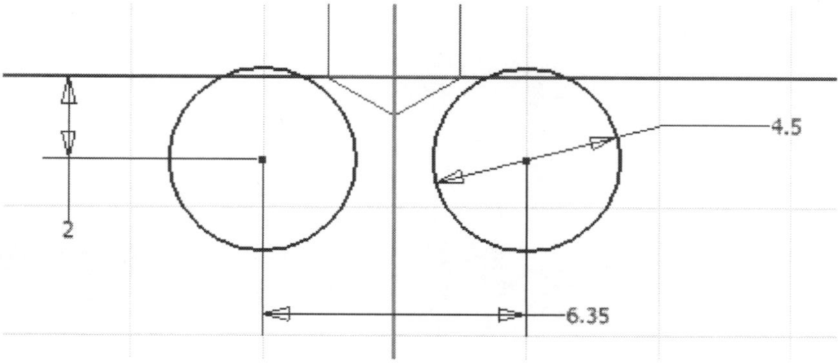

Figure 5–33

4. Finish the sketch.

Task 2: Create the coil.

1. In the *3D Model* tab>Create panel, click (Coil). The Properties panel opens.
2. Select one of the sketched circles as the profile.
3. Activate the *Axis* field, if not already active, and select **Work Axis1**. Flip the pitch direction for the coil, if required, so the path extends along the part.
4. Click to set the operation to cut away material.
5. In the *Method* field, select **Pitch and Height**. Set the *Pitch* to **25 mm** and the *Height* to **75 mm**.
6. Ensure that the **Close Start** and **Close End** options remain unselected.
7. Click (Apply). The model displays as shown in Figure 5–34.

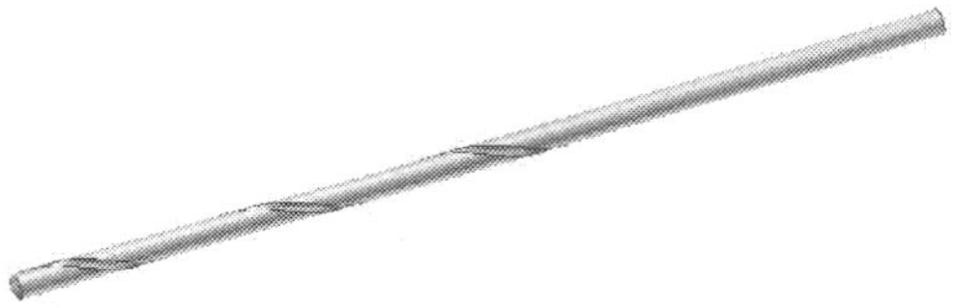

Figure 5–34

8. Continue to use the Properties panel and select the other circular profile and the same axis to create another coil using the same settings.
9. Click **OK** to complete the coils. The model displays as shown in Figure 5–35 and both Coil features are added to the Model browser list.

Figure 5–35

10. Save and close the model.

End of practice

Chapter Review Questions

1. Which of the following best describes an Area Loft? (Select all that apply.)
   a. It enables you to only create geometry between only two sketched sections.
   b. It enables you to control the shape of the geometry using Rail references.
   c. It enables you to control the area of a section.
   d. It enables you to control intermediate points along a center line.

2. An area value can be assigned to either the start section or the end section of an Area Loft.
   a. True
   b. False

3. When the Driven ( ) option is selected in the Section Dimensions dialog box, which section type(s) is not available (i.e., driven by the model geometry)?
   a. Section Position
   b. Section Size
   c. Both Section Position and Section Size

4. What does the Guide sweep enable you to control? (Select all that apply.)
   a. Control the orientation of the profile along the path of the sweep.
   b. Control the shape of the profile by referencing two curves.
   c. Control the scale and twist of the sweep.
   d. Control the shape of the sweep using the normal from a reference surface.

5. What sweep option enables you to control the twist of the sweep using a surface?
   a. Path
   b. Guide using Rail
   c. Guide using Surface

6. To create the coil geometry shown in Figure 5–36, the **Close Start** was enabled and the **Close End** was not enabled.

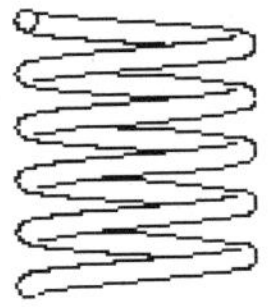

Figure 5–36

   a. True
   b. False

7. If a sketched line is being used as the axis of revolution for a Coil feature, it must exist as an independent feature and must be created prior to initiating the creation of the coil.
   a. True
   b. False

Command Summary

Button	Command	Location
	**Coil**	• **Ribbon:** *3D Model* tab>Create panel
	**Loft**	• **Ribbon:** *3D Model* tab>Create panel
	**Sweep**	• **Ribbon:** *3D Model* tab>Create panel

Chapter 6

Generative Shape Design

The Generative Shape Design tool available in the Autodesk® Inventor® software enables designers to set design criteria for a mass reduction target in a model. Based on assigned materials, constraints, and loads, the system returns a design suggestion that can be used to manipulate the model geometry to reduce its mass. Although this tool recommends a new shape, the manipulation is done manually using standard 3D modeling features. Once modified, stress analysis tools should be used on the model to ensure that it meets structural requirements.

Learning Objectives

- Create a Shape Generator study that sets a goal to meet a mass reduction target.
- Assign criteria in a Shape Generator study to accurately define a model's working environment.
- Promote a Shape Generator study to the modeling environment.

6.1 Shape Generator

The Shape Generator tool in Autodesk Inventor enables you to design light-weight models based on specified requirements. First, you must start with an Inventor model that approximates the overall volume or shape that is required. After setting the requirements and running the Shape Generator, you are presented with a 3D mesh design that you can use as a guide to redesign your initial geometry. Figure 6–1 shows the progression of a model from its initial design, through Shape Generator, to the final design.

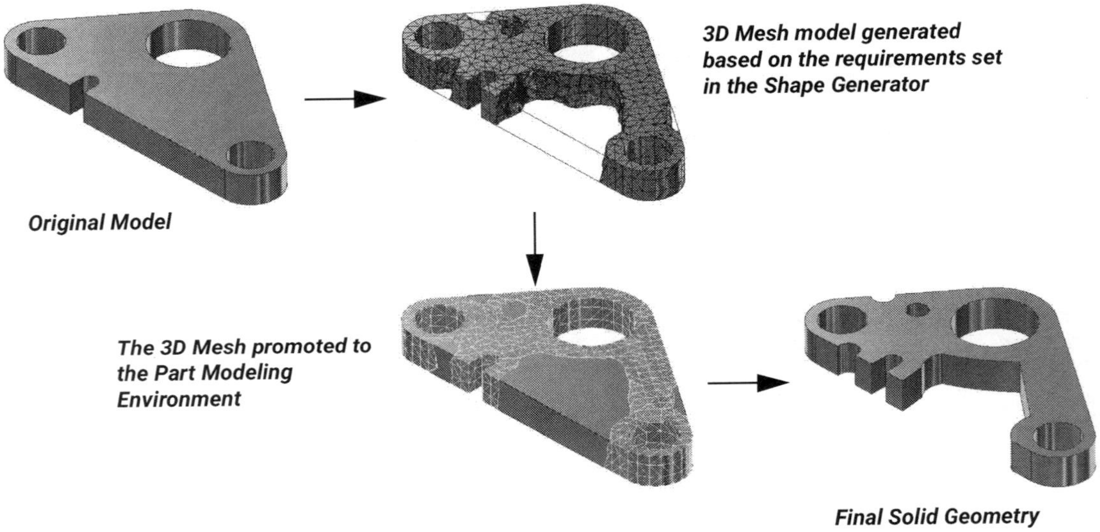

Figure 6–1

How To: Generate a Design Using Shape Generator

1. Open the model in the Shape Generator environment.
2. Define the material specification.
3. Apply constraints and loads that will represent the stresses that the part will encounter.
4. Define the Shape Generator Settings.
5. (Optional) Set zones that will be preserved during the analysis.
6. (Optional) Define symmetry in the model, if required.
7. Run the Shape Generator study.
8. Modify the initial design using the Shape Generator's 3D mesh as a guide for making modifications.

Preparing a Model for Shape Generator

Prior to initiating the Shape Generator tool, ensure that the Autodesk Inventor model represents the overall volume and shape of the intended geometry. The model should contain any required contact points (such as holes) that will represent pin locations and surfaces that will sustain forces.

Hint: Environment Support

Shape generator is only supported for single-body part modeling. It cannot be used for multi-body part or assembly design.

Opening Shape Generator

To open the Shape Generator environment, in the *3D Model* tab>Explore panel, click

(Shape Generator). Click **OK** if prompted to review the learning tool. The *Analysis* tab opens as shown in Figure 6–2.

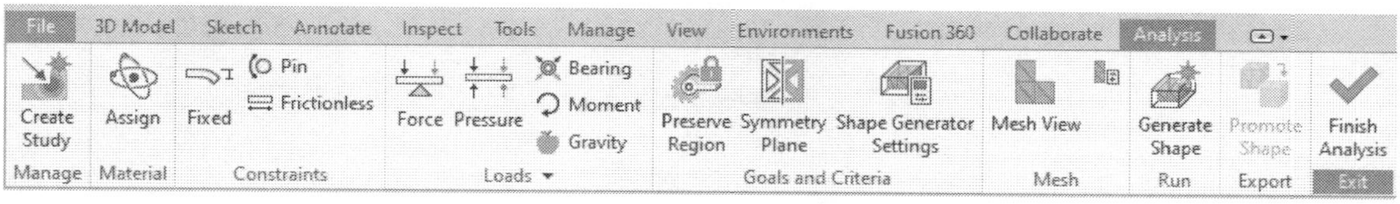

Figure 6–2

By default, a Shape Generator study is added to the Model browser once the *Analysis* tab is opened. The commands on this tab enable you to do the following:

- Create multiple shape generator analyzes and manage them.
- Assign material to an analysis.
- Assign constraints and loads to an analysis to define how the model is loaded in its working environment.
- Set goals and criteria for the analysis. This involves defining regions in the model that should not be changed as well as symmetry planes. Additionally, you set the criteria against which the design will be optimized. For example, reduce weight by x% to achieve a specific weight.
- Generate the optimized shape.
- Export the 3D mesh of the optimized shape to the modeling environment.

__Note:__ While in the study, you can select __Modeling__ at the top of the Model browser to review the features in the design while remaining in the analysis.

To create additional Shape Generator studies, in the Manage panel, click (Create Study), select **Shape Generator** in the Create New Study dialog box, and click **OK**.

Hint: Shape Generator in the Stress Analysis Environment

The Shape Generator functionality can also be accessed in the Stress Analysis environment.

In the *3D Model* tab> Simulation panel, click (Stress Analysis). Once in the *Analysis* tab, click (Create Study), select **Shape Generator** as the study type in the Create New Study dialog box and click **OK**.

Material Assignment

In the Material panel, click (Assign) to open the Assign Materials dialog box, shown in Figure 6–3.

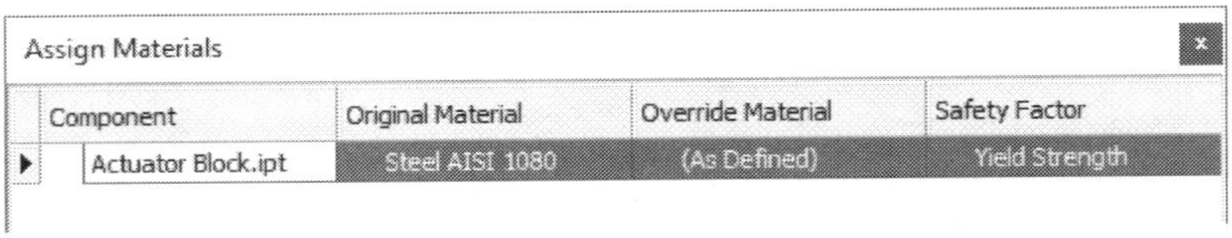

Figure 6–3

- Maintain the **(As Defined)** option in the Override Material drop-down list to run the generator using the original material that was set in the modeling environment.
- Select an alternate material type in the Override Material drop-down list to study an alternative material.
- Select **Materials** to open and use the Material browser to define materials.
- Set the Safety Factor based on the **Yield Strength** or the **Ultimate Tensile Strength**.
- The material information is stored in the **Material** node for the active study. Each study that is set up in the Shape Generator environment can use a unique material setting.

Applying Constraints

You can assign constraints to the model to accurately define the translational or rotational degrees of freedom that exist in its working environment. **Fixed**, **Pin**, and **Frictionless** constraints can be assigned.

How To: Add Constraints

1. In the *Analysis* tab>Constraints panel, select the type of constraint to be assigned. Alternatively, you can right-click on the **Constraints** node in the Model browser and select the constraint type.

Constraint Type	Description
(Fixed)	Removes all degrees of freedom on a face, edge, or vertex.
(Pin)	When used with cylindrical surfaces, it prevents faces from moving or deforming in combinations of radial, axial, or tangential directions.
(Frictionless)	When used with flat or cylindrical surfaces, it prevents the surface from moving or deforming in the normal direction relative to the surface.

2. In the applicable Constraint dialog box, select (Location) and select the location to which the constraint is being assigned. Select faces, edges, or vertices, as required.

3. Click >> on the dialog box to access the additional constraint settings for each constraint type. The options in this portion of the dialog box enable you to further customize the constraint.
   - The **Display Glyph** option is used to enable/disable the visibility of the constraint glyph on the model.
   - A custom constraint name can be assigned, if required.
   - To apply a Fixed constraint with non-zero displacement, click **Use Vector Components** and enter X, Y, or Z values, as required.
   - For cylindrical surfaces, **Pin** constraints can be fixed radially, axially, or tangentially, as required. The default is to be fixed radially and axially.

4. Click **OK** to assign and close the dialog box. Alternatively, click **Apply** to assign the constraint and continue adding additional constraints of the same type.

Once added to the model, constraints are listed in the **Constraints** node in the Model browser. To edit them, right-click on the constraint name and select **Edit <Constraint Type>**.

Applying Loads

To accurately determine a shape using shape generator, you can assign loads that represent the applied load on the model. **Force**, **Pressure**, **Bearing**, **Moment**, **Gravity**, **Remote Force**, and **Body** loads can be assigned.

How To: Add Loads

1. In the *Analysis* tab>Loads panel, select the type of load to be assigned. Alternatively, you can right-click on the **Loads** node in the Model browser and select the load type.

Load Type	Description
(Force)	Assigns a force to a face, edge, or vertex. The force points to the inside of the part. You can assign the direction reference planar to a face or along a straight edge or axes.
(Pressure)	Assigns a pressure load to a face. Pressure is uniform and acts normal to the surface at all locations on the surface.
(Bearing)	Assigns a bearing load to a cylindrical face. By default, the load is along the axis of the cylinder and the direction of the load is radial.
(Moment)	Assigns a moment load to a face. You can assign the direction reference using a planar face, or along a straight edge or axes. The moment is applied around the direction to the selected face.
(Gravity)	Assigns the gravity load normal to the selected face or parallel with the selected edge.
(Remote Force)	Assigns a force at a specific point outside or inside the model. This option is located in the expanded Loads panel.
(Body)	Assign linear acceleration or angular velocity and acceleration for the model using a planar or cylindrical face as the input. This option is located on the expanded Loads panel. You can only apply one Body load per Shape Generator study.

2. In the applicable Load dialog box, select and select the reference to which the load is being assigned. Select faces, edges, or vertices, as required.
   - A glyph displays on the model indicating the direction in which the load is applied. To change the direction, click in the *Direction* area and select an alternate reference or flip the direction.

3. Define the magnitude of the load.
    - Click for Force, Bearing, Moment, Gravity, Remote Force, and Body loads to assign the magnitude values using vector components.
4. Click on the dialog box to access additional settings for each load type. The options in this portion of the dialog box enable you to further customize the load.
    - The **Display Glyph** option can be enabled/disabled to control the load glyph display, as required.
    - The scale and color of the glyph display can be modified.
    - A custom name can be assigned for the load, if required.
5. Click **OK** to assign and close the dialog box. Alternatively, click **Apply** to assign the load and continue adding additional loads of the same type.

Once loads are added to the model they are listed in the **Loads** node in the Model browser. To edit them, right-click on the constraint name and select **Edit <Force Load>**.

Hint: Multiple Loads on a Face

Consider using the **Split** command to split a single face if the face experiences multiple loading situations.

Shape Generator Settings

The Shape Generator settings enable you to define the design criteria. To open the Shape Generator Settings dialog box (shown in Figure 6–4), click (Shape Generator Settings). By default, the 3D mesh model will be generated to maximize stiffness; however, you can also define the following additional criteria:

- Reduce the mass by a specified percentage or reduce it to a specific value.
- Define a specific member size that must be maintained during 3D mesh creation. This helps ensure that the mesh does not generate a wall thicknesses that can not be manufactured or might fail structural testing.

- The *Mesh Resolution* area provides a slider and a *Value* field that can be used to set the mesh resolution. A finer setting results in a smoother, higher quality mesh; however, it requires increased run time.

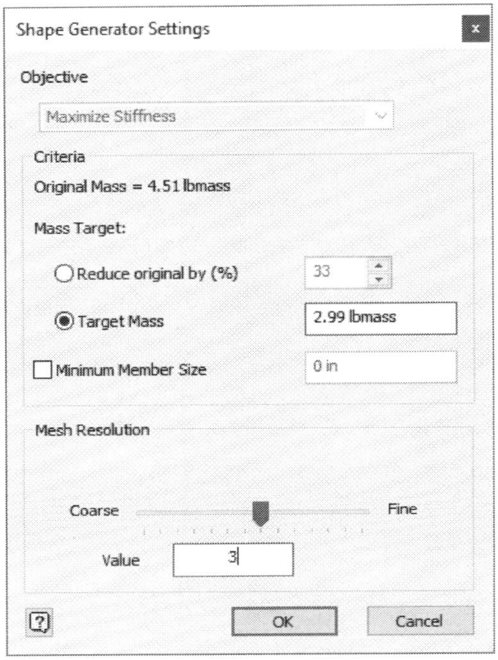

Figure 6–4

Preserving Regions

In most models, there will be regions of the design that should not be removed when generating a suggested 3D mesh. For example, specific areas around bolt holes or other supporting features may need to be maintained to allow the model to function as required.

How To: Preserve an Area on the Model

1. In the Goals and Criteria panel, click  (Preserve Region).
2. In the Preserve Region dialog box, click  and select a face on the model. Based on the selection of the face, a default preserved region boundary will appear on the model.
    - If a planar face is selected, a bounding box displays around the face, as shown in Figure 6–5.

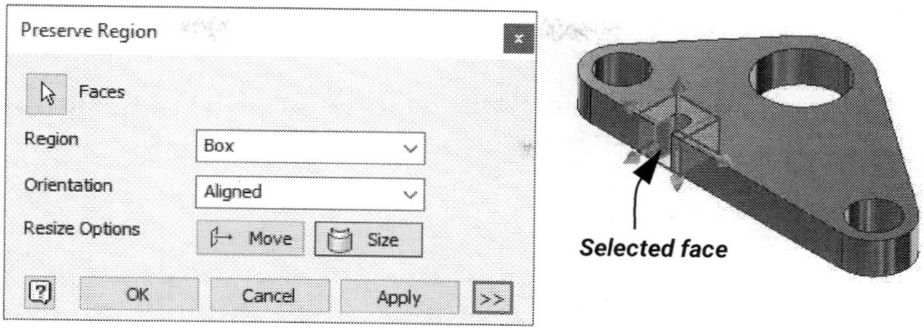

Figure 6–5

- If a cylindrical face is selected, a bounding cylinder displays around the face, as shown in Figure 6–6.

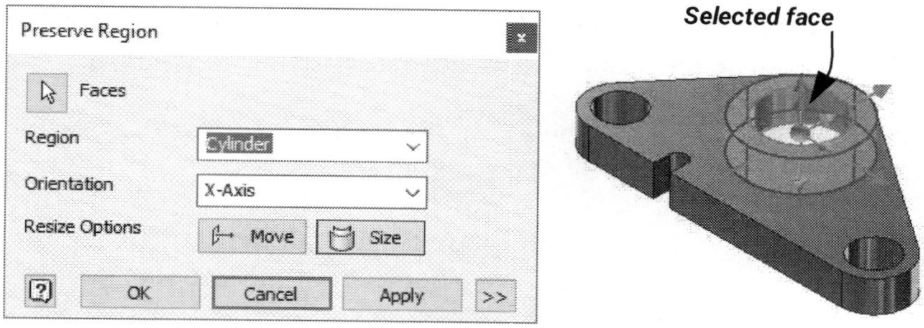

Figure 6–6

- If the assumption of **Box** or **Cylinder** is not correct, you can switch the option in the Region drop-down list.

3. Refine the location and size of the bounding shape.
   - Select **Move** and drag the center point of the displayed triad to reposition the bounding shape on the model.
   - Select **Size** and activate and drag any of the handles that radiate from the bounding shape.
   - Click >> to enter specific values for the center point and the bounding shape dimensions.
4. (Optional) In the expanded portion of the dialog box (>>) you can modify the glyph color, control its visibility, or enter a custom name for the preserved region.
5. Click **OK** to create the preserved region. Alternatively, click **Apply** to create the region and continue creating additional regions.

Once preserved regions are added to the model they are listed in the **Preserved Regions** node in the Model browser. To edit them, right-click on the constraint name and select **Edit Preserved Region**.

Assigning Symmetry

Symmetry planes can be assigned in the model to force the Shape Generator to produce a 3D mesh result that is symmetric about a selected plane or up to three planes (XY, XZ, or YZ).

How To: Assign Symmetry

1. In the Goals and Criteria panel, click (Symmetry Plane).
2. By default, the symmetry planes are placed at the center of mass and are aligned with the global coordinate system. If required, use any of the following to modify the location of the default symmetry planes:
   - To align the symmetry plane with a local UCS, click (Local UCS) and select an active UCS. The symmetry plane is created in the local XY plane of the UCS.
   - To place at the center of mass, click (Center of mass). The UCS and symmetry plane are placed at the center of mass of the part.
   - To place at the center of the bounding box of the part, click (Center of bounding box). The UCS and symmetry plane are placed at the center of bounding box of the part.
3. Toggle the active planes (), as required, to define the model symmetry. Active planes appear red in the model.
4. (Optional) Click to toggle the display of the symmetry glyph and assign a name for symmetry definition.

5. Click **OK** to close the dialog box. The Symmetry Plane dialog box and a single symmetry plane are shown in Figure 6–7.

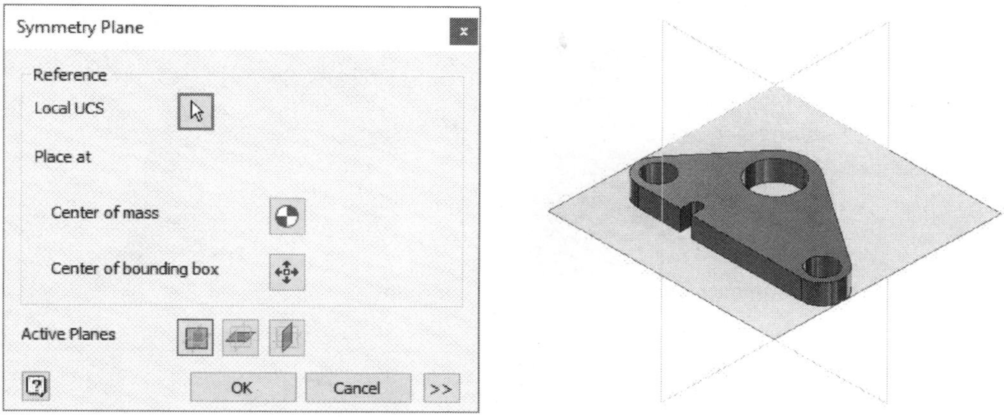

Figure 6–7

Once symmetry planes are added to the model, they are listed in the **Symmetry Planes** node in the Model browser. To edit them, right-click on the constraint name and select **Edit Symmetry Plane**.

Run the Shape Generator

Once the analysis has been set up, click  (Generate Shape) to open the Generate Shape dialog box, as shown in Figure 6–8. Click **Run** to start the shape generator. The expandable area at the bottom of the dialog box reports warnings or errors while the process is being run.

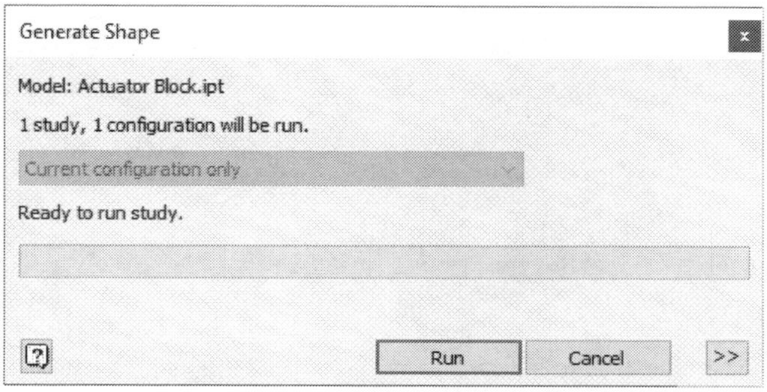

Figure 6–8

Once shape generation is complete, you are presented with a recommended 3D mesh model that can be used to guide your model design. Figure 6–9 shows the original model and a resultant mesh model after constraints, loads, and criteria were set.

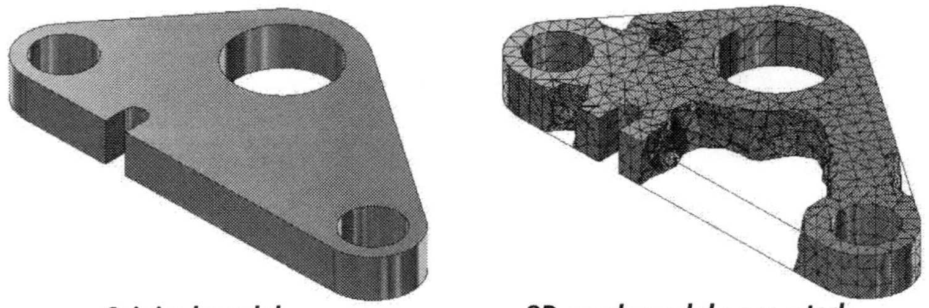

Original model

3D mesh model generated using Shape Generator

Figure 6–9

Promote the 3D Mesh Model

Once the mesh model has been generated, it can be promoted to the modeling environment to be used as a guide for making modeling changes to the geometry. In the Export panel, click  (Promote Shape) and select whether to copy the 3D mesh model directly to the part modeling environment (**Current Part File**) or to an STL file (**STL File**) that can be imported separately. Once the 3D mesh model is displayed, in the part modeling environment, you can use it as a guide to remove material from the part geometry.

Figure 6–10 shows an example of the promoted 3D mesh model in the part modeling environment and the final geometry based on suggested areas to be removed.

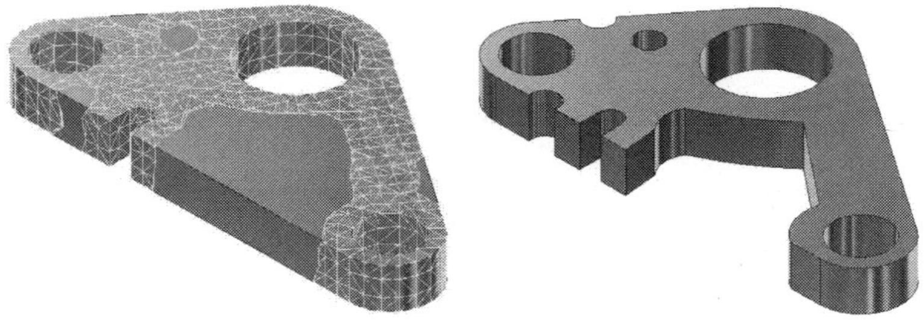

3D model promoted to the part modeling environment

Final solid geometry

Figure 6–10

Consider the following when using a 3D mesh model to make changes to your design:

- When making geometry changes to the model, consider using lines and arcs where possible to help ensure that the final geometry is manufacturable.
- Not all geometry needs to be removed. This is a recommendation based on the criteria set.
- Consider using the Stress Analysis environment to further analyze the structural integrity of the final geometry. The constraints and loads set in Shape Generator can be reused in the Stress Analysis environment.

Hint: Visual Style

Consider using the Wireframe visual style when using the 3D mesh model to make design changes. This enables you to see how the mesh model looks inside the solid geometry.

Practice 6a
Generating a Design Using Shape Generator

Practice Objectives

- Create a Shape Generator study that sets a goal to meet a mass reduction target.
- Assign material, constraint, and load criteria in a Shape Generator study to accurately define a model's working environment.
- Set regions in the model that will not be removed after the Shape Generator study is complete.
- Define a symmetry plane in the model.
- Promote a Shape Generator study to the modeling environment.

In this practice, you will open a model that represents the overall shape and volume of an actuator mounting block that exists in a top-level assembly. The Shape Generator tool will be used to suggest modeling changes that helps to reduce the mass of the model to under 3 lbs. You will define the material, constraints, loads, preserved regions, and a symmetry plane prior to running the study. Figure 6–11 shows the model's progress through the practice.

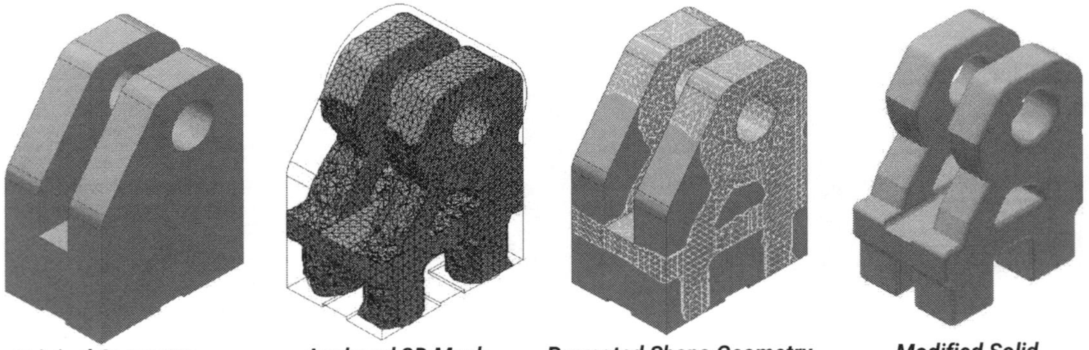

Original Geometry ***Analyzed 3D Mesh*** ***Promoted Shape Geometry*** ***Modified Solid Geometry***

Figure 6–11

Task 1: Open an existing part model in the Shape Generator environment.

1. Open **Actuator Block.ipt** from the practice files folder.
2. Change the model display to **Shaded with Hidden Edges** to better visualize the interior of the model.
3. In the *3D Model* tab> Explore panel, click (Shape Generator).

4. Click **OK** if prompted with the Shape Generator dialog box. This provides an introduction to the tool and the option to learn more from the Help documentation. If this was previously disabled, you will not be shown this dialog box.

5. The *Analysis* tab becomes the active tab and the model and Model browser display as shown in Figure 6–12. While in the study, you can select **Modeling** at the top of the Model browser to review the features in the design while remaining in the analysis. The overall shape of the model was created using the part modeling features.

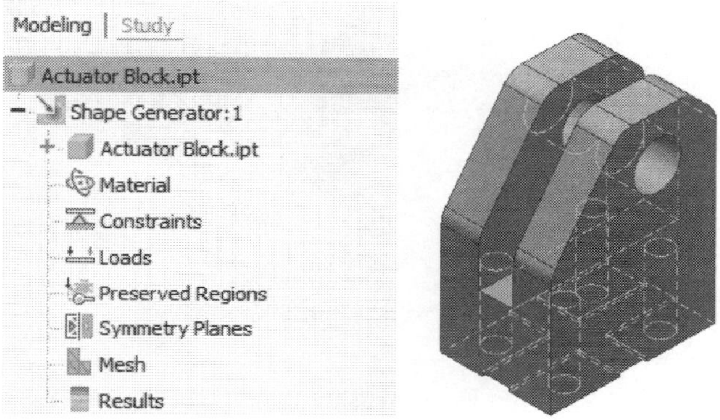

Figure 6–12

Task 2: Define the material specification.

1. In the Material panel, click  (Assign) to open the Assign Materials dialog box, as shown in Figure 6–13.

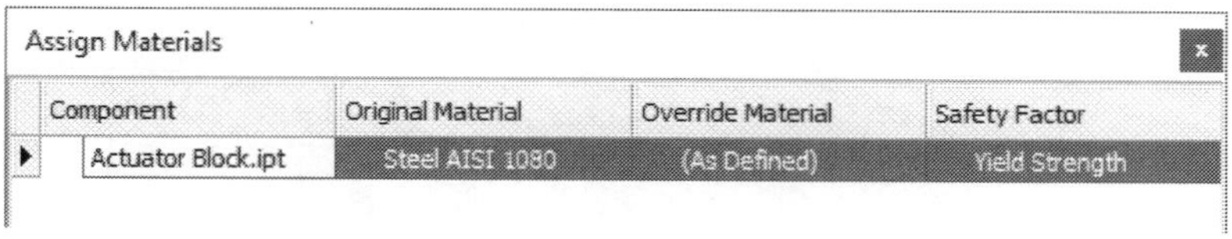

Figure 6–13

2. Maintain the **(As Defined)** option in the Override Material drop-down list. This uses the material that was defined when the model was created.

3. Click **OK**.

Task 3: Apply constraints and loads that will represent the stresses that the part will encounter.

1. In the *Analysis* tab>Constraints panel, click  (Pin). Pin constraints prevent faces from moving or deforming in combinations of radial, axial, or tangential directions.

2. Ensure that the  (Location) button is active and select the cylindrical surface shown in Figure 6–14.

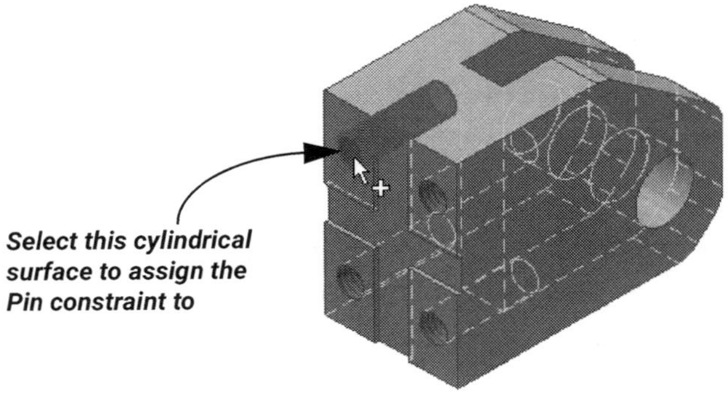

Figure 6–14

3. Click **Apply** to assign the constraint and leave the dialog box open. The Pin glyph displays on the model.
4. Continue to apply three additional Pin constraints to the remaining 3 support holes on the bottom of the model. Once assigned, the model and Model browser should display as shown in Figure 6–15.

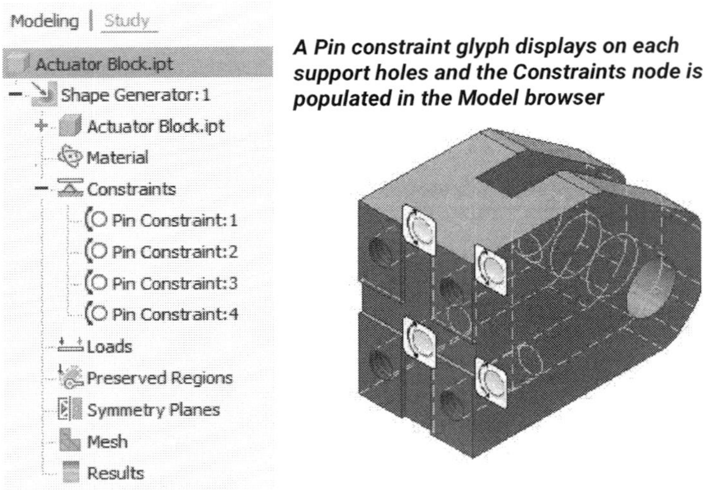

Figure 6–15

5. Click **Cancel** to close the dialog box.
6. Change the view display to **Shaded** if you had been working in an alternate view style.
7. In the *Analysis* tab>Loads panel, click  (Bearing).

8. Ensure that the (Faces) button is active and select the two cylindrical faces shown in Figure 6–16 as the reference faces to which the **Bearing** load is being assigned (blue faces).

9. By default, the load is along the axis of the cylinder and the direction of the load is radial.

   Click in the *Direction* area and select the face shown in Figure 6–16 as the direction reference (green face). A glyph displays on the model indicating the direction in which the load is applied.

   ***Note:** To assign the load based on vector directions, expand the dialog box and enter the values in the additional fields that are provided.*

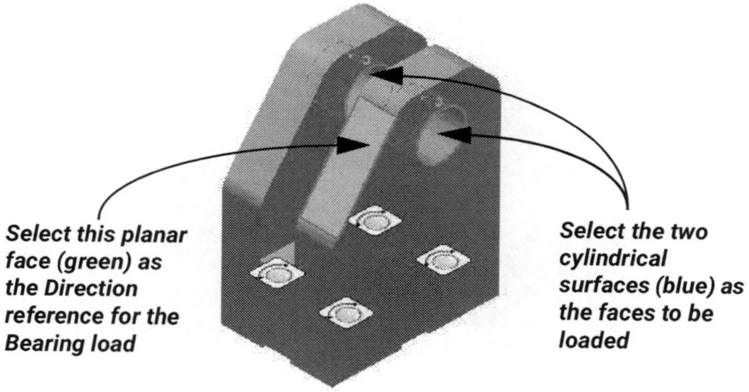

Figure 6–16

10. Set the load *Magnitude* to **5000 N**, as shown in Figure 6–17.

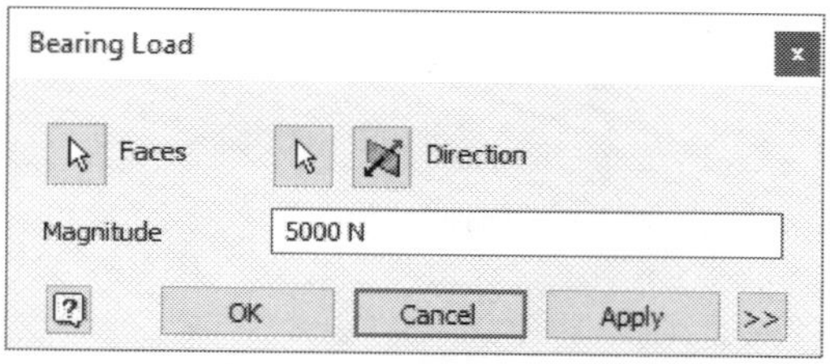

Figure 6–17

11. Click on the dialog box to access the additional settings. Enter **Bearing** as the custom name for the load.

12. Click **OK** to assign the load and close the dialog box. The **Bearing** load has been added to the **Loads** node.

Task 4: Define the Shape Generator settings.

The current mass of the model is 4.51 lbs. The design goal in this model is to reduce the weight to under 3 lbs.

1. To open the Shape Generator Settings dialog box, click (Shape Generator Settings).
2. Select **Target Mass** and enter **2.99lbmass**, as shown in Figure 6–18.
3. Maintain the *Mesh Resolution* slider at **3.000**, as shown in Figure 6–18.

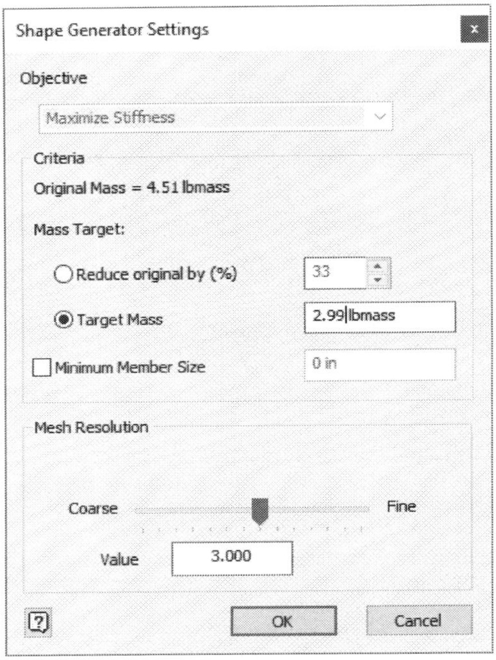

Figure 6–18

4. Click **OK**.

Task 5: Set zones that will be preserved

1. In the Goals and Criteria panel, click (Preserve Region).

2. In the Preserve Region dialog box, click (Location) and select one of the cylindrical faces used in placing the **Bearing** load.

3. The Preserve Region dialog box updates to create a cylindrical region. Use the arrows on the various sides of the cylindrical bounding box to drag it, as shown in Figure 6–19. Ensure that the preserved area extends the width of the part and preserves the material above and around the holes.

   Note: *Before dragging, reorient the model using the ViewCube to ensure the proper size of the region.*

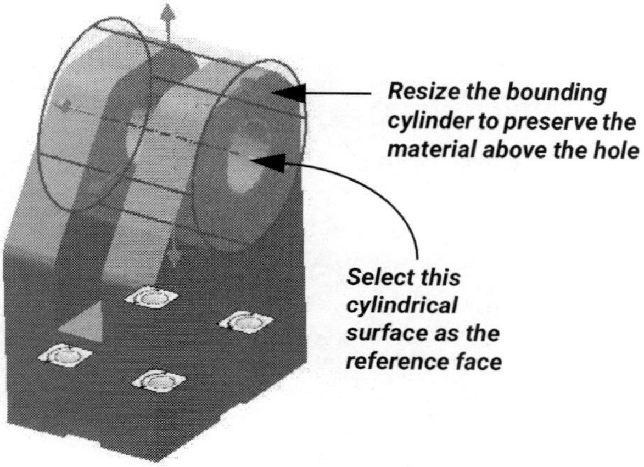

Figure 6–19

4. Click **OK**.
5. Reorient the model to the **BOTTOM** view using the ViewCube.
6. In the Model browser, expand the **Constraints** node. Right-click on **Pin Constraint1** and clear the **Visibility** option, as shown in Figure 6–20. This removes the glyph from the model display.

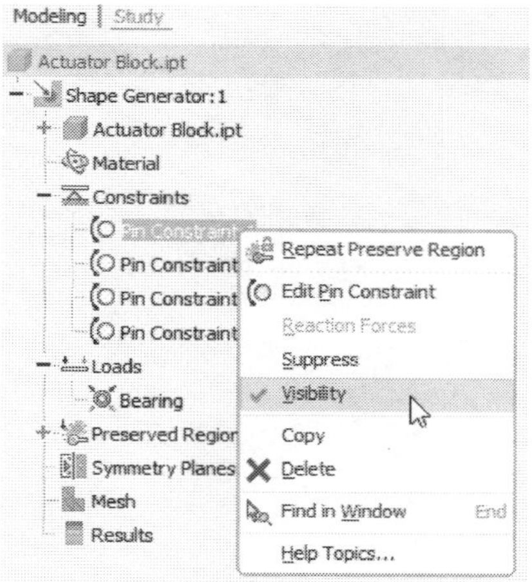

Figure 6–20

7. Clear the glyph display for the other three Pin constraints.

8. In the Goals and Criteria panel, click  (Preserve Region).

9. Ensure that  (Location) is active and select the edge of the circular hole, as shown in the BOTTOM view in Figure 6–21.

10. Click  to expand the dialog box. In the *Region Dimensions* area, set the *Radius value* to **0.4 in** and the *Length* value to **1.1 in**. Ensure that the length is extending into the model, as shown in the FRONT view in Figure 6–21. In the *Center Point* area, set the *Y* value to **.55 in**.

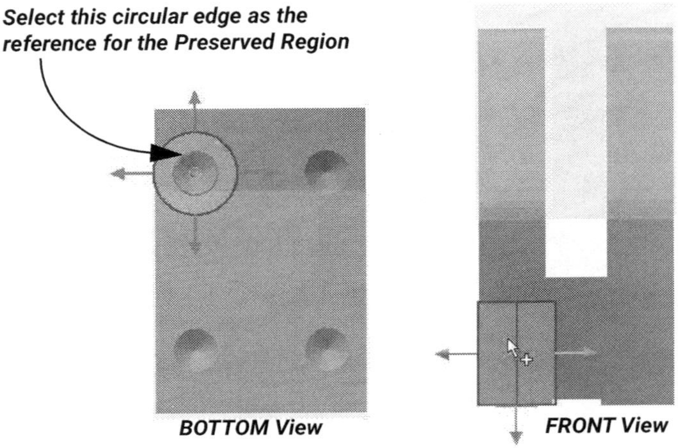

Figure 6–21

11. Create three identical preserved regions on the other support holes. The model should display as shown in Figure 6–22.

Figure 6–22

One additional preserve area is required to ensure that material is not removed that will affect the stability along the X axis.

12. Click  (Preserve Region), if the dialog box is not already open.
13. Select the planar face that connects the two symmetric sides. Using the ViewCube, reorient the model to size the bounding box similar to that shown in Figure 6–23. The box should extend the width of the model and extend into the preserve areas for the support holes (approx, 0.354 in). Click **OK** to create the preserved area.

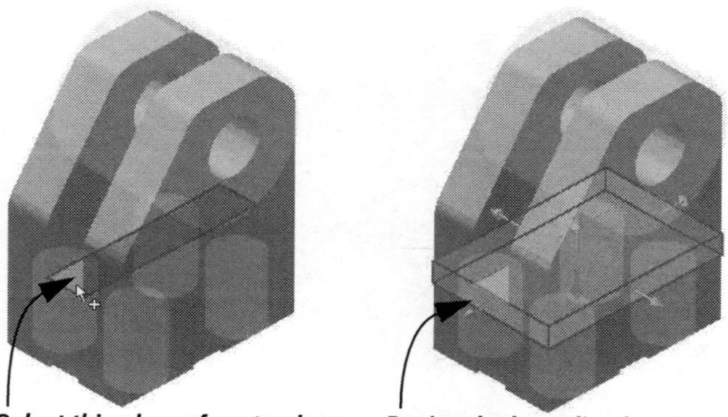

Figure 6–23

14. All six preserved areas are listed in the **Preserved Regions** node in the Model browser.

Task 6: Define symmetry in the model.

The model is symmetric about the YZ plane. This should be assigned as criteria to ensure that the 3D mesh model is symmetric.

1. In the Goals and Criteria panel, click  (Symmetry Plane).
2. By default, the symmetry planes are placed at the center of mass and are aligned with the global coordinate system. No change is required to reposition the planes for this model.

3. Toggle the active planes so that the YZ plane is the only plane highlighted in red, as shown in Figure 6–24.

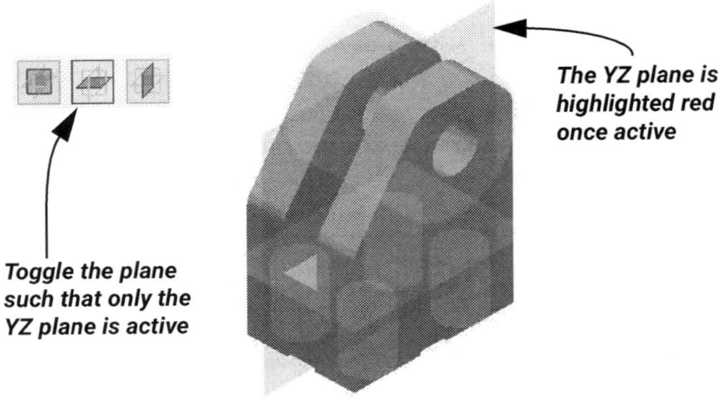

Figure 6–24

4. Click **OK** to assign the symmetry plane.

Task 7: Run the Shape Generator and promote the study.

Now that the analysis has been set up, you can run the shape generator and promote the study to the model environment.

1. Click  (Generate Shape) to open the Generate Shape dialog box.
2. Click **Run** to start the shape generator analysis.

   Note: *The analysis may take a few minutes to complete. The run time will vary depending on your computer. Warnings may be presented as the geometry is optimized.*

3. Once complete, a 3D mesh should be returned, similar to that shown in Figure 6–25.

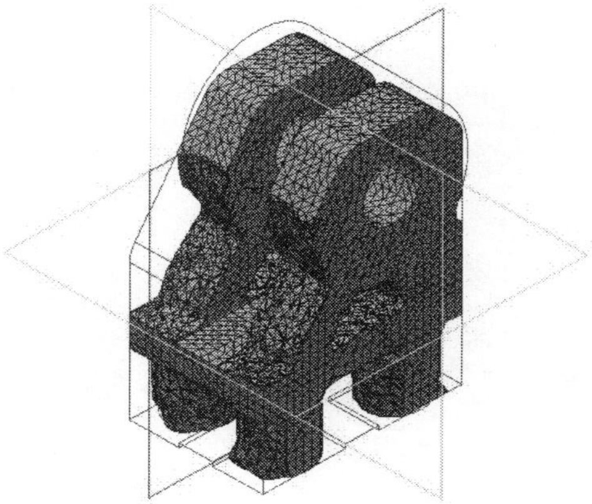

Figure 6–25

4. In the Export panel, click (Promote Shape) and select **Current Part File** to promote the optimized 3D mesh directly to the part model. Click **OK**.
5. Click **OK** in the Promote Shape dialog box that displays. This dialog box, indicates that shape promotion was successful and provides recommended steps. The 3D mesh displays embedded in the solid geometry, as shown in Figure 6–26 with the **Shaded with Edges** view display.

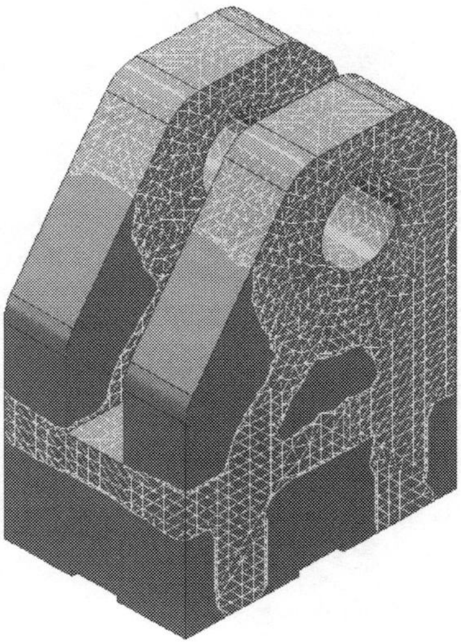

Figure 6–26

Task 8: Modify the initial design using the Shape Generator's 3D mesh.

1. Open **Actuator Block_Final.ipt**. This model already has been optimized using Shape Generator and sketches that approximate the material removal have been created for you.

   Note: *If time permits, try to create the sketches in your own model.*

2. Using the **Side Cut Profiles** and **Front Cut Profile** sketches, create the geometry shown in Figure 6–27.

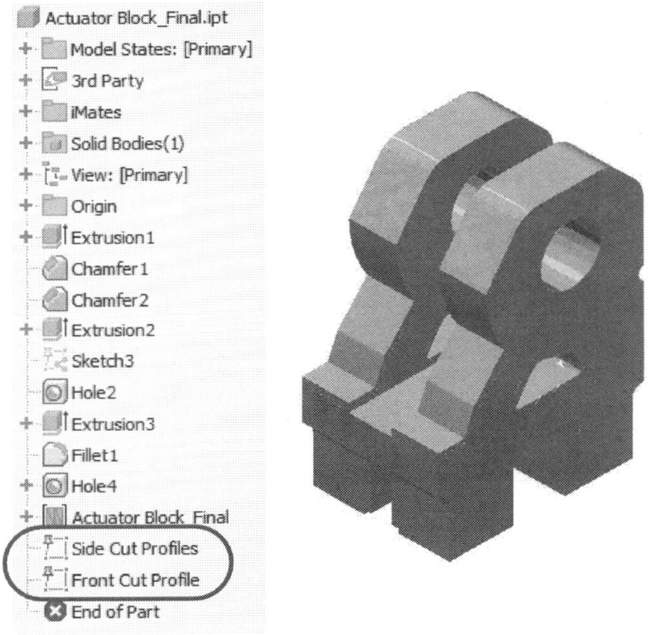

Figure 6–27

3. Open the model's iProperties dialog box and update its physical properties. Note that the mass is still slightly over 3 lbs.
4. To further reduce the mass of the model, you can add fillets to the edges of the geometry, modify the sketches that were used to remove the material, and/or change to a lower weight steel. Ultimately, the changes that are made must still be analyzed for structural integrity to ensure it can withstand its loads; however, the Shape Generator has provided a satisfactory starting point.
5. Save the model and close the window

End of practice

Chapter Review Questions

1. The Shape Generator tool automatically modifies the initial geometry of the model when it is promoted to the part modeling environment.
   a. True
   b. False

2. In which Autodesk Inventor working environment can you gain access to the Shape Generator tool? (Select all that apply.)
   a. Part Modeling
   b. Assembly Modeling
   c. Drawing
   d. Presentation
   e. Stress Analysis

3. Only a single shape generation study can be set up in a model.
   a. True
   b. False

4. Which of the following constraints can be added to the model to accurately describe how it is constrained in its working environment? (Select all that apply.)
   a. Bearing
   b. Fixed
   c. Force
   d. Frictionless
   e. Gravity
   f. Moment
   g. Pin
   h. Pressure

5. Which of the following cannot be controlled using the additional options in the expandable load creation dialog boxes? (Select all that apply.)
    a. The location reference of the load.
    b. The direction reference for a load.
    c. The magnitude of the load broken down into vector components.
    d. The assignment of a custom load name.
    e. The display of the load glyph in the model.
    f. The scale of the load glyph when it is displayed in the model.

6. Which of the following are valid when setting the criteria for a Shape Generator analysis? (Select all that apply.)
    a. The volume of the model is set to reach a target value.
    b. The mass of the model is set to reach a target value.
    c. The volume of the model is reduced by a set percentage value.
    d. The mass of the model is reduced by a set percentage value.

7. A cylindrical face that is selected as the reference for a preserved region cannot use the **Box** option to define its boundary.
    a. True
    b. False

8. How many planes can be selected during a Shape Generator analysis to define symmetry in a model?
    a. 1
    b. 2
    c. 3
    d. Unlimited

Command Summary

Button	Command	Location
	**Assign (material)**	• **Ribbon:** *Analysis* tab>Material panel • **Context Menu:** In Model browser with Material node selected
	**Bearing Load**	• **Ribbon:** *Analysis* tab>Loads panel • **Context Menu:** In Model browser with Loads node selected
	**Body Load**	• **Ribbon:** *Analysis* tab>Loads panel • **Context Menu:** In Model browser with Loads node selected
	**Create Study**	• **Ribbon:** *Analysis* tab>Manage panel
	**Finish Analysis**	• **Ribbon:** *Analysis* tab>Exit panel
	**Fixed Constraint**	• **Ribbon:** *Analysis* tab>Constraints panel • **Context menu:** In Model browser with Constraints node selected • **Context menu:** In graphics window
	**Force Load**	• **Ribbon:** *Analysis* tab>Loads panel • **Context Menu:** In Model browser with Loads node selected • **Context menu:** In graphics window
	**Frictionless Constraint**	• **Ribbon:** *Analysis* tab>Constraints panel • **Context Menu:** In Model browser with Constraints node selected
	**Generate Shape**	• **Ribbon:** *Analysis* tab>Run panel • **Context Menu:** In Model browser with Study node selected
	**Gravity Load**	• **Ribbon:** *Analysis* tab>Loads panel • **Context Menu:** In Model browser with Loads node selected
	**Mesh View**	• **Ribbon:** *Analysis* tab>Mesh panel • **Context Menu:** In Model browser with Study node selected • **Context menu:** In graphics window

Button	Command	Location
	**Moment Load**	• **Ribbon:** *Analysis* tab>Loads panel • **Context Menu:** In Model browser with Loads node selected
	**Pin Constraint**	• **Ribbon:** *Analysis* tab>Constraints panel • **Context Menu:** In Model browser with Constraints node selected
	**Preserve Region**	• **Ribbon:** *Analysis* tab>Goals and Criteria panel
	**Pressure Load**	• **Ribbon:** *Analysis* tab>Loads panel • **Context Menu:** In Model browser with Loads node selected
	**Promote Shape**	• **Ribbon:** *Analysis* tab>Export panel
	**Remote Force Load**	• **Ribbon:** *Analysis* tab>Loads panel • **Context Menu:** In Model browser with Loads node selected
	**Shape Generator**	• **Ribbon:** *3D Model* tab>Explore panel
	**Shape Generator Settings**	• **Ribbon:** *Analysis* tab>Goals and Criteria panel
	**Stress Analysis**	• **Ribbon:** *3D Model* tab>Simulation panel
	**Symmetry Plane**	• **Ribbon:** *Analysis* tab>Goals and Criteria panel

Chapter 7

Introduction to Surfacing

The Autodesk® Inventor® software enables you to combine traditional surface modeling with advanced parametric modeling technology to create seamless, hybrid surface-solid models. Features such as extrudes, revolves, lofts, or sweeps can also be used to create surfaces or solids.

Learning Objectives

- Set the Surface Output type so that features are created as surfaces.
- Create a planar surface by referencing a closed sketched profile.
- Create a three-dimensional surface that is defined by a series of planar and non-planar edges.
- Create a surface that is normal, tangent, or along a vector.
- Combine individual surface features into one quilted surface that can be used as a single surface for modeling.
- Add or remove material to a model by referencing a surface that defines the shape of the material to be added/removed.
- Create a surface that is offset by a specified amount from the face of a solid feature or another surface.
- Create solid geometry using surface geometry.
- Control whether a surface is displayed in a drawing view.

7.1 Introduction to Surfaces

A surface is a non-solid, zero-thickness feature that can define a contoured shape. Surfaces help capture the design intent of complex shapes that are not easily defined using solids. Surfaces can also be used as references to help create other features (solid and non-solid). The term "quilt" is often used to describe surface features and can refer to a single surface feature or a group of stitched (combined) surface features. Surface features can be used to do the following:

- Create surface models that can be converted to solid models.
- Create a "skin" over an imported wireframe model.
- Create complex solid cuts and extrusions.
- Create a solid form.
- Define complex curves.

A feature created using surfaces is shown in Figure 7–1.

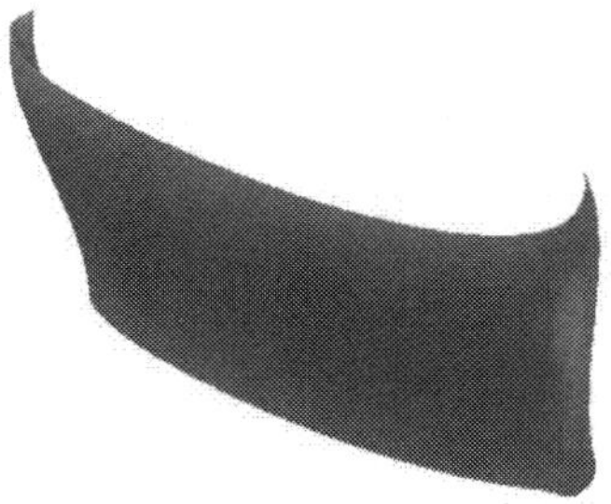

Figure 7–1

Surfaces display in the Model browser with symbols specific to their type, as shown in Figure 7–2. They are also listed in the **Surface Bodies** node at the top of the Model browser.

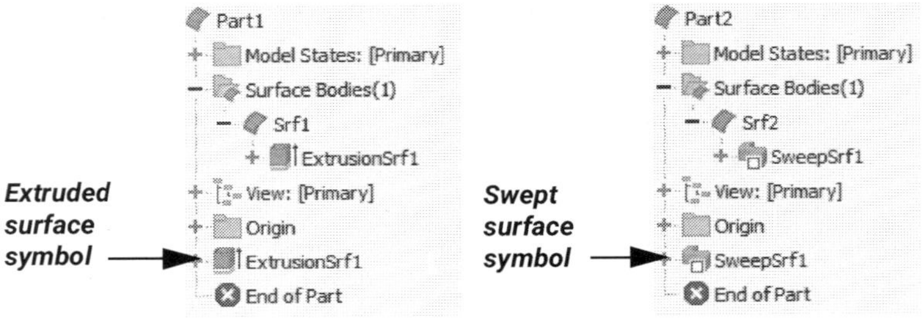

Figure 7–2

7.2 Basic Surfaces

When creating most features (such as extrudes, lofts, revolves, sweeps, and coils), you can specify if the feature is created as a solid or a surface. For extrudes, revolves, sweeps, and coils, you can switch between solid mode and surface mode by toggling the button at the top of the Properties panel, as shown in Figure 7–3, to toggle the surface mode on or off.

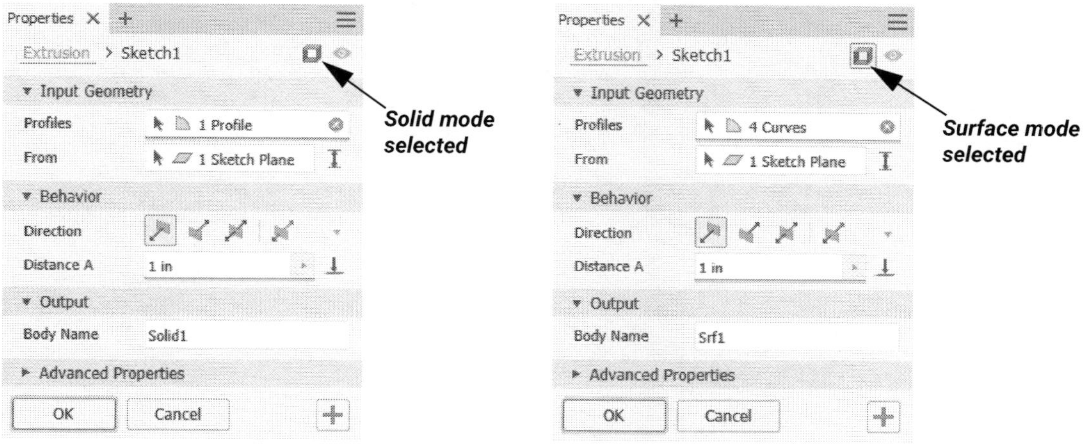

Figure 7–3

For lofts, you toggle between solid mode and surface mode by selecting (Solid) and (Surface) in the *Output* area of the feature dialog box, as shown in Figure 7–4.

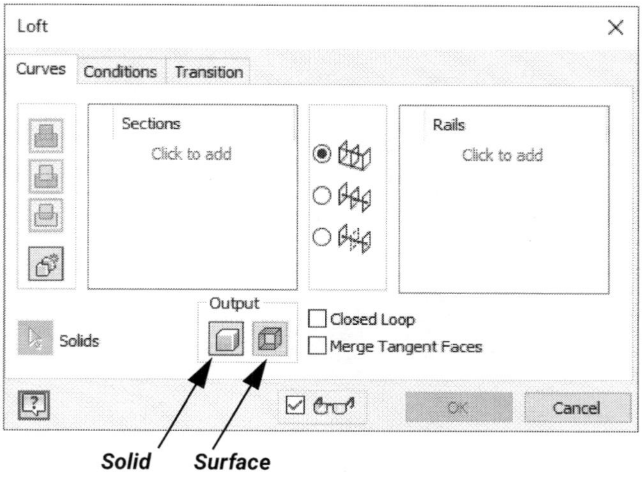

Figure 7–4

- Creating a solid requires a closed profile, but a surface can be created using an open or closed profile. Defining the remaining options for a surface is the same as creating a solid feature.
- All surfaces created in a part model are created as their own surface bodies, and are independently listed in the **Surface Bodies** node of the Model browser. Even if surfaces are combined, they create a new body in the list.

7.3 Patch Surfaces

Boundary patch surfaces are surfaces created from closed 2D or 3D sketches, or existing closed boundary edges. Examples of a 2D and two 3D patch surfaces are shown in Figure 7–5.

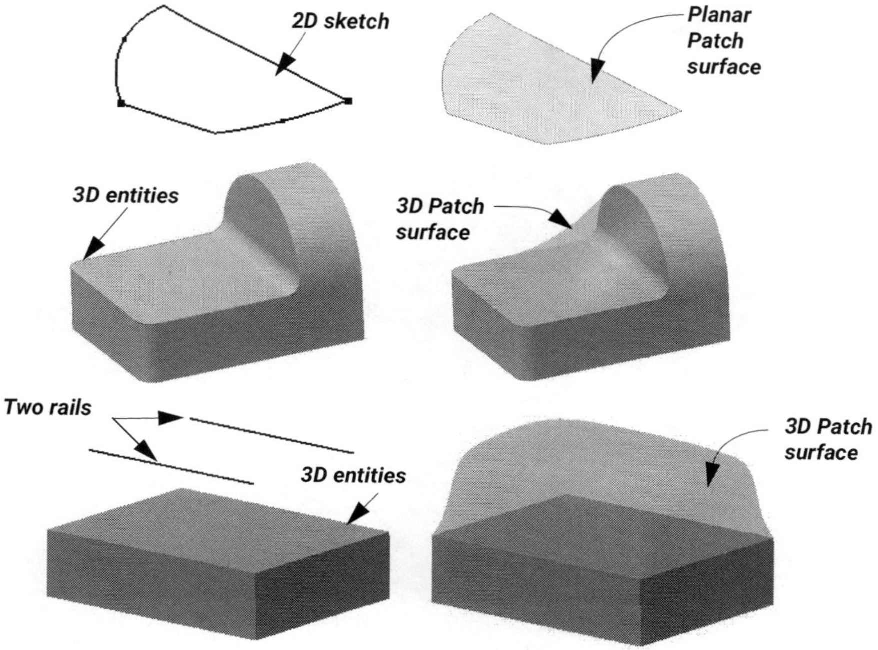

Figure 7–5

How To: Create Patch Surface

1. In the *Surface* panel, click (Boundary Patch). The Boundary Patch dialog box opens.
2. Select a closed 2D or 3D sketch, or select edges on existing objects to form a closed profile. When selecting the edges to form a patch, consider using **Automatic Edge Chain** to select adjacent edges together instead of individually selecting them.
3. (Optional) If edges are selected, you can assign a boundary condition (e.g., Free, Tangent, Curvature Continuous, or G2) to the edge and its adjacent surfaces in the *Condition* area.
4. To further refine the shape of the patch surface, click (Guide Rails) and select curves or points to drive the shape of the patch.
5. Click **OK** to create the surface.

- Surface patches are identified by the symbol in the Model browser.

7.4 Ruled Surfaces

The **Ruled Surface** option enables you to create normal, tangent, and vector surfaces. A ruled surface is a surface where a straight line lies at every point on the surface. Common uses for this type of surface includes creating parting surfaces for mold design, creating surfaces that can split a body, or adding pockets.

How To: Create a Ruled Surface

1. Click (Ruled Surface) to open the Ruled Surface dialog box, as shown in Figure 7–6.

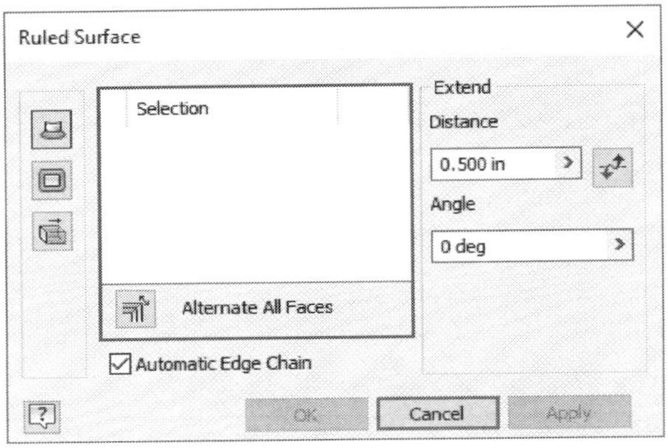

Figure 7–6

2. On the left-hand side of the dialog box, select the type. The dialog box options vary depending on the type of ruled surface you select.

   - Click (Normal) to create a ruled surface that remains normal along the edge reference.
   - Click (Tangent) to create a ruled surface that remains tangent along the edge reference.
   - Click (Vector) to create a ruled surface that follows a direction vector along the edge reference.

   Note: *For Tangent and Normal ruled surfaces, select* ***Automatic Edge Chain*** *so that when selecting an edge, any edge that is tangent to it is also selected. Clear this option to select individual edges.*

3. Define references to create the ruled surface.
   - For Tangent or Normal, select an edge reference to create the surface. Multiple edges can be selected. The references are listed in the *Edges Selection* area.
   - For Vector, select an edge or sketch to define the path and a vector to define the direction. The direction vector can be a face, edge, or axis. If a sketch is being used, it must already exist in the model.
4. Enter a value in the *Distance* field to extend the edge(s) or sketch.
   - Select  (Flip) to reverse the extension direction.
   - Select  (Alternate All Faces) to reverse the faces that are being used to define the directions.
5. (Optional) Enter an *Angle* value for the ruled surface.
6. Click **OK** to complete the ruled surface.

Figure 7–7 shows examples of the three types of ruled surfaces.

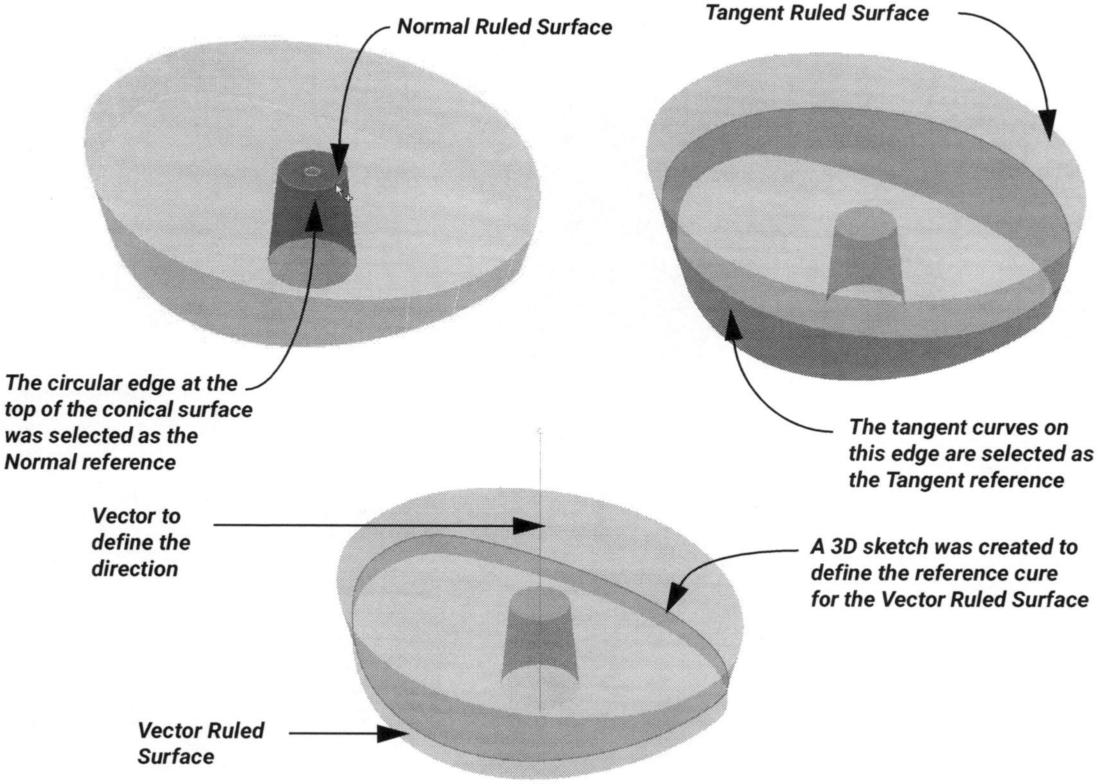

Figure 7–7

7.5 Stitch Surfaces

A Stitch surface combines individual surface features into one surface feature. This option is useful when you want to split a part or surface, solidify a group of enclosed surfaces, or replace a face with a single item. When you stitch a group of surfaces together, you form a quilt. The quilt can be converted to a solid if it forms a closed volume.

How To: Stitch Surfaces to Form a Quilt

1. In the Surface panel, click (Stitch) to create a quilt. The Stitch dialog box opens as shown in Figure 7–8.

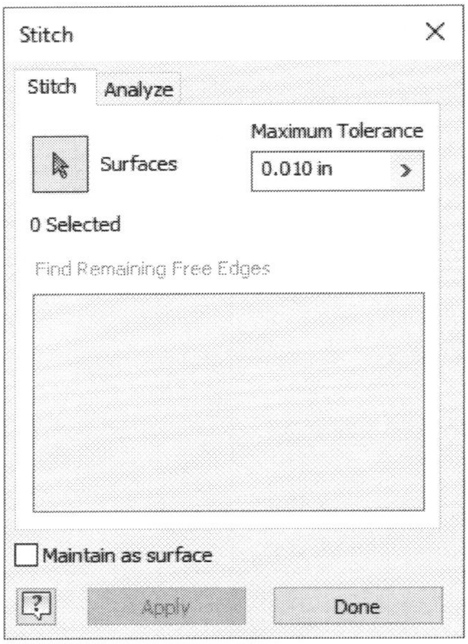

Figure 7–8

2. Select the surfaces to create a quilt. The edges you are stitching must be the same size and adjacent to each other.
3. Click **Apply** to apply the feature. Continue stitching surfaces together or click **Done** to finish.

- Stitched quilts are listed in the Model browser, as shown in Figure 7–9, and a surface is added to the **Surface Bodies** node.

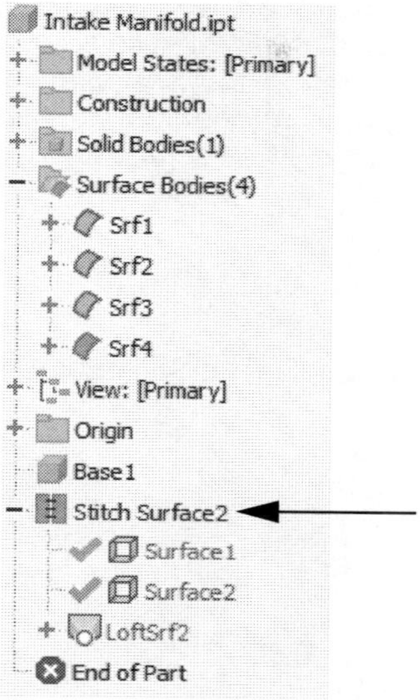

Figure 7–9

- To edit a stitched (quilt) surface, right-click it and select **Edit Feature**. When editing, you can add more surfaces to form larger quilts.

7.6 Sculpting with Surfaces

Sculpt can be used to add or remove material from a solid body using surfaces and work planes. Use Sculpt to create complex or stylized solid shapes that would be difficult to create using solid features. The selected surfaces and work planes, along with all the automatically selected solid faces of the model, are used to create a fully enclosed boundary that defines the solid volume to be added or removed. Unlike the split and stitch options, sculpt surface references do not need to be trimmed.

How To: Add or Remove Material Using Sculpt

1. In the Surface panel, click (Sculpt). The Sculpt dialog box opens, as shown in Figure 7–10.

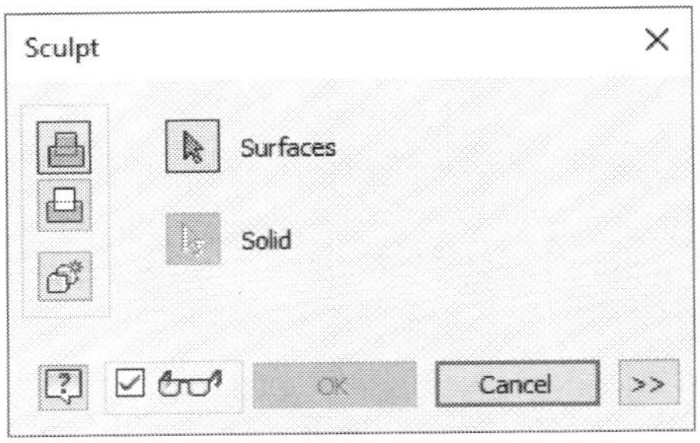

Figure 7–10

2. Click (Add) or (Remove).
3. If material is added as a result of the sculpt, you can click to create a new solid body from the resulting sculpted geometry.
4. Select the surfaces and work planes to form the boundary to add or remove. An example where one surface is selected and two solid faces are automatically selected is shown in Figure 7–11.

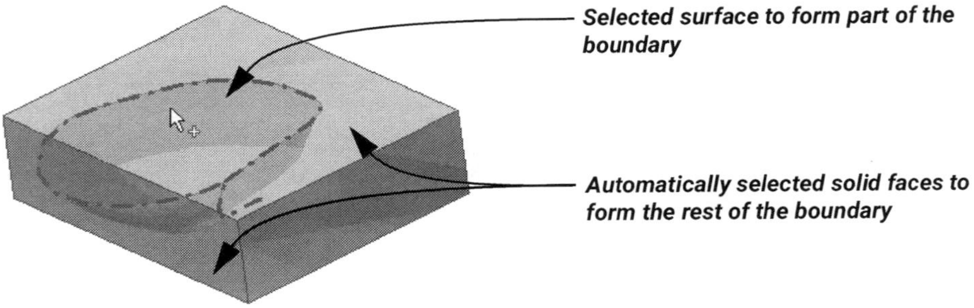

Figure 7–11

5. Define the direction, as required, by clicking >> and using the direction drop-down list for each individual surface, as shown in Figure 7–12. When adding material, the arrow indicates what will be added. When removing material, the arrow indicates what will be removed.

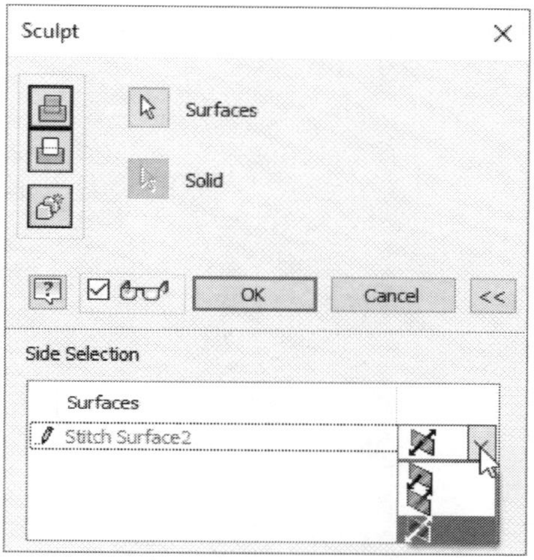

Figure 7–12

6. Click **OK** to complete the feature. An example of material removed using the sculpt feature is shown in Figure 7–13.

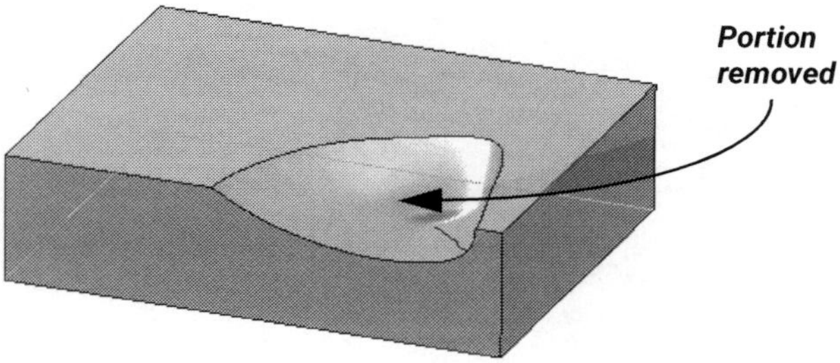

Figure 7–13

7.7 Thickening Solids and Offsetting Surfaces

Thickening and offsetting enables you to change the thickness of a part or surface or create offset surfaces from part faces or other surfaces. If you add thickness to a surface, it will become a solid. This option works only in the part environment. Surfaces in the construction environment cannot be thickened or offset. An offset surface created from a solid feature face and then thickened is shown in Figure 7–14.

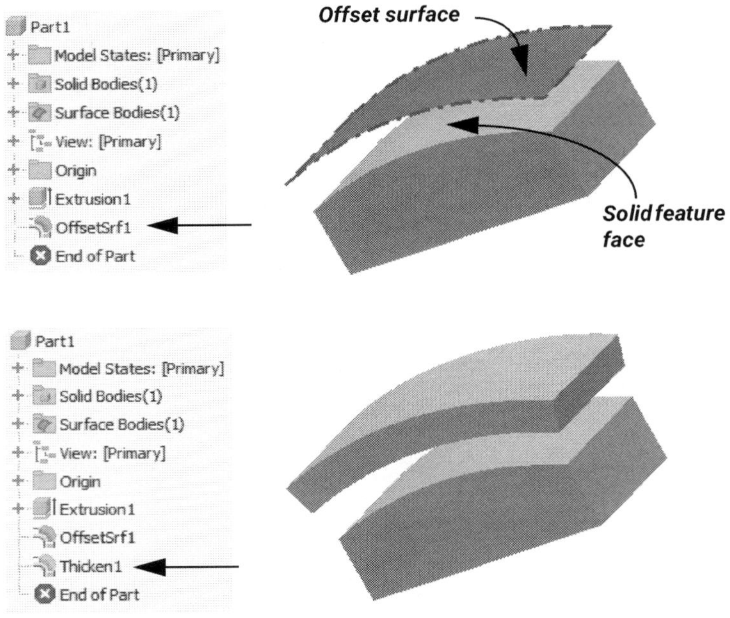

Figure 7–14

How To: Thicken a Solid or Offset a Surface

1. In the Modify panel, click (Thicken/Offset) to change the thickness of a part or surface, or to create offset surfaces from part faces or other surfaces.
2. Define whether the new feature will be a thickened solid or an offset surface by toggling the (Surface Mode) option on or off at the top of the panel, as required. The Properties panel opens, as shown in Figure 7–15 for each option.

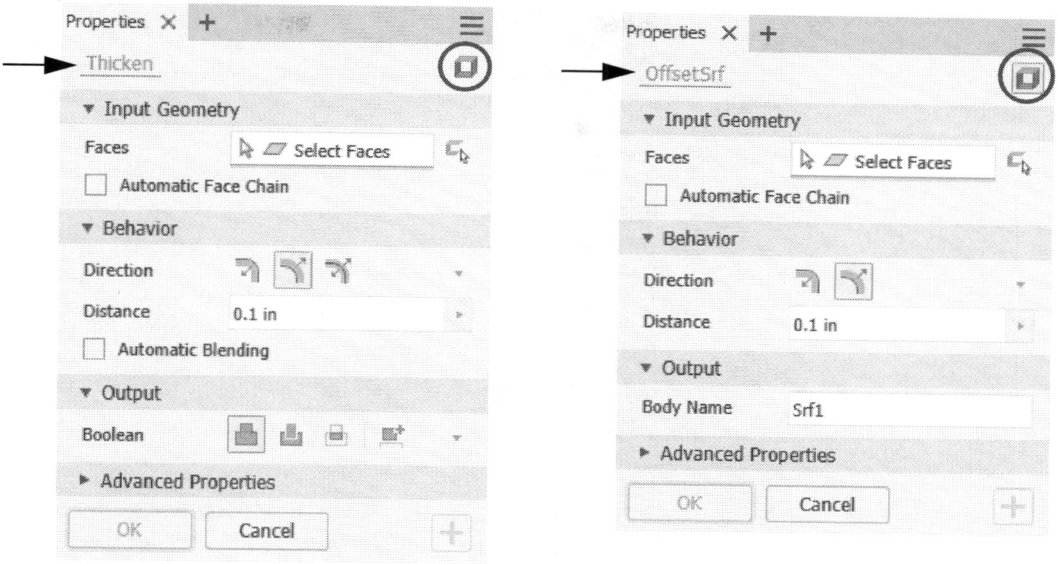

Figure 7–15

3. Select **Thicken** or **OffsetSrf** (default feature names) at the top of the Properties panel to assign a name for the feature.
4. Select a reference surface face to thicken or offset from. To enable Quilt selection, click .
   - For face/quilt selection, you can enable the **Automatic Face Chain** option to automatically select faces adjacent and tangent to the selected reference. This should be selected before selecting the face.
5. Define the options in the *Behavior* area:
   - Define the direction that the new feature is created in.
   - Enter an offset distance value.
   - If a solid face is selected, the **Automatic Blending** option is available, to blend the feature with any other interfering feature. If a surface feature is selected to be thickened, **Automatic Blending** becomes unavailable.
6. Define the options in the *Output* area:
   - Define whether material is added or removed using the Boolean options.
   - If the resulting feature is a solid, you can click  to create a new solid body from the resulting thickened geometry.

7. (Optional) In the *Advanced Properties* area, enable **Allow Approximation** to allow the system to deviate from the specified thickness when creating the surface. This can be used when a precise solution does not exist. If enabled, you can select *Type* and *Tolerance* options, as shown in Figure 7–16.

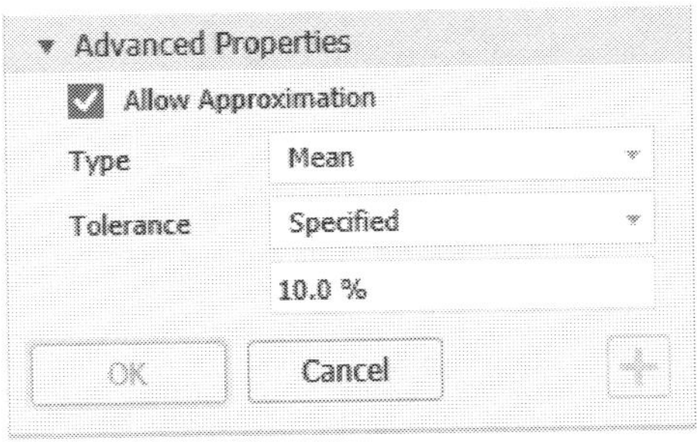

Figure 7–16

- The *Types* include **Mean**, **Never too thin**, and **Never too thick**. **Mean** divides the thickness to fall both above and below the specified distance. **Never too thin** preserves the minimum distance. **Never too thick** preserves the maximum distance.
- The *Tolerance* can be set to affect the computation time when approximating a thickening. **Optimized** minimizes computation time by using a reasonable tolerance. The **Specified** option takes more time and uses a specified tolerance %.

8. Click **OK** to complete the operation.
   - To continue creating additional thicken features without closing the panel, click  (Apply) and define the references as needed. Once all geometry has been completed, click **OK**.

7.8 Surfaces in Drawing Views

When solid and surface geometry are included in a model, the surfaces are not automatically shown in drawing views. In these situations, you must set the view so that it includes surfaces. To include surfaces in views, in the Drawing View dialog box, select the *Recovery Options* tab and select **Include Surface Bodies**, as shown in Figure 7–17. If the **Include Surface Bodies** option was disabled when the view was created, it can be enabled by editing the drawing view.

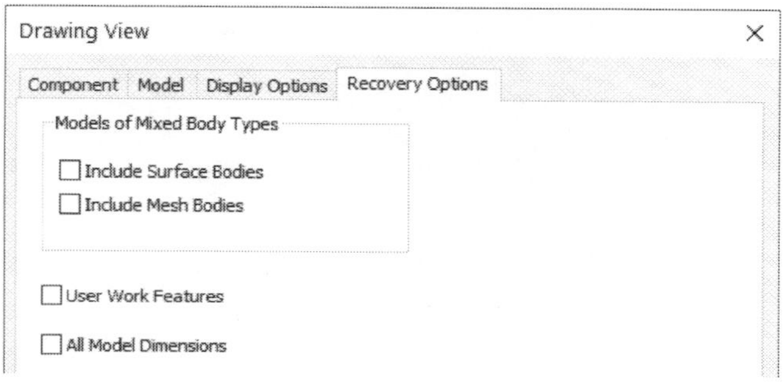

Figure 7–17

Once views with the **Include Surface Bodies** option are placed, you can individually control surface visibility for each view directly in the Model browser.

- To control the display of individual surfaces in a view, expand the view containing the surface in the Model browser and in the **Surface Bodies** node, right-click on the required surface and clear/select **Visibility**, as required, as shown in Figure 7–18. By default, if the surface displays (is visible) in the model, it also displays in the drawing view.

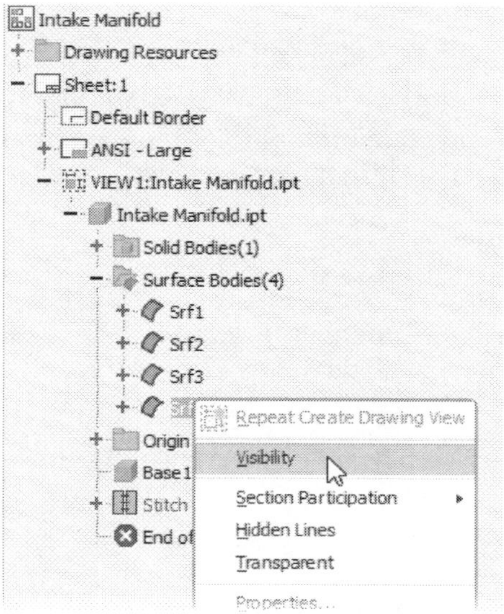

Figure 7–18

- To control the visibility all surfaces that exist in a part at once, in the Model browser, expand the view node, right-click on the required part name, and clear/select **Include All Surfaces**, as required, as shown in Figure 7–19. Alternatively, you can right-click on the Surface Bodies folder and clear/select **Visibility** to control the visibility of all surfaces at once. By default, if the surface displays (is visible) in the model, it also displays in the drawing view.

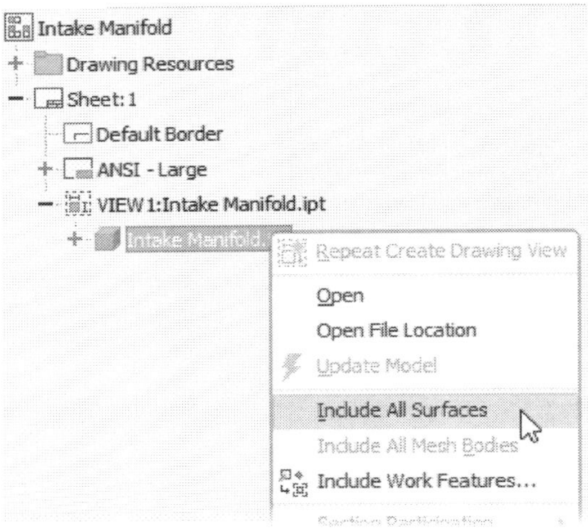

Figure 7–19

Consider the following:

- If a surface is added to the model, the drawing view only updates to reflect the display of the new surface if the **Include Surface Bodies** recovery option was originally set when the view was created.
- If a surface is deleted, the drawing view updates.
- Construction surfaces cannot be included in a drawing view. If you want to include a construction surface, you must first promote it to the Part environment. Surfaces included in a **Repaired Geometry** node display in a drawing view.

Surfaces in Child Views

When a child view (such as a Projected or Auxiliary view) is created, it is generated based on the same surface display setting in the parent view. However, once the view is created, including or excluding surfaces on a parent view does not have any effect on existing child views. Both views are independent in terms of the surface display settings.

For section and breakout views, hatching is only visible on solids, not surfaces.

Annotating Surfaces in a Drawing

You can modify surface edge properties, such as line type, line weight, and color. Right-click on the surface or on the surface edge and select **Properties**. The Edge Properties dialog box opens as shown in Figure 7–20.

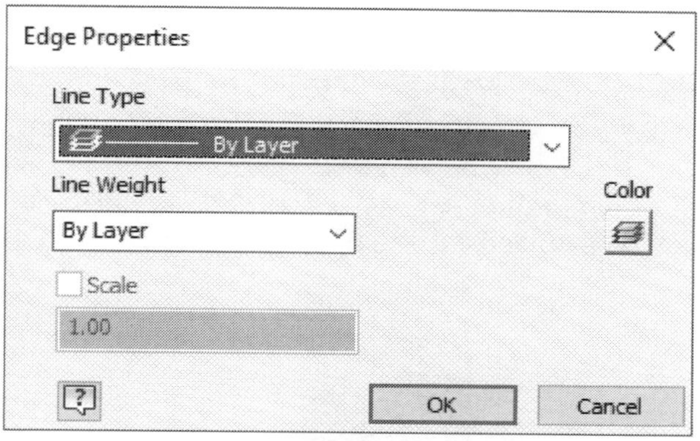

Figure 7–20

Annotations can be applied to surface edges once a surface is included in a view.

Practice 7a
Creating a Surface I

Practice Objectives

- Create an extruded surface for use as the termination plane for a solid cut.
- Mirror, fillet, and shell the geometry to achieve the required results.

In this practice, you will create a surface and use it to define an extruded cut on a bottle. You will also fillet and mirror the extruded cut and finally shell the bottle part. The resulting model is shown in Figure 7–21.

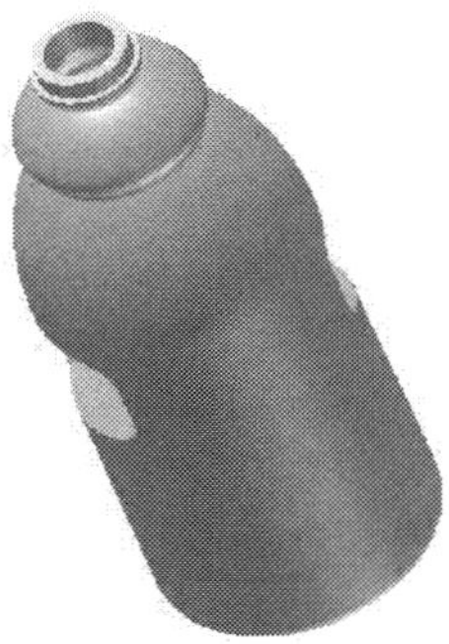

Figure 7–21

Task 1: Create the extrusion.

In this task, you use the unconsumed sketch (**Sketch3**) to create a surface extrusion. Later in this practice, you use this surface as a termination plane for a solid cut.

1. Open **surface.ipt**.
2. The model contains **Sketch3**, an unconsumed sketch. Zoom and rotate as required to view this sketch.
3. Change the display mode to Wireframe display so that you can see the portion of the sketch inside the part, or hover over **Sketch3** in the Model browser to display it.
4. Start the **Extrude** option and click at the top of the Properties panel to toggle to surface mode.
5. Select **Sketch3** as the profile and set the distance to **101.6 mm**. Extrude symmetrically on each side of the sketch plane.

6. Complete the feature. The model displays as shown in Figure 7–22.

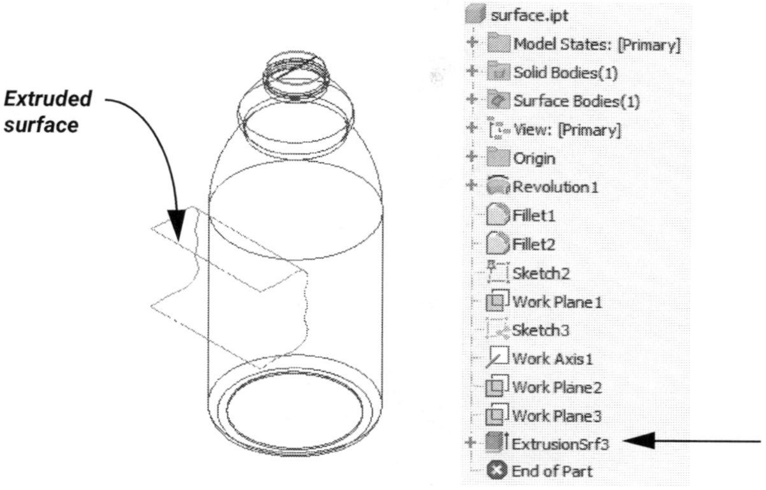

Figure 7–22

Task 2: Sketch the cut profile and create the cut.

1. Create a sketch on Work Plane3. Sketch and dimension the geometry shown in Figure 7–23. The location of the outside vertical lines are symmetric about the Work Axis1.

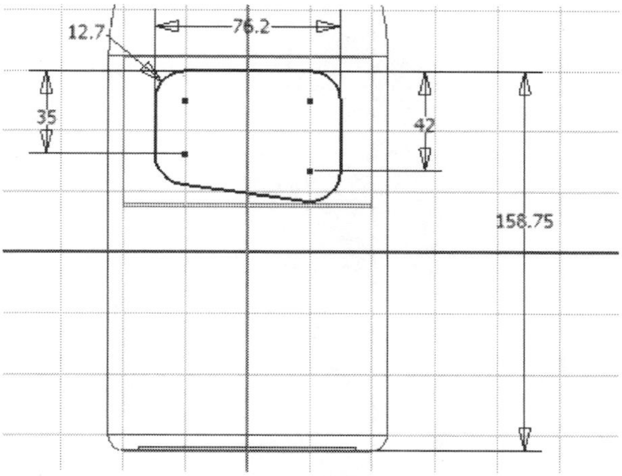

Figure 7–23

2. Start **Extrude** and toggle off surface mode using the icon at the top of the Properties panel. This ensures the geometry is created as a solid.

3. Select the new sketch as the profile. Create the feature as a cut and set it to cut through to the surface feature.

4. Expand the *Advanced Properties* area and set the *Taper angle* to **-30 degrees**.
5. Complete the feature. Toggle off any visible work features and the surface. The model displays as shown in Figure 7–24.

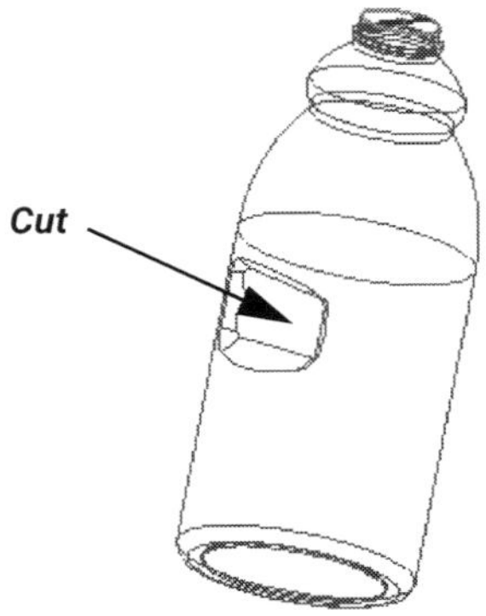

Figure 7–24

6. Fillet the inside edge of the cutout with a radius of **3.175 mm**.
7. Mirror the features (surface extrusion, cut, and fillet) about the XY plane.
8. The mirrored surface is created as its own surface body. In the Model browser, expand the **Surface Bodies** node, right-click on **Srf2**, and clear the **Visibility** option.
9. Shell the bottle with a *Thickness* of **5 mm** removing the top face of the bottle. The shaded model displays as shown in Figure 7–25.

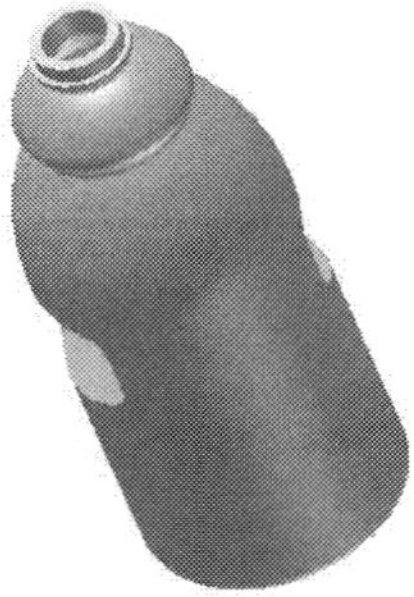

Figure 7–25

10. Save and close the model.

End of practice

Practice 7b
Creating a Surface II

Practice Objectives

- Create a lofted surface that transitions between the edges on two alternate surfaces.
- Stitch the resulting lofted surface to the existing surfaces in the model to create a single surface and form a quilt.
- Create solid geometry from the stitched geometry using the Thicken/Offset command.

In this practice, you will create the portion of the model shown in Figure 7–26 by creating a Loft surface, stitching it together with two adjacent surfaces and finally thickening this surface to create solid geometry.

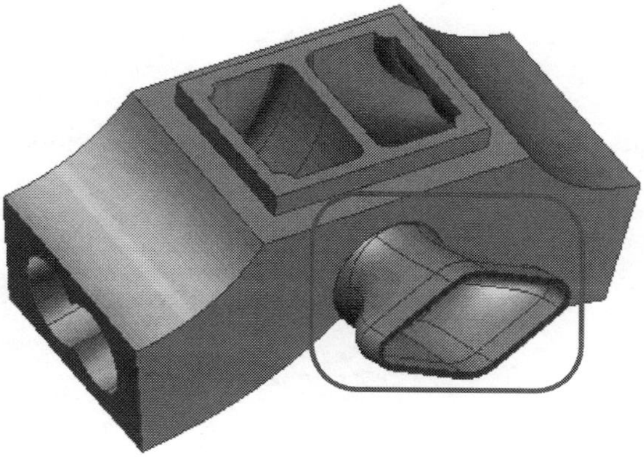

Figure 7–26

Task 1: Create a loft surface.

1. Open **Intake Manifold.ipt**. You should see two surfaces listed in the **Surface Bodies** node of the Model browser. You will create a loft between these surfaces.
2. Start the creation of a loft. The Loft dialog box opens.
3. In the Loft dialog box, in the *Output* area, click  (Surface) to create a surface.
4. In the *Sections* area, click **Click to add**.
5. Select the circular surface's edge. You might need to enable **Edge Chains** in the shortcut menu.

6. In the *Sections* area, click **Click to add** again and select the edge on the other surface, as shown in Figure 7–27.

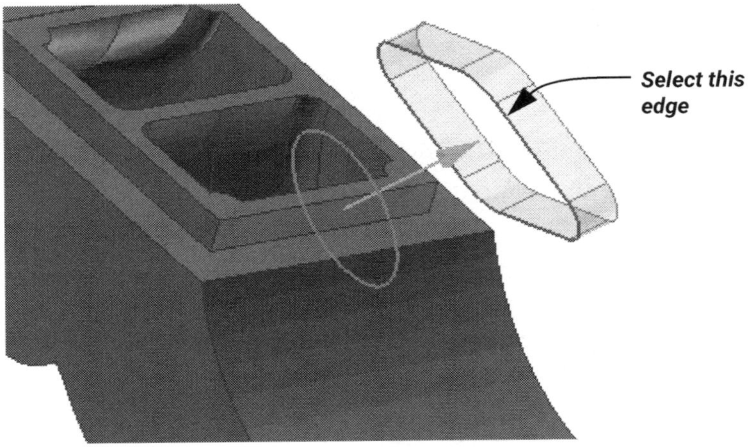

Figure 7–27

7. Select the *Conditions* tab.
8. Change both conditions from free to tangent, as shown in Figure 7–28.

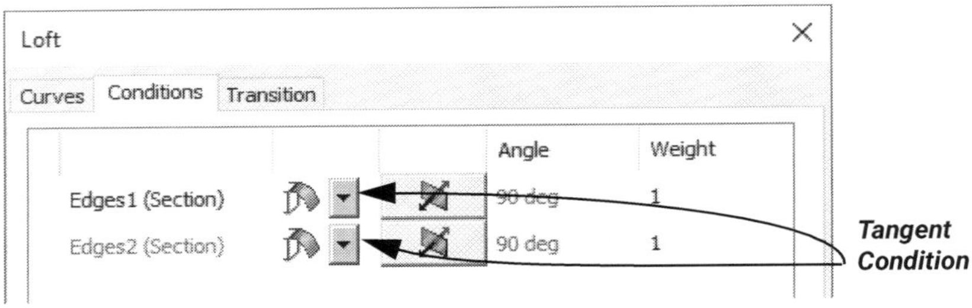

Figure 7–28

9. Click **OK** to complete the loft definition. The loft surface displays as shown in Figure 7–29.

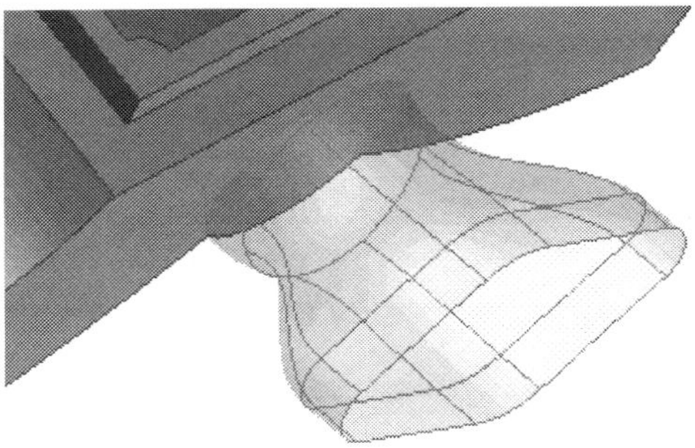

Figure 7–29

Task 2: Stitch surfaces together.

1. In the Surface panel, click (Stitch). The Stitch dialog box opens.
2. Select the Loft surface and its two adjacent surfaces, as shown in Figure 7–30.

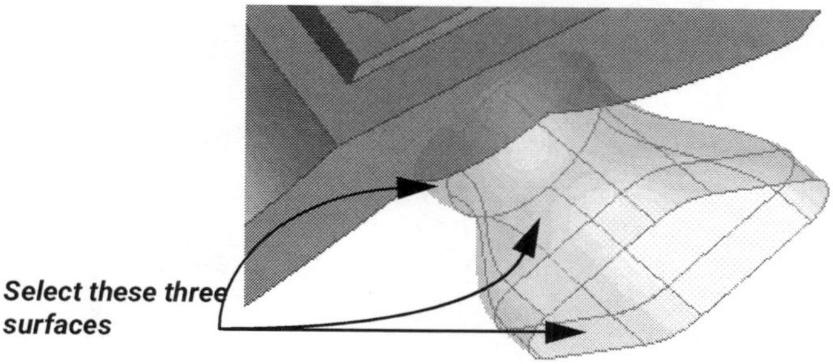

Figure 7–30

3. Click **Apply** and **Done**. In the Model browser, in the **Surface Bodies** node, a fourth surface is added.

Task 3: Use the Thicken/Offset option.

1. In the Modify panel, click (Thicken/Offset). The Properties panel displays.
2. Click to enable Quilt selection.
3. Select the newly created stitched surface and set the *Distance* to **2 mm**.
4. Click **OK**. Toggle off visibility for the stitched surface. The model displays as shown in Figure 7–31.

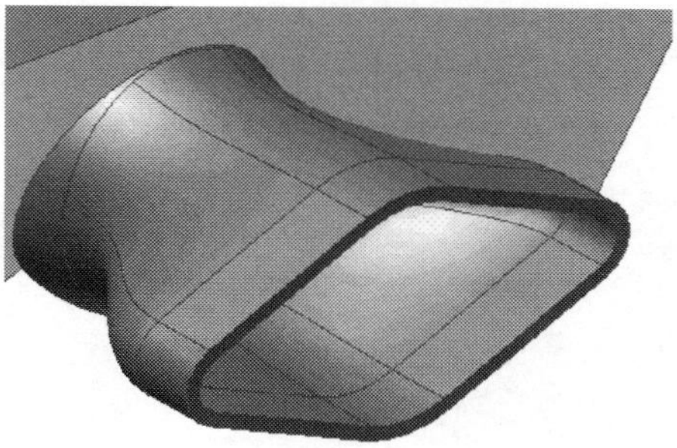

Figure 7–31

5. Save the part and close the window.

End of practice

Practice 7c
Sculpting a Surface

Practice Objectives

- Add material to the model by referencing a surface that defines the shape of the material to be added.
- Remove material from the model by referencing a surface that defines the shape of the material to be removed.

In this practice, you use a sculpt feature to add and remove material, as shown in Figure 7–32.

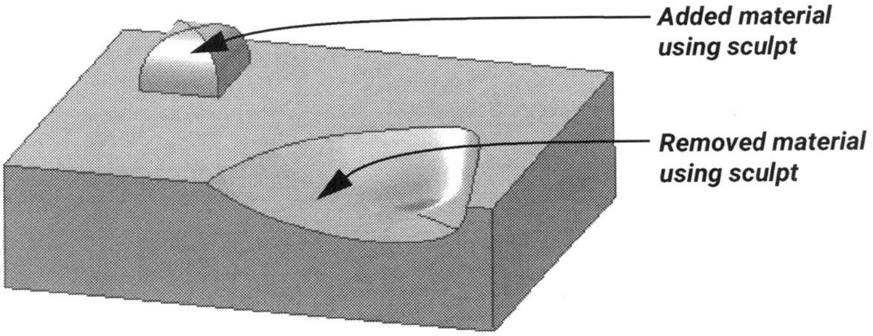

Figure 7–32

Task 1: Add material using the sculpt option.

1. Open **sculpt.ipt**.
2. Toggle on the visibility of the surface called **Add surface**. The surface displays as shown in Figure 7–33.

Figure 7–33

3. In the Surface panel, click (Sculpt).
4. Select the surface called **Add surface**.
5. Click **OK** to complete the feature. The model displays as shown in Figure 7–34. The material in the Add surface feature has been added to the model. Once the feature is complete, note that the Add surface feature has automatically had its visibility removed.

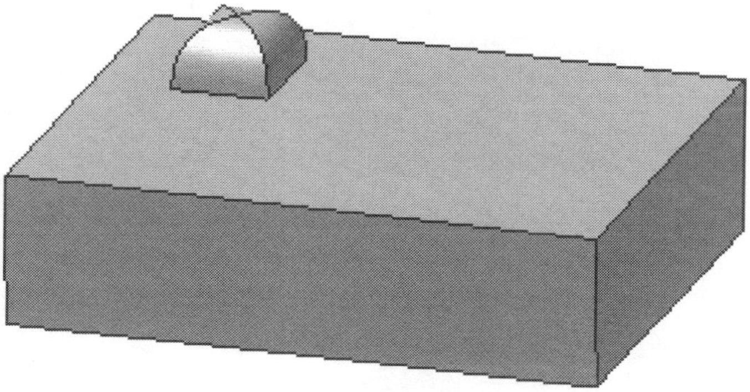

Figure 7–34

Task 2: Remove material using the sculpt option.

1. Toggle on the visibility of the surface called **Remove surface**. The surface displays as shown in Figure 7–35.

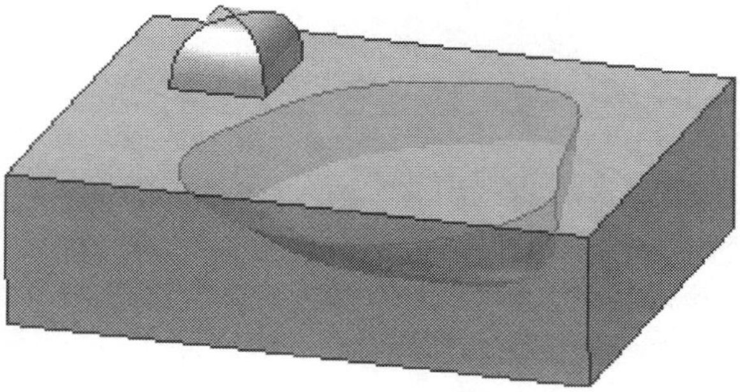

Figure 7–35

2. In the Surface panel, click (Sculpt).
3. Click (Remove).
4. Select the surface called **Remove surface**.

5. Click >> to expand the dialog box, as shown in Figure 7–36.

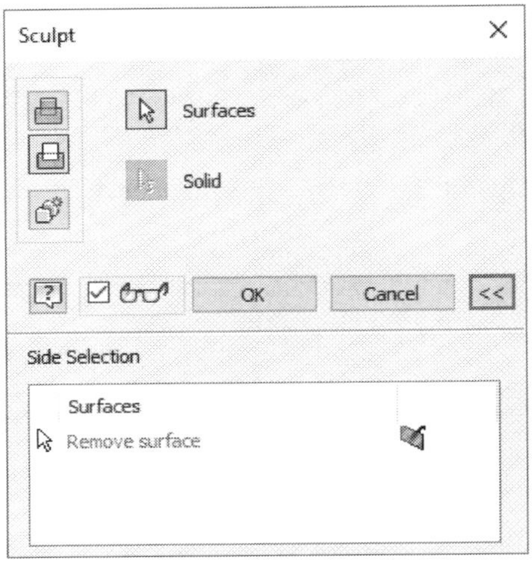

Figure 7–36

6. Select the direction column to access the drop-down list that defines the side of material to be removed. The portion to be removed is highlighted in red. Verify the side containing the smaller portion of material is removed, as shown in Figure 7–37.

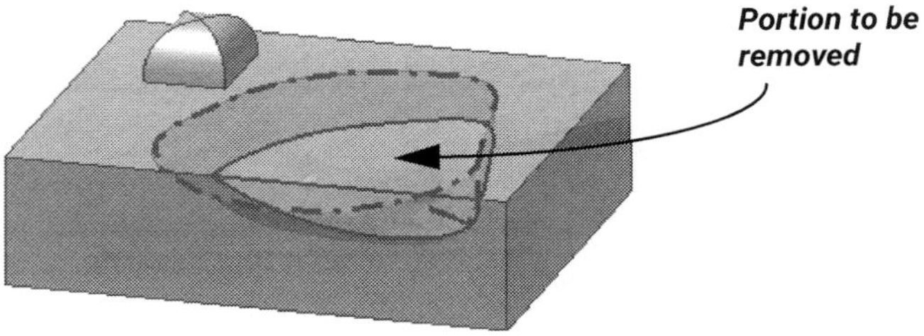

Figure 7–37

7. Click **OK**. The model displays as shown in Figure 7–38.

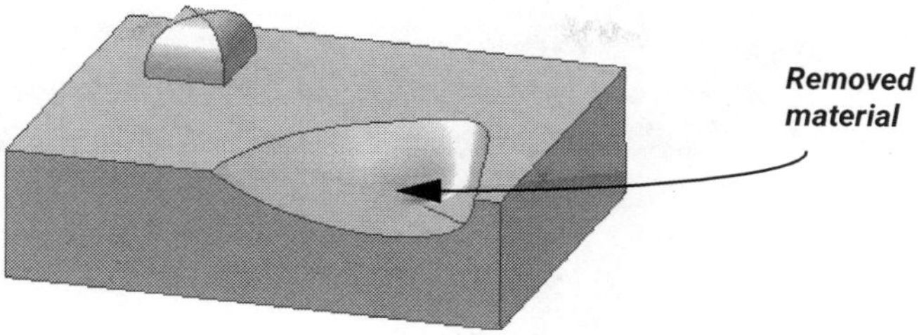

Figure 7–38

8. Save and close the model.

End of practice

Practice 7d
Ruled Surface Creation

Practice Objective

- Create normal, tangent, and vector ruled surfaces.

In this practice, you will learn how to use the **Ruled Surface** command to create normal, tangent, and vector ruled surfaces to complete a model. To complete the practice, you will use the **Stitch** and **Thicken** commands to create solid geometry from surface geometry. The completed geometry is shown (in a top and bottom view) in Figure 7–39.

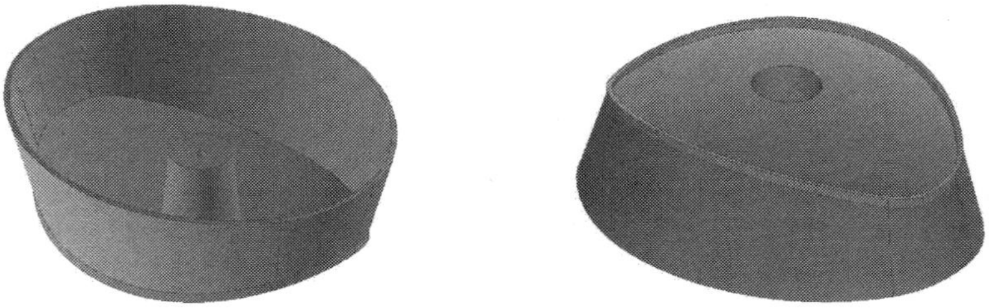

Figure 7–39

Task 1: Create a ruled surface using the Normal type.

1. Open **Ruled_Surface.ipt** from the practice files folder.

2. In the *3D Model* tab>Surface panel, click  (Ruled Surface). The Ruled Surface dialog box opens, as shown in Figure 7–40.

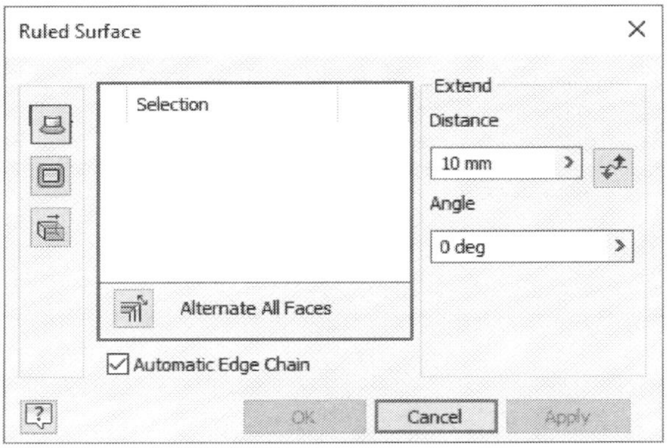

Figure 7–40

3. In the Ruled Surface dialog box, ensure that (Normal) is selected, if not already set.

   Note: *The* ***Shaded with Edges*** *Visual Style setting was assigned to improve the clarity of the images.*

4. Select the circular edge, as shown in Figure 7–41.
5. Set the *Distance* to **10 mm**, if not already set as the default value. The surface that is previewed should be pointing inwards as shown in Figure 7–41. If not, flip the orientation using the button.

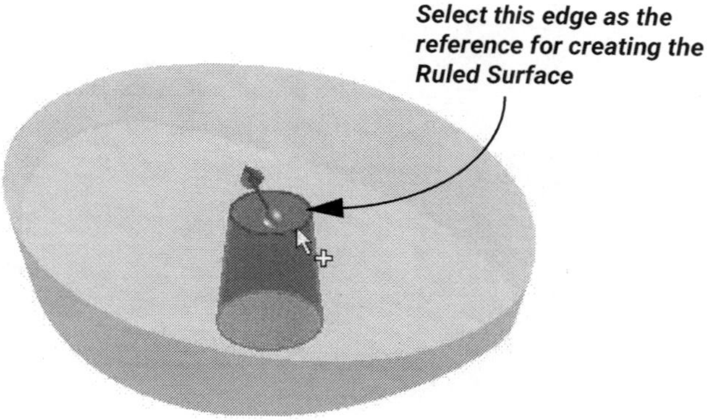

Figure 7–41

6. Click **Apply** to create the surface and leave the dialog box open to create additional surfaces.
7. In the **Top** view, zoom in on the surface. Note that the new ruled surface is perpendicular to the conical surface that is adjacent to it, not parallel to the bottom of the model. Figure 7–42 shows a sectioned view through the XY plane to visualize the ruled surface.

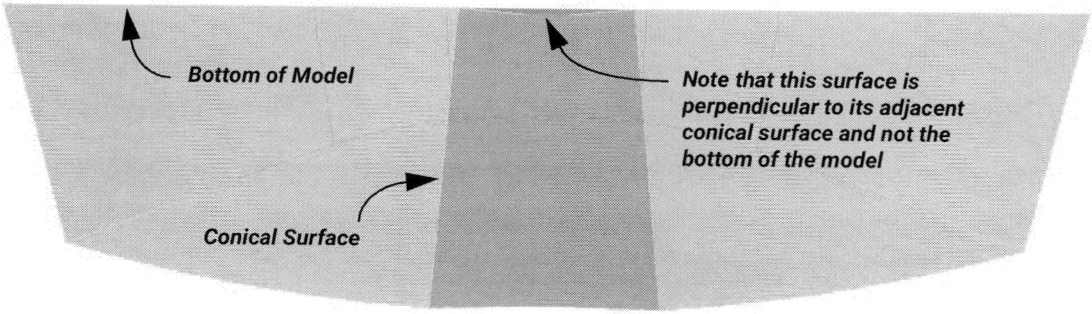

Figure 7–42

Task 2: Create a ruled surface using the Tangent type.

1. With the Ruled Surface command still active, in the Rule Surface dialog box, select  (Tangent).
2. Set the *Distance* to **25 mm** and ensure that **Automatic Edge Chain** is selected.
3. Select the edge shown in Figure 7–43.
4. The preview of the tangent ruled surface displays, as shown in Figure 7–43. Click **Apply** to create the surface. Leave the dialog box open to create additional surfaces.

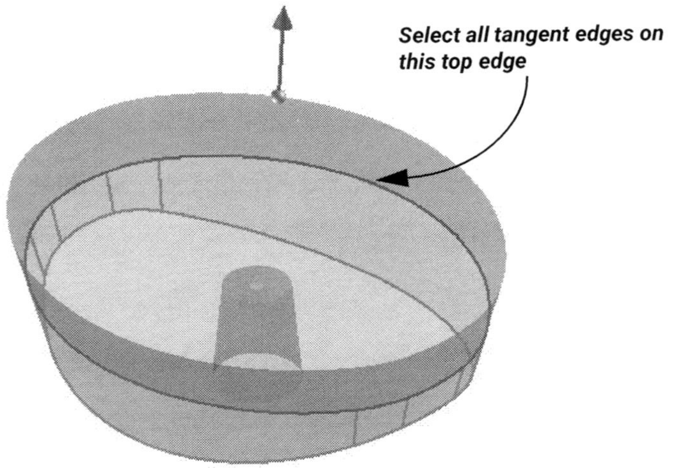

Figure 7–43

Task 3: Create a ruled surface using the Vector type.

1. Select  (Vector) to activate the ruled surface option.

2. Ensure that **Automatic Edge Chain** is selected and select the lower edge of the outer surface, as shown in Figure 7–44.

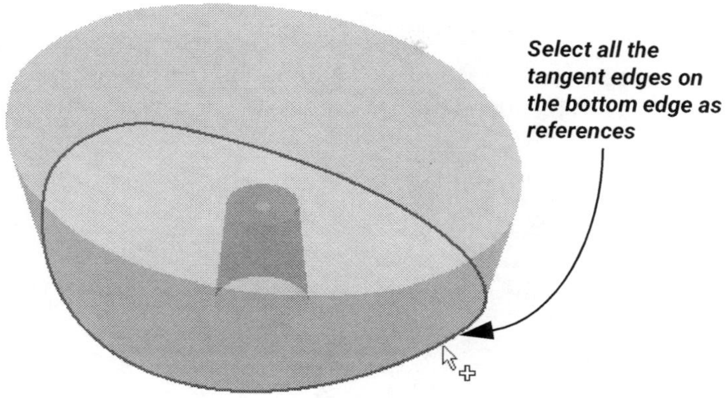

Figure 7–44

3. Select  (Vector), if not already active. Expand the origin folder and select the **Z Axis** as the direction vector.
4. Set the *Distance* to **5 mm** and flip the surface creation direction, if required. A preview of the ruled surface displays, as shown in Figure 7–45.

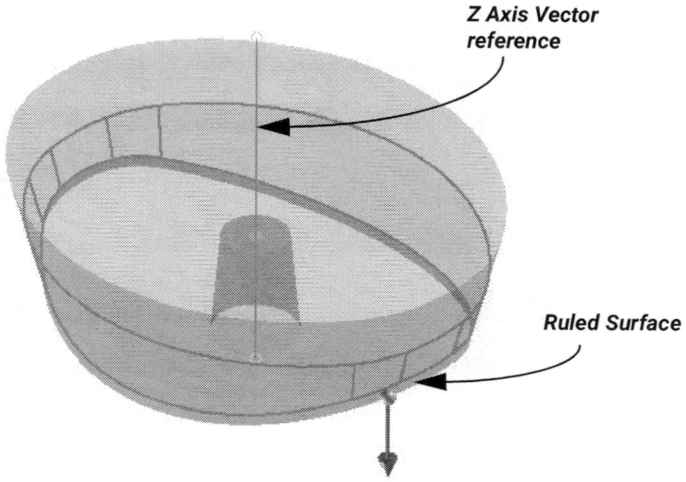

Figure 7–45

5. Click **OK** to create the surface.

Task 4: Thicken the surfaces to create a solid part.

1. In the *3D Model* tab>Surface panel, click (Stitch).
2. Select the five surfaces shown in Figure 7–46 to add to the new quilt. Do not select the vector ruled surface, as this causes the stitch to fail.

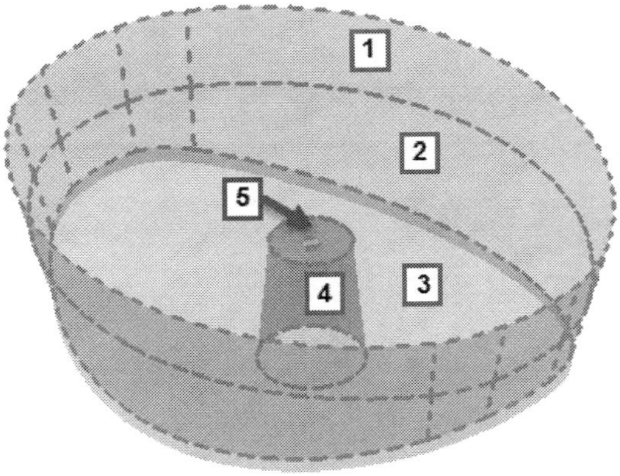

Figure 7–46

3. Click **Apply** to create the stitched surface quilt.
4. Click **Done** to complete the command. The surface updates and the edges between the tangent ruled surface and its selection have disappeared.
5. In the *3D Model* tab>Modify panel, click (Thicken/Offset).
6. In the Properties panel, click to enable Quilt selection and select the newly created quilt.
7. Set the *Distance* to **2.5 mm**.
8. Flip the thicken direction, if required, so that the material is created to the inside of the part.
9. Click **OK** to thicken the part and create a new solid body.
10. Start the Thicken/Offset command again. Ensure that (Join) and (Quilt selections) are active and the *Distance* value remains at **2.5 mm**.
11. Select the last ruled surface quilt that was created with the Vector option. Flip the direction to create the solid geometry to the inside of the surface, if required.
12. Click **OK** to thicken the quilt and complete the command.

13. In the *View* tab>Visibility panel, expand the Object Visibility drop-down list and clear the **Construction Surfaces** selection. Figure 7–47 shows the completed model from the top and bottom.

Figure 7–47

14. Save and close the part.

End of practice

Chapter Review Questions

1. Which of the following statements is true regarding surface features? (Select all that apply.)
   a. The profile of the surface must be closed.
   b. Only a single surface body can exist in a model.
   c. When creating an extruded surface, Join and Cut options are not available.
   d. When creating an extruded surface, the depth extent options are the same as those for extruding a solid.

2. Which of the following options can be used to create a planar surface from a closed 2D sketch?
   a. Extrude
   b. Loft
   c. Stitch
   d. Sculpt
   e. Thicken/Offset
   f. Boundary Patch

3. Which of the following options can be used to add or remove solid material from a model by referencing a surface body? (Select all that apply.)
   a. Extrude
   b. Loft
   c. Stitch
   d. Sculpt
   e. Thicken/Offset
   f. Boundary Patch

4. The **Thicken/Offset** option enables you to add solid geometry to a model by referencing either a surface or solid face.
   a. True
   b. False

5. Which of the following options can be used to combine two or more surfaces together?
    a. Extrude
    b. Loft
    c. Stitch
    d. Sculpt
    e. Thicken/Offset
    f. Boundary Patch

6. Which of the following are valid Ruled Surface creation options? (Select all that apply.)
    a. Normal
    b. Tangent
    c. Loft
    d. Vector

7. Which of the following best describes how excluding a surface in a drawing view affects its children views?
    a. When the visibility of a surface in a parent view is cleared, the visibility of that surface in all of its existing children views are updated to reflect the change.
    b. When the visibility of a surface in a parent view is cleared, the visibility of that surface in all of its existing children views do not change and the surface remains displayed.

Command Summary

Button	Command	Location
N/A	**Include all Surfaces**	• **Context menu**: In Model browser with model name selected
	**Boundary Patch**	• **Ribbon:** *3D Model* tab>Surface panel
N/A	**Properties (edge Properties for surface in a drawing)**	• **Context menu** with surface selected in the required view
	**Ruled Surface**	• **Ribbon:** *3D Model* tab>Surface panel
	**Sculpt**	• **Ribbon:** *3D Model* tab>Surface panel
	**Stitch**	• **Ribbon:** *3D Model* tab>Surface panel
	**Thicken/ Offset**	• **Ribbon:** *3D Model* tab>Modify panel

Chapter

8

Additional Surfacing Options

There are a number of tools in the Autodesk® Inventor® software that enable you to manipulate surfaces that have been created in a model. Understanding these tools and how they can be used to obtain the required surface and solid geometry enables you to create robust models.

Learning Objectives

- Remove portions of a surface using a reference surface or work plane.
- Increase the extent of a surface by extending it at a selected edge so that the surface maintains the curve directions of the edges adjacent to the selected edge.
- Increase the extent of a surface by stretching it at a selected edge so that the surface remains normal to the edge.
- Create a new solid face by replacing an existing solid face with surface geometry.
- Remove existing surfaces or solid faces from the model to aid in surface modeling.
- Copy surfaces to a Repaired Geometry node so that they can be opened and manipulated in the Repair environment.
- Copy surfaces from one model into another in the context of an assembly.

8.1 Extend and Trim Surfaces

Trim Surface

The **Trim Surface** option enables you to trim an existing surface feature using another surface feature or work plane.

How To: Trim a Surface

1. In the *3D Model* tab>Surface panel, click (Trim).
2. Select geometry to represent the cutting tool. In Figure 8–1, the cutting tool represents another surface.

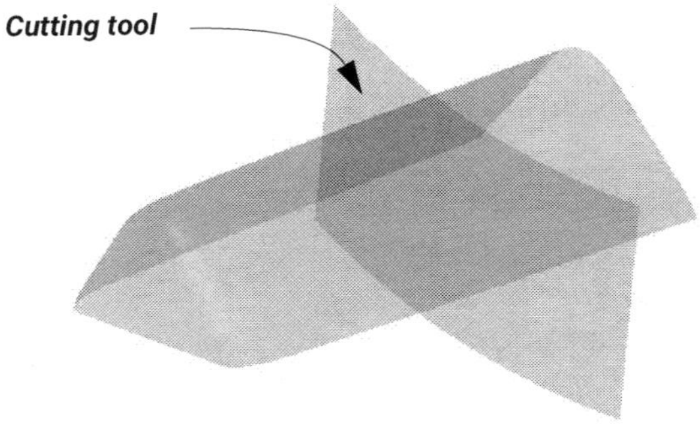

Figure 8–1

3. Select the portion of the surface you want to remove, as shown in Figure 8–2. Once the portion to be removed is selected, it is highlighted in green. You can click in the Trim Surface dialog box to invert the selection, if required.

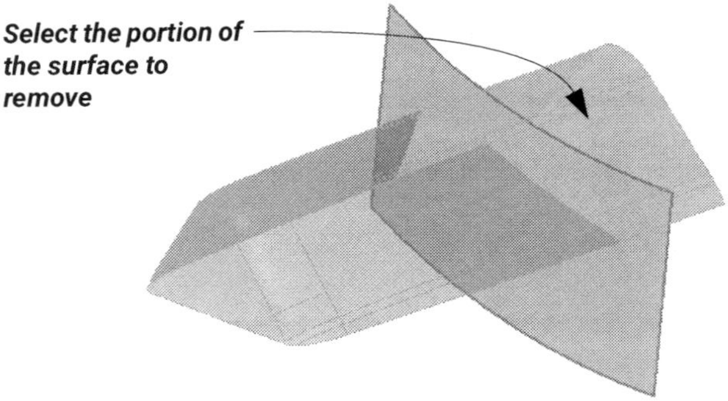

Figure 8–2

4. Click **OK** to complete the feature. Figure 8–3 shows the resulting surface after trimming.

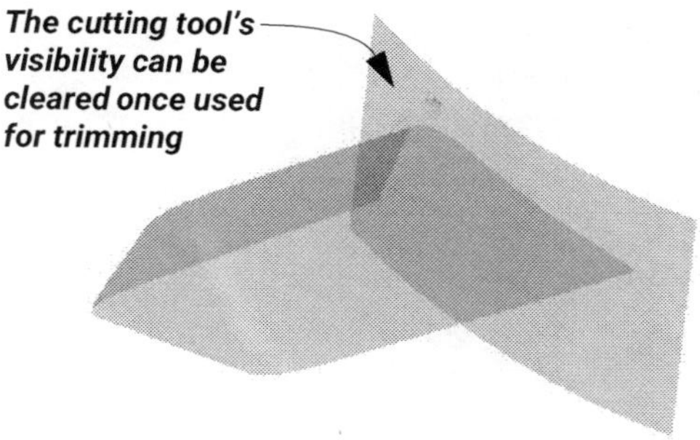

Figure 8–3

Extend Surface

Extend Surface enables you to increase the size of surfaces in one or more directions. You can specify a distance to increase by or a termination face to which the surface is extended to.

How To: Extend a Surface

1. In the *3D Model* tab>Surface panel, click (Extend). The Extend Surface dialog box opens as shown in Figure 8–4.

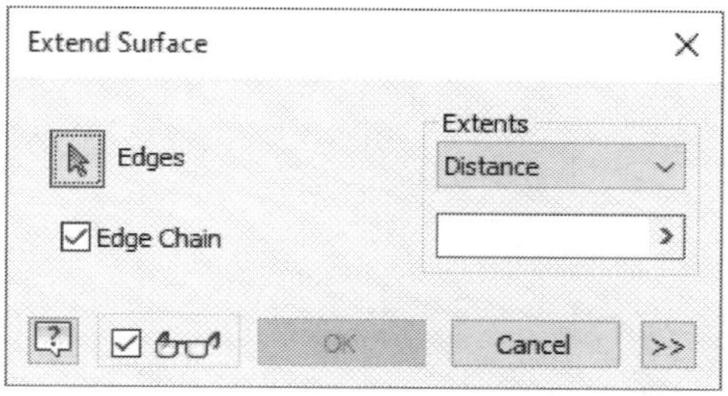

Figure 8–4

2. Select one or more edges to extend, as shown in Figure 8–5.

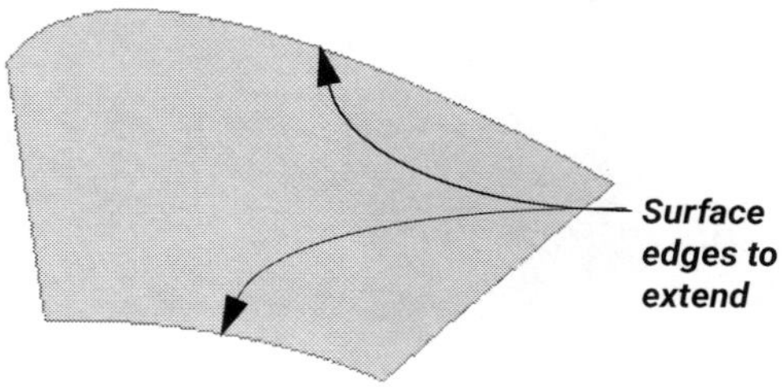

Figure 8–5

3. Enter a distance or specify a termination reference.

4. Click [>>] to expand the dialog box. Select **Extend** to extend the selected edges along the same curve direction as the adjacent edges, as shown on the left side in Figure 8–6. Select **Stretch** to extend the selected edges in a straight line from the adjacent edges, as shown on the right side in Figure 8–6.

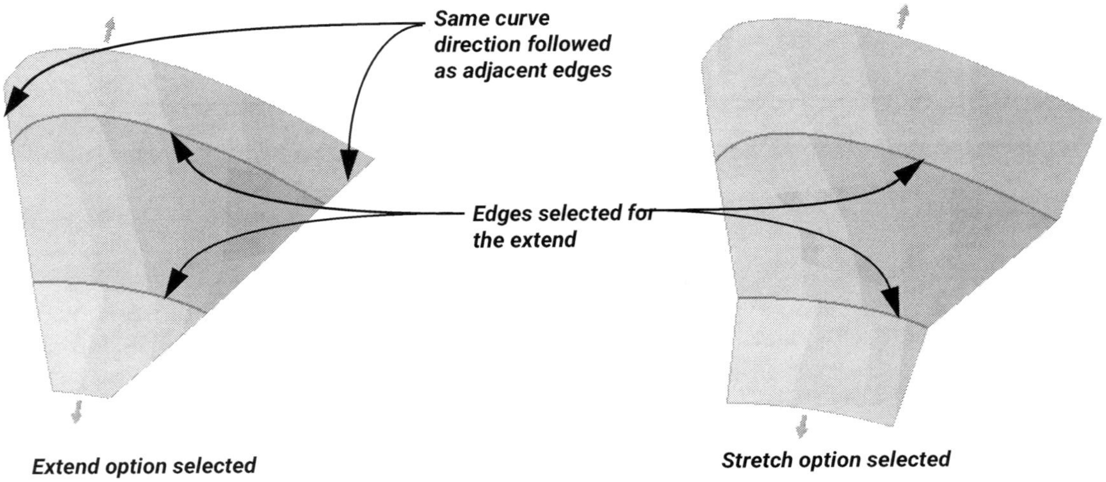

Figure 8–6

5. Click **OK** to complete the feature.

8.2 Replace Face with a Surface

The **Replace Face** option enables you to replace any face of a part with another surface. This is useful for creating parts using simple surfaces. Figure 8–7 shows a face replaced with a surface on the right side. When you replace a face with a face defined by a surface, you create a feature relationship between features. You can toggle off the visibility of the surface, but you cannot delete it. If you delete the surface, the new face is also deleted.

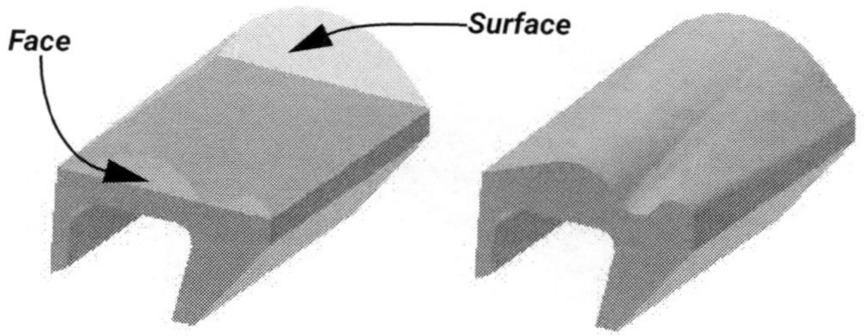

Figure 8–7

How To: Replace a Face with a Surface

1. In the *3D Model* tab>Surface panel, click (Replace Face). The Replace Face dialog box opens as shown in Figure 8–8.

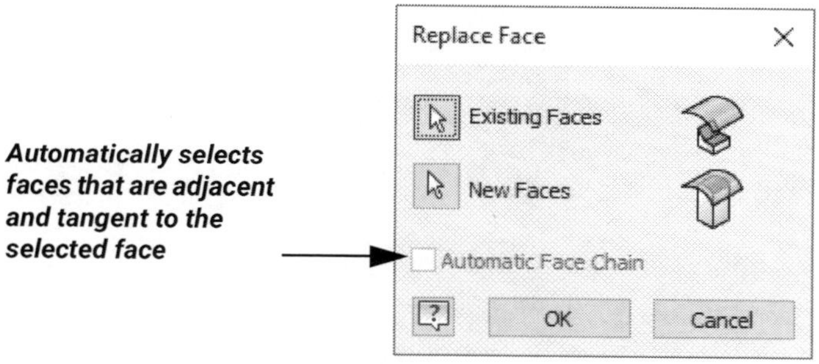

Figure 8–8

2. Select the existing part face that is to be replaced.
3. Click (New Faces) and select the replacing surface. The new face must completely intersect the part face.
4. Click **OK** to complete the feature.

8.3 Delete Faces

The **Delete Face** option enables you to remove unwanted surfaces, solid pieces, and hollow areas from a model in the part environment. This is useful when doing hybrid solid/surface modeling. For instance, a loft operation may have created an unwanted "dent" in the object. You can clean it up by deleting the face(s), creating a new lofted surface with the required shape, then stitching everything back together to form a solid.

How To: Delete Faces

1. In the *3D Model* tab>Modify panel, click (Delete Face). The Properties panel opens, as shown in Figure 8–9.

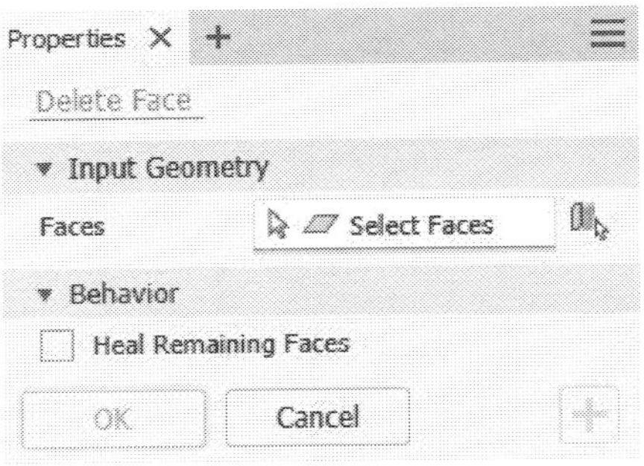

Figure 8–9

2. Select **Delete Face** (default feature name) at the top of the Properties panel to assign a new name for the feature.
3. Select the faces to delete. If a face on a solid is deleted, the solid becomes a surface.
   - Toggle the option to select individual faces (off) or select multiple faces as a lump or void (on) when defining the input geometry.
   - A lump is a solid piece, such as a portion that remains after a Cut operation, that splits a part into multiple pieces. A void is a hollow area in a part.
4. If required, select **Heal Remaining Faces** when a face on a solid is deleted and you want the system to extend the adjacent faces to keep the part a solid.

   Note: *Healing can be valuable if you remove the face created by a chamfer. This option extends the sides to restore the edge. This option is not available with the lump or void selection option toggled on.*

5. Click **OK** to complete the feature. To continue deleting faces without closing the panel, click (Apply) and select additional faces as needed. Once all changes have been completed, click **OK**.

8.4 Copy Surfaces

The **Copy Object** option can be used to copy surfaces as follows:

- Copy geometry in an assembly from one part to another part. You can then use the copied geometry as reference geometry to create new geometry.
- Copy a surface to a Repaired Geometry node so that it can be opened and manipulated in the Repair environment.

  Note: *The Repair environment has options to repair surface geometry for use in the Part environment. This is discussed in Working with Imported Surfaces.*

How To: Copy Objects

1. If you are using **Copy Object** to copy information between components you must first assemble the components in a temporary assembly.
2. In the assembly, activate the component into which you will be copying the surface geometry.
3. In the *3D Model* tab>expanded Modify panel, click (Copy Object) to copy surfaces to the Part environment. The Properties panel opens, as shown in Figure 8–10.

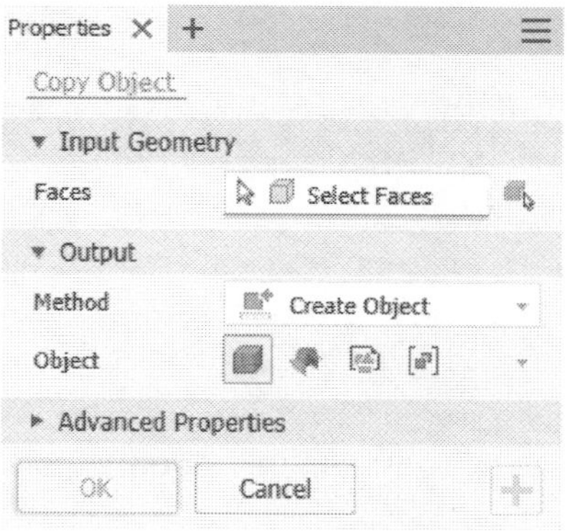

Figure 8–10

4. Select **Copy Object** (default feature name) at the top of the Properties panel to assign a new name for the feature.
5. Toggle the (Body Selection) option, as required, to select individual faces (off) or select an entire body (on) when defining the input geometry to be copied.

6. Define the Output option for how the face will be copied. The available methods include the following:

   - **Create Object** - Enables you to use the selected face(s) to create a new object. When this option is used, you must select how the object is to be copied using one of the following Object options:

(Surface)	Copies the selected face/body as a surface feature to the active part model.
(Composite)	Copies the selected faces/bodies as a single composite feature to the part model.
(Solid)	Copies the selected body as a solid feature to the active part model. This is only available when bodies are selected.
(Repaired Geometry)	Copies the selected geometry as a Repaired Geometry body that can be used to access the Repair environment.
(Group)	Copies the selected geometry as a group to a new Construction folder in the Model browser.

   - **Join Existing** - Enables the selection of a target composite feature or group to copy to. Once the option is selected, the *Existing* field appears enabling you to select the existing reference.

7. (Optional) In the *Advanced Properties* area, enable or disable the **Delete Original** option to define whether the face being copied is deleted once the Copy operation is complete.

8. Click **OK** to complete the feature.

   - To continue copying faces/bodies without closing the panel, click (Apply) and select additional faces/bodies as needed. Once all copies have been completed, click **OK**.
   - Surfaces and bodies copied from one part to another remain adaptive in the new part, unless the option is explicitly cleared in the Model browser after it is copied.

Practice 8a
Extending Surfaces

Practice Objectives

- Increase the extent of a surface by extending the surface at a selected edge, such that the extended surface maintains the curve directions of the edges adjacent to the selected edge.
- Increase the extent of a surface by stretching the surface at a selected edge, such that the stretched surface remains normal to the edge.

In this practice, you extend a surface using the two available extend options: **Extend** and **Stretch**, as shown in Figure 8–11.

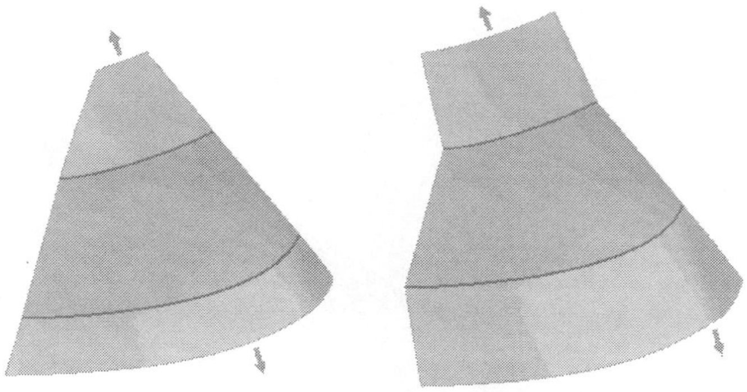

Extend *Stretch*

Figure 8–11

Task 1: Use the Extend Surface option.

1. Open **extend surface.ipt**.
2. In the *3D Model* tab>Surface panel, click  (Extend).
3. Verify that **Distance** is selected in the *Extents* drop-down list.

4. Reorient the model and select the edges shown in Figure 8–12.

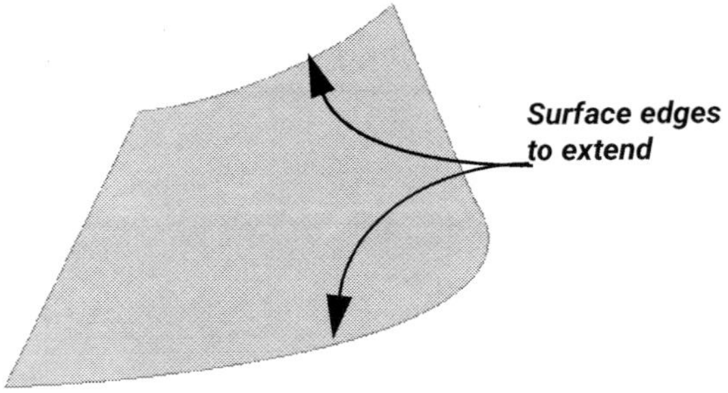

Figure 8–12

5. Set the *Distance* to **15**.

6. Click [>>] to expand the dialog box. Verify that **Extend** is selected to extend the selected edges along the same curve direction as the adjacent edges. The preview displays as shown in Figure 8–13.

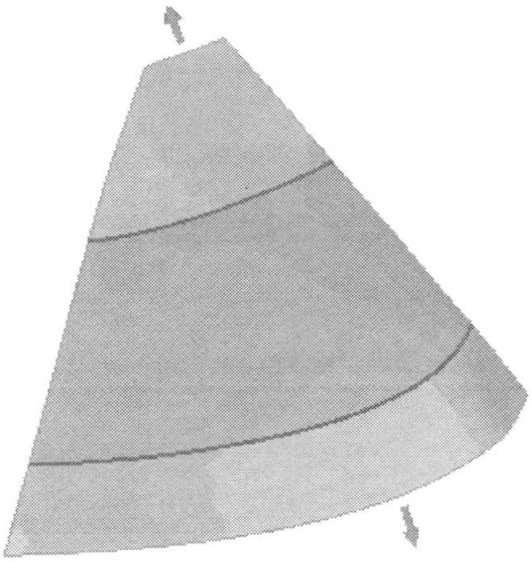

Figure 8–13

7. Select **Stretch** to extend the selected edges in a straight line from the adjacent edges, as shown in Figure 8–14.

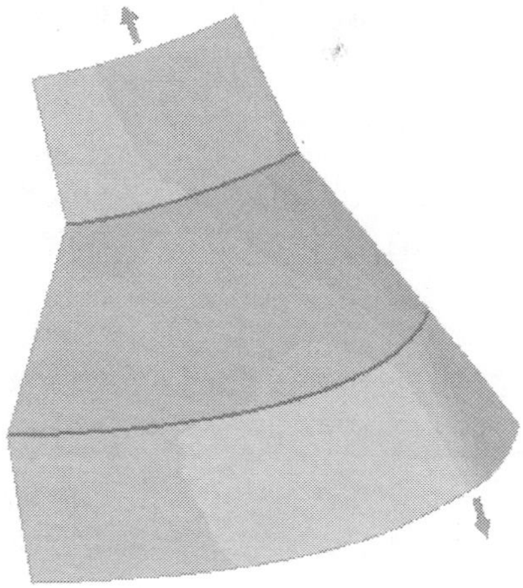

Figure 8–14

8. Click **OK** to complete the extend.
9. Save and close the model.

End of practice

Practice 8b
Copying Surfaces

Practice Objectives

- Copy the geometry of one part model into another part model in the context of an assembly.
- Using copied surface geometry, replace an existing solid face with the copied surface geometry to create a new solid face.

In this practice, you copy a surface to another part in an assembly, and use the surface to replace a face on that part. The resulting component is shown in Figure 8–15.

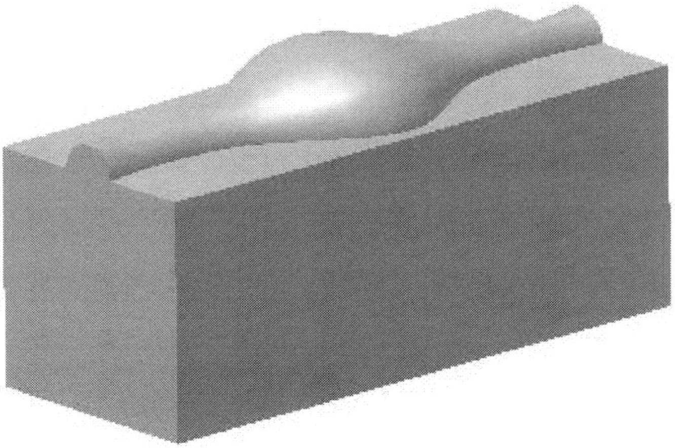

Figure 8–15

Task 1: Create a new assembly file.

1. Create a new assembly file using the Metric template.
2. Place one instance of **blank.ipt**. Right-click and select **Place Grounded at Origin**. The first component in the assembly is grounded at the origin (0,0,0).
3. Place one instance of **shape.ipt**.
4. Show the assembly degrees of freedom (*View* tab>Visibility panel>click  (Degrees of Freedom)).

5. Fully constrain **shape.ipt** as shown in Figure 8–16. The model is displayed in wireframe.

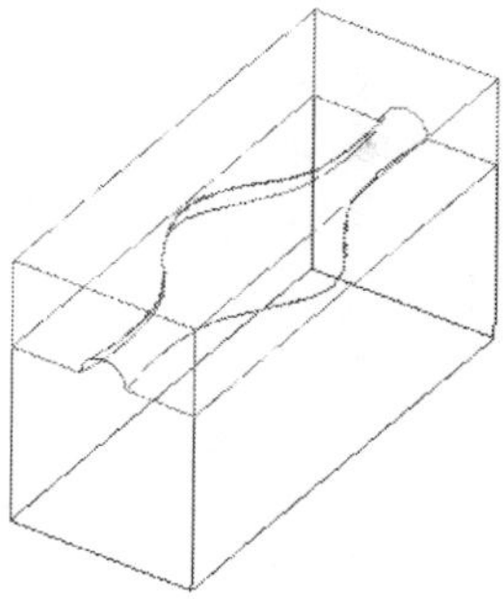

Figure 8–16

Task 2: Copy shape.ipt.

1. Activate **blank.ipt** in the assembly.

2. In the *3D Model* tab>expanded Modify panel, click (Copy Object) to copy *shape.ipt* into **blank.ipt**.

3. Ensure that is selected to enable Body selection. Select the **Shape** component in the graphics window.

4. Ensure that the Method is set as **Create Object** and the (Composite) option is selected.

5. Click **OK** to copy the object into blank.ipt. Update the assembly, if required. The Model browser displays as shown in Figure 8–17.

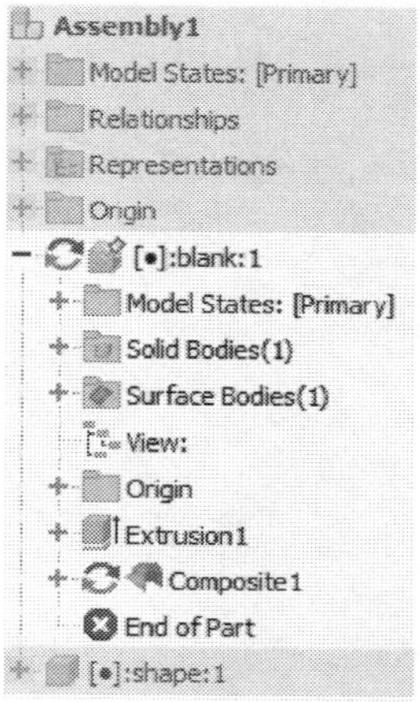

Figure 8–17

Task 3: Replace the part face with the copied surface.

In this task, you open the blank component in a separate window and replace the blank component's top face with the copied surface.

1. Open **blank.ipt** in a separate window. The part displays as shown in Figure 8–18. Surfaces from **shape.ipt** have been added.

Figure 8–18

2. In the *3D Model* tab>Surface panel, click (Replace Face) to replace a face in the part with the copied surface.
3. Select blank.ipt's top rectangular face as the existing face.
4. Click (New Faces). Select the curved face and its two adjacent flat faces, as shown in green in Figure 8–19. Be sure to select all three faces.

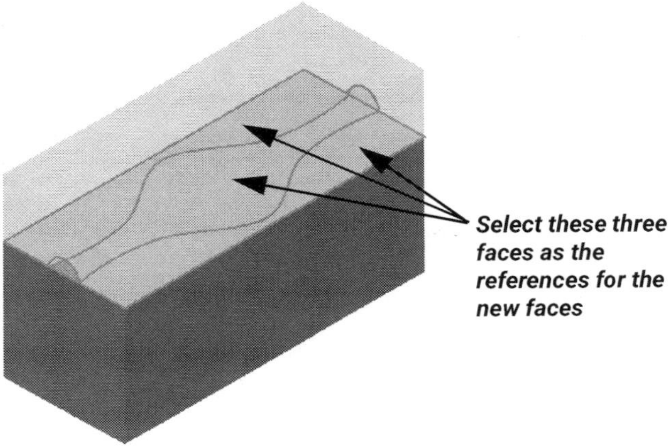

Figure 8–19

5. Click **OK**. Toggle off the visibility of the copied surface (**Composite1**). The blank part displays as shown in Figure 8–20.

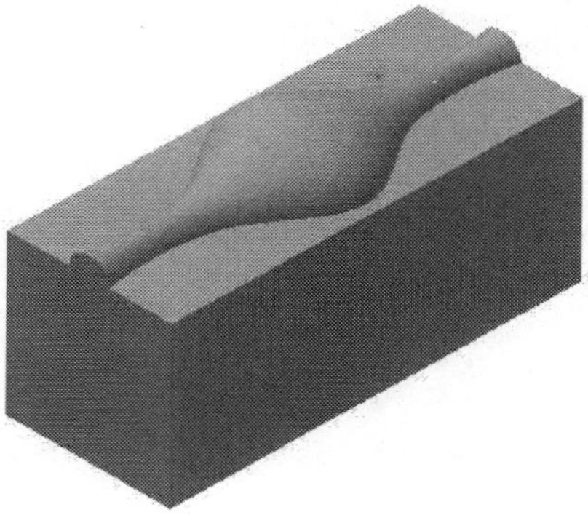

Figure 8–20

6. Save the part and assembly. If changes are made to shape.ipt, the assembly can be updated and the change will reflect in the **blank.ipt** component. If the assembly is not kept the associativity between the two components is lost and if changes are made to shape.ipt they are not reflected in **blank.ipt**.
7. Close the window.

End of practice

Practice 8c
Deleting a Surface

Practice Objectives

- Combine adjacent surfaces to form a single quilted surface that can be easily selected as a reference when creating other features.
- Remove an existing surface from the model.
- Create a surface that is defined by a series of edges to create a three-dimensional surface.
- Create solid geometry from a surface using the Thicken/Offset command.

In this practice, you create a thicken feature using an imported surface. Based on the surface geometry, it cannot be created with the required thickness. To resolve the error, you will delete the problem surface and create a new boundary surface. The resulting model, after a successful thicken feature is added, is shown in Figure 8–21.

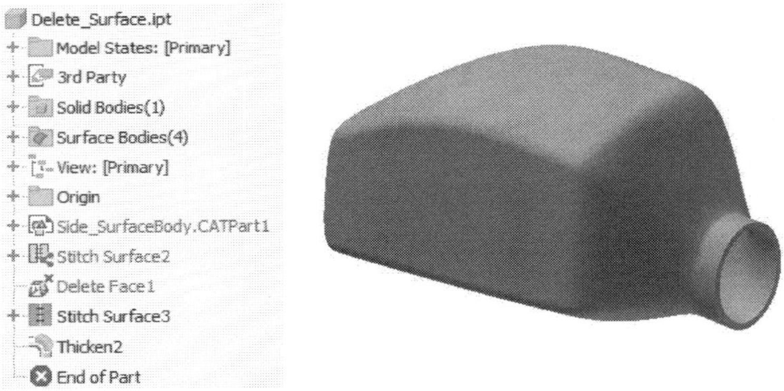

Figure 8–21

Task 1: Open a part file.

1. Open **Delete_Surface.ipt**. Note that in the Model browser, a surface is listed in the **Surface Bodies** node. This surface has been imported from another CAD system.

Task 2: Stitch surfaces together.

1. In the Surface panel, click (Stitch). The Stitch dialog box opens.

2. Select the surface body, as shown in Figure 8–22. All of the surfaces in the body are selected.

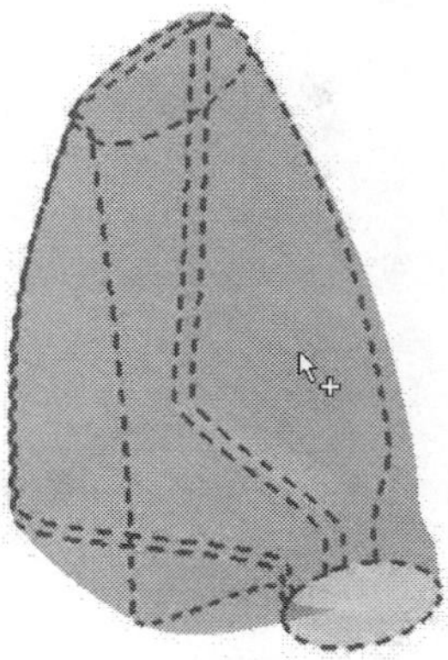

Figure 8–22

3. Click **Apply** and **Done**. In the Model browser, in the **Surface Bodies** node, a second surface is added.

Task 3: Use the Thicken/Offset command.

1. In the Modify panel, click  (Thicken/Offset). The Properties panel opens.
2. Select  to enable Quilt selection and select the stitched surface.
3. Select the stitched surface and enter a distance of **4 mm**.
4. Click **OK**. The Create Thicken feature dialog box opens indicating that the feature cannot be created due to the geometry. The 4 mm value is the minimum acceptable wall thickness for this model. A smaller value will work, however, will not meet the design requirement.
5. Click **Cancel** to close the dialog box.

Task 4: Delete a face on the model.

To resolve the failure, you will delete a surface face from the imported geometry and then recreate a new surface that will accept the required wall thickness.

1. In the *3D Model* tab>Modify panel, click 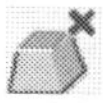 (Delete Face).
2. Verify that  is not active to ensure that individual faces can be selected.

3. Select the four faces as shown in Figure 8–23.

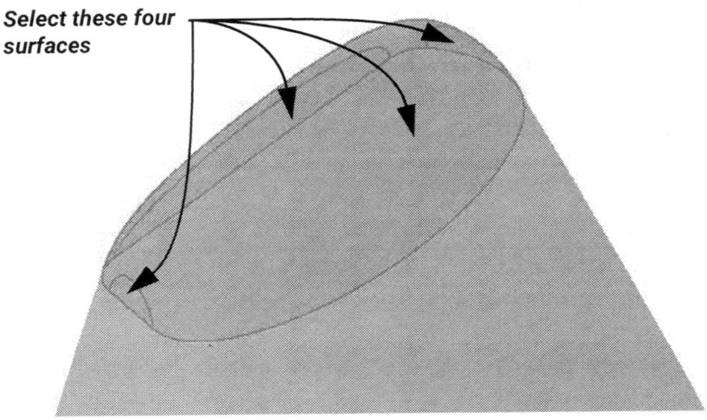

Figure 8–23

4. Click **OK**.

Task 5: Create a boundary patch.

1. In the *3D Model* tab>Surface panel, click  (Patch).
2. Select **Automatic Edge Chain** if it is not already selected. This enables you to select all the adjacent edges together instead of selecting them individually.
3. Select the circular edges bounding the face that was just deleted. A flat face immediately previews on the model, as shown in Figure 8–24.

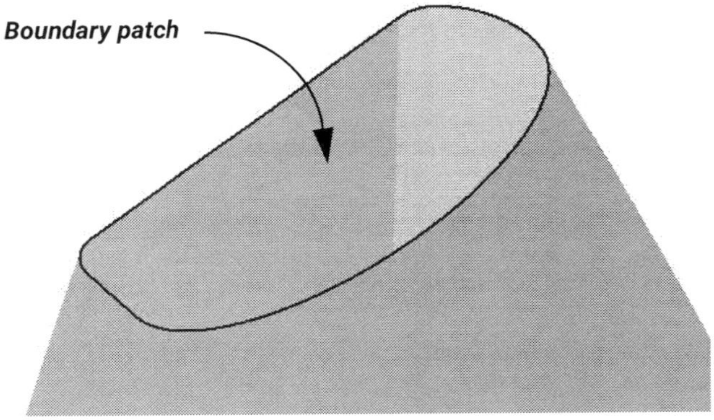

Figure 8–24

4. In the Boundary Patch dialog box, in the *Condition* area, in the selected edge drop-down list, click (Smooth G2), as shown in Figure 8–25, for the edges that defines the patch. This creates a smooth continuous condition between the patch and adjacent faces on the selected edge.

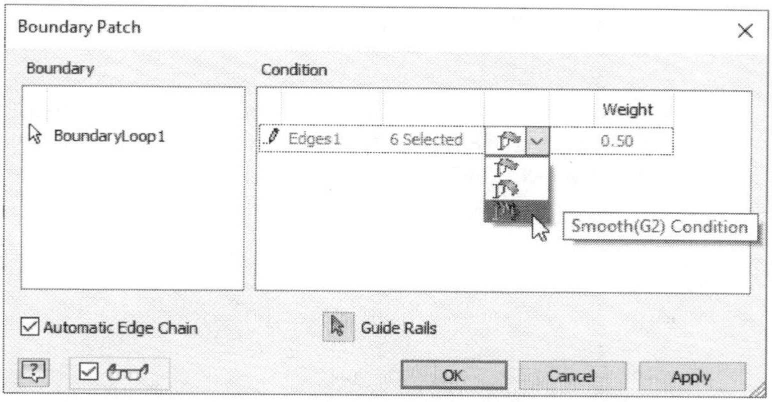

Figure 8–25

5. Maintain the default *Weight* value of **0.5**. Click **OK**. The model displays as shown in Figure 8–26.

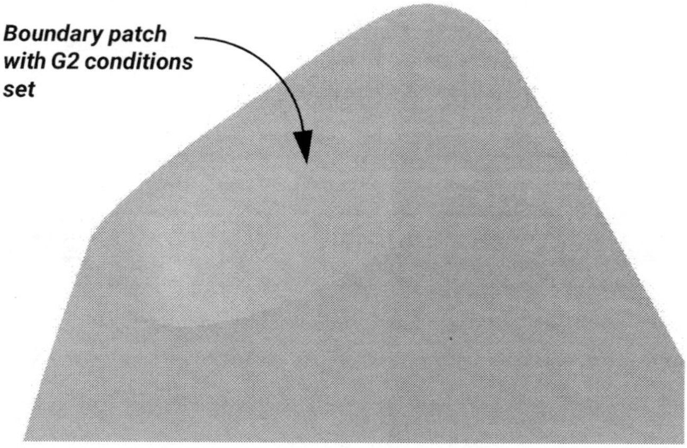

Figure 8–26

Task 6: Stitch surfaces to create a solid.

1. In the *3D Model* tab>Surface panel, click (Stitch).
2. Select the new surface and the existing stitched surface. Click **Apply** and **Done**.

Task 7: Use the Thicken/Offset option.

1. In the Modify panel, click (Thicken/Offset). The Properties panel opens.
2. Select to enable Quilt selection and select the stitched surface.
3. Set the *Distance* to **4 mm**.
4. Click **OK**. The solid geometry is created with a 4 mm thickness, as shown in Figure 8–27. By deleting the end portion of the surface geometry and simplifying it with the creation of a boundary patch that was G2 continuous with its adjacent surface, the geometry was able to be created.

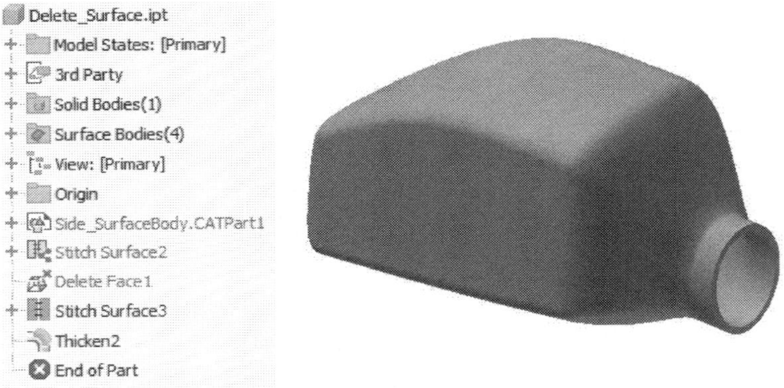

Figure 8–27

5. Save the model and close the window.

End of practice

Practice 8d
Creating a Solid from Surfaces

Practice Objectives

- Trim a surface using another reference surface as the cutting tool.
- Remove an existing surface from the model.
- Create surfaces that are defined by a series of edges to create a three-dimensional surface.
- Create solid geometry by stitching surfaces together.

In this practice, you will create solid geometry using imported surfaces as its foundation. Based on the surface geometry that is provided, you will trim it and create new surfaces to generate solid geometry. To complete the model, you will shell it. After the solid has been created, the completed model will display as shown in Figure 8–28.

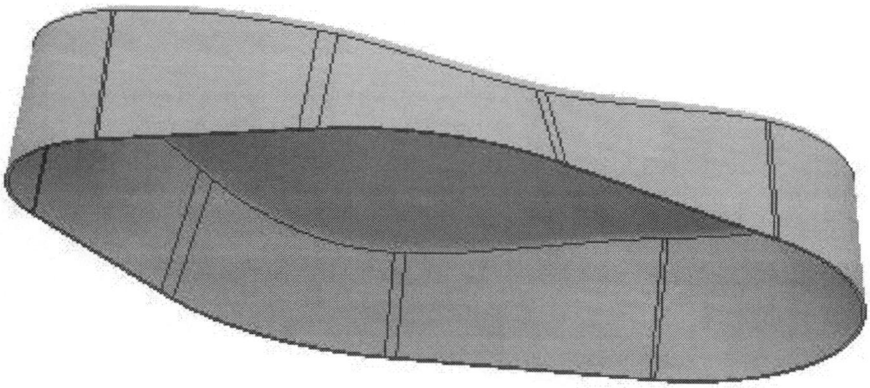

Figure 8–28

Task 1: Trim a surface.

1. Open **Surface_to_Solid.ipt**. Note that in the Model browser, two surfaces are listed in the **Surface Bodies** node. These surfaces have been imported from another CAD system.

2. In the *3D Model* tab>Surface panel, click  (Trim).

3. Select the **Top** surface as the cutting tool, as shown in Figure 8–29.
4. Select the portion of the surface you want to remove, as shown in Figure 8–29. Once the portion to be removed is selected, it is highlighted in green. To invert the selection, in the Trim Surface dialog box, click , as required.

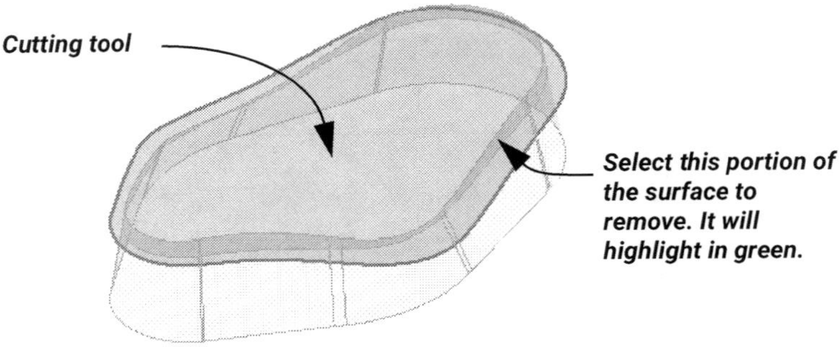

Figure 8–29

5. Click **OK** to trim the surface.

Task 2: Delete a surface.

1. In the *3D Model* tab>Modify panel, click (Delete Face).
2. Verify that is not active to ensure that individual faces can be selected.
3. Select the surface shown in Figure 8–30 to delete.

   Note: *In the Autodesk Inventor software, the edges of surfaces will display as yellow. The images in this practice show as black for the purposes of printing clarity.*

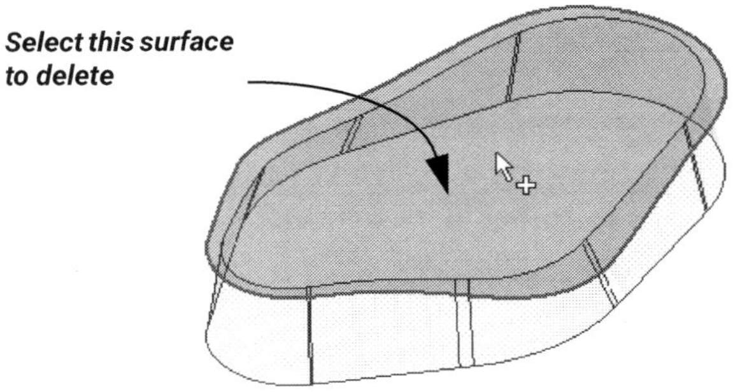

Figure 8–30

4. Click **OK** to delete the surface.

Task 3: Create a boundary patch.

1. In the *3D Model* tab>Surface panel, click (Patch).
2. Ensure that **Automatic Edge Chain** is selected. This option enables you to select all of the adjacent edges together, instead of selecting them individually.
3. Select the chain of edges that were generated by the **Trim** option in Task 2. A flat face immediately previews on the model, as shown in Figure 8–31.

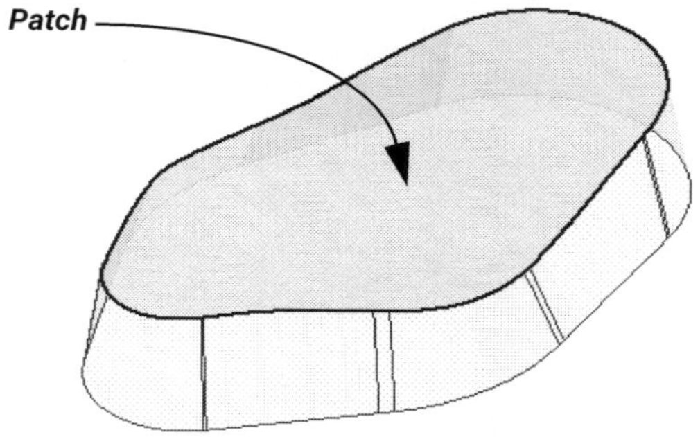

Figure 8–31

4. In the Boundary Patch dialog box, in the *Condition* area, in the selected edge drop-down list, click (Tangent Condition) (as shown in Figure 8–32) for the edges that define the patch. This creates a tangent condition between the patch and adjacent faces on the selected edge.

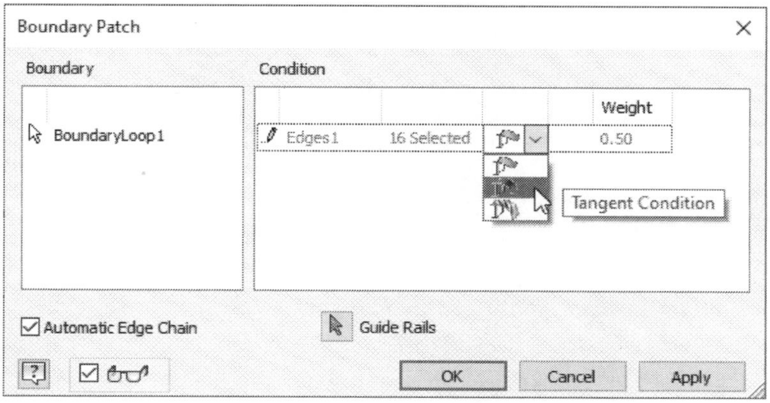

Figure 8–32

5. Set the *Weight* value to **0.2** to change the influence of tangency on the geometry. Reducing this value creates a flatter surface because tangency is maintained over a shorter distance. Click **OK**. The model appears as shown in Figure 8–33.

   Note: *To further refine the shape of the boundary patch, a guide rail curve or a point can also be selected to control its shape.*

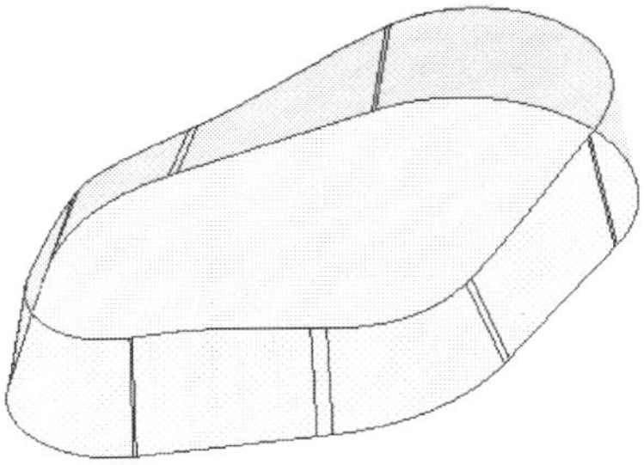

Figure 8–33

The remainder of the practice has you create a shelled solid from the imported and modified surfaces. Simply using the Thicken/Offset command does not provide for a flat lip on the bottom edge because a thickened solid remains normal to the surface, as shown in Figure 8–34. Alternatively, you will create an additional surface and then use it to create the solid geometry.

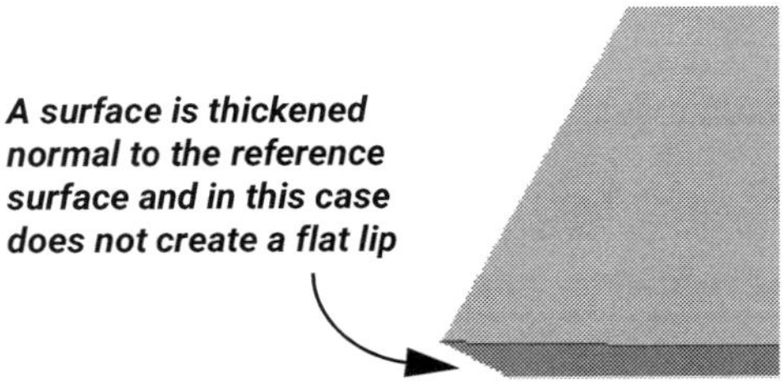

Figure 8–34

Task 4: Create solid geometry from the surfaces.

1. In the *3D Model* tab>Surface panel, click  (Patch).

2. Select the edges along the Bottom surface, as shown in Figure 8–35.

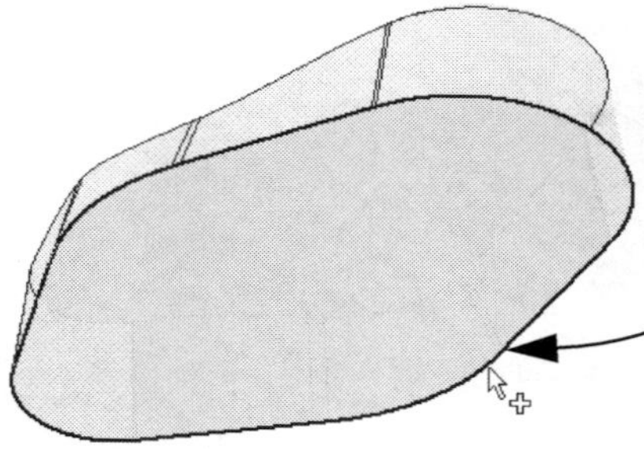

Figure 8–35

3. Click **OK**.
4. In the Surface panel, click (Stitch). The Stitch dialog box opens.
5. Select all three surfaces in the model by dragging a selection window around them. Maintain the default tolerance value and click **Apply**. The stitched surfaces form a watertight area, and therefore automatically generate a solid, as shown in Figure 8–36. Close the Stitch dialog box.

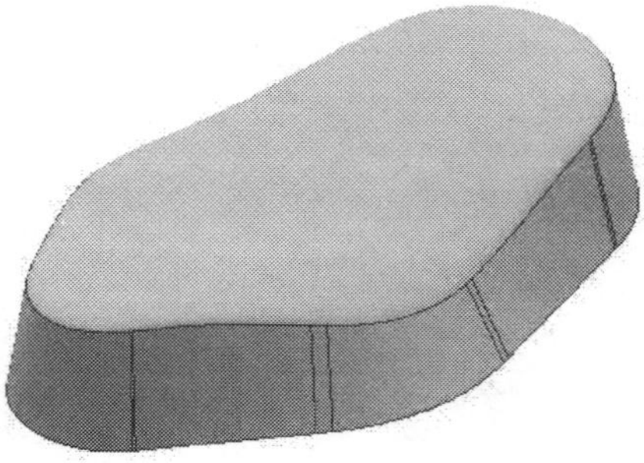

Figure 8–36

Task 5: Add a shell to complete the solid geometry.

1. In the Modify panel, click (Shell). The Shell dialog box opens.
2. Ensure that the shell is being created on the inside of the model.
3. Select the bottom flat surface as the surface to be removed.
4. Set the shell *Thickness* to **.125 in**.

5. Click **OK**. The solid geometry is created as shown in Figure 8–37.

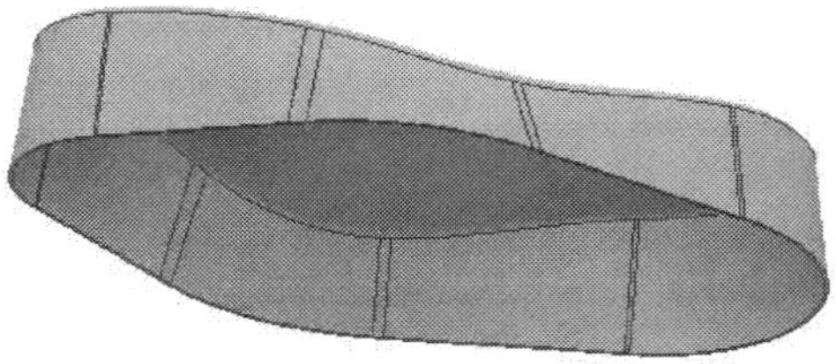

Figure 8–37

6. Save the model and close the window.

End of practice

Practice 8e
Modifying Geometry with Surface Tools

Practice Objectives

- Remove existing surfaces from the model so that the removed faces are automatically replaced by new surfaces.
- Thicken solid faces on the model to modify the geometry.

In this practice, you will be provided a model that has been imported from another CAD system. In reviewing the model, you will note a design error and a geometry change that is required. Using the **Delete Face** and **Thicken/Offset** options, you will fix these issues so that the geometry appears as shown in Figure 8–38.

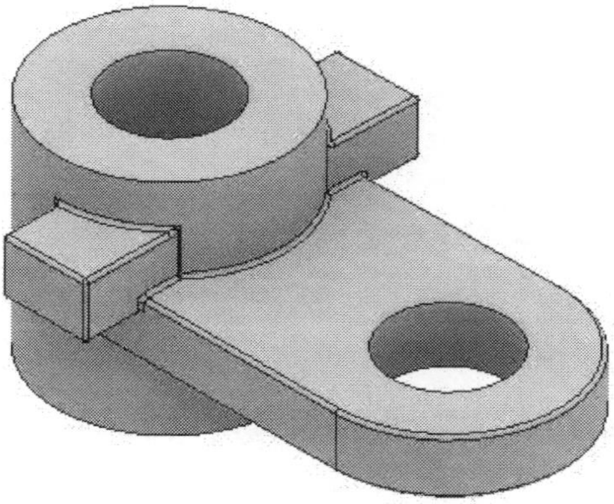

Figure 8–38

Task 1: Delete faces on the model.

The keyway that is in the geometry is not required. The **Delete Face** option can be used to remove this.

1. Open **Delete_Face.ipt**. Note that in the Model browser, a single solid is listed in the **Solid Bodies** node and in the feature list. This solid has been imported from another CAD system.
2. In the *3D Model* tab>Modify panel, click (Delete Face).
3. Verify that is not active to ensure that individual faces can be selected.

4. Select the three faces shown in the highlighted keyway in Figure 8–39.

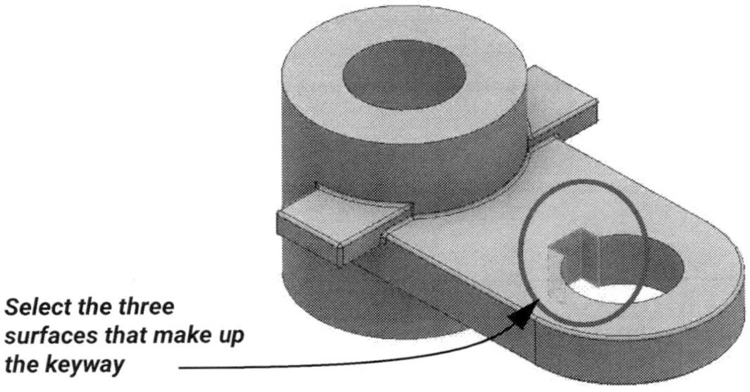

Figure 8–39

5. Click **OK**. In the Model browser, note that the geometry is now listed in the **Surface Bodies** node. The removal of these faces has converted the solid model to surface geometry because it is no longer watertight.

To create a solid you could patch the openings with surface geometry and use **Sculpt** to create the solid. As an alternative, you will use a tool in the **Delete Face** command to heal the area where the faces were removed.

6. Double-click on the **Delete Face1** feature in the Model browser to edit the feature.
7. In the *Behavior* area, select **Heal Remaining Faces** in the Properties panel.
8. Click **OK**. Note how using this option creates surfaces to replace those that were removed.

Task 2: Delete additional faces on the inside of the model.

A modeling error was made in the original geometry and it must be corrected.

1. Rotate the model to view the hole shown in Figure 8–40. Note that there is a modeling error and that a rectangular extrusion exists in the hole.

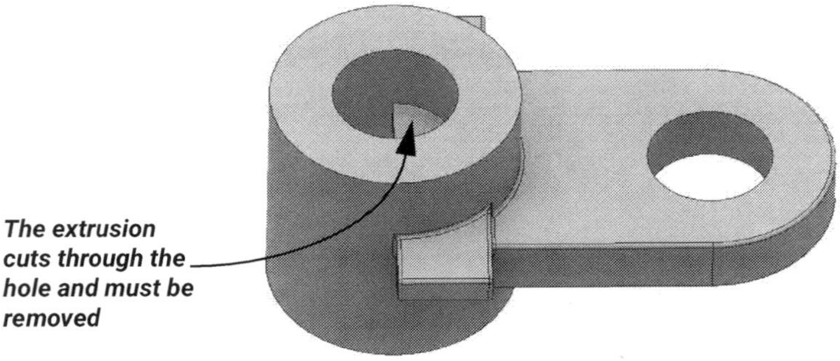

Figure 8–40

2. Similar to the previous task, use the **Delete Face** command so that the three faces that must be removed are automatically healed. The final solid geometry should display as shown in Figure 8–41.

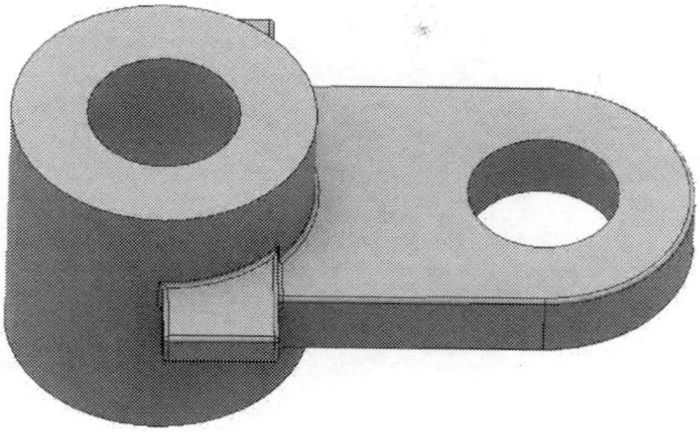

Figure 8–41

Task 3: Use the Thicken/Offset option to change the model geometry.

1. In the Modify panel, click (Thicken/Offset). The Properties panel opens.
2. Ensure that the (Surface Mode) option is off at the top of the panel. This ensures that the thicken feature will be added as solid geometry.
3. Ensure that is disabled to allow solid faces to be selected.
4. Select the solid face shown in Figure 8–42 to be thickened.

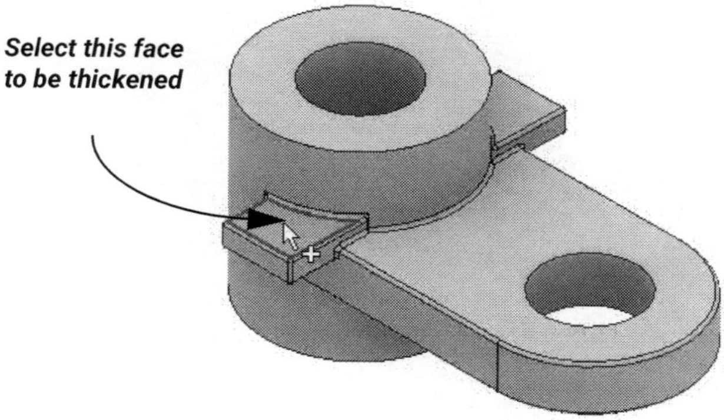

Figure 8–42

5. Enter a *Distance* value of **0.25 in**.
6. Ensure that **Automatic Blending** is disabled.

7. Click **OK**. The geometry is created as shown in Figure 8–43. Note how the thicken feature did not take into account the fillet geometry adjacent to the selected face.

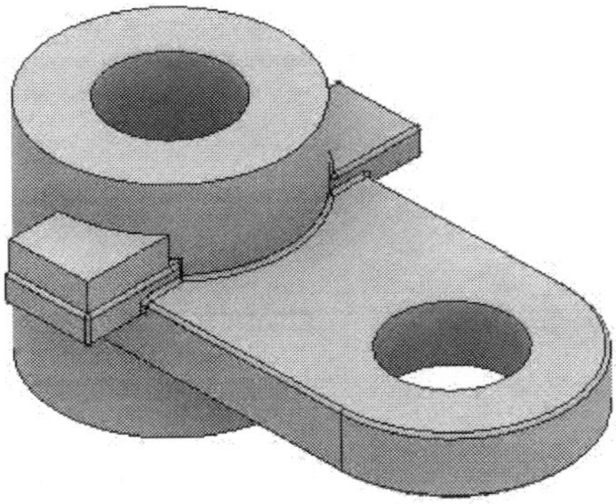

Figure 8–43

8. Edit the **Thicken1** feature.
9. Select **Automatic Blending** to enable it and click **OK**. The geometry updates as shown in Figure 8–44.

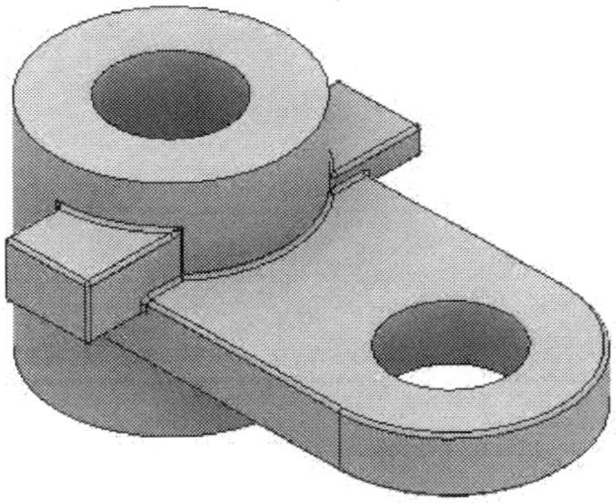

Figure 8–44

10. Open the Parameters dialog box. Because this geometry was imported from a third-party software, the only dimension in the dialog box is the thicken feature's *Distance* value (d0). Close the Parameters dialog box.

11. Create a second thicken feature and select the face of the fin on the other side of the model. Instead of entering another *Distance* value, enter **d0**. This ensures that if the initial thicken distance is modified, both sides will update to maintain the original design intent. Also ensure that **Automatic Blending** is enabled, as shown in Figure 8–45.

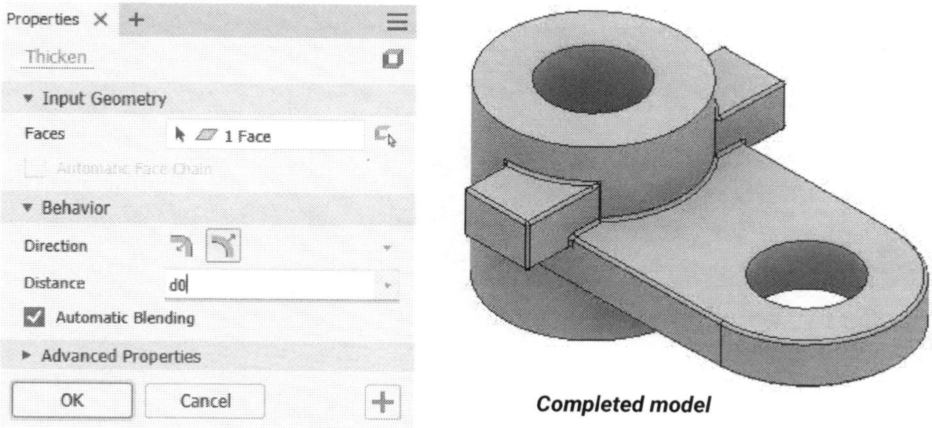

Completed model

Figure 8–45

12. Click **OK**.
13. Modify the **d0** value in the Parameters dialog box and ensure that both sides update as expected.
14. Save the model and close the window.

End of practice

Chapter Review Questions

1. Which **Extend** surface option is used to extend the arc shown in Figure 8–46?

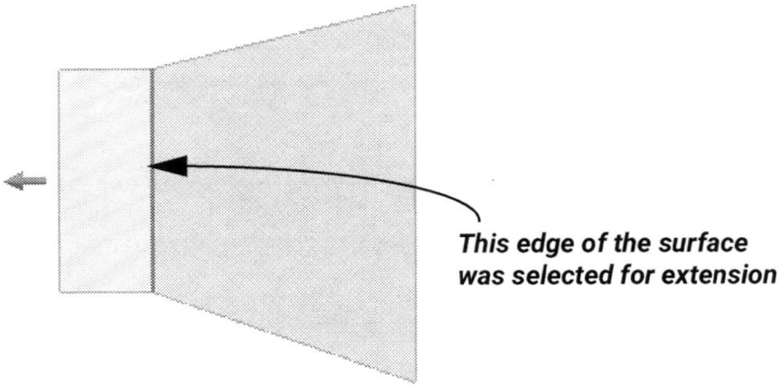

Figure 8–46

   a. Extend
   b. Stretch

2. Which option can be used to remove surface geometry on either side of an intersecting plane or surface?
   a. Trim
   b. Stitch
   c. Sculpt
   d. Patch
   e. Delete Face
   f. Replace Face

3. Which option can be used to edit existing geometry in a model with an intersecting surface?
   a. Trim
   b. Stitch
   c. Sculpt
   d. Patch
   e. Delete Face
   f. Replace Face

4. The **Delete Face** command can only be used to remove an existing surface in the model and not a solid face.
   a. True
   b. False

5. Which of the following statements are true regarding using the **Copy Object** option to copy surfaces between components? (Select all that apply.)
   a. To copy a surface between models, right-click on the surface in the source model and select Copy Object. Then open the new model, right-click, and select Paste.
   b. To copy surfaces between models, assemble them and use the Copy Object command in the target model.
   c. When using the Copy Object command, you must use the *Faces* field to assign individual surfaces in the source model.
   d. Once a surface is copied between components. Changes to the original surface can never be reflected in the new model.

6. Match the command in the left column to its icon in the right column.

Command	Icon	Answer
a. Trim		
b. Extend		
c. Replace Face		
d. Delete Face		
e. Copy Object		

Command Summary

Button	Command	Location
	**Copy Object**	• **Ribbon:** *3D Model* tab>expanded Modify panel
	**Delete Face**	• **Ribbon:** *3D Model* tab>Modify panel
	**Extend (Surface)**	• **Ribbon:** *3D Model* tab>Surface panel
	**Replace Face**	• **Ribbon:** *3D Model* tab>Surface panel
	**Trim (Surface)**	• **Ribbon:** *3D Model* tab>Surface panel

Chapter 9

Part Model States

Model states enable you to save configured states of components (parts and assemblies). They can be incorporated into your part designs for many uses, including creating families of parts or simplified versions of parts for design work, capturing manufacturing processes, or for FEA analysis. This chapter covers part model states.

Learning Objectives

- Understand the uses for model states in part files.
- Create model states in part files.
- Opening parts in their model states.
- Documenting model states in drawing views and tables.

9.1 Part Model States

Part model states have multiple uses, including creating manufacturing stages, simplifying the display of a part for design work, or creating configurations of parts that represent various products. The model state shown on the far left in Figure 9–1 is the Primary model state for the part. It was created by default and includes all non-suppressed features. Model State 1, 2, and 3 have different features suppressed (holes), sizes (overall length and hole size), and materials.

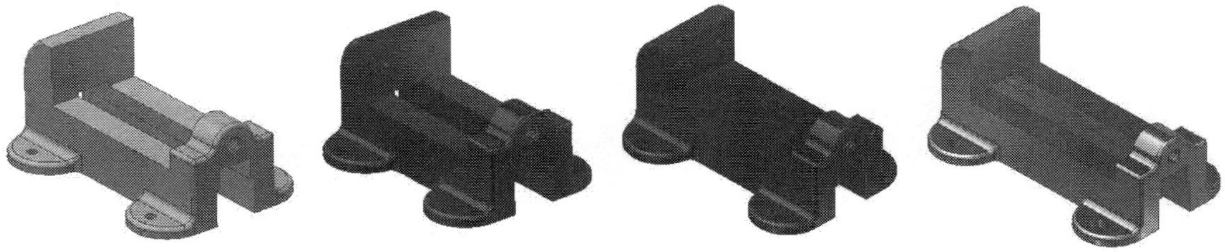

Primary Model State ***Model State 1*** ***Model State 2*** ***Model State 3***

Figure 9–1

How To: Create a Model State

1. In the Model browser, right-click on the **Model States** node and select **New**.
   - If prompted, click **OK** to the message regarding the edit member scope setting. This is an informational message only.
   - The model state (as shown in Figure 9–2) is created as a copy of the active model state and is immediately activated.

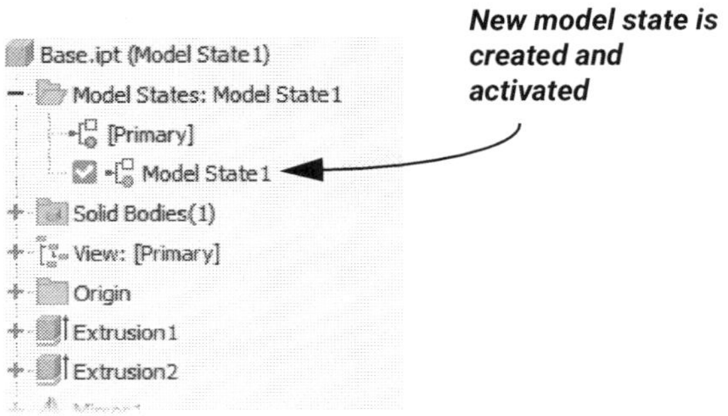

Figure 9–2

__Note:__ Alternatively, you can right-click on a model state you want to copy and select __Copy__ to create a new model state based on an existing one.

2. Verify the edit scope setting is appropriate for the model state customization that you will be doing. This setting determines if the change will affect only the active model state or all model states. By default, the edit scope is set for the current model state only and the (blue pencil) icon appears adjacent to its name.

   - By enabling the scope ( ) to affect all model states (as shown in Figure 9–3), you can ensure the change is made to all model states. When enabled, the (blue pencil) icon appears adjacent to all model state names, indicating they will all be edited.

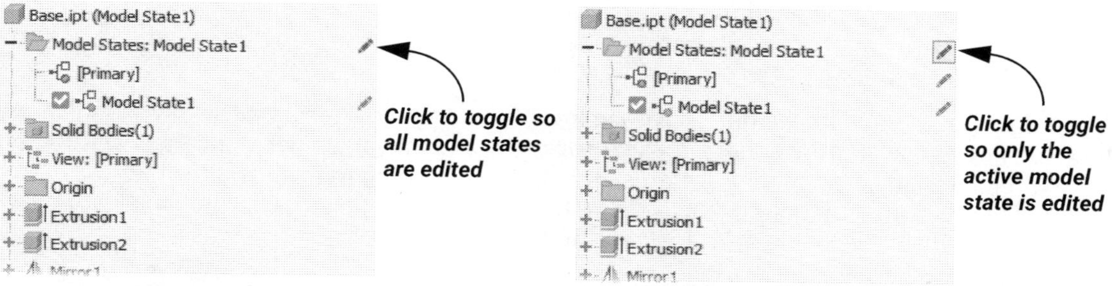

Default edit scope: Changes affect only the active model state

The (blue pencil) icon appears adjacent to the model states that will be affected by a change

Figure 9–3

*Note: The **Delete** operation is global and affects all model states regardless of the edit scope setting. To delete a feature or component from a model state, you must activate it and set it as suppressed.*

3. With the new model state active, modify the part's configurable attributes as follows to customize the model state. Once modified, each configurable attribute is assigned a column in the file's internal model state spreadsheet.

   - Suppress/unsuppress features in the model state.
   - Modify the iProperties, as required, for the active model state. In the Model browser, right-click the model state name or the model name and select **iProperties**.
   - Modify parameters, as required, for the active model state. In the Parameters dialog box (fx), modify parameter values, as required, for the active model state. Alternatively, by showing dimensions in the graphics window and modifying them, you can also change dimension values as an alternative to locating them in the Parameters dialog box.
   - Assign materials to each model state.

4. Rename the model state using a descriptive name by clicking it twice (not double-clicking) in the Model browser and entering the new name.

5. (Optional) Once you have created one model state, you can use standard spreadsheet functionality to create additional model states or add customizable attributes. To open the spreadsheet, right-click on the **Model States** node in the Model browser and select **Edit via Spreadsheet**. Edit as required, save, and close. The model states update to reflect any new model states or edits to existing model states.
6. Save the assembly to save the new model state.

You can make changes to the model states once created. To do this, ensure the required model state is active, verify the edit scope setting is as required for the change, and manipulate the part. Once edits are done, ensure the file is saved.

Model States vs. iParts

The Model State functionality (introduced in Inventor 2022) provides an alternative to the iPart functionality. Unlike iParts, model states are all saved and managed in the one part or assembly file. With the introduction of model states, the Model State functionality and the iPart functionality become mutually exclusive. The Model State functionality is enabled by default in all new parts. If you are using previously created parts consider the following:

- If the part does **not** contain pre-existing iParts, the Model State functionality is enabled.

  Note: *To return to iPart functionality, only a Primary model state can exist in the file. To switch, on the Manage tab, click*  *(Create iPart) and create an iPart member. Once complete, the Model States node is removed from the Model browser and is replaced with an iPart table.*

- If the part contains pre-existing iParts, the Model State functionality is **not** enabled.
- The process of converting an iPart table to model states is manual. You can either delete the iPart table and recreate the configurations using model states or you can use spreadsheets, as follows:
  1. Open the part, right-click on the **Table** node in the Model browser, and select **Edit via Spreadsheet**.
  2. With the spreadsheet open, copy the data or save the file to a temporary location.
  3. Delete the iPart table. A **Model States** node appears in the Model browser, indicating that it is active.
  4. Create a new model state in the file.
  5. Right-click on the **Model States** node and select **Edit via Spreadsheet**.
  6. Copy the data from iPart table into the model states table to provide a starting point for your model states table.
     - Note that the syntax is not the same in the two tables. For example, model states tables use **Compute** and **Suppress** for feature inclusion and iPart tables use **Include** and **Exclude**. Edits will be required for the model states table to be recognized and generate the required configurations.

Hint: Model States and Autodesk Vault

Model states offer capabilities similar to those found in iParts/iAssemblies; however, all configurations are stored in a single file instead of multiple files. Additional Vault integration functionality is available for model states if your Vault Professional implementation includes items. If your Vault implementation does not include items, any file that contains model states will display the primary model's properties (e.g., iProperties, parameters, etc.). If you require separate files that can be managed and released, consider using iParts and iAssemblies. For more information, see "Working with Model States and Vault Files" in the Vault Help documentation.

9.2 Opening Parts Using Model States

Part files can be opened so that a specific model state is active. This can save time in locating and enabling the required model state, or it can ensure that future design changes are not mistakenly added to the wrong model state after a model is opened.

How To: Open a Part in a Model State

1. In the Open dialog box, select the part and click **Options**. The File Open Options dialog box opens.
2. Select the required model state from the Model State drop-down list, as shown in Figure 9–4.

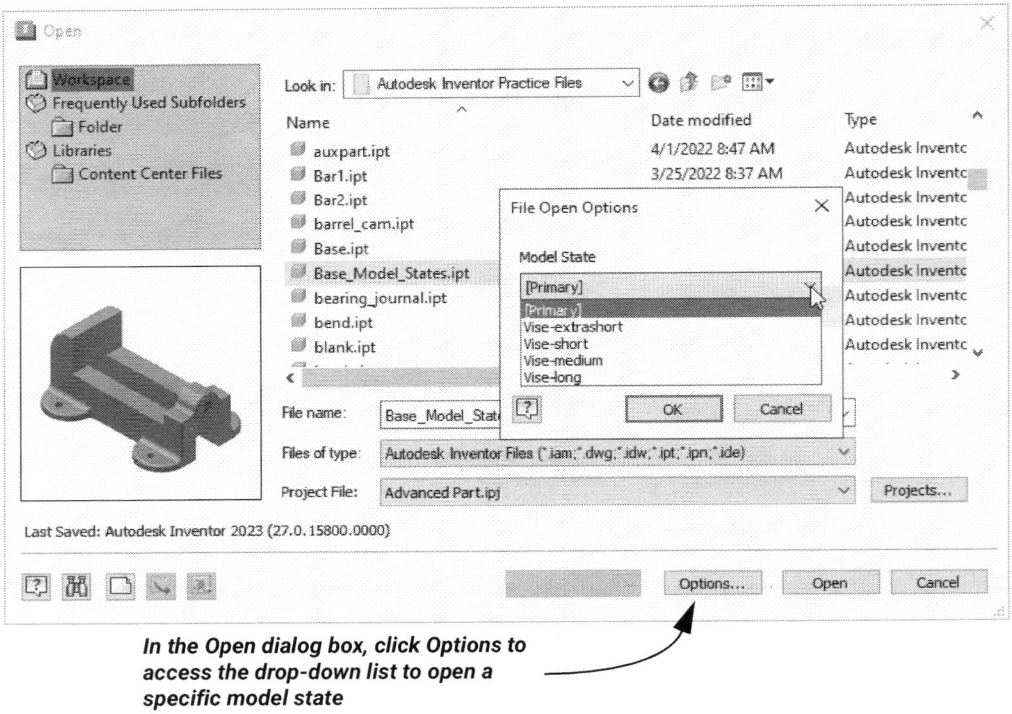

Figure 9–4

3. Click **OK** in the File Open Options dialog box.
4. Click **Open** in the Open dialog box. The part opens with the selected model state activated.

Note: *This process can also be used when placing components that have model states in an assembly.*

Hint: Setting the Default Model State for Opening

By default, assemblies are set to open the model state that was active when the part was last saved. Maintaining this setting helps reduce the chance that you might open the Primary model state in error. You control this setting in the Application Options.

1. In the Application Options dialog box, select the *File* tab and click **File Open**.
2. Select the required option in the Model State drop-down list. Maintain the default **Last Active** option to always open parts based on the model state that was active the last time they were saved. Select **Primary** to always open the Primary model state of the part.

9.3 Using Model States in Drawings

Drawing Views

Any model state can be selected for use while creating base drawing views. When modifying the parent view, you can also change the model state that is active by editing the view. When creating a base view, select the required model state name from the drop-down list, as shown in Figure 9–5. To change the model state that is used in a base view, right-click on the view, select **Edit View**, and select a new model state name. All views that reference it will also update. Hint: If you want an isometric drawing view to have a different model state than a 2D base view, create the isometric view as a new base view and orient it as needed.

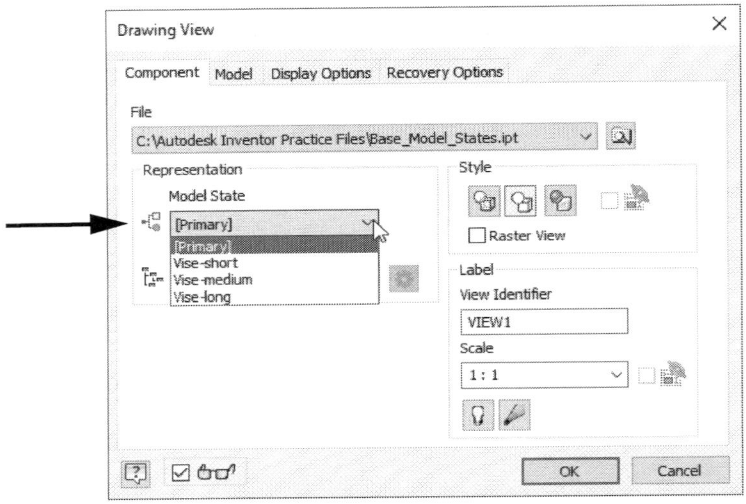

Figure 9–5

General Tables

A general table can be used to show all of the model state details for a drawing model's configurations. To create this table, complete the following steps:

1. Click (General Table) on the *Annotate* tab to open the Table dialog box.
2. Select the drawing view that will be the source for the table. The view can be the primary or a model state configuration of the assembly.
3. In the *Columns and Rows* area, select (Column Chooser).
4. In the Table Column Chooser dialog box, select the columns that you would like to include in the table from the *Available Columns* list and move them to the *Selected Columns* list using the **Add** option. The list will include all the configurable items that were modified in the model states (e.g., dimensions, parameters, etc.)

5. Click **OK** twice to create the table and add it to the drawing.
6. (Optional) To customize the column names, double-click on the table to edit it, right-click on the column name, and select **Format Column**. In the Format Column dialog box, you can disable the **Name From Data Source** option and enter a custom name for the column.

Figure 9–6 shows the columns that were added to the general table and the resulting drawing table that was created. In the table, the column headers were customized to have descriptive names using the procedure described in Step 6 above.

TABLE				
Member	Material	Length	Mounting Holes	Mounting Hole Size
[Primary]	Cast Steel	184.15 mm	Compute	8 mm
Vise-short	Copper, Cast	164.15 mm	Suppress	8 mm
Vise-medium	Iron, Cast	184.15 mm	Compute	8 mm
Vise-long	Cast Steel	204.15 mm	Compute	12 mm

The general table can show all the customized items in the model states. The column headers have been modified and the hole size removed for the suppressed Vise-short model state.

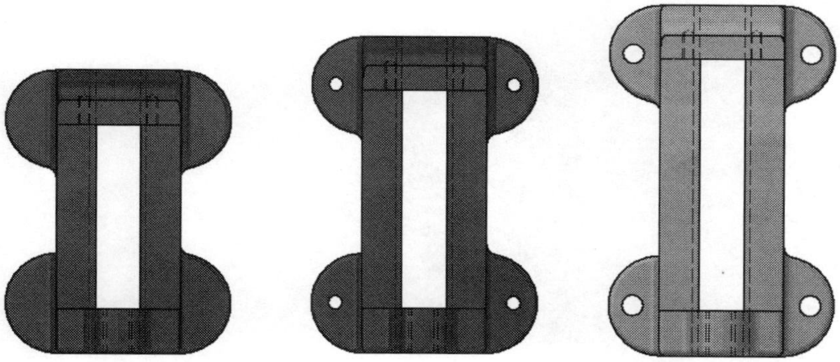

Figure 9–6

Consider the following when working in a drawing with model states:

- If a design change is made to a model state that is used in a drawing view, it will update to reflect the change when next opened. Any associated parts lists or general tables will also update.
- The model state assigned to a view can be switched by editing the view and selecting an alternate in the Model State drop-down list.
- A view can be modified to replace its reference model (and its model state) using the  (Replace Model Reference) option on the *Manage* tab. In the Replace Model Reference dialog box, select the file that is being replaced, select , select a new file, and click **Options**. In the File Open Options dialog box, select the required model state. Once the file is replaced, the view and tables will update.

Practice 9a
Part Model States

Practice Objective

- Create model states that represent various configurations of a part file.

In this practice, you will use model states to create multiple design variations in the model shown in Figure 9–7. You will vary dimensions, feature inclusion, materials, and iProperties.

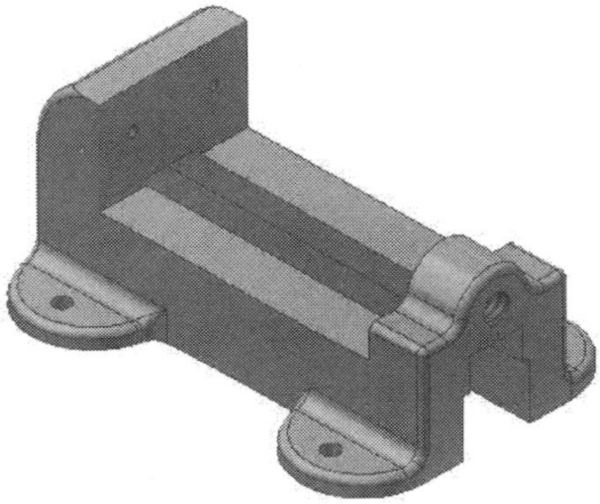

Figure 9–7

Task 1: Open a part file.

1. Open **Base_Model_States.ipt**.
2. In the Model browser, expand the **Model States** node, as shown in Figure 9–8. Note that a Primary model state has been created and is active by default.

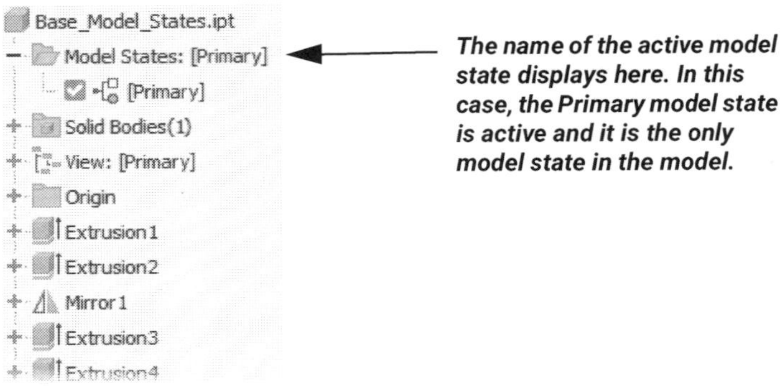

Figure 9–8

Task 2: Create model states with various size configurations.

In this task, you will create the design variations shown in Figure 9–9 using three model states.

Vise-short ***Vise-medium*** ***Vise-long***

Figure 9–9

1. Right-click on the **Model States: Primary** node and select **New**. A new model state is added to the list, called **Model State1**, and it becomes the active model state.
2. Click **OK** in the message window that appears explaining that you click Toggle Edit Scope to switch between Edit Member Scope settings. This will be explained later in this practice.
3. In the Model browser, click twice (do not double-click) on **Model State1** and rename it as **Vise-short**.
4. Create two additional model states called **Vise-medium** and **Vise-long**. The Model browser should appear as shown in Figure 9–10.

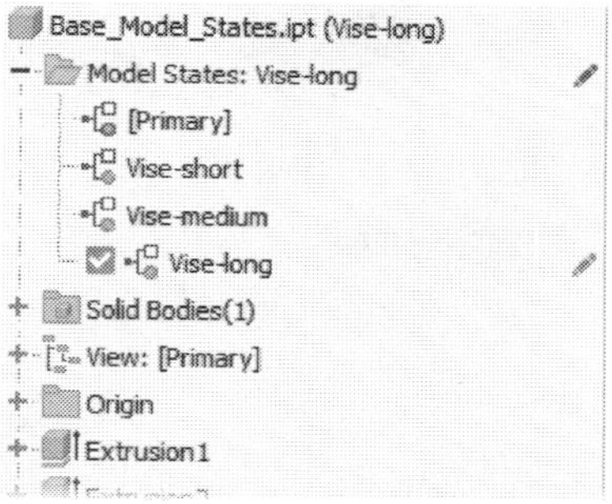

Figure 9–10

5. Double-click on the **Vise-short** model state to activate it.
6. In the Quick Access Toolbar, click (Parameters) to open the Parameters dialog box. Alternatively, by showing dimensions in the graphics window and modifying them, you can also change dimension values as an alternative to locating them in the Parameters dialog box.
7. Scroll through the list and locate the **d5** model parameter. This is the dimension that drives the length of the model and the sizes for the different model states.

8. Enter **Length** for the name of the d5 model parameter to make it easier to locate and change.
9. Modify the *Length* parameter value to **164.15 mm**. Click **Done** to close the Parameters dialog box. Note that the model's length updated to this smaller value.
10. Activate the **Vise-medium** model state.
11. Open the Parameters dialog box and note that the *Length* value is still set at **184.15 mm** for this model state. No change is required to this model state. Click **Done**.
12. Activate the **Vise-long** model state.
13. Open the Parameters dialog box and modify the *Length* value to **204.15 mm** for this model state. Click **Done**. A long version of the model is created in this model state.
14. Switch between the model states to review their size differences.
15. Save the part.

Task 3: Customize a feature's inclusion and size in the model states.

In this task, you will further customize the three model states such that a feature is either included or not and so its size will vary. The complete design variations are shown in Figure 9–11.

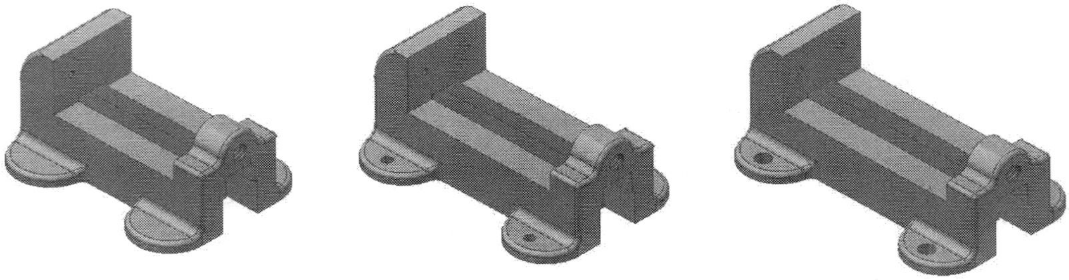

Vise-short ***Vise-medium*** ***Vise-long***

Figure 9–11

1. Activate the **Vise-short** model state, if not already active.
2. Click the (gray pencil) icon adjacent to the **Model States:Vise short** node to set the edit scope to all model states. The (blue pencil) icon appears adjacent to all of the model states, indicating that they are being edited. Click **OK** to confirm that the Edit Factory Scope is enabled.
3. In the Model browser, right-click on the **Hole4** feature and select **Suppress Features**. The mounting holes are removed from the model state.
4. Activate the **Vise-medium** model state. Note that the holes are also removed in this model state. No changes were required in this model state. The suppression of the holes occurred in this model state because the edit scope setting was set incorrectly and the change affected all model states. The same is true for the **Vise-long** model state.

5. Right-click on the **Hole4** feature again and select **Unsuppress Features**.
6. Activate the **Vise-short** model state.
7. Click the (gray pencil) icon adjacent to the Model States**: Vise short** node name to toggle off the edit scope for all model states. The (blue pencil) icon should now only appear adjacent to the active model state.
8. Suppress **Hole4** in this model state and verify the hole still exists in the other model states.
9. Activate the **Vise-long** model state, if not already active. The holes are required in this model state; however, they must have a larger diameter.
10. In the Quick Access Toolbar, click *fx* to open the Parameters dialog box. Scroll to the bottom of the *Model Parameter* list. The **d90** dimension is associated with the Hole4 feature (as shown in the *Consumed by* column). This is the hole diameter value.
11. Change the d90 parameter name to **Mounting_Hole_Dia**.
12. Enter **12 mm** as the new value for the hole in the Vise_long model state. Click **Done** to close the Parameters dialog box.
13. The **Vise-long** model state now has larger diameter mounting holes. Toggle between the three model states to verify the holes are correctly displaying.
14. Save the part.

Task 4: Customize the material that is used in each model state.

In this task, you will set the material that will be used in each of the three model states, as shown in Figure 9–12.

Vise-short - Copper, Cast ***Vise-medium - Iron, Cast*** ***Vise-long - Cast Steel***

Figure 9–12

1. Activate the **Vise-short** model state.
2. The material will be unique in each model state so the edit scope setting should be set to only affect the Vise-short model state. Ensure that the (blue pencil) icon only appears adjacent to this model state's name.

3. Cast Steel is the material that was assigned to the Primary model when it was created. In the Quick Access Toolbar, select **Copper, Cast**, as shown in Figure 9–13.

   Note: *Material choices were made so that their appearances vary, making the material differences easily identifiable.*

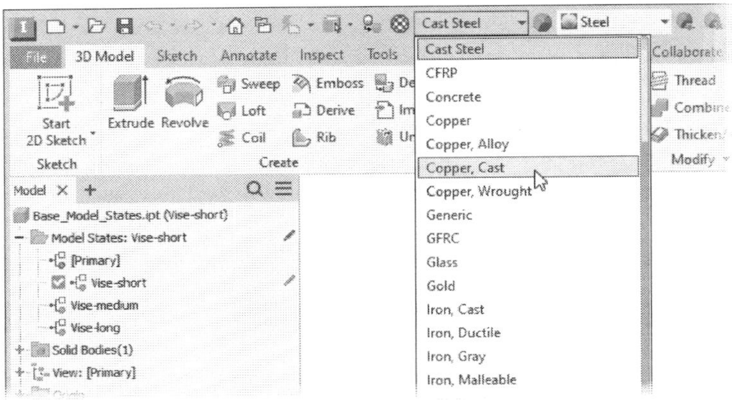

Figure 9–13

4. Activate the **Vise-medium** model state and assign the **Iron, Cast** material.
5. No material change is required for the Vise-long model state. It should remain as **Cast Steel**.
6. Save the part.

Task 5: Customize an iProperty in each model state.

In this task, you will set a unique iProperty in each of the three model states.

1. Activate the **Vise-short** model state.
2. Right-click on either the model name or the model state name and select **iProperties**. Select the *Project* tab and enter **Vise-short** for the *Part Number*. Click **OK** to assign and close the dialog box.

3. Instead of editing the remaining iProperties using the iProperties dialog box, you will edit them using the internal spreadsheet for the model states. Right-click **Model States: Vise-short** and select **Edit via Spreadsheet**, as shown in Figure 9–14.

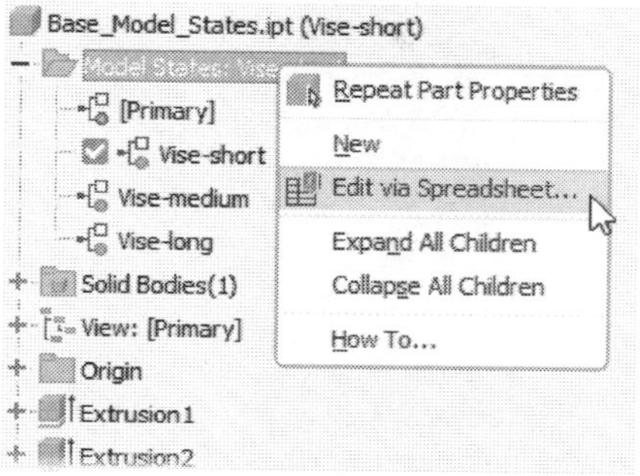

Figure 9–14

4. Click **OK** to acknowledge that the changes will take affect after the spreadsheet is closed.
5. Expand the columns and note how each row has columns and values that are driving each model state.
6. Edit the table as shown in Figure 9–15 to assign the *Part Number* iProperties to the other model states and add a fourth model state called **Vise-extrashort**. Note that a hole diameter was assigned to the new model state so that if the hole was unsuppressed, it would not fail.

	A	B	C	D	E	F
1	Member	Length	Hole4	Mounting_Hole_Dia	Material [Physical]<mat	Part Number [Project]
2	[Primary]	184.15 mm	Compute	8 mm	Cast Steel	Base
3	Vise-short	164.15 mm	Suppress	8 mm	Copper, Cast	Vise-short
4	Vise-medium	184.15 mm	Compute	8 mm	Iron, Cast	Vise-medium
5	Vise-long	204.15 mm	Compute	12 mm	Cast Steel	Vise-long
6	Vise-extrashort	154.15 mm	Suppress	8 mm	Cast Steel	Vise-extrashort
7						

Figure 9–15

7. Save and close the spreadsheet.

8. The new model state is added to the Model browser. Select it and drag and drop it above the Vise-short model state, as shown in Figure 9–16. Model states can be reordered as needed by dragging and dropping the model state names. You can also reorder the model states by reordering the rows in the spreadsheet.

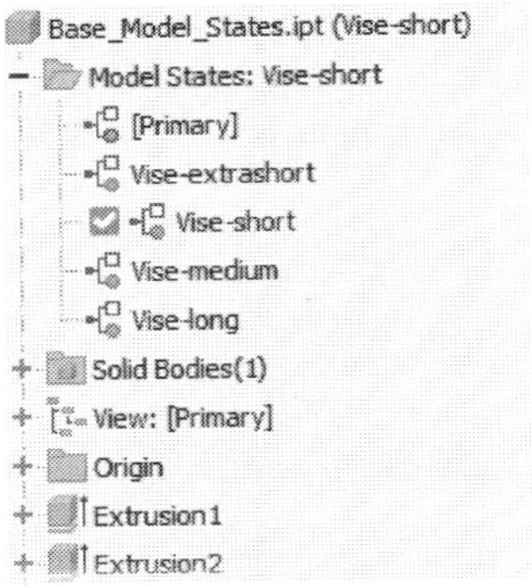

Figure 9–16

9. Activate the **Vise-extrashort** model state to verify its size and material, and review the iProperties dialog box to verify it has the correct *Part Number* iProperty (Vise-extrashort) value set.
10. Save the part and close the window with the **Vise-extrashort** model state active.

Task 6: Open the Base_Model_States model using a model state.

1. In the Quick Access Toolbar, click . The Open dialog box opens.
2. Select **Base_Model_States.ipt** and click **Options** at the bottom of the dialog box. The File Open Options dialog box opens.
3. In the File Open Options dialog box, note that the **Vice-extrashort** model state is set to open by default. This is because the Application Option for opening files is set to open with the last active model state.

   Note: *To change the Application Option that controls how model states are opened, in the Application Options dialog box>File tab, click* ***File Open*** *and select the required option in the Model State drop-down list.*

4. Click **OK** and then in the Open dialog box, click **Open**. The model is opened with the **Vise-extrashort** model state activated.
5. Close the part.

End of practice

Chapter Review Questions

1. The Model State functionality in a part model is mutually exclusive with which of the following Inventor part-level functionalities?
   a. iParts
   b. Design Views

2. Which of the following statements regarding part model states are true? (Select all that apply.)
   a. Model states can be created in a model to vary dimensions of the model geometry.
   b. Model states are assigned the same iProperties as the primary model and cannot be changed.
   c. The Edit via Spreadsheet option can be used to begin the creation of all model states and their configurations from the Primary model state.
   d. Part files can be opened so that a model state is immediately active.
   e. To remove a feature from an active model state, right-click and select Delete on the feature in the Model browser.

3. Once a drawing view has been created to represent a model state configuration, it must be deleted and recreated to switch configurations.
   a. True
   b. False

4. In your office environment, if you open a part file that was created for you and it has iParts associated with it, will the Model States node be available?
   a. Yes
   b. No

5. If **Hole1** is suppressed in the **Vise-short** model state shown in Figure 9–17, will it be suppressed in the Vise-long model state?

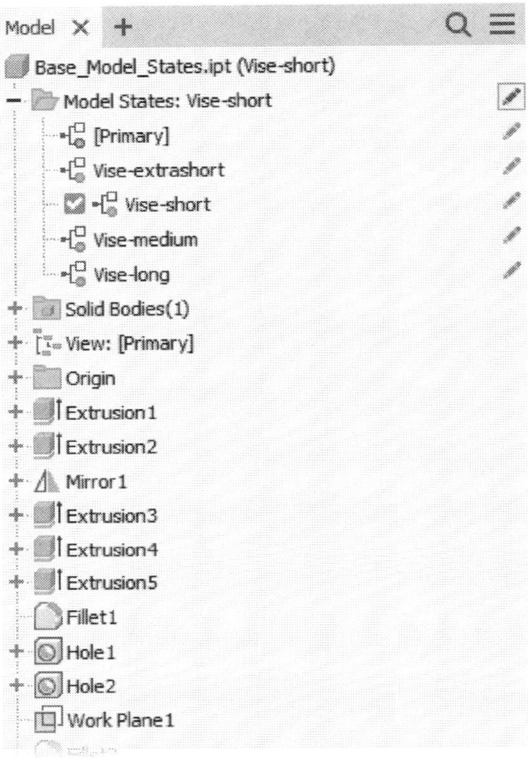

Figure 9–17

a. Yes
b. No

Command Summary

Button	Command	Location
N/A	**New (model state)**	• **Model browser:** *Right-click on the Model States node.*

Chapter 10

Copying Between Parts (iFeatures)

The Autodesk® Inventor® software provides several methods to copy features between models. One of these methods involves the use of iFeatures. This duplication technique helps to reduce the amount of time spent duplicating a collection of features or components that are used repeatedly in an individual model or across several models.

Learning Objectives

- Create an iFeature by selecting the features, parameters, and placement elements to define the iFeature.
- Place an iFeature by defining its placement plane, size values, and precise positioning to fully locate it in a model.
- Use the Copy command to duplicate features in a model or between models.
- Create a table-driven iFeature that includes variations that can be retrieved during the placement of the iFeature.
- Edit the size, position, and sketch location of an iFeature that has been placed in a model.
- Edit a source iFeature file to make changes to its initial definition.

10.1 Creating iFeatures

When you create parts, you may require the same type of feature in multiple parts. By using iFeatures, you can save any sketched feature for use in other part files. Using iFeatures saves time and helps ensure consistency between parts. iFeatures are stored in files with the extension .IDE. By default, they are stored in the *C:\Users\Public\Public Documents\Autodesk\Inventor 2024\Catalog* directory. Several predefined iFeatures are installed with the Autodesk Inventor software and are stored in this directory.

Use the following general steps to create an iFeature:

1. Start the creation of an iFeature.
2. Select features to save as iFeatures.
3. Set the parameter size.
4. Define the iFeature position geometry.
5. Save the iFeature.

Step 1 - Start the creation of an iFeature.

Open the part that contains the sketches/features to use. In the *Manage* tab>Author panel, click (Extract iFeature). The Extract iFeature dialog box opens, as shown in Figure 10–1.

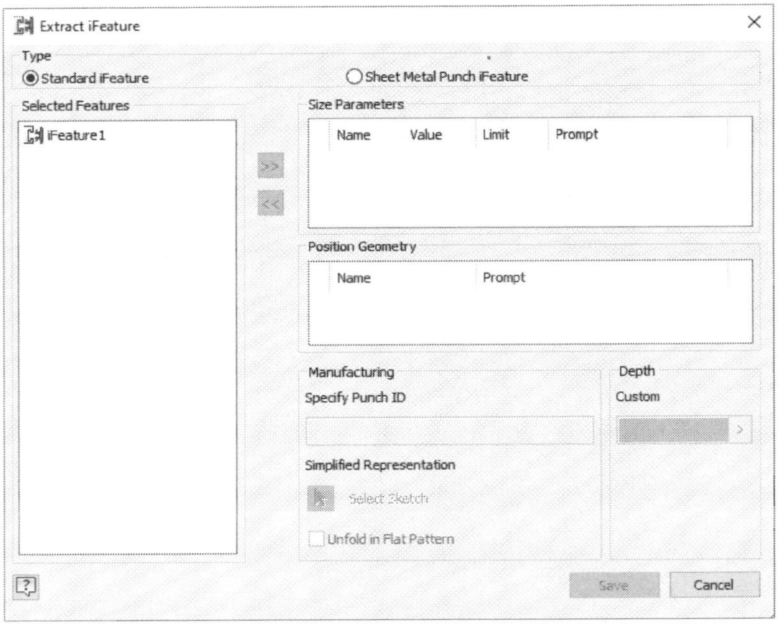

Figure 10–1

Step 2 - Select features to save as iFeatures.

Select sketches (consumed or unconsumed) and features in the Model browser or graphics window that are to become iFeatures. If the selected feature has dependent features, they are automatically selected. All elements used to create the selected feature appear below the name of the iFeature in the *Selected Features* area, as shown in Figure 10–2. You can use any or all of the part features in the iFeature.

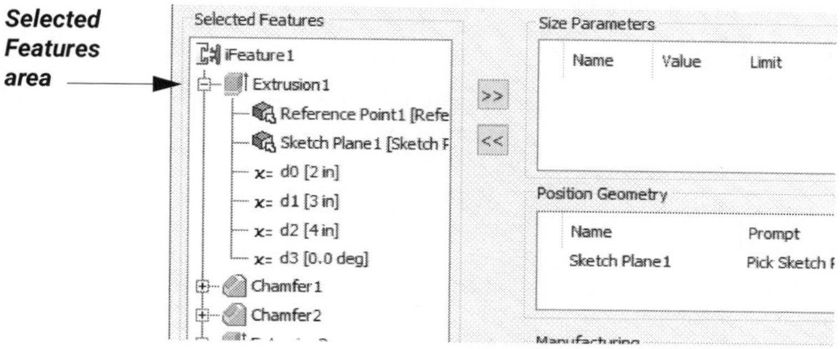

Figure 10–2

The dialog box auto populates the *Size Parameters* and *Position Geometry* areas with any renamed parameters. To add other feature parameters that are to be used in the iFeature, select them in the *Selected Features* area and use the >> icon to transfer the parameters one by one. To add all parameters associated with a feature, select the feature and select **Add All Parameters** in the shortcut menu. Figure 10–3 shows all Extrusion1 parameters transferred to the *Size Parameters* area.

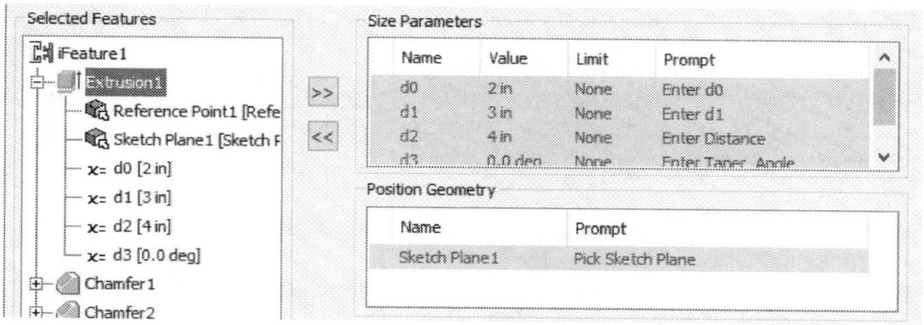

Figure 10–3

To remove a feature from a list, select the feature and select **Remove Feature** in the shortcut menu. To remove parameters, use the << icon to return the parameters to the *Selected Features* area, or select **Remove All Parameters** in the shortcut menu.

Step 3 - Set the parameter size.

Once the feature parameters are transferred to the *Size Parameters* area of the dialog box you can control the size of the iFeature by applying a range or limits to the parameters. The *Size Parameters* area consists of four columns, described as follows:

Name		Lists the name of the parameter that describes a dimension of the feature. You can change the name of the parameter by selecting on it. Use a name that is descriptive to help when reusing the iFeature.
Value		Displays the default value for the parameter.
Limit		Enables you to restrict the values of parameters using the following three options:
	None	Any value is acceptable.
	Range	Set the allowable range for the value by entering the upper and lower values and the operator.
	List	Enables you to create a group of acceptable values and set the default value of the parameter.
Prompt		Enables you to set the text that displays in a dialog box when the iFeature is inserted. It can clarify the use of the value or describe restrictions.

Step 4 - Define the iFeature position geometry.

In the Extract iFeature dialog box, the *Position Geometry* area specifies the elements in the iFeature that are used to locate it on a part. The Sketch Plane is automatically added to this area. You can add or remove other items, such as constraints from the feature, using the >> and << icons.

> **Note:** *An iFeature should contain geometry that is only dependent on the geometry in the iFeature itself. Do not use Origin work features. Horizontal and vertical constraints can make it difficult to place an iFeature, because those terms are relative to the part where the feature is placed. Use parallel and perpendicular constraints instead.*

The *Position Geometry* area consists of two columns, described as follows:

Name	Names the position geometry. You can change it here, but it does not change the name in the *Selected Features* area.
Prompt	Defines the text prompt that is provided when the iFeature is inserted. You can enter information that prompts you where to select on the existing part to place the iFeature.

You might need to customize position geometry (for example, combine two location geometries, or make one position independent of the other). Right-click on the position in the *Position Geometry* area and select **Combine Geometry**, then select another position to combine. To make positions in a combined geometry independent, right-click on the combined position and select **Make Independent**.

Step 5 - Save the iFeature.

Once the iFeature is defined and its locating position determined, click **Save**. The Save As dialog box opens. Enter a unique name for the iFeature and click **Save** and close the dialog box. All iFeatures are saved with the extension .IDE.

By default, iFeatures are saved in the *Catalog* folder (*C:\Users\Public\Public Documents\Autodesk\Inventor 2024\Catalog*) or you can create a new subfolder to further organize the files. When saving to the default location, if a prompt displays that the location is not in the active project, add the path to the project. Alternatively, save to a folder in the workspace.

> ***Note:*** *To rename an iFeature so that its name in the Model browser is descriptive, right-click on the iFeature# at the top of the Selected Features column and select* ***Rename****. Enter a new name. This name identifies the iFeature whenever it is placed. Renaming the iFeature is different from naming the iFeature's .IDE filename.*

10.2 Inserting iFeatures

An iFeature reduces the time spent on duplicating a collection of features or components that are used repeatedly in the same or in different models. An iFeature can be placed in the same part in which it was created or it can be placed in any other part, as shown in Figure 10–4.

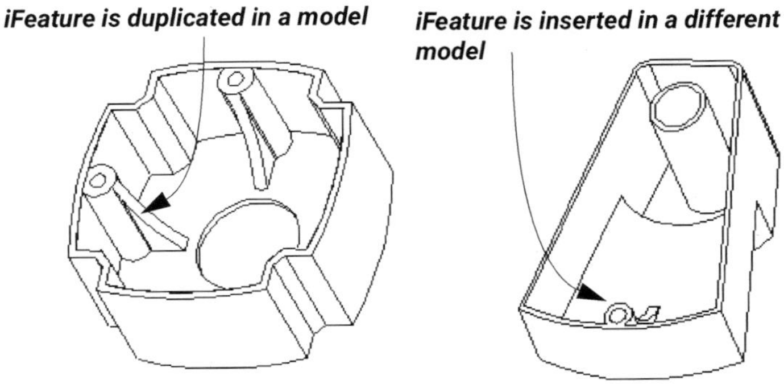

Figure 10–4

Use the following general steps to place an iFeature:

1. Start the placement of the iFeature.
2. Select the position of the iFeature.
3. Determine the size of the iFeature.
4. Determine the precise position.
5. Complete the insertion.

Step 1 - Start the placement of the iFeature.

In the *Manage* tab>Insert panel, click (Insert iFeature). Click **Browse** and browse to the iFeature, select, and open the iFeature. By default, iFeatures are saved in the *Catalog* folder (*C:\ Users\Public\Public Documents\Autodesk\Inventor 2024\ Catalog*).

As an alternative to initiating the **Insert iFeature** option and selecting an iFeature, you can select an iFeature directly from the ribbon, or you can also drag an iFeature from Windows Explorer to the main window. All iFeatures stored in the Catalog are listed in the drop-down list, as shown in Figure 10–5. Scroll through the list and select the iFeature.

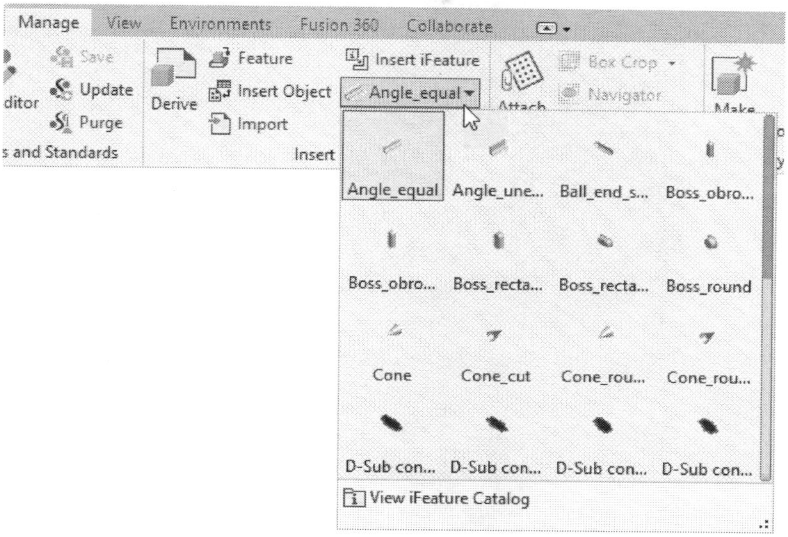

Figure 10–5

Step 2 - Select the position of the iFeature.

Once the iFeature is open, a green symbol on the left side of the Insert iFeature dialog box shows you that you are in the Position step. The Position step enables you to select a planar face or work plane to locate the feature. Once you select the plane, you can select the rotation or the position symbol, shown in Figure 10–6, to rotate or move the iFeature, as required.

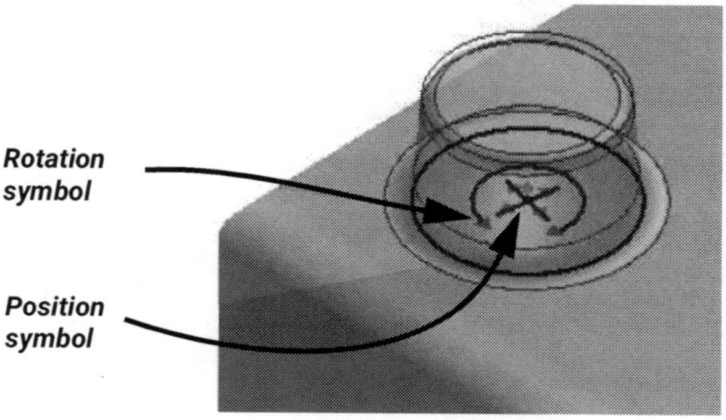

Figure 10–6

Alternatively, you can enter a rotation angle in the dialog box. Click [flip icon] to flip the direction of the iFeature. A checkmark displays to the left of the name of the feature or sketch when the placement for the iFeature is fully defined, as shown in Figure 10–7.

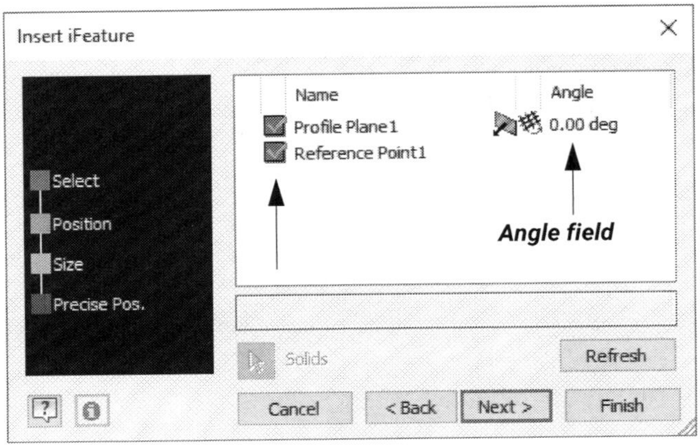

Figure 10–7

Step 3 - Determine the size of the iFeature.

Once the position is defined, click **Next** to move to the Size step. The Size step lists the names and default values of the parameters of the iFeatures. An example is shown in Figure 10–8.

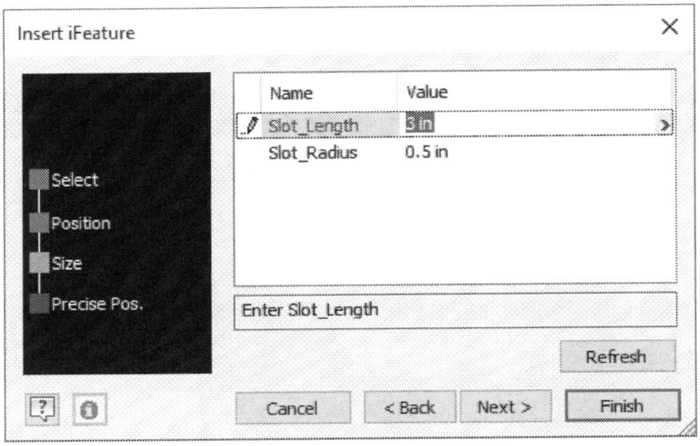

Figure 10–8

Select a value to change it. Once you change the size, click **Refresh** in the dialog box to update the display of the iFeature.

Step 4 - Determine the precise position.

Once the sizes are defined, click **Next** to move to the Precise Pos. step. The Insert iFeature dialog box displays as shown in Figure 10–9.

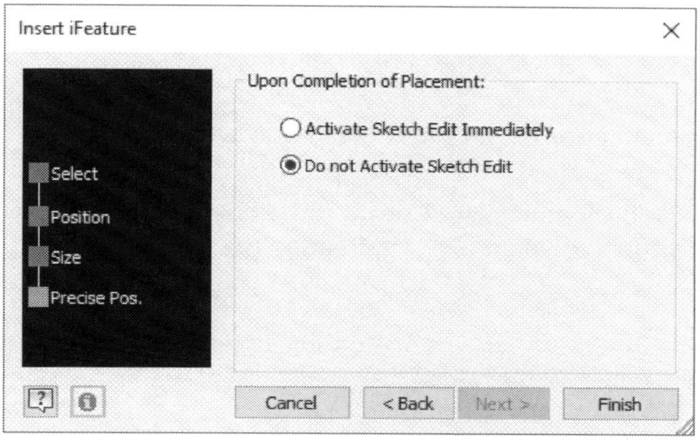

Figure 10–9

The Precise Pos. step determines what happens when the operation is complete.

- If you select **Activate Sketch Edit Immediately**, **Edit Sketch** is activated so that you can locate the sketch precisely before you continue with the part.
- If you select **Do not Activate Sketch Edit**, **iFeature** is added without accessing the sketch environment.

You can move back and forth through the steps using **Next** and **Back**, or by selecting the steps in the tree graphic.

Step 5 - Complete the insertion.

Once the location and size of the iFeature are defined, click **Finish** to complete the operation. Depending on the option that was selected in the Precise Pos. step, the sketch environment might open to refine the iFeature's placement.

No link exists between the .IDE file and the iFeature once the iFeature is placed. Therefore, changes to the .IDE file do not affect iFeatures that are already placed. Even if you insert a revised iFeature into a file that contains an older version of the feature, the original iFeature is not affected. To update a placed iFeature, delete the old iFeature and insert the new one.

10.3 iFeatures vs. Copy Feature

Some features in your models can be simply copied and pasted as a means of duplicating them within or to another model. For those features that cannot be copied, you can use iFeatures. In general, features that have sketched sections can be copied; however, features that are located on surface or reference edges (e.g., holes, fillets, shells) cannot be copied.

How To: Copy and Paste a Feature

1. Verify that the **Select Features** filter is enabled and select the feature in the model or the Model browser.
2. Once selected, right-click and select **Copy**. If the **Copy** option is not available, this action is not permitted and you should consider recreating the feature or using an iFeature.
3. Activate the model that is to be the target model, if it is not already the active model.
4. Right-click and select **Paste**. A Paste Features dialog box similar to that shown in Figure 10–10 opens, indicating the references required to place the feature.

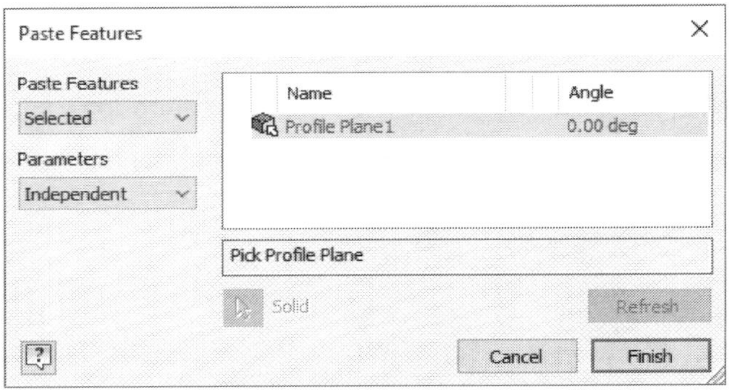

Figure 10–10

5. Select a *Parameters* option. This enables you to define whether the copied feature is dependent or independent. If the feature is copied in the same model, you can select whether or not the new feature is dependent on the source feature. If you are copying to a new model, the copied feature can only be independent.
6. Define the placement reference for the copied feature.
7. Click **Finish**. Depending on the placement references that were defined, you might need to further edit the feature to fully locate it in the model.

10.4 Table-Driven iFeatures

iFeatures are made up of parameters independent of each other, unless they are related by an equation. Table-driven iFeatures provide additional control by presetting these parameters to permitted values. For example, a threaded stud can be an iFeature. The diameter of the stud may have several preset values, and each diameter, preset lengths. Not all lengths apply to all of the diameters; therefore, you can change the iFeature to allow only certain lengths. Through the use of keys in a Table-driven iFeature you can logically group the iFeature members to enable quicker access to the required configuration.

Use the following general steps to create a table-driven iFeature:

1. Open the iFeature file.
2. Select the configurable attributes.
3. Create the table.
4. Set up keys.
5. Complete the table.

Step 1 - Open the iFeature file.

Open an iFeature. In the iFeature panel, click  (iFeature Author Table). The dialog box opens as shown in Figure 10–11.

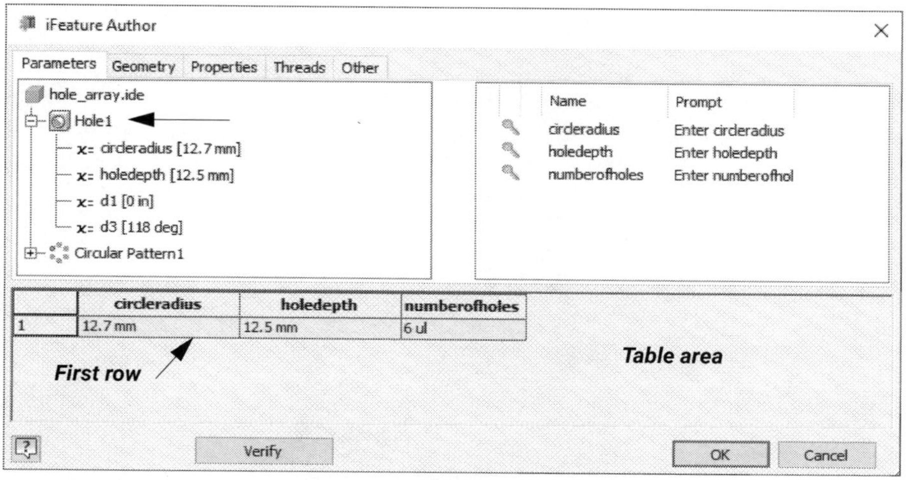

Figure 10–11

Step 2 - Select the configurable attributes.

The tabs in the iFeature Author dialog box contain the configurable attributes that can be varied to create the different iFeature configurations.

Tabs	Description
Parameters	Contains the parameters used in the part and they are listed under the features in which they belong. Parameters that have names other than d# are listed automatically in the Selected Parameters list.
Geometry	Displays the geometry used to position the iFeature. You can change the names and prompts for the geometry in this tab.
Properties	Lists the properties of the feature. Any custom properties in an iFeature can be made available in the Part files in which they are inserted. In the *Properties* tab, expand the **Custom** node and select the required custom parameter, then add it to the table as a property using the arrow icons. Once a property has been moved to the right side of the dialog box, you can set keys on these properties.
Threads	Enables you to include thread variables. Each thread variable is defined as a key. Designations such as UNC are case-sensitive.
Other	Enables you to create additional columns in the table. These columns do not control the size of the part, but can be used as keys in the table.

> ***Note:*** *To create a custom property in an iFeature, open the iFeature, right-click on the iFeature name in the Model browser, and select* ***iProperties****. Select the Custom tab and create any custom properties that are required.*

You can insert the iFeature with any of the attribute values that were set in the iFeature Author dialog box. For example, you can insert an iFeature with the hole depth parameter values shown in Figure 10–12.

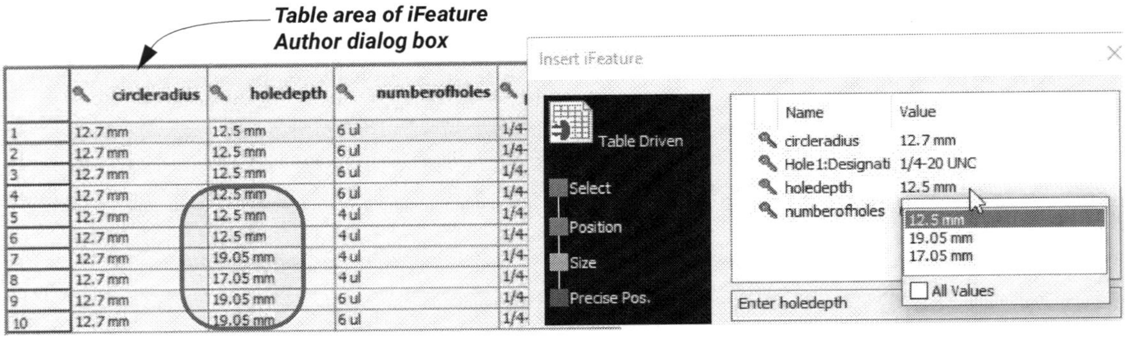

Figure 10–12

Step 3 - Create the table.

Each row in the table represents a different version of the iFeature. To add more versions, right-click in the first row and select **Insert Row**. Select the table cells and enter the attribute values for each cell. Once filled in, the table area displays similar to that shown in Figure 10–13.

Alternatively, it is possible to edit the iFeature table in a spread sheet format using (Edit Using Spread Sheet).

	circleradius	holedepth	numberofholes	Hole1: Designation
1	12.7 mm	12.5 mm	6 ul	1/4-20 UNC
2	12.7 mm	12.5 mm	6 ul	1/4-20 UNC
3	12.7 mm	12.5 mm	6 ul	1/4-24 UNS
4	12.7 mm	12.5 mm	6 ul	1/4-24 UNS
5	12.7 mm	12.5 mm	4 ul	1/4-20 UNC
6	12.7 mm	12.5 mm	4 ul	1/4-20 UNC
7	12.7 mm	19.05 mm	4 ul	1/4-20 UNC
8	12.7 mm	17.05 mm	4 ul	1/4-20 UNC
9	12.7 mm	19.05 mm	6 ul	1/4-20 UNC
10	12.7 mm	19.05 mm	6 ul	1/4-20 UNC

Figure 10–13

Step 4 - Set up keys.

An iFeature contains attribute values that define each iFeature member. Keys enable you to group iFeature members according to their attribute values in a hierarchical manner. This sorts the iFeature members more logically, enabling quicker access to the required configuration. A key symbol displays in front of each attribute in the iFeature Author dialog box.

Toggle the key symbols on (blue) and off (gray) to define a particular attribute as a key. For the attributes you set as keys, assign the key order (starting from 1 as the first key). The attribute set as Key 1 is the first attribute that is used for sorting or grouping the iFeature members. If Length was the first key, then all the iFeature members will be sorted according to length. To change the order of key numbers, or to assign a key number to an attribute, right-click it and select **Key** and the required number, as shown in Figure 10–14.

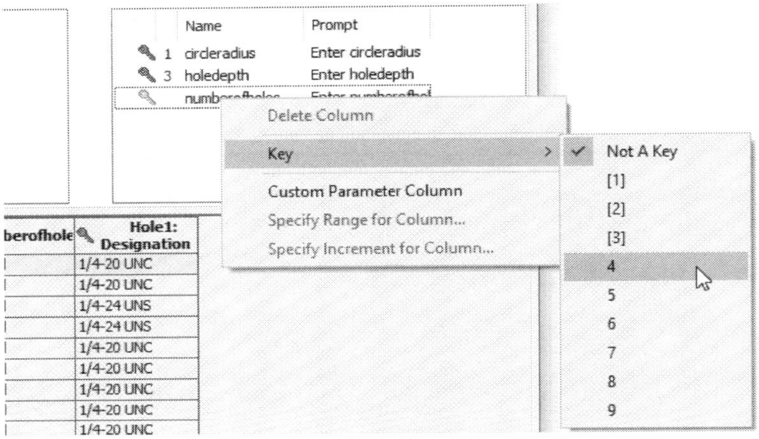

Figure 10–14

> ***Note:*** *You can customize the name displayed in the Model browser for an iFeature to show the Key1 parameter name and its value. Select the* ***Use Key 1 as Browser Name column*** *in the Application Options dialog box (iFeature tab). This helps identify which iFeature value set is used.*

If five members had the same length of 500 mm, then all five would be listed under that length (length = 500 mm) in the Model browser. Next, the members are sorted according to the second key, for example width. The five members with length = 500 mm would be grouped according to width. If two of those members had widths of 100 mm and the other three had widths of 150 mm, then they would be sorted under width = 100 mm and width = 150 mm. The sorting continues until no more keys are defined.

Step 5 - Complete the table.

Once the table is defined, click **OK** to complete the operation.

10.5 Editing iFeatures

iFeatures can be edited once placed in a file or you can open the original iFeature's .ide file to make changes to the source file.

Editing the Inserted iFeature

Once the iFeature is inserted, you can only edit its size, position, and sketch location on the sketch plane. To edit the size and position, right-click on the iFeature and select **Edit iFeature**. To edit the sketch location, right-click on the iFeature and select **Edit Sketch**. You can add dimensions and constraints; however, not change its dimensions.

Editing the source iFeature File

You might need to change the iFeature file (.IDE) once it has been created. To do so, open the iFeature file in a separate window. The iFeature panel displays as shown in Figure 10–15. The  (Edit iFeature) option enables you to modify sizes and position.

Figure 10–15

To view stored iFeatures, including standard predefined iFeatures, in the iFeature panel, click  (View Catalog). The Catalog viewer displays in a standard Windows Explorer view, as shown in Figure 10–16.

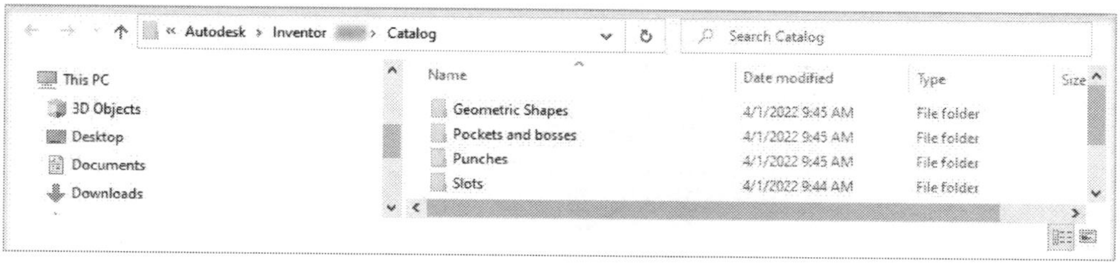

Figure 10–16

Click  (iFeature Author Table) to create or modify iFeature tables. If an iFeature table is used, you can use 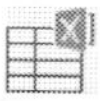 (Edit Using Spread Sheet) to edit the values in a spread sheet format. Tables are covered in more detail in the table-driven iFeatures topic.

Editing the iFeature Image

When an iFeature is created, it is assigned the default icon image ( ). This image identifies the iFeature in the Model browser of any part that you place it in, as well as in the ribbon when selecting the iFeature from the Insert panel. You may want to change the iFeature image to help identify it in the Model browser. To do this, open the iFeature file in a separate window and in the iFeature panel, click (Change Icon). The Edit Icon dialog box opens as shown in Figure 10–17.

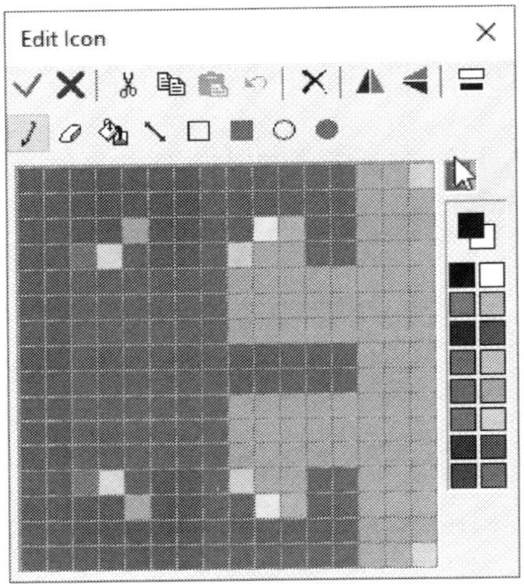

Figure 10–17

Using the colors and the tools in the dialog box, create a new image to represent the iFeature. To obtain a white background, you must use the Magenta color in all areas that are required to be displayed as white. Once the icon is complete, save the .IDE file. The new icon will display once you restart the Autodesk Inventor software.

Placement Help

You can create a separate document to help describe, to future users of the iFeature, how it is to be placed and used in a model. To attach a placement help file, open the iFeature's .IDE file and on the *Tools* tab>Insert panel, click (Insert Object). Select **Create from File** and click **Browse** to browse to the document. Click **Open** when you have selected the required document.

The placement help file can be added as a linked or an embedded object. Embedded objects are not dependent on the external file, whereas linked files are dependent. Click **OK**. The file displays in the Model browser, as shown in Figure 10–18.

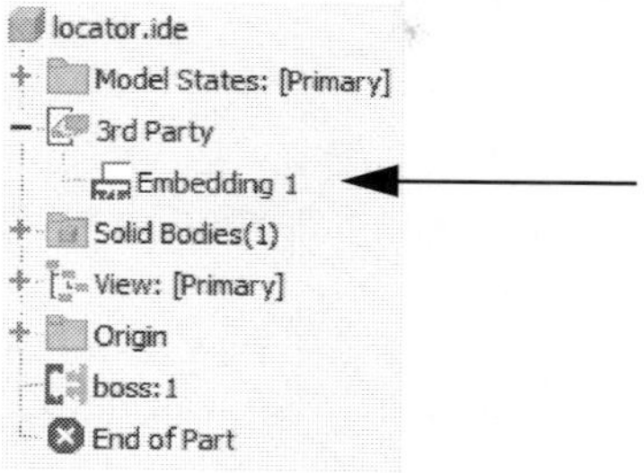

Figure 10–18

In the Model browser, right-click on the placement help file and select **Placement Help** to set this as the placement help document. Save the iFeature file.

To open the placement help file, double-click on the file in the Model browser.

Practice 10a
Create and Insert an iFeature

Practice Objectives

- Assign parameter names and equations to existing dimensions in a model to prepare for iFeature creation.
- Create an iFeature from existing geometry so that a limit and range is established for selected iFeature dimensional values and an appropriate prompt is defined for the placement plane.
- Insert a placement help file to be used as a reference for locating an iFeature in a model.
- Insert an iFeature into a new part file.

In this practice, you create an iFeature. You set the limits for the iFeature's sketch diameter and set a range for one of the features' height. You then place help text in the iFeature file to help insert it. The completed model is shown in Figure 10–19.

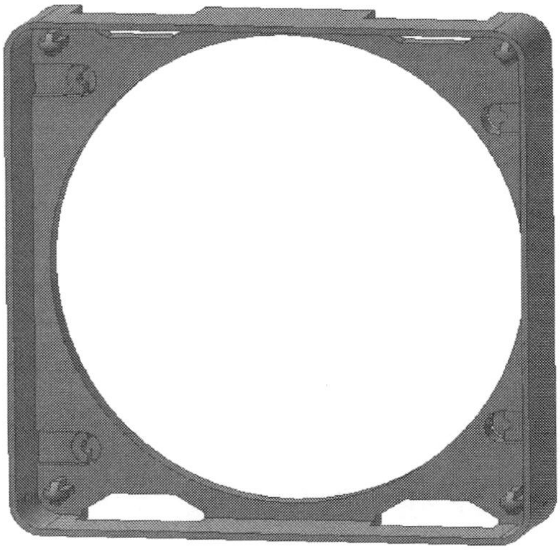

Figure 10–19

Task 1: Change the name of model parameters.

iFeatures are created from existing features or sketches. To make it easier to create the iFeature, use parameters that have descriptive names and apply those parameters to items in the sketches and features that will become your iFeature. Creating an iFeature with default parameters (such as d0) can be confusing to identify. In this task, you change the name of model parameters (dimensions).

1. Open **createif.ipt**. The model displays as shown in Figure 10–20.

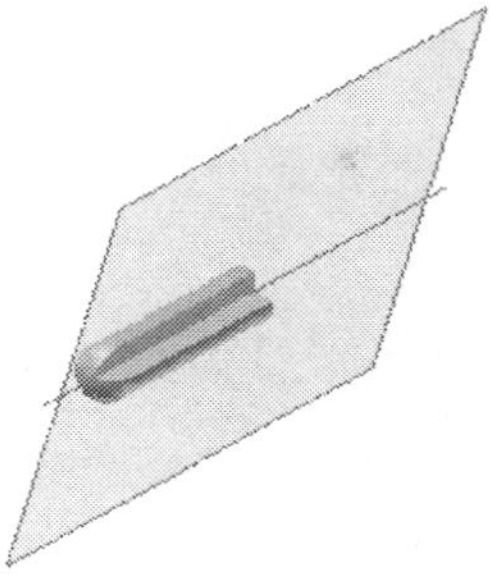

Figure 10–20

2. In the *Manage* tab>Parameter panel, click *fx* (Parameters) to open the Parameters dialog box.
3. Change the names of parameters as follows:
   - *d1* to **diameter**
   - *d2* to **height**

Plan your iFeatures so that a minimum number of parameters are required. If a dimension is always half of another dimension, use an equation rather than forcing you to enter both numbers.

4. Change the equations as follows. The Parameters dialog box displays as shown in Figure 10–21.
   - *d0* to **diameter/3**
   - *d4* to **diameter/2**

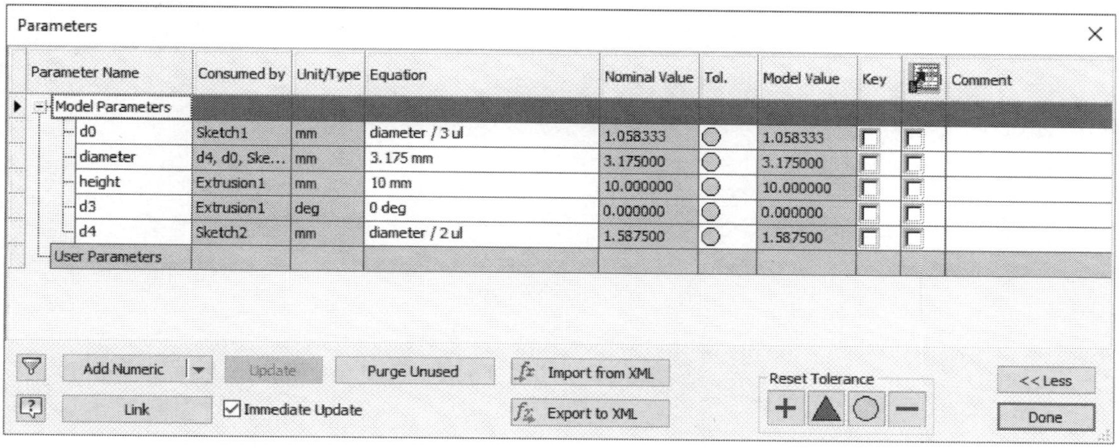

Figure 10–21

5. Click **Done** to close the dialog box.

Task 2: Create an iFeature.

1. In the *Manage* tab>Author panel, click (Extract iFeature) to open the Extract iFeature dialog box.
2. Select **Extrusion1** in the Model browser. The *Selected Features* area displays **Extrusion1**, **Revolution1**, and the work features because the other features are children. The renamed parameters are automatically entered in the *Size Parameters* area and the **Extrusion1** sketch plane is displayed in the *Position Geometry* area. The Extract iFeature dialog box displays as shown in Figure 10–22.

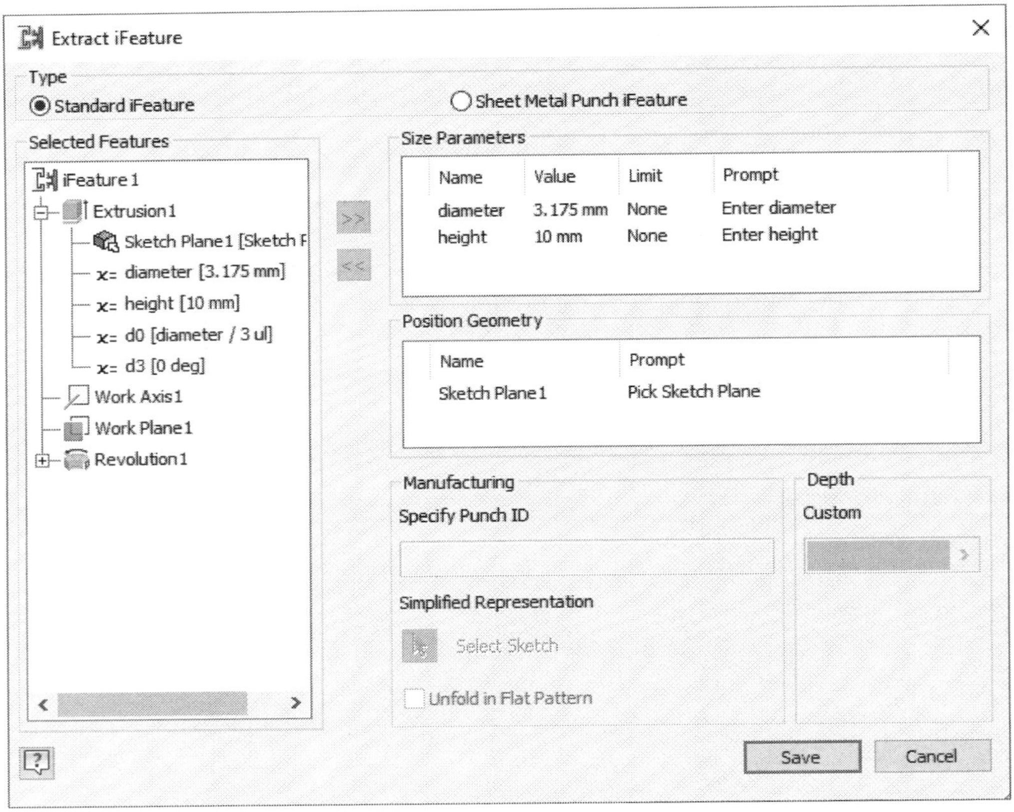

Figure 10–22

3. Note that the Limit for both parameters is set to **None**. Select **None** for the diameter parameter, and select **List** in the drop-down list. The List Values for the diameter dialog box opens.

4. Select **Click here to add value** at the bottom of the list and add the following diameters: **1.5875**, **4.7625**, **6.35**, **9.525**.
5. Set **4.7625** as the *Default*, as shown in Figure 10–23.

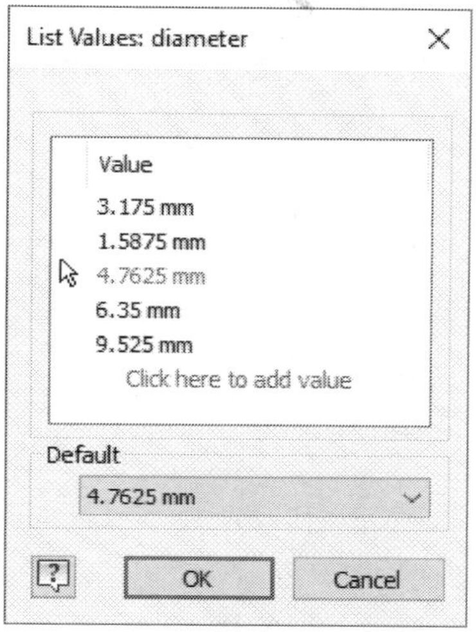

Figure 10–23

6. Click **OK** to close the dialog box.
7. Select **None** for the height parameter, and select **Range** in the drop-down list. The Specify Range for the height dialog box opens.
8. Set the *Range* to **2.5<10<25**, as shown in Figure 10–24.

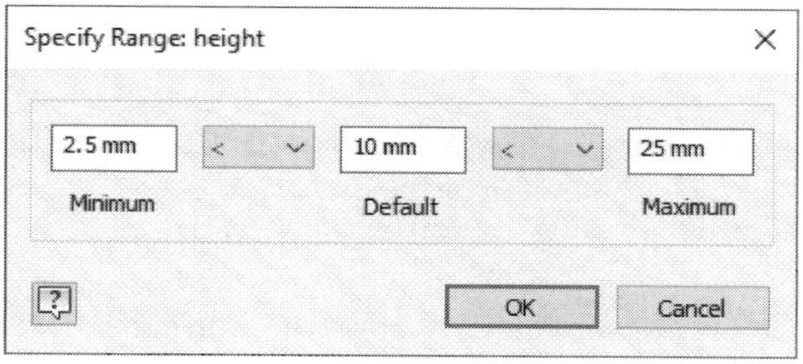

Figure 10–24

9. Click **OK** to close the dialog box.

10. Change the *Prompt* for **Sketch Plane1** to **Pick plane for base of locator**, as shown in Figure 10–25.

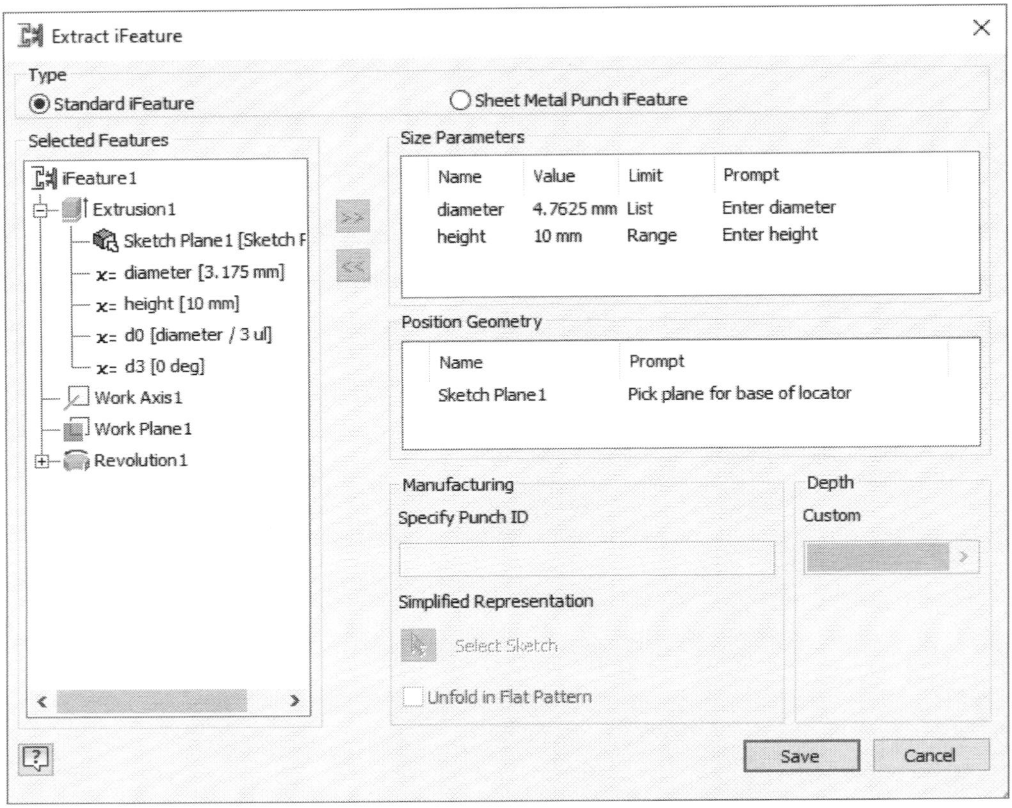

Figure 10–25

11. Right-click on **iFeature1** at the top of the *Selected Features* pane and select **Rename**. Enter **boss** as the new name. This name will be used to identify the iFeature in the Model browser whenever it is placed.

    Once the iFeature is defined and its locating position is determined, it can be saved. By default, it is saved in the *Catalog* folder. Alternatively, you can create a new folder in the *Catalog* folder or you can save the file to your Workspace. In this exercise you will be creating a folder and saving to the Workspace.

12. In the Extract iFeature dialog box, click **Save**. The Save As dialog box opens.
13. In the Save As dialog box, note that you are in the default *Catalog* folder. Select **Workspace** in the left-hand frame of the dialog box. This takes you directly to your project's home directory.
14. Right-click in the white area, and select **New>Folder**. Create a new folder called **Custom iFeatures**. Store your iFeatures in this folder.

15. Double-click on the new folder, type the name **locator** for the iFeature filename, and click **Save** to save the iFeature. iFeatures are saved with the extension .IDE.

    Note: *Renaming the iFeature is different from naming the iFeature's .IDE filename.*

16. Close the **createif.ipt** file. You do not need to save the changes, since they are already saved in the catalog.

Task 3: Insert a placement help file in iFeature.

1. Open the file **locator.ide** that you just created and saved to the *Custom iFeatures* folder in your active project.
2. In the *Tools* tab>Insert panel, click (Insert Object) to open the Insert Object dialog box.
3. Select **Create from File** and click **Browse** to browse to the **locator.doc** file in your practice files folder. Click **Open**. This file is a Placement Help file that can be added as a linked or an embedded object. Embedded objects are not dependent on the external file, whereas linked files are dependent.
4. Click **OK**. Expand the **3rd Party** node and the file displays in the Model browser, as shown in Figure 10–26.

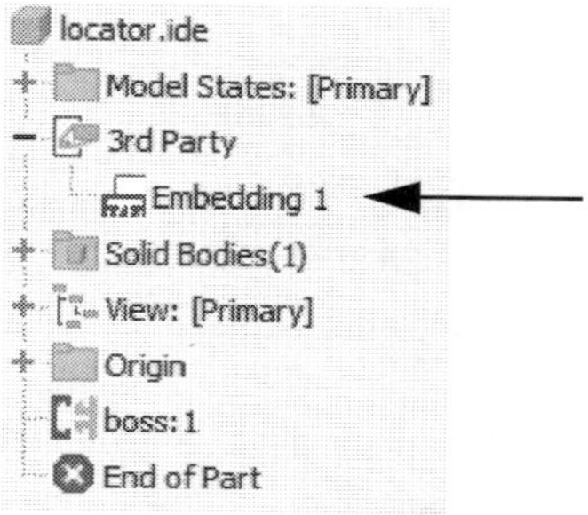

Figure 10–26

5. Right-click on **Embedding 1** in the Model browser, and select **Placement Help** to set this as the placement help document.
6. Save the iFeature file and close the window. You cannot insert an open iFeature.

Task 4: Insert an iFeature.

In this task, you insert and place the locator.ide file into a part.

1. Open **fanbase.ipt** from the top-level practice files folder.
2. In the *Manage* tab>Insert panel, click (Insert iFeature).

3. Browse to and open the **locator.ide** file.

The green symbol in the graphic on the left side of the Insert iFeature dialog box indicates that you are in the Position step. This step enables you to select a face to locate the feature. Once you select the face, you can select the rotation or the position symbol to rotate or move the part. Alternatively, you can type the rotation angle in the fields.

4. Select the face shown in Figure 10–27 as the position plane. A checkmark displays to the left of the name of the feature or sketch when the placement for the iFeature has been fully defined.

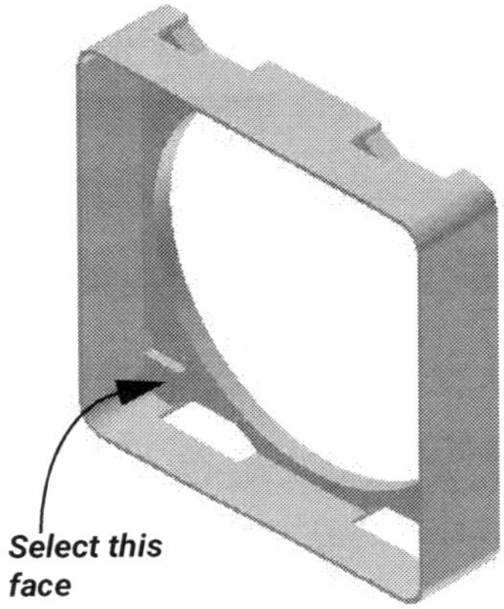

Figure 10–27

5. Once the position is defined, click **Next** to move to the Size step. The Size step lists the names and default values of the parameters for locator.ide, as shown in Figure 10–28.

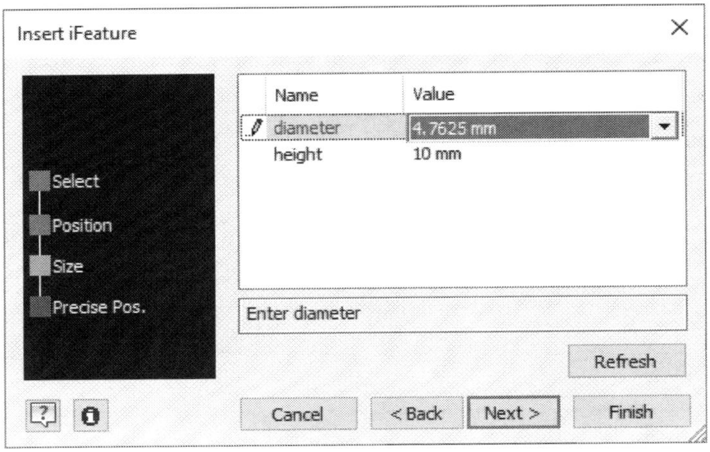

Figure 10–28

6. Note that the diameter *Value* column shows the default, **4.7625 mm**.

7. Enter **8 mm** in the height *Value* column. Remember the height range is between 2.5 mm and 25 mm.
8. Click **Next** to move to Precise Pos. step.
9. Click to open **locator.doc**, as shown in Figure 10–29. Read the instructions on how to locate the **locator.ide** and close it.

   Note: *The Precise Pos. step determines what happens when the command is completed.*

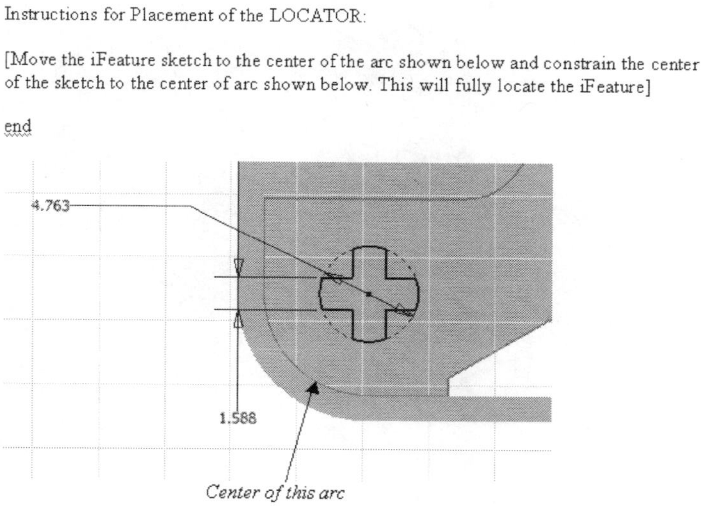
Instructions for Placement of the LOCATOR:

[Move the iFeature sketch to the center of the arc shown below and constrain the center of the sketch to the center of arc shown below. This will fully locate the iFeature]

end

Figure 10–29

10. Select **Activate Sketch Edit Immediately** to activate the sketch environment.
11. Click **Finish** to complete the operation.

12. Locate the iFeature sketch according to the instructions and exit the sketch. Consider using the Horizontal or Vertical constraints to constrain the sketch rotationally. The locator displays on the model, as shown in Figure 10–30. The placement help file displays in the **fanbase.ipt** part Model browser, where you can open or edit it.

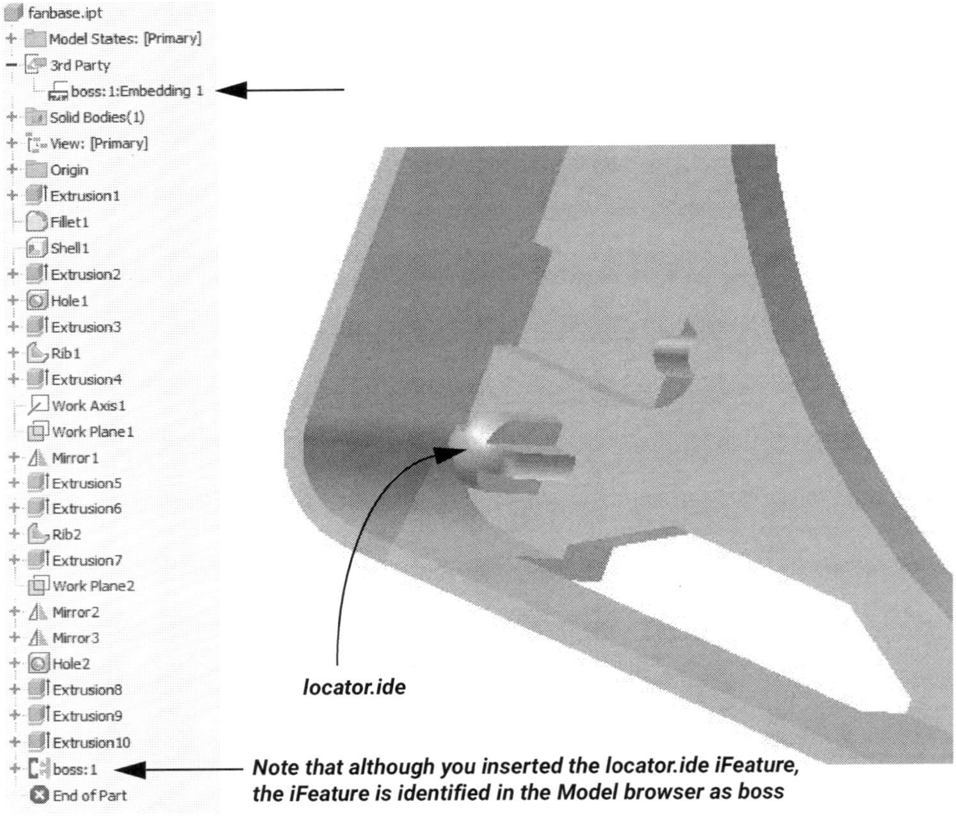

Figure 10–30

There is no link between the .IDE file and the iFeature once placed. Therefore, changes to the .IDE file do not affect existing iFeatures. Even if you insert a revised iFeature into a file that contains an older version of the feature, the original iFeature is not affected. To update an existing iFeature, delete it and insert the new one.

13. Insert three instances of **locator.ide** in the three corners of **fanbase.ipt**. Select the same plane as before for the position. Try to set the height of the feature to **30 mm**. Since it is outside the specified range, the value is not allowed. Change the diameter; note that you can select from the values you specified in the list.

14. Save and close the model.

End of practice

Practice 10b
Table-Driven iFeature

Practice Objectives

- Create an iFeature that is driven by a table defining the possible variations that can be retrieved during placement.
- Insert a table driven iFeature into a new part file.
- Edit a placed iFeature to change the table instance that was inserted into a new part file.

In this practice, you create a table-driven iFeature from a hole pattern, and use the iFeature in a part. The final model displays as shown in Figure 10–31.

Figure 10–31

Task 1: Create an iFeature.

1. Open **circle.ipt**.

2. In the *Manage* tab>Author panel, click (Extract iFeature) to open the Extract iFeature dialog box.

3. In the Model browser, select **Hole1** (**Circular Pattern2** is automatically selected with **Hole1** because it is a child of Hole1). The Extract iFeature dialog box displays as shown in Figure 10–32.

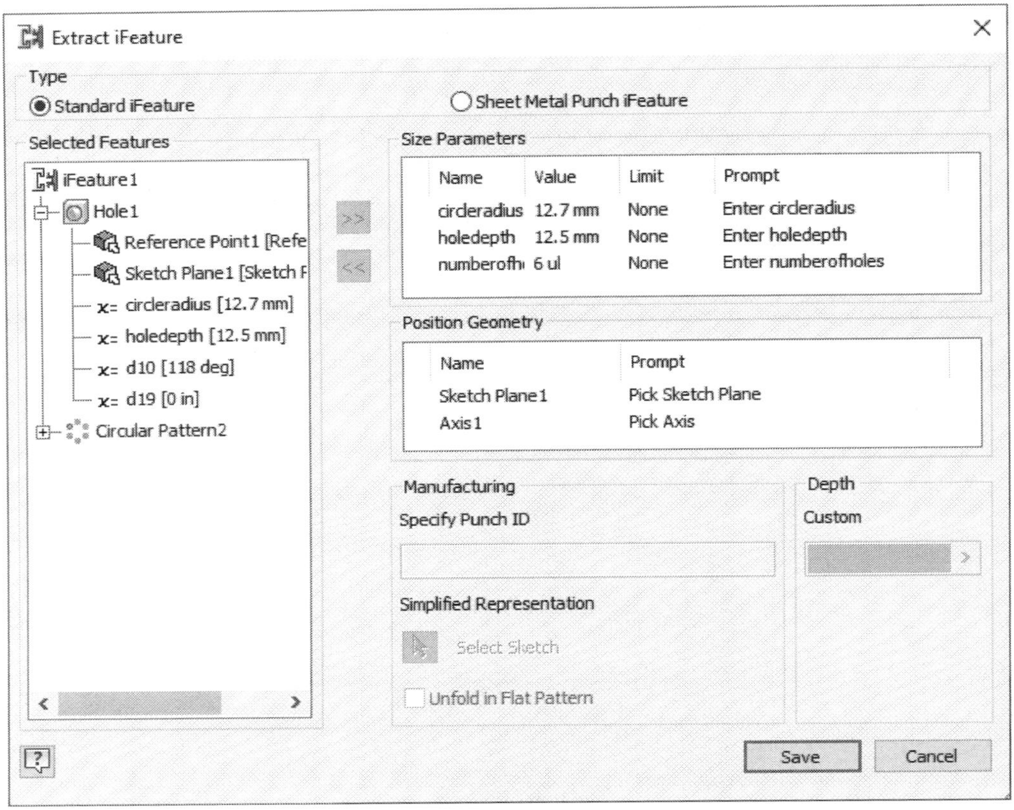

Figure 10–32

4. At the top of the *Selected Features* pane, right-click on **iFeature#** and select **Rename**. Enter **hole_array** as the new name.
5. In the Extract iFeature dialog box, click **Save**.
6. In the Save As dialog box, note that you are in the default *Catalog* folder. Select **Workspace** in the left-hand frame of the dialog box. This takes you directly to your project's home directory.
7. Save the file as **hole_array** in the *Custom iFeatures* folder that you created in the previous exercise.
8. Close **circle.ipt**. You do not need to save the changes, since they are already saved in the catalog.

Task 2: Create a table-driven iFeature.

1. Open the file **hole_array.ide** that you just created and saved in the *Custom iFeatures* folder in your active project. The iFeature file only contains the selected features, as shown in Figure 10–33.

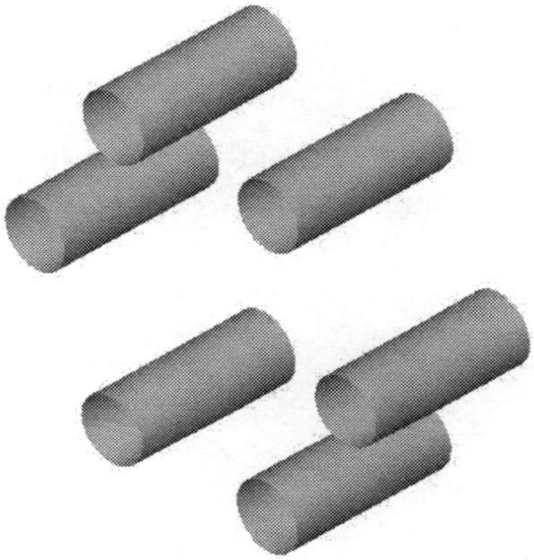

Figure 10–33

2. In the *iFeature* tab>iFeature panel, click (iFeature Author Table). The dialog box opens as shown in Figure 10–34. The named parameters and their values are already listed.

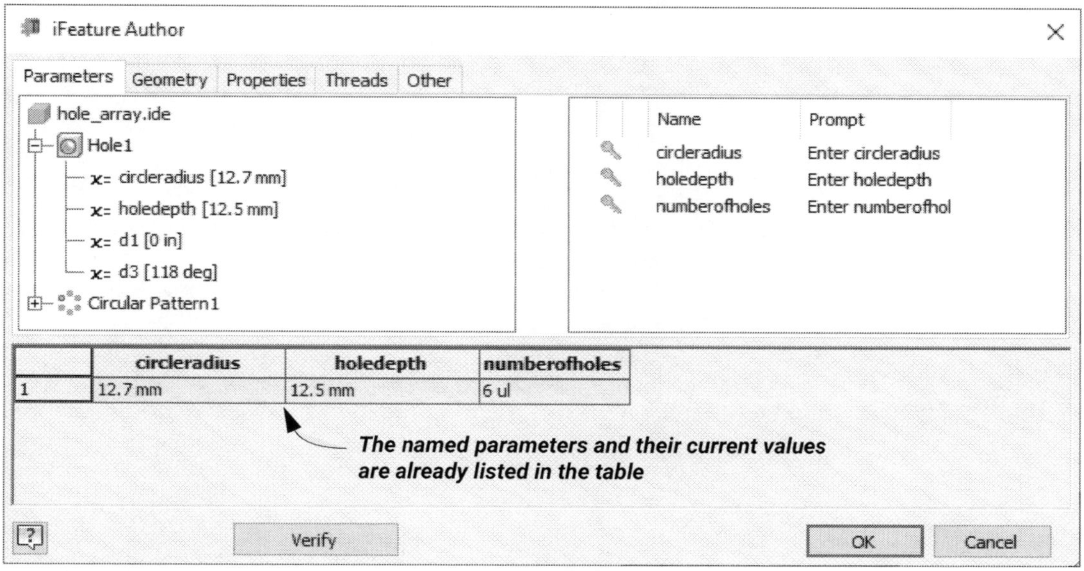

Figure 10–34

3. Select the *Threads* tab and copy **Hole1: Designation** from the left to the right side using the >> icon to add it as a column in the table.
4. Select the *circleradius* column header, right-click, and select **Key>1** in the shortcut menu. Then, do the following:
    - Assign Key 2 to the *Hole1:Designation* column.
    - Assign Key 3 to the *holedepth* column.
    - Assign Key 4 to the *numberofholes* column.
5. Select the first row and select **Insert Row** in the shortcut menu. Add 8 additional rows for a total of 10 rows. Edit the table values as shown in Figure 10–35.

	circleradius	holedepth	numberofholes	Hole1: Designation
1	12.7 mm	12.5 mm	6 ul	1/4-20 UNC
2	12.7 mm	12.5 mm	6 ul	1/4-20 UNC
3	12.7 mm	12.5 mm	6 ul	1/4-24 UNS
4	12.7 mm	12.5 mm	6 ul	1/4-24 UNS
5	12.7 mm	12.5 mm	4 ul	1/4-20 UNC
6	12.7 mm	12.5 mm	4 ul	1/4-20 UNC
7	12.7 mm	19.05 mm	4 ul	1/4-20 UNC
8	12.7 mm	17.05 mm	4 ul	1/4-20 UNC
9	12.7 mm	19.05 mm	6 ul	1/4-20 UNC
10	12.7 mm	19.05 mm	6 ul	1/4-20 UNC

Figure 10–35

6. Click **OK** to close the iFeature Author dialog box.
7. Save and close **hole_array.ide**.

Task 3: Insert the iFeature.

1. Open **drivenif.ipt**.
2. In the *Tools* tab>Options panel, click (Application Options). Select the *iFeature* tab and verify that **Use Key 1 as Browser Name column** is enabled. By enabling this option, you can customize the name displayed in the Model browser for an iFeature to show the Key1 parameter name and its value. Close the dialog box.
3. In the *Manage* tab>Insert panel, click (Insert iFeature). Alternatively, you can use the menu below this option to open iFeatures that are stored in the *Catalog* folder.
4. Select and open **hole_array.ide**.

5. Select the face shown in Figure 10–36 as the position plane. Select the Axis row and select one of the cylinders as **Axis1**. A checkmark displays to the left of the sketch plane and axis name indicating their placement has been fully defined.

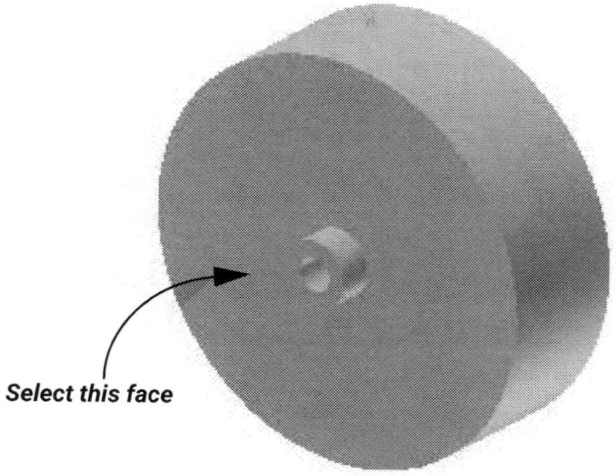

Figure 10–36

6. Once you define the position, click **Next** to move to the Size step.
7. Accept the defaults in the *Size* area. Click **Next** to move to the Precise Pos. step.
8. Select **Do not Activate Sketch Edit**.
9. Click **Finish** to complete the operation.

   Note: *As of the release of this material (May 2023), the addition of the iFeature was causing a failure. When the iFeature is initially displayed, it is unexpectedly snapping to the central axis of the part. To resolve this issue, the following workaround has been found. Keep in mind that the preview of the iFeature placement is not always the same as the actual geometry placement. You can always make changes to its position once it is placed.*

10. Cancel the iFeature placement in the failure dialog box.
11. In the *Manage* tab>Insert panel, click **Insert iFeature** ( ) and open **hole_array.ide**.
12. Select the same face (Figure 10–36) as the position plane.
13. Select the Axis row and select one of the cylinders as **Axis1**.
14. Select the Move grip that is positioned on the central axis and drag the iFeature away and place it away from the central axis, while still remaining on the geometry.
15. Once you define the position, click **Next**.
16. Accept the defaults in the *Size* area. Click **Next**.
17. Select **Do not Activate Sketch Edit**.

18. Click **Finish** to complete the operation. The model displays similar to that shown in Figure 10–37. The circle diameter is dependent on where you placed the Move grip. You can edit the feature and add dimensions to place the holes as required.

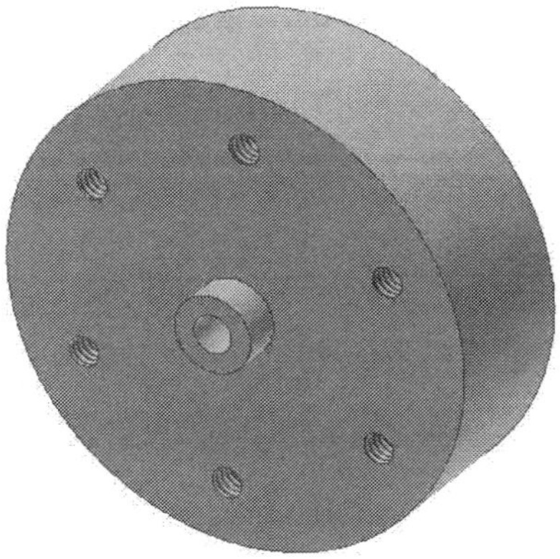

Figure 10–37

19. In the Model browser, expand the iFeature, right-click the Table node and select **Edit iFeature**. The Insert iFeature dialog box opens.
20. Enter a new *numberofholes* value, as shown in Figure 10–38.

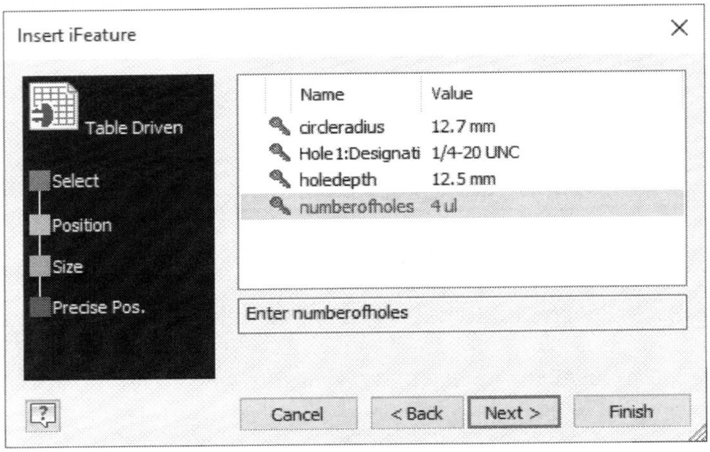

Figure 10–38

21. Click **Finish** to complete the operation. The model displays with four holes.
22. Save and close the model.

End of practice

Practice 10c
(Optional) Slotted Hole iFeature

Practice Objectives

- Create an iFeature ensuring that all of the required geometry is included in the iFeature for accurate placement.
- Insert an iFeature into a new part file and vary the dimensional sizes to produce a required result.

In this practice, you will create an iFeature of a slotted hole. When placing the iFeature you will vary its angle and size. Minimal instructions are provided. Refer to the material for iFeatures if required. The completed model is shown in Figure 10–39.

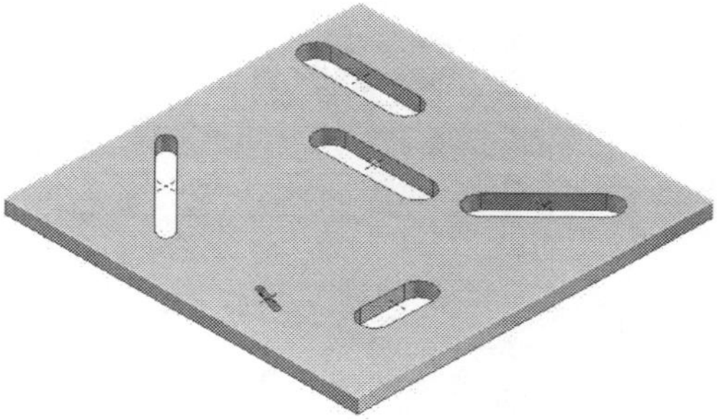

Figure 10–39

Task 1: Create a part with a slotted hole.

1. Create a new part based on the **Standard (in).ipt** template. Create the part as a ½" thick plate measuring 12" x 12", as shown in Figure 10–40.

Figure 10–40

2. Start a new sketch on one of the large faces of the plate and randomly place six points using the (Point) option. It is not required to constrain or dimension these points. Finish the sketch. The model displays similar to that shown in Figure 10–41.

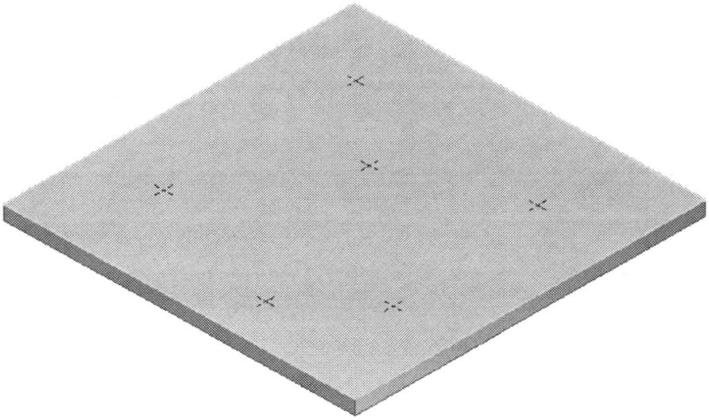

Figure 10–41

3. Start a new sketch on the same face as the sketch from Step 2. Do not just edit the previous sketch. Use the **Project Geometry** tool to project a point created in Step 2, as shown in Figure 10–42.

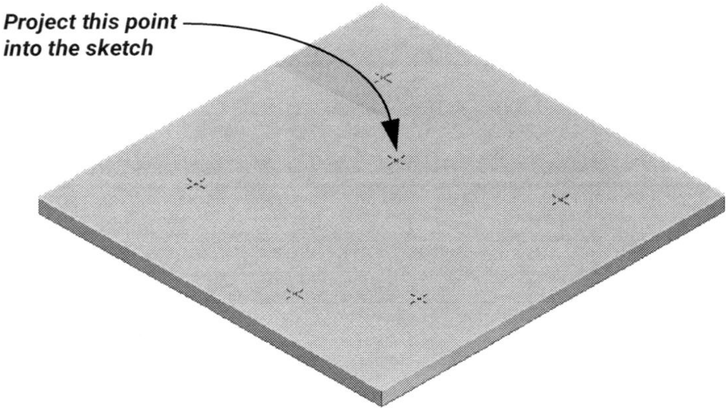

Figure 10–42

4. Sketch a slot, similar to that shown in Figure 10–43. Constrain the projected point to the midpoint of the center-to-center line. When editing the two values, enter **Slot_Length=3** and **Slot_Radius=.5** to rename the parameters, while at the same time editing the values of the parameters.

   Note: *Renaming parameters while you are editing their values prevents you from having to open the Parameters dialog box to reassign names.*

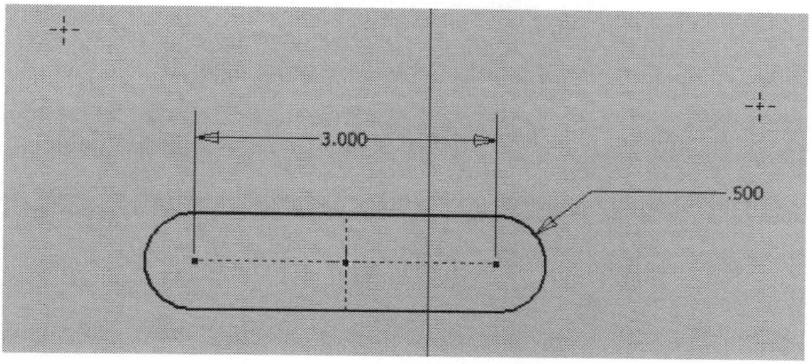

Figure 10–43

5. Finish the sketch.
6. Create the slotted cut shown in Figure 10–44 using **Extrude**. Extrude the slot **Through All** of the model.

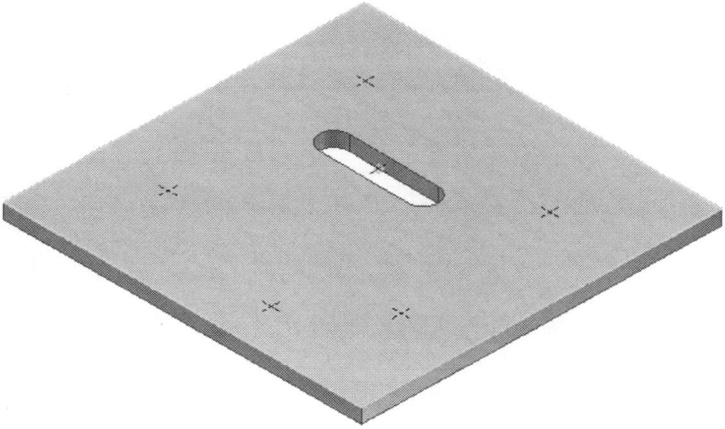

Figure 10–44

Task 2: Create an iFeature.

1. In the *Manage* tab>Author panel, click (Extract iFeature) to open the Extract iFeature dialog box.
2. Select the extrude (slot) feature.
3. Because the point was used as a reference in the slot sketch, it is available as a reference for the slot iFeature. In the *Selected Features* area, select **Reference Point1** and transfer it to the right area to add the work point to the iFeature.
4. Reorder the *Position Geometry* by dragging **Profile Plane1** above **Reference Point1**, as shown in Figure 10–45.
5. In the *Selected Features* area, right-click on **iFeature#** and select **Rename**. Enter **slot** as the new name.

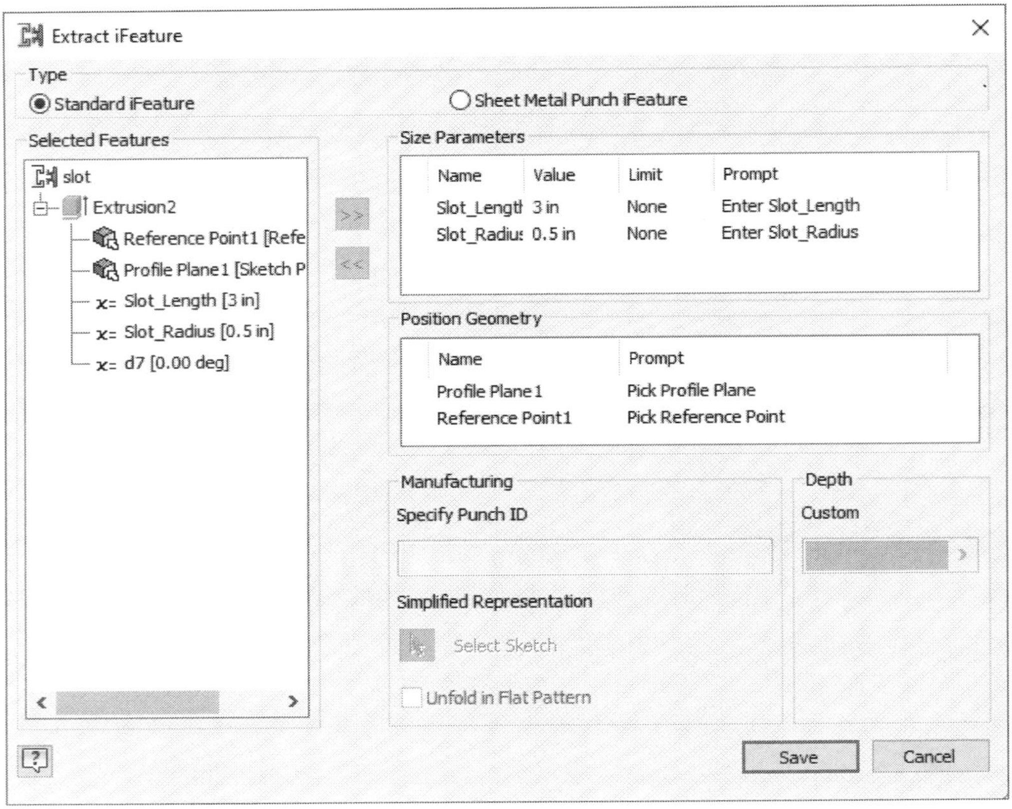

Figure 10–45

6. Save the iFeature to your *Custom iFeature* folder as **slot.ide**.

Task 3: Insert the iFeature.

In this task, you insert a number of instances of the slot.ide feature in the same model.

1. In the *Manage* tab>Insert panel, click (Insert iFeature) and open **slot.ide**.
2. Select the profile plane and slot center points to place the slots, as shown in Figure 10–46. You will need to add separate features for each instance. To rotate the slot on the profile plane, in the Insert iFeature dialog box, enter an *Angle*. To vary the sizes, you need to enter new values for the radius and length, as required. Keep in mind that the preview of the iFeature placement is not always the same as the actual geometry placement. You can always make changes to its position once it is placed.

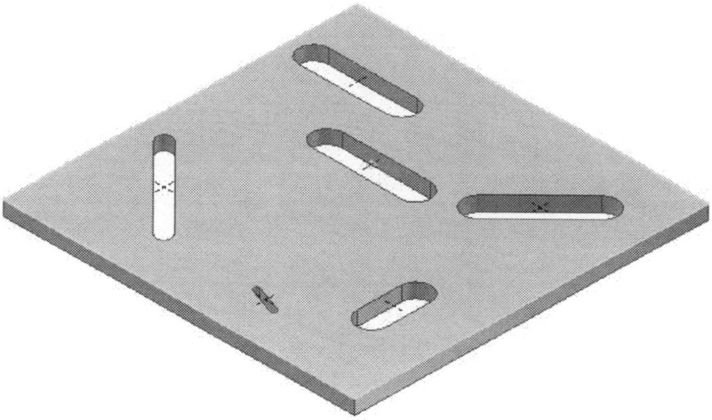

Figure 10–46

3. Save and close the model.

End of practice

Chapter Review Questions

1. Renamed model parameters are automatically included as variable size parameters when creating an iFeature.
   a. True
   b. False

2. Which file extension type is used to store an iFeature?
   a. .IDW
   b. .IDE
   c. .IPN
   d. .IPT

3. Which of the following are valid menu options that can be used when defining limits on the parameter size of an iFeature? (Select all that apply.)
   a. Range
   b. List
   c. User Entry
   d. None

4. If you insert a revised iFeature into a file that contains an older version of the feature, the original iFeature is automatically updated.
   a. True
   b. False

5. Which of the following statements are true regarding the **Copy** option used to copy features? (Select all that apply.)
   a. It can only be used to copy features in the same model.
   b. It can be used to copy a chamfer from one edge and duplicate it on another edge.
   c. It can be used to create a copy of a sketched extrusion.
   d. A copied feature can always be created independent of the original; however, there are restrictions on when a dependent copy is possible.

6. The table for a table-driven iFeature is created during iFeature creation in a part mode.
   a. True
   b. False

Command Summary

Button	Command	Location
	**Change Icon**	• **Ribbon:** *iFeature* tab>iFeature panel
N/A	**Copy (features)**	• **Context menu: In Model browser with feature name selected**
	**Edit iFeature**	• **Ribbon:** *iFeature* tab>iFeature panel • **Context menu** from the Model browser
	**Edit Using Spread Sheet**	• **Ribbon:** *iFeature* tab>iFeature panel
	**Extract iFeature**	• **Ribbon:** *Manage* tab>Author panel
	**iFeature Author Table**	• **Ribbon:** *iFeature* tab>iFeature panel • **Context menu:** In the graphics window
	**Insert iFeature**	• **Ribbon:** *Manage* tab>Insert panel
	**Insert Object**	• **Ribbon:** *Tools* tab>Insert panel
	**View Catalog**	• **Ribbon:** *iFeature* tab>iFeature panel

Chapter 11

iParts

The Autodesk® Inventor® iPart functionality enables you to create variations in your part designs quickly and easily. This provides an alternative to the Model State functionality. iParts can also be used to create similar models, instead of recreating the same model repeatedly with slight variations. Once a part has been created with iPart members, the members can also be documented in a drawing using tables.

Learning Objectives

- Create an iPart that can generate different configurations of a model.
- Group iPart attributes into keys to logically sort the members for quick access.
- Insert standard or custom iParts into an assembly based on specified Keys, Tree, or Table lists for the iPart factory.
- Replace an iPart in an assembly with a new iPart instance.
- Modify an iPart factory using the Edit Table or Edit via Spreadsheet options to add or modify parameters and attributes.
- Specify whether an edit made to an iPart should reflect only in the active member or in all members.
- Use a table-driven iPart to create an iFeature.
- Use a drawing table to clearly document the members and attributes of an iPart.

11.1 iPart Creation

Many similar parts are used in creating assemblies. For example, one bolt may differ from another bolt only in its length. Rather than create several bolts that are identical in all ways but length, you can create one iPart to cover all lengths. Like other part files, iPart files have the extension .IPT. The iPart in Figure 11–1 shows three configurations of a cover plate.

Figure 11–1

iPart files are called iPart Factories. The factory produces parts based on the part geometry and attribute values stored in a table. The new parts created by an iPart factory are unique files. By default, a part file is not created until the iPart is placed in an assembly.

Hint: iParts vs. Model States

iParts offer capabilities similar to those found in Model States to quickly create multiple configurations of a model. One major difference is that with iParts, all configurations are stored as individual files once generated, whereas model states are stored within a single file.

Use the following general steps to create an iPart:

1. Create or open a part with parameters.
2. Start the creation of an iPart.
3. Select the configurable attributes.
4. Add iPart members.
5. Verify the table.
6. Set up keys.
7. (Optional) Assign custom parameters.
8. Complete the operation.
9. Verify iPart instances in the Model browser.
10. (Optional) Generate iPart Members

Step 1 - Create or open a part with parameters.

Create or open a part. To make it easier to create the iPart, use parameters that have descriptive names and apply those parameters to items in the features that will become your attributes. Consider the following:

- Plan your iPart so that a minimum number of parameters are required. If a dimension is always half of another dimension, use an equation rather than input both numbers.
- Consider what design variations are required and can be created. The parameters and dimensions that control this are used to create the iPart.

Step 2 - Start the creation of an iPart.

In the *Manage* tab>Author panel, click (Create iPart). The iPart Author dialog box opens, as shown in Figure 11–2.

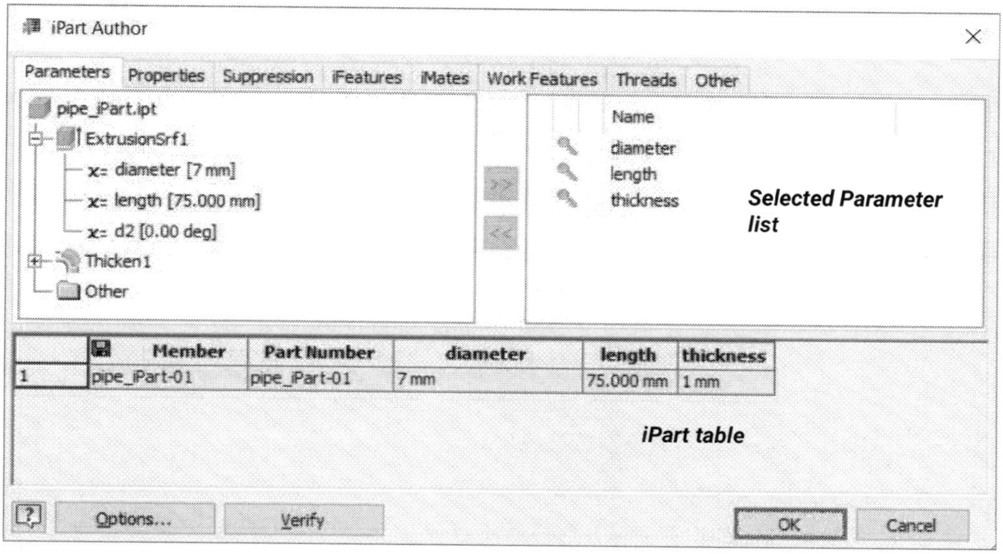

Figure 11–2

Step 3 - Select the configurable attributes.

The tabs in the iPart Author dialog box contain the configurable attributes that can be varied to create the different iPart configurations. Any parameter that has been renamed is automatically added as a configurable attribute. Use the >> and << buttons to add and remove additional parameters, as required.

The iPart Author tabs are described as follows:

Tabs	Description
Parameters	Contains the parameters used in the part, which are listed under the features in which they belong.
Properties	Enables you to add feature information, such as the part number or the name of the manufacturer.
Suppression	Enables you to specify individual features to compute or suppress for each instance of the part.
iFeatures	Enables you to specify which table-driven instance of an iFeature to include in the iPart, or set the suppression status. Add the **Table Replace** item and assign rows from the iFeature to instances in the iPart.
iMates	Enables you to include iMates. You can specify to do any of the following: include, suppress, set offset values, specify matching name, and specify sequence number.
Work Features	Enables you to specify work features to include.
Threads	Enables you to add thread variables to the iPart. Designations such as UNC are case-sensitive.
Other	Enables you to create additional columns in the table. These columns do not control the size of the part, but can be used as keys in the table.

Step 4 - Add iPart members.

Right-click on the first row, and select **Insert Row**. Continue adding rows, as required. Each additional row is an additional iPart member or configuration.

The columns in the table shown in Figure 11–3 list the parameter names and other attributes added from the tabs. Each row lists the values for one iPart instance. Select each table cell and enter the required attribute value.

	Member	Part Number	diameter	length	thickness
1	Pipe-7x75x1	Pipe-7x75x1	7 mm	75.000 mm	1 mm
2	Pipe-7x80x1	Pipe-7x80x1	7 mm	80.000 mm	1 mm
3	Pipe-7x85x1	Pipe-7x85x1	7 mm	85.000 mm	1 mm
4	Pipe-7x75x1_1	Pipe-7x75x1_1	7 mm	75.000 mm	1.1 mm
5	Pipe-7x80x1_1	Pipe-7x80x1_1	7 mm	80.000 mm	1.1 mm
6	Pipe-7x85x1_1	Pipe-7x85x1_1	7 mm	85.000 mm	1.1 mm
7	Pipe-8x75x1	Pipe-8x75x1	8 mm	75.000 mm	1 mm
8	Pipe-8x80x1	Pipe-8x80x1	8 mm	80.000 mm	1 mm
9	Pipe-8x85x1	Pipe-8x85x1	8 mm	85.000 mm	1 mm
10	Pipe-8x75x1_1	Pipe-8x75x1_1	8 mm	75.000 mm	1.1 mm
11	Pipe-8x80x1_1	Pipe-8x80x1_1	8 mm	80.000 mm	1.1 mm
12	Pipe-8x85x1_1	Pipe-8x85x1_1	8 mm	85.000 mm	1.1 mm

Figure 11–3

- The row highlighted in green is the default part used when placing the iPart in an assembly. To change the default row, right-click on the required row and select **Set As Default Row**.
- To suppress a feature in a part, enter one of the following in the *iPart* table cell: Suppress, S, s, Off, OFF, off, 0.
- To compute the feature, enter one of the following in the cell: Compute, C, c, U, u, ON, on, On, 1.
- When entering values that require either **Exclude** or **Include**, the first letter in each word can be entered as lowercase, but the entire word is required to be a valid entry.

***Note:** Alternatively, you can use Excel to add new iPart members. This enables you to use some of the built-in Excel functionality, such as copy, paste, formulas, and sorting. To do so, click **OK**, right-click on Table in the Model browser, and select **Edit via Spreadsheet**.*

Step 5 - Verify the table.

To ensure all entered values are valid, click **Verify**. Invalid values highlight in the table in yellow. Correct all invalid values before continuing.

Step 6 - Set up keys.

Keys enable you to group iPart members according to their attribute values in a hierarchical manner. This sorts the iPart members logically, enabling quicker access to the required configuration.

If you do not assign keys, it can be much more difficult to find a specific configuration. Without creating any keys, configurations are listed as follows:

In the...	The configurations are listed...
iPart table	According to the order of the columns in the iPart table, as shown in Figure 11–4.
Model browser	According to the member name, as shown in Figure 11–5.
Place Standard iPart dialog box	Separately at the top-level branch, as shown in Figure 11–6.

	Member	Part Number	diameter	length	thickness
1	Pipe-7x75x1	Pipe-7x75x1	7 mm	75.000 mm	1 mm
2	Pipe-7x80x1	Pipe-7x80x1	7 mm	80.000 mm	1 mm
3	Pipe-7x85x1	Pipe-7x85x1	7 mm	85.000 mm	1 mm
4	Pipe-7x75x1_1	Pipe-7x75x1_1	7 mm	75.000 mm	1.1 mm
5	Pipe-7x80x1_1	Pipe-7x80x1_1	7 mm	80.000 mm	1.1 mm
6	Pipe-7x85x1_1	Pipe-7x85x1_1	7 mm	85.000 mm	1.1 mm
7	Pipe-8x75x1	Pipe-8x75x1	8 mm	75.000 mm	1 mm
8	Pipe-8x80x1	Pipe-8x80x1	8 mm	80.000 mm	1 mm
9	Pipe-8x85x1	Pipe-8x85x1	8 mm	85.000 mm	1 mm
10	Pipe-8x75x1_1	Pipe-8x75x1_1	8 mm	75.000 mm	1.1 mm
11	Pipe-8x80x1_1	Pipe-8x80x1_1	8 mm	80.000 mm	1.1 mm
12	Pipe-8x85x1_1	Pipe-8x85x1_1	8 mm	85.000 mm	1.1 mm

Figure 11–4

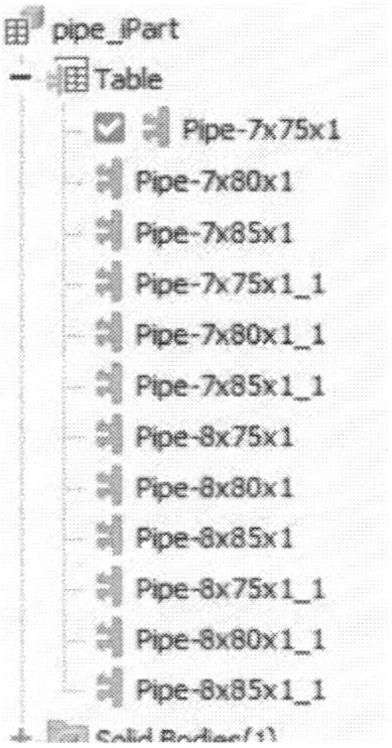

Figure 11–5

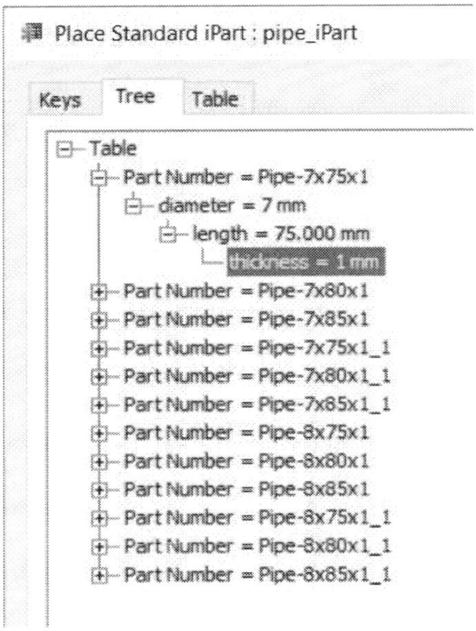

Figure 11–6

By assigning keys, you are able to organize these configurations into a logical and hierarchical structure, as shown in Figure 11–7. In the example shown, the iParts have been assigned keys for their diameter and thickness. This enables you to quickly expand the branches to find a required configuration, or easily view all of the different lengths that are available for a specific diameter and thickness.

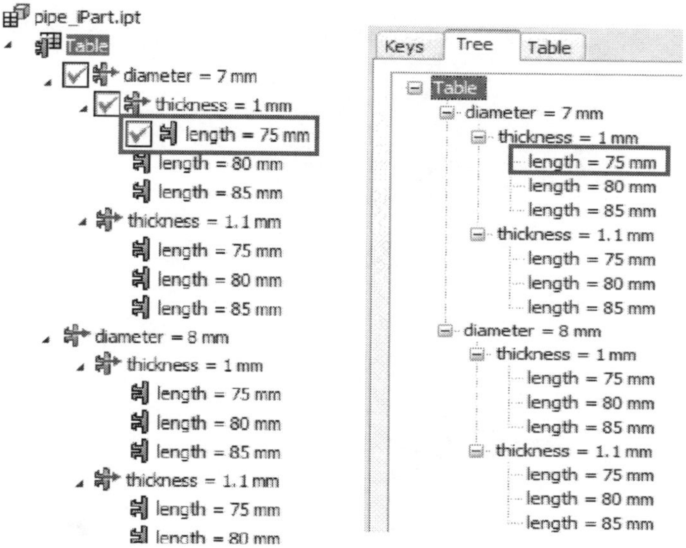

Figure 11–7

To organize in this way you specify keys when you create the iPart factory. A key symbol displays in front of each parameter, as shown in Figure 11–8.

- Blue keys indicate that the attribute is set as a key.
- Gray keys indicate that the attribute is not used as a key.

Note: *Not all attributes need keys. If the assigned keys already narrow down the configurations to one, then no remaining keys are required.*

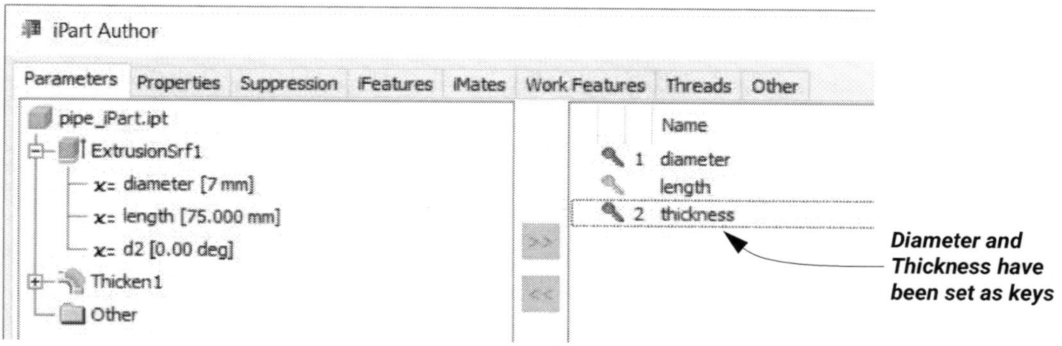

Figure 11–8

- The number next to the key indicates the hierarchy: 1 is the first key used for sorting, followed by 2, etc. Use the most descriptive or logical attribute as the first key.
- Up to nine keys can be used in a part factory. Click on a key to toggle it on or off.
- To change the order of key numbers, or to assign a key number to a parameter, in the *Name* column or table, right-click on the parameter and select **Key**. Select the required key number, as shown in Figure 11–9. You can also select a key to assign it to the next non-assigned key value.

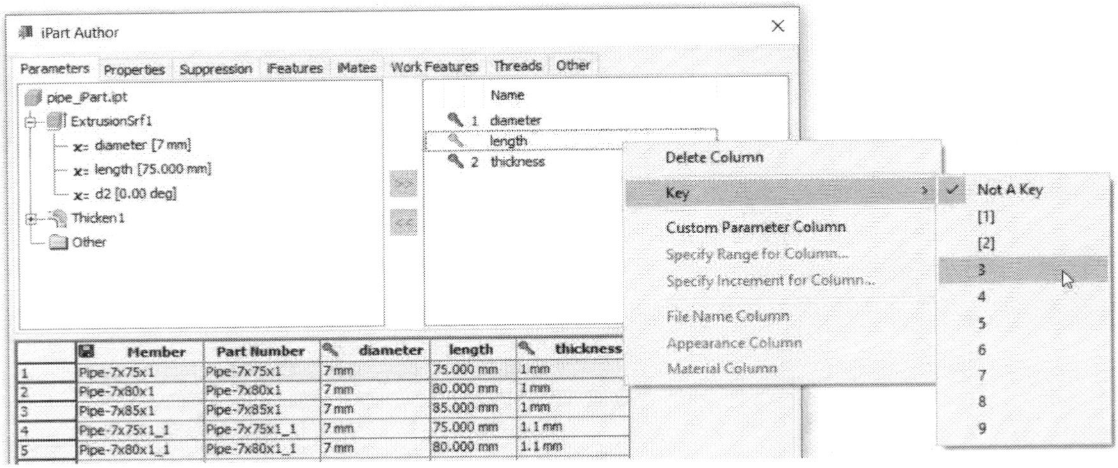

Figure 11–9

Step 7 - (Optional) Assign custom parameters.

Parameters can be set up so that when you are placing the iPart factory member in an assembly, you are prompted to enter its value. When a custom parameter is assigned, the iPart is considered a custom iPart or custom iPart factory. A keyed column cannot be set as a custom column.

To assign a custom parameter, right-click on the parameter's heading and select **Custom Parameter Column**, as shown in Figure 11–10. Once assigned, the entire column turns blue, indicating that it is custom. It can be disabled later, if required, by clearing the **Custom Parameter Column** option.

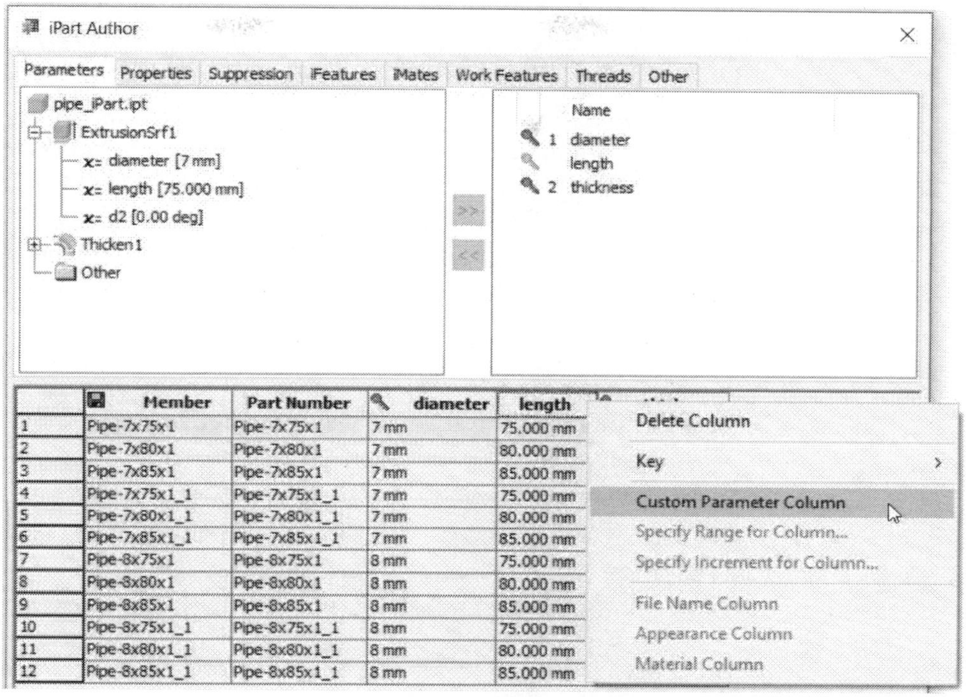

Figure 11–10

Step 8 - Complete the operation.

Once the iPart is defined, click **OK** to complete iPart creation. The iPart Table node is listed at the top of the Model browser. The **Model States** node that appears by default is replaced with the iPart **Table** node after an iPart is created in the model.

Step 9 - Verify iPart instances in the Model browser.

After you have defined the iPart Factory, the table is listed in the Model browser. The members can be listed by their name or by key. Right-click on **Table** in the Model browser and select **List by Keys** or **List by Member Name** to customize the display of the members to either option.

Expand the table to see the configurations of the part defined in the table (organized according to the key attribute(s) you defined). The left side of Figure 11–11 shows the members displayed by key. The member name display is shown on the right side.

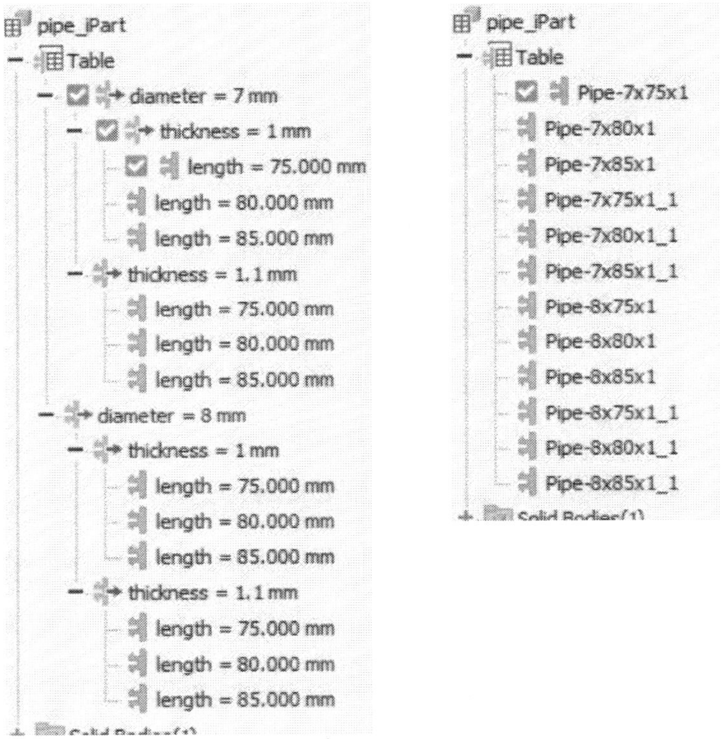

Figure 11–11

The active iPart member is marked with a checkmark. Double-click on the most-nested branches to activate that configuration (or right-click and select **Activate**). The most-nested branches are not expandable (i.e., an arrowhead symbol does not exist next to it in the Model browser).

Step 10 - (Optional) Generate iPart Members

Once the iPart is created, you can create the member when it is used in an assembly or you can generate all the files at once.

How To: Generate All the Files at Once

1. In the Model browser, right-click on **Table** and select **List By Member Name**. If you selected **List By Keys**, you must select the most nested member names.
2. Hold <Shift> and select all member names.
3. Right-click and select **Generate Files**, as shown in Figure 11–12.

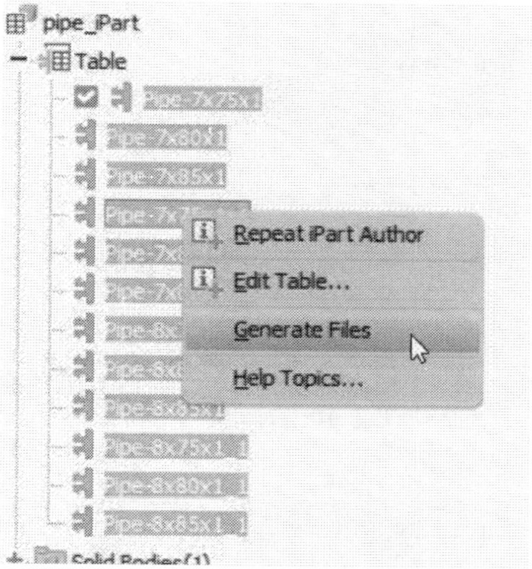

Figure 11–12

The iPart members are created in a folder with the same name as the iPart file. In the above example, a folder called ***hex_bolt*** was created and contains four files.

> **Note:** *If a Custom Parameter column is specified in the table, you will not be able to generate files. This is because the parameter is a required entry when the component is placed in an assembly; therefore, generating the files does not prompt you for user entry.*

11.2 iPart Placement

Inserting iParts in assemblies is similar to inserting parts, except you must specify a member to use. The procedure varies depending on if they are a standard factory (does not contain any custom cells) or from a custom iPart factory (contains at least one custom cell).

When selecting iPart members for placement, the three tabs provide different ways of listing the same iPart members. This helps you quickly find the part you are looking for.

- The *Keys* tab, as shown in Figure 11–13, lists members in the order specified in the iPart Factory along with their current values. Click on a value to select a different standard value or to change a custom value. After the value for one attribute is selected, only the valid corresponding values will be listed for the other attributes.

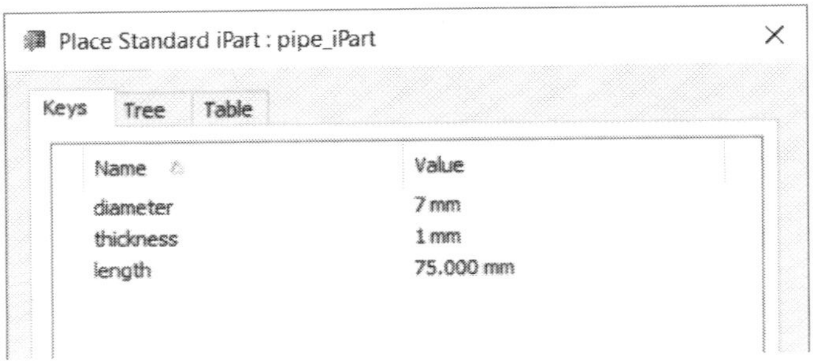

Figure 11–13

- The *Tree* tab, as shown in Figure 11–14, lists the values for each instance of the iPart. Expand the tree to see and select the instances of the part defined in the table (organized according to the key attributes).

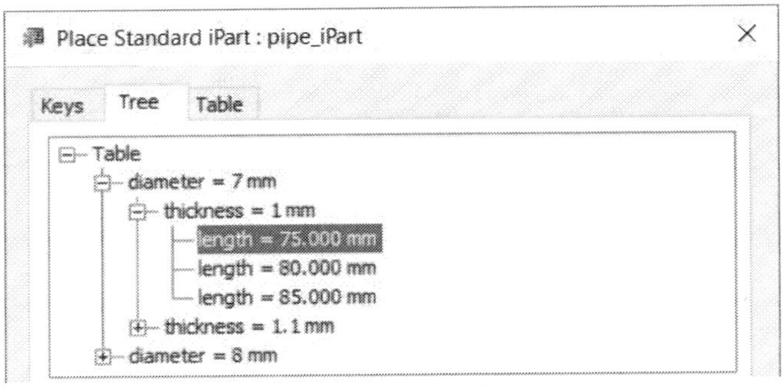

Figure 11–14

- The *Table* tab, as shown in Figure 11–15, lists the values for each instance of the iPart in the iPart Factory. Right-click on a column header to select ascending or descending sort order.

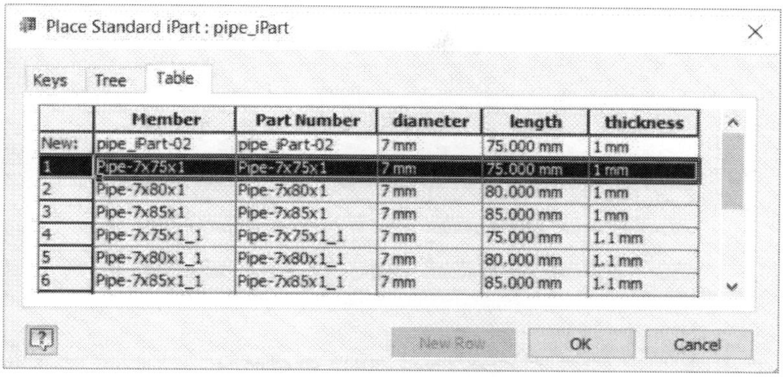

Figure 11–15

Placing a Standard iPart

How To: Place a Standard iPart

1. In the *Assemble* tab>Component panel, click  (Place).
2. Select and open the iPart. The Place Standard iPart dialog box opens.
3. Select an iPart member using one of the following methods:
   - Select the current value in the *Keys* tab.
   - Select an instance from the *Tree* tab.
   - Select a row in the *Table* tab.
4. Select a point on the screen to place the component.
5. Repeat Steps 1 to 3 to place any additional iPart members.
6. Right-click and select **OK**.
7. Constrain the component in the assembly, as required.

When you place a standard iPart for the first time, the Autodesk Inventor software creates a new directory in the same directory as the iPart factory. The directory is created using the same name as the iPart factory. As you place iParts from the factory, each part is created and it is added to the folder.

Placing a Custom iPart

How To: Place a Custom iPart

1. In the *Assemble* tab>Component panel, click (Place).
2. Select and open the iPart. The Place Custom iPart dialog box opens, as shown in Figure 11–16. The right column contains the values you can customize.

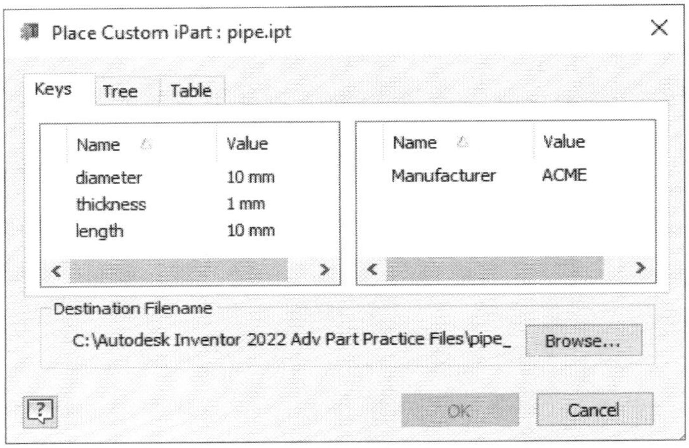

Figure 11–16

3. Select an iPart member using one of the following methods:
   - Select the current value in the *Keys* tab.
   - Select an instance from the *Tree* tab.
   - Select a row in the *Table* tab.
4. Set the values for the custom items as required.
5. (Optional) Click **Browse** to change the *Destination Filename* for the new part. Standard iParts are named by default.
6. Select a point on the screen to place the component.
7. Right-click and select **OK**.
8. Constrain the component in the assembly, as required

Replacing an iPart

How To: Replace iPart Components

1. In the Model browser, expand the component, right-click on the **Table** node and select **Change Component**.
2. Select the new iPart instance to use.
3. Click **OK** to replace the instance.

11.3 Editing an iPart Factory

Edit Table

How To: Edit the iPart Factory

1. Open the iPart factory as you would open any part file.
2. In the Model browser, right-click on the **Table** node in the Model browser and select **Edit Table** to open the iPart Author dialog box.
3. Add or change the entries in the dialog box, and click **OK**.
4. Save the changes to the file.

Alternatively, in the Model browser, right-click on the **Table** node in the Model browser and select **Edit via Spreadsheet** to access the spreadsheet in Excel. You can add equations and relate the cells to each other. Changes that are made to an iPart Factory reflect in the iPart instances already placed in assemblies once their assembly has been updated.

Adding Features to an iPart

When adding features to an existing iPart, considering the scope of the change is important. Consider whether the new feature should reflect in only the active factory member (**Edit Member Scope**) or reflect in all factory members (**Edit Factory Scope**). In the Author panel, the **Edit Member Scope** and **Edit Factory Scope** options, as shown in Figure 11–17, enable you to control the scope of change.

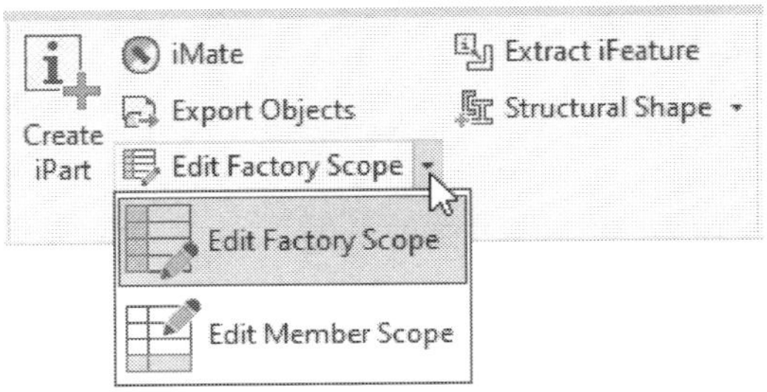

Figure 11–17

- By default, the scope is automatically set to change the entire factory (**Edit Factory Scope**), which means that if a feature is added, it is added to all members and no changes are made to the iPart table.
- If **Edit Member Scope** is specified and a feature is added, the feature and any dimensional parameters used to create it are automatically added to the table. The feature's cell for the active member will be marked to **Compute**. Other members are automatically **Suppressed**, but can be modified if required.

11.4 Creating iFeatures from Table-Driven iParts

Table-driven iParts, in their entirety, can be used to create a table-driven iFeature. This enables you to create an iFeature directly from a whole table-driven iPart. The entire table of data for the iPart is included in the new iFeature. You do not need to manually enter all instances of the iPart into the table.

How To: Create a Table-Driven iFeature from a Table-Driven iPart

1. Create a table-driven iPart using the standard workflow.
2. In the *Manage* tab>Author panel, click (Extract iFeature). The Extract iFeature dialog box opens.
3. In the Model browser, select the required features, or select those directly from the model geometry. To select the entire iPart, select the base feature first, and all following features will automatically be selected. Assign any of the *Size Parameters* or *Position Geometry*, as shown in Figure 11–18.

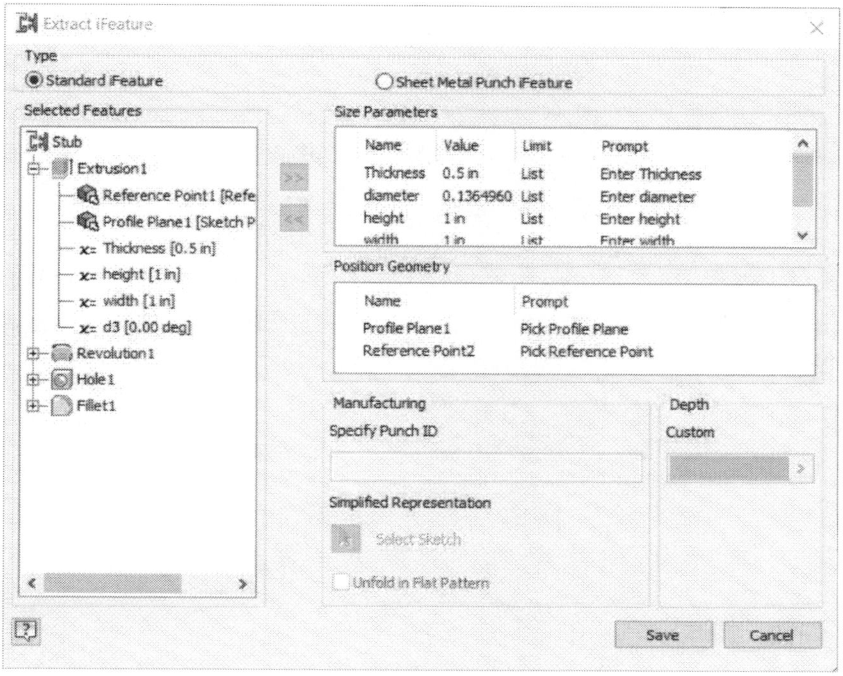

Figure 11–18

4. Save the iFeature in the catalog directory. The iFeature can be placed using the same techniques as placing any iFeature.

11.5 Tables for Factory Members

You can create tables for iParts and iAssemblies to show factory members and their attributes, as shown in Figure 11–19.

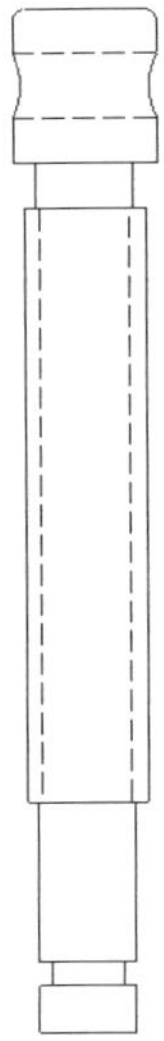

Table		
Member	Part Number	vise_screw_length
Short	Vise_Screw-01	138.75 mm
Medium	Vise_Screw-02	158.75 mm
Long	Vise_Screw-03	178.75 mm

Figure 11–19

How To: Create a Table for iPart Factory Members

1. Open or create a drawing that contains a view of an iPart member.
2. Select the *Annotate* tab>Table panel and click (General). The Table dialog box opens.
3. Select a drawing view containing the required iPart for which you want to create a table. The Table dialog box updates, as shown in Figure 11–20.

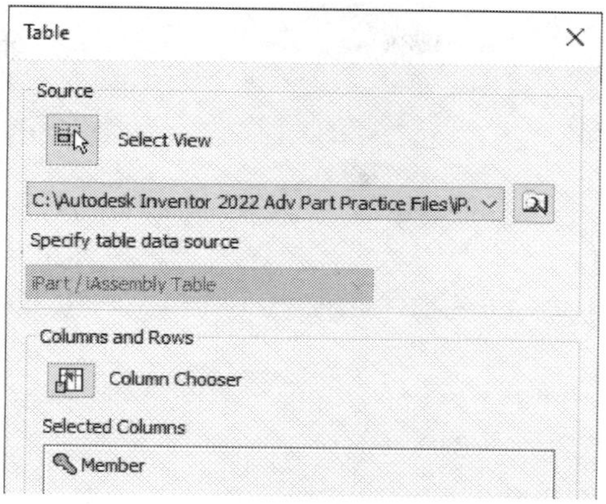

Figure 11–20

4. Click (Column Chooser). The Table Column Chooser dialog box opens, as shown in Figure 11–21.

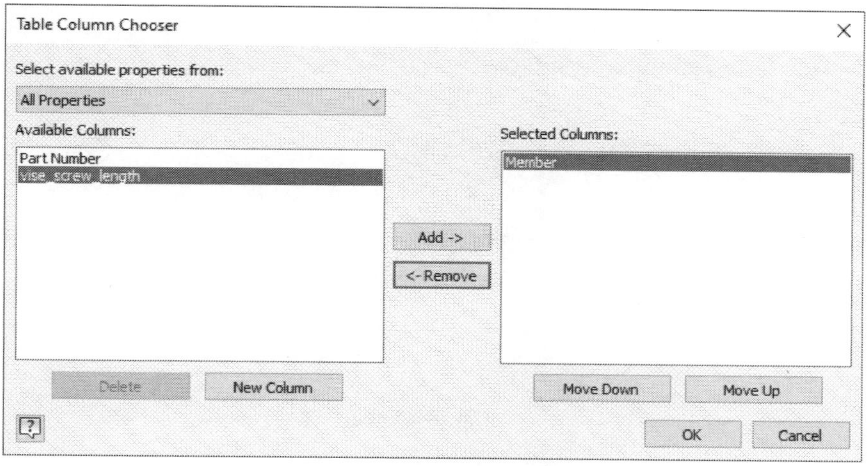

Figure 11–21

5. Customize the columns that will be displayed in the table and click **OK**.
   - Move the required column properties from the *Available Columns* list to the *Selected Columns* list to create it as a column in the table and display the attribute value for each factory member.
   - You can reorder the column properties in the *Selected Columns* list as required by clicking **Move Down** and **Move Up**.
6. Click **OK** to close the Table dialog box.
7. Move the cursor to the required location and click to place the table. The table populates with the columns and attributes of the iPart factory members.

Practice 11a
Bolt iPart Factory

Practice Objectives

- Create an iPart factory using custom parameters to show different configurations of the part.
- Group iPart attributes into Keys to sort the iPart members logically, enabling quick access to the configuration.
- Add a new feature to the model and edit the member scope to define how the new feature will appear in the iPart.
- Generate the members of the iPart factory to create new part models.

In this practice, you rename part parameters so they have a descriptive name and are easily identifiable. You then establish logical relationships between these parameters so that only a small number of parameters control them all. Using these parameters, you then create an iPart factory to quickly produce multiple bolt parts. The hex_bolt you will be working with is shown in Figure 11–22.

Figure 11–22

Task 1: Change parameter names.

In this task, you change the bolt dimension (parameter) names to descriptive names. You also relate the parameters.

1. Open **hex_bolt.ipt**.
2. In the *Manage* tab>Parameters panel, click f_x (Parameters) and change the parameter names as follows:

- d0 = stub_len
- d6 = major_dia
- d7 = minor_dia
- d9 = h_width
- d10 = h_height
- d23 = thread_len
- d24 = grip_len

3. Enter the following equation for the thread_len parameter:

   - thread_len = stub_len - grip_len

   This equation calculates the length of the thread when the stub length is changed.

4. Close the Parameters dialog box.

Task 2: Create an iPart factory.

1. Note the **Model States** node at the top of the Model browser. The Model State functionality provides an alternative to the iPart functionality. The Model State functionality is enabled by default in all new parts.

2. In the *Manage* tab>Author panel, click (Create iPart) to enable iPart creation in the model, instead of using Model States. The iPart Author dialog box opens. Note that the named parameters are already listed in the column on the right side and in the lower table.

3. Insert three more rows to the table by right-clicking on row **1** and selecting **Insert Row**. Enter the values shown in the Figure 11–23.

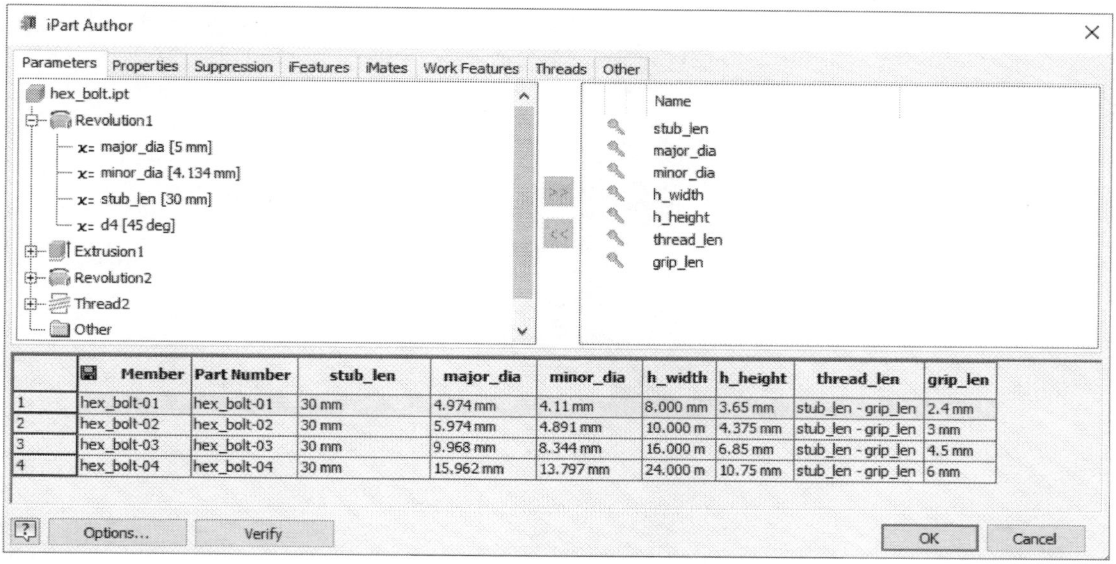

	Member	Part Number	stub_len	major_dia	minor_dia	h_width	h_height	thread_len	grip_len
1	hex_bolt-01	hex_bolt-01	30 mm	4.974 mm	4.11 mm	8.000 mm	3.65 mm	stub_len - grip_len	2.4 mm
2	hex_bolt-02	hex_bolt-02	30 mm	5.974 mm	4.891 mm	10.000 m	4.375 mm	stub_len - grip_len	3 mm
3	hex_bolt-03	hex_bolt-03	30 mm	9.968 mm	8.344 mm	16.000 m	6.85 mm	stub_len - grip_len	4.5 mm
4	hex_bolt-04	hex_bolt-04	30 mm	15.962 mm	13.797 mm	24.000 m	10.75 mm	stub_len - grip_len	6 mm

Figure 11–23

4. Select the *Threads* tab and add **Thread2:Designation** to the right column. The attribute is also added in the iPart table as a new column.

5. Enter the values shown in Figure 11–24 for the Thread Designation.

	Member	Part Number	stub_len	major_dia	minor_dia	h_width	h_height	thread_len	grip_len	Thread2: Designation
1	hex_bolt-01	hex_bolt-01	30 mm	4.974 mm	4.11 mm	8.000 mm	3.65 mm	stub_len - grip_len	2.4 mm	M5x0.8
2	hex_bolt-02	hex_bolt-02	30 mm	5.974 mm	4.891 mm	10.000 m	4.375 mm	stub_len - grip_len	3 mm	M6x1
3	hex_bolt-03	hex_bolt-03	30 mm	9.968 mm	8.344 mm	16.000 m	6.85 mm	stub_len - grip_len	4.5 mm	M10x1.5
4	hex_bolt-04	hex_bolt-04	30 mm	15.962 mm	13.797 mm	24.000 m	10.75 mm	stub_len - grip_len	6 mm	M16x2

Figure 11–24

Task 3: Assign keys.

1. In the *Threads* tab, next to **Thread2:Designation**, click to assign it as Key 1. The key turns blue.
2. Assign Keys 2 and 3 to **stub_len** and **major_dia**, consecutively.
3. Click **OK** to close the iPart Author dialog box.
4. In the Model browser, note that the **Model States** node has been removed and a Table is listed. Expand the **Table** node. To configure the Model browser to display the iPart configurations listed by keys, right-click on **Table** and select **List by Keys**. If the Model browser is already displayed by keys, **List by Keys** will not be available. Expand the branches for the first thread designation, as shown in Figure 11–25.

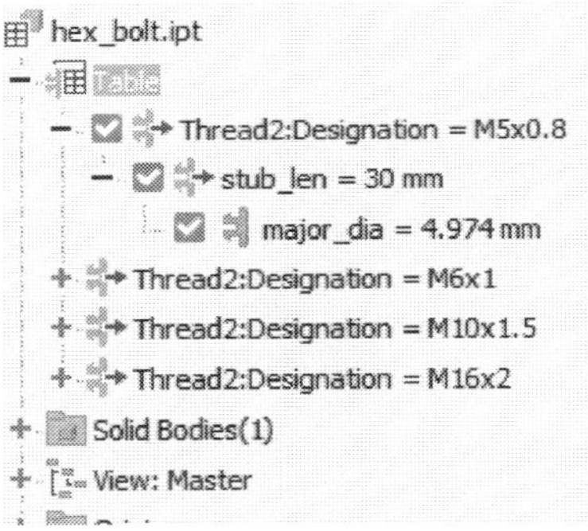

Figure 11–25

Note: *If your iPart table is created with recognizable part numbers as the Member name, you might want to consider setting the Table to* ***List by Member Name*** *so you can easily activate a member of the iPart family.*

5. To activate another iPart configuration, expand it in the Model browser until it cannot expand further and double-click on the last key describing the configuration. This single iPart can be used in assemblies to add different configurations of the bolt.
6. Save the model.

Task 4: Add a feature to the iPart.

1. Review the Author panel and note that the (Edit Factory Scope) is enabled. This is the default option, as shown in Figure 11–26.

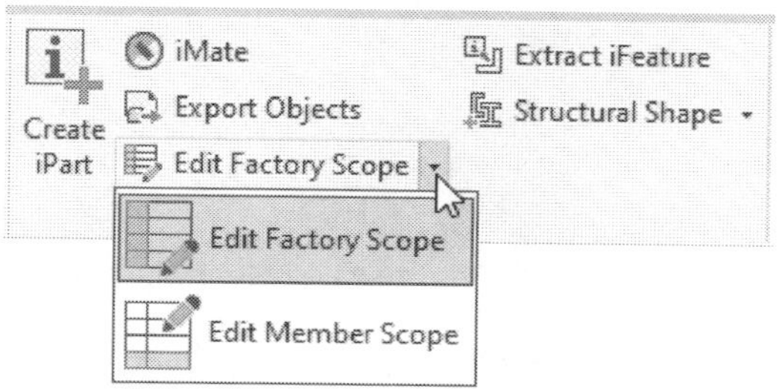

Figure 11–26

2. Create a cut feature similar to that shown in Figure 11–27 on the active factory member.

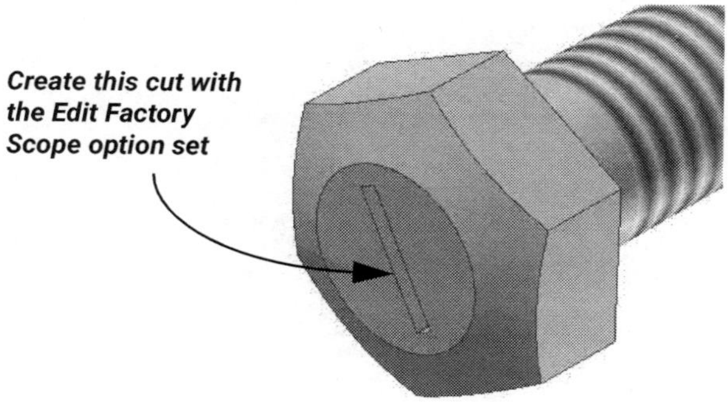

Figure 11–27

3. In the Model browser, right-click on **Table** and select **List By Member Name**.
4. Double-click on the three other factory members to verify that this feature has been added to all members. If the values for the cut must be varied for each member, use the standard editing tools to add the parameters and modify them in the table.
5. Activate **hex_bolt-01**.

6. In the *Manage* tab>Author panel, click (Edit Member Scope), as shown in Figure 11–28.

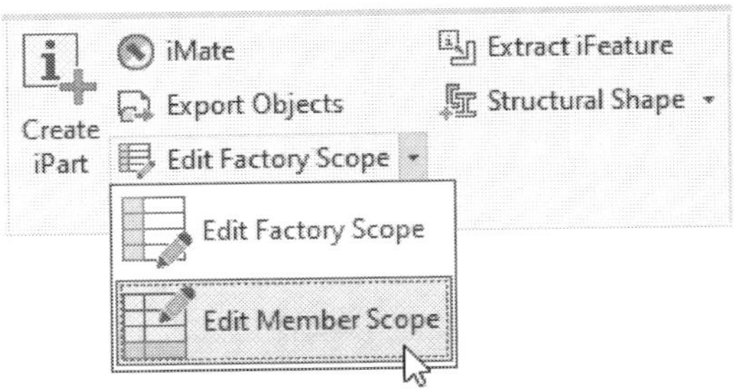

Figure 11–28

7. Create a cut feature similar to that shown in Figure 11–29. For this practice, use similar dimensions to those used to create the previous cut.

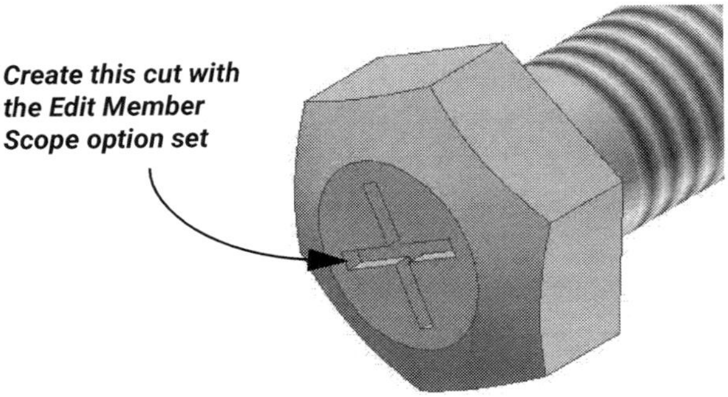

Figure 11–29

Note: Consider setting up equations to ensure that the dimensions of both cuts are the same, or use sketching techniques to build both sketches into a single sketch but use it to create two extrusions.

8. Double-click on the three other factory members to verify that this feature has not been added to the other members. It is only shown in the **hex_bolt-01** member because this was the active member when the feature was created.
9. Activate **hex_bolt-01**.
10. Right-click on **Table** in the Model browser and select **Edit Table** to open the iPart Author dialog box.
11. Note the new column shown in Figure 11–30. Note that **Suppress** is assigned for the cut in **hex_bolt-02**, **hex_bolt-03**, and **hex_bolt-04**, and the cut is computed in **hex_bolt-01**. The Suppress/Compute settings can be modified, if required. The values of the sketch dimensions can also be included or removed from the table, if required, to control the size of the cuts in each factory instance. If the dimensions were added, remove them from the table by selecting them and selecting << to move them back to the parameters list.

d_len	grip_len	Thread2: Designation	d29	d30	Extrusion3
- grip_len	2.4 mm	M5x0.8	3.5 mm	0.75 mm	Compute
- grip_len	3 mm	M6x1	3.579 mm	0.449 mm	Suppress
- grip_len	4.5 mm	M10x1.5	3.579 mm	0.449 mm	Suppress
- grip_len	6 mm	M16x2	3.579 mm	0.449 mm	Suppress

Figure 11–30

12. Click **OK** to close the iPart Author dialog box.

Task 5: Generate the members of the factory.

1. Verify that the Model browser is still set to **List By Member Name**.
2. Hold <Shift> and select all four member names.
3. Right-click and select **Generate Files**, as shown in Figure 11–31.

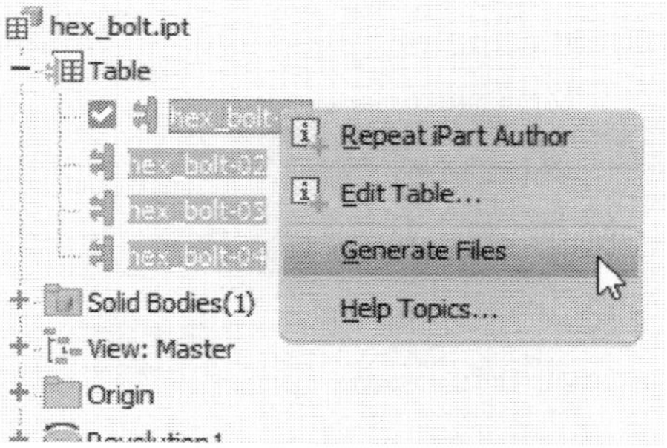

Figure 11–31

4. If you did not previously save the iPart file, you are prompted to save the file prior to file generation. Open Windows Explorer and review the four files in the new *Hex_Bolt* folder in the practice files directory.
5. Return to the Autodesk Inventor software.

Task 6: Assign a custom parameter.

Although values have been assigned to the *grip_len* parameter for each iPart member, the values might need to vary depending on the current requirements when the hex_bolt is placed in an assembly. In this case, the column will be set as custom. The default values that were provided in the table will be used; however, designers will still have the option to enter custom values, if required.

1. In the Model browser, right-click on **Table** and select **Edit Table**. The iPart Author dialog box opens.

2. Right-click on the *grip_len* column header and select **Custom Parameter Column**, as shown in Figure 11–32. The column will turn purple, indicating that it is a custom column.

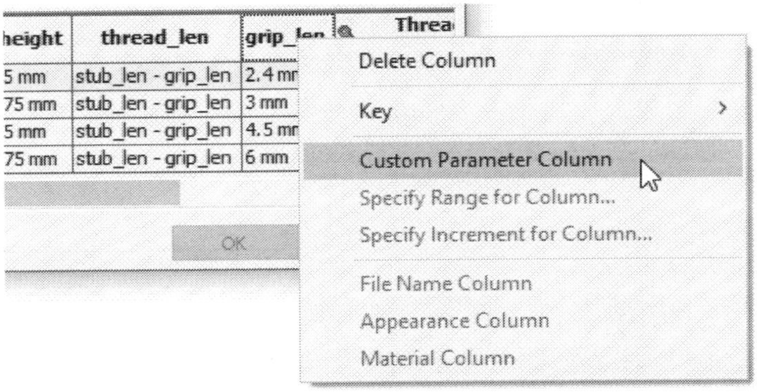

Figure 11–32

3. Click **OK** to close the iPart Author dialog box.

   Note: *If a Custom Parameter Column is specified in the table, you are not able to generate files using the* ***Generate Files*** *command. You can only generate files when the part is assembled. This is because the parameter is a required entry when the component is placed in an assembly, and using the* ***Generate Files*** *command does not prompt you for user entry.*

4. The iPart factory is ready to be placed. Save the file with the name **hex_bolt_iPart** and close the window.

End of practice

Practice 11b
Create an iPart Factory

Practice Objectives

- Create an iPart factory using user parameters to show different configurations of the part.
- Modify and edit the iPart factory parameters and attributes in Autodesk Inventor software and Microsoft Excel.
- Place an iPart into an assembly file.
- Replace an iPart component in an assembly file with another instance from its factory.

In this practice, you create two user-defined parameters for a light-switch cover and assign them to part dimensions. To sort the instances of the part, you create an iPart factory to produce cover parts for varying combinations of switches and jacks. You edit the cover part and add a new row and column to the iPart factory via a spreadsheet. Finally, you place and constrain one instance in an assembly file. The final assembly is shown in Figure 11–33.

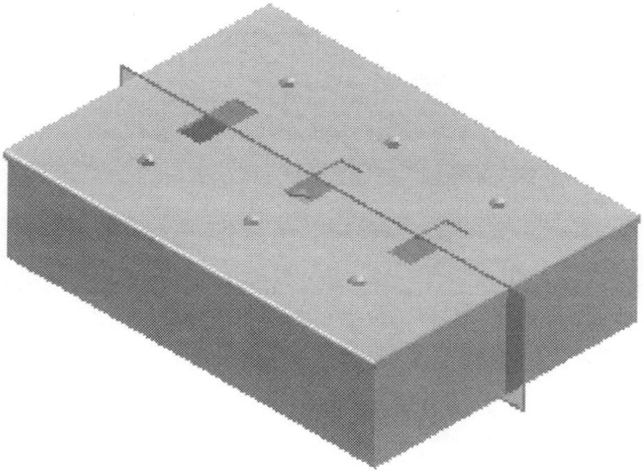

Figure 11–33

Task 1: Create user-defined parameters.

In this task, you create two user-defined parameters and assign these parameters to part dimensions to sort various instances of the cover part.

1. Open **cover.ipt**. The model displays as shown in Figure 11–34.

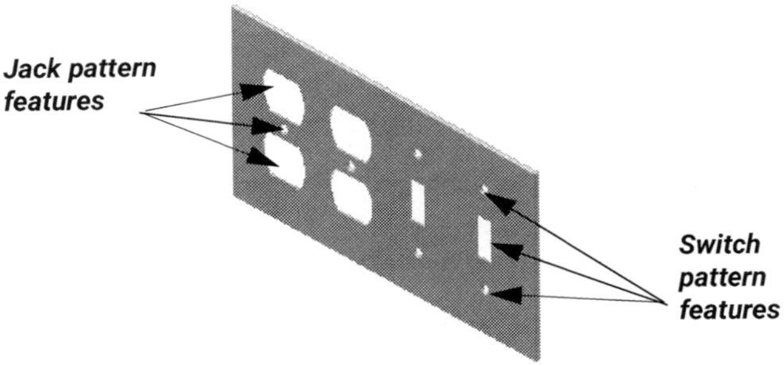

Figure 11–34

2. Use the Model browser to examine the cover part features and pattern numbers for the switch and jack pattern features.
3. In the *Manage* tab>Parameters panel, click (Parameters). The Parameters dialog box opens.
4. Click **Add Numeric** and create two user-defined unitless (ul) parameters called **switches** and **jackpairs**, as shown in Figure 11–35.

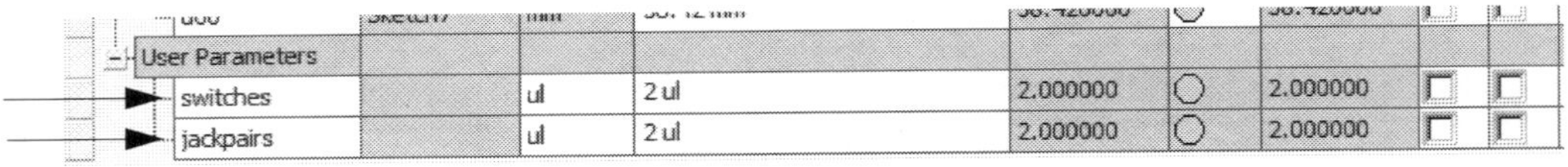

User Parameters								
switches		ul	2 ul	2.000000		2.000000		
jackpairs		ul	2 ul	2.000000		2.000000		

Figure 11–35

5. Change the equation for the d0 dimension to the following to make it equal to the overall length of the part:
   - 25.4+(45.72*(switches+jackpairs))
6. Change the equation for the d18 dimension to **switches**.
7. Change the equation for the d50 dimension to **jackpairs**. The d18 and d50 dimensions are pattern numbers for the switches and jackpairs in the cover part.
8. Click **Done** to close the Parameters dialog box.
9. Update the model, if required.

10. Show the dimensions for the **Extrusion1**. Change the dimension display to **Expression.** The model displays as shown in Figure 11–36.

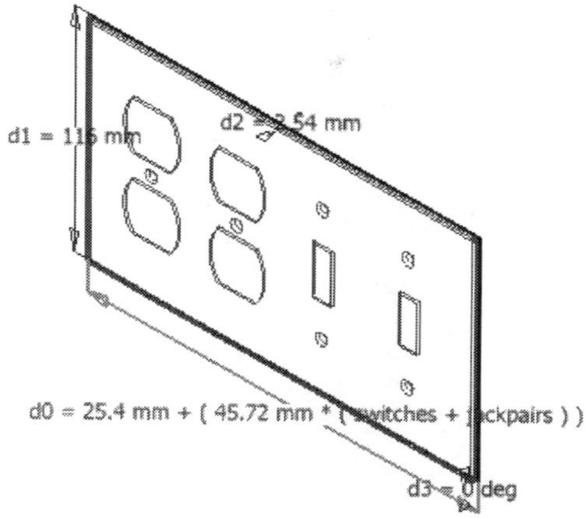

Figure 11–36

Task 2: Create an iPart factory.

In this task, you create an iPart factory to sort the various instances of the cover part by pattern numbers for the switches and jackpairs.

1. Suppress the **switch pattern** and **jack pattern** features.
2. Note the **Model States** node at the top of the Model browser. The Model State functionality provides an alternative to the iPart functionality. The Model State functionality is enabled by default in all new parts.
3. In the *Manage* tab>Author panel, click (Create iPart) to enable iPart creation in the model, instead of using Model States. The iPart Author dialog box opens. Note that the named parameters are already listed in the column on the right side of the table.
4. Select the key symbol next to the parameter **switches** in the right side panel. Key 1 is automatically assigned, the key turns blue, and a number 1 displays beside it.
5. Select the key symbol next to **jackpairs** to set it as Key 2. The key turns blue and a number 2 appears beside it.
6. Select the *Suppression* tab. The suppressed features are already listed in the column on the right side of the table.
7. Add **switch, switch holes, jacks**, and **jack holes** to the column on the right side. The features are also added as columns at the bottom of the table.

8. Right-click on row 1 and select **Insert Row**. Insert additional rows and edit the entries as shown in Figure 11–37.
   - To suppress a feature in a part in the iPart table, enter one of the following entries in a cell: Suppress, S, s, Off, OFF, off, 0.
   - To compute the feature, enter one of the following entries in the cell: Compute, C, c, U, u, ON, on, On, 1.

	Member	Part Number	switches	jackpairs	switch pattern	jack pattern	switch	switch holes	jacks	jack holes
1	cover-01	cover-01	1 ul	3 ul	Suppress	Compute	Compute	Compute	Compute	Compute
2	cover-02	cover-02	2 ul	1 ul	Compute	Suppress	Compute	Compute	Compute	Compute
3	cover-03	cover-03	3 ul	0 ul	Compute	Suppress	Compute	Compute	Suppress	Suppress
4	cover-04	cover-04	1 ul	1 ul	Suppress	Suppress	Compute	Compute	Compute	Compute
5	cover-05	cover-05	0 ul	1 ul	Suppress	Suppress	Suppress	Suppress	Compute	Compute
6	cover-06	cover-06	3 ul	2 ul	Compute	Compute	Compute	Compute	Compute	Compute

Figure 11–37

9. Right-click on row 6 and select **Set As Default Row**.
10. Click **OK** to close the iPart Author dialog box. The cover part displays as shown in Figure 11–38. The features are computed according to the conditions you set in the table.

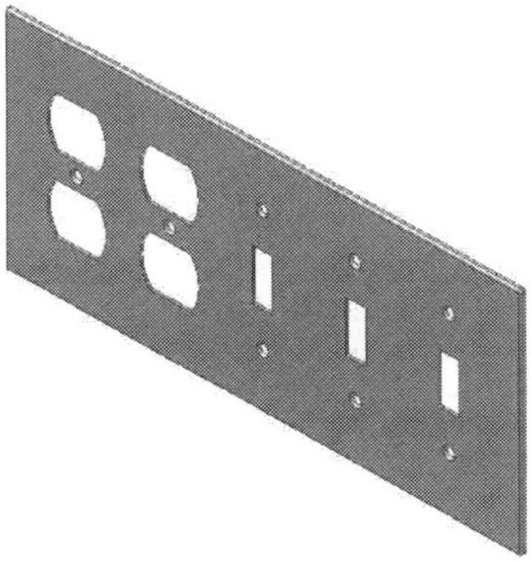

Figure 11–38

11. Save the model.

Task 3: Edit the iPart factory.

1. In the Model browser, note that the **Model States** node has been removed and a Table is listed. Expand **Table** and ensure that the table display is as shown in Figure 11–39, showing all the keys and not model names. If not, right-click on **Table** and select **List by Keys**. Expand **switches = 3**. The Model browser displays as shown in Figure 11–39.

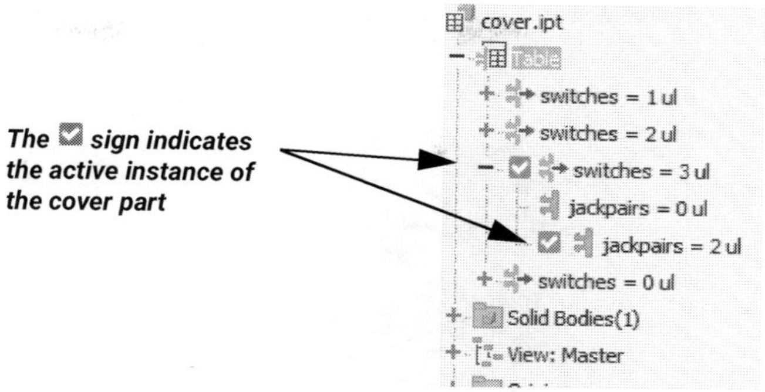

Figure 11–39

2. In the Model browser, expand **switches = 2 ul** and double-click on the **jackpairs = 1ul** node. The part displays as shown in Figure 11–40.

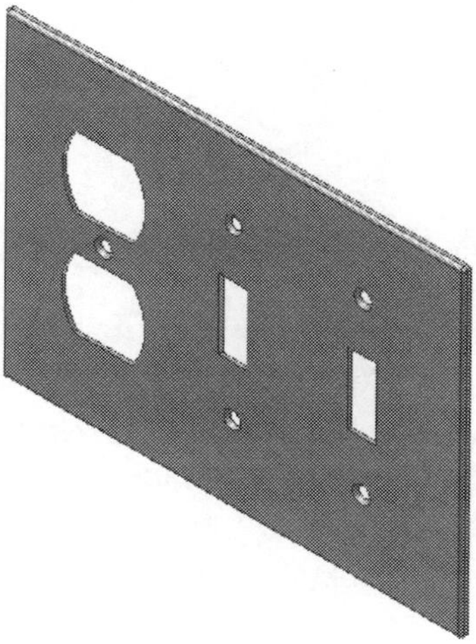

Figure 11–40

3. In the Model browser, right-click on **Table** and select **Edit Table**. The iPart Author dialog box opens.

4. Make row 3(cover-03) the default and click **OK**. The cover part displays as shown in Figure 11–41.

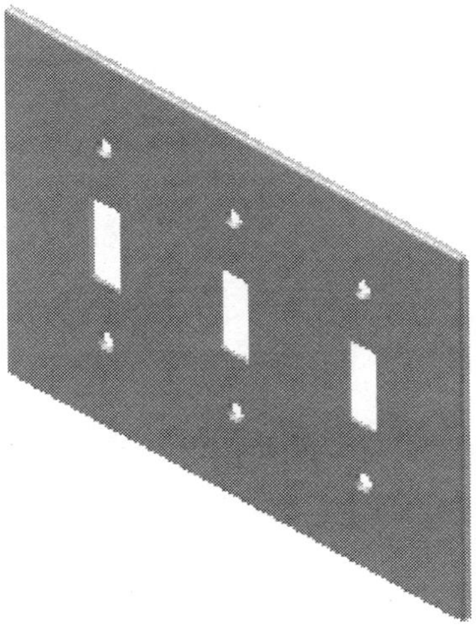

Figure 11–41

Task 4: Edit the iPart factory via spreadsheet.

In this task, you add a row to the iPart table using a spreadsheet. You also add a column to the table to calculate the overall length of various instances.

1. In the Model browser, right-click on **Table** and select **Edit via Spreadsheet**. Click **OK** to confirm that the changes made via the Spreadsheet will take effect after the Excel process is closed.
2. Edit the iPart table in Microsoft Excel to remove the "ul" dimension from columns C and D, as shown in Figure 11–42.

	A	B	C	D	E	F	G	H	I	J
1	Member<c	Part Number [F	switches<	jackpairs<	switch pattern	jack pattern	switch	switch holes	jacks	jack holes
2	cover-01	cover-01	1	3	Suppress	Compute	Compute	Compute	Compute	Compute
3	cover-02	cover-02	2	1	Compute	Suppress	Compute	Compute	Compute	Compute
4	cover-03	cover-03	3	0	Compute	Suppress	Compute	Compute	Suppress	Suppress
5	cover-04	cover-04	1	1	Suppress	Suppress	Compute	Compute	Compute	Compute
6	cover-05	cover-05	0	1	Suppress	Suppress	Suppress	Suppress	Compute	Compute
7	cover-06	cover-06	3	2	Compute	Compute	Compute	Compute	Compute	Compute

Figure 11–42

3. Add a row to the table with the values shown in Figure 11–43. The values are shown in row 8 of the table.

	A	B	C	D	E	F	G	H	I	J
1	Member<c	Part Number [F	switches<	jackpairs<	switch pattern	jack pattern	switch	switch holes	jacks	jack holes
2	cover-01	cover-01	1	3	Suppress	Compute	Compute	Compute	Compute	Compute
3	cover-02	cover-02	2	1	Compute	Suppress	Compute	Compute	Compute	Compute
4	cover-03	cover-03	3	0	Compute	Suppress	Compute	Compute	Suppress	Suppress
5	cover-04	cover-04	1	1	Suppress	Suppress	Compute	Compute	Compute	Compute
6	cover-05	cover-05	0	1	Suppress	Suppress	Suppress	Suppress	Compute	Compute
7	cover-06	cover-06	3	2	Compute	Compute	Compute	Compute	Compute	Compute
8	cover-07	cover-07	4	2	Compute	Compute	Compute	Compute	Compute	Compute

Figure 11–43

4. Save the Microsoft Excel file and close excel to return to cover.ipt.
5. Activate the new row. The cover part displays as shown in Figure 11–44.

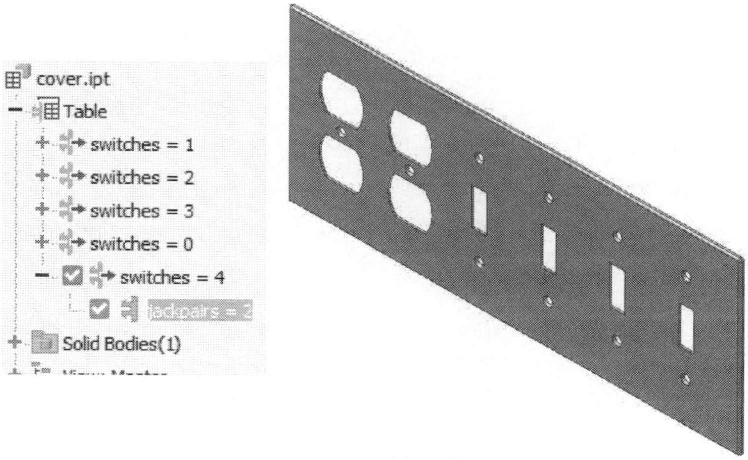

Figure 11–44

6. Open the iPart table using Microsoft Excel and add a column called **Overall Length** to the table.

7. Enter the formula below in each cell of the new column by replacing the "switches" and "jackpairs" with the corresponding C# and D#, as shown in Figure 11–45. Verify that none of the values under the switches and jackpairs columns contain "ul". The formula for the overall length is shown below. The table displays as shown in Figure 11–45.

   - 25.4+(45.72*(switches+jackpairs))

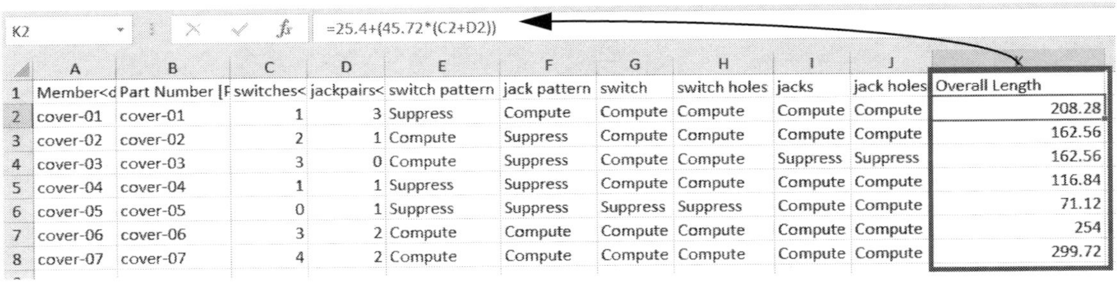

K2 =25.4+(45.72*(C2+D2))

	A	B	C	D	E	F	G	H	I	J	K
1	Member<d	Part Number [F	switches<	jackpairs<	switch pattern	jack pattern	switch	switch holes	jacks	jack holes	Overall Length
2	cover-01	cover-01	1	3	Suppress	Compute	Compute	Compute	Compute	Compute	208.28
3	cover-02	cover-02	2	1	Compute	Suppress	Compute	Compute	Compute	Compute	162.56
4	cover-03	cover-03	3	0	Compute	Suppress	Compute	Compute	Suppress	Suppress	162.56
5	cover-04	cover-04	1	1	Suppress	Suppress	Compute	Compute	Compute	Compute	116.84
6	cover-05	cover-05	0	1	Suppress	Suppress	Suppress	Suppress	Compute	Compute	71.12
7	cover-06	cover-06	3	2	Compute	Compute	Compute	Compute	Compute	Compute	254
8	cover-07	cover-07	4	2	Compute	Compute	Compute	Compute	Compute	Compute	299.72

Figure 11–45

8. Save and close the Excel file and return to the part.
9. Edit the table.
10. Right-click the heading of the *Overall Length* column and select **Key>3** to assign Key 3 to the overall length column.
11. Make row 3 default. Close the dialog box.
12. In the Model browser, expand **Table** (change the Table to list by keys, if required). The overall length for each instance displays in the Model browser, as shown in Figure 11–46.

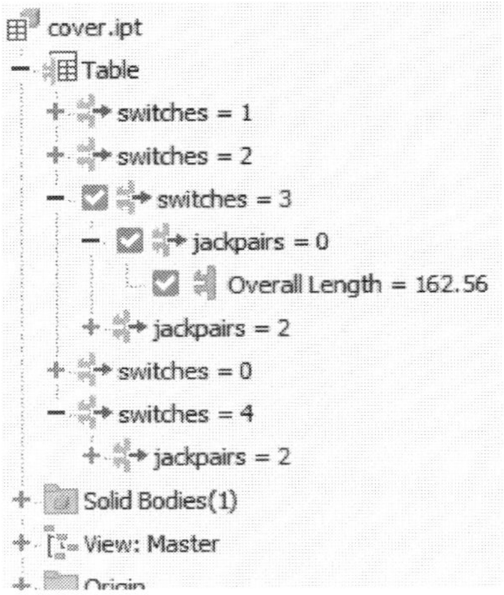

Figure 11–46

13. Save Copy As the part with the name **cover_iPart** and close the window. Do not save cover.ipt. This enables you to retain the original cover part.

Task 5: Place the cover_iPart.

1. Create a new assembly file using the **Standard (mm).iam** template.
2. Place one instance of the **box_cover.ipt** part in the assembly. Right-click and select **Place Grounded at Origin** to place the first file in the assembly at (0, 0, 0).
3. Place one instance of the **cover_iPart.ipt** Component. The dialog box opens, as shown in Figure 11–47, showing the default key parameter values you previously set.

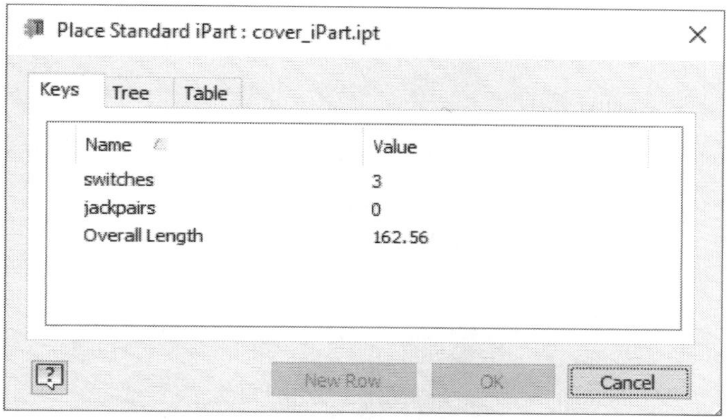

Figure 11–47

4. Select a point on the screen, right-click and select **OK**.
5. When you place the first standard iPart, Inventor creates a subdirectory in the same directory as the iPart factory. The subdirectory is created using the same name as the iPart factory. As you place iParts from the factory, each part is created and added to the folder. Open Windows Explorer and review the *cover_iPart* folder in the practice files directory.
6. Fully constrain the cover_iPart. The assembly displays as shown in Figure 11–48.

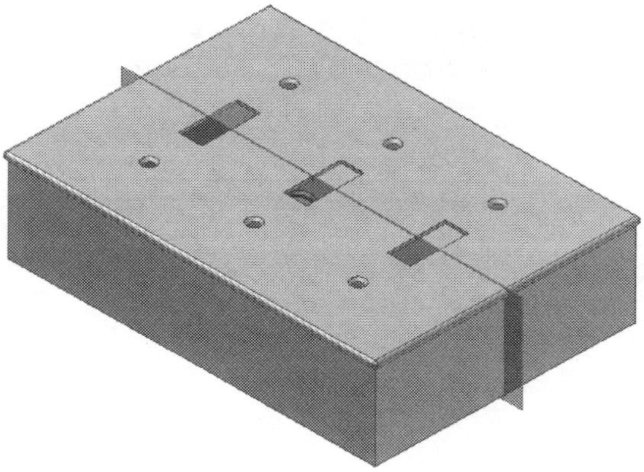

Figure 11–48

Task 6: Change the cover-03 component in the assembly.

1. In the Model browser, expand **cover-03**, right-click on **Table** and select **Change Component**. The Place Standard iPart dialog box opens.

   Note: *You can select iPart factory components to use in an assembly using any of the three tabs: Keys, Tree, and Table. In this situation, it was easier to review the table for the correct length and select the required configuration.*

2. The only other component that will fit with the current size of the box_cover is **cover-02**. Select the *Table* tab, select **cover-02** (row 2) and click **OK**. The assembly displays as shown in Figure 11–49.

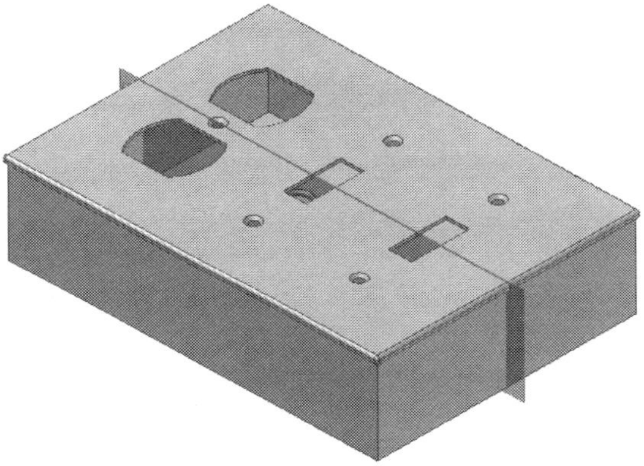

Figure 11–49

   To further automate this assembly, you can design it using Adaptivity or iAssemblies so that selecting a different cover_iPart causes an update in the cover_box.

3. Save the assembly as **assembly_iPart** and close the window.

End of practice

Practice 11c
iParts in Assemblies

Practice Objective

- Place an iPart into an assembly by modifying a custom parameter and editing the iPart to include a new configuration.

In this practice, you modify an iPart table in the hex-bolt part to create a configuration that can be used in an assembly with the plate and switch covers. The final assembly is shown in Figure 11–50.

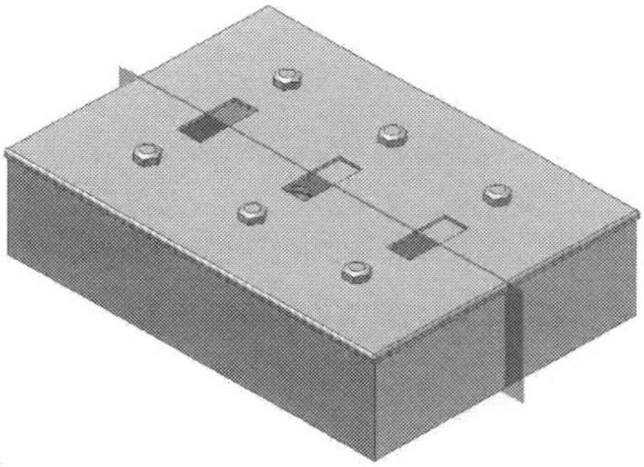

Figure 11–50

Task 1: Open an assembly file and measure the diameter of a hole.

1. Open **outlet.iam**. The model displays as shown in Figure 11–51.

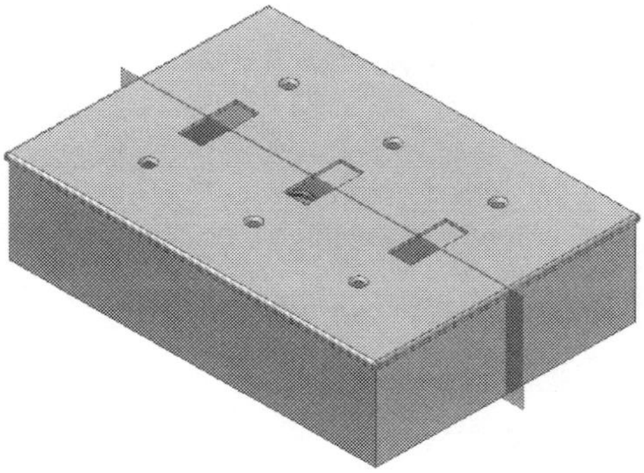

Figure 11–51

2. Measure the diameter of a hole in the cover component. This value will be used to create a new entry in the **hex_bolt_ipart_final.ipt** that fit the holes.

Task 2: Create a new entry for the hex_bolt to fit the assembly.

1. Open **hex_bolt_ipart_final.ipt**.
2. Add an entry of **M5x0.8** to the Designation with a diameter that can be used in the assembly. Verify that the configuration can be generated and opens.
3. Place **hex_bolt_ipart_final** into the outlet assembly using the configuration that you just created. The Place Custom iPart dialog box opens, enabling you to enter a custom value for the *grip_len* parameter. This parameter was set as a custom parameter in the iPart file. Click in the *Value* cell beside **grip_len** and enter **3** as the custom value, as shown in Figure 11–52. Select the appropriate **major_dia** for the hole.

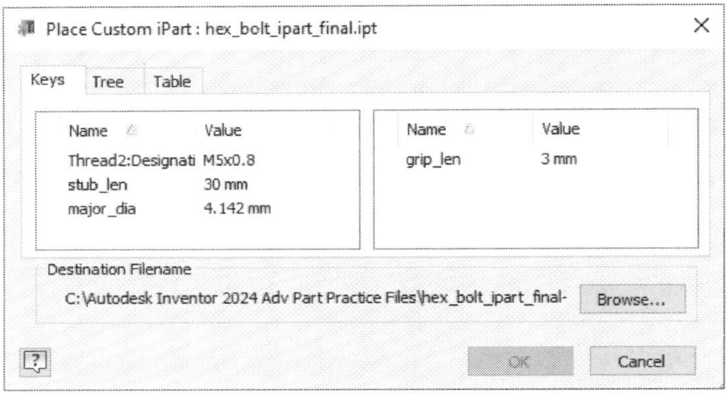

Figure 11–52

4. Assemble the remaining five bolts. The final assembly displays as shown in Figure 11–53.

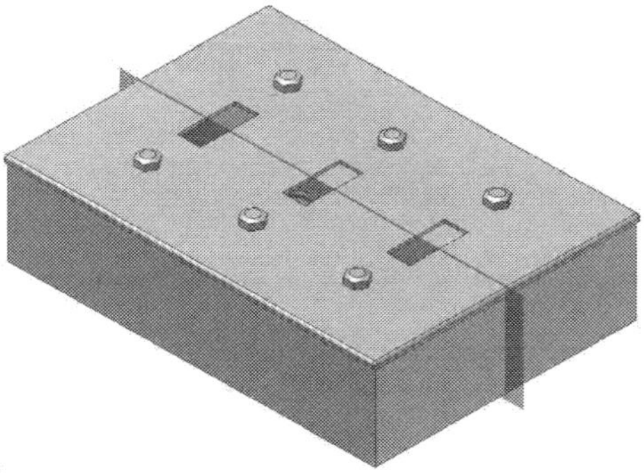

Figure 11–53

5. Save all files and close the window.

End of practice

Practice 11d
iPart Member Tables

Practice Objectives

- Replace the iPart factory instance that is displayed in a drawing view with another instance.
- Place an iPart member table in a drawing to display its factory members and their attributes.

In this practice, you will practice switching a view of an iPart to an alternate member. In addition, you will create a table of the iParts, as shown in Figure 11–54.

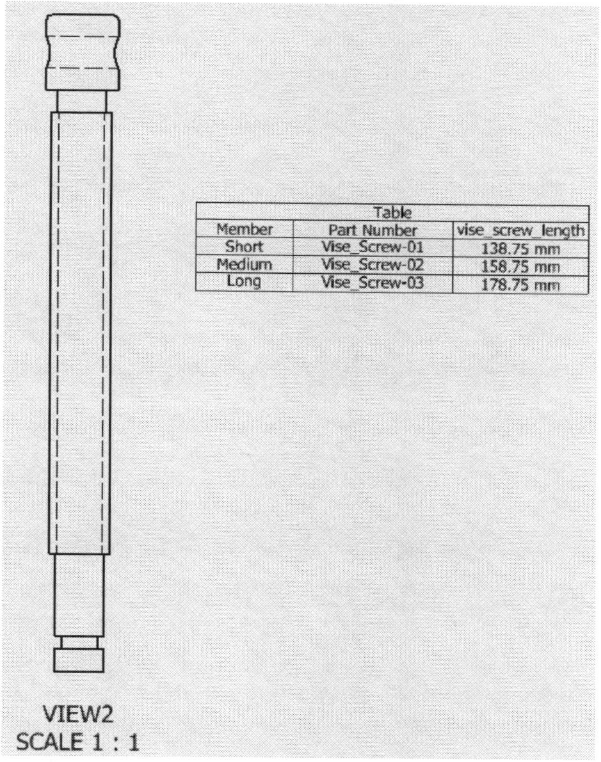

Table		
Member	Part Number	vise_screw_length
Short	Vise_Screw-01	138.75 mm
Medium	Vise_Screw-02	158.75 mm
Long	Vise_Screw-03	178.75 mm

Figure 11–54

Task 1: Switch the views to display an alternate iPart member.

1. Open **Vise_screw.dwg** from the *iPart Table* folder. The drawing displays as shown in Figure 11–55. The views reference **Short.ipt**, which is a member of Vise_Screw iPart. The three members of the iPart factory vary only in length.

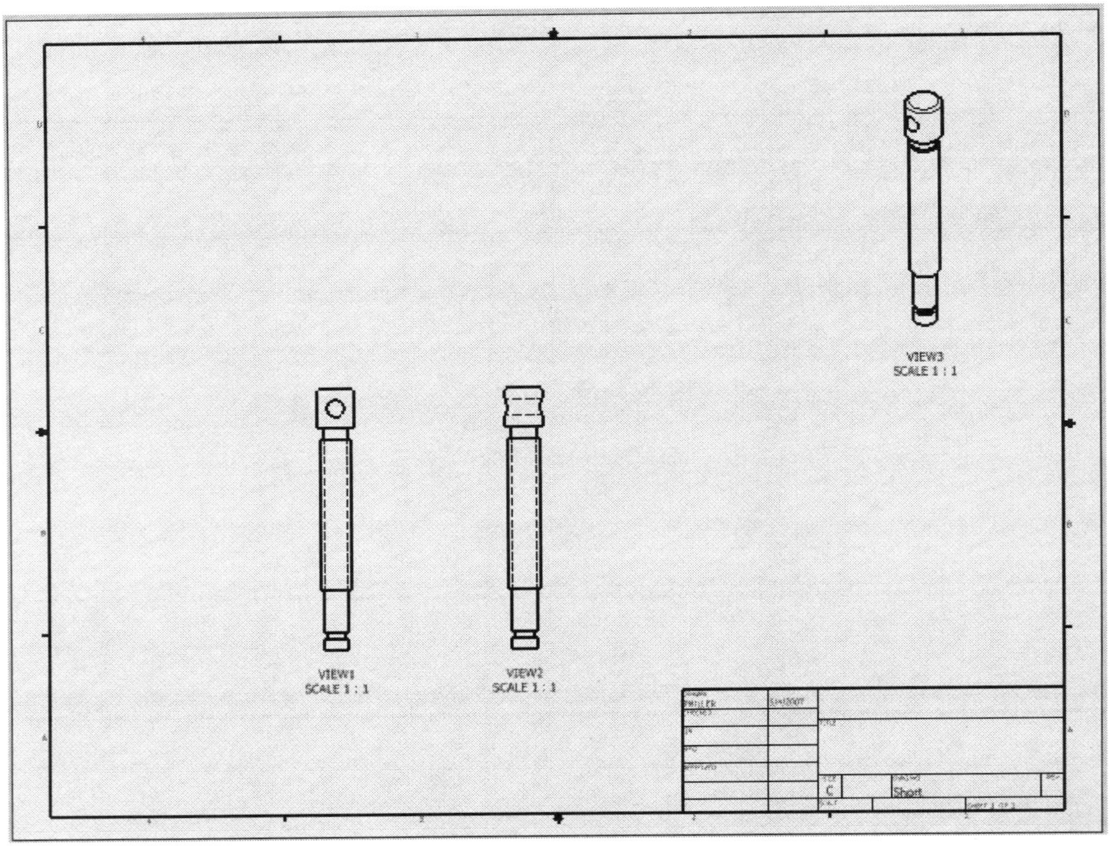

Figure 11–55

2. Right-click the isometric view (View 3, top right corner) and select **Edit View**. The Drawing View dialog box opens.

3. Select the *Model* tab. The *Member* area displays a list of the available iPart members you can display in the drawing views, as shown in Figure 11–56.

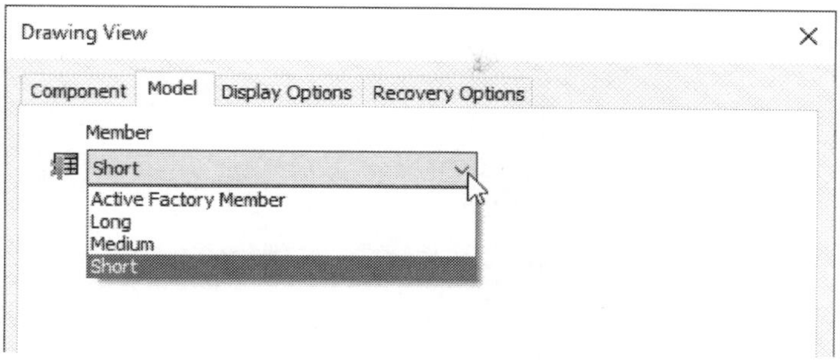

Figure 11–56

4. In the Member drop-down list, select **Long** and click **OK**. The views all update to display the newly selected iPart member.
5. Select the View labels and move them below their view.

Task 2: Create a table for the iPart.

1. In the *Annotate* tab>Table panel, click (General). The Table dialog box opens.
2. Select **VIEW2**. The Table dialog box updates as shown in Figure 11–57.

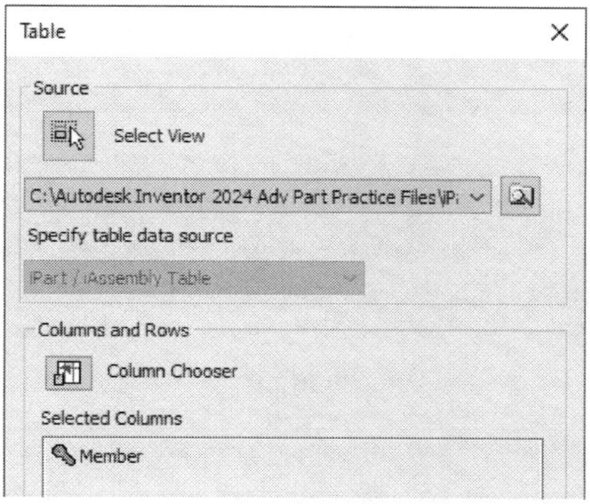

Figure 11–57

3. Click (Column Chooser). The Table Column Chooser dialog box opens.
4. With **Part Number** selected in the *Available Columns* area, click **Add** to move the column property to the *Selected Columns* area.

5. Add the **vise_screw_length** property to the *Selected Columns* area as well. The Table Column Chooser displays as shown in Figure 11–58.

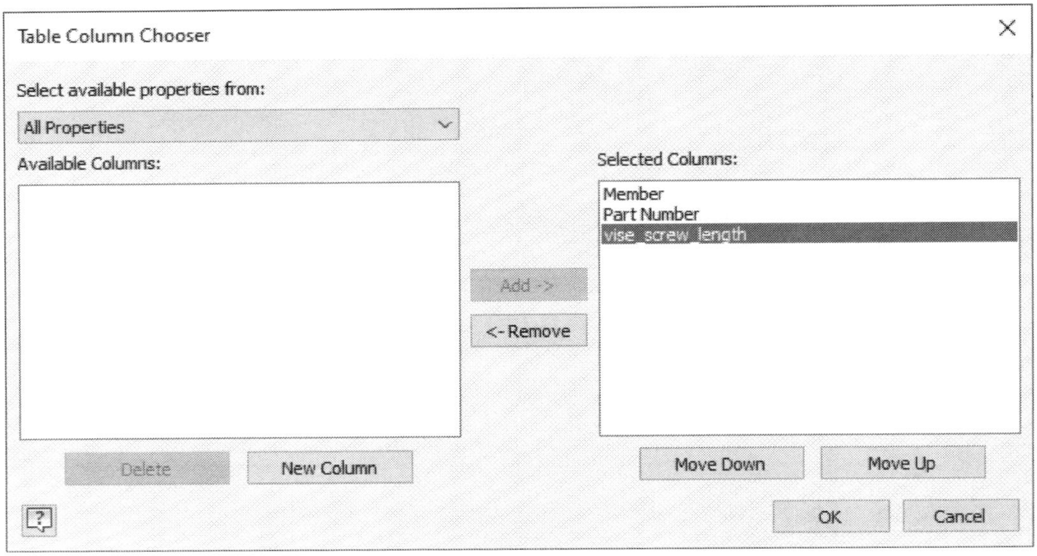

Figure 11–58

6. Click **OK** to close the Table Column Chooser dialog box.
7. Click **OK** to close the Table dialog box.
8. Move the cursor to the right of **VIEW2** and click to place it. The table populates with the columns and attributes of the iPart factory members and displays as shown in Figure 11–59.

Table		
Member	Part Number	vise_screw_length
Short	Vise_Screw-01	138.75 mm
Medium	Vise_Screw-02	158.75 mm
Long	Vise_Screw-03	178.75 mm

Figure 11–59

9. Save and close the drawing.

End of practice

Chapter Review Questions

1. Which of the following best describes the difference between a standard iPart Factory and a custom iPart Factory?
   a. Custom iPart Factories include parameters that enables you to enter values when the iPart file is opened. In standard iPart Factories, all values for all parameters are preset.
   b. Custom iPart Factories include parameters that enables you to enter values when the iPart is placed in an assembly. In standard iPart Factories, all values for all parameters are preset.
   c. Both custom and standard iPart Factories include parameters that enables you to enter values when the iPart Factory file is used.
   d. None of the above.

2. Which of the following tabs in the iPart Author should be accessed to add features to the table so that they can be suppressed in iPart members?
   a. Parameters
   b. Properties
   c. Suppression
   d. iFeatures
   e. iMates
   f. Other

3. Which of the following can be entered in an iPart table to suppress a feature in a part? (Select all that apply.)
   a. Suppress
   b. Compute
   c. S
   d. C
   e. 0
   f. 1
   g. Off
   h. On

Refer to Figure 11–60 when answering Questions 4. and 5. below:

	Member	Part Number	stub_len	major_dia	minor_dia	grip_len	Thread2: Designation
1	hex_bolt_ipart_final-01	hex_bolt_ipart_final-01	30 mm	4.974 mm	4.11 mm	2.4 mm	M5x0.8
2	hex_bolt_ipart_final-02	hex_bolt_ipart_final-02	30 mm	5.974 mm	4.891 mm	3 mm	M6x1
3	hex_bolt_ipart_final-03	hex_bolt_ipart_final-03	30 mm	9.968 mm	8.344 mm	4.5 mm	M10x1.5
4	hex_bolt_ipart_final-04	hex_bolt_ipart_final-04	30 mm	15.962 mm	13.797 mm	6 mm	M16x2
5	hex_bolt_ipart_final-05	hex_bolt-05	30 mm	4.142 mm	3.98 mm	3 mm	M5x0.8

Figure 11–60

4. How many Keys have been set in the iPart Factory shown in Figure 11–60?

a. 1

b. 3

c. 7

d. None

5. Which parameter in the iPart Factory shown in Figure 11–60 is custom?

a. Part Number

b. stub_len

c. grip_len

d. Thread2:Designation

e. None

6. The equations that are entered in Excel cannot be changed in the iPart Author dialog box.

a. True

b. False

7. Which command should be used when adding a new feature that is only required in the active factory member?

a. Edit Member Scope

b. Edit Factory Scope

8. Which of the following drawing **Annotation** options can you use to document the members of an iPart factory in a drawing?

    a. Parts List

    b. Revision Table

    c. General Table

    d. Hole Table

Command Summary

Button	Command	Location
N/A	**Change Component**	• **Context menu**: In Model browser with Table selected
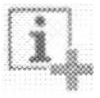	**Create iPart**	• **Ribbon:** *Manage* tab>Author panel
N/A	**Edit Factory Scope**	• **Ribbon:** *Manage* tab>Author panel
N/A	**Edit Member Scope**	• **Ribbon:** *Manage* tab>Author panel
N/A	**Edit Table**	• **Context menu**: In Model browser with Table selected
N/A	**Edit via Spreadsheet**	• **Context menu**: In Model browser with Table selected
	**Extract iFeature**	• **Ribbon:** *Manage* tab>Author panel
	**General (table)**	• **Ribbon:** *Annotate* tab>Table panel
	**Place (Component)**	• **Ribbon:** *Assemble* tab>Component panel

Chapter 12

Introduction to Freeform Modeling

A Freeform Modeling workflow enables you to create complex, visually appealing shapes without the complex work that is required when using a Parametric Modeling workflow.

Learning Objectives

- Create freeform geometry base shapes, faces, and converted geometry.
- Edit freeform base geometry by manipulating existing geometry or adding new elements to the base shape.

12.1 Creating Freeform Geometry

Using conventional modeling techniques to create organic, highly shaped, and visually appealing models is often difficult and time-consuming. Freeform modeling is an alternate modeling approach for these types of surfaces. It enables you to create shapes that can be manipulated directly, without needing to use parametric constraints. These tools can be combined with parametric tools, where required.

Creating Standard Freeform Shapes

To begin the modeling process you must create the shape that is going to form the base geometry. Select the type that provides you with the best overall shape for the required geometry. The available shapes are shown in Figure 12–1.

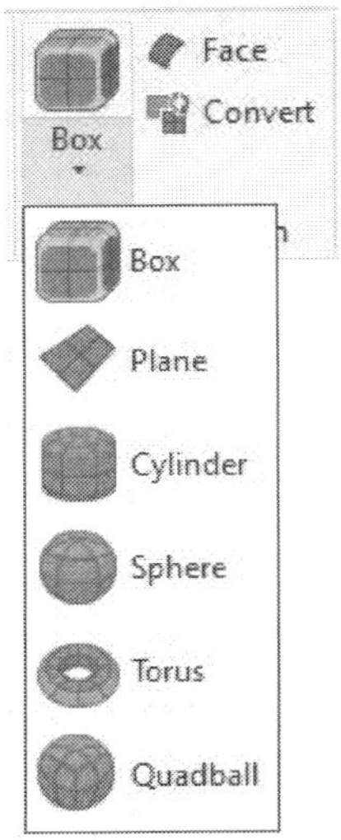

Figure 12–1

The overall procedure for creating the freeform shapes is similar and all of them use dialog boxes to define their geometry.

How To: Create a Base Freeform Shape

1. In the *3D Model* tab>Create Freeform panel, select the type of freeform shape to create. Figure 12–2 shows the dialog boxes that are used to create each shape type.

Figure 12–2

2. Select a work plane or planar face on which to place the freeform shape.
3. Select the center of the freeform shape.
   - Select the projected model origin to locate the shape at the origin center point.
   - If creating a freeform shape on an existing face, geometry points are projected from the model and can be selected as the center point reference.
   - If no reference point exists, you can also select anywhere on the plane.

4. Manipulate the size of the freeform shape using any of the following techniques:
   - Drag the arrowheads that display on the model. The active arrowhead is displayed in gold. Select any of the other arrowheads to activate them for dragging. Figure 12–3 shows the default shape and arrowheads available for a Box and Cylinder.
   - Enter values for the freeform size in its creation dialog box, as shown in Figure 12–3.

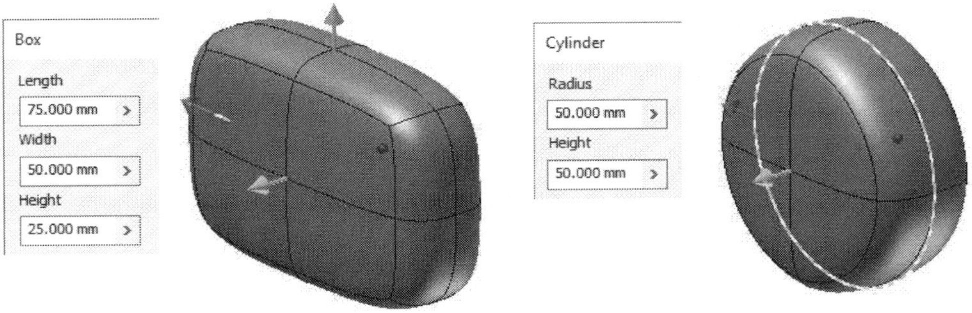

Figure 12–3

5. Enter the number of faces that are to be added in all directions, as shown in Figure 12–4.

The freeform shape is more refined when more faces are added. Note that using too many sides can create too much control.

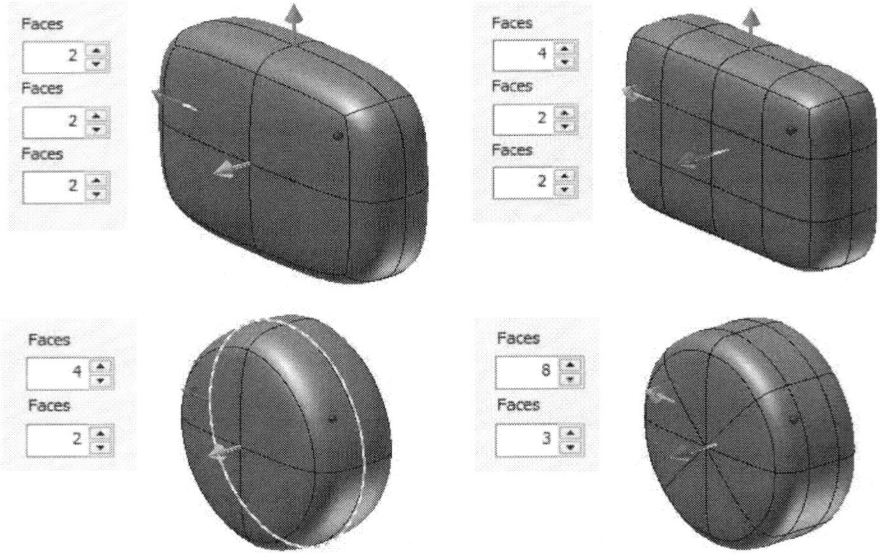

Figure 12–4

   - For a Sphere freeform, you enter the number of faces in the longitudinal and latitudinal directions. For the Quadball freeform, only a single face field is provided.

6. Assign symmetry by selecting the appropriate axis/directions in the creation dialog box.
   - Hover the cursor over each option to display the symmetry plane that will be used.
   - Once assigned, black edges display as a dashed yellow edge to identify the symmetry lines.

> **Hint: Defining Symmetry**
>
> If symmetry is required in the model after the base freeform shape is created, you can use (Symmetry) in the Symmetry panel to explicitly assign symmetry between selected faces.

7. For the Box and Cylinder freeform shapes, select the direction in which the freeform shape is to be created relative to the placement plane by clicking and .
8. Click **OK**.

Figure 12–5 shows the available shapes. Each have been manipulated using the options in their creation dialog boxes. The Model browser shown on the left is the same regardless of the type of shape created. It indicates that a **Form** feature has been added to the model.

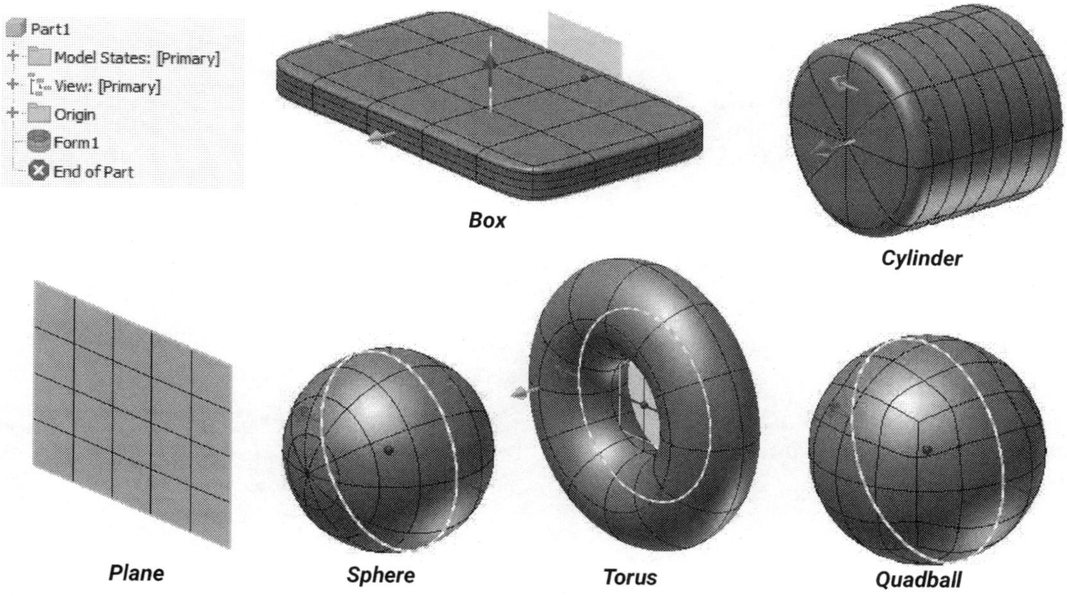

Figure 12–5

Note: *To create additional freeform shapes once in Freeform mode, select the geometry type from the Freeform tab>Create Freeform panel.*

Creating a Face Freeform

A **Face** freeform enables you to create an irregular, planar, or non-planar face as the base freeform geometry. It can also be used to close a gap.

How To: Create a Face

1. In *3D Model* tab>Create Freeform panel, select (Face). The Face dialog box opens as shown in Figure 12–6.

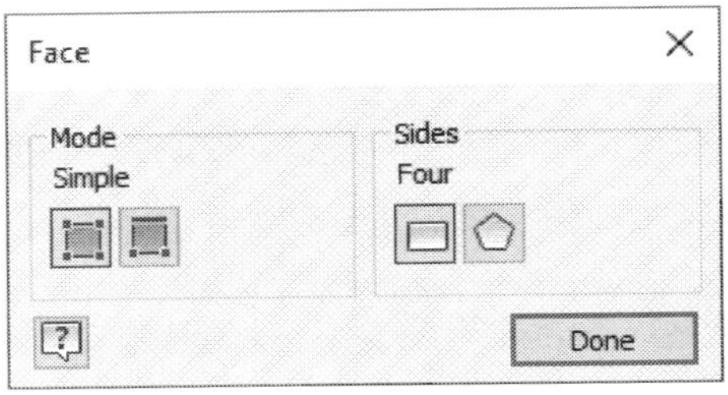

Figure 12–6

2. Set how the face is to be created using the options in the *Mode* area:
   - Select (Point) to select individual points to define the face.
   - Select (Edge) to select an edge and two points to define the face.
3. Define the number of corners in the face in the *Sides* area:
   - Select (Four) to create a face with four boundary points.
   - Select (Multiple) to create a face with any number of points. To complete the face, you must select the first selected point a second time.
4. Select points to define the face. By default, if points are selected individually without referencing existing entities, the points create a planar face.
5. Click **Done** to complete the face.

   Note: *To create additional faces once you are in Freeform mode, select (Face) from the Freeform tab>Create Freeform panel.*

Converting Geometry to a Freeform

Existing solid faces and surface 3D geometry can be converted into a freeform object using **Convert**. Once converted, it copies the shape of the original geometry and becomes freeform geometry, enabling you to use all of the editing tools to further manipulate the shape of the model.

How To: Convert to Freeform Geometry

1. In the *3D Model* tab>Create Freeform panel, click (Convert). The Convert to Freeform dialog box opens, as shown in Figure 12–7.

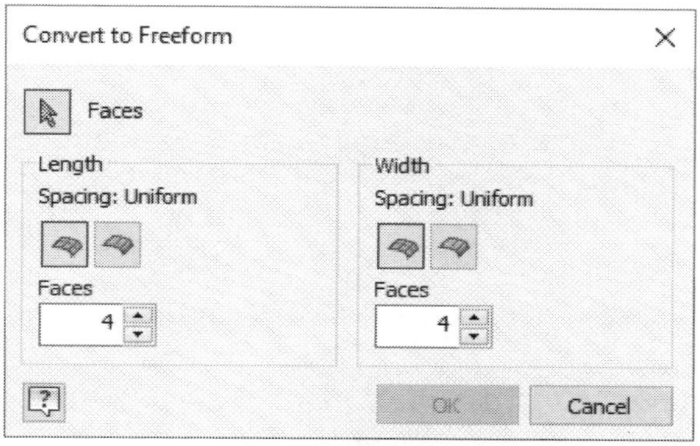

Figure 12–7

2. Select faces on a solid or surface model.
3. Define how the faces will be created in the converted freeform geometry for Length:
    - Select (Uniform) to create the converted geometry with uniform spacing and enter the number of faces to be created.
    - Select (Curvature) to create the converted geometry with curvature and enter a deviation value to define how it should be divided in the Length.

    Note: *If the resulting shape is different from the original, increase the number of faces to more closely match it.*

4. Set values in the *Width* area to define how the faces will be created in the converted freeform geometry. The available options are the same as in *Length*.
5. Click **OK** to complete the conversion to freeform geometry.

    Note: *To convert additional faces once in Freeform mode, select (Convert) from the Freeform tab>Create Freeform panel.*

The solid geometry shown in Figure 12–8 was selected for conversion. Once converted, you can use the editing tools in the freeform environment to manipulate the shape, as required.

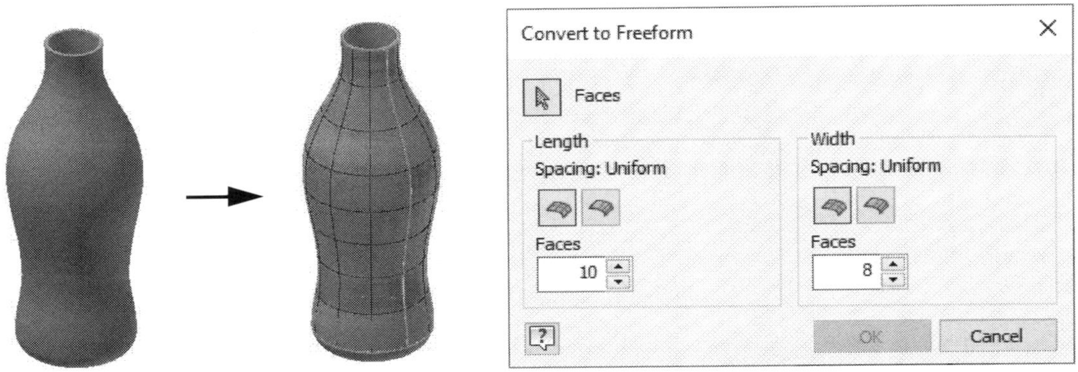

Figure 12–8

Once the freeform base solid, face, or converted freeform geometry has been created, the Freeform environment is active, as shown in Figure 12–9. All of the commands outside the *Freeform* tab are unavailable.

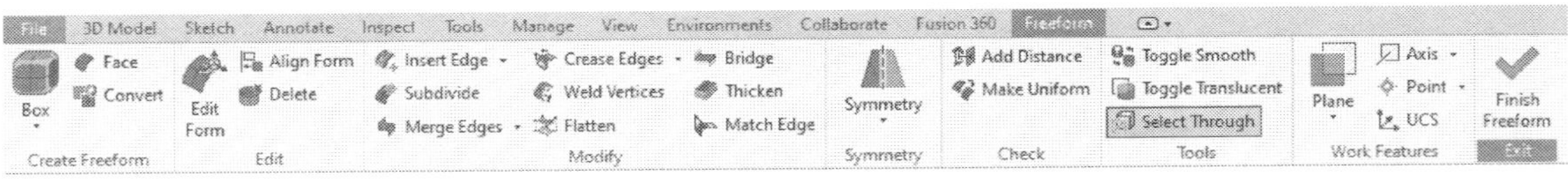

Figure 12–9

Hint: Toggle Smooth

Use the (Toggle Smooth) option located in the Tools panel to toggle the freeform from a smooth to blocky mode display type, as shown in Figure 12–10. When in Blocky mode, the performance is faster. The model is still smooth once it has been toggled off or when Freeform mode is off.

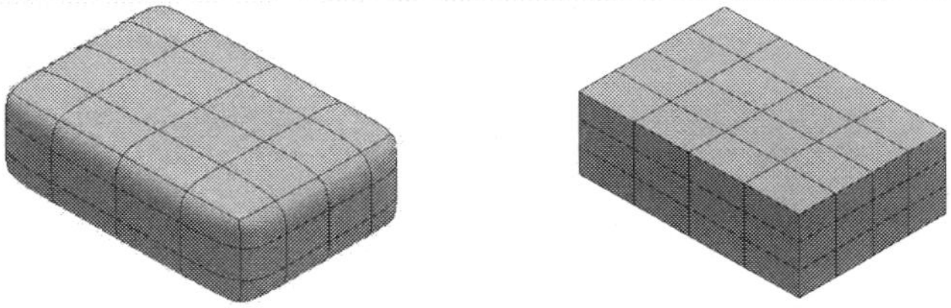

Box displayed in Smooth Mode ***Box displayed in Blocky Mode***

Figure 12–10

Deactivating and Activating Freeform Mode

To exit the Freeform environment, either:

- Click  (Finish Freeform) in the Exit panel.
- Right-click and select **Finish Freeform** in the marking menu.

Once closed, the ribbon updates and you can access the parametric modeling tools and the Model browser adds a **Form** feature to the list of features. To reactivate the Freeform environment, right-click on the **Form** feature node and select **Edit Freeform** (shown in Figure 12–11), or double-click on the **Form** node.

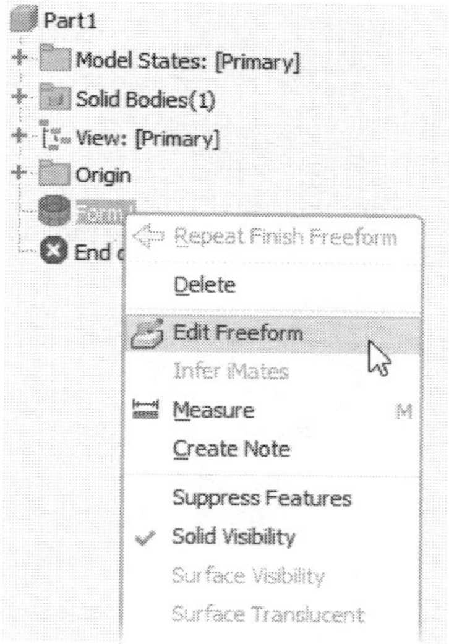

Figure 12–11

12.2 Editing Freeform Geometry

The *Freeform* tab provides editing tools (shown in Figure 12–12) that enable you to further refine the freeform geometry. As changes are made to the geometry they are all incorporated into the Form feature. Feature history is not recorded to account for each of the edits. While in the same session you can undo actions, but once the model has been saved the undo history is cleared.

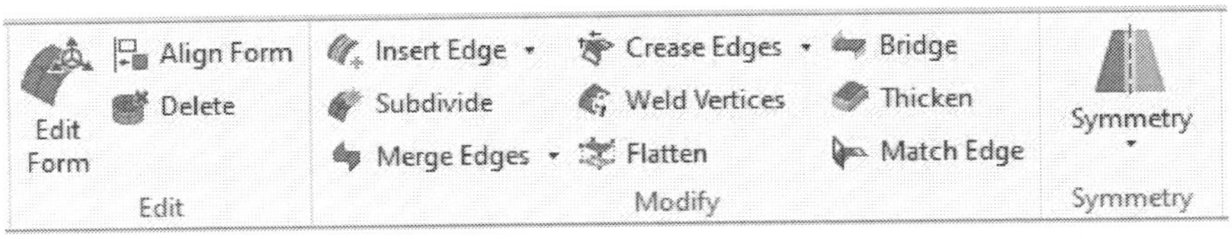

Figure 12–12

The mesh that overlays the geometry is used for editing. The overall mesh consists of points that are connected by edges and the enclosed edges are called *faces*. While editing you can select points, edges, faces, loops, or bodies for editing. The Box freeform shown in Figure 12–13 identifies what each of the entity types refer to in the model.

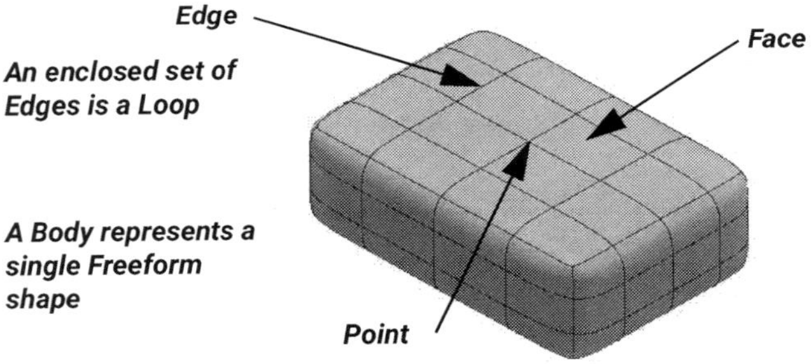

Figure 12–13

The following describes how you can use the available editing tools to manipulate the freeform shape.

Edit Form

The **Edit Form** command in the Freeform panel is the primary command that is used to manipulate geometry. It enables you to select point, edges, faces, bodies, or loops to access a manipulator triad that can be dragged to change the shape of the freeform.

How To: Edit Elements

1. In the *Freeform* tab>Edit panel, click  (Edit Form). The Edit Form dialog box opens, as shown in Figure 12–14.

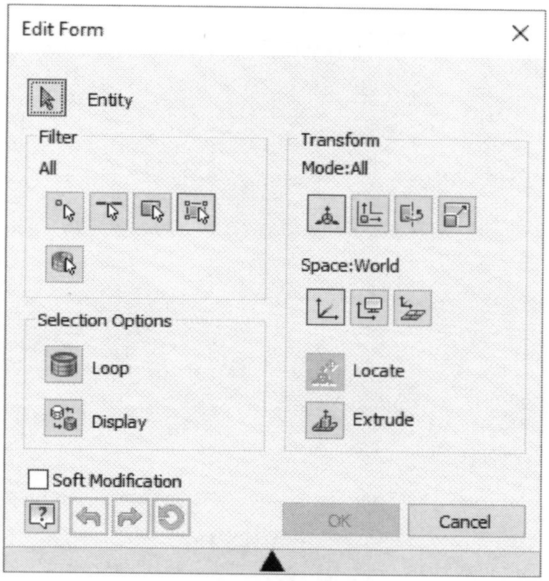

Figure 12–14

2. In the *Filter* area, select the element type that is to be manipulated. To select multiple entities for simultaneous manipulation, hold <Shift> while selecting. The options include the following:

Icon	Description
	When selected, only points are available for selection.
	When selected, only edges are available for selection. To automatically select the loop to which the selected edge belongs, click  (Loop), right-click and select **Select Loop**, or double-click on the edge.
	When selected, only faces are available for selection.
	When selected, points, edges, and faces are all available for selection.
	When selected, a body is available for selection.

Once an element has been selected, a manipulator triad displays, as shown in Figure 12–15. The triad center is placed on the selected reference entity that is displayed in blue.

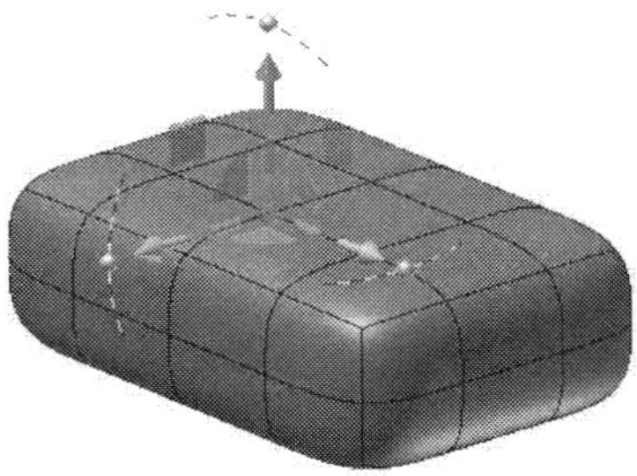

Manipulator triad on a point

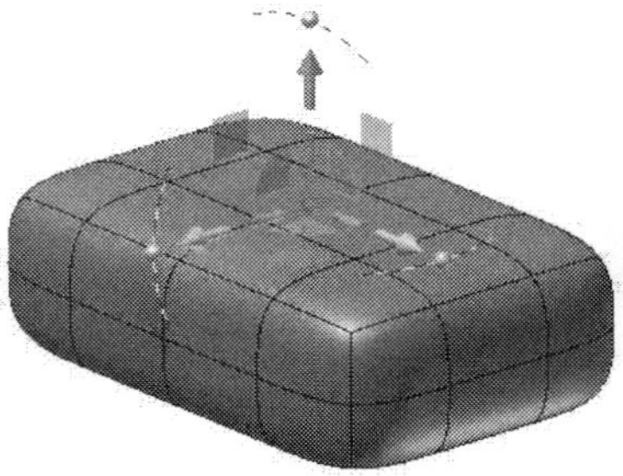

Manipulator triad on an edge

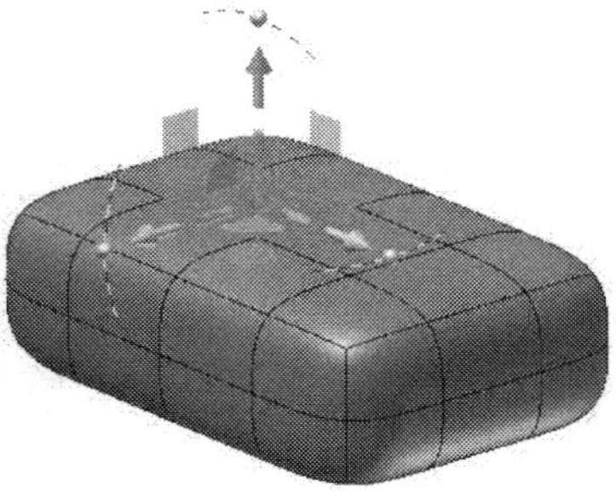

Manipulator triad on a face

Manipulator triad on a body

Manipulator triad on a loop

Figure 12–15

3. (Optional) Filter the manipulator types that are displayed on the triad using the *Mode* settings in the *Transform* area. The available options enable you to determine whether it displays controls for ( ) Translation, (Rotation), (Scaling) or all of the controls at the same time ( ), as shown in Figure 12–16. The default setting is to show all of the manipulator types.

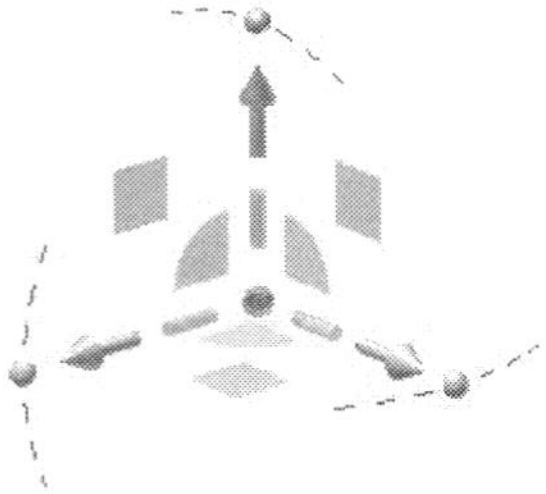

All types

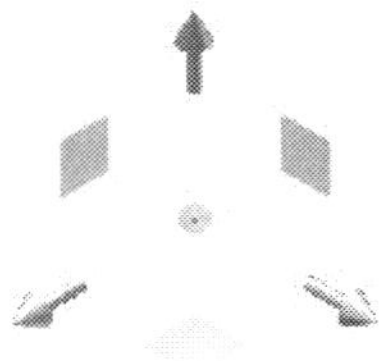

Translation

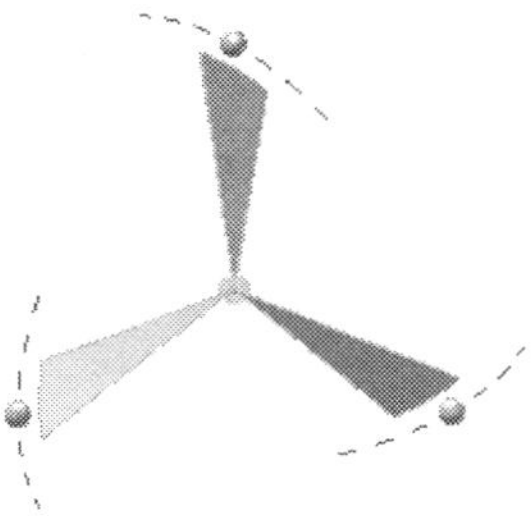

Rotation

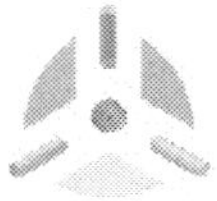

Scale

Figure 12–16

4. Define the *Space* setting in the *Transform* area. It enables you to control the orientation of the manipulator triad.

    - Use (World) to set the orientation with the model origin orientation.
    - Use (View) to set the orientation relative to the current view of the model.
    - Use (Local) to set the orientation relative to the selected object.

    ***Note:** Alternatively, you can select **Locate** in the mini-toolbar to reset the triad's location.*

5. (Optional) Click (Locate) to reset the location of the manipulator triad on the geometry (not the element). Once active, select a new edge or point to locate the triad.

    - Faces cannot be selected as new references.

6. Select the remaining options as required:

    - Click (Display) to toggle the model display from a smooth to blocky display style.
    - Click (Extrude) in the *Transform* area to set the editing tool to entirely extrude a selected face instead of transforming it. If used, additional edges, faces, and points are created, as shown in Figure 12–17.

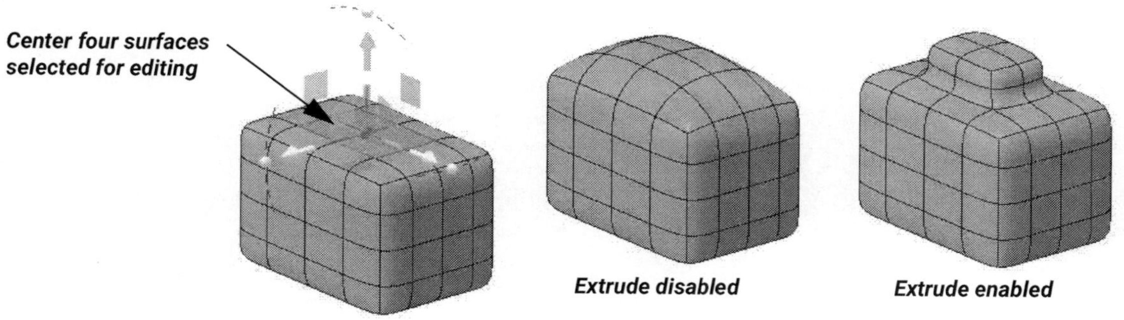

Figure 12–17

    - Click **Soft Modification** to enable the edit actions to have a more gradual impact on adjacent surfaces. When enabled, you are provided additional controls to define the *Type* and *Falloff* for the modification. **Soft Modification** is not available if the **Extrude** option is being used.
    - Click (Reset) to clear all of the edits.
    - Use (Undo) and (Redo) to clear or redo edits.

7. Reposition the geometry using either of the following:
    * Select the controls directly on the triad to reposition the geometry. Each control on the triad enables you to manipulate the geometry in a different way. Figure 12–18 shows the controls and describes their uses. You can only manipulate one triad at a time.

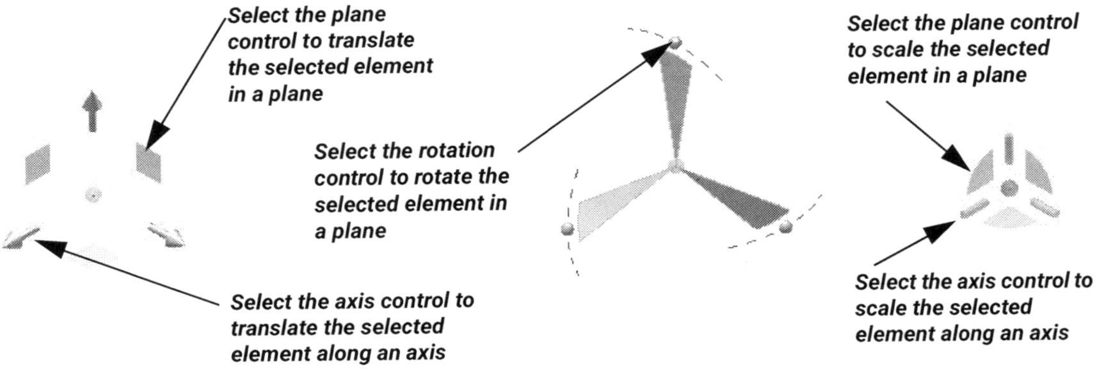

Figure 12–18

* Enter values in the mini-toolbar entry field. The available field depends on the active triad control. For example, if the Y axis is selected for translational movement, 

 is available in the mini-toolbar for entry. This value is not parametric and is not tied to the model.

8. Ensure the  (Entity) option is active and select a new element on the freeform model to make changes to it. Continue to select and edit elements, as required.
9. Click **OK** to complete the edit.

Figure 12–19 shows the final geometry after multiple edits were made to a Box and Cylinder freeform shape.

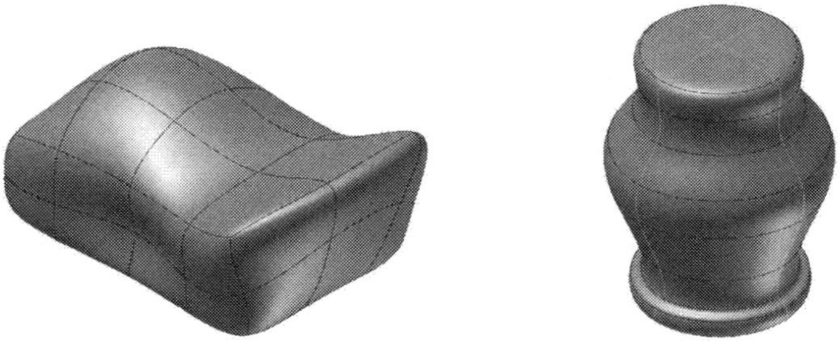

Box freeform ***Cylinder freeform***

Figure 12–19

Working with Edges

There are a number of different editing tools on the Modify panel that can be used to modify the edges of freeform geometry. These tools include the following:

- Insert Edge
- Merge Edges
- Unweld Edges
- Crease Edges
- Uncrease Edges
- Match Edge

Insert Edge

Additional edges can be added to a freeform using the **Insert Edge** command. By adding edges you can provide additional references (edges and the points at the end of edges) that can be modified to refine the shape of the model.

How To: Insert a New Edge(s)

1. In the *Freeform* tab>Modify panel, click  (Insert Edge). The Insert Edge dialog box is shown in Figure 12–20.

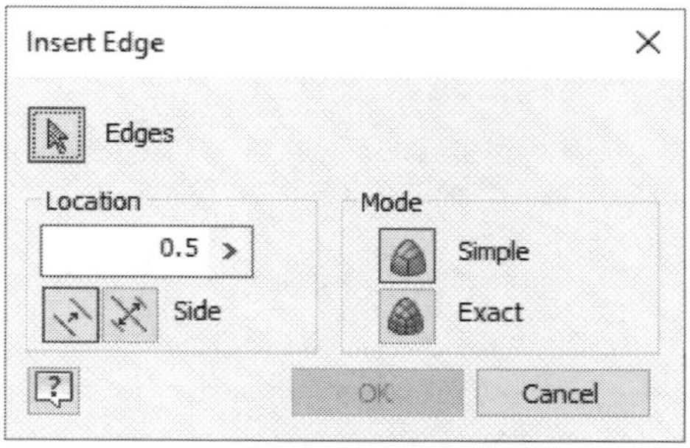

Figure 12–20

2. Click  (Edges) and select an existing edge in the model as a reference.
3. Enter an offset value in the *Location* area to define where the new edge is going to be located relative to the referenced edge. If the new edge is not created on the correct side, enter a negative value to switch sides.

4. Click (Single) or (Both) to create a new single edge at the defined location or to create edges on both sides of the reference, respectively.
5. Set the mode that should be used to define the final geometry once the edge is inserted.
    - Click (Simple Mode) to add the new edge exactly as specified. The shape might change to add the edge.
    - Click (Exact Mode), which while adding the new edge as specified, also adds any additional edges that might be required to enable the model to retain its current shape.
6. Click **OK** to insert the edge.

The images shown in Figure 12–21 show how two edges are inserted and how the overall shape changes when the edges are added.

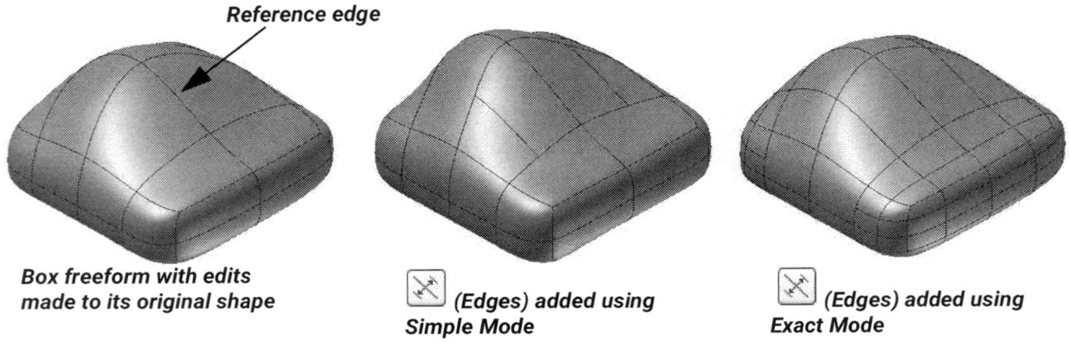

Figure 12–21

Merge Edges

Use the **Merge Edges** command to merge two open freeform edges. This can be used to blend between two freeform bodies or two edges in a single body, if the geometry permits.

How To: Merge Edges

1. In the *Freeform* tab>Modify panel, click (Merge Edges). The Merge Edge dialog box is shown in Figure 12–22.

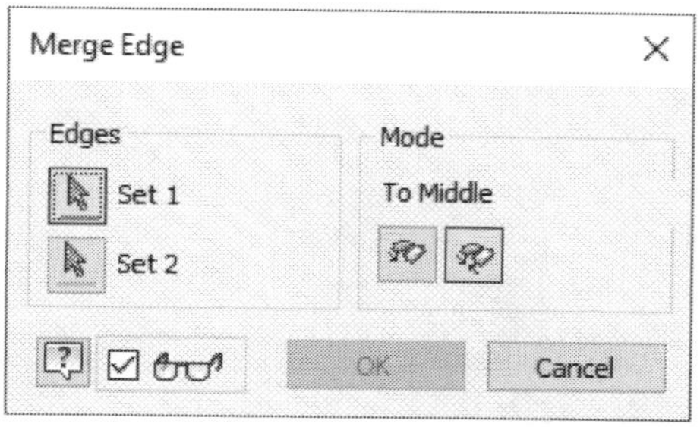

Figure 12–22

2. Click (Set 1) and select an existing edge in the model as a reference.
3. Click (Set 2), and select a second open edge to merge to. If the geometry can be created based on your selections, a preview of the geometry displays.
4. Set the *Mode* options to control the final geometry, as required.
    - Use (To Edge) to blend to the second edge selection.
    - Use (To Middle) to blend to the midpoint of the two edge selections.
5. Click **OK** to complete the merge.

Figure 12–23 shows how two edges are merged.

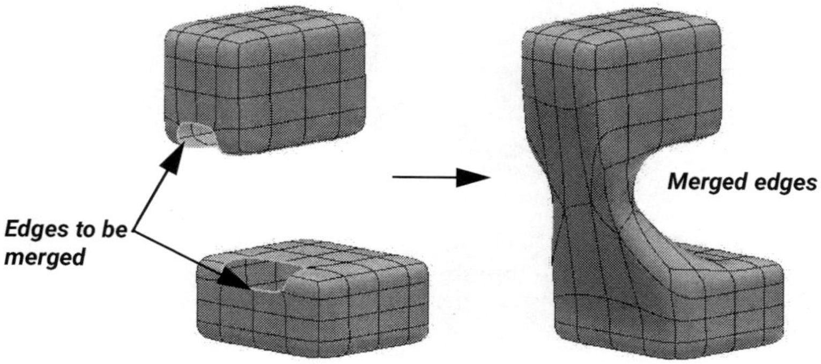

Figure 12–23

Unweld Edges

The  (Unweld Edges) option in the Modify panel enables you to select edges to separate them from the remaining freeform body. To unweld, simply select the edge or loop of edges and click **OK**. Once unwelded, multiple bodies are created that can be moved independently, as shown in Figure 12–24.

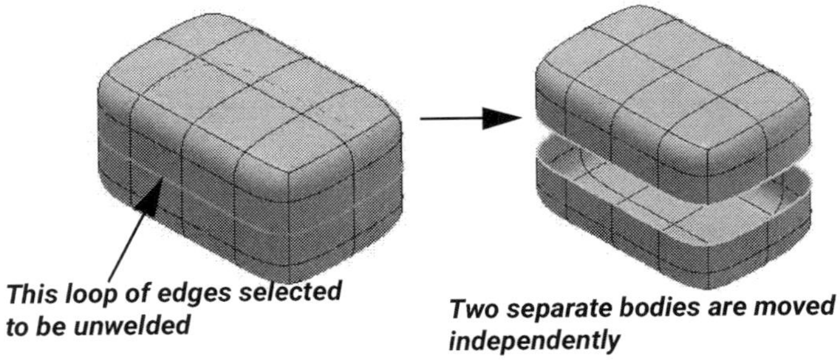

Figure 12–24

Crease/Uncrease Edges

The  (Crease Edges) option in the Modify panel enables you to create non-curvature continuous edges on a freeform body by selecting and moving an edge. In Figure 12–25, the two edges were set to allow creasing. Once set, they display as gray. To crease an edge, simply select the edge or loop of edges and click **OK**.

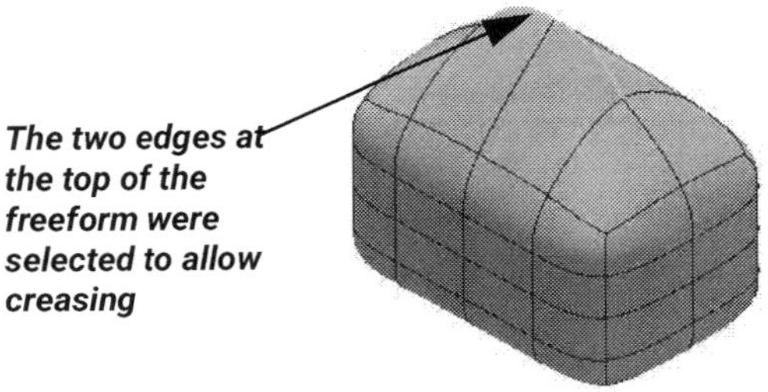

Figure 12–25

To clear the crease setting, click  (Uncrease Edges) and select the edges to be cleared. The crease is immediately removed and the geometry updates.

Match Edge

When designing a freeform shape, there might be a design requirement that it must match an existing solid edge or a defined sketch. To match the edge of a freeform with a geometrically constrained edge or sketch, you can use the **Match Edge** command.

How To: Match a Freeform Edge with a Geometrically Constrained Edge

1. Click (Match Edge) in the Modify panel to open the Match Edge dialog box, shown in Figure 12–26.

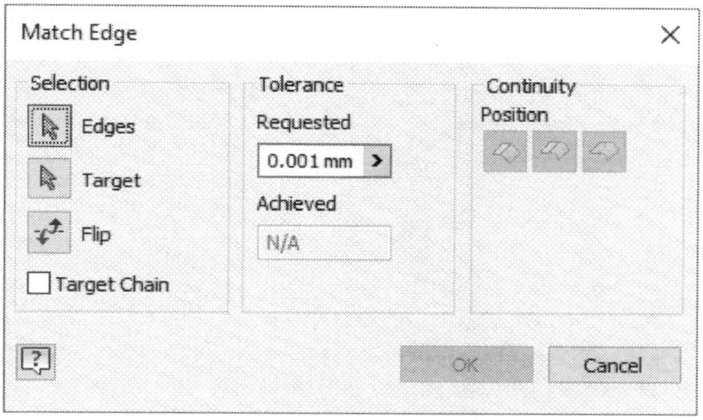

Figure 12–26

2. Click (Edges) and select the freeform edge(s) that are to be modified to match the existing constrained geometry. If you are matching a fully enclosed entity, the freeform references must also be fully enclosed.
3. Click (Target) and select the existing edge/sketch in the model to match.
4. (Optional) Click (Flip), as required, to flip the direction of the match once the references are selected.
5. In the *Tolerance* area, enter the tolerance to attempt to meet. The freeform shape attempts to create a match with this value. If it cannot, you are prompted with an *Achieved* value. The *Requested* value must be less than the *Achieved* value for the match to be successful.
6. (Optional) If the match edge is a NURB surface edge, you have access to set continuity options to further define the shape. The options enable you to maintain G0, G1, or G2 continuity with the reference.
7. Click **OK** to match the edges.

The images in Figure 12–27 represent a cylinder freeform in which three of its edges were matched to three parametric sketches.

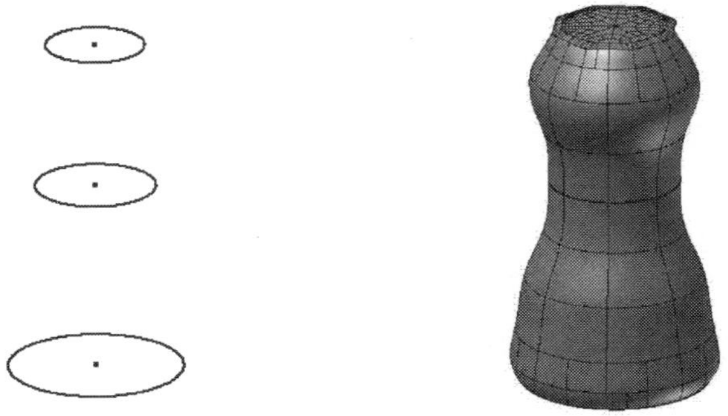

Three parametric sketches that define the top, middle, and bottom sizes of the model

Match Edge used to match the edges at the top, middle, and bottom of the freeform with the parametric sketches

Figure 12–27

If the referenced edge that was used for matching changes, you can rematch the edge by expanding the Matches folder in the Form feature, right-clicking, and selecting Rematch, as shown in Figure 12–28. **Rematch** can be used, when required, to ensure that the match is maintained. This behavior does not happen automatically.

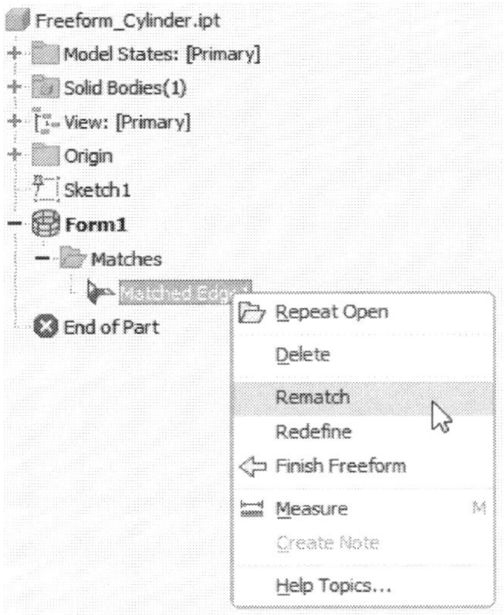

Figure 12–28

Working with Faces

The faces that make up a freeform mesh can also be manipulated to change the shape of freeform geometry. The **Subdivide** and **Bridge** commands enable you to manipulate a face.

Subdivide

The **Subdivide** command enables you to add additional faces to the model. The additional faces can help to refine the shape of the model.

How To: Subdivide an Existing Face

1. In the Modify panel, click (Subdivide) to open the Subdivide dialog box, shown in Figure 12–29.

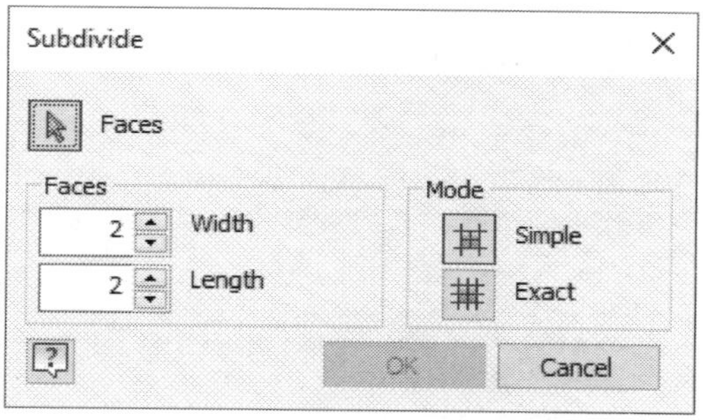

Figure 12–29

2. Click (Faces) and select an existing face in the model as a reference. Hold <Shift> to select multiple faces for editing.
3. In the *Faces* area, enter values to define how the selected face is going to be subdivided.
4. Set the mode to be used to define the final geometry once the face is subdivided:
   - Click (Simple mode) to subdivide exactly as specified. The shape may change to add faces.
   - Click (Exact mode), which while adding the face as specified, also adds any additional faces that might be required to enable the model to retain its current shape.
5. Click **OK** to insert the face(s).

The images in Figure 12–30 show how nine faces were added (**3** in *Length* and **3** in *Width*) on a reference face using both the **Simple** and **Exact** mode options.

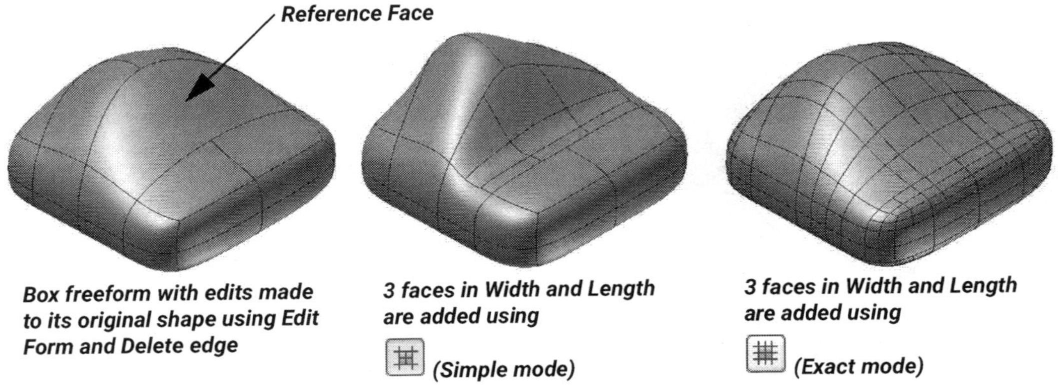

Figure 12–30

Bridge

When using multiple freeform bodies in a model, you can use the **Bridge** command to connect the space between the two shapes. Bridge can also be used to join multiple gaps in a single body.

How To: Create Bridge Geometry Between Existing Faces or Edges

1. Click (Bridge) in the Modify panel. The Bridge dialog box opens as shown in Figure 12–31.

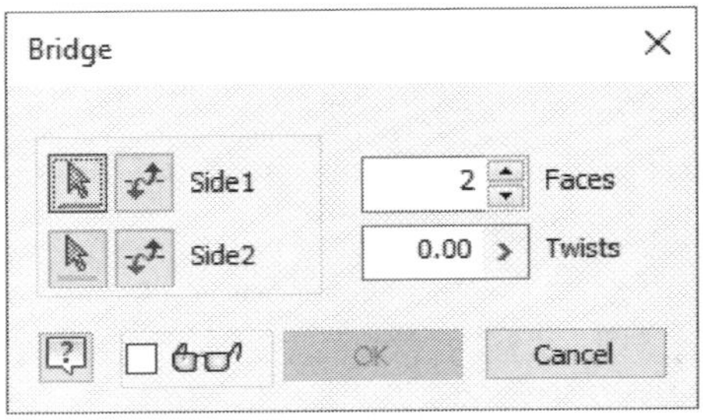

Figure 12–31

2. Click (Side1) and select existing faces or edges on the freeform model where the bridge geometry is going to begin.

3. Click  (Side2) and select existing freeform faces or edges to which the bridge geometry is going to merge.

   Note: *Multiple faces can be selected for both the Side1 and Side2 references.*

4. Enter a value in the *Faces* area to define the number of faces that the new bridge geometry is going to be subdivided into.
5. (Optional) Enter a value in the *Twists* area to define how many complete rotations there are going to be on the bridge geometry.
6. Click **OK** to create the bridge geometry.

The images in Figure 12–32 show how two separate cylindrical freeform shapes are bridged by new geometry and how it can be used in a single body to create a hole.

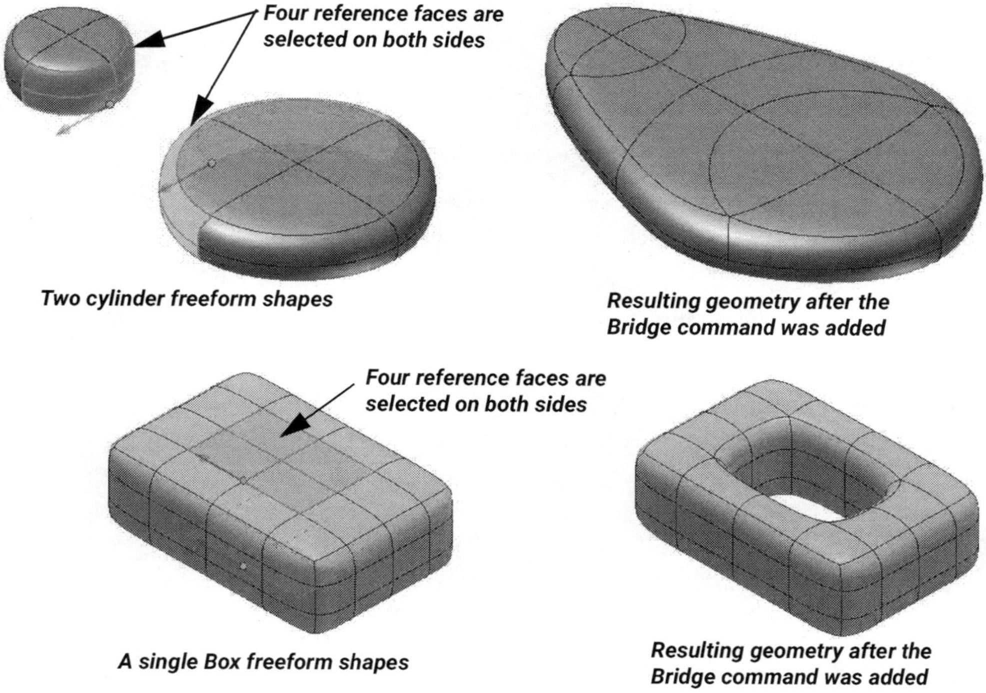

Figure 12–32

Working with Points

The points that define the edges and faces can also be modified using tools on the Modify panel. These tools include the following:

- Insert Point
- Weld Vertices
- Flatten

Insert Point

Similar to inserting edges, points can be inserted using a similar workflow. An edge is defined when multiple points are inserted, which also defines a new face.

How To: Insert Points

1. In the Modify panel, click (Insert Point).
   - By default, the **Insert Point** command is located in the **Insert Edge** drop-down list. Subsequently, the most recent command used is displayed.
2. Select points on edges to place new points.
3. Select the *Mode* to define the shape of the new points and subsequent edges. The **Simple** and **Exact** options are the same as for when inserting edges.
4. Click **OK**.

The new point breaks the edge and creates multiple edges to fully define any adjacent faces.

Weld Vertices

The **Weld Vertices** option enables you to combine two selected vertices. Consider using this option to combine vertices once edges are merged to refine the faces that are generated.

How To: Weld Vertices

1. In the Modify panel, click (Weld Vertices).
2. Select two points to weld.
3. Select one of the following *Weld Mode* options to customize the geometry that results from welding the vertices.
   - Select (Vertex to Vertex) to merge two selected vertices. The first vertex is moved to the position of the second vertex.

- Select (Vertex to Midpoint) to move two selected vertices to the midpoint between the selections.
- Select (Weld to Tolerance) to combine multiple vertices within a specified tolerance. Select the vertices and then set the *Tolerance* value.

4. Click **OK** to weld the points.

Flatten

The **Flatten** option enables you to select multiple vertices and force them to flatten to a single plane. You must select more than three vertices to be able to flatten.

How To: Flatten Points

1. In the Modify panel, click (Flatten).
2. Select all the points to flatten.
3. In the *Direction* area, select an option to define how the points will flatten. The options include:
   - Use (Auto Fit) to move points to a single plane that passes through the vertices.
   - Use (Plane) to move points through a specified plane.
   - Use (Parallel Plane) to move points parallel to a selected plane.
4. Click **OK** to flatten the selected points.

Figure 12–33 shows how the **Flatten** option was used to flatten multiple vertices so that they are parallel with a selected plane.

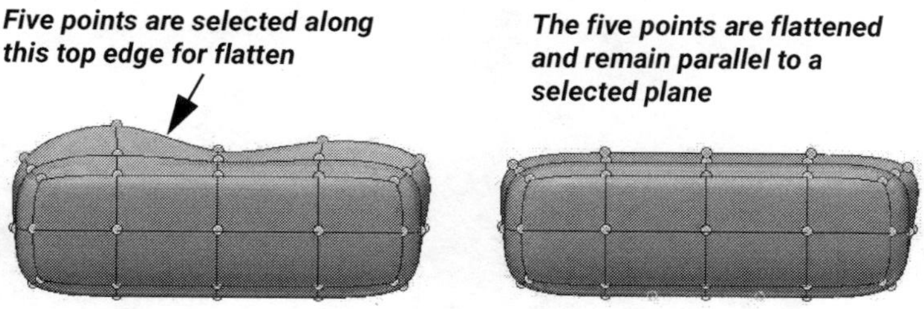

Figure 12–33

Thickening Freeform Geometry

The **Thicken** command can be used with freeform geometry to:

- Convert an open surface to a solid with soft or sharp edges.
- Create an offset surface.
- Create an interior or exterior wall if the selected freeform body is solid.

How To: Thicken a Freeform Body

1. In the Modify panel, click (Thicken)
2. In the *Type* area, select how the thickened geometry is capped. This is only available when thickening an open body. The possible options include:
    - Use (Sharp) to create a flat face to bridge the offset.
    - Use (Soft) to create a new face that is rounded to bridge the offset.
    - Use (No Edges) to leave an open gap between the thickened geometry.
3. Enter a thickness value.
4. Select the direction of the offset. The options include normal to the selected body or in a selected direction. To define a direction, you must select an axis.
5. Click **OK** to thicken the selected body.

Figure 12–34 shows geometry that has been thickened when the selected body is open.

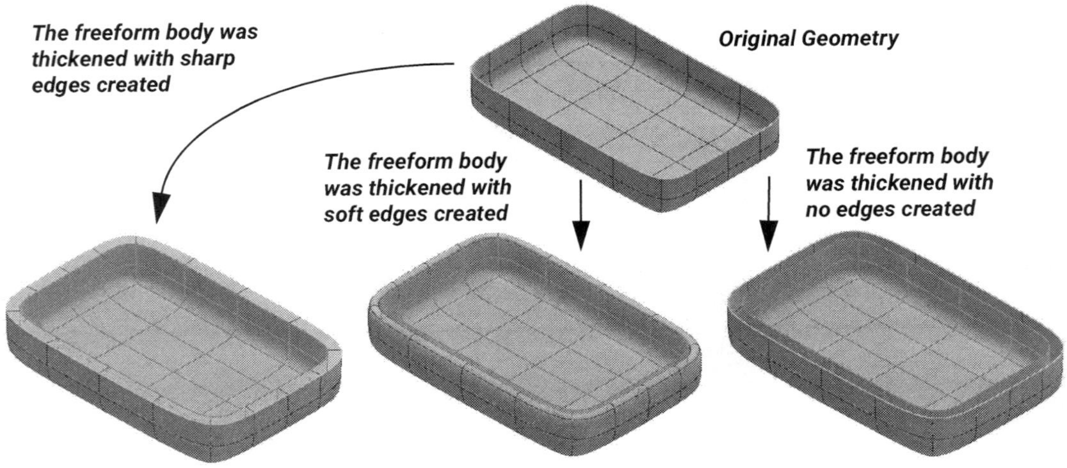

Figure 12–34

Hint: Reviewing Internal Geometry

When the **Thicken** command is used, geometry can be created internally. Click (Toggle Translucent) to better visualize the internal geometry.

Controlling Symmetry

When the base freeform shape was created, symmetry could have been defined for the overall geometry. The **Symmetry** option enables you to define internal symmetry between selected faces on the freeform body after the base freeform creation.

How To: Apply Symmetry Between Faces

1. In the Symmetry panel, click (Symmetry). The Symmetry dialog box is shown in Figure 12–35.

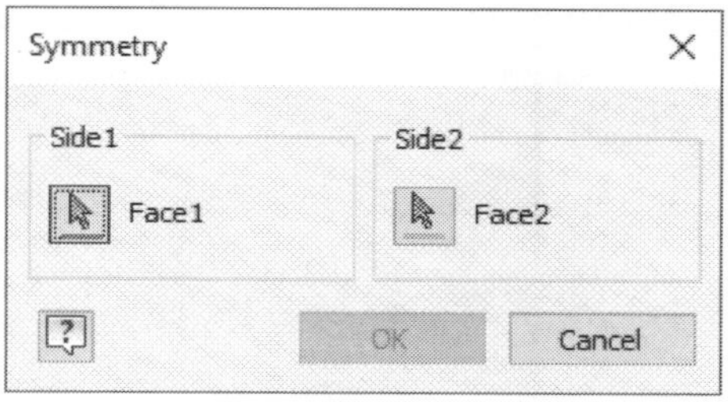

Figure 12–35

2. Click (Face1) and select the face on side 1 as the reference for symmetry. The reference displays in blue on the model.
3. Click (Face2) and select the face that is to be symmetric on the other side of the model. The reference displays in green on the model.
4. Click **OK** to assign symmetry.

   Note: *If symmetry cannot be assigned based on the references that are selected, you are prompted to retry making selections.*

The two images shown at the top of Figure 12–36 indicate how changes are made to the base freeform to which symmetry has not been assigned. The two images shown at the bottom indicate how two faces that have been assigned to be symmetric are updated when a change is made to one of the faces.

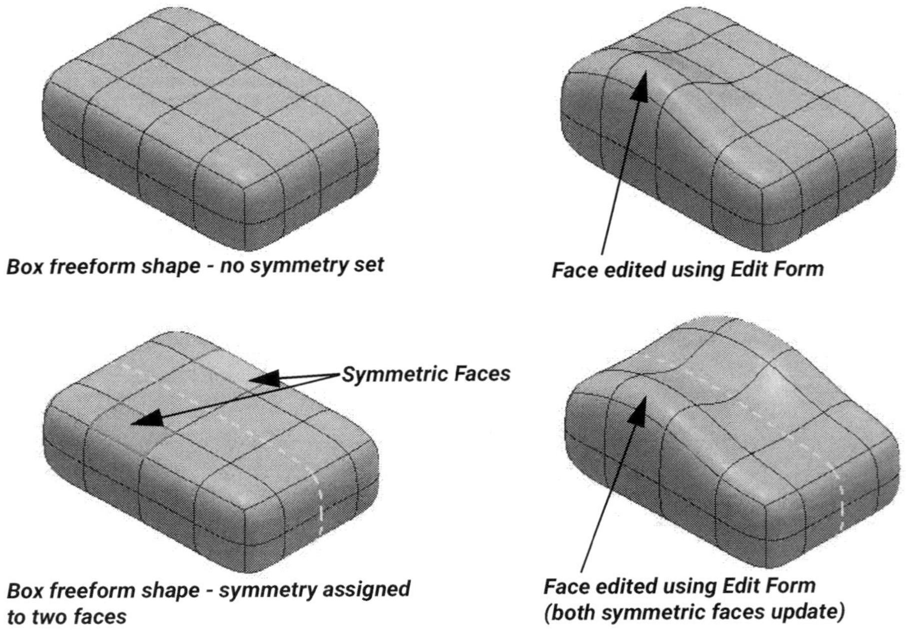

Figure 12–36

- Symmetry that has been explicitly assigned between faces or that was assigned when the base freeform geometry was created, can be cleared by clicking (Clear Symmetry) in the expanded Symmetry drop-down list.

Mirroring Freeform Geometry

The (Mirror) command on the expanded Symmetry drop-down list enables you to mirror an entire freeform body about a selected plane.

How To: Complete the Mirror

1. In the Symmetry panel, click (Mirror).
2. Click (Body) and select the body that is to be mirrored. Only bodies can be selected for mirroring.

3. Click (Mirror Plane) and select a plane to mirror about.
4. If the mirrored body has an open edge and is to be merged with the original body, click **Weld** and enter a tolerance value. Based on the tolerance value, the two bodies will be merged, if possible.
5. Click **OK** to complete the mirror.

Hint: Repositioning a Freeform Body

When modeling or mirroring the location of the body relative to a required plane, the body's location may not be as required. To move the body, use either of the following commands:

- Use the **Edit Form** command. Select the entire body and use the translation arrows to move it.
- Use the **Align Form** command. With (Vertex) enabled select a vertex on the freeform body and then select a target plane to align to. If the geometry has defined symmetry, the (Symmetry Plane) option is used by default and you can align the symmetry plane to a target plane.

Deleting Entities

The mesh layout of a freeform shape may include too many points, edges, and faces. The **Delete** option enables you to delete points, edges, loops of edges, faces, and entire bodies. To open the Delete dialog box (shown in Figure 12–37), click (Delete) in the Edit panel.

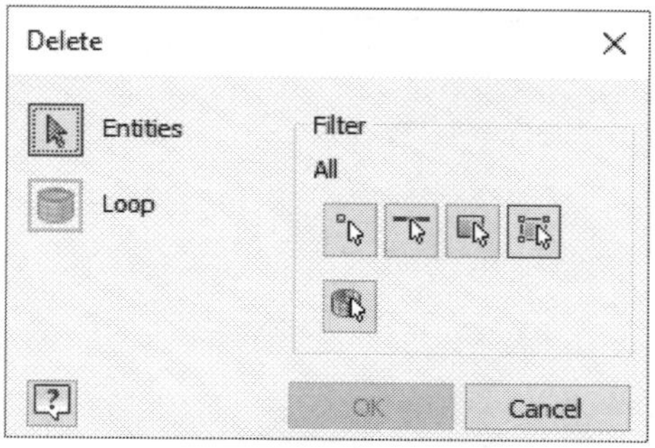

Figure 12–37

To delete entities, simply select them and click **OK**. Consider using the options in the *Filter* area to control the type of entities allowed for selection. As an alternative, you can right-click on an entity and select **Delete**. A feature history is not recorded, so keep in mind that once the freeform is finished, edits can't be undone. Figure 12–38 shows how the **Delete** command is being used to delete points, edges, and faces on a freeform shape.

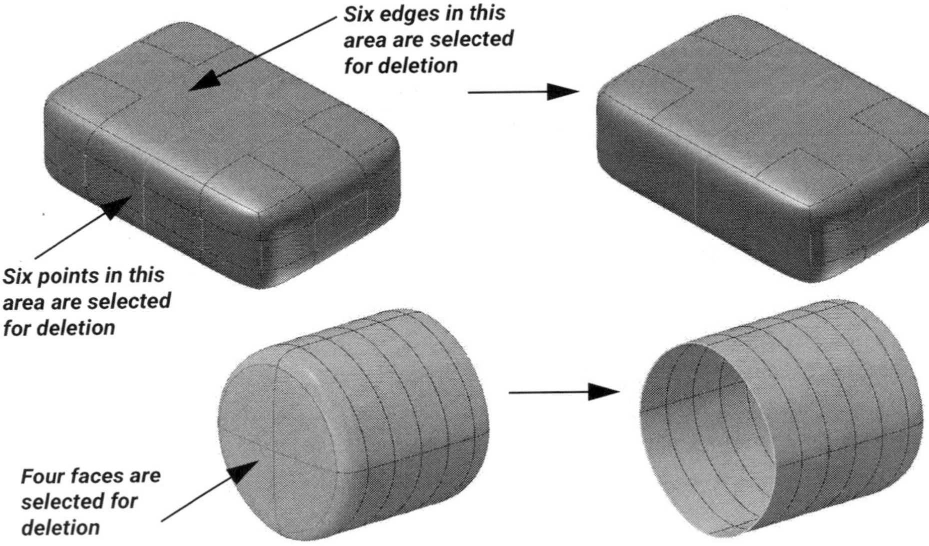

Figure 12–38

Hint: Selecting Faces

Toggle the (Select Through) option on the Tools panel to control how faces in a selection window are selected. When on, the selection includes hidden faces. When toggled off, the selection only includes the visible faces that fall in the selection window.

Practice 12a
Box Freeform Modeling

Practice Objectives

- Create freeform base geometry using the **Box** command.
- Toggle the view display from a smooth to block visual display style.
- Edit freeform base geometry so that points, edges, and faces are translated and rotated.
- Subdivide, delete, and insert elements on freeform base geometry to permit changes to the shape of the geometry.

In this practice, you will learn how create a box-shaped freeform model and to navigate the Freeform modeling environment. Using the Edit Form and additional editing tools, you will manipulate the shape of the box.

Task 1: Create a Box freeform shape.

1. Create a new part with the default mm template.

2. In the *3D Model* tab>Create Freeform panel, click  (Box). The Box dialog box opens (as shown in Figure 12–39), providing options that enable you to define the shape of the Box freeform geometry.

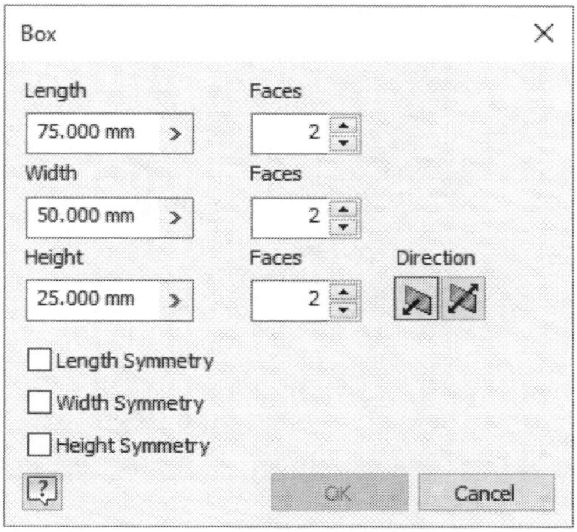

Figure 12–39

3. The Origin planes are temporarily displayed in the graphics window (as shown in Figure 12–40), so that you can select the sketch plane.

Figure 12–40

4. Hover the cursor over the origin planes in the graphics window. Note that the names display directly on the work planes in the graphics window.
5. Locate and select the XZ Plane as the sketch plane.
6. Use the ViewCube to return the model to its default orientation, if not already set.
7. By default, the Origin Center Point is projected onto the sketch plane. Select the center point as the base point for the Box.
8. You can enter values for the *Length*, *Width*, and *Height* or select manipulator arrowheads on the geometry. Select the X-direction arrowhead (*Length*) and drag it to enlarge the box. Drag it until the box is approximately **100 mm**.

   Note: *To display the Origin 3D Indicator in the graphics window to help identify directions, open the Application Options dialog box and enable* ***Show Origin 3D Indicator*** *on the Display tab.*

9. Select the Z-direction arrowhead (*Width*) and drag it to a size of approximately **60 mm**.
10. In the Box dialog box, set the *Height* value to **25**.
11. Ensure that exact values are entered for *Length*, *Width*, and *Height*, as shown in Figure 12–41.
12. Ensure that  (Direction) is selected to create the freeform above the XZ plane.
13. Select **Width Symmetry** to maintain symmetry on both sides of the XY plane.

14. To define the number of faces on each plane of the model, enter the *Face* values in the Box dialog box, as shown in Figure 12–41. Once all of the settings have been set, the model updates as shown on the right.

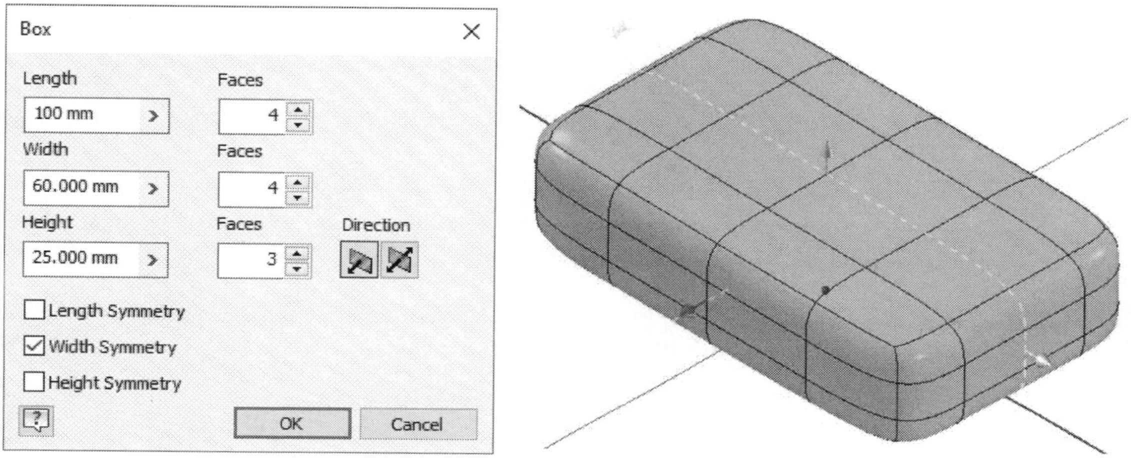

Figure 12–41

15. Click **OK** to complete the Box. The *Freeform* tab is activated.

16. In the *Freeform* tab>Tools panel, click  (Toggle Smooth). The model switches from a smooth display to a block display style, as shown in Figure 12–42. This is a display type only, which can increase performance speed. The model is still smooth when it is toggled off or when Freeform mode is off.

Figure 12–42

17. Click  (Toggle Smooth) again to return to the smooth display style.

Task 2: Edit the freeform geometry.

1. In the Edit panel, click  (Edit Form). The Edit Form dialog box opens as shown in Figure 12–43.

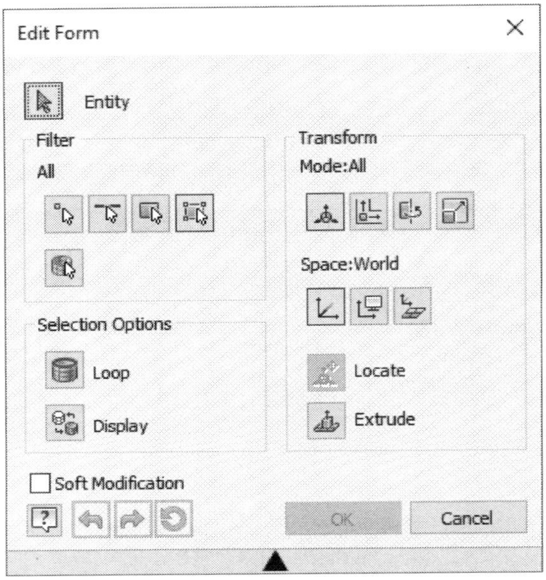

Figure 12–43

2. Note that in the *Filter* area,  (All) is set as the default option. If it is not selected, do so. This enables you to select any point, edge, or face on the model. Hover the cursor over the points, edges, and faces in the model. Note that you can select any of them. Selecting the other options filters the selection to points only, edges only, or faces only, which can be useful when working with complex freeform geometry with large mesh structures.
3. Select the vertex shown in Figure 12–44 to be translated.

4. Select the Y-axis manipulator arrowhead (as shown in Figure 12–44) and drag upwards similar to that shown.

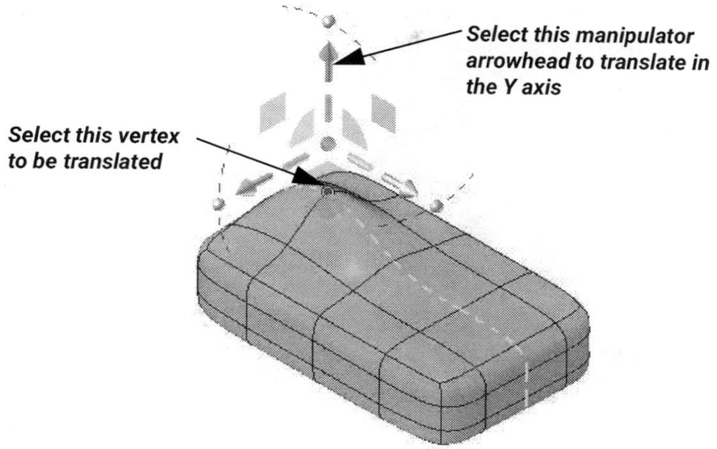

Figure 12–44

5. In the Edit Form dialog box, ensure the (Entity) option is active and select the face shown in Figure 12–45 to be translated.
6. Select the Y-axis manipulator arrowhead (as shown in Figure 12–45), and drag upwards similar to that shown. Note that both sides update together. This is because the **Width Symmetry** option was used when the box was created.

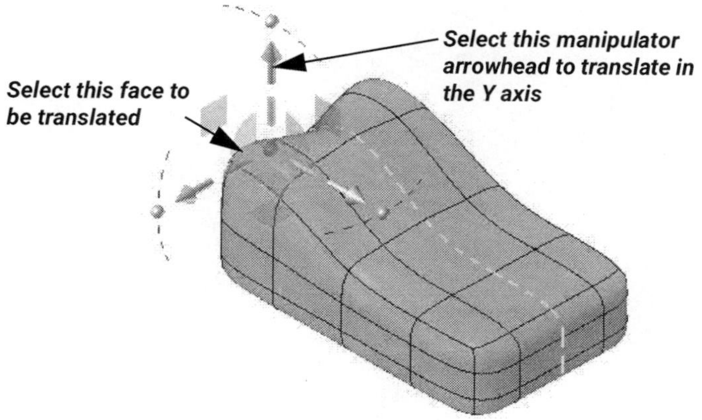

Figure 12–45

7. In the Edit Form dialog box, ensure the (Entity) option is active and select the face shown in Figure 12–46 to be translated.
8. Select the manipulator wheel shown in Figure 12–46 and drag upwards to rotate the face in the XY plane. Note that both sides update together.

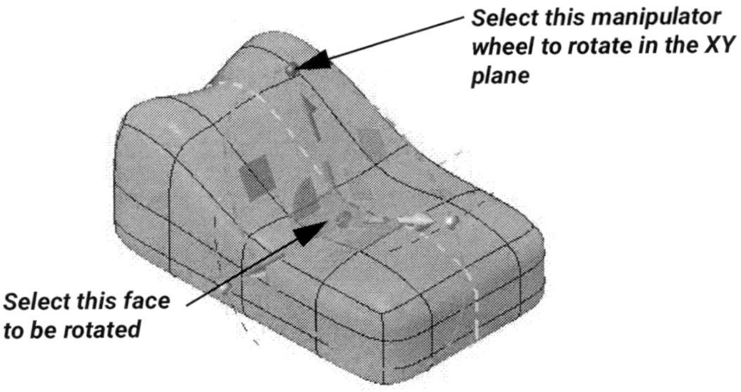

Figure 12–46

9. In the Edit Form dialog box, ensure the (Entity) option is active and select the front edge shown in Figure 12–47 to be translated.
10. Select the X-axis manipulator shown in Figure 12–47 and drag outward in the X axis. Both sides update together.

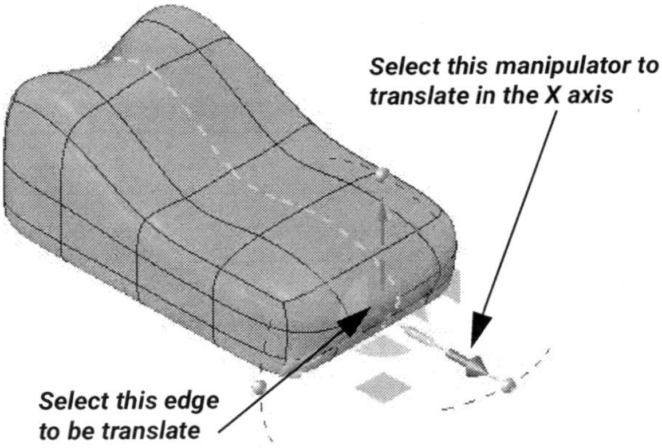

Figure 12–47

11. In the Edit Form dialog box, click to undo the last change to the model.

12. Select the same edge again, if not still selected and click (Loop) in the *Selection Options* area of the Edit Form dialog box. Alternatively, right-click and select **Select Loop**. The loop in which the edge exists highlights. Drag the same manipulator handle. The model displays similar to that shown in Figure 12–48. The entire loop of edges translate forward.

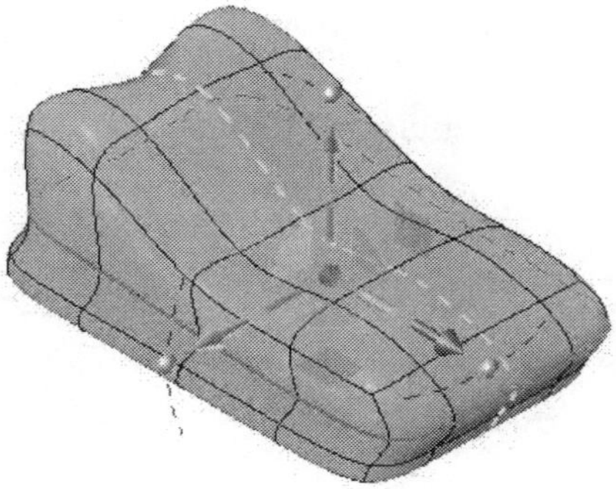

Figure 12–48

13. Click to complete the edit.

    Note: *In Freeform mode, all of the parametric model commands are not available.*

14. Save the file as **Freeform_Box.ipt**. Note that the model cannot be saved in Freeform mode. Click **Cancel**.

15. In the *Freeform* tab>Exit panel, click (Finish Freeform). Alternatively, right-click in the graphics window and select **Finish Freeform** in the marking menu. Note that the model displays as solid geometry, similar to that shown in Figure 12–49.

    Note: *The default visual display for new models is Shaded with Edges. To clear the display of the edges, you can change to the Shaded display style.*

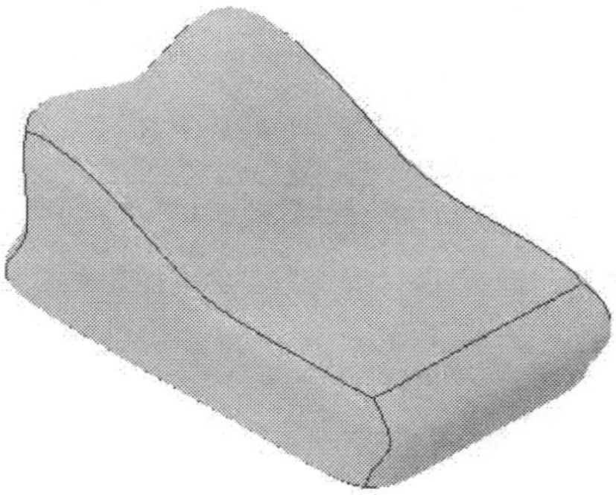

Figure 12–49

16. Save the file as **Freeform_Box.ipt**.

Task 3: Use Edit tools to further customize the meshed structure of the freeform.

1. In the *3D Model* tab, note that all of the parametric model commands are now available. You can continue to design the model using the familiar parametric commands. To further edit the freeform geometry, right-click on the **Form1** feature in the Model browser and select **Edit Freeform**.
2. The middle portion needs to be subdivided to include more faces. In the Modify panel, click (Subdivide) to open the Subdivide dialog box.
3. Click (Faces) if it is not already active, and select the face shown in Figure 12–50. Note that the symmetry setting that was assigned during Box creation still persists.
4. Accept the default value for the number of faces in the *Width* and *Length* fields, as shown in Figure 12–50.
5. For the *Mode* setting, maintain (Simple).

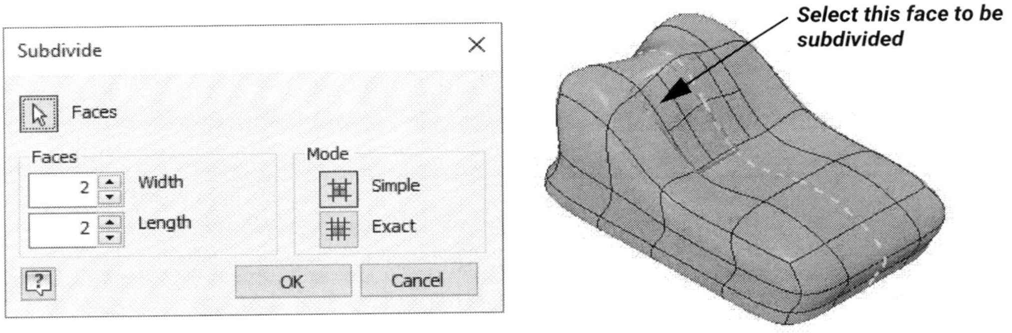

Figure 12–50

6. Click **OK** to insert the face(s). Note that the geometry changed slightly to permit the subdivision. This was acceptable. If the change is not acceptable, click (Exact) in the Subdivide dialog box when creating it. The geometry shape will stay the same but additional faces are added to maintain the shape.
7. In the Freeform panel, click (Edit Form).

8. Select one of the edges generated by the subdivide action, (as shown in Figure 12–51) and click (Loop) or right-click and select **Select Loop** to automatically select all of the adjacent edges.

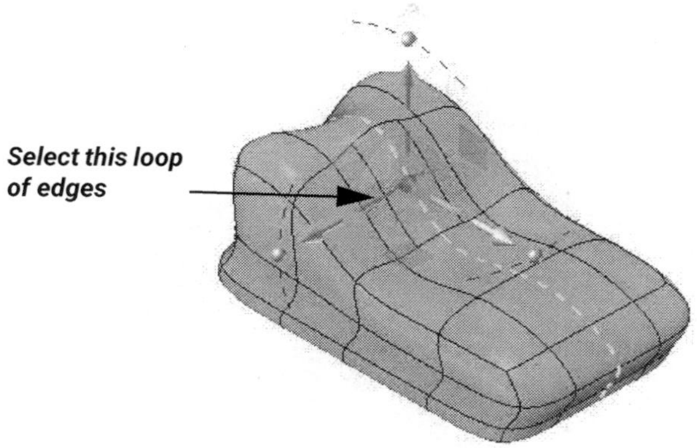

Figure 12–51

9. In the Edit Form dialog box, in the *Transform* area, click (View). The triad changes to only display two axis manipulators, as shown in Figure 12–52.

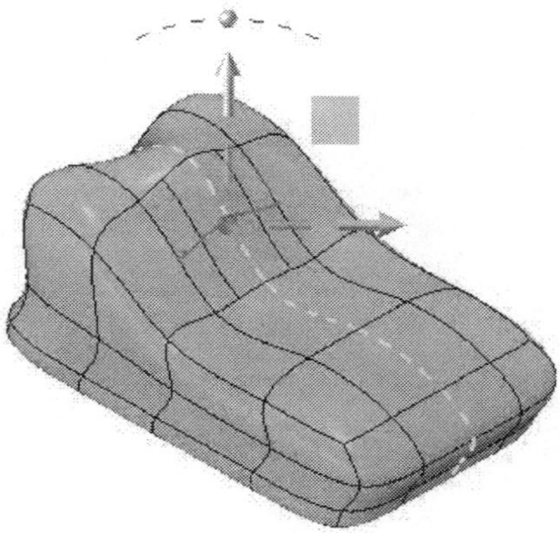

Figure 12–52

10. In the ViewCube, select the **FRONT** view. Note that the triad updates to display the Manipulators in the new orientation, while retaining the X and Y directions for the view.

11. Right-click in the graphics window and select **Previous View**. The edge remains selected. If it does not, select the loop again.

12. In the *Transform* area, click (Local) to change the triad location to the Local orientation. Drag the manipulators to create the geometry shown in Figure 12–53.

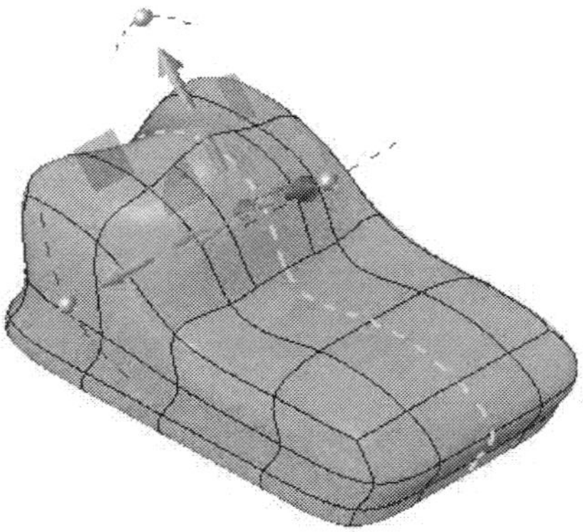

Figure 12–53

13. Click **OK** to complete the edit.

Task 4: Delete edges from the freeform geometry.

1. Now that the reshaping is done you can delete edges in the area that was subdivided. In the Edit panel, click (Delete).
2. In the Delete dialog box, click (Edge) and select the four edges shown in Figure 12–54.

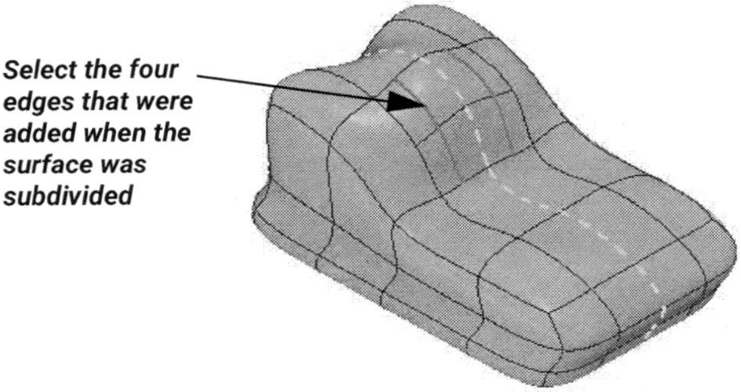

Figure 12–54

3. Click **OK** to delete the edges. The model updates as shown in Figure 12–55. Alternatively, because the Box was created symmetrically in the width direction, selecting two edges on one side would also have deleted the edges on the other side.

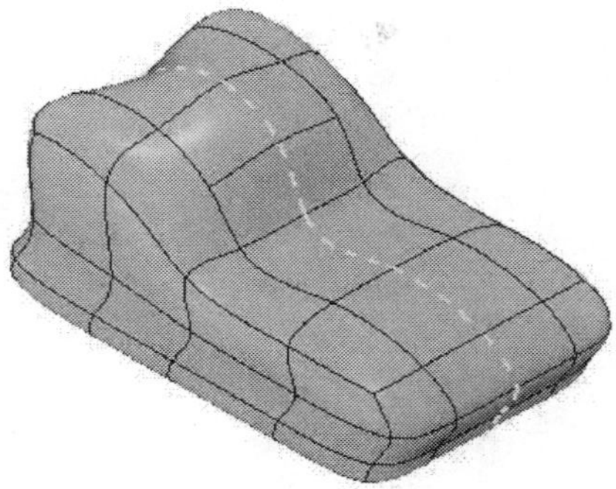

Figure 12–55

Task 5: Insert edges on freeform geometry.

1. In the Modify panel, click (Insert Edge). The Insert Edge dialog box opens.

2. Click (Edges) if it is not already active, and select the edge shown in Figure 12–56. A preview of the new edge displays immediately.

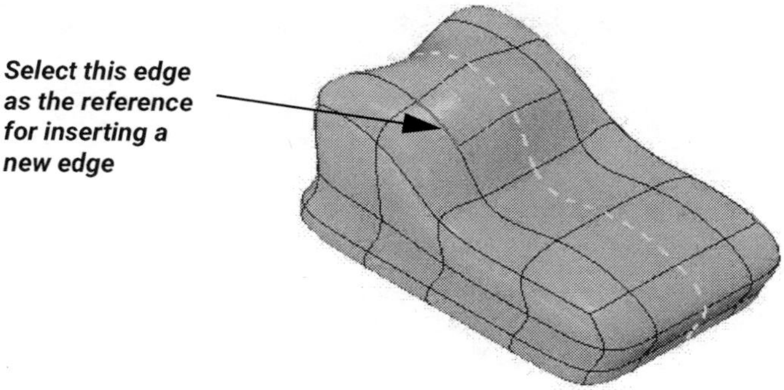

Figure 12–56

3. In the *Location* area, set the offset value to **0.2**. The edge moves closer to the reference edge.

4. Return the value to **0.5** to create the new edge midway between the reference edge the next edge.

5. In the *Mode* area, click (Exact). If Simple mode had been used the geometry would change to create the edge. In this situation the exact shape must be retained so Exact mode is used.
6. Click **OK** to insert the edit. The new edge is created, but to keep both symmetry and the existing shape, more edges have been added, as shown in Figure 12–57.

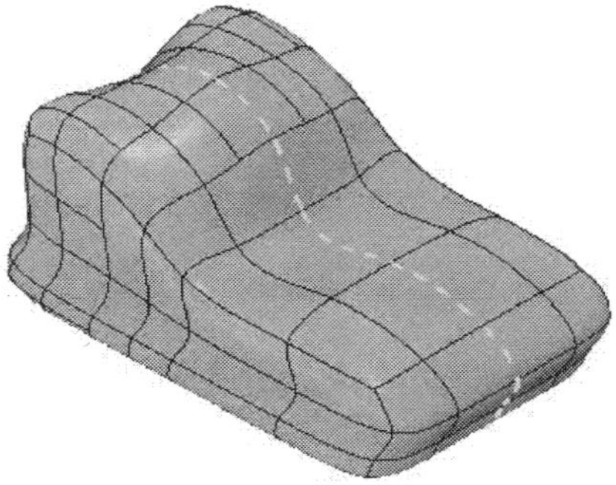

Figure 12–57

7. In the *Freeform* tab>Exit panel, click (Finish Freeform). Alternatively, right-click in the graphics window and select **Finish Freeform** in the marking menu.
8. Save the file and close the window.

End of practice

Practice 12b
Cylinder Freeform Modeling

Practice Objectives

- Create freeform base geometry using the **Cylinder** command.
- Match edges on the freeform base geometry to that of parametric sketch geometry.
- Assign symmetry to faces on the freeform base geometry.
- Cancel assigned symmetry between faces on the freeform base geometry.
- Use the **Edit Form** command to scale elements on the freeform base geometry.

In this practice, you will learn how to create a Cylinder as the freeform base geometry. You will also assign symmetry so that when editing faces on the cylinder, the change is also mirrored on the model. Additionally, you will use the **Match Edge** command to assign an edge on the freeform model equal to that of a parametric sketch.

Task 1: Create a sketch that will be referenced by a freeform cylinder.

1. Create a new part using the default mm template.
2. In the *3D Model* tab>Sketch panel, click  (Start 2D Sketch).
3. Select the XY Plane as the sketch plane.
4. Create a circle with a diameter of **70 mm** centered on the projected Origin Center Point.
5. Complete the sketch.
6. Toggle off the dimension visibility for the sketch.

Task 2: Create a freeform cylinder.

1. In the *3D Model* tab>Create Freeform panel, click (Cylinder). The Cylinder dialog box (shown in Figure 12–58) opens, providing options for defining the shape of the Cylinder freeform geometry.

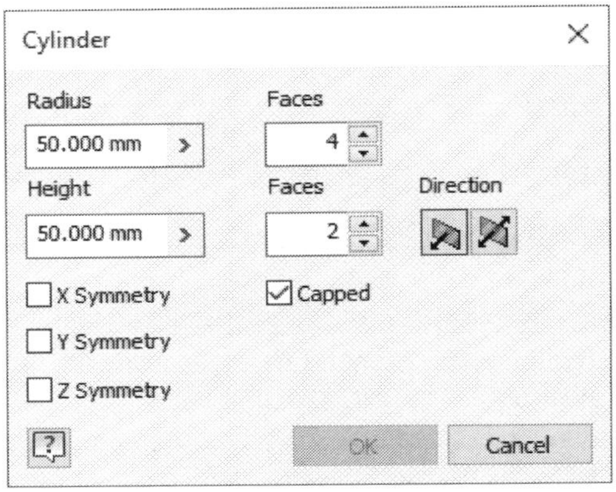

Figure 12–58

2. Locate and select the XY Plane as the sketch plane.
3. Select the projected Origin Center Point as the base point for the Cylinder.
4. In the Cylinder dialog box, click to ensure that the freeform geometry is centered on both sides of the sketch plane.
5. You can enter values for the *Radius* and *Height* or select the manipulator arrowheads on the geometry. Using either technique, create the cylinder so that its *Radius* is **40** and its *Height* is **200**.
6. Symmetry will be assigned using the **Symmetry** command in the editing tools. Ensure that symmetry is not specified in the Cylinder dialog box.
7. To define the number of faces on each plane of the model, enter the *Face* values shown on the left in Figure 12–59.

8. Ensure that **Capped** is selected. Once all of the settings have been set, the model updates as shown on the right in Figure 12–59.

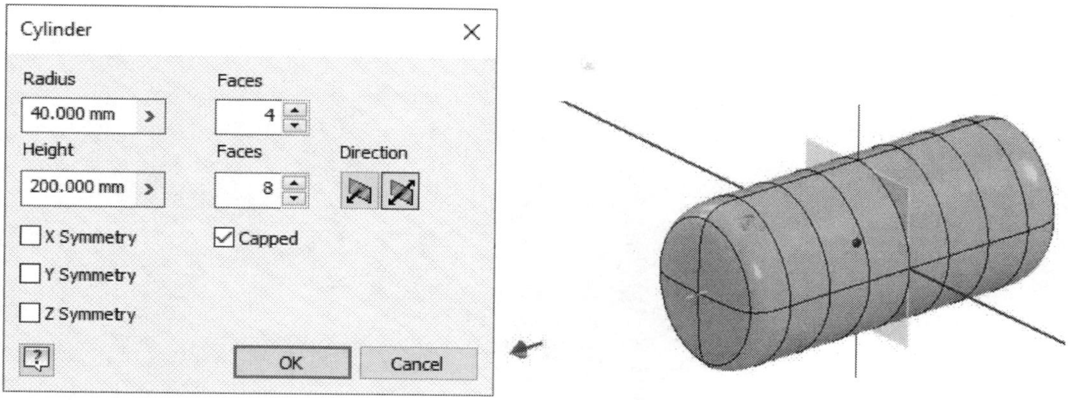

Figure 12–59

9. Click **OK** to complete the Cylinder.

Task 3: Match an edge on the freeform geometry with the sketch.

1. In the Modify panel click (Match Edge). The Match dialog box opens as shown in Figure 12–60.

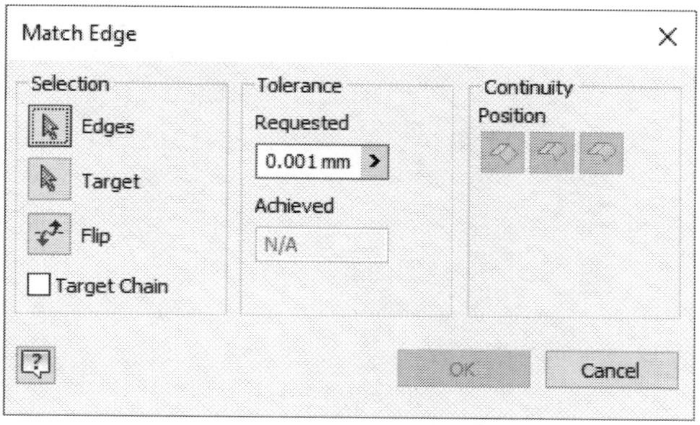

Figure 12–60

2. Click (Edges) if it is not already active, and select the freeform edges shown in Figure 12–61 to match the circular sketch. Alternatively, you can double-click one edge to select the loop.

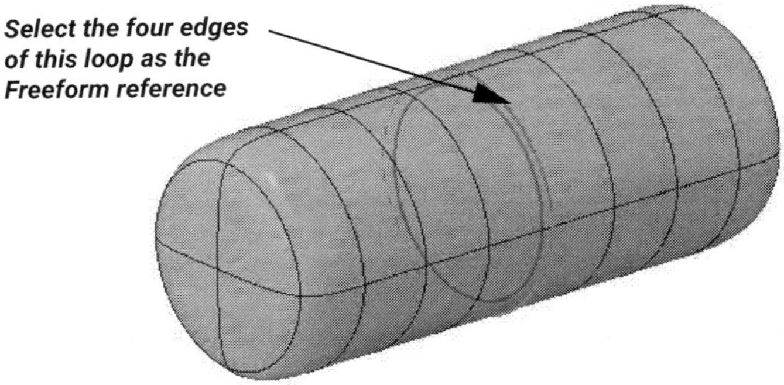

Figure 12–61

Note: *If you are matching a fully enclosed entity, the freeform references must also be a fully enclosed loop.*

3. Click (Target) and select the existing circular sketch as the Match reference.
4. Maintain the default tolerance value.
5. Click **OK** to match the edges. The freeform geometry updates as shown in Figure 12–62.

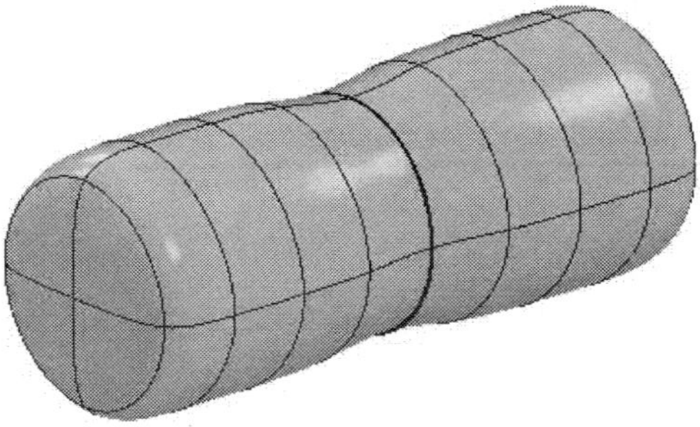

Figure 12–62

Task 4: Assign Symmetry to the freeform geometry and edit the symmetric faces.

1. In the Edit panel, click (Edit Form). The Edit Form dialog box opens as shown in Figure 12–63.

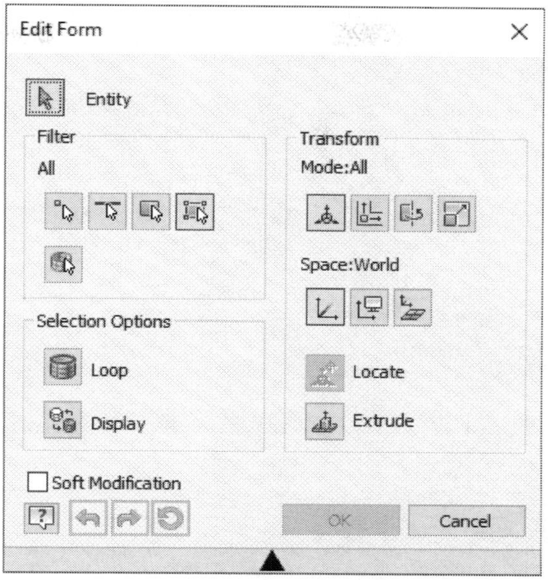

Figure 12–63

2. Reorient the model as shown in Figure 12–64.

3. In the *Filter* area, ensure that either (All) or (Face) is selected and select the face shown in Figure 12–64 to be translated.

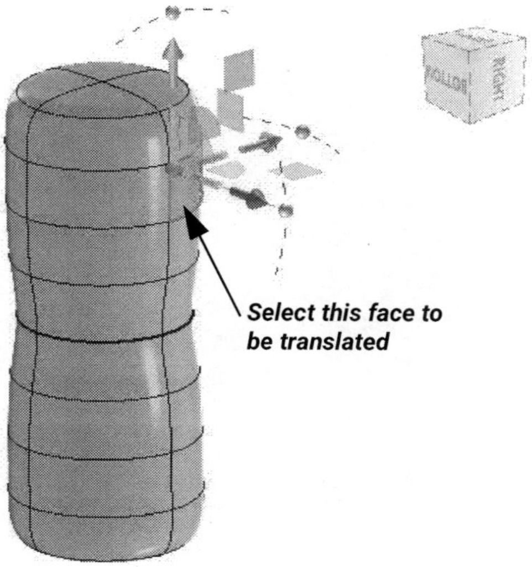

Figure 12–64

4. In the Edit Form dialog box, in the *Transform* area, click (View). The triad changes to only display two axis manipulators.
5. In the ViewCube, select the edge between the Right and Bottom sides, as shown in Figure 12–65.

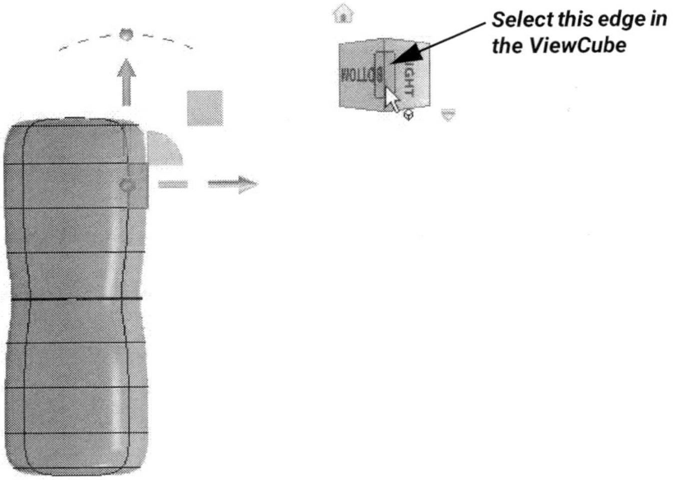

Figure 12–65

6. Select the X-axis manipulator arrowhead and drag it to the right, similar to that shown in Figure 12–66.

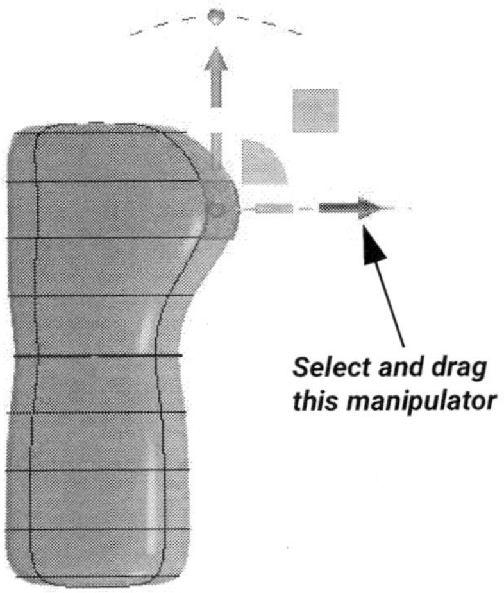

Figure 12–66

7. In the Edit Form dialog box, click (Reset) to reset any of the changes made in the command. Click **Yes** to confirm the reset.

8. Click **Cancel** to close the Edit Form dialog box.

9. In the Symmetry panel, click (Symmetry). The Symmetry dialog box is shown in Figure 12–67.

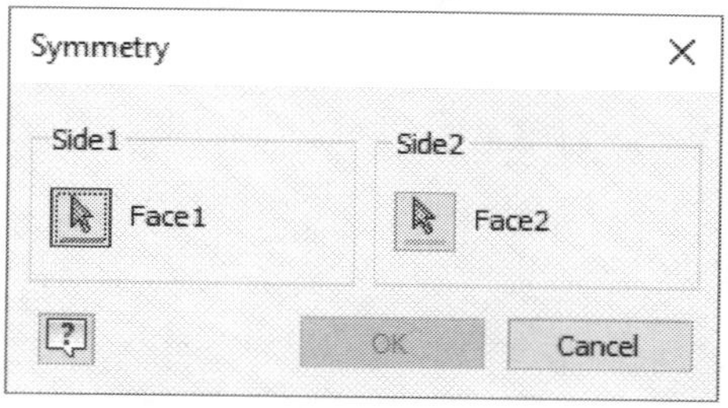

Figure 12–67

10. Click (Face1) if it is not already active, and select the face shown in Figure 12–68. The reference displays in blue.

11. Click (Face2) and select the face shown in Figure 12–68 as the symmetric reference on the other side of the model. The reference displays in green on the model.

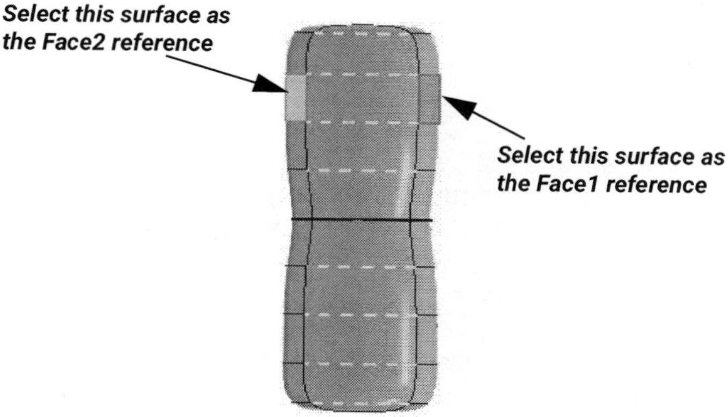

Figure 12–68

12. Click **OK** to assign the symmetry.

13. Use the **Edit Form** command again to translate the face that was just translated in the X-axis direction. Now that symmetry has been assigned with this surface, its symmetric face is also selected. Ensure that (View Space) is set and that the ViewCube is oriented as was previously set.

14. Drag the X-axis manipulator to translate the face inward, as shown on the left in Figure 12–69. Both symmetric faces update.
15. Activate entity selection in the dialog box and select the surface below it and translate it inwards, as shown on the right in Figure 12–69. Note that it also reacts as symmetric.

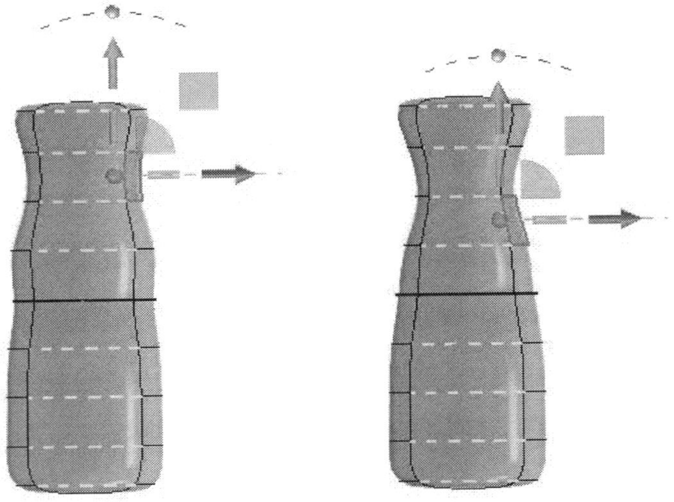

Figure 12–69

16. Complete the edit.
17. In the Symmetry panel, expand the Symmetry drop-down list, and click  (Clear Symmetry). Select the cylindrical body to clear its symmetry. Selecting this option clears all of the assigned symmetry as well as any symmetry assigned during freeform creation.

Task 5: Ensure that the matched edges in the freeform remain matched.

1. Rotate the model as shown on the left in Figure 12–70. Note that the edge that was matched is no longer matched. The edits that were made have moved it. Matching does not maintain the relationship.

   Note: *The degree to which the edges are mismatched is dependent on the edits that were made.*

2. In the Model browser, expand **Form1** and the *Matches* folder. Right-click on **Matched Edge 1** and select **Rematch**. The matches edges are shown in Figure 12–70.

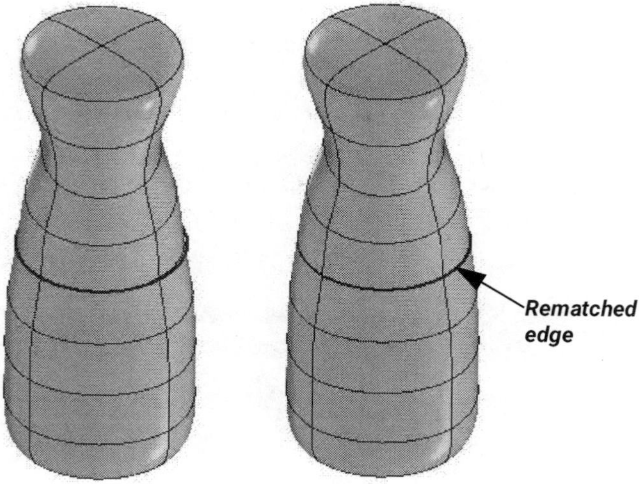

Figure 12–70

Task 6: Scale a face in the freeform geometry.

1. Start the **Edit Form** command.
2. In the *Transform* area, click (Scale) to only display the scaling triad.
3. Select the face and scale manipulator in the Z axis, as shown in Figure 12–71, and drag upward to scale the face.

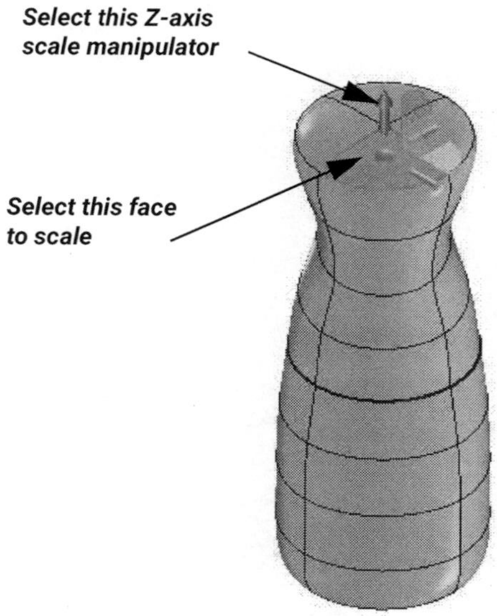

Figure 12–71

4. Complete the edit.
5. Use the ViewCube to orient the model to the **Bottom** view and note that the scaling has changed the geometry on the face that was selected.
6. Right-click in the graphics window and select **Previous View**.
7. In the *Freeform* tab>Exit panel, click ✔ (Finish Freeform). Alternatively, right-click in the graphics window and select **Finish Freeform** in the marking menu.
8. Save the file as **Freeform_Cylinder.ipt** and close the window.

End of practice

Practice 12c
(Optional) Bridging Freeform Geometry

Practice Objective

- Create two freeform base geometry forms and use the **Bridge** command to generate additional geometry between the forms.

In this practice, you will create two cylinder freeform base shapes in the model to help when creating the required freeform geometry. Once created, you will use the **Bridge** command to create additional geometry between the two cylinders.

Task 1: Create a freeform cylinder.

1. Create a new part using the default mm template.
2. Use the Cylinder freeform feature to create the freeform, similar to that shown in Figure 12–72. Locate the cylinder on the XY Plane and use the projected Origin Center Point as the base point for the Cylinder.

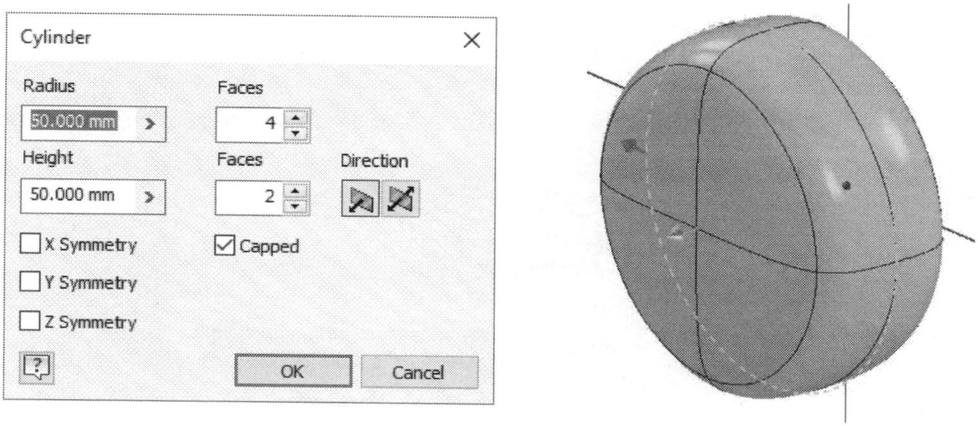

Figure 12–72

3. In the *Freeform* tab>Create Freeform panel, use the **Cylinder** freeform feature to create a second freeform, similar to that shown in Figure 12–73. Select the same plane, but use an origin point that is offset from the initial cylinder.

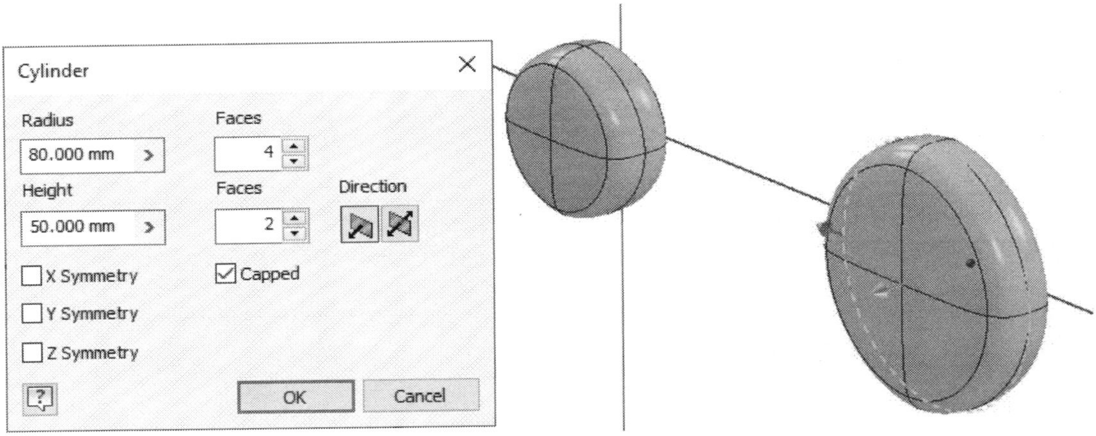

Figure 12–73

Task 2: Create geometry between the two cylinders.

1. In the Modify panel, click (Bridge).

2. Click (Side1), if it is not already active, and select the four faces shown in Figure 12–74.

3. Click (Side2) and select the four faces shown in Figure 12–74.

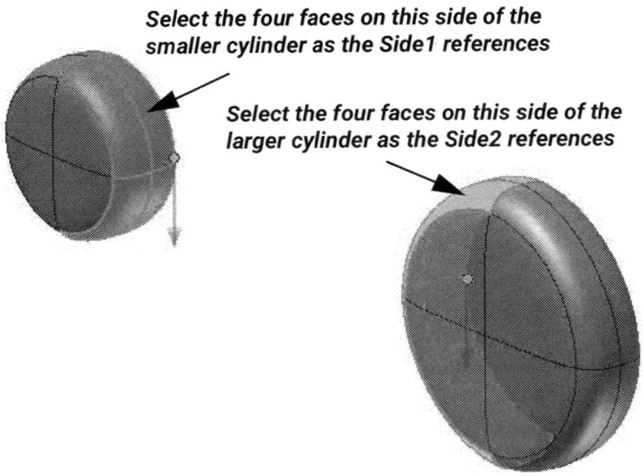

Figure 12–74

4. Maintain the default faces for the number of faces and the twist.
5. Click **OK** to create the bridge geometry. The geometry displays as shown in Figure 12–75. Additional **Edit Form** actions can be performed on the new freeform feature, as required.

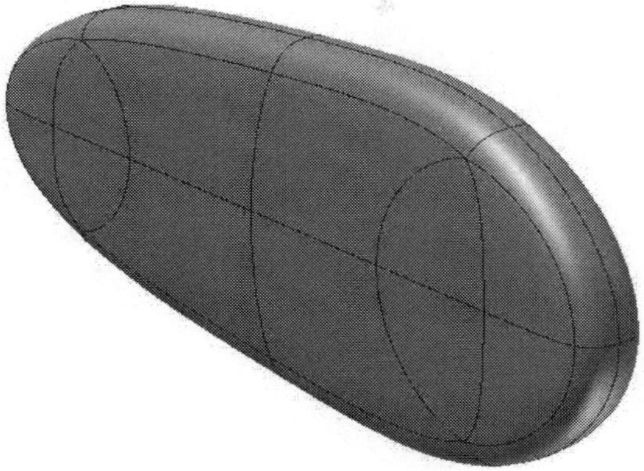

Figure 12–75

6. Exit the Freeform environment.
7. Save the file as **Freeform_Bridge.ipt** and close the window.

End of practice

Chapter Review Questions

1. When modeling in the Freeform environment you can create parametric sketches for use with the **Match Edge** command.
   a. True
   b. False

2. Which of the following standard freeform shapes enables you to assign symmetry in the width, length, and height when creating the freeform base shape?
   a. Box
   b. Cylinder
   c. Sphere
   d. Torus
   e. Quadball
   f. Plane

3. The Quadball standard freeform shape enables you to assign faces along the longitude and latitude of the resulting shape.
   a. True
   b. False

4. Which of the following statements are true regarding symmetry in freeform geometry? (Select all that apply.)
   a. Symmetry can only be assigned when the base freeform shape is created.
   b. Symmetry can only be assigned using the Symmetry command by selecting faces on the freeform geometry.
   c. All of the symmetry assigned on the base freeform shape can be removed using the Clear Symmetry command.
   d. Faces adjacent to a face that was selected as a symmetry reference also update to reflect the symmetry.

5. When using the **Edit Form** command, which of the following describe the manipulator controls that are available when the triad displays as shown in Figure 12–76? (Select all that apply.)

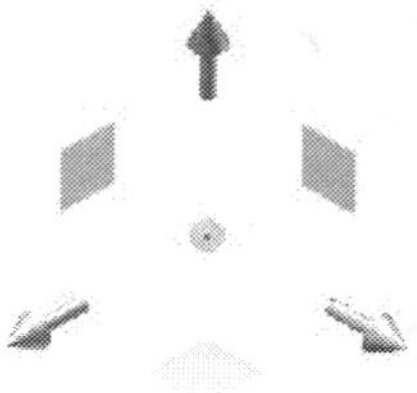

Figure 12–76

a. Translate in X, Y, or Z axis
b. Translate in plane
c. Rotate in plane
d. Scale in X, Y, or Z axis
e. Scale in plane

6. Which of the Space settings provides you with two manipulators that can be used to manipulate the freeform geometry?

a.  (World)

b.  (View)

c.  (Local)

7. Which of the following editing commands enable you to add additional elements (points, edges, or faces) to existing freeform geometry? (Select all that apply.)

a. Insert Edge
b. Insert Point
c. Subdivide
d. Crease Edges
e. Bridge
f. Match Edge

8. The **Flatten** command enables you to select multiple points and make them parallel to a selected plane.
   a. True
   b. False

9. When subdividing a face,  (Simple mode) forces the freeform geometry to remain exactly the same once the faces have been subdivided.
   a. True
   b. False

10. Which of the following commands can be used to create the geometry between two freeform shapes? (Select all that apply.)
    a. Insert Edge
    b. Subdivide
    c. Merge Edges
    d. Bridge
    e. Match Edge

Command Summary

Button	Command	Location
	**Align Form**	• **Ribbon:** *Freeform* tab>Edit panel
	**Box**	• **Ribbon:** *3D Model* tab>Create Freeform panel • **Ribbon:** *Freeform* tab>Create Freeform panel
	**Bridge**	• **Ribbon:** *Freeform* tab>Modify panel
	**Clear Symmetry**	• **Ribbon:** *Freeform* tab>Symmetry panel
	**Convert**	• **Ribbon:** *3D Model* tab>Create Freeform panel • **Ribbon:** *Freeform* tab>Create Freeform panel
	**Crease Edges**	• **Ribbon:** *Freeform* tab>Modify panel
	**Cylinder**	• **Ribbon:** *3D Model* tab>Create Freeform panel • **Ribbon:** *Freeform* tab>Create Freeform panel
	**Delete**	• **Ribbon:** *Freeform* tab>Edit panel
	**Edit Form**	• **Ribbon:** *Freeform* tab>Edit panel
	**Face**	• **Ribbon:** *3D Model* tab>Create Freeform panel • **Ribbon:** *Freeform* tab>Create Freeform panel
	**Finish Freeform**	• **Ribbon:** *Freeform* tab>Exit panel • **Context menu:** In the graphics window
	**Flatten**	• **Ribbon:** *Freeform* tab>Modify panel
	**Insert Edge**	• **Ribbon:** *Freeform* tab>Modify panel
	**Insert Point**	• **Ribbon:** *Freeform* tab>Modify panel
	**Match Edge**	• **Ribbon:** *Freeform* tab>Modify panel
	**Merge Edges**	• **Ribbon:** *Freeform* tab>Modify panel
	**Mirror**	• **Ribbon:** *Freeform* tab>Symmetry panel

Button	Command	Location
	**Plane**	• **Ribbon:** *3D Model* tab>Create Freeform panel • **Ribbon:** *Freeform* tab>Create Freeform panel
	**Quadball**	• **Ribbon:** *3D Model* tab>Create Freeform panel • **Ribbon:** *Freeform* tab>Create Freeform panel
	**Select Through**	• **Ribbon:** *Freeform* tab>Tools panel
	**Sphere**	• **Ribbon:** *3D Model* tab>Create Freeform panel • **Ribbon:** *Freeform* tab>Create Freeform panel
	**Subdivide**	• **Ribbon:** *Freeform* tab>Modify panel
	**Symmetry**	• **Ribbon:** *Freeform* tab>Symmetry panel
	**Thicken**	• **Ribbon:** *Freeform* tab>Modify panel
	**Toggle Smooth/ Blocky**	• **Ribbon:** *Freeform* tab>Tools panel
	**Toggle Translucent**	• **Ribbon:** *Freeform* tab>Tools panel
	**Torus**	• **Ribbon:** *3D Model* tab>Create Freeform panel • **Ribbon:** *Freeform* tab>Create Freeform panel
	**Uncrease Edges**	• **Ribbon:** *Freeform* tab>Modify panel
	**Unweld Edges**	• **Ribbon:** *Freeform* tab>Modify panel
	**Weld Vertices**	• **Ribbon:** *Freeform* tab>Modify panel

Chapter 13

Importing and Editing CAD Data

The Autodesk® Inventor® software supports the import of files from many different types of 3D CAD programs. In some cases, an associative link can be maintained between the source file and the Autodesk Inventor software. Once a CAD file has been imported, the geometry is brought into an Autodesk Inventor file where it can be further manipulated using tools available in the software. Understanding the editing tools that are available to further manipulate the imported geometry is essential to ensuring the efficient creation of the required model.

Learning Objectives

- Import CAD data into the Autodesk Inventor software.
- Export CAD data from the Autodesk Inventor software in an available export format.
- Use the Edit Base Solid environment to edit solids that have been imported into the Autodesk Inventor software.
- Create Direct Edit features in a model that move, resize, scale, rotate, and delete existing geometry in both imported and native Autodesk Inventor files.
- Index a supported point cloud data file, and attach and edit it for use in a file.

13.1 Importing CAD Data (AnyCAD)

You can import supported file formats using the AnyCAD import functionality. This enables you to either open the files as reference models or convert the files and break the link to the original data. The Autodesk Inventor software can open the file formats shown in Figure 13–1.

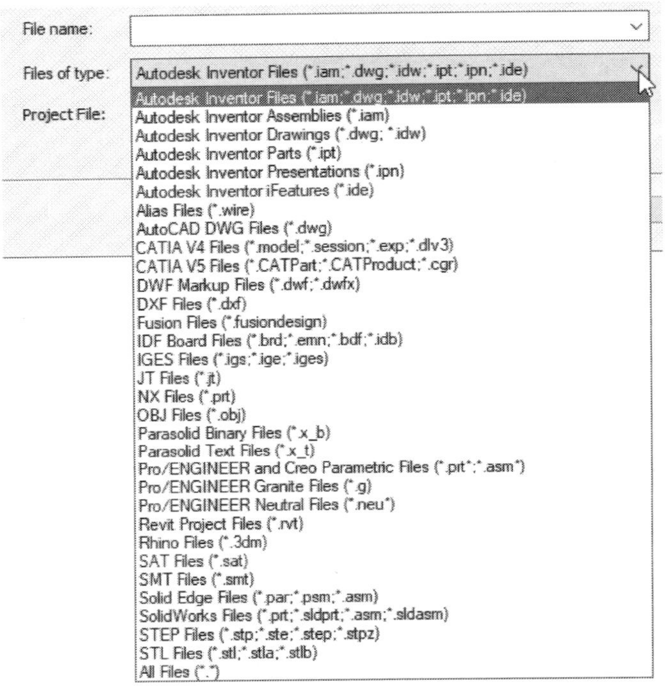

Figure 13–1

***Note:** For more details on the specific formats and versions of other CAD software products that are supported for import, search the Autodesk Inventor Help for "Importing Files".*

How To: Import Data

1. In the **File** menu, Home page, or Quick Access Toolbar, select **Open**. The Open dialog box displays.
2. In the Files of type drop-down list, select the file format that is to be imported.
3. Select the file to import and click **Open**. The Import dialog box opens.
    - If a part file is imported, a new Autodesk Inventor part file is created.
    - If an assembly is imported, a new Autodesk Inventor assembly is created.

- The available options in the dialog box vary depending on the file format that is being imported.

In the example shown in Figure 13–2, a CATIA part file and an .IGS file were selected, as indicated by the filenames at the top of the dialog boxes.

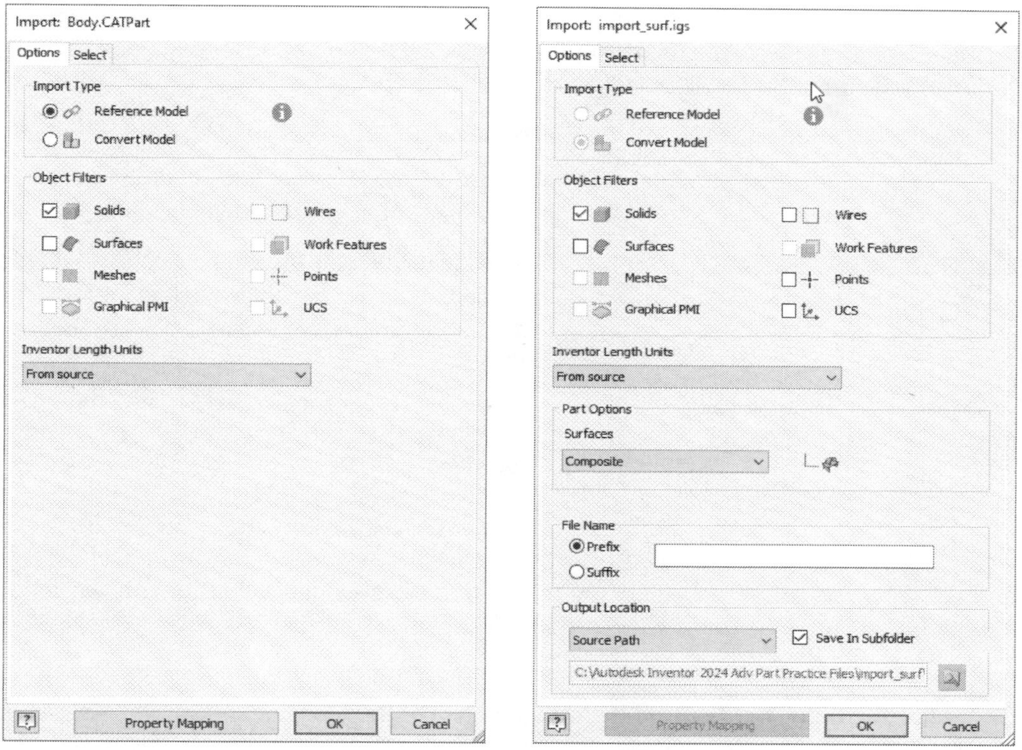

Figure 13–2

4. In the *Import Type* area, select how the data will be imported:
   - Select **Reference Model** to import the data so that a reference is maintained to the source file. If this option is used, when changes are made to the source file, you can update the model in Autodesk Inventor to reflect the changes.
   - Select **Convert Model** to import the geometry and break the link with the original model.
5. In the *Object Filters* area, select the data type to import (e.g., Solids, Surfaces, Meshes, Wires, Work Features, Points, or UCS).
6. In the *Inventor Length Units* area, specify the type of length unit to use for the imported geometry. The options enable you to maintain the same units as the data being imported (**From source**), or select from a list of standard units (e.g., inch, foot, millimeter, meter, etc).

7. Depending on the *Import Type*, proceed as follows:
    - If the data is being imported using the **Reference Model** option, there are no additional options that are available. Continue to Step 10.
    - If the data is being imported using the **Convert Model** option, continue to Step 8.
8. In the *Assembly Options* and *Part Options* areas, select how the assembly structure and surfaces are to be imported using the drop-down lists. The options vary depending on the file format being imported as follows:

File Format	Drop-down List	Options
Parts	• Surfaces	• **Individual:** Surfaces are brought in individually. • **Composite:** A single composite feature.
IGES or STEP files	• Surfaces	• **Individual:** Surfaces are brought in individually. • **Composite:** A single composite feature. • **Stitch:** Automatically stitches surfaces together on import.
Assemblies	• Structure • Surfaces	• **Assembly:** The original assembly structure is maintained. • **Individual part:** Each component is imported as individual parts. • **Composite Part:** Each part in an assembly is a composite. • The Part surface options that are available for assemblies are the same as those available for parts.

9. By default, the name of the new file that contains the imported geometry is the same as the imported filename. In the *File Names* area, enter a prefix or suffix to append to the default name in the *Name* field. Additionally, you can browse to a new directory or accept the default file location for the new file.
10. In the *Select* tab, click **Load Model** to add the model data to the dialog box and display a preview of the model.
11. (Optional) Click the circular node associated with each node to toggle its inclusion. By default, all nodes are included ( ). When the node is displayed, the geometry is excluded. To toggle multiple surfaces, select them and use the appropriate Status symbol at the top of the Import dialog box.
    - The ability to include or exclude geometry depends on the type of part or assembly that is being imported.
12. (Optional) You can map properties from CATIA, Solidworks, NX, STEP, and Pro-ENGINEER/ Creo to standard Autodesk Inventor properties using the **Property Mapping** option. Select the file type that you want to map the Autodesk Inventor properties to fill the values, as required. Click **Save**.

13. Once the options are set, click **OK** to open the imported solid in the Autodesk Inventor software.

Once data is imported as a reference, the source files are required whenever the Inventor file is active. If the source file is missing, you can use the Resolve Link dialog box to search for the file. This is the same tool used to located missing part files in an assembly file.

Hint: Importing into an Existing File

You can import CAD Data into existing files using the following options:

- In an open part file, in the *3D Model* tab>Create panel, click (Import). The **Import** command is also available on the *Manage* tab>Import panel.
- In an assembly file, in the *Assemble* tab>expanded Place commands, click (Place Imported CAD Files).

13.2 Exporting Geometry

To export files, select **Save As>Save Copy As** in the **File** menu. The export file formats that are available for part, assembly, and drawing files are shown in Figure 13–3.

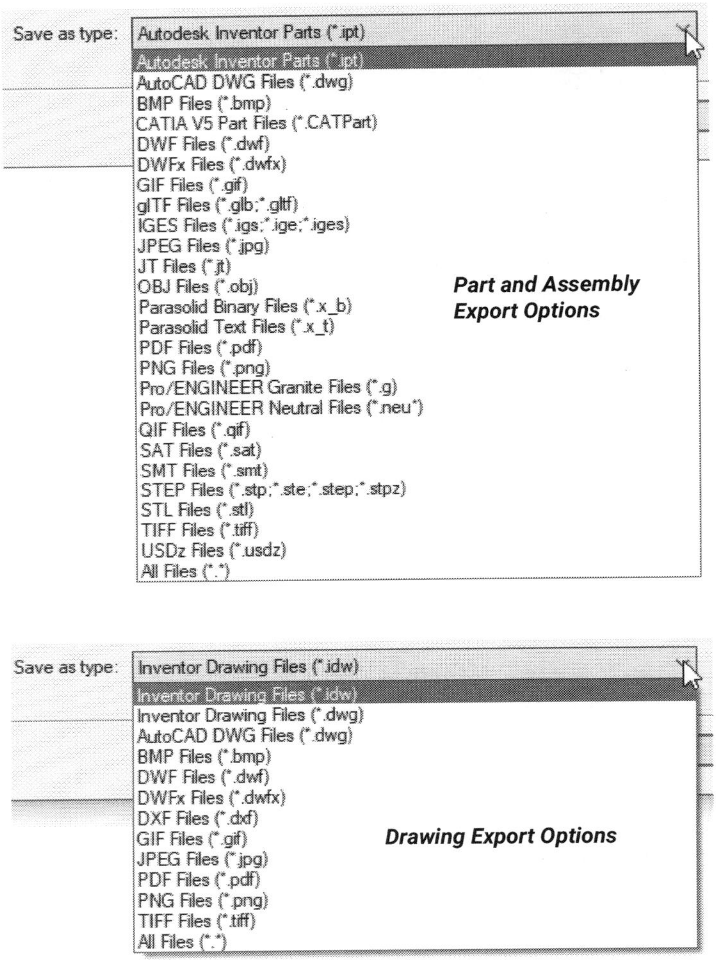

Figure 13–3

Consider the following when exporting:

- Presentation files can be exported to the following file formats: .DWF, .DWFX, .BMP, .PDF, .PNG, .GIF, .JPG and .TIFF.
- Image files can also be exported by selecting **Export>Image** in the **File** menu.

- Sketches or planar faces can be exported to .DWG or .DXF by right-clicking on a sketch and selecting **Export Sketch As**, or by selecting a planar face, right-clicking on it, and selecting **Export Face As**.
- If you save a file as a .BMP file, a snapshot of the part, assembly, presentation, or drawing file is created as the file displays on the screen.
- SAT files are generally used to translate from a program that uses an ACIS kernel to another. It can also be used to include sketches in the file.
- Sheet metal flat patterns can be exported to .SAT, .DWG, or .DXF formats by right-clicking and selecting **Save Copy As**.
- The .STL file format provides options that enable you to control the facets quality, format, and structure of the file so that an accurate prototype of a part or an assembly file can be sent to a 3D printer.
- The IGES file format enables you to export part geometry and base surfaces and assign them to different layers. Note that only the surfaces visible in the model when exported are included in the exported IGES file.
- Exporting an assembly as a Step file saves all of the files in a single file.
- Exporting as JT allows for the export of Product Manufacturing Information (PMI), including semantic PMI data. Quality Information Framework (QIF) files can also be exported containing PMI data.

13.3 Editing the Base Solid

To edit a solid base feature that has been imported, right-click on the base feature in the Model browser and select **Edit Solid**. The *Edit Base Solid* tab displays, as shown in Figure 13–4, providing the editing options for imported solids.

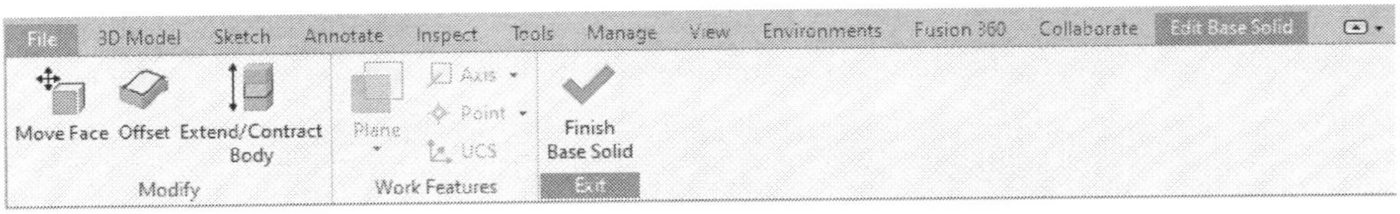

Figure 13–4

Move Face

The 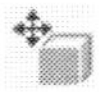 (Move Face) options enable you to select faces to be moved. There are three move options in the mini-toolbar  drop-down list: **Free Move**, **Direction and Distance**, and **Points and Plane**, as shown in Figure 13–5.

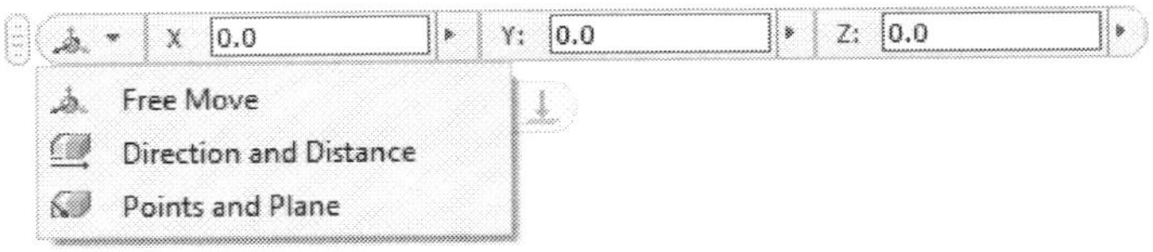

Figure 13–5

Figure 13–6 shows the mini-toolbar for the **Free Move** option. The hole face can be dragged or assigned to an X, Y, Z location.

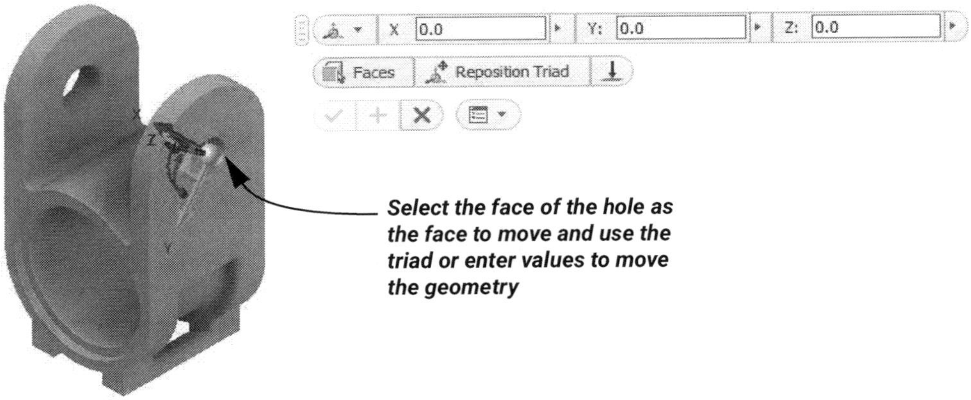

Figure 13–6

Figure 13–7 displays the mini-toolbar for the **Direction and Distance** option. The hole face can be moved relative to the selected distance reference.

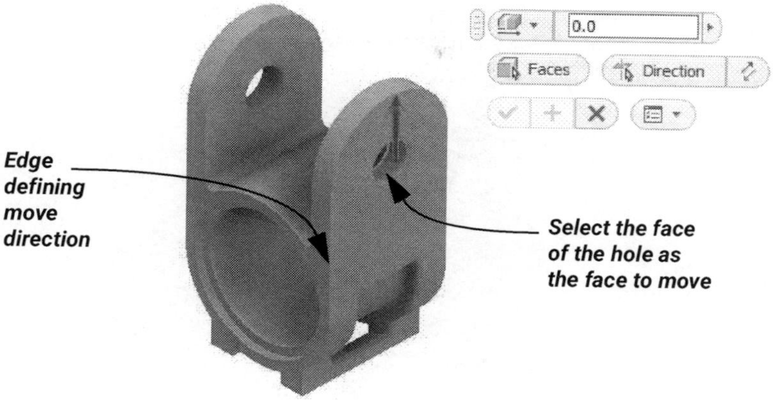

Figure 13–7

Figure 13–8 displays the mini-toolbar for the **Points and Plane** option. The hole face can be moved to a selected point.

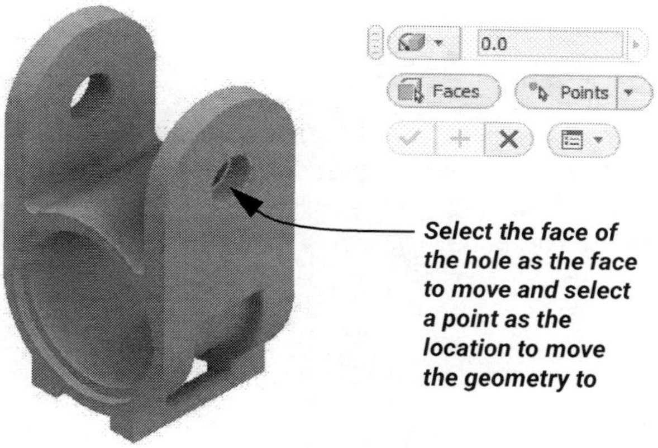

Figure 13–8

Offset

The  (Offset) option enables you to offset the existing face by a specified value or by dynamically pressing and pulling the face, as required. The face shown on the left in Figure 13–9 is selected and offset to change its thickness.

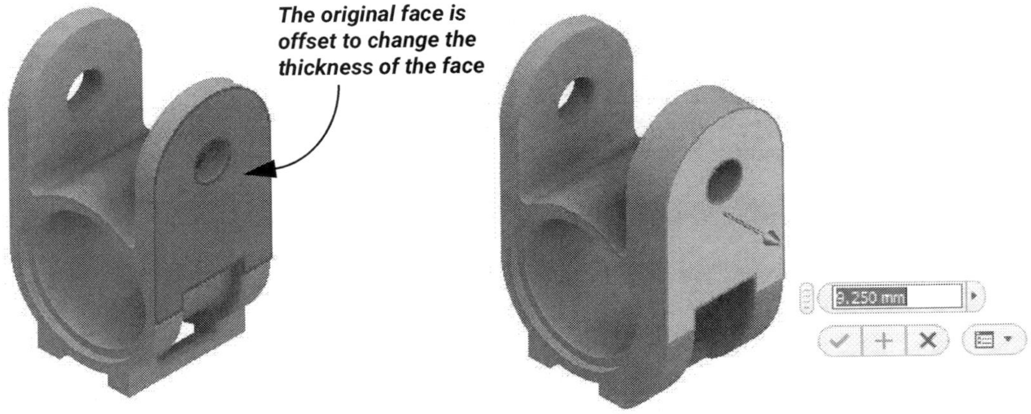

Figure 13–9

Extend or Contract Body

The  (Extend/Contract Body) option enables you to resize an imported solid in a direction perpendicular to a selected plane. In Figure 13–10, a plane was selected at the bottom of the part as the reference for an extension. The imported geometry is extended by the specified distance.

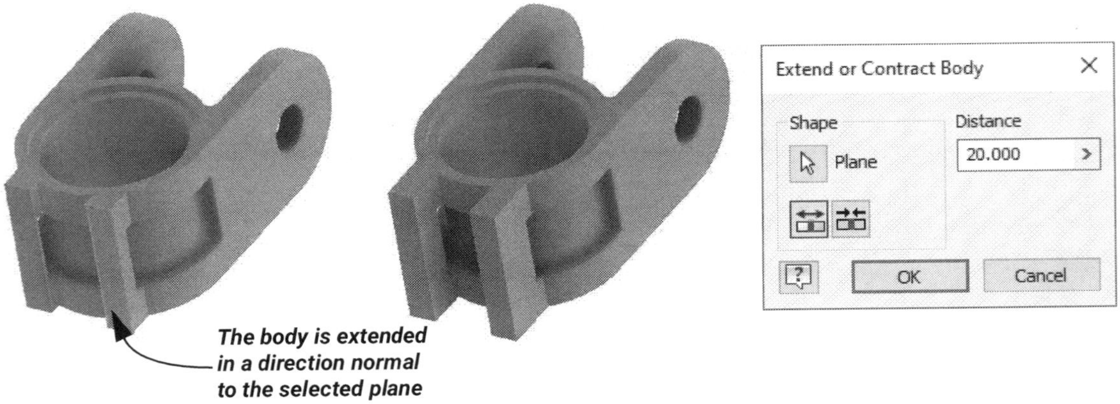

Figure 13–10

Delete Faces

To delete faces from the imported solid, select the faces and select **Delete** in the shortcut menu. In Figure 13–11, a face is selected and deleted from the imported solid. The geometry updates to account for the deleted face.

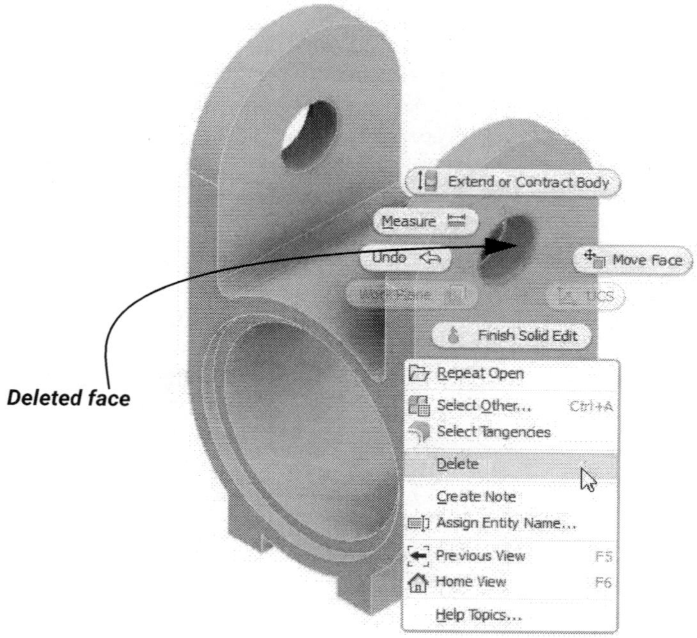

Figure 13–11

13.4 Direct Edit

Direct Edit is a method of editing both imported data and native Autodesk Inventor parametric models. These tools enable you to delete and adjust the size, scale, shape, and location of features by directly manipulating geometry in the model.

Uses of Direct Edit include:

- Incorporating quick yet precise changes to parametric data without changing the initial feature settings. The edits can still be considered parametric because they are added to the Model browser and can be edited.
- Making changes to imported Base Solid data.

To start the **Direct Edit** command, in the *3D Model* tab>Modify panel, click  (Direct). Alternatively, you can right-click on imported geometry in the Model browser and select **Direct Edit**. The Direct Edit mini-toolbar opens, which provides access to all of the Direct Edit tools, as shown in Figure 13–12. These tools are activated in the top row of the mini-toolbar and the remaining tools in the mini-toolbar update to support the selected editing type.

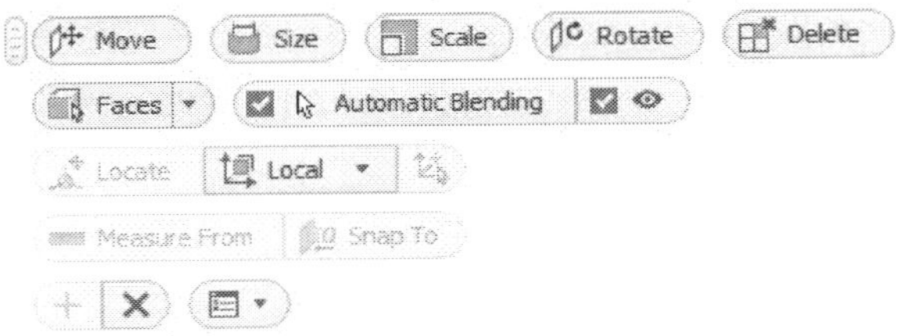

Figure 13–12

Move

How To: Move Geometry

1. In the mini-toolbar, click **Move**. The tools in the mini-toolbar update, as shown in Figure 13–13, to permit the moving of the geometry.
2. Use the Geometry Type drop-down list to select the geometry type that is going to be selected for moving. The options include faces and solids. Select the geometry in the model that you want to move. A triad displays on the model to define the move direction, as shown in Figure 13–13.

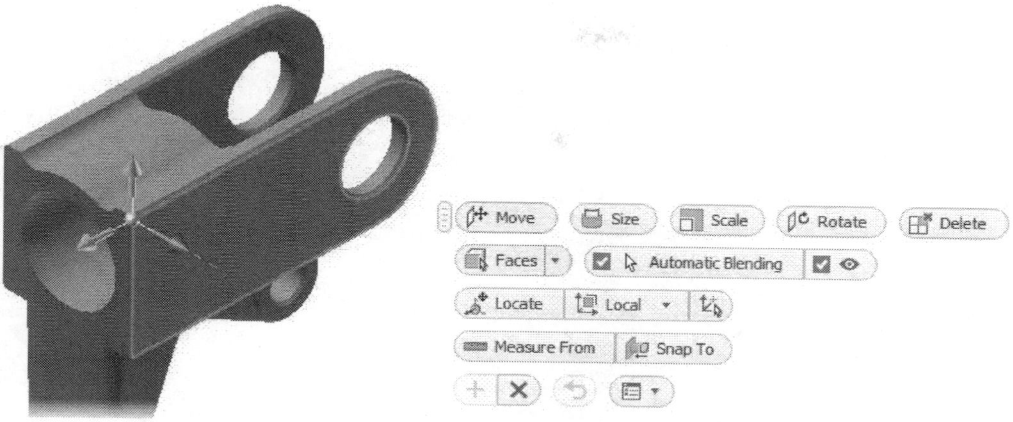

Figure 13–13

3. Enable/disable the **Automatic Blending** option, as required.
   - Enable the **Automatic Blending** option to ensure that when a face is moved, it takes into account any adjacent tangential faces and creates new blends, if required.
   - Disable the **Automatic Blending** option to ensure that adjacent tangential faces are not taken into account when a face is moved. If a face is moved to a location that prevents any adjacent blends from being created, the move operation will fail and the  icon will displays in the mini-toolbar.
4. The triad location in the model displays based on the location where the selection was made (identified with a green dot). The commands on the third line of the mini-toolbar enable you to manipulate the triad's location:
   - Click **Locate** to select a new location on the selected face. Hover the cursor over the selected face until the required placement location is highlighted in green and select to move it.
   - Click **Locate** or **World** to reorient the direction of triad axis based on the selected object (local) or the model origin (world), respectively.
   - When a local system is used, click  to realign the triad to other geometry in the model.

5. Select the arrow head on the appropriate triad axis to move the selected face or solid in that direction. To define the move with more accuracy, use either of the following:

   - Click **Measure From** to specify a start point and display an *Offset* field to accurately enter an offset value. In the example shown in Figure 13–14, the midpoint on the back edge was selected as a measurement reference and a value was entered.

Figure 13–14

   - Click **Snap To** to select a specific reference point on the geometry to which to move.

6. Click [+] to apply the operation. [Move icon] displays on the model indicating a **Move** operation was added to the Direct Edit feature. The Model browser also updates to indicate that a **Move** operation was added, as shown in Figure 13–15.

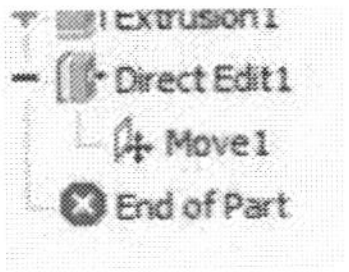

Figure 13–15

7. Continue to incorporate other direct edit manipulations in the model or click [X] to close the **Direct Edit** command.

Size

How To: Resize Geometry

1. In the mini-toolbar, click **Size**. The tools in the mini-toolbar update to permit the resizing of geometry, as shown in Figure 13–16.

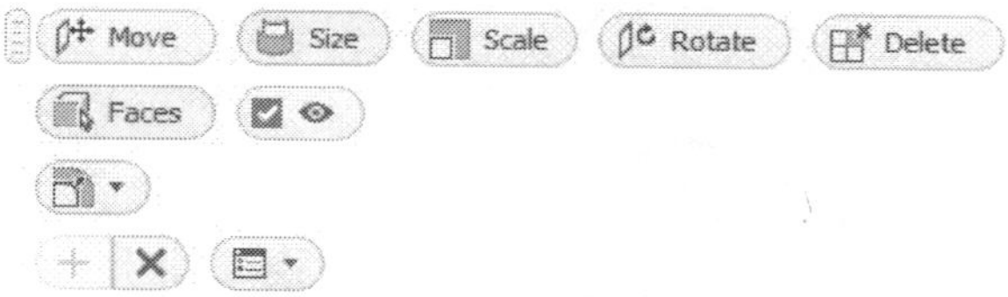

Figure 13–16

2. Select a face(s) in the model to resize it.
3. Drag the arrow or enter a value in the value field to define the new size. The face shown in Figure 13–17 is being resized.

Figure 13–17

4. Depending on the selected reference, the Modifier drop-down list, shown in Figure 13–18, provides control over how the selected face is resized. For example, **Offset** enables you to enter a distance, **Diameter** is used to change the size of cylindrical faces, and **Radius** changes the size of radial faces.

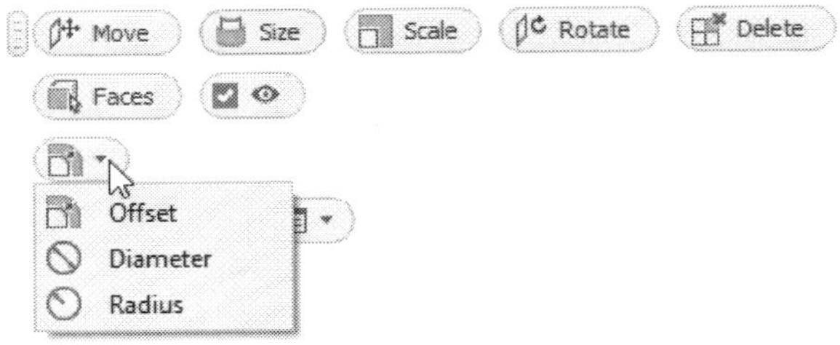

Figure 13–18

5. Click  to apply the operation.  displays on the model indicating that resizing was done to the face and added to the Direct Edit feature. The Model browser also updates to indicate that a **Size** operation was added to the Direct Edit feature, as shown in Figure 13–19.

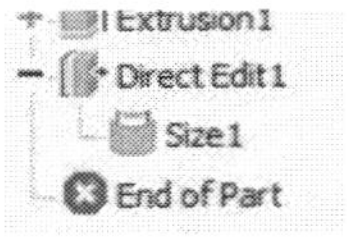

Figure 13–19

6. Continue to incorporate other direct edit manipulations to the model or click  to close the **Direct Edit** command.

Scale

How To: Scale Geometry

1. In the mini-toolbar, click **Scale**. The tools in the mini-toolbar update to permit the scaling of geometry, as shown in Figure 13–20.

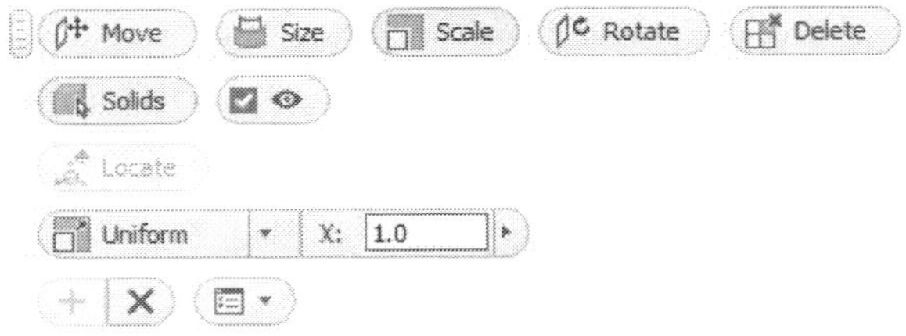

Figure 13–20

2. Select the solid that you want to scale.
3. In the drop-down list on the third line of the mini-toolbar select whether the scaling will be **Uniform** or **Non Uniform**.
4. The triad location appears at a system-defined location on the model. The commands on the second line of the mini-toolbar enable you to manipulate the triad's location:
   - Click **Locate** to select a new location on the face. Hover the cursor over the face until an acceptable placement location is highlighted in green and select to move it.
   - Click **Local** or **World** to reorient the direction of the triad axis based on the selected object (local) or the model origin (world), respectively. This option is only available if the scaling is set to **Non Uniform**.
   - When a local system is used, click to realign the triad to other geometry in the model. This option is only available if the scaling is set to **Non Uniform**.
5. Drag the arrow or enter a value in the value field(s) to define the scaling value. For a non-uniform scaling, you can enter values in all three directions. Figure 13–21 shows uniform scaling.

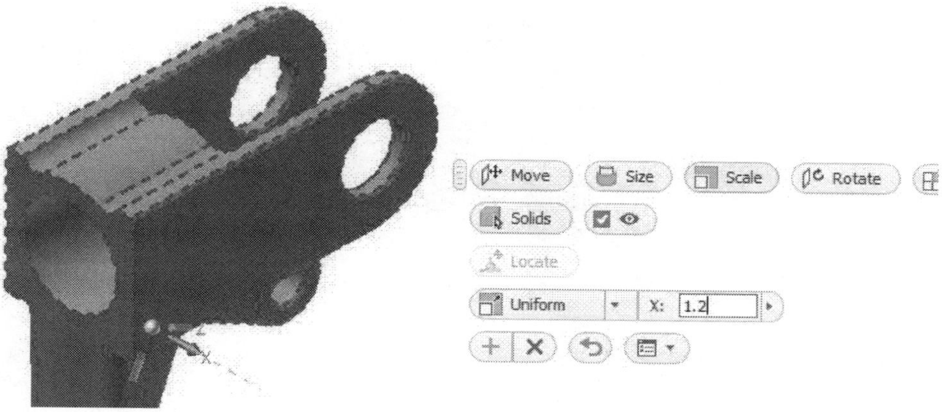

Figure 13–21

6. Click to apply the operation. displays on the model indicating that a scaling operation was added to the Direct Edit feature. The Model browser also updates to indicate that a **Scale** operation was added to the Direct Edit feature, as shown in Figure 13–22.

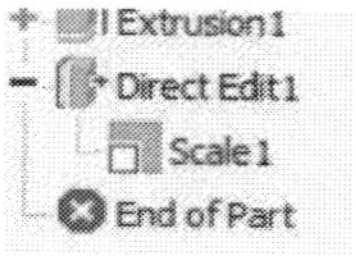

Figure 13–22

7. Continue to incorporate other direct edit manipulations to the model, or click to close the **Direct Edit** command.

Rotate

How To: Rotate Geometry

1. In the mini-toolbar, click **Rotate**. The tools in the mini-toolbar update to permit the rotation of geometry, as shown in Figure 13–23.

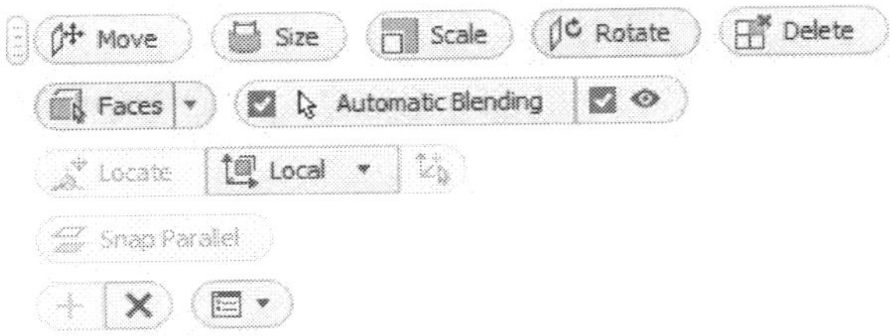

Figure 13–23

2. Use the Geometry Type drop-down list to select the geometry type that is going to be selected for rotating. The options include faces and solids. Select the geometry in the model that you want to rotate. A triad displays on the model to define the rotate direction, as shown in Figure 13–24.

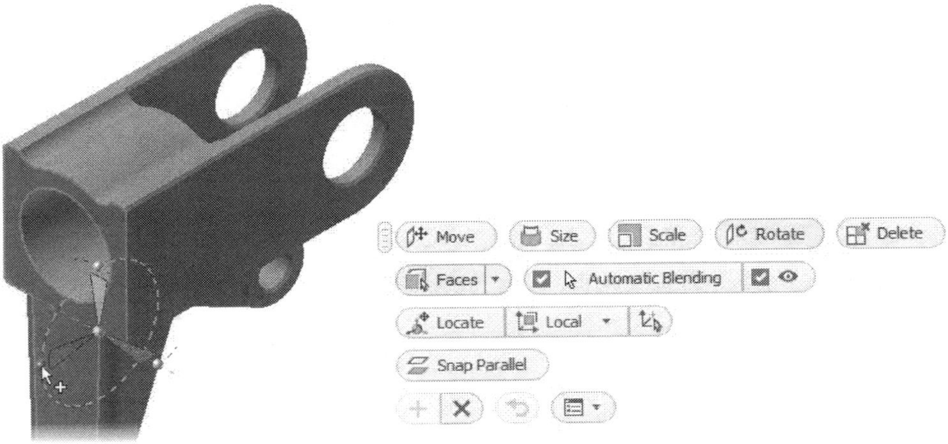

Figure 13–24

3. Enable/disable the **Automatic Blending** option, as required.
   - Enable the **Automatic Blending** option to ensure that when a face is rotated, it takes into account any adjacent tangential faces and creates new blends, if required.
   - Disable the **Automatic Blending** option to ensure that adjacent tangential faces are not taken into account when a face is rotated. If a face is rotated into a new location that prevents any adjacent blends from being created, the rotate operation will fail and the 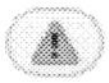 icon will appear in the mini-toolbar.
4. The triad location in the model displays based on the location on the face or solid at which you select the geometry (identified with green dot). The commands on the third line of the mini-toolbar enable you to manipulate the triad's location prior to rotation:
   - Click **Locate** to select a new location on the selected face. Hover the cursor over the selected face until an acceptable placement location is highlighted in green and select to move it.
   - Click **Local** or **World** to reorient the direction of the triad axis based on the selected object (local) or the model origin (world), respectively.
   - When a local system is used, click  to realign the triad to other geometry in the model.
5. Select the rotation wheel on the appropriate triad axis to rotate the selected face or solid in that direction. To define the rotation with more accuracy, click **Snap Parallel** to specify another plane to which the selected face should be set parallel, as shown in Figure 13–25.

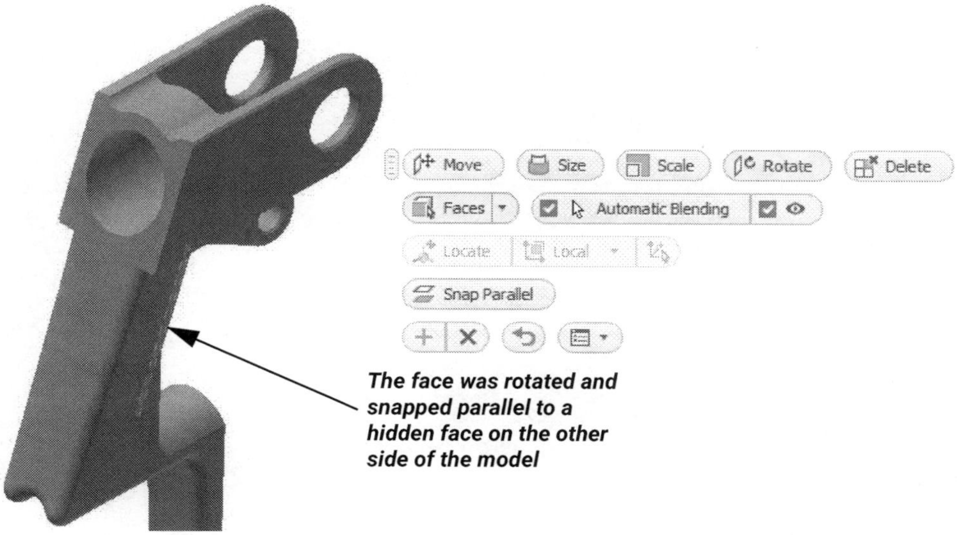

Figure 13–25

6. Click [+] to apply the operation. The rotate icon displays on the model indicating that a **Rotation** operation was added to the Direct Edit feature. The Model browser also updates to indicate that a **Rotation** operation was added to the Direct Edit feature, as shown in Figure 13–26.

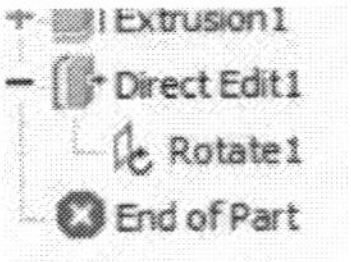

Figure 13–26

7. Continue to incorporate other direct edit manipulations to the model or click [X] to close the **Direct Edit** command.

Delete

How To: Delete Geometry

1. In the mini-toolbar, click **Delete**. The tools in the mini-toolbar update to permit the deleting of geometry, as shown in Figure 13–27.

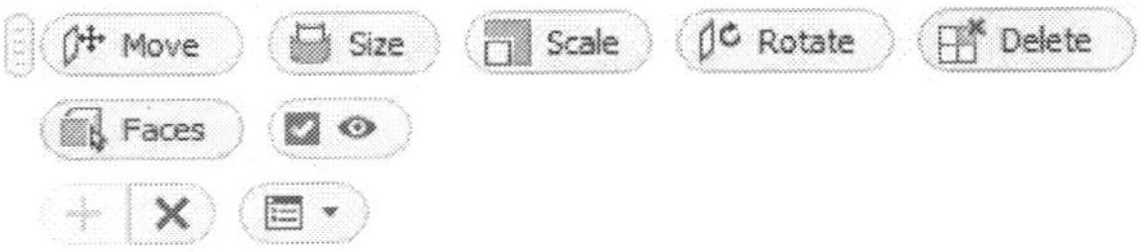

Figure 13–27

2. Select a face in the model to delete it.

3. Click [+] to apply the operation. The delete icon displays on the model indicating that a deletion was made in the model. The Model browser also updates to indicate that a **Delete** operation was added to the Direct Edit feature, as shown in Figure 13–28.

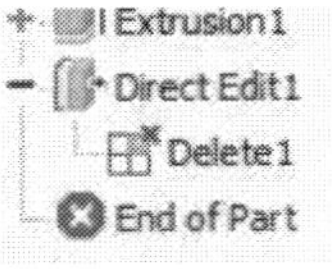

Figure 13–28

Continue to incorporate other direct edit manipulations to the model or click [X] to close the **Direct Edit** command.

Hint: Direct Edit Operation Failures

When adding a **Direct Edit** operation, ⚠ might display in the mini-toolbar after the reference has been selected. It indicates that the operation cannot be done on this reference. For example, surfaces can only be deleted if the geometry still forms a solid after deletion. The face generated from the hole geometry can be deleted, but an outside face of the model cannot. To delete an outside face, consider using the **Delete Face** command in the Modify panel. This command coverts the model to a surface model once an outside face is deleted.

To undo a failed face selection, click (Reset) to reset the operation or hold <Ctrl> and select the failing face again to remove it from the selection.

Once changes have been made with **Direct Edit** you can decide whether to edit, delete, or apply the edits to the parametric feature history (if available). This is done while the Direct Edit feature is active by right-clicking on the operation symbol that was added to the model, as shown in Figure 13–29.

Figure 13–29

13.5 Attaching Point Cloud Data

In addition to the file formats that can be directly opened/imported into the Autodesk Inventor software, you can also attach a point cloud dataset to a new or existing Autodesk Inventor file.

A point cloud file contains a large number of individual vertices that represent the surface of an object(s). The vertices are generally defined with an X, Y, and Z coordinate. The point cloud file is created by a 3D scanning device and can consist of many different file formats. Once imported, the scanned point cloud file can be used to verify fit and function in a top-level assembly file. Figure 13–30 shows an example of a scanned pump system. This piping system could be brought into an assembly model that contains other details of the design.

Figure 13–30

To attach a point cloud file to an Autodesk Inventor file, it must be first opened in the Autodesk® ReCap™ software, indexed, and then saved for import into the Autodesk Inventor software.

The point cloud files that can be indexed in the Autodesk ReCap software are shown in Figure 13–31.

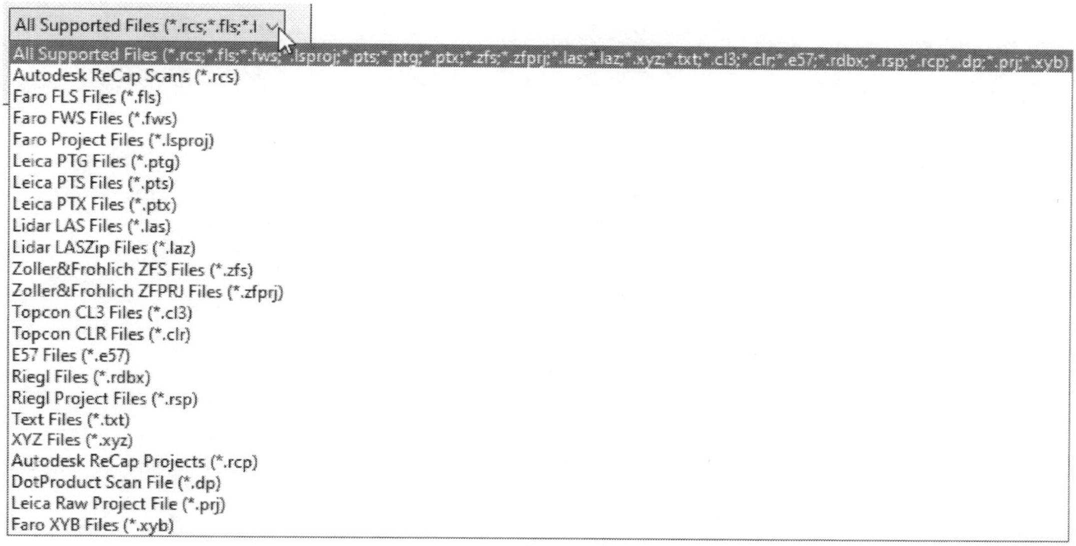

Figure 13–31

How To: Index a Point Cloud File

1. Launch the Autodesk ReCap software.
2. Close the Welcome screen.
3. In the top left corner of the interface, select **new project** to create a new project file to index the point cloud data.
4. Select **import point cloud** to create the project by importing data.
5. Enter a name for the project. A default path for the project is listed below the project name. Select the default path to open the Browse for Folder dialog box and assign a new folder path.
6. Click **proceed** once the project name and folder have been confirmed.
7. On the Import files page, select **select files to import** to open the Import Point Clouds dialog box. Browse to and select a supported point cloud file. Click **Open**.
8. Select **launch project** in the lower right-hand corner to open the project and indexed data in the Autodesk ReCap software. Once opened, you can use additional tools to manipulate and work with the data. The project is saved in the *Project* directory and the indexed data is saved in the *Project* directory\\<*project name*> folder as an .RCS file.

   Note: *Refer to the Autodesk ReCap Help for more information about customizing imported Point Cloud Data.*

How To: Attach a Point Cloud File in a Model

1. In the *Manage* tab>Point Cloud panel, click (Attach).
2. In the Select Point Cloud File dialog box, select the indexed file (.RCS or .RCP) to attach. Click **Open**.
3. Select a location in the Autodesk Inventor file to place the point cloud data. The Attach Point Cloud dialog box opens enabling you to customize the attachment point and rotation values, and to adjust the density, as shown in Figure 13–32.

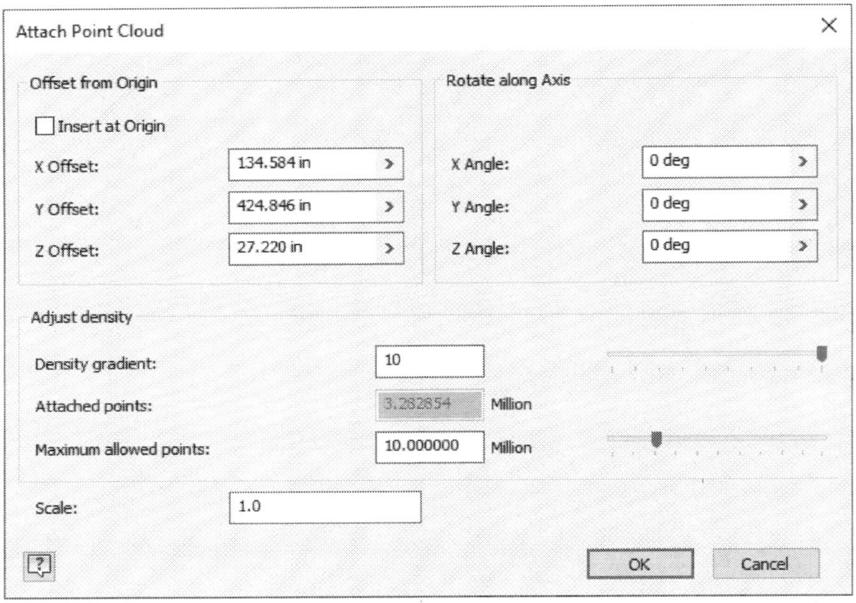

Figure 13–32

4. Click **OK** to attach the point cloud. Once imported, the Model browser updates to include a Point Clouds node that lists the imported file, as shown in Figure 13–33.

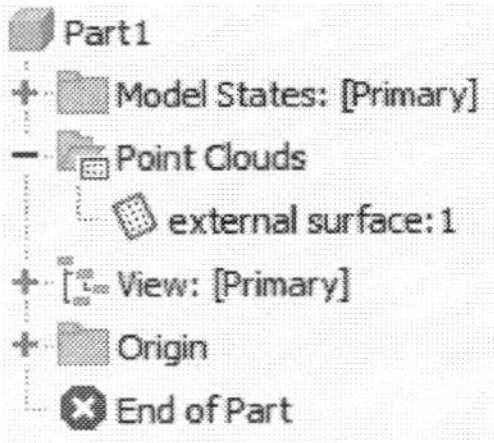

Figure 13–33

Once the point cloud data has been imported, you can use the commands in the Point Cloud panel (as shown in Figure 13–34) to work with the data.

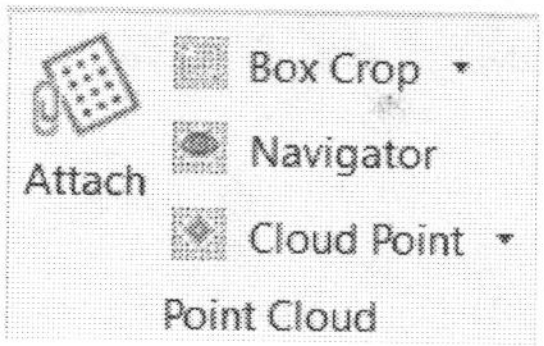

Figure 13–34

- Crop the point cloud data to remove unnecessary data from the file. To crop, click (Box Crop) in the Point Cloud panel and draw a bounding box around the area that is to be kept. Select an arrow on any of the six sides of the bounding box and drag to change the position of its wall or enter an explicit value, as shown in Figure 13–35. Continue to activate each wall and modify as required, to create the required bounding box. Click to crop.

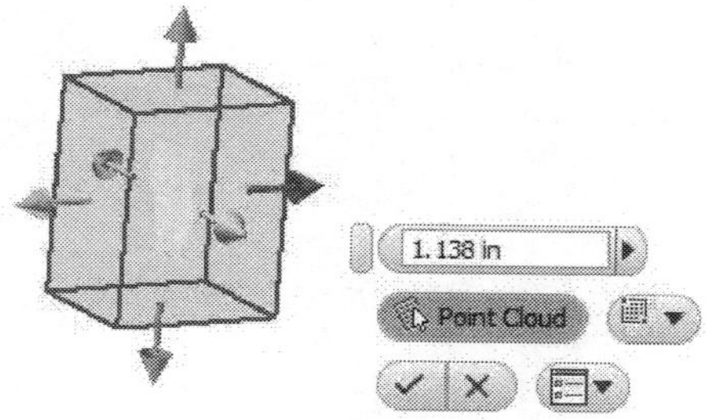

Figure 13–35

- Use the **Uncrop** command to remove the previous crop operation and return all of the point cloud data to the file. To uncrop, expand the **Box Crop** command and click (Uncrop) in the Point Cloud panel.
- Open the Point Cloud Navigator dialog box to control the visibility status of any attached point cloud data. To open the dialog box, click (Navigator) in the Point Cloud panel and click next to the data file to toggle its visibility off. Click to toggle its visibility back on. Its visibility can also be toggled off in the Model browser.
- Add a work point to the model by using a point cloud point as a reference. To create a work point on an existing cloud point, click (Cloud Point) in the Point Cloud panel and select a point. Work points can be used to create additional geometry in the model.
- Add a Work Plane to the model by using points in the point cloud as references. To create a Work Plane, click (Cloud Plane) in the Point Cloud panel and select in the model to create the plane. The plane is inferred from a set of points in the point cloud.

Practice 13a
Opening a CATIA Assembly

Practice Objectives

- Open a CATIA assembly file in Autodesk Inventor by referencing the source data.
- Incorporate changes made to the CATIA model in the Autodesk Inventor model.

In this practice, you will open a CATIA assembly file using the **Reference Model** option. By importing the CAD data in this way, changes made in the source model update in the Autodesk Inventor assembly. A change in a CATIA model is made, and you will update the change in the assembly. The final model is shown in Figure 13–36.

Figure 13–36

Task 1: Import a CATIA assembly file in Autodesk Inventor.

1. In the Quick Access Toolbar, click .
2. In the Open dialog box, navigate to the *SparkPlug* folder in the practice files folder.
3. In the Files of type drop-down list, select **CATIA V5 Files**.

   ***Note:** Alternatively, the CATIA assembly could be placed in an existing assembly using **Place Imported CAD Files** on the Component panel.*

4. Select **SparkPlug.CATProduct** and click **Open**. The Import dialog box opens.
5. Select **Reference Model** from the *Import Type* area. This assembly is required for use in an Autodesk Inventor assembly model. If changes are made in the source model, the changes must be updated in the Inventor version of the file.
6. In the *Object Filters* area, ensure that only **Solids** is selected. Clear any other options.

7. In the *Inventor Length Units* area, ensure that **From source** is selected. The dialog box updates as shown in Figure 13–37.

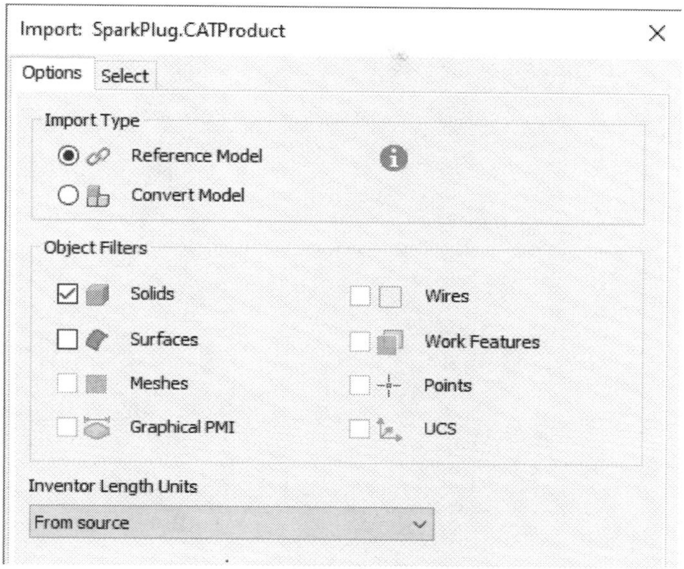

Figure 13–37

8. In the *Select* tab, click **Load Model**. A preview of the CATIA assembly displays in the graphics window and the components of the assembly are listed.

9. Click the circular node associated with the **Wire.1** component to toggle its status to (Excluded). Leave all of the other components as (Included), as shown in Figure 13–38.

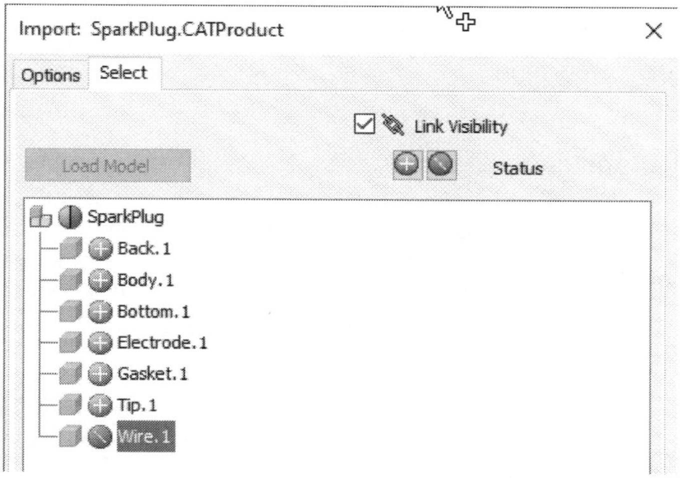

Figure 13–38

10. Click **OK** to close the dialog box and import the geometry. The assembly is listed in the Model browser, as shown in Figure 13–39.

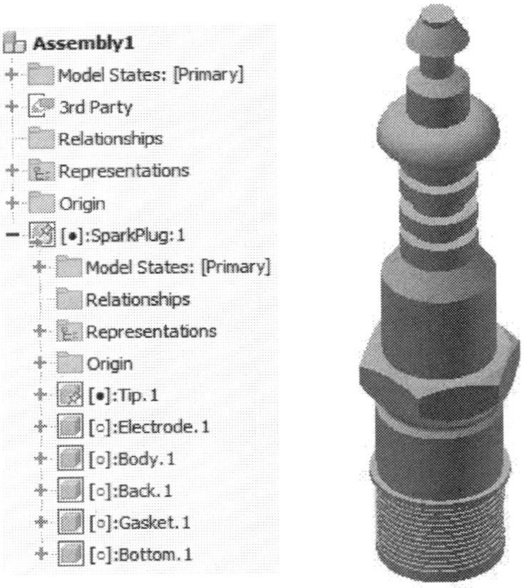

Figure 13–39

11. Save the assembly as **Sparkplug.iam** in the *SparkPlug* folder.

Task 2: Edit the imported options.

1. In the Model browser, right-click on **SparkPlug:1** and select **Edit Import** to open the Import dialog box that was used to import the files.
2. In the *Select* tab, select adjacent to the **Wire.1** component to include it in the imported geometry.
3. Click **OK** to confirm the change. Note that the component is now listed in the Model browser.

Task 3: Edit the imported model geometry.

In this portion of the practice, you will simulate making a design change in the original CATIA model. To do this, you will rename a file that has been provided to you so that it is used instead of the existing file. This file has had modifications made to it in CATIA. By renaming, you are simulating that the change was made locally to the CATIA file.

1. In Windows Explorer, navigate to your practice files folder and open the *SparkPlug* folder.
2. Select the **Body.CATPart** file and rename it to **Body_OLD.CATPart**.
3. Select the **Body_Updated.CATPart** file and rename it to **Body.CATPart**.
4. Return to the Autodesk Inventor software.

5. Note in the Model browser that the icon displays next to the **SparkPlug:1** imported geometry node (it might take a moment to update). In the Quick Access Toolbar, click (Local Update) to update the imported geometry with the change that was made in the source model. The model appears as shown in Figure 13–40.

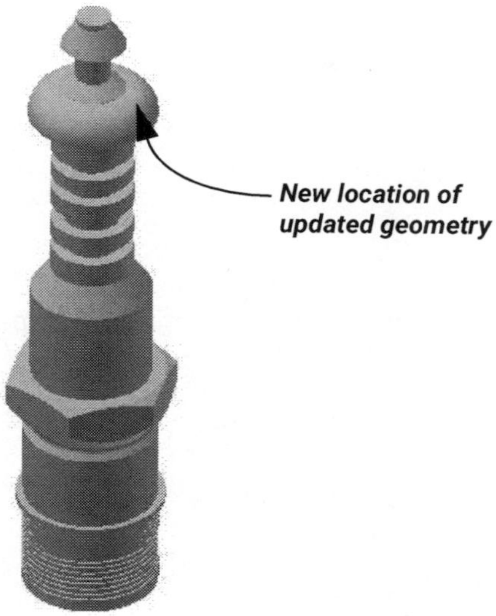

Figure 13–40

6. In Model browser, right-click on **SparkPlug:1** and note the **Suppress Link** and **Break Link** options. These options can be used to either temporarily break the link with the source CATIA model (**Suppress Link**) or permanently break the link (**Break Link**).
7. Save the file and close the window.

End of practice

Practice 13b
Opening STEP Files

Practice Objectives

- Open a STEP file in the Autodesk Inventor software.
- Edit the imported STEP data to delete a face, move a face, and change its size.
- Add parametric Autodesk Inventor features to the imported geometry.

In this practice, you will open auxpart.stp and edit the solid base model to make changes to the imported data. You will also add standard Autodesk Inventor features (fillets) to the model and illustrate that the fillet is parametric although the imported geometry is not. The final model is shown in Figure 13–41.

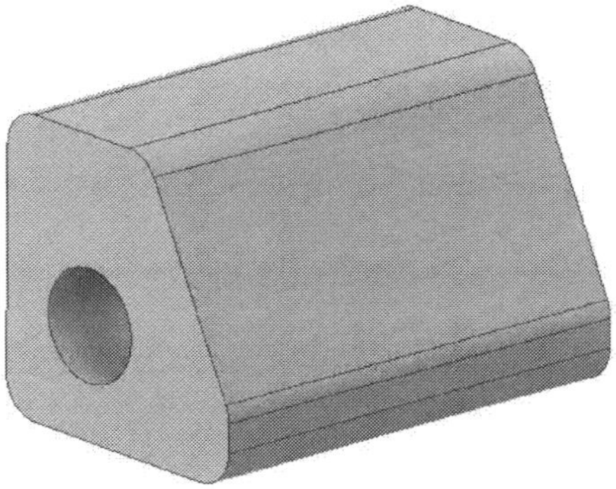

Figure 13–41

Task 1: Open a part file.

1. In the Quick Access Toolbar, click .
2. In the Open dialog box, in the Files of type drop-down list, select **STEP Files**.
3. Select **auxpart.stp** from the top-level practice files folder. Click **Open**. The Import dialog box opens.
4. Select **Convert Model** from the *Import Type* area to import the file.
5. In the *Object Filters* area, ensure that **Solids** is selected. Clear any other options, if required.
6. In the *Inventor Length Units* area, ensure that **From source** is selected.
7. In the *Part Options* area, select **Composite** from the Surfaces drop-down list.

8. Click **OK** to close the dialog box and import the geometry. The geometry is listed as **Base1** in the Model browser, as shown in Figure 13–42. The imported solid is a single feature with no associativity between it and the original file.

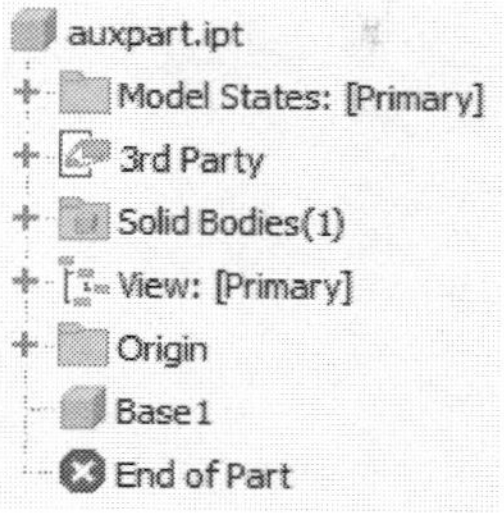

Figure 13–42

Task 2: Edit the imported model geometry.

1. In the Model browser, right-click on **Base1** and select **Edit Solid**. The *Edit Base Solid* tab displays. The panels available provide editing options for imported solids.
2. Select the surface of the hole, as shown in Figure 13–43.

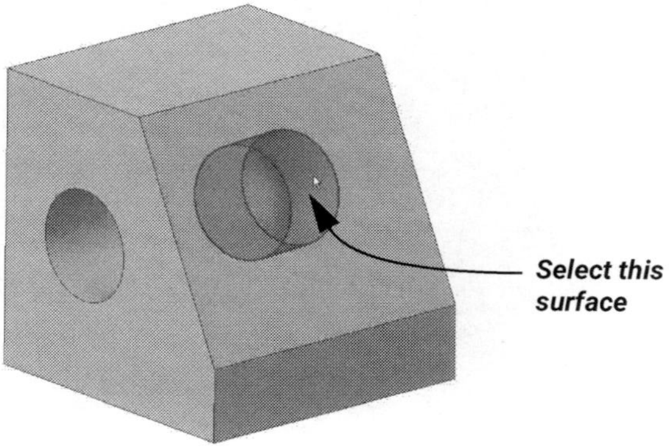

Figure 13–43

3. Right-click and select **Delete** to remove the hole.
4. In the Modify panel, click (Move Face). The Move Face mini-toolbar opens. The **Move Face** option enables you to select one or more faces on the imported solid to move them in a specified direction.

5. In the mini-toolbar, expand the  drop-down list and select **Direction and Distance,** as shown in Figure 13–44.

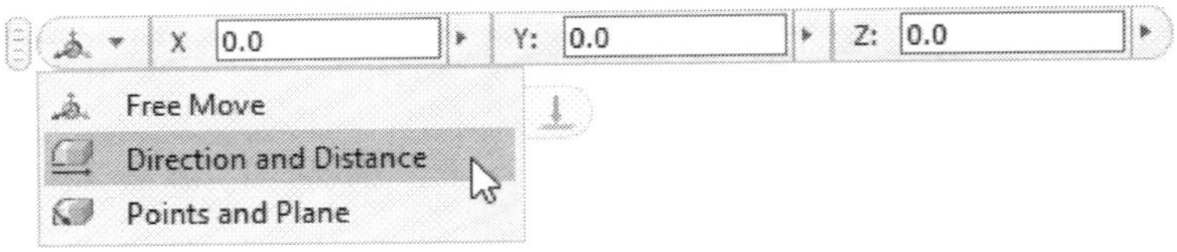

Figure 13–44

6. In the mini-toolbar, the **Faces** option is selected by default. Select the hole face as shown in Figure 13–45.
7. In the mini-toolbar, click **Direction** and select the edge indicated in Figure 13–45 to define the direction for the move. If required, click  to flip the direction of the arrow, as shown in Figure 13–45.

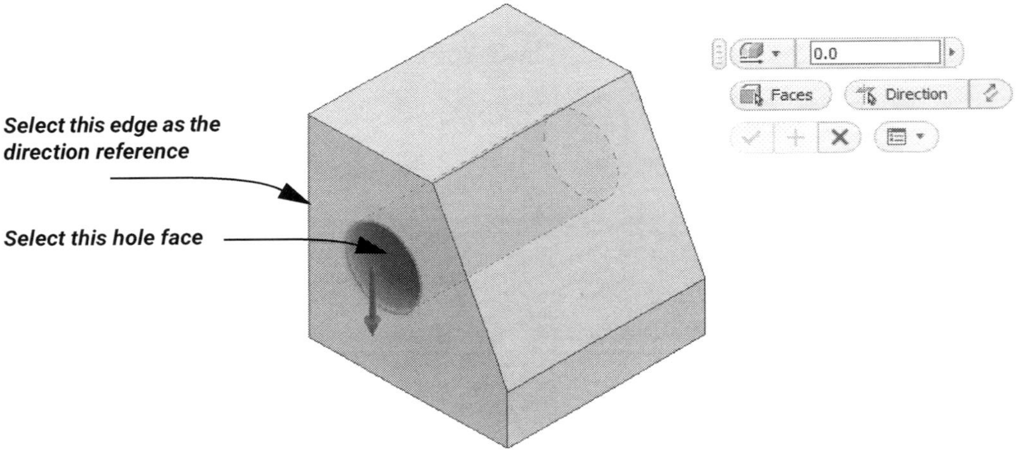

Figure 13–45

8. In the *Distance* field, enter **0.25**. Complete the move. The part displays as shown in Figure 13–46.

Figure 13–46

9. In the Modify panel, click  (Extend/Contract Body). This option resizes an imported solid in a direction perpendicular to a selected plane. The Extend or Contract Body dialog box opens as shown in Figure 13–47.

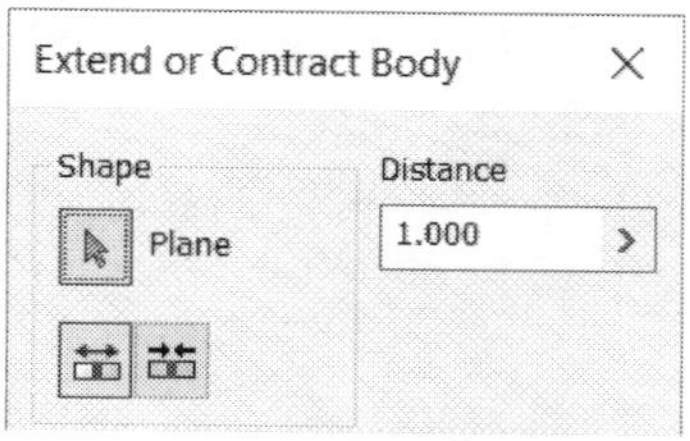

Figure 13–47

10. Select the face shown in Figure 13–48 as the reference plane for the extension.

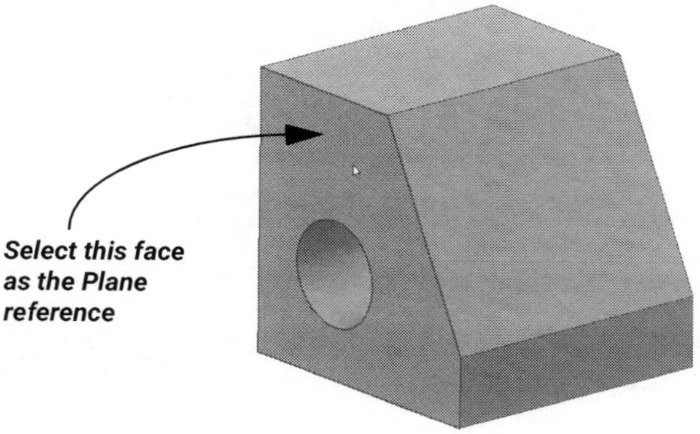

Figure 13–48

11. In the *Distance* field, enter **2** and click  (Expand) to expand the solid part.

12. Click **OK**. The part displays as shown in Figure 13–49. The imported geometry is extended in length by the specified distance.

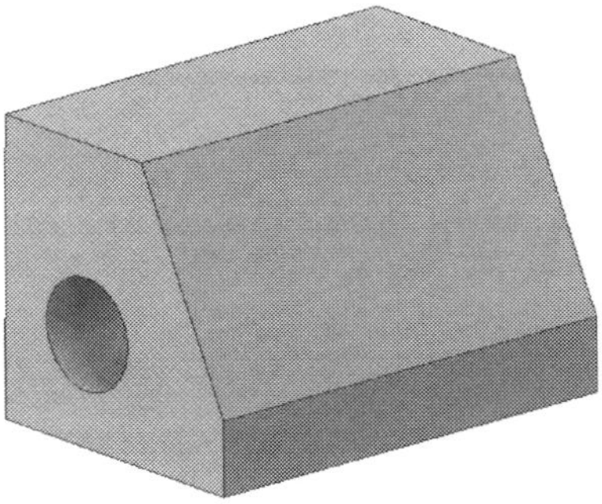

Figure 13–49

13. In the Exit panel, click  (Finish Base Solid).
14. Add fillets to the horizontal edges of the model using the default radius value.
15. In the Model browser, right-click on **Fillet1** and select **Show Dimensions**.
16. Set the new *Radius* to **0.25** and press <Enter>.
17. Update the model to incorporate the dimension change. The part displays as shown in Figure 13–50. Note that the fillet is parametric although the imported geometry is not.

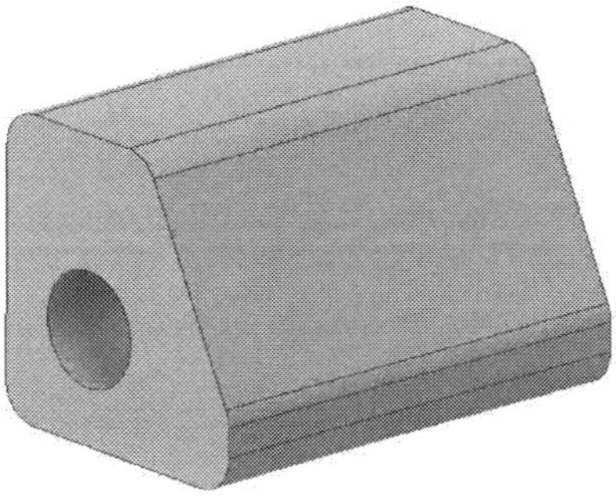

Figure 13–50

18. Save the part and close the window.

End of practice

Practice 13c
Direct Edit

Practice Objectives

- Open a CATIA part model and review the base solid geometry that was imported.
- Edit the base solid geometry using the **Direct Edit** option to move, resize, rotate, and delete faces on imported geometry.

In this practice, you will learn how to use the **Direct Edit** option to edit base solid geometry that was imported into the Autodesk Inventor software. Faces will be deleted, moved, resized, and rotated to obtain the required modified geometry. To complete the practice, you are also provided with a native Autodesk Inventor file to edit using the Direct Edit tools.

Task 1: Open a CATIA model.

1. Open the **Cover.CATPart** model from the practice files folder. The Import dialog box opens.
2. In the *Import Type* area, select **Convert Model** to import the geometry and break the link with the original model.
3. In the *Object Filters* area, ensure that **Solids** is selected. Clear any other options, if required.
4. In the *Inventor Length Units* area, ensure that **From source** is selected.
5. In the *Part Options* area, select **Composite** from the Surfaces drop-down list.
6. Click **OK** to close the dialog box and import the geometry. The Model browser shows that a base feature called Casting has been imported, as shown in Figure 13–51.

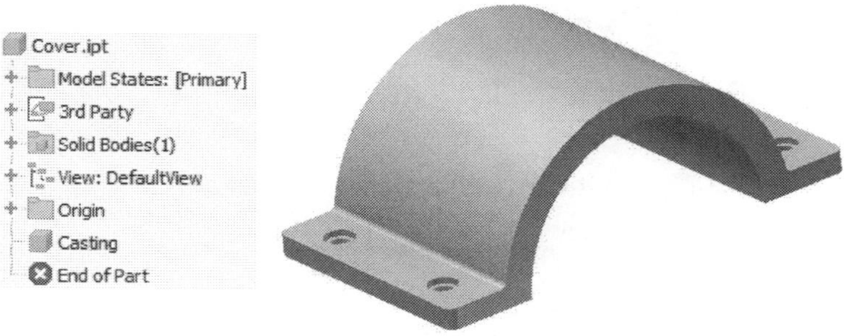

Figure 13–51

Task 2: Edit the Base Solid that was imported to move a face.

1. In the *3D Model* tab>Modify panel, click (Direct). The Direct Edit mini-toolbar opens, as shown in Figure 13–52.

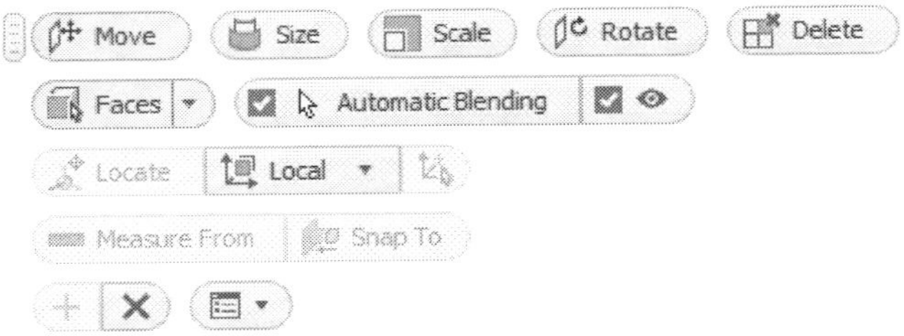

Figure 13–52

2. Ensure that **Move** is selected in the mini-toolbar. Hover the cursor over the face shown in Figure 13–53 as the face to be moved. Hold <Ctrl> to maintain this surface while locating the control point. Hover the cursor over different vertices on the face before selecting. The highlighted green dot determines where the triad will be located for moving. Ensure that you click in the area shown to place the triad and begin moving the face.

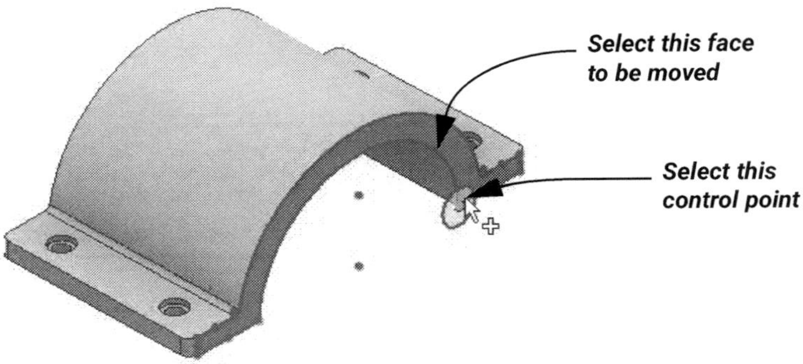

Figure 13–53

3. By default, the X axis (local to the model) is active, as indicated by the gold colored X axis on the triad. Drag the face outward by dragging the arrowhead, as shown in Figure 13–54.

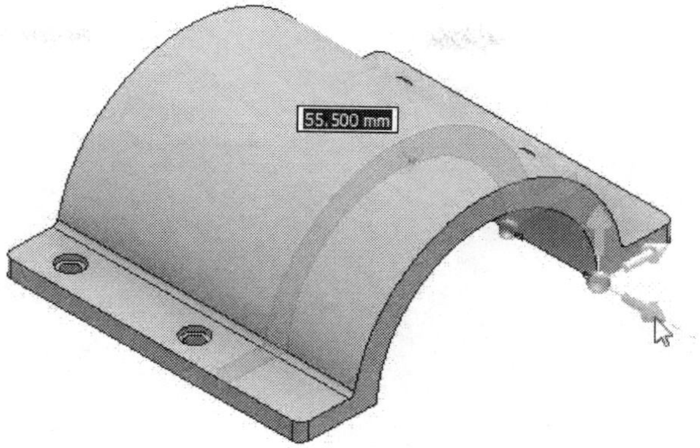

Figure 13–54

4. Enter **50** as the value by which the face will be moved and click [icon] to complete the Move operation.

5. Note that [icon] displays on the model, indicating that the move exists in the Direct Edit feature, as shown in Figure 13–55. **Move1** also displays in the Model browser in the Direct Edit feature.

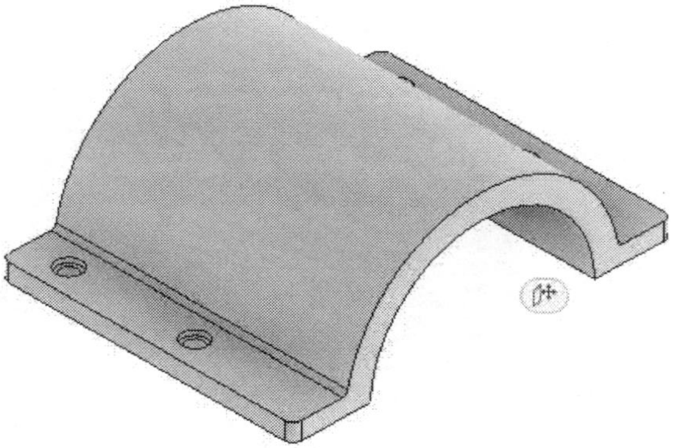

Figure 13–55

6. Right-click on [icon] and select **Edit Operation** to edit the Move operation that was just added.

7. Instead of entering a specific value to move the face, the required depth is to be measured relative to the back surface. Click **Measure From** and select the edge shown in Figure 13–56. Enter **180** as the value.

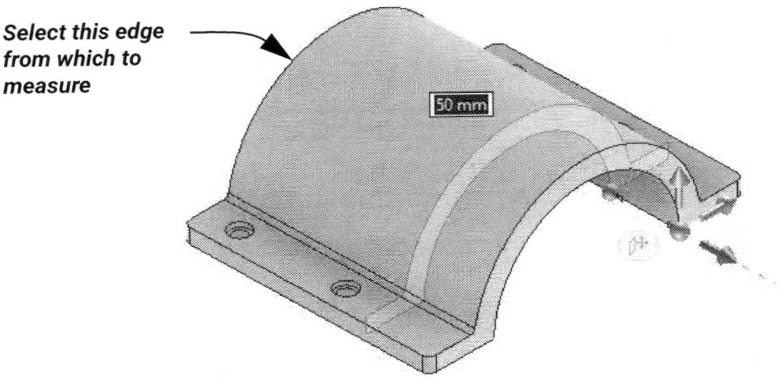

Figure 13–56

8. Click to complete the changes.
9. Select the face shown in Figure 13–57 and move it **20 mm**. Do the same on the opposite face. Once the two Move operations have been added, the model displays as shown in Figure 13–57.

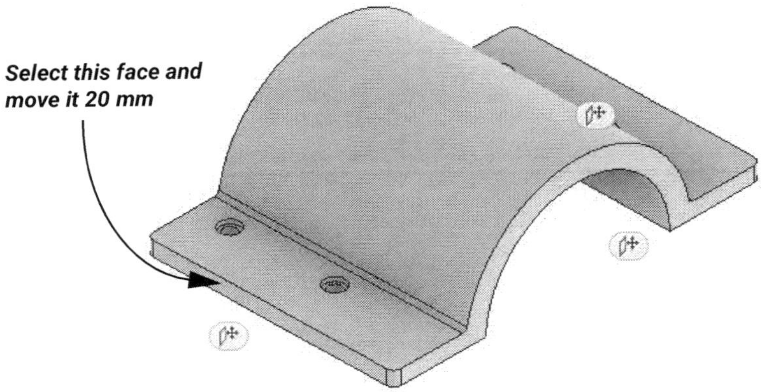

Figure 13–57

Task 3: Edit the position and size of the holes.

1. In the mini-toolbar, select **Delete** to activate the Delete operation.

2. Select the four faces that were created in the holes as counterbores. Two of these faces are shown in Figure 13–58, but select all four.

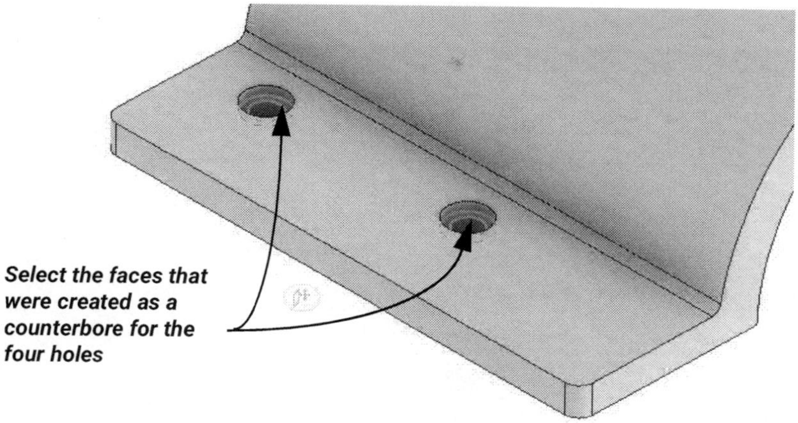

Figure 13–58

3. Click [+] to complete the operation. Four operations have now been added to the Direct Edit feature.
4. Click **Size** and select the surface of the hole shown in Figure 13–59.
5. Drag the triad arrow head. Enter **-6** to enlarge the diameter by an exact value, as shown in Figure 13–59.

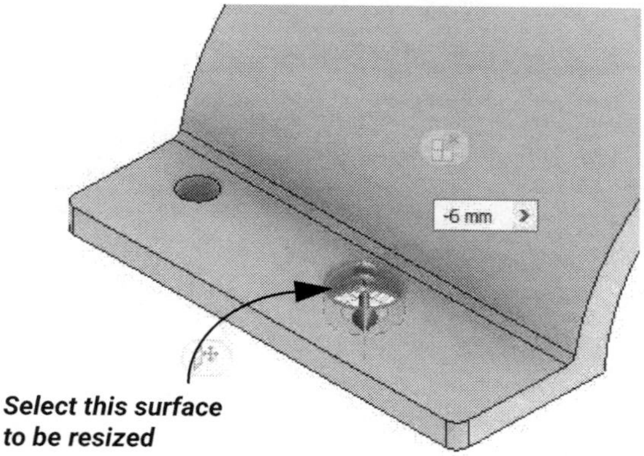

Figure 13–59

6. Click [+] to complete the operation.
7. With **Size** still active, select the inside face of the hole that you just resized.
8. Expand [icon] and select **Diameter**.

9. Select the hole faces in the three remaining holes, as shown in Figure 13–60. This sets the size of the three selected faces to that of the previously modified hole.

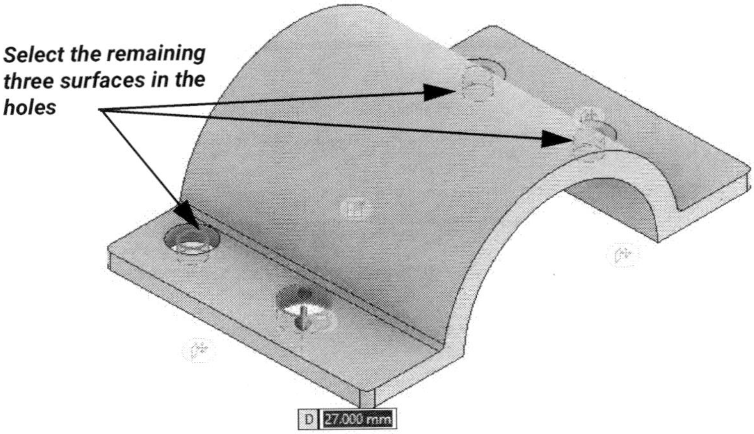

Figure 13–60

10. Click [+] to complete the operation.
11. Click **Move** and select the surface of the hole shown in Figure 13–61. Ensure that the highlighted green point is at the center of the circle to enable you to move the center of the hole.

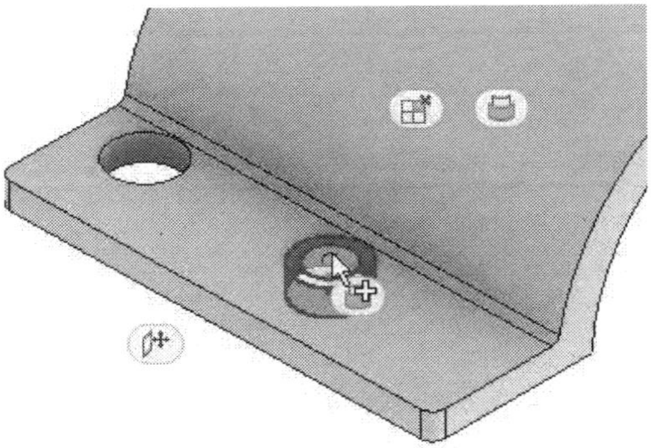

Figure 13–61

12. Ensure the X-axis arrow on the triad is selected.

13. Click **Measure From** and select the front edge (midpoint) of the model, as shown in Figure 13–62. Enter **-25 mm** as the value. Do not press <Enter>.

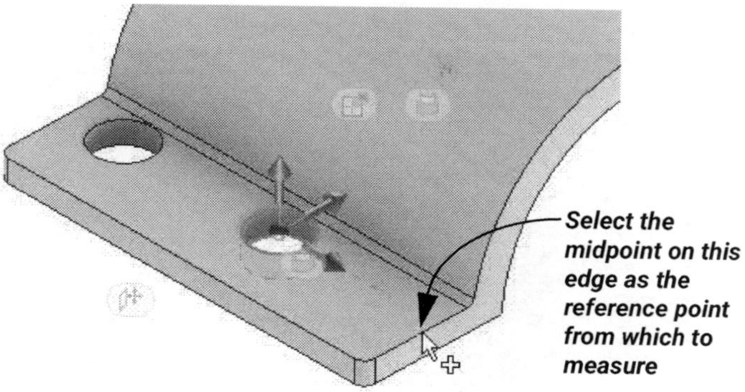

Figure 13–62

14. Select the Y-axis arrow on the triad.

15. Click **Measure From** and select the side edge as shown in Figure 13–63. Enter **25 mm** as the value and press <Enter> to complete the operation.

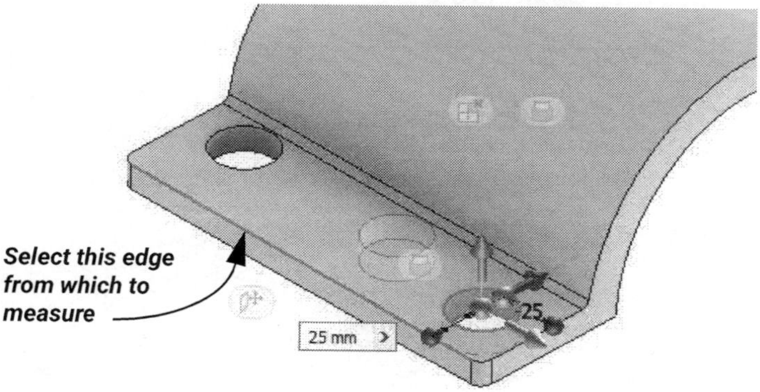

Figure 13–63

16. Adjust the positions of the other three holes in the model so that they are positioned in the same way from their nearest edges. The model should display similar to that shown in Figure 13–64.

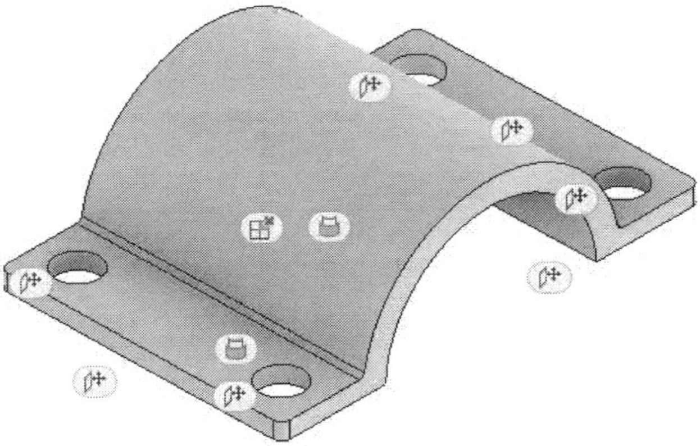

Figure 13–64

Task 4: Rotate faces and scale the model.

1. Click **Rotate** and hover the cursor over the surface shown in Figure 13–65. Holding <Ctrl>, continue to move the mouse and ensure that the highlighted green point is at the center of the edge shown. Press the left mouse button to select it. You are now able to rotate as required from this point.

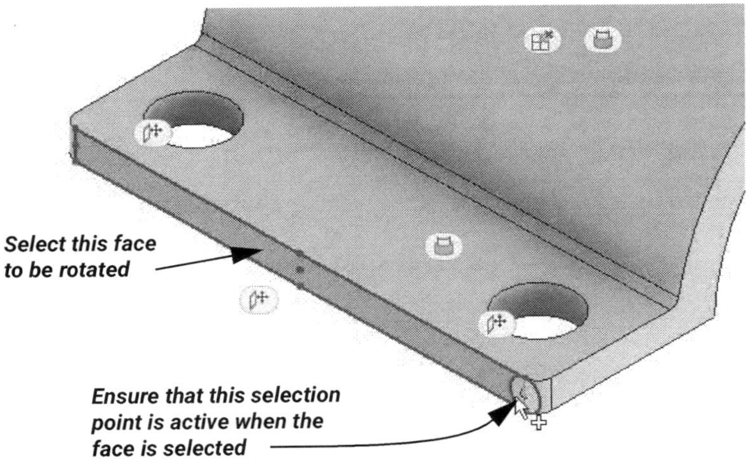

Figure 13–65

2. Rotate the wheel as shown in Figure 13–66. Drag the triad to **20.00 deg**. Alternatively, you can enter the value. Press <Enter>.

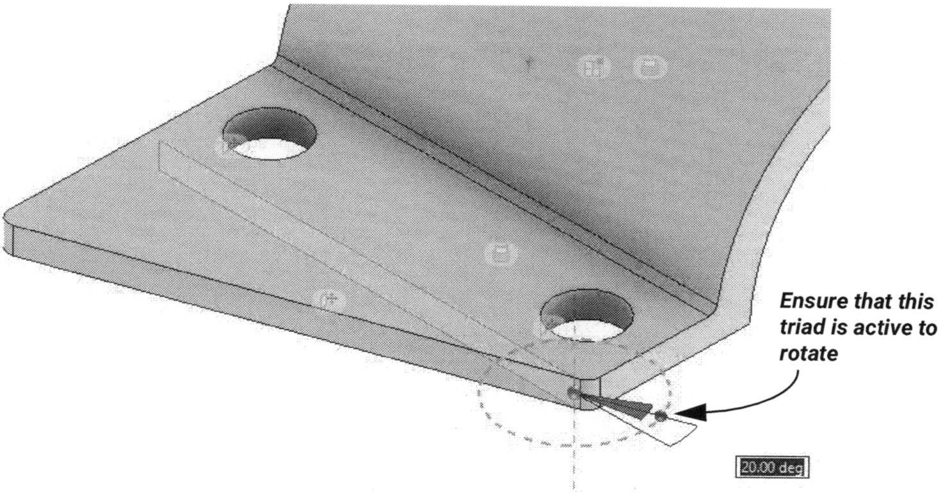

Figure 13–66

3. Rotate the opposite edge in the same way. Review the Model browser and note that all of the operations are listed in the Direct Edit feature.

4. Click  to cancel the Direct Edit feature. The model displays as shown in Figure 13–67.

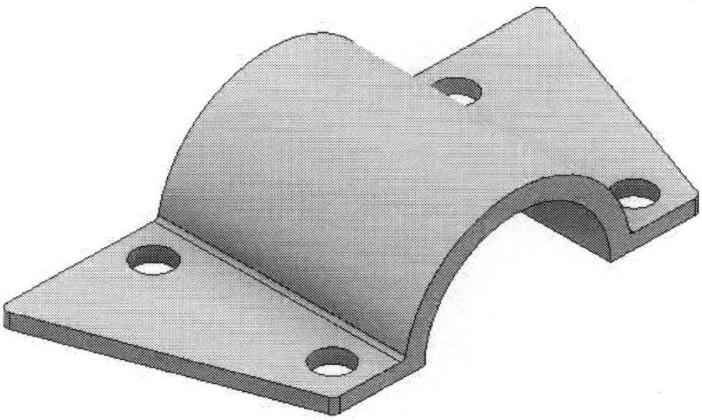

Figure 13–67

5. Note that the Model browser lists the Direct Edit feature and that the operations are no longer displayed. To edit or review the operations you must edit the feature.
6. Double-click on the **Direct Edit** feature in the Model browser.

7. Right-click on (icon) in the graphics window and select **Delete** (as shown in Figure 13–68) to remove the operation from the model.

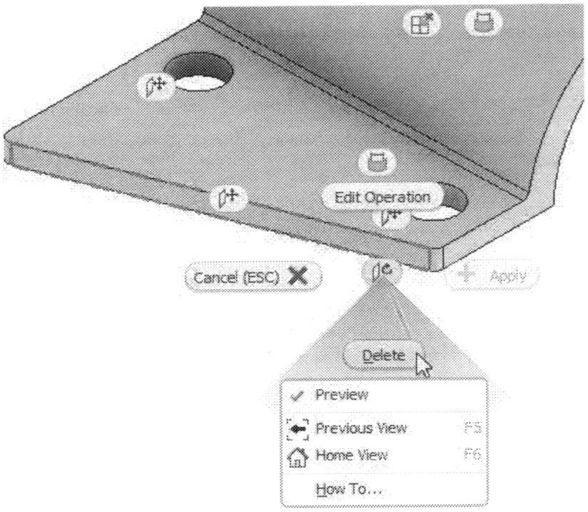

Figure 13–68

8. Remove the second **Rotate** operation.
9. Click **Scale** and select the solid body shown in Figure 13–69.

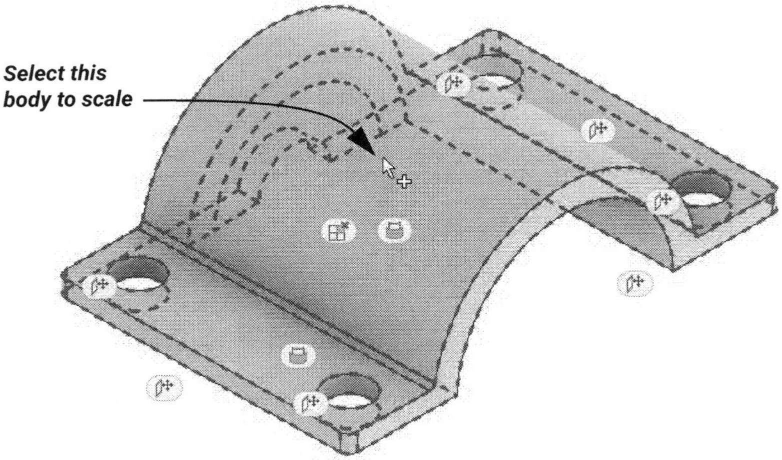

Figure 13–69

10. Ensure that the X-axis manipulator is active. Enter **2** in the entry field and press <Enter> to scale the model.

11. Click (icon) to cancel the Direct Edit feature.

12. Save the model and close the window.

Hint: Using Direct Edit with Referenced CAD Models

It is not recommended to add Direct Edit features to a CAD model that has been imported and maintains its link to the source CAD model. This is because the Direct Edit feature may fail if the model changes in the source CAD tool.

End of practice

Chapter Review Questions

1. Which of the following two Import Type opens should be used to ensure that a link to the source file is maintained and that changes that are made to the imported data can be updated?
   a. Reference Model
   b. Convert Model

2. Which of the statements are true regarding the Import dialog box when importing CAD data from another software package? (Select all that apply.)
   a. If a part file is imported, a new Autodesk Inventor part file is created.
   b. If an assembly is imported, a new Autodesk Inventor assembly is created.
   c. When importing a part into the Autodesk Inventor software, you can set the Part options to recognize each feature as a separate body.
   d. All geometry in the CAD file must be imported. Once imported, you can remove geometry as required.

3. Which of the following menu options enable you to export a .DWG file as a .BMP file? (Select all that apply.)
   a. File>Save>Save
   b. File>Save As>Save As
   c. File>Save As>Save Copy As
   d. File>Save As>Save Copy as Template
   e. File>Export>Image

4. Which commands can be used to edit the Base geometry shown on the left in Figure 13–70 to create the geometry shown on the right in Figure 13–70? (Select all that apply.)

Figure 13–70

a. Move Face
b. Offset
c. Extend/Contract Body
d. Delete

5. The **Extend/Contract Body** option in the Edit Base Solid ribbon enables you to resize selected features on an import solid.

a. True
b. False

6. How many **Delete** operations were completed on the model on the left side in Figure 13–71 to obtain the model shown on the right side in Figure 13–71?

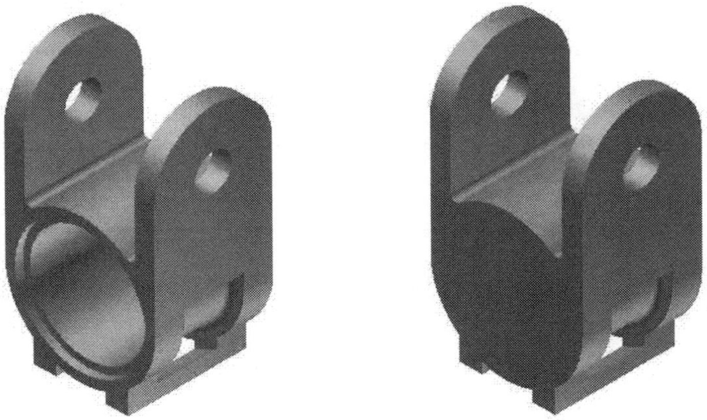

Figure 13–71

   a. 1
   b. 2
   c. 4
   d. None, delete would not obtain this final geometry.

7. Which of the following are Direct Edit tools that are available in the Direct Edit mini-toolbar? (Select all that apply.)
   a. Move
   b. Size
   c. Define Envelopes
   d. Rotate
   e. Remove Details
   f. Delete
   g. Scale

8. The green dot that is highlighted on a face that is being relocated using the **Direct Edit** command indicates where the triad is placed.
   a. True
   b. False

9. Which of the following enables you to define the measurement reference point when using **Direct Edit**?

   a. Measure From

   b. Snap To

   c. 

   d. Snap Parallel

10. Which of the following icons displays in the Direct Edit mini-toolbar when a face in the exterior geometry on the model is selected for deletion?

    a. 

    b. 

    c. 

    d. 

11. Which software product should you use to index the point cloud data before importing it into the Autodesk Inventor software?

    a. Autodesk® Revit®

    b. Autodesk® Inventor®

    c. Autodesk® ReCap™

    d. Autodesk® Alias®

Command Summary

Button	Command	Location
N/A	**Delete Face**	• **Context menu:** In graphics window
	**Direct Edit**	• **Ribbon:** *3D Model* tab>Modify panel • **Context menu:** In graphics window
NA	**Export Face As**	• **Browser: right-click on a face**
	**Export Image**	• **File menu: Export**
NA	**Export Sketch As**	• **Browser: right-click a sketch**
	**Extend/ Contract Body**	• **Ribbon:** *Edit Base Solid* tab>Modify panel
	**Import**	• **Ribbon:** *3D Model* tab>Create panel • **Ribbon:** *Manage* tab>Import panel • **Ribbon:** *Assemble* tab>expanded Place commands
	**Move Face**	• **Ribbon:** *Edit Base Solid* tab>Modify panel
	**Offset**	• **Ribbon:** *Edit Base Solid* tab>Modify panel
	**Open**	• **Home Page** • **Quick Access Toolbar** • **File menu**
	**Save Copy As**	• **File menu: Save As**

Chapter 14

Working with AutoCAD Data

There are several ways to incorporate AutoCAD® DWG files in an Autodesk® Inventor® file. The method you use depends on your project requirements. You can open the file directly in the Autodesk Inventor software for review. You can also import and convert the AutoCAD DWG into an Inventor DWG file, where all links to the original AutoCAD DWG file are lost. Alternatively, you can import and use an AutoCAD DWG as an associative underlay in an Autodesk Inventor file. Understanding the process and results of each method helps you identify which is the best for your situation.

Learning Objectives

- Open an AutoCAD DWG file directly into an Autodesk Inventor part file and review the data.
- Use the DWG/DXF File Wizard and its options to import files into an Autodesk Inventor file.
- Use an AutoCAD DWG file in an Autodesk Inventor part file so that the geometry created in Inventor remains associative with the AutoCAD DWG file.

14.1 Opening AutoCAD Files

When an AutoCAD DWG file is selected for opening, you can either open the file directly or import it so that it is converted to an Autodesk Inventor DWG file. These two options represent two of the methods that can be used to view and use AutoCAD DWG files in the Autodesk Inventor software.

Opening DWG Files

By default, when a DWG file is opened using the Open dialog box, the file is opened directly in Autodesk Inventor. The file remains in a native AutoCAD DWG format, enabling you to view, plot, and measure the file contents. Objects display exactly as they do in AutoCAD. If changes to the DWG file are required, you should make the changes directly in the AutoCAD software. Figure 14–1 shows an example of the YA-Base.dwg AutoCAD file that has been opened in Autodesk Inventor. You can double-click on each of the nodes in the Model browser to activate the opened model, sheet, or layouts.

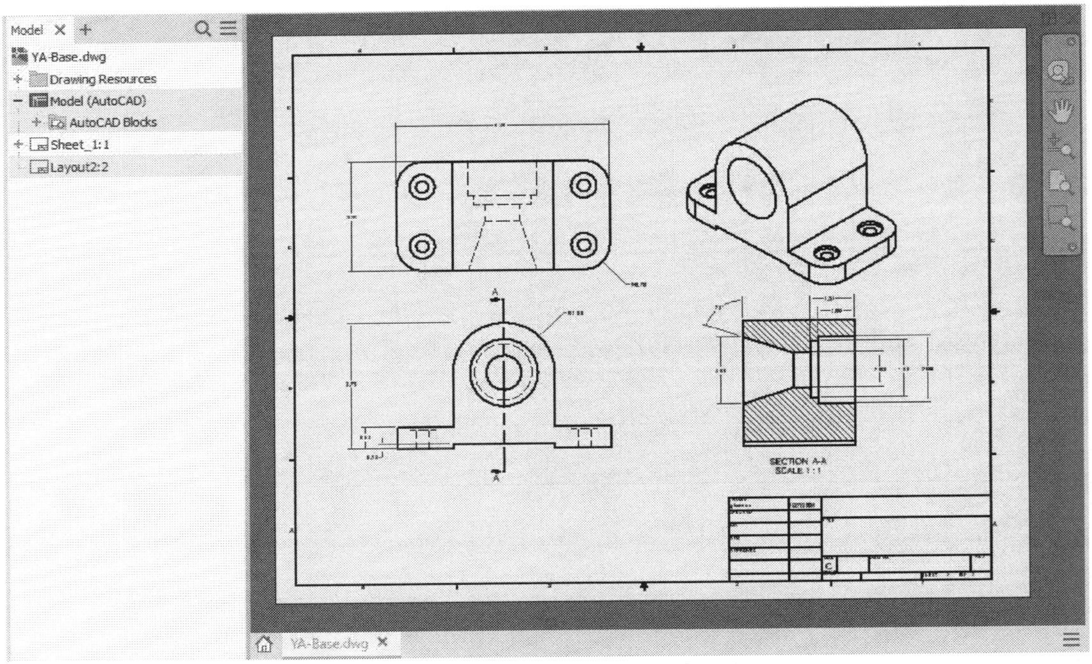

Figure 14–1

Importing DWG Files

To convert the AutoCAD DWG to a native Autodesk Inventor DWG file, the DWG/DXF File Wizard is used. The data is imported and any associative link between the source and new file are lost. When importing, you have the ability to customize many options as well as the layers that are imported.

How To: Import an Autodesk DWG File Using the DWG/DXF File Wizard

1. In the **File** menu, Home page, or the Quick Access Toolbar, select **Open**. The Open dialog box opens.
2. Select **AutoCAD DWG Files** from the Files of type drop-down list. DXF files can also be imported using the wizard
3. Select the Autodesk file to import, and click **Options**.
4. In the File Open Options dialog box, select **Import**, as shown in Figure 14–2, and click **OK**.

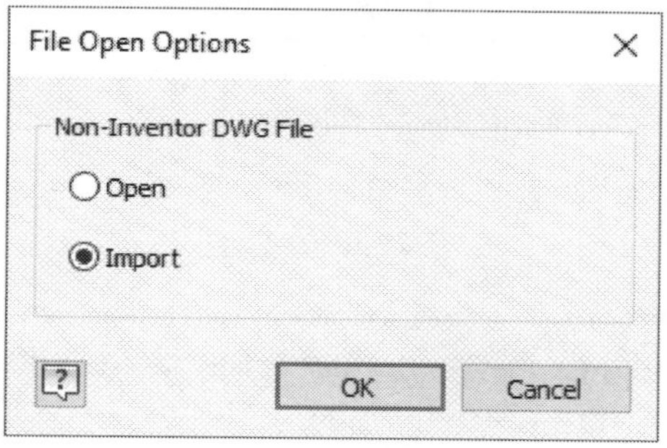

Figure 14–2

Note: *Consider using the* ***Import DWG*** *option in the expanded* ***Open*** *command on the* ***File*** *menu to avoid using the File Open Options dialog box.*

5. Click **Open**. The DWG/DXF File Wizard dialog box opens similar to that shown in Figure 14–3.

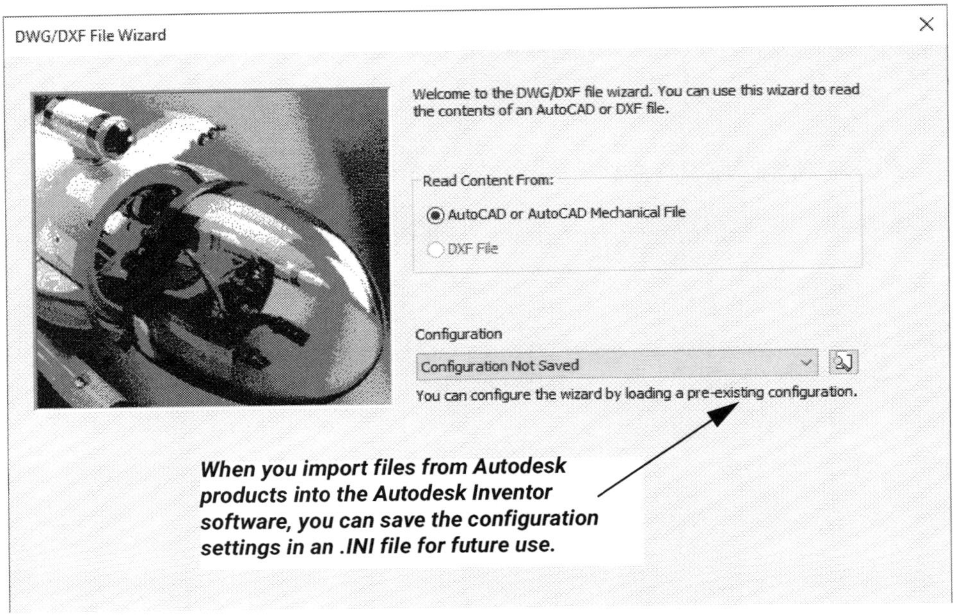

Figure 14–3

6. In the *Read Content From* area, verify that the correct file format is selected for import. Specify a configuration file to use, as required. To use the settings defined in the selected configuration file or to accept the default file settings, click **Finish**. To continue defining import options, click **Next**.

   The Layers and Objects Import Options dialog box opens. The dialog box varies depending on the file format being imported. Figure 14–4 shows the options for the import of a DXF, AutoCAD DWG, or AutoCAD Mechanical DWG file.

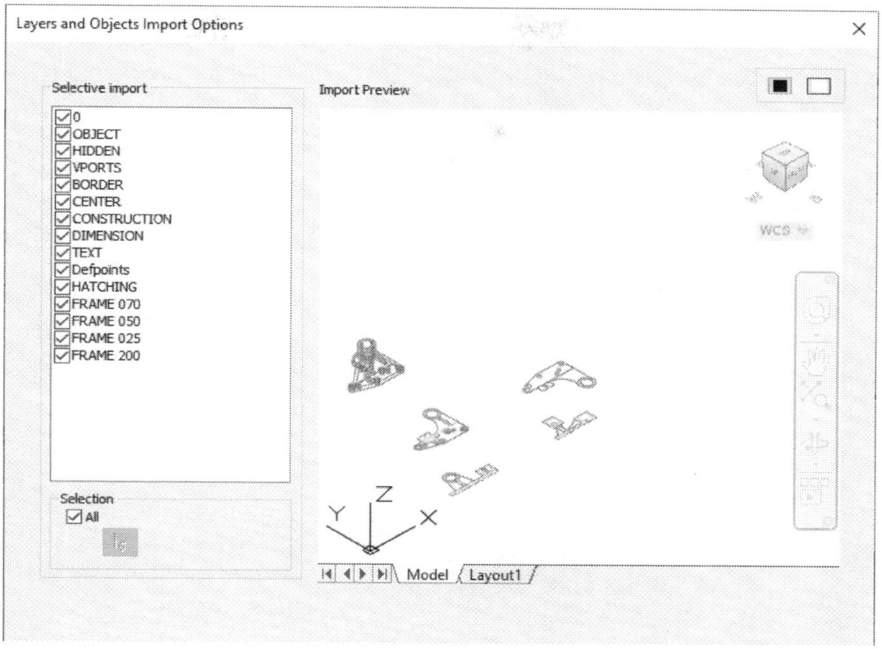

Figure 14–4

7. The Layers and Objects Import Options dialog box enables you to specify what data to translate.

   For an AutoCAD DWG file:

   - Use the *Import Preview* area to view the data. Right-click or use the Navigation toolbar to access view manipulation options or the right-click to access file options.
   - Select the data to import by selecting layers to include from the *Selective import* area or select specific entities to include by deactivating the **All** option in the *Selection* area and selecting entities in the *Import Preview* area.

   For a Mechanical Desktop DWG file:

   - Use **Parts and Assemblies** to import parts and assemblies into the Autodesk Inventor software, as required.
   - Use **All Layouts as Drawings with Views** to import AutoCAD layouts into drawing views and annotations.
   - Use the **Selected Layout as Drawings with Draft Views** options to import the selected layout into an Autodesk Inventor drawing. This option is only available when a layout tab is selected and the **All Layouts as Drawings with Views** option is cleared.

8. Click **Next** when finished defining the options. The Import Destination Options dialog box opens.

9. The Import Destination Options dialog box for Mechanical Desktop DWG files also differs from the dialog box for DXF and other DWG files. Figure 14–5 shows the options that are available during the import of a DXF, AutoCAD DWG, or AutoCAD Mechanical DWG file.

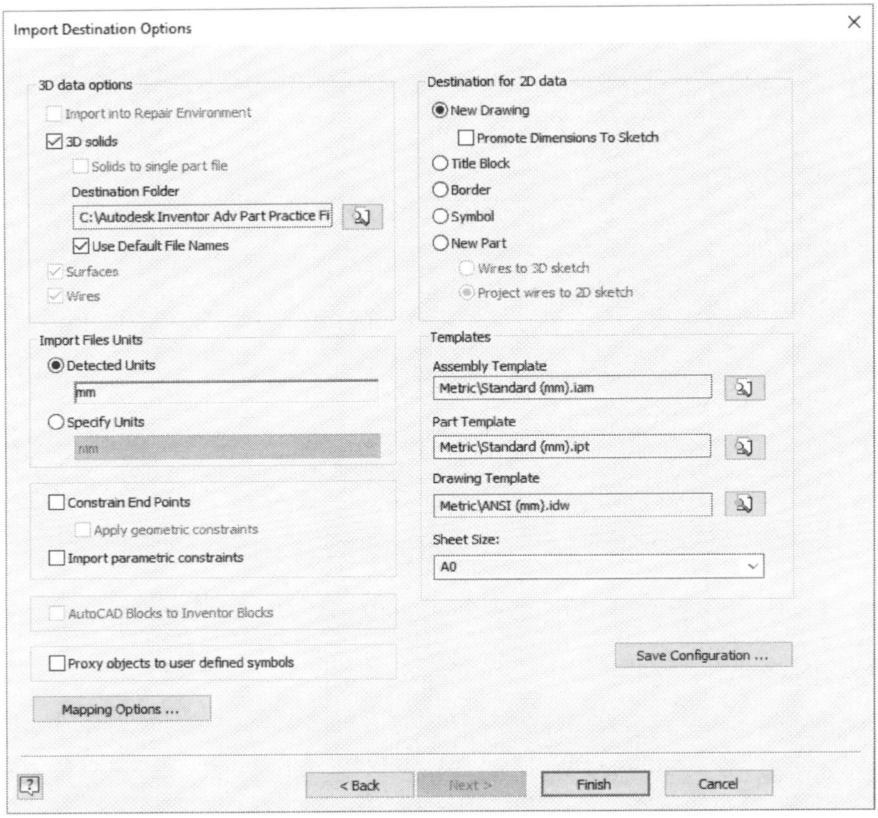

Figure 14–5

For DXF and other non-Mechanical Desktop DWG files, the available options are:

- Activate the **3D solids** option to import the 3D solids from AutoCAD, otherwise, they are not included. If **Surfaces** or **Wires** exist in the imported file, you can select these options, if required on import. Selecting a destination folder specifies the directory in which new Autodesk Inventor files are created as a result of importing 3D solids. Select **Use Default File Names** to automatically name new files based on the name of the DWG file.
- Specify the units to use in the *Import Files Units* area.
- Select **Constrain End Points** to apply endpoint constraints. Clear this option to manually assign them. Use **Apply geometric constraints** to fully constrain the sketch.
- Select **Import parametric constraints** to translate 2D constraints into a sketch.
- Select **AutoCAD Blocks to Inventor Blocks** to import AutoCAD blocks as sketch blocks when opened in an Autodesk Inventor sketch.

- Select **Proxy objects to user defined symbols** to import proxy objects from AutoCAD for use as custom symbols.
- Click **Mapping Options** to set the mapping of layers and fonts. Select the **Map all layers and dimensions to a single sketch** option in the Mapping Options dialog box to avoid creating as many sketches as you have layers.
- Select **New Drawing** to import the 2D data on the layouts into a new drawing file. Imported 2D geometry is placed in sketches attached to a draft view. Dimensions are placed in the sketch containing the associated geometry. Unassociated dimensions, symbols, and other annotations are imported onto the drawing sheet. Blocks are imported as sketched symbols and placed in the *Drawing Resources* folder.
- Select **Promote Dimensions To Sketch** to import dimensions as sketch dimensions on a sheet in a drawing file. The promoted dimensions are associative and change if the sketch geometry is modified.
- Select **Title Block** to import 2D data from the selected layers into a new title block
- Select **Border** to import 2D data from the selected layers into a new border.
- Select **Symbol** to import 2D data from the selected layers into a sketched symbol under the *Drawing Resources* folder in a new drawing file. An instance of the sketched symbol is also placed on the first sheet in the drawing.
- Select **New Part** to import 2D geometry from model space or paper space into a sketch in a new part. Associated dimensions are imported into the sketch, but unassociated dimensions, symbols, and other annotations are not imported.
- Select the drawing, part and assembly template files to use when new files are created during import. Also, specify the sheet size to use for new drawings.
- Click **Save Configuration** to reuse the same import settings in the future.

For Mechanical Desktop DWG files, many of the Import Destination options are the same as those available when importing DXF and other non-Mechanical Desktop DWG files. The options that are different include the following:

- Specifying **Referenced components only** or **All component definitions** for assemblies. You can also control whether to discard the .IAM file for any single part assemblies.
- Specifying whether to **Translate body only** or **As features**. For Mechanical Desktop files with unsupported features you can select the additional options.
- Importing only the selected file or external files as well for drawings with view options.
- Specifying the options for mapping mechanical symbols.
- Overwriting duplicate files that are found or using the existing file that is found.

10. Click **Finish** when you are done setting the import options and to begin the import.

    Note: *The settings you define in this wizard can be saved as a configuration file and used during future imports.*

Depending on the information in the AutoCAD file, the import produces different results in the form or model layouts, sheets, and imported base geometry. Consider the following:

- If you want to use 2D AutoCAD data to create features in a part, you can import the DWG file into a new part file (.IPT) or into a sketch in an active part. Alternatively, you can open the DWG and copy views to help create solid geometry. Dwg Underlays can also be used and are discussed in the next section.
- Materials applied in an AutoCAD DWG are maintained in the Autodesk Inventor software after translation. To view the materials, set the Visual Style for the part to **Realistic**.
- For AutoCAD 3D solids, they are imported as Autodesk solid bodies into an Autodesk Inventor part file (.IPT). When multiple solids are translated, a part file is created for each body and an assembly file that contains references to each part is created. AutoCAD 3D solids are not parametric, so they are brought in as non-parametric solid bodies without separately defined features (i.e., boundary representations).

14.2 DWG File Underlays

Importing an AutoCAD DWG file into a part file enables you to import an associative underlay by referencing the AutoCAD DWG. The DWG underlay can be imported on one or more work planes or faces, enabling you to project it into sketches and use it to create associative geometry. If changes are made in the source DWG file, the change can be updated in the Inventor file. Additionally, in assembly files, you can use constraints and joints to create relationships between a DWG underlay and a part.

Importing a DWG File as an Underlay

How To: Import an Autodesk DWG File as an Associative Underlay

1. Start a new part file using a template and save the file.
2. In the *3D Model* tab>Create panel, click (Import). Select and open an AutoCAD DWG file.
   - If the file was not saved, a prompt displays indicating that this may cause problems in resolving links between the files.
3. Select an origin plane or planar face to import the file onto.
4. Select a origin point reference to locate the DWG file.
5. Click **OK** when prompted that inserting an AutoCAD DWG produces an associative underlay. The DWG file is listed in the Model browser as an independent node.

- To redefine the placement plane and origin point, right-click on the file in the Model browser and select **Redefine**, as shown in Figure 14–6. Select a new plane and origin point.

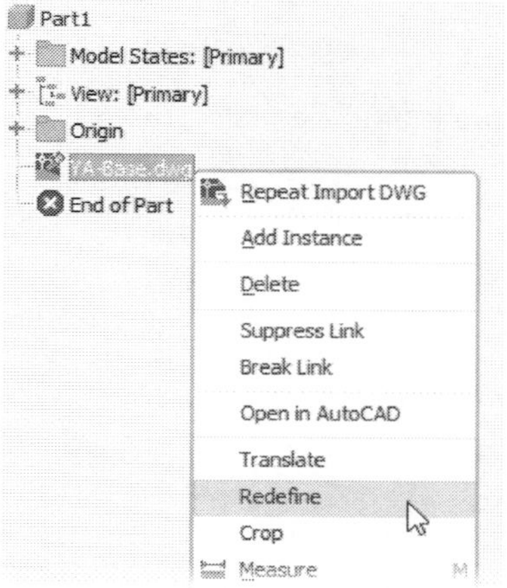

Figure 14–6

- To open the DWG file in AutoCAD, right-click on the underlay file name in the Model browser and select **Open** in AutoCAD.

Controlling Layer Visibility

Once a DWG file has been imported as an underlay, you can control its layer visibility.

How To: Control the Layer Visibility

1. Right-click on the DWG file in the Model browser and select **Layer Visibility**. The Layer Visibility dialog box opens, as shown in Figure 14–7.

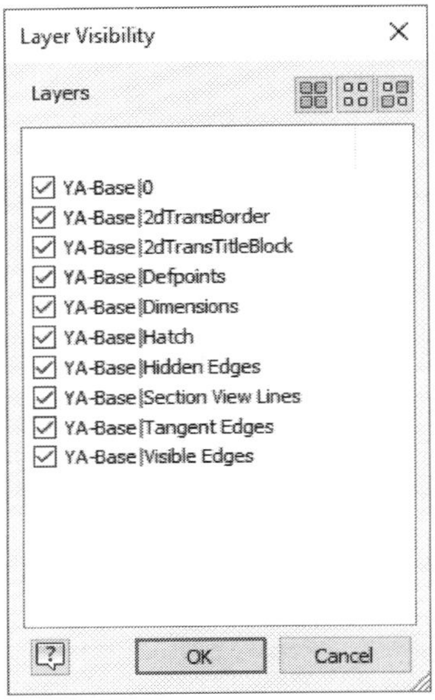

Figure 14–7

2. Toggle on/off the layer names to customize the data that will be imported.
   - Use the filter settings at the top of the dialog box to quickly clear, select all, or invert the selected layers.
   - The visibility of any of the layers can be controlled at any time using this dialog box.
3. Click **OK** to close the Layer Visibility dialog box.

Moving an Underlay

If the imported file does not display in the correct location relative to the model's origin, it can be translated.

How To: Move a DWG Underlay

1. Right-click on the DWG file in the Model browser and select **Translate**. A translation triad is displayed on the selected origin point.
2. Using the mini-toolbar, move the AutoCAD DWG file relative to the model's origin, as required:
   - In the mini-toolbar, click **Locate** and select a new reference on the imported DWG file to reposition the triad.
   - In the mini-toolbar, click **Snap To** and select the Origin Center Point or another point to align the DWG underlay as required in the model.
3. Click  to complete the translation.

   Note: *The* ***Translate*** *command is not available to modify the location of an underlay placed in an assembly. To rotate it on the placement plane, you can expand the* ***Relationships*** *node in the Model browser and modify the* ***Angle 2*** *constraint, as required. As a workaround, insert the underlay into a part file, position it, and then insert the part into the assembly.*

Cropping an Underlay

An imported DWG underlay can be cropped to simplify the amount of detail that is displayed. Cropping can also help improve performance.

How To: Crop Entities in a DWG Underlay

1. Right-click on the DWG file in the Model browser and select **Crop.**
2. In the graphics window, drag a bounding box around the entities that you want to keep.
3. Right-click in the graphics window and select **OK (Enter)** to complete the crop. Any geometry that was not included in the selected area is automatically removed.

- Once an DWG underlay file is cropped, a **Crop** node is added to the Model browser.
- Only one crop can be made to a file, thus if a change is required, you must delete the crop element. To delete a Crop, right-click on the element in the Model browser and select **Delete**.

Using an Underlay to Create Geometry

To use the imported underlay to create solid geometry that remains associative to the AutoCAD DWG file, consider the following along with your standard sketching and feature creation techniques:

- Start the creation of a new sketch. In the *Sketch* tab>Create panel, expand the Project Geometry options and select  (Project DWG Geometry). By projecting the DWG geometry you can maintain the reference between the sketch and the DWG file. Use the filter options in the mini-toolbar to project single geometry (), connected geometry (), or a DWG Block (). Click  to close the mini-toolbar and cancel the Project DWG Geometry command.
- When projected, all of the entities are fully constrained. Consider creating Driven Dimensions to identify key dimensions in the underlay that can be used to drive solid geometry. For the example shown in Figure 14–8, the Driven Dimension can now be used to define the depth of the model.

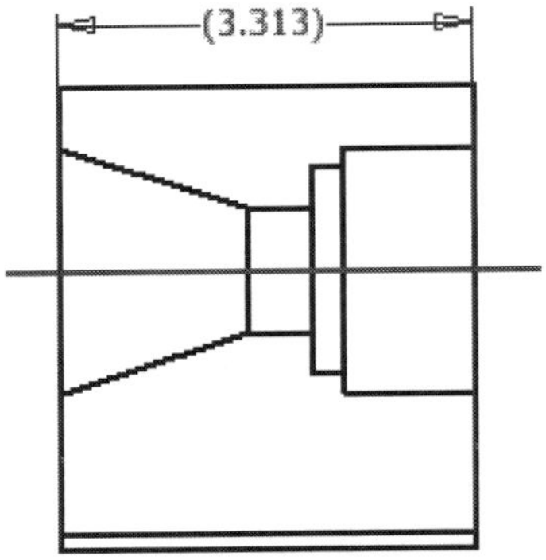

Figure 14–8

- In the Model browser, right-click on the imported DWG file to access the **Suppress Link** and **Break Link** options. These options can be used to either temporarily break the link with the source DWG file (**Suppress Link**) or permanently break the link (**Break Link**).

An imported AutoCAD DWG file can also be used as a layout reference to assemble components in an Inventor assembly file. For the example shown in Figure 14–9, the factory floor layout is an AutoCAD DWG file that can be used for assembly references in a top-level assembly.

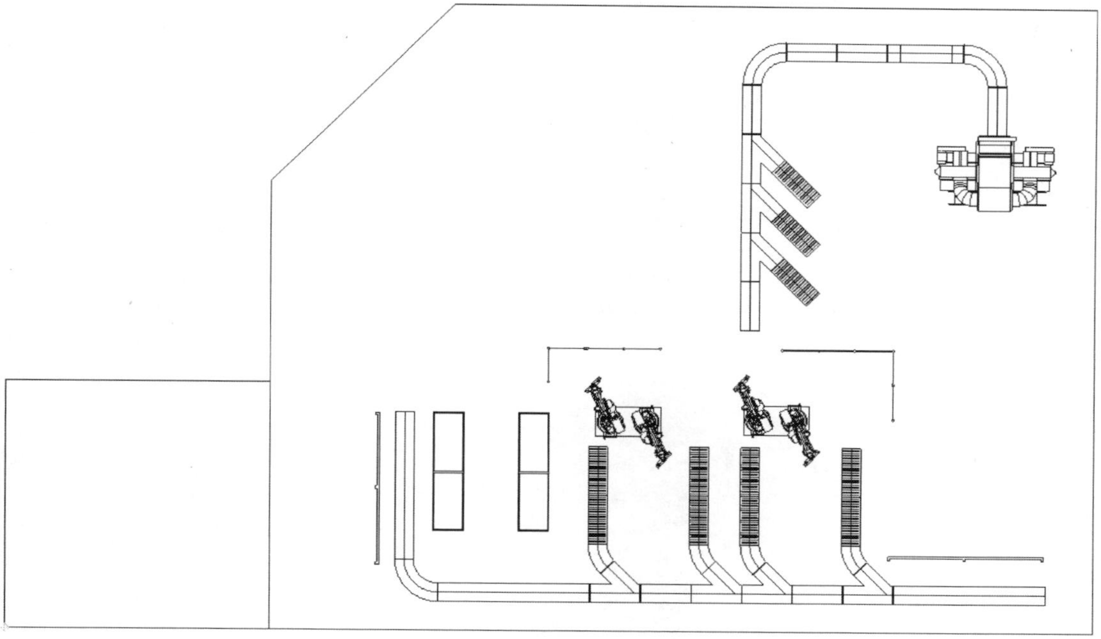

Figure 14–9

- The underlay is placed in an assembly file as a placed component. Many of the right-click menu options that are available in the part environment to edit the underlay are also available in an assembly.

Hint: Associative DWG Underlays in Drawings

To include a DWG underlay in a drawing view, right-click on the Associative DWG file associated with the view and select **Include**, as shown in Figure 14–10. Once included, you can add text, dimensions, manage layers, or edit line types to appropriately annotate the underlay geometry.

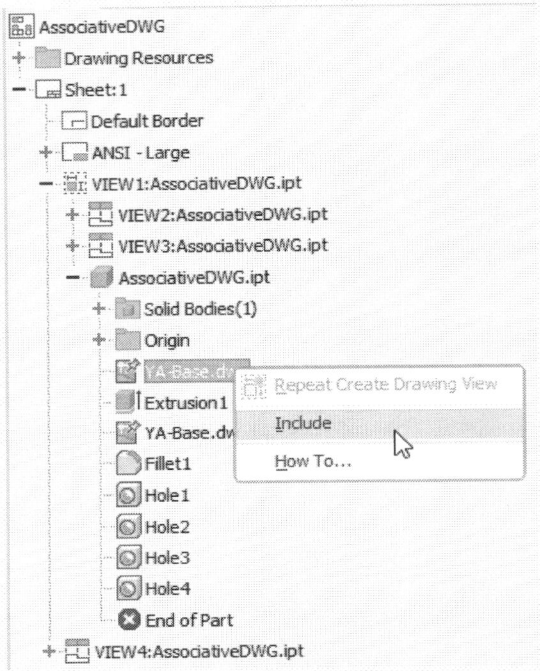

Figure 14–10

Hint: AutoCAD Mechanical Files as DWG Underlays

AutoCAD Mechanical files can be imported as DWG files. If imported into an assembly file, constraints can be used to constrain the drawing. Note that cropped AutoCAD Mechanical geometry cannot be selected. Do not crop the DWG file.

Practice 14a
Import an AutoCAD DWG File into Autodesk Inventor

Practice Objective

- Use the DWG/DXF File Wizard to import an AutoCAD DWG file into an Autodesk Inventor part file and work with the data.

In this practice, you will import an AutoCAD DWG file directly into Autodesk Inventor. The AutoCAD DWG file contains a 3D AutoCAD model and a 2D layout. Once imported, you will review the file and use copy and paste techniques to copy non-associative 2D drawing data into a new Inventor model. The AutoCAD 3D model and drawing are shown in Figure 14–11.

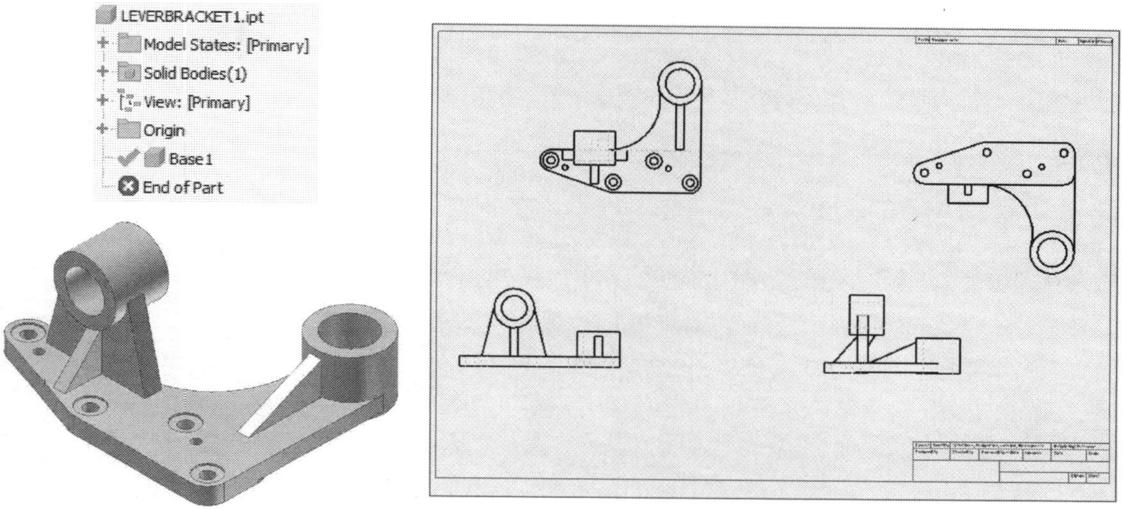

Figure 14–11

Task 1: Import the AutoCAD DWG file.

1. In the Quick Access Toolbar, click [icon].
2. In the File of type drop-down list, select **AutoCAD Dwg Files**.
3. Select **LEVERBRACKET.dwg** and click **Options**. The File Open Options dialog box opens. It enables you to directly open the DWG file in the Autodesk Inventor software or you can import the file. In this practice you will import the drawing.
4. Select **Import** and click **OK**.

5. Click **Open**. The DWG/DXF File Wizard displays.
6. In the *Read Content From* area, keep the **AutoCAD or AutoCAD Mechanical File** option selected. Leave the **Configuration** option set to **Configuration Not Saved** as you have not yet saved a configuration file.
7. Click **Next**. The Layers and Objects Import Options dialog box opens. A preview of the AutoCAD 3D Solid geometry and its views are shown.

   Note: *You can also zoom in and out using the scroll wheel.*

8. In the dialog box, in the top right corner, click to change the background to white. You can use the Navigation Bar or right-click on the background of the preview window to access the view orientation and manipulation options (e.g., pan, zoom). Manipulate the model as required. The Layers and Objects Import Options dialog box is shown in Figure 14–12.

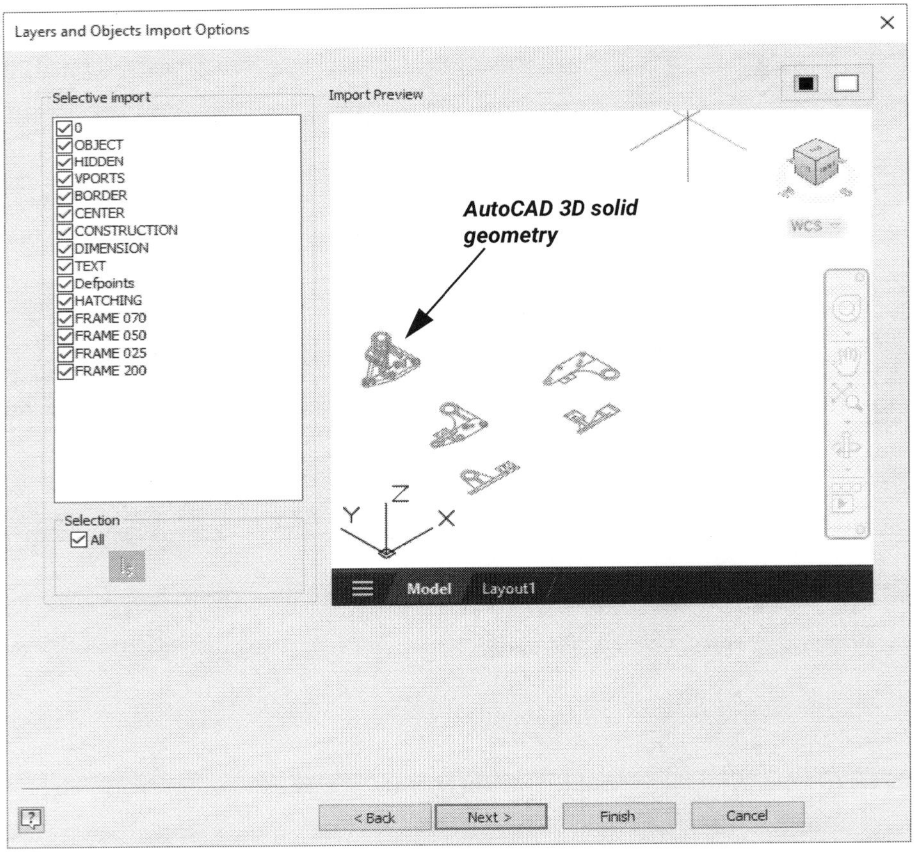

Figure 14–12

9. In the Navigation Bar, click [icon] to fit the entire drawing in the *Import Preview* area.
10. Clear **OBJECT**. Note that the model entities are removed.
11. Clear **HIDDEN** to remove the hidden lines.
12. Select **OBJECT** and **HIDDEN** again so that those entities will be imported.
13. To import specific entities from the DWG, in the *Selection* area, you can clear the **All** option and select individual entities to import. Leave the **All** option selected.
14. Select the *Layout1* tab to review the layout that will be imported.
15. Return to the *Model* tab.
16. Click **Next**. The Import Destination Options dialog box opens.
17. Activate **3D solids** to import the AutoCAD 3D solids that exist in the DWG file. Clear the **Solids to single part file** option, if selected.
18. In the *3D data options* area, verify that the *Destination Folder* field is set to the practice files directory. This is the directory where the new files will be created as a result of the import. Also verify that **Use Default File Names** is activated.
19. Select **New Drawing** to import the 2D data on the layouts into a new Autodesk Inventor drawing file. Imported 2D geometry is placed in sketches attached to a draft view. Dimensions are placed in the sketch containing the associated geometry. Unassociated dimensions, symbols, and other annotations are imported onto the drawing sheet. Blocks are imported as sketched symbols and placed in the *Drawing Resources* folder. The **Promote Dimensions To Sketch** option imports dimensions as sketch dimensions on a sheet in a drawing file. The promoted dimensions are associative and so they will change if the sketch geometry is modified. Deactivate **Promote Dimensions To Sketch**, if enabled.
20. In the *Templates* area, next to the Assembly Template, click [icon]. In the *Metric* tab, select **Standard(mm).iam**. Click **OK**.
21. For the Part Template, in the *Metric* tab, select **Standard(mm).ipt**. Click **OK**.
22. For the Drawing Template, in the *Metric* tab, select **ANSI(mm).idw**. Click **OK**.
23. For the *Sheet Size*, select **A0**.
24. Click **Save Configuration** and enter **AutoCAD 3D Solid using metric** as the filename. Save it in the practice files directory.
25. Click **Finish** to begin the import. The DWG data is imported as a new part and drawing file.
26. Activate the LEVERBRACKET1 part file window by selecting it from the tabs along the bottom of the graphics window.
27. Return to the model's Home view using the ViewCube.
28. The color is imported from the source AutoCAD file. Change the default appearance to **Steel** using the Appearance Override drop-down list in the Quick Access Toolbar, to display the model in a better color.

29. The model displays as shown in Figure 14–13. The model is a solid feature, but it is a boundary representation (rather than being made up of several features). You can now edit the solid using **Edit Solid** or **Direct Edit,** or add and remove material from the solid and use any of the edges and faces as references as you would a regular native Autodesk Inventor solid.

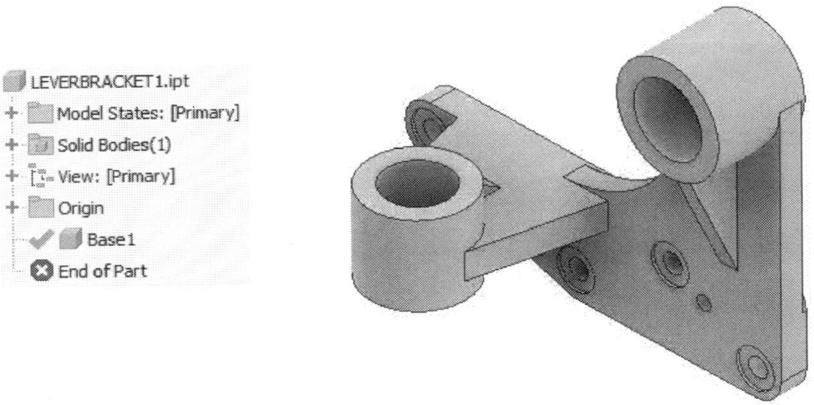

Figure 14–13

30. Save the part file using the default name.

Task 2: Review and edit the imported drawing.

1. In the **Drawing1.dwg** drawing, expand the *Drawing Resources* folder and **Sketch Symbols** node. Right-click on **ISO A2 title block** and select **Insert**. Place the title block anywhere on the drawing.
2. Click **OK** to leave the title block entries blank. Right-click and select **Cancel** to cancel placing additional title blocks.
3. The title block is small compared to sheet. To change the size, right-click on the title block, select **Edit Symbol**, enter **2** for the *Scale*, and click **OK**.
4. Use the green dot at the center of the title block to drag it to fit. Select any geometry on a view and drag it to reposition all of the views on the drawing sheet. You might have to also reposition the title block. The drawing displays as shown in Figure 14–14.

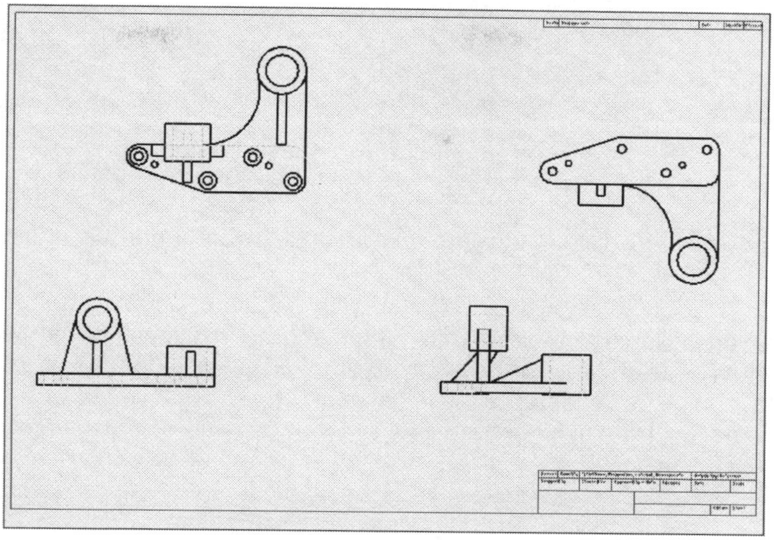

Figure 14–14

5. In the Model browser, expand the **Sheet:1** and the **ImportDraftView** branches. The 2D entities were imported into sketches, so the drawing views are actually sketched entities rather than views, unlike those in regular native Autodesk Inventor drawings.
6. Save the drawing as **Leverbracket2.idw** and save it in the practice files directory. Close the files.

End of practice

Practice 14b
Open AutoCAD DWG Data to Create a Solid

Practice Objective

- Open an AutoCAD DWG file directly into an Autodesk Inventor part file and work with the data.

In this practice, you will open an AutoCAD DWG file in Autodesk Inventor. You will review the contents of the DWG file and use some of its 2D data to create a sketch in new Autodesk Inventor file that can be used to create the initial geometry for an Inventor model. The geometry that will be created is shown in Figure 14–15.

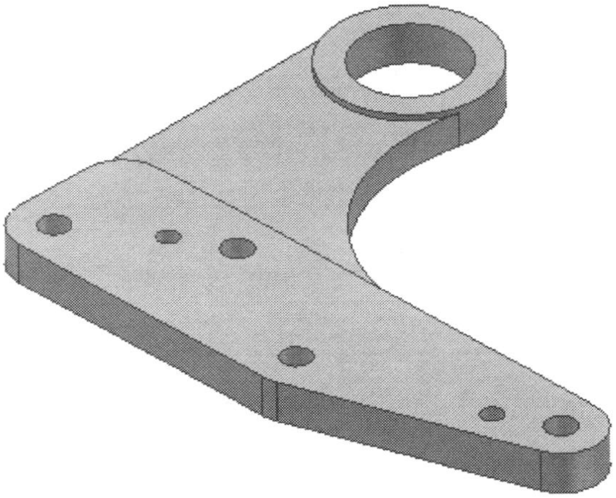

Figure 14–15

Task 1: Open an AutoCAD DWG and view the data in Autodesk Inventor.

1. In the Quick Access Toolbar, click .
2. Select **LEVERBRACKET.dwg** and click **Options**. The File Open Options dialog box opens.
3. By default, **Open** is already selected. If not, select **Open** and click **OK**.
4. Click **Open**. The **Leverbracket.dwg** file and the Browser display as shown in Figure 14–16.

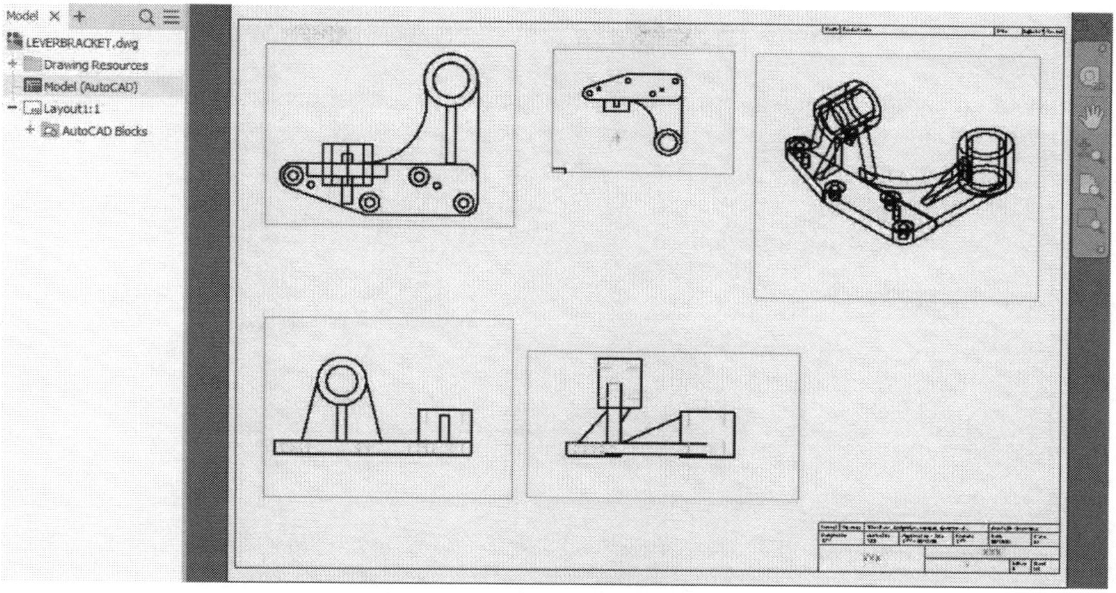

Figure 14–16

5. In the Model browser, double-click on the **Model (AutoCAD)** node.

   Note: *If you receive an error indicating that properties have been updated outside of the session, click* ***No****. In the next window, click* ***Accept****. These errors are software related and random, occurring only in some 2024 installs. It does not affect what is shown in Inventor and you can complete the next steps without error.*

6. To change the display color of the background, in the Model browser, right-click on **Model** and select **Background Color**. Change the color to white, if not already set as white. The model displays as shown in Figure 14–17.

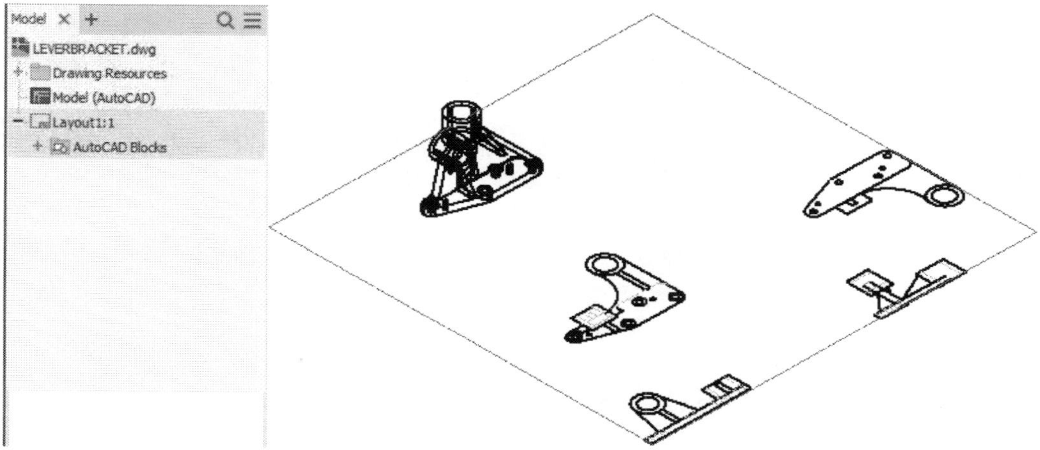

Figure 14–17

Task 2: Use the AutoCAD DWG data to create an Autodesk Inventor part file.

1. Select and drag a selection box around the top right view, as shown in Figure 14–18.

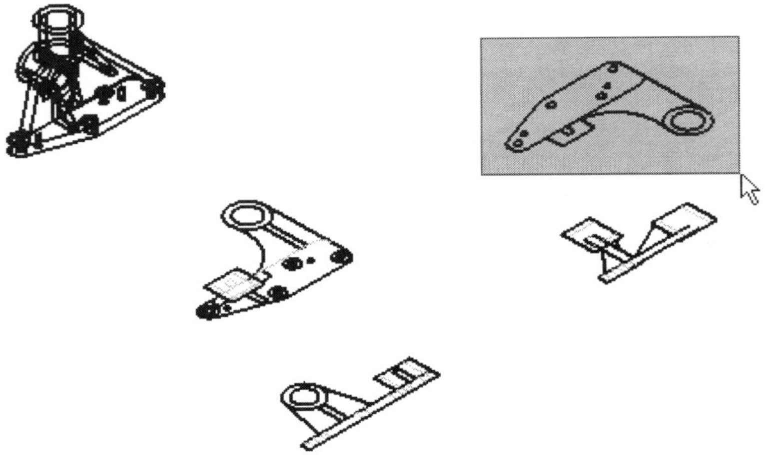

Figure 14–18

2. Right-click and select **Copy**.
3. Start a new part file using the **Standard (mm).ipt** metric template.
4. Create a sketch on the XZ plane. Once you are placed in the Sketch environment, right-click and select **Paste**. Place the entities in the sketch.
5. In the Navigation Bar, click  (Zoom All) to refit the model.
6. Use the **Rotate** and **Move** tools to move the entities relative to the origin center, as shown in Figure 14–19.

   Note: *You need to either create construction lines and a point at the intersection of the construction lines. Alternatively, you can create a point at the virtual intersection of the horizontal and vertical entities, and then constrain the point horizontally and vertically. Once all the reference items are created you can move the entities to the projected origin center.*

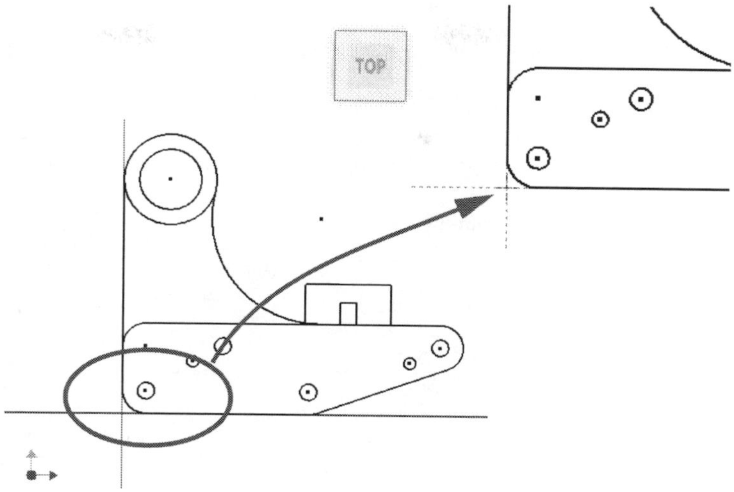

Figure 14–19

7. Project YZ and XY and locate the geometry's horizontal bottom and vertical left side entities to lie on these projected planes.
8. For simplicity, dimension the remaining entities using **Auto Dimension**. Normally, it is recommended to place dimensions based on your required design intent, but for this practice you use this tool to quickly progress to creating geometry. Finish the sketch.
9. Create an Extrude and select the three closed sections of the sketch and the six holes to obtain the solid in Figure 14–20. Extrude the feature **16 mm** and flip the creation direction below the sketch plane.

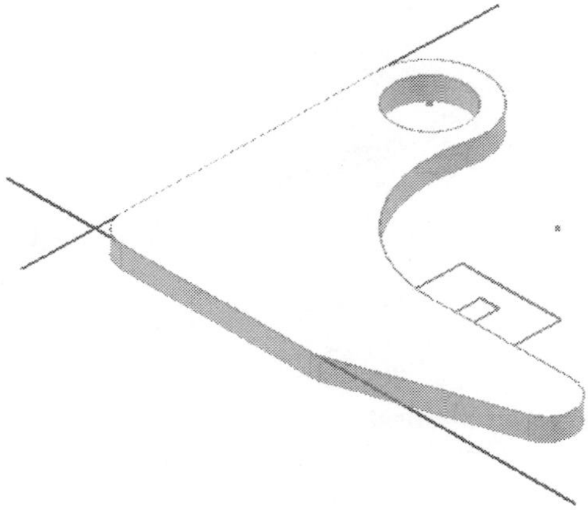

Figure 14–20

10. Expand **Extrusion1**. Right-click on **Sketch1** and select **Share Sketch**. Alternatively, you can select and drag **Sketch1** above the Extrusion to share it. By sharing the sketch it copies the sketch outside the extrusion for use with other features.

11. Toggle on the **Visibility** for the shared sketch, if it is off.
12. Extrude the two additional closed sections by **3 mm**, as shown in Figure 14–21.
    - **Hint:** When extruding the larger section, you also need to select the six holes to create the solid or select near an exterior edge of the section. This enables you to then use the circular sections to create separate features later in the design process.

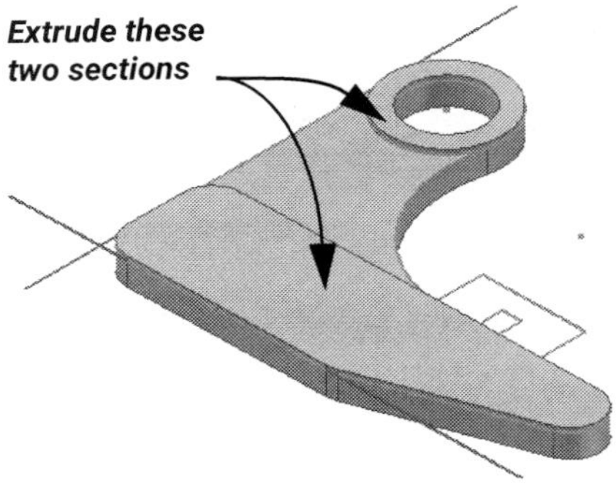

Figure 14–21

13. Create extruded cuts to represent the holes, as shown in Figure 14–22. The holes cut through the entire model. As an alternative, you could also have edited the sketch and added points to the centers of the holes. The points could then have been created with the **Hole** command to create the holes with the required diameters.

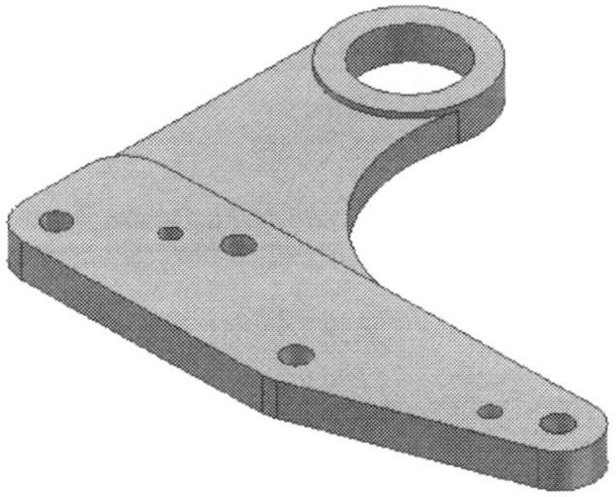

Figure 14–22

14. Save the part.

Up to this point, the method used to create the model is only one interpretation of how the model can be created. There are many other alternatives. For example, you can use the copied entities and create individual sketches for each feature, dimension and constrain them as required, and remove links to the original copied entities. Whichever method you use, consider your design intent and what information you need to communicate how the model is manufactured. Ultimately, because the data was copied from the AutoCAD file, it does not maintain any associative link.

Task 3: (Optional) Continue modeling the solid geometry.

After you have finished creating all of the practices in this chapter, continue to model the geometry for the leverbracket part that was originally created in the AutoCAD software. You can take measurements, as required, using the imported model that you created in Task 1. You need to create additional sketch planes and copy entities from the .DWG file to create the remaining geometry. In some situations you might want to consider creating features on your own instead of using copied entities.

End of practice

Practice 14c
Import Associative DWG Data into a Part File

Practice Objective

- Open an AutoCAD DWG file directly into an Autodesk Inventor part file and work with the data.

In this practice, you will import an AutoCAD DWG file into an Autodesk Inventor file as an underlay. You will control the layer visibility and its location in the file so that the underlay can be used to project geometry onto sketches. The sketch geometry will then be used to create a 3D model. The geometry that will be created is shown in Figure 14–23.

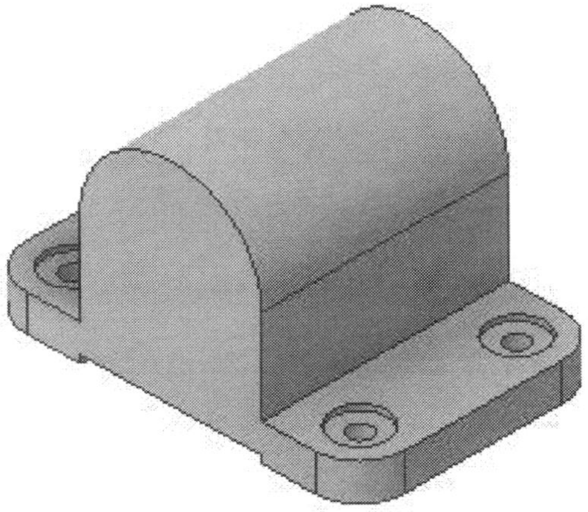

Figure 14–23

Task 1: Create a new Autodesk Inventor model and import AutoCAD data.

1. Start a new part file using the **Standard (in).ipt** template.
2. Save the file as **AssociativeDWG.ipt**.
3. In the *3D Model* tab>Create panel, click (Import).
4. In the Import dialog box, expand the Files of type drop-down list and select **AutoCAD DWG Files (*.dwg)**.
5. Select **YA-Base.dwg** from the practice files folder and click **Open**.
6. Select the XY Origin plane as the plane to import the DWG file to.
7. Select the projected Origin Center Point as the center point for the import.

8. If you had not previously saved the file as **AssociativeDWG.ipt**, you will be prompted that the file is unsaved and this may cause problems in resolving links between the files. Click **OK**.
9. Click **OK** when prompted that inserting an AutoCAD DWG produces an associative underlay.
10. If you had not previously saved the files, save it now as **AssociativeDWG.ipt.**
11. Review the three 2D views. Note that the side view is a section view.

Task 2: Set the Layer Visibility on the AutoCAD DWG file.

1. Right-click on **YA-Base.dwg** in the Model browser and select **Layer Visibility**. The Layer Visibility dialog box opens.
2. In the filter settings at the top of the dialog box, click (Clear All) to clear all the layers from being displayed.
3. Select **YA-Base|Hidden Edges**, **YA-Base|Tangent Edges**, and **YA-Base|Visible Edges**.
4. Click **OK** to close the Layer Visibility dialog box. The visibility of any of the layers can be controlled at any time using this dialog box.

Task 3: Crop the AutoCAD DWG file.

1. Right-click on **YA-Base.dwg** in the Model browser and select **Crop**.
2. Drag a bounding box around the two views shown in Figure 14–24. The box defines which entities in the underlay file will remain in the file.

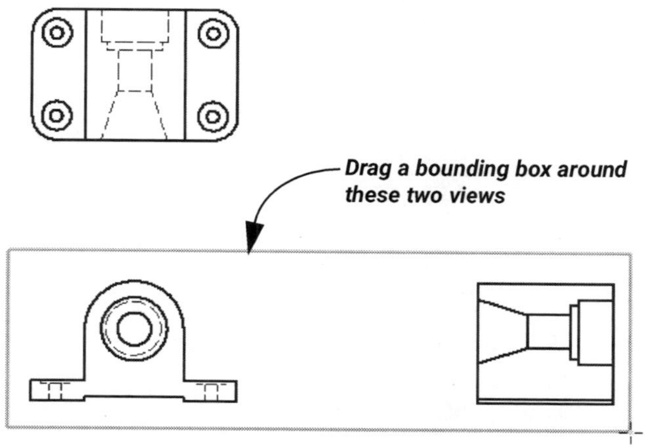

Figure 14–24

3. Right-click and select **OK (Enter)** to remove the entities outside the bounding box from view.

Task 4: Translate the AutoCAD DWG file relative to the model's origin.

1. Expand the **Origin** node in the Model browser and toggle on the visibility of the Center Point.
2. Using the Navigation Bar, select **Zoom All** to refit the model so that both the Origin Center Point and the drawing are displayed on the screen. If you are using a white background you may have difficulty seeing the yellow origin center point. Hover the cursor over the origin planes in the Model browser to display them in the model to understand where the origin point is located.
3. Right-click on **YA-Base.dwg** in the Model browser and select **Translate**.
4. A triad displays on the Origin Center Point. Click **Locate** in the mini-toolbar. Select the center point of the internal hole, as shown in Figure 14–25.

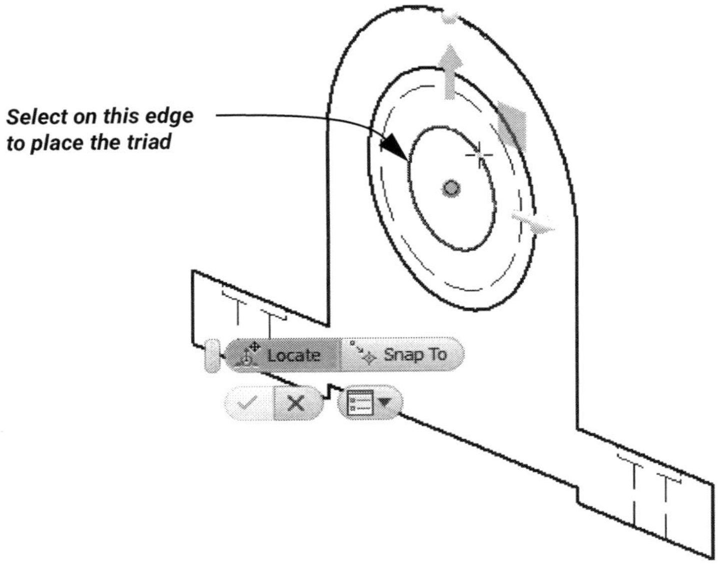

Figure 14–25

5. Click ✓ to close the mini-toolbar and complete the translation.
6. Return the model to its Home View using the ViewCube.

Task 5: Create associative geometry from the DWG file.

1. Create a new 2D sketch on the XY plane.
2. In the *Sketch* tab>Create panel, expand the Project Geometry options and select (Project DWG Geometry).

3. In the mini-toolbar, select (Project Connected Geometry) and select on an outside edge in the Front view, as shown on the left in Figure 14–26. All connected edges are projected. Project the outside loop of single edges ( ) on the section view, as shown on the right of Figure 14–26.

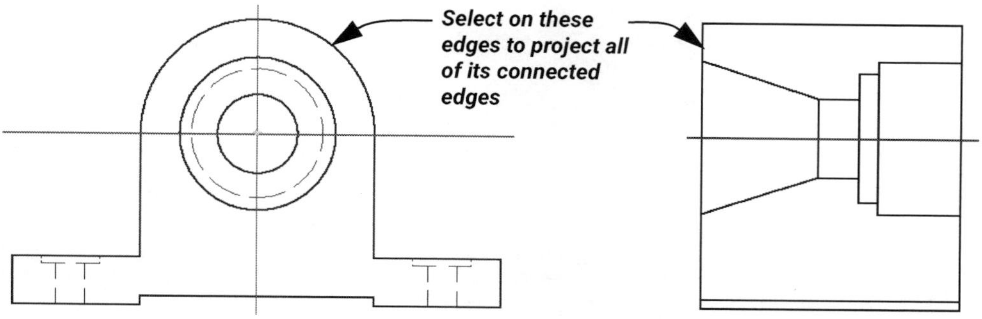

Figure 14–26

4. Click to close the mini-toolbar and cancel the Project DWG Geometry command.
5. Create a dimension on the side section view to define the depth of the model. Once placed, you will be prompted that the dimension will over-constrain the sketch. Click **Accept** to place the dimension as a Driven Dimension, as shown in Figure 14–27.

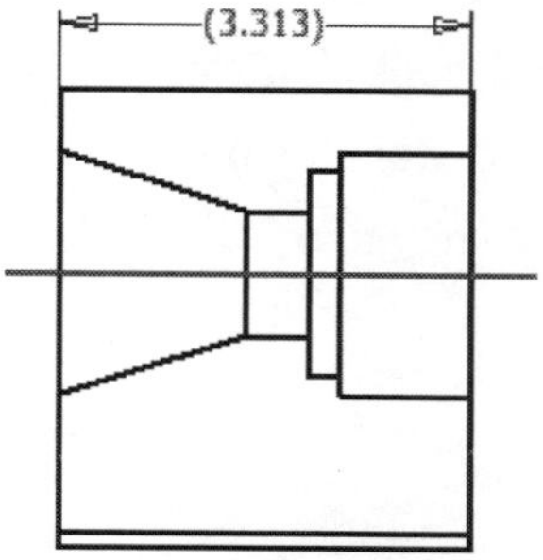

Figure 14–27

6. Finish the sketch.
7. Right-click in the graphics window and click **Dimension Display>Name** to display the name of the dimension value.

8. Create an Extrude and select the section shown in Figure 14–28. Enter **d1** (or name of your Driven Dimension) as the value for the extruded depth (*Distance A*).

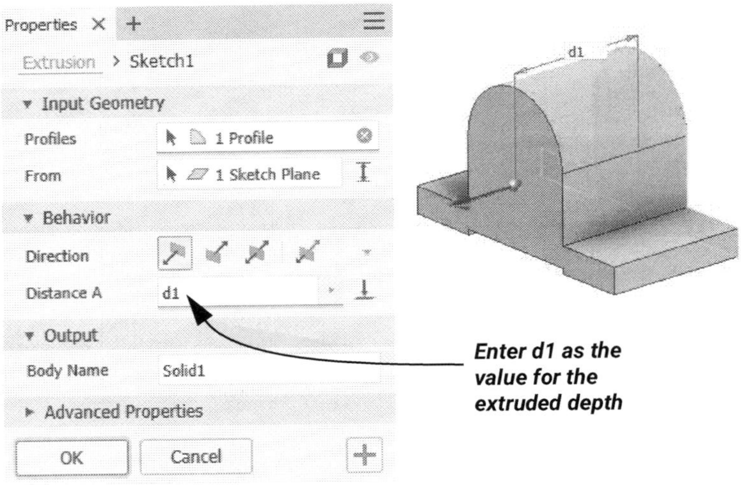

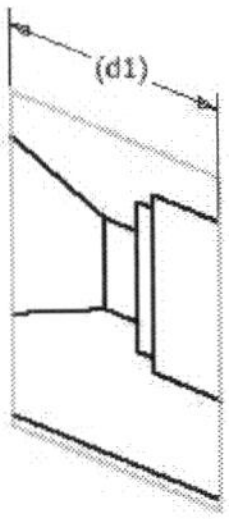

Figure 14–28

9. Complete the feature.

Task 6: Insert the DWG on another plane and create additional geometry.

1. In the *3D Model* tab>Create panel, click (Import).
2. In the Import dialog box, select **YA-Base.dwg** from the practice files folder and click **Open**.
3. Select the plane and origin point shown in Figure 14–29 as the references to import the DWG file.

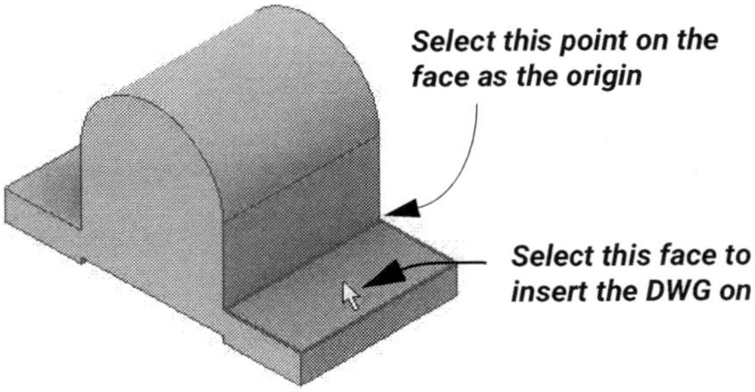

Figure 14–29

4. When prompted that inserting an AutoCAD DWG produces an associative underlay, click **OK**.

5. Right-click on the newly imported **YA-Base.dwg** in the Model browser and select **Layer Visibility**. The Layer Visibility dialog box opens. Note that the same visibility settings are set. Click **OK** to close the Layer Visibility dialog box.
6. In the Navigation Bar, select **Zoom All** to refit the model to see the solid geometry and the new underlay.
7. Right-click on newly imported **YA-Base.dwg** in the Model browser and select **Translate**.
8. A triad appears, by default, on the point that was selected on the placement face. Click **Locate** in the mini-toolbar. Select the point shown in Figure 14–30 on the newly imported underlay.

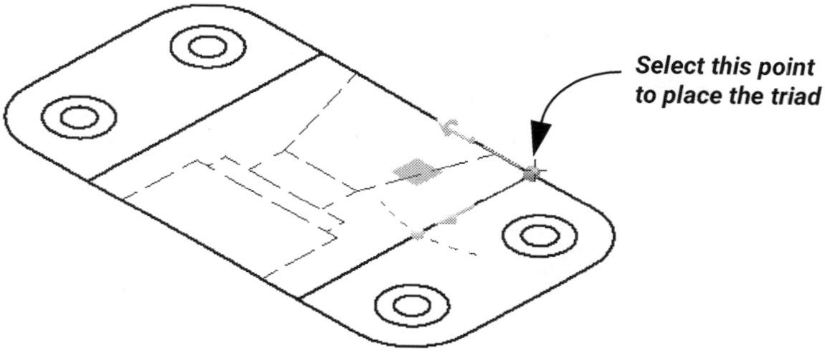

Figure 14–30

9. Click ✓ to close the mini-toolbar and complete the translation.
10. Both underlays are on different planes and are visible. Right-click on the first **YA-Base.dwg** and clear the **Visibility** option. You can toggle the display of underlays on and off as required.
11. Create a new sketch on the same face that was used to place the latest DWG underlay file.
12. In the Create panel, click (Project DWG Geometry).
13. In the mini-toolbar, ensure that (Project Single Geometry) is selected and select the four arcs on the outside corners of the view shown in Figure 14–31 to project them.
14. Project one large and one small circle, as shown in Figure 14–31. Close the mini-toolbar or cancel the command.

15. Create the three Driven Dimensions shown in Figure 14–31.

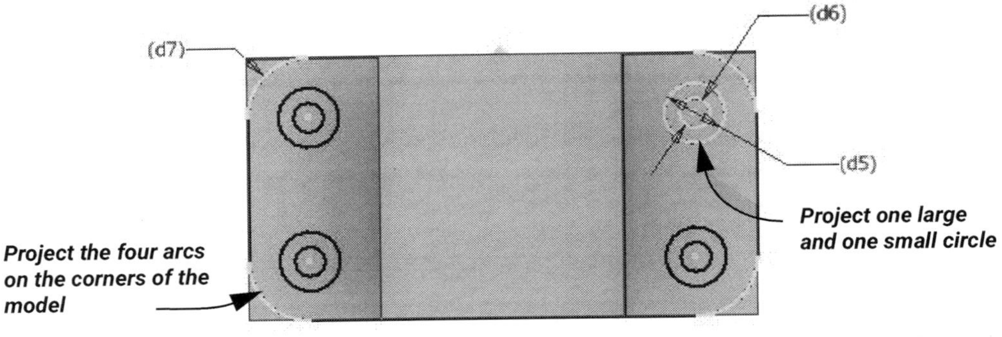

Figure 14–31

16. While in the same sketch, project the required edges and create the reference dimension shown in Figure 14–32.

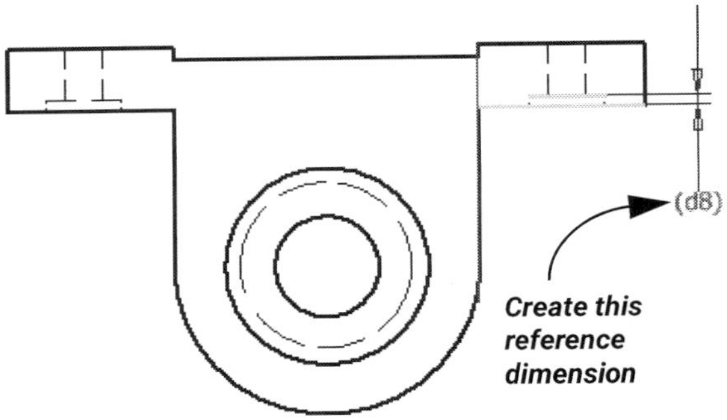

Figure 14–32

17. Finish the sketch.

18. Create a fillet.

Note: *The dimension name may vary depending on the order that you created the Driven Dimensions in the sketch.*

19. Select the four vertical edges on the outside of the model. Enter **d7** (or name of your Driven Dimension) as the value of the fillet, as shown in Figure 14–33. This ensures the size of the fillet is driven by the projected geometry.

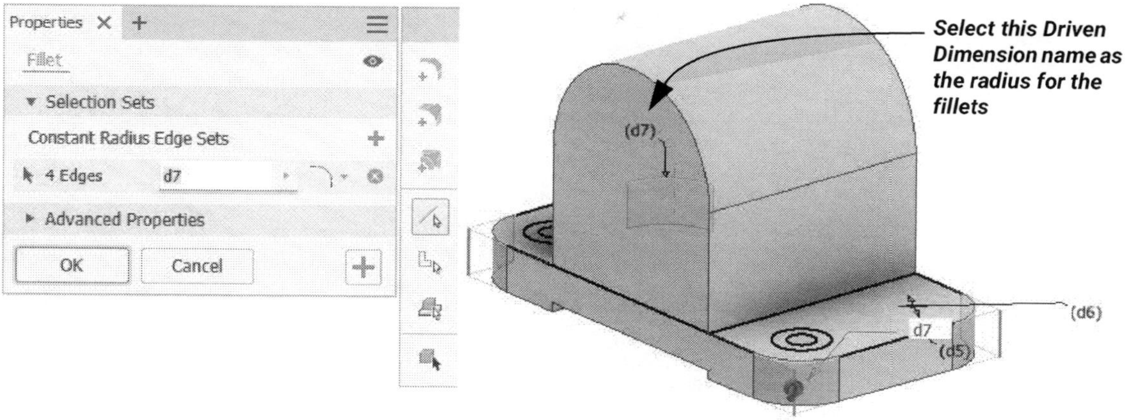

Figure 14–33

20. Complete the feature.

21. Create a concentric hole by selecting the placement plane and concentric reference shown in Figure 14–34. Note: If you cannot select the placement face, turn off the visibility of the sketch so that points are not defined by default as the placement type.

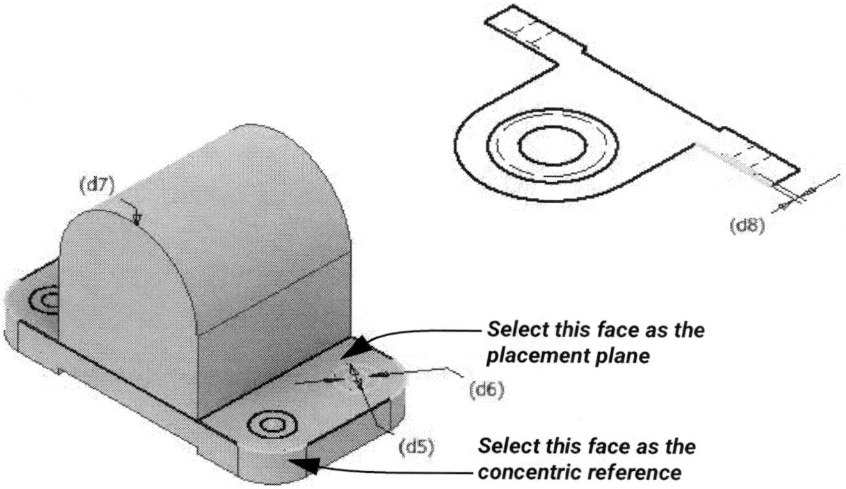

Figure 14–34

22. Enter the dimension values for the hole using the driven dimensions that were created in the sketch, as shown in Figure 14–35. Ensure that you enter the correct dimension name to match the counterbore dimensions. Create the hole as **Through All**.

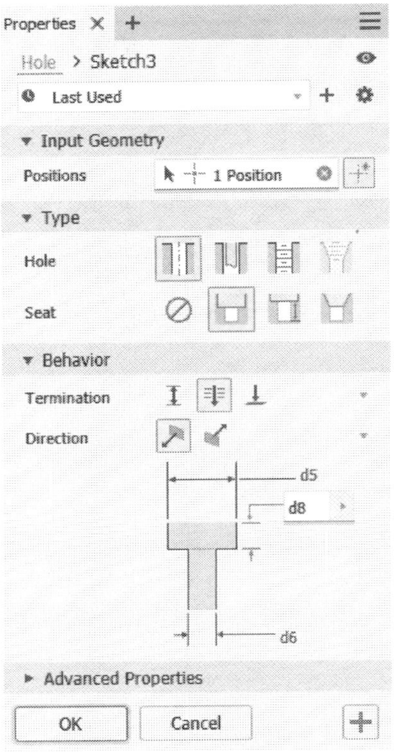

Figure 14–35

23. Complete the feature.
24. Create the additional three counterbore holes using the same settings and driven dimensions.
25. Toggle off the visibility of the second imported DWG underlay and the sketch, if visible. The model displays as shown in Figure 14–36.

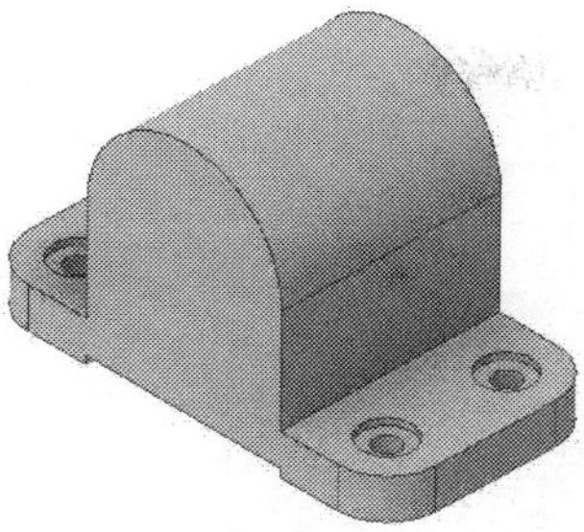

Figure 14–36

26. Save the file.

Task 7: Replace the YA-Base.dwg with a modified version.

1. Open Windows Explorer and navigate to the *Updated DWGs* folder within the top-level practice files folder.
2. Copy **YA-Base.dwg** from the *Updated DWGs* folder into the top-level practice files folder. Confirm that you want to replace the original file with the copied version. This new file has had changes made to the file to increase the size of the holes and the depth of the model.

   Note: *A copy of the original YA-Base.dwg file, called* ***YA-Base_ORIGINAL.dwg****, is in the Updated DWGs folder, if required.*

3. Return to Autodesk Inventor and review the **AssociativeDWG.ipt**. The Model browser indicates that **YA-Base.dwg** has been updated, as shown by the lightning bolt icons in Figure 14–37.

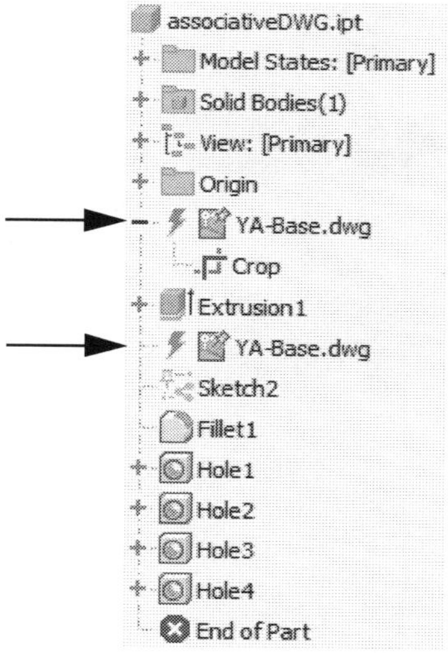

Figure 14–37

4. In the Quick Access Toolbar, select (Local Update). Note that the model updates as shown in Figure 14–38.

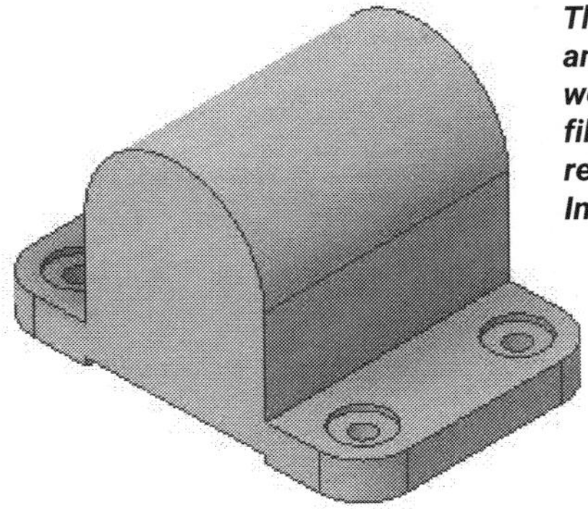

The depth of the model and the size of the holes were updated in the DWG file. The changes are reflected in the Autodesk Inventor model.

Figure 14–38

5. In the Model browser, right-click on either of the **YA-Base.dwg** files and note the **Suppress Link** and **Break Link** options. These options can be used to either temporarily break the link with the source DWG file (**Suppress Link**) or permanently break the link (**Break Link**).
6. Save the model and close the window.

Task 8: (Optional) Continue modeling the solid geometry.

After you have finished creating all of the practices in this chapter, continue to add the geometry from the DWG file into the Autodesk Inventor model. The only remaining feature is a revolved cut. To create this, consider creating a workplane and project the section that is to be revolved. Alternatively, edit one of the sketches and add more Driven Dimensions that can be used to drive additional hole features.

End of practice

Practice 14d
Associative DWG Layout

Practice Objective

- Assemble the underlay part file as the base grounded component and reference it to place and create components.

In this practice, you will begin by creating a new part file that imports an AutoCAD DWG file for use as an underlay. The underlay is imported so that associativity is maintained between the files. The part file is then used in an assembly to constrain and create new components in the assembly. To complete the practice, a change is made in the original DWG file and the updates are shown to reflect in the assembly file. The geometry that will be created is shown in Figure 14–39.

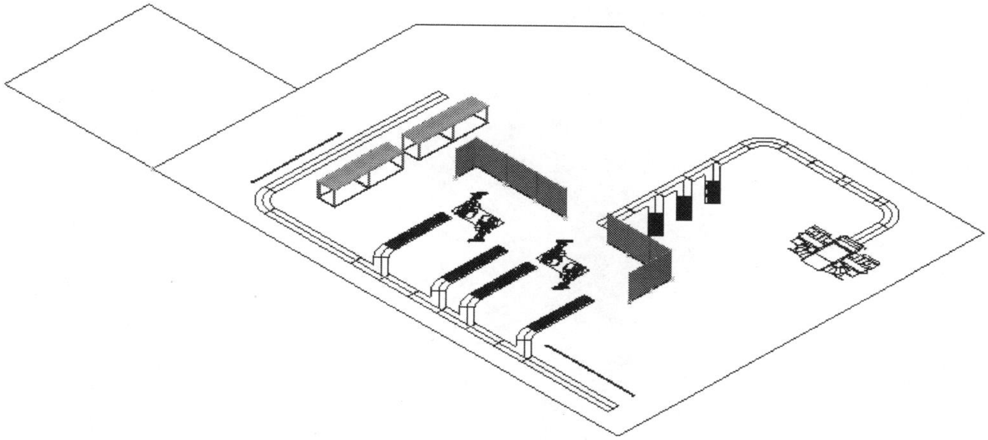

Figure 14–39

Note: *You are able to place a DWG underlay directly into an assembly using the* ***Place*** *option. Unfortunately, placing the underlay in this way does not provide an option to translate the underlay, as is available in the Part environment. As an alternative, if translation is required, you can insert the underlay into a Part file and place the part file into an assembly using assembly constraints to constrain the part, as required. In this practice, you must translate the placement point so that inserting it into a part and then assembling it will be the process used.*

Task 1: Create a new Autodesk Inventor model and import AutoCAD data.

1. Start a new part file using the **Standard (in).ipt** template.
2. Save the new file as **FactoryLayout.ipt**.

3. In the *3D Model* tab>Create panel, click (Import).
4. In the Import dialog box, expand the Files of type drop-down list and select **AutoCAD DWG Files (*.dwg)**.
5. Select **Layout Example.dwg** from the practice files folder and click **Open**.
6. Select the XZ Origin plane as the plane to import the DWG file.
7. Select the projected Origin Center Point as the center point for the import.
8. Click **OK** when prompted that inserting an AutoCAD DWG produces an associative underlay. If you had previously not saved the file, you will be notified that saving is also required.
9. Review the factory layout. The orientation of the drawing should be rotated 180 degrees and the origin point needs to be repositioned. In the next task you will reorient the imported DWG file.

Task 2: Translate the AutoCAD DWG file relative to the model's origin.

1. Expand the **Origin** node in the Model browser. Toggle on the visibility of the Center Point and note where it is located.
2. Right-click on **Layout Example.dwg** in the Model browser and select **Translate**.
3. A triad displays on the Origin Center Point. Select the rotation handle shown in Figure 14–40 to enable the rotation of the imported DWG file.

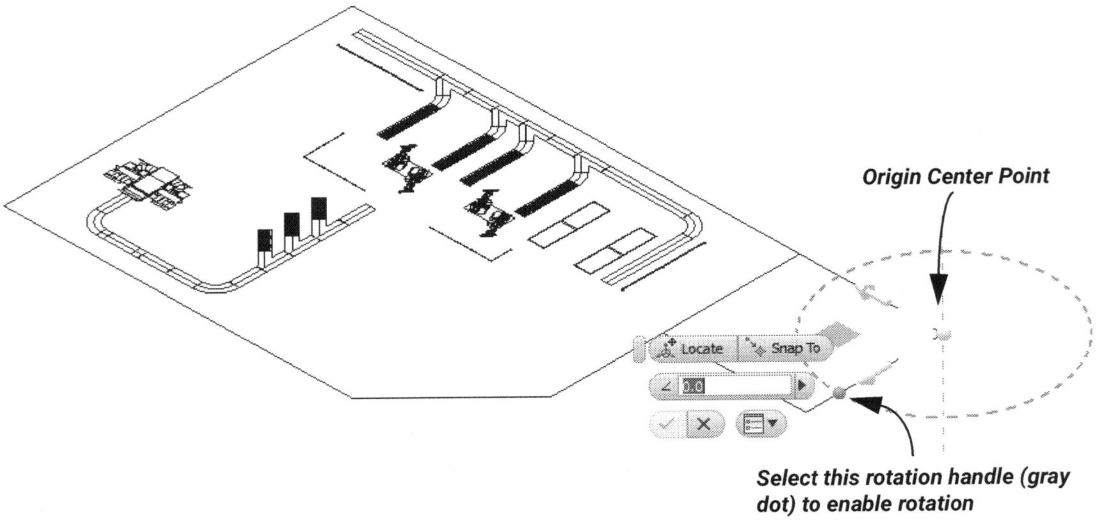

Figure 14–40

4. Begin dragging the handle and enter **180** to rotate the DWG file. Do not press <Enter>.
5. Click **Locate** in the mini-toolbar and select the point where the two rooms join, as shown in Figure 14–41.

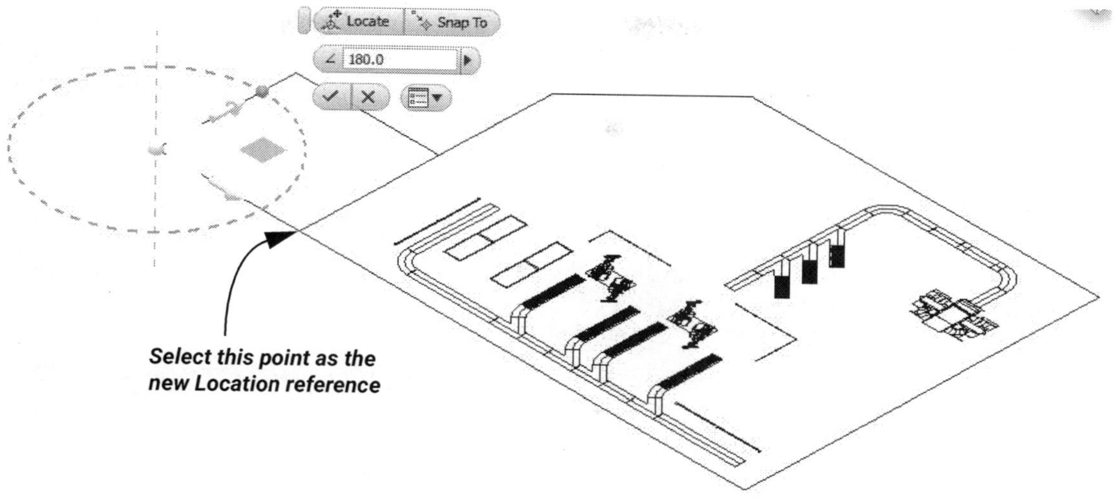

Figure 14–41

6. Click **Snap To** in the mini-toolbar and select the Origin Center Point in the Model browser to align the DWG underlay and the reference point on the drawing.

7. Click  to close the mini-toolbar and complete the translation. The model should display as shown in Figure 14–42.

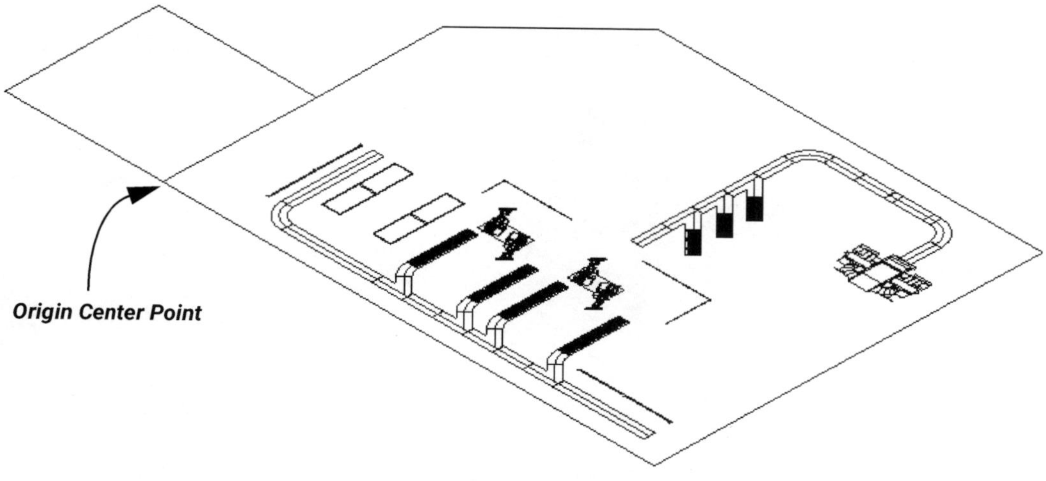

Figure 14–42

Task 3: Set the Layer Visibility for the AutoCAD DWG file.

1. Right-click on **Layout Example.dwg** in the Model browser and select **Layer Visibility**. The Layer Visibility dialog box opens. This dialog box enables you to control the DWG layers that are displayed in the Autodesk Inventor model.
2. Select **Layout Example|Slab** in the list and note how additional entities are added to the view. As these are not required, you can leave this option cleared.
3. Select **Layout Example|Walls-Interior** to clear the option. Note how all of the entities are cleared. In this drawing all of the entities have been added to this layer. Select **Layout Example|Walls-Interior** again to enable the option.
4. Click **OK** to close the Layer Visibility dialog box. The visibility of layers can be controlled at any time using this dialog box.
5. Save the model.

Task 4: Use the associative DWG file as a reference for assembling and creating components in an assembly.

1. Start a new assembly file using the **Standard (in).iam** template.
2. Place one instance of **FactoryLayout.ipt** into the assembly file. Right-click and select **Place Grounded at Origin** to assemble the part as the base model and ground it.
3. Press <Esc> to cancel the assembly of additional instances of the file.
4. Place a single instance of **Table.iam** into the assembly file, as shown in Figure 14–43.

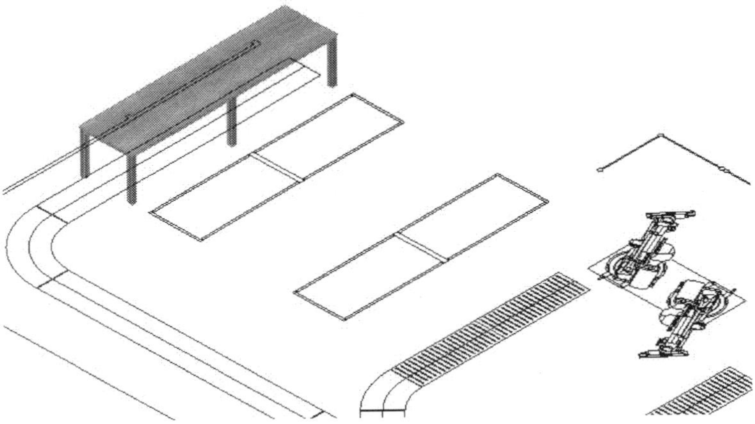

Figure 14–43

5. In the *Assembly* tab>Relationships panel, click 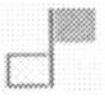 (Constrain).

6. Using the Place Constraint dialog box, assign the following constraints to fully locate the table relative to the **FactoryLayout.ipt** file:
    - Add two Mate constraints that align the edges of the table legs and the border of the table's layout in the X and Z directions, as shown in Figure 14–44.

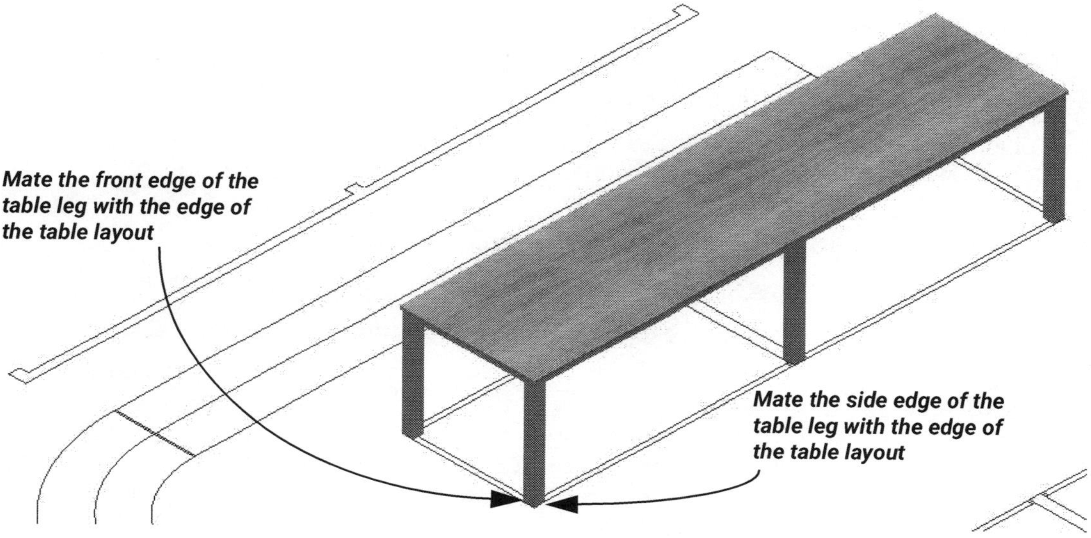

Figure 14–44

7. Close the Place Constraints dialog box.
8. Place a second instance of **Table.iam** and constrain it to the other table layout. The final assembly should display as shown in Figure 14–45.

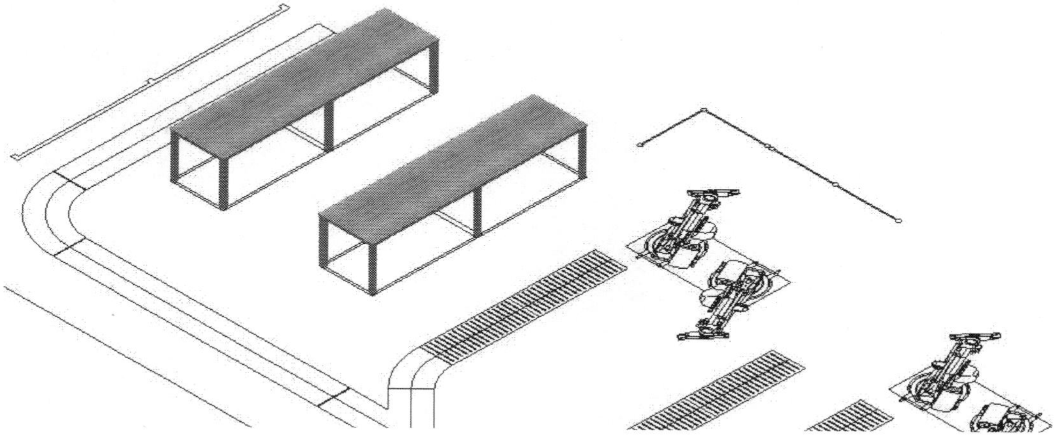

Figure 14–45

9. Save the file as **Factory.iam**.

Task 5: Create part geometry using the AutoCAD DWG underlay as a reference.

1. In the *Assembly* tab>Component panel, click (Create) to start a new part file in the context of the assembly.
2. In the Create In-Place Component dialog box, enter **Screen.ipt** as the name of the new file and assign **Standard(in).ipt** as the part template to be used. Click **OK**.
3. Select the XZ plane of the assembly as the sketch plane reference for the new part. **Screen.ipt** becomes the active component in the assembly (if not, activate it).
4. In the *3D Model* tab>Sketch panel, click (Start 2D Sketch).
5. Select the YZ plane in the Screen model as the sketching plane for the sketch.
6. In the *Sketch* tab>Create panel, expand the **Project Geometry** option, and select (Project DWG Geometry).
7. In the mini-toolbar, ensure that (Project Single Geometry) is selected. Select the 13 circular entities described in Figure 14–46. If the entire entity is not selected, it cannot be extruded in a later step.

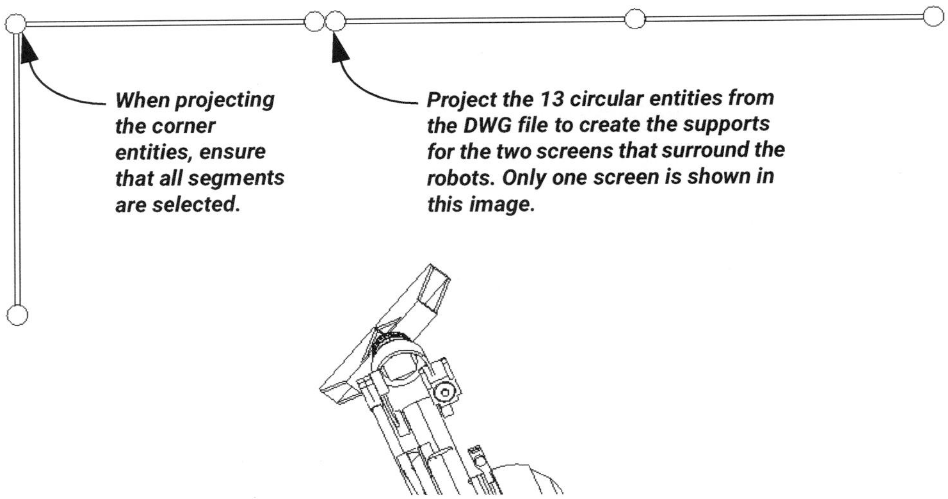

Figure 14–46

8. Finish the sketch and rename the sketch as **Supports**.
9. Create a second sketch on the YZ plane and start the (Project DWG Geometry) option.

10. In the mini-toolbar, select (Project Connected Geometry) and project the 9 rectangles that are used to define the screen geometry between the supports, as shown in Figure 14–47.

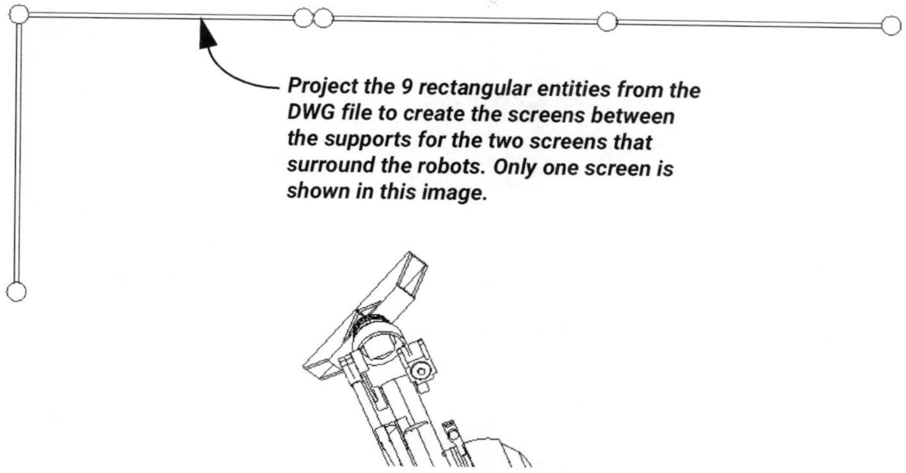

Figure 14–47

11. Finish the sketch and rename the sketch as **Screens**.
12. Use the **Extrude** command to create the screen geometry shown in Figure 14–48.
    - Extrude the 13 circular entities in the Supports sketch to a height of **72 in**.
    - Extrude the 9 rectangular entities in the Screens sketch to a height of **70 in**.

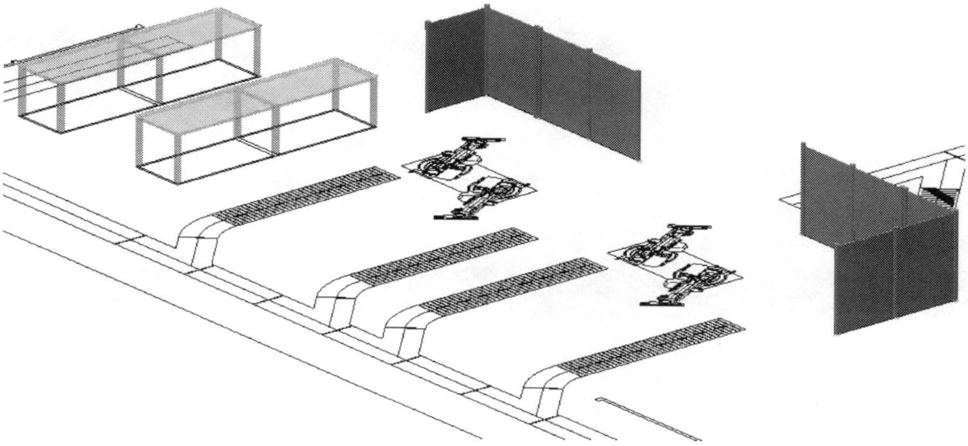

Figure 14–48

13. Reactivate the top-level assembly.
14. Save the assembly and the newly created part file.

Task 6: Update the DWG underlay and the associated geometry.

1. Open Windows Explorer and navigate to the *Updated DWGs* folder within the top-level practice files folder.
2. Copy **Layout Example.dwg** from the *Updated DWGs* folder into the top-level practice files folder. Confirm that you want to replace the original file with the copied version. This new file has had changes made to relocate the tables and change the size of one of the screens.

   Note: *A copy of the original Layout Example.dwg file, called* ***Layout Example_ORIGINAL.dwg****, is in the Updated DWGs folder, if required.*

3. Return to Autodesk Inventor and note that the (Local Update) option is available in the Quick Access Toolbar and that the **FactoryLayout** underlay is showing as out-of-date in the Model browser. Click (Local Update) to update the assembly, as shown in Figure 14–49.

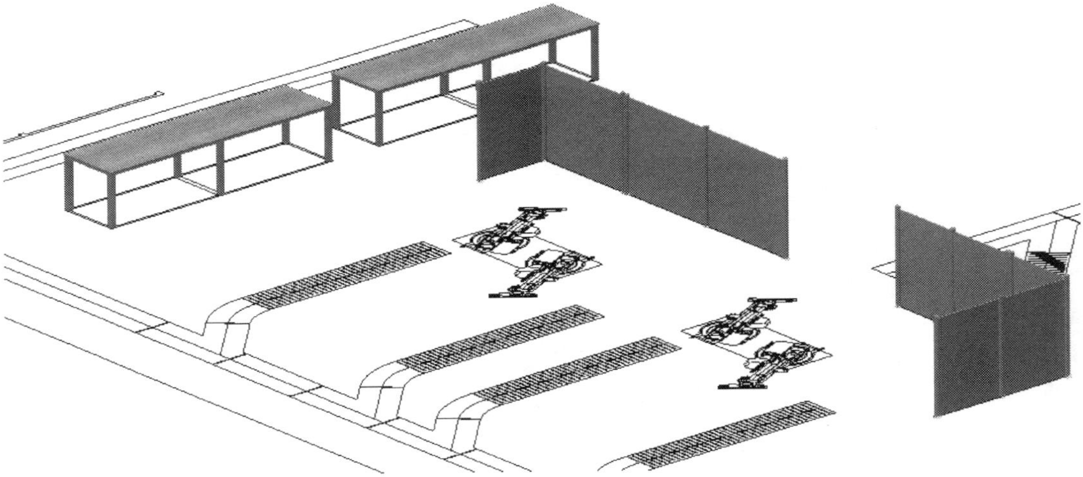

Figure 14–49

4. Save the assembly and close the files.

End of practice

Chapter Review Questions

1. When using an AutoCAD .DWG file in Autodesk Inventor, which of the following Open Options should be used to view, plot, and measure the file contents?
   a. Open
   b. Import

2. Which of the following Open Options should be used to create a single solid-body base feature when an AutoCAD 3D DWG file is required for use in Autodesk Inventor?
   a. Open
   b. Import

3. Which of the following are true statements regarding importing AutoCAD DWG data as an underlay in Autodesk Inventor? (Select all that apply.)
   a. The DWG data can only be imported onto a single plane in the model.
   b. The layers in the DWG underlay can be set to display only specific layers.
   c. Use the Project Geometry command to project and use DWG data in a sketch.
   d. The DWG data that is imported remains unassociated with the source data.
   e. The visibility of the DWG underlays can be controlled using the Visibility option.
   f. An imported AutoCAD DWG file can also be used as a layout reference to assemble components.
   g. An imported AutoCAD DWG file can be displayed in a drawing view of the Inventor file.

4. Which of the following best describe how the **Translate** command can be used? (Select all that apply.)
   a. The Translate command enables you to relocate the DWG underlay on the same plane.
   b. The Translate command enables you to relocate the DWG underlay onto another plane.
   c. The Translate command enables you to snap the DWG underlay to the origin center point on the same plane.

5. You can crop an imported DWG underlay in multiple locations to simplify the data that displays.
   a. True
   b. False

6. Which of the following three methods for incorporating AutoCAD DWG data in Autodesk Inventor enables you to review sheets in the DWG file?
   a. Selecting Open in the File Open Options dialog box.
   b. Selecting Import in the File Open Options dialog box.
   c. Creating a new part file and selecting Import in the *3D Model* tab>Create panel.

Command Summary

Button	Command	Location
	**Import**	• **Ribbon:** *3D Model* tab>Create panel
	**Options (import options)**	• Open dialog box
	**Project DWG Geometry**	• **Ribbon:** *Sketch* tab>Create panel

Chapter 15

Analyzing a Model

The ability to analyze models prior to manufacturing is a valuable tool in digital prototyping. The Autodesk® Inventor® software offers a variety of basic tools that can be used to verify such things as continuity, draft, curvature, and cross-sections in model geometry. Understanding how to use these tools during the design process helps to ensure that there are fewer issues prior to finalizing a model or sending it to a more complex analysis software tool.

Learning Objectives

- Conduct a Zebra analysis that evaluates continuity between surfaces.
- Conduct a Draft analysis that enables you to visually evaluate whether the applied draft values in a model are within a specified range.
- Conduct a Curvature analysis that evaluates whether continuity exists between surfaces based on the results of flow lines.
- Conduct a Gaussian, Mean Curvature, or Maximum Curvature analysis for points on a surface.
- Conduct a Cross Section analysis that displays the model sectioned through a single plane.
- Conduct a Cross Section analysis that displays the model sectioned through a series of planes and also identifies areas of the model that conflict with specified maximum and minimum wall thickness values.

15.1 Analysis Types

There are five analysis types that are available to analyze model geometry. These types are Zebra, Draft, Curvature, Surface, and Section.

Zebra Analysis

A Zebra analysis projects parallel lines onto a model to determine if continuity between surfaces exists.

- If the stripes are parallel, the surface/face is flat.
- If the stripe edges do not line up, then the two surfaces are not tangent.
- If the stripe edges line up, but display a sharp angle, then the boundary is tangent but not curvature continuous.
- If the stripe edges are continuous (no sharp angles) across the boundary of two surfaces, then the transition is curvature continuous.

Figure 15–1 shows the three continuity options.

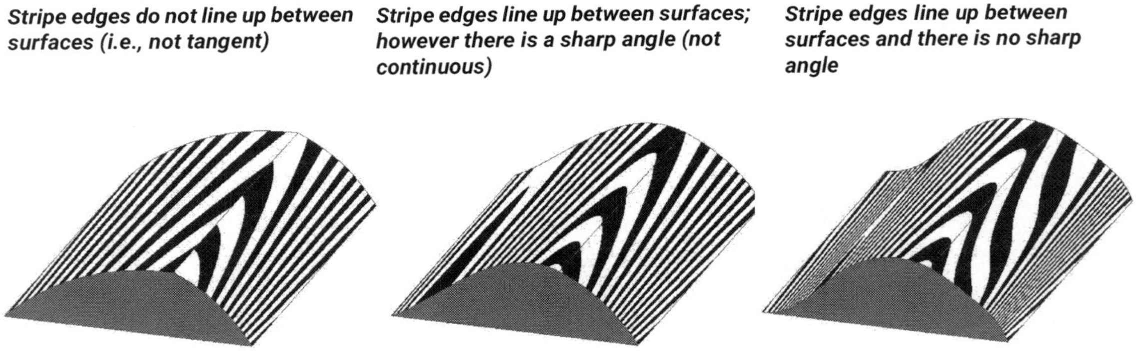

Figure 15–1

Draft Analysis

A Draft analysis determines if the drafts that have been added to the model are satisfactory for manufacturing. Based on a draft's maximum and minimum permissible values, a color gradient is displayed so that you can compare it to the model.

- If the draft falls within the permissible range (i.e., faces with adequate draft angles), the color of the selected faces/ surfaces can be distinguished in the color gradient.
- If the colors on the model are outside the gradient, the draft angle is outside the range and further analysis of the surface should be done.

Figure 15–2 shows an example of a model whose draft angle is within the permissible range.

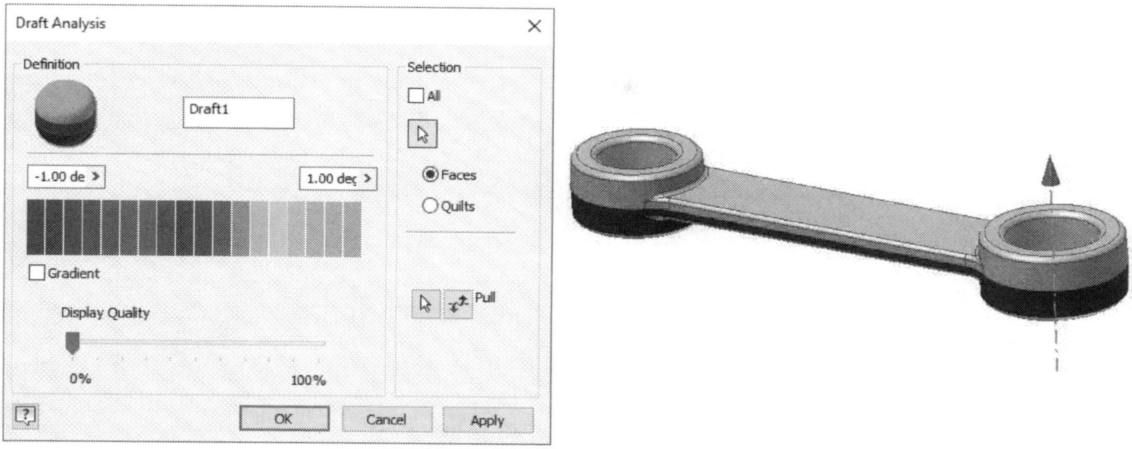

Figure 15–2

Curvature Analysis

An edge is generated where two surfaces meet, and a vertex is generated where two curves meet. The term continuity refers to how the faces/surfaces or end points meet. A Curvature analysis enables you to visually analyze the results of continuity calculations for flow lines (curvature comb) on selected faces or quilts or between them. The connections between curves and surfaces are described as follows:

<table>
<tr><td>G-1</td><td>Curves or surfaces <u>do not</u> share a common end point. There is no continuity.
</td></tr>
<tr><td>G0</td><td>Curves or surfaces <u>do</u> share a common end point. They are not tangent to one another.
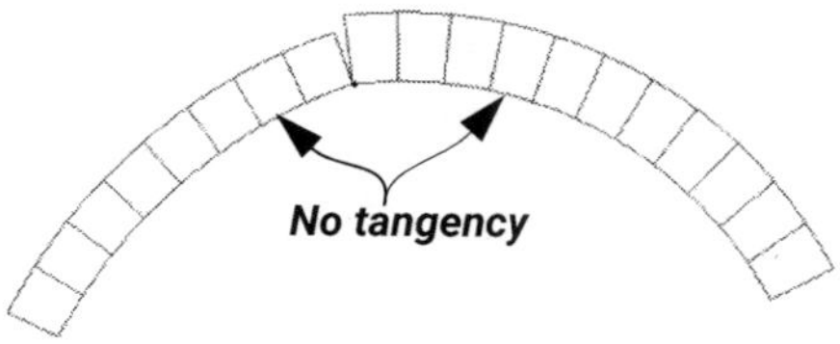
</td></tr>
</table>

G1	Curves or surfaces are tangent to each other and share a common boundary, but have differing curvature magnitudes at their intersection. 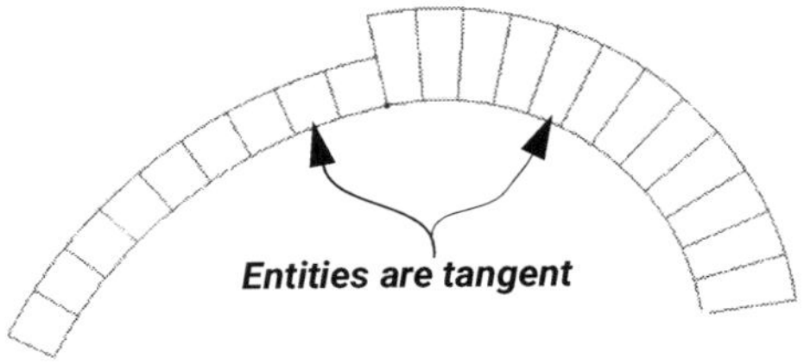
G2	Curves or surfaces are tangent to each other and have a common curvature at their shared boundary. G2 continuity produces a smooth connection. G2 continuity is usually only required for surfaces in which light reflection is an issue. 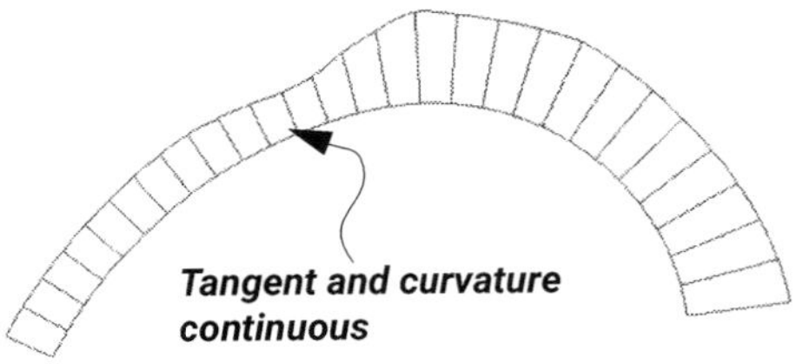

Surface Analysis

Surface analysis tools provide three analysis types: Gaussian, Mean Curvature, and Maximum Curvature, as shown in Figure 15–3.

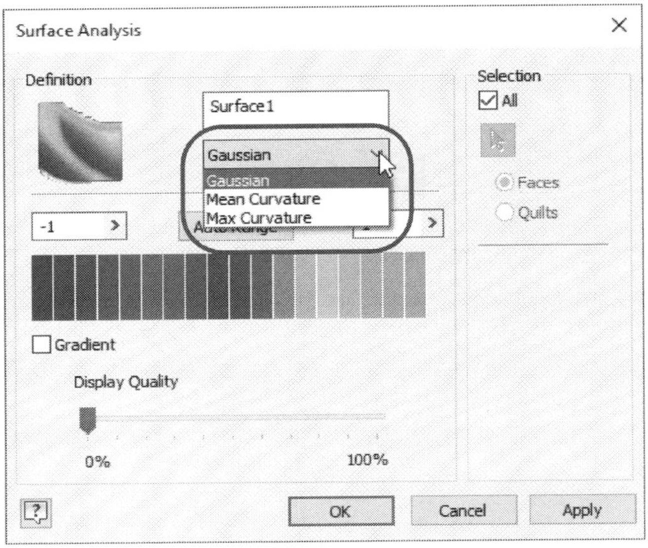

Figure 15–3

The three surface analysis types are described as follows:

- A **Gaussian** analysis is the product of the minimum curvature and maximum curvature for a given point on a surface. It is used to locate areas of high and low surface curvature and values can be either positive or negative. Minimum curvature values display in blue and maximum values display in green. All other values are assigned a color between blue and green. The Gaussian curvature for planar and cylindrical surfaces are zero because the curvature is always zero in at least one direction. Figure 15–4 shows a Gaussian Curvature analysis performed on two different parts.

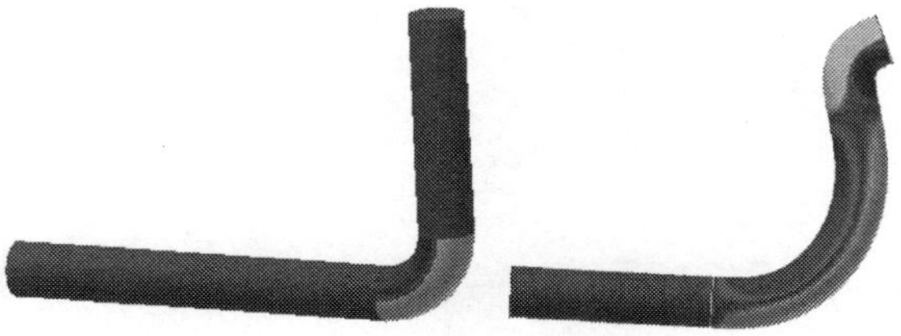

Figure 15–4

- The **Mean Curvature** surface analysis provides information on the curvature of the u and v surfaces. Similar to a Gaussian analysis, it displays the results using a color gradient.
- The **Maximum Curvature** surface analysis shows the largest normal curvature at every point on the surface. Similar to a Gaussian analysis, it displays the results using a color gradient.

Cross Section Analysis

A Cross Section (Section) analysis obtains information about a cross-section through a part. You can perform two types of analyses: Simple and Advanced.

- A simple section analysis displays the model as a cutaway view of the part based on the selected plane and enables visual inspection. This view is similar to the slice graphics option, as shown in Figure 15–5.

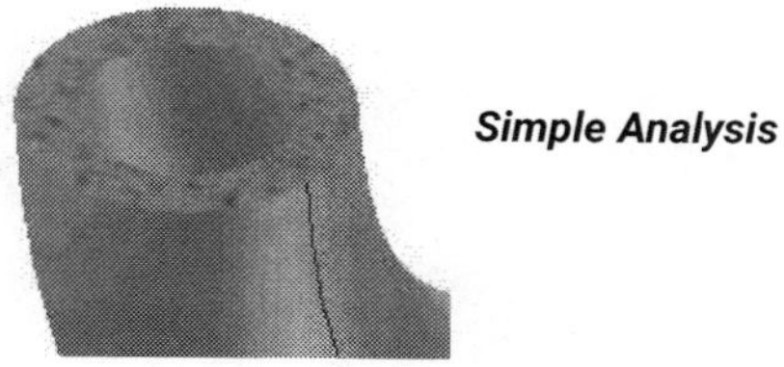

Figure 15–5

- An advanced section analysis enables you to define multiple section planes by either selecting or creating them. It can also verify the maximum and minimum wall thickness and area. For an advanced section analysis, areas in a section that are thicker than the maximum highlight in red on the model and are listed in the *Results* area. Areas thinner than the minimum part thickness highlight in blue on the model and are listed in the *Results* area. A sample Advanced Section analysis is shown in Figure 15–6, where the part contains one cross-section that is too thick, one that is within the thickness range, and one that is too thin.

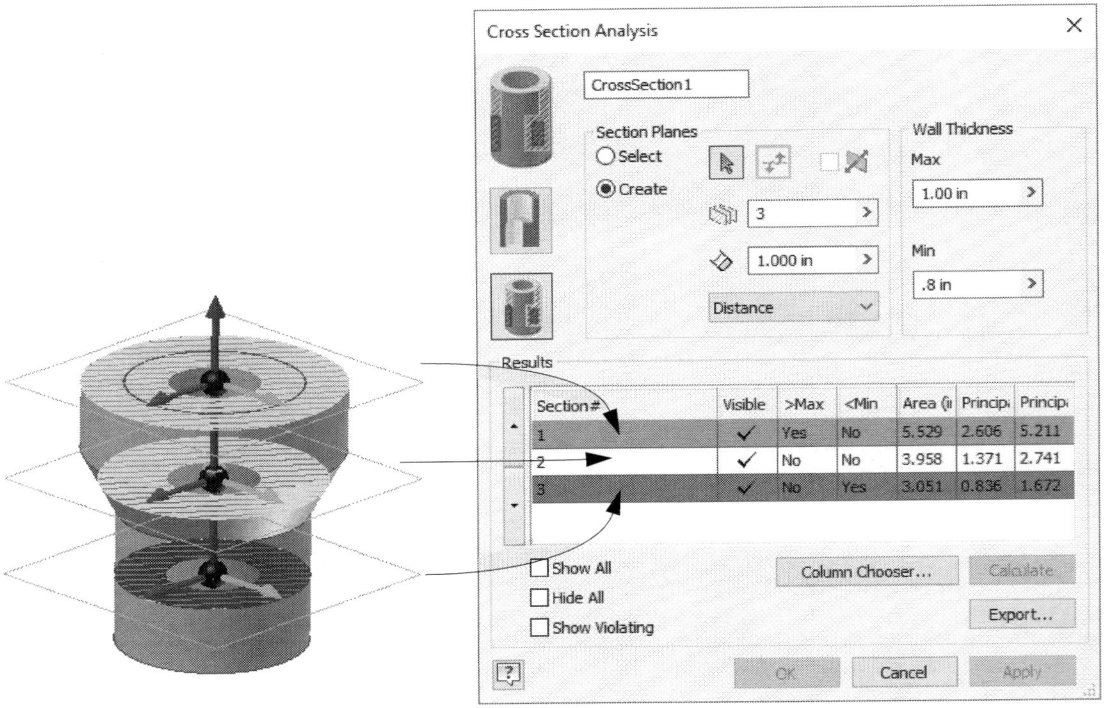

Figure 15–6

15.2 Analysis Procedures

Regardless of which analysis tool you use, the procedure for analyzing a model is similar. Use the following general steps to perform an analyses on a model:

1. Start the analysis.
2. Select the references.
3. Define the options.
4. Complete and review the analysis.
5. Display or edit an existing analysis.

Step 1 - Start the analysis.

In the *Inspect* tab>Analysis panel, select the required analysis type, as shown in Figure 15–7.

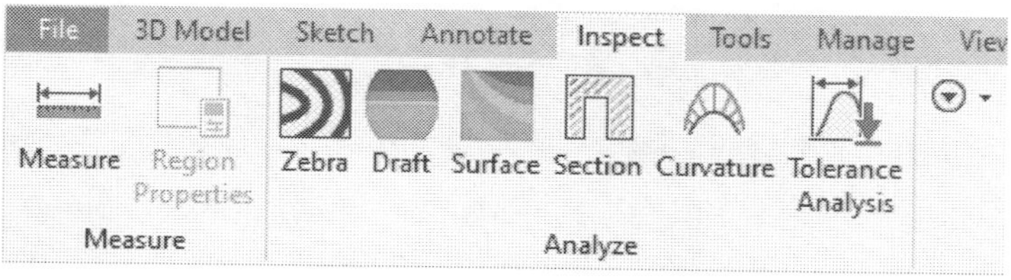

Figure 15–7

The corresponding dialog box opens. For all analyses, specify a name for the analysis or use the default.

- For a Surface Analysis, you must also select the type of surface analysis: **Gaussian**, **Mean Curvature**, or **Max Curvature**.
- For a Section Analysis you must also select the type of section analysis as **Simple** or **Advanced**.

Step 2 - Select the references.

Reference selection is required to define which geometry on the model is to be analyzed.

- For the Zebra, Draft, Curvature, and Surface analyses you must select surfaces to analyze. The default is to analyze all surfaces; however, you can clear the **All** option and select either **Faces** or **Quilts**, as shown in Figure 15–8. If either **Faces** or **Quilts** are to be used you must select the entities to analyze. For a Draft analysis, you must also select a reference for the pull direction.

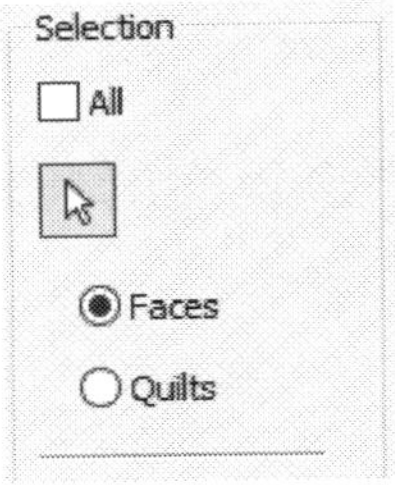

Figure 15–8

- For a Section analyses, select a plane that cuts through the part at the required angle.
  - For a Simple Section analysis, an offset can be added from the plane by entering an offset value or by clicking and dragging it in the graphics window. The options for a simple section analysis are shown in Figure 15–9.

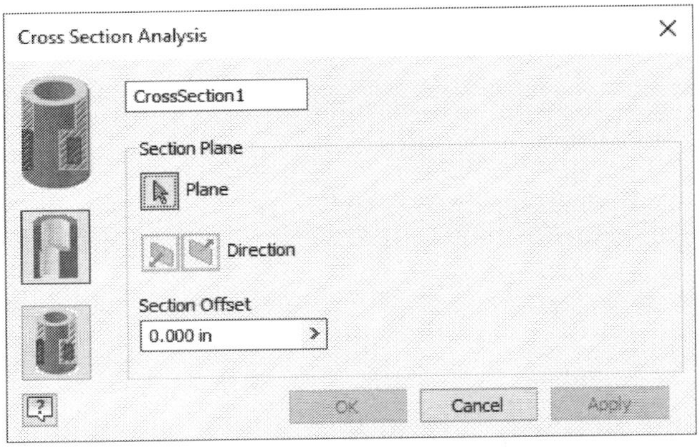

Figure 15–9

- For an Advanced Section analysis, specify the number of sections and the section spacing (i.e., the distance between sections), as shown in Figure 15–10.

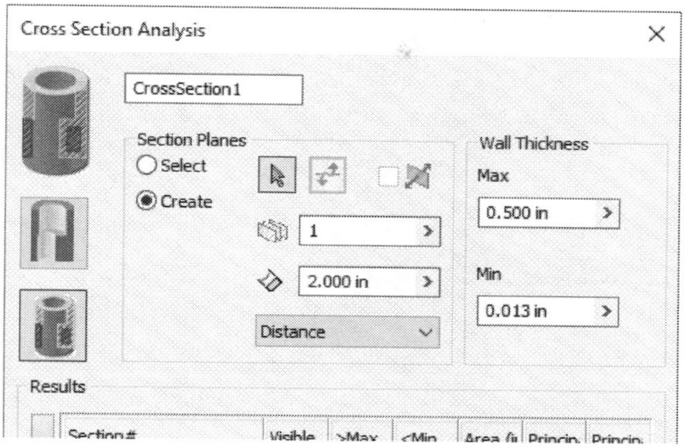

Figure 15–10

Step 3 - Define the options.

Once you have selected references for the analysis, you can define the options.

Zebra Analysis

For a Zebra analysis, select one of the three direction icons as shown in Figure 15–11. Select the direction that most clearly shows the transition between surfaces. You can leave it with the default direction first, define the other options, apply the analysis, and then edit the analysis to change the direction, as required. Adjust the Thickness, Density, Opacity, and Display Quality values to modify the proportion of white to black, number of stripes, transparency, and resolution for the zebra pattern, respectively.

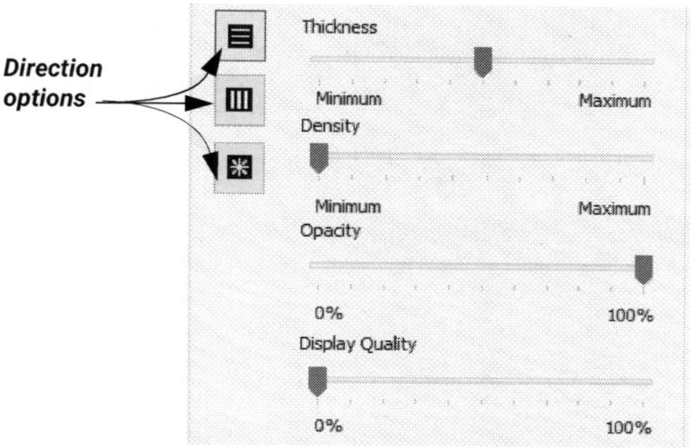

Figure 15–11

Draft Analysis

Enter minimum and maximum angles, as shown in Figure 15–12. Selected faces or quilts that fall between the specified angles will display in a color corresponding to the measured angle, based on the pull direction. Activate the **Gradient** option to display the color band as a continuous gradient, rather than discrete color bands. Adjust the display quality to control the quality of the color shown on the selected faces and quilts.

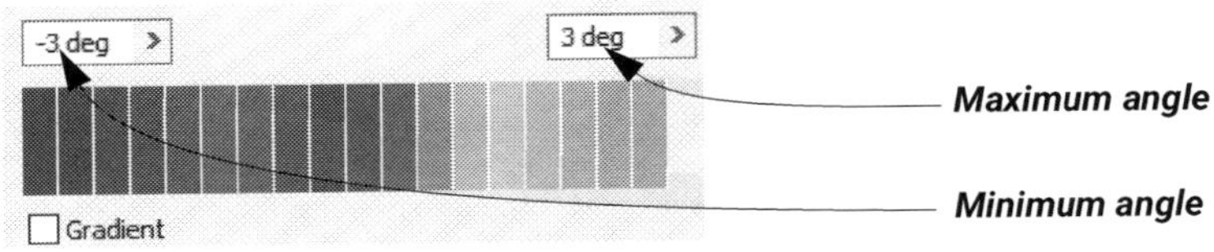

Figure 15–12

Curvature Analysis

To control the visual display of a curvature analysis you must manipulate the Comb Density, Comb Scale, and Surface Density. The  (Comb Density) option controls the spacing between the spines. The  (Comb Scale) option controls the scale or length of the spines. The  (Surface Density) controls the density of the sample curves for interior faces. In the Direction section, specify having the curvature comb display in Direction1, Direction2, or both. The options are shown in Figure 15–13.

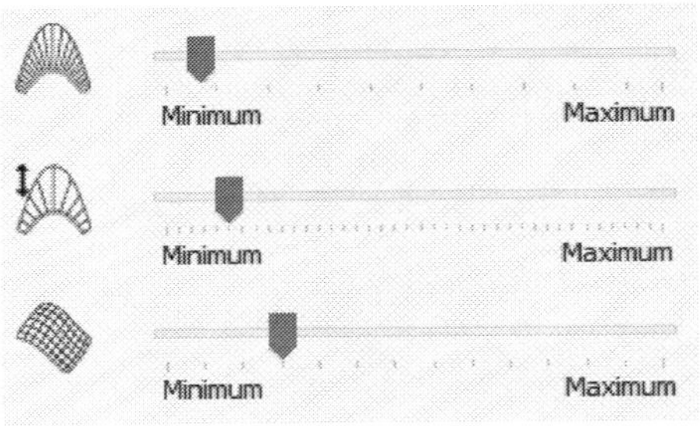

Figure 15–13

Surface Analysis

Enter minimum and maximum curvature ratio values, as shown in Figure 15–14. Selected faces or quilts that fall between the specified curvature ratios display in a color corresponding to the measured curvature ratio. Click **Auto Range** to set the minimum curvature ratio to the smallest value found on the selected faces and the maximum curvature ratio to the largest value found on the selected faces. Activate the **Gradient** option to display the color band as a continuous gradient, rather than discrete color bands. Adjust the display quality to control the quality of the color shown on the selected faces and quilts.

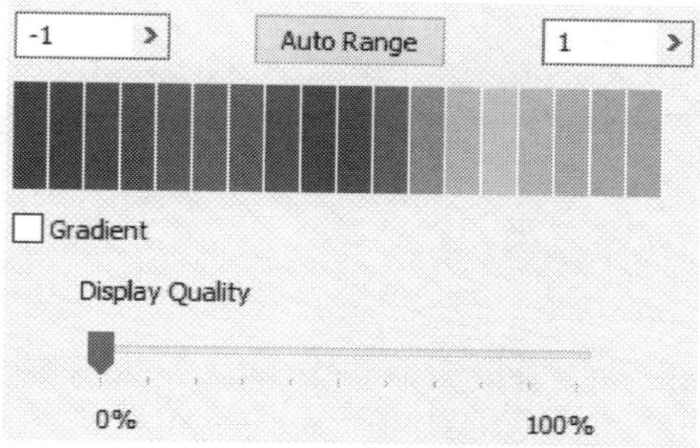

Figure 15–14

Cross Section Analysis

With a Simple Section analysis, you can only change the section offset value and the direction. For Advanced, additional options enable you to specify minimum and maximum thicknesses, as shown in Figure 15–15.

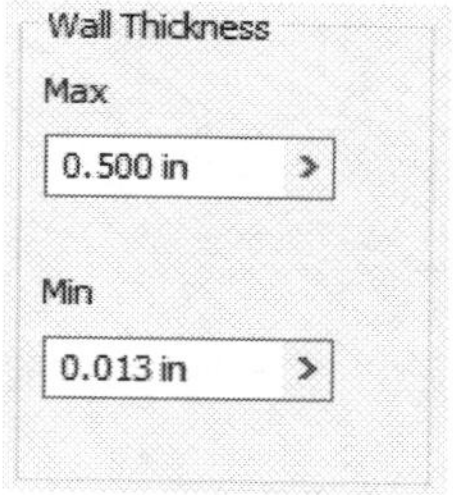

Figure 15–15

Step 4 - Complete and review the analysis.

Click **Apply** to run the analysis. The analysis is added to the Model browser. Review the results to ensure that they display as required.

- Rotate the model, as required, to better view the results. Rotating the model for a Zebra analysis is particularly helpful in determining how well the stripe edges line up.

You might want to clarify or adjust the results by changing the direction(s) selected for a Zebra or Curvature analysis, or you might want to adjust the minimum and maximum values for a Draft, Gaussian, or Section analysis. Make adjustments, as required, and click **Apply**. Continue adjusting, as required, and click **Cancel.**

Step 5 - Display or edit an existing analysis.

To display an analysis you already created, double-click on it in the *Analysis* folder in the Model browser. The analysis result displays on the model. To toggle off the visibility of all analyses, right-click on the *Analysis* folder and select **Analysis Visibility**, as shown in Figure 15–16.

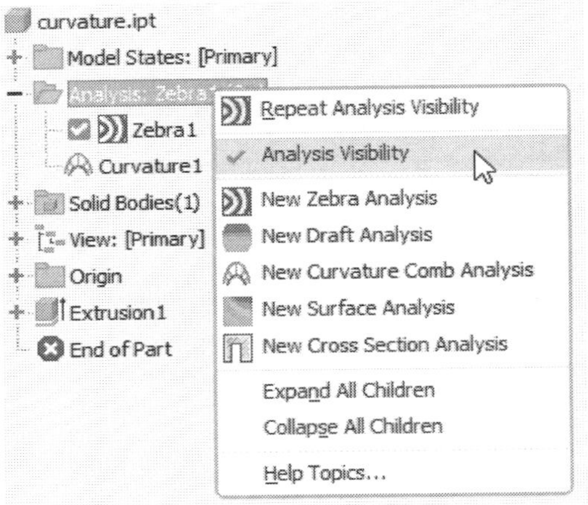

Figure 15–16

To edit an analysis you already created, right-click on it in the Model browser and select **Edit**.

Practice 15a
Analyzing Continuity

Practice Objectives

- Conduct a Zebra analysis that evaluates whether continuity exists between adjacent surfaces based on the results of stripes applied to the surfaces.
- Conduct a Curvature analysis that evaluates whether continuity exists between adjacent surfaces based on the results of flow lines that extend normal to the surfaces.

In this practice, you will analyze a model using the Zebra and Curvature analysis tools. The Zebra analysis enables you to investigate the continuity between adjacent faces or quilts, while the Curvature analysis investigates the curvature of a face or quilt, as well as between boundaries.

Task 1: Perform a Zebra analysis.

Perform a Zebra analysis to determine if continuity exists between surfaces.

1. Open **zebra.ipt**. Rotate the part to appear similar to that shown in Figure 15–17.

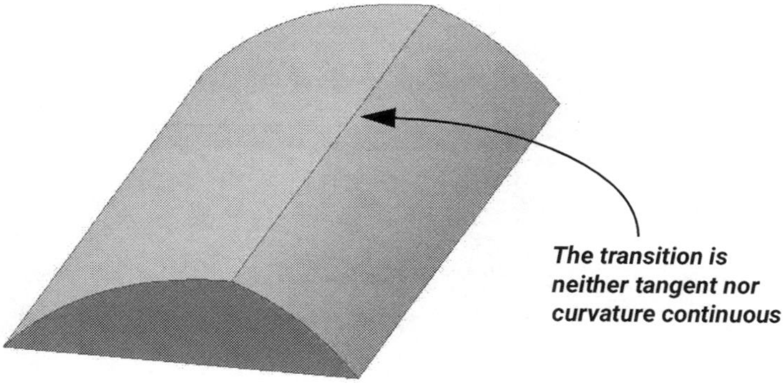

Figure 15–17

2. In the *Inspect* tab>Analysis panel, click  (Zebra). The Zebra Analysis dialog box opens.

3. Keep the default name of **Zebra1**. In the *Selection* area, clear the **All** option. Select the two curved faces in the model.
4. Set the *Thickness* slider halfway between Minimum and Maximum, the *Density* slider at approximately 75%, the *Opacity* at 100%, and the *Display Quality* at 100%, as shown in Figure 15–18.

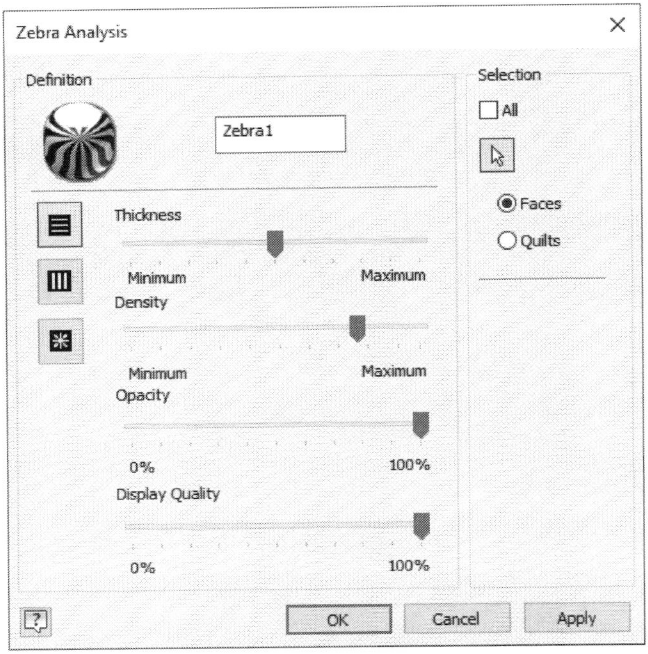

Figure 15–18

5. Click **Apply** to run the analysis while leaving the dialog box open. The model displays similar to that shown in Figure 15–19. Note how the stripes on any one face do not line up with the stripes on the adjacent face The orientation of the model affects the display of the results. Try and spin the model so that you obtain something similar to that shown.

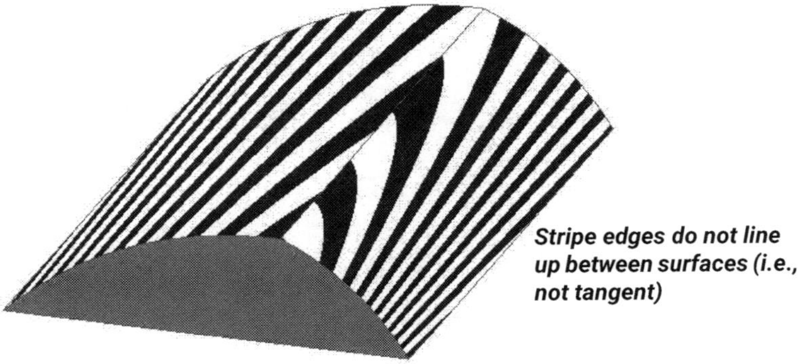

Figure 15–19

6. Close the Zebra Analysis dialog box. The analysis is listed in the Model browser, as shown in Figure 15–20.

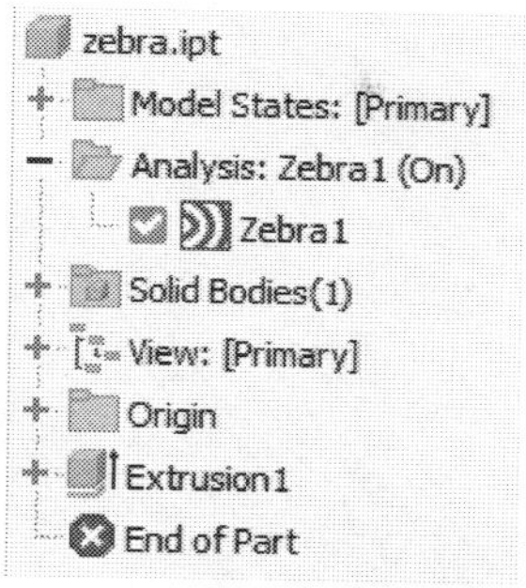

Figure 15–20

7. In the Model browser, right-click on **Analysis:Zebra1 (On)** and select **Analysis Visibility**. This toggles off the display of the stripes on the model; however, the analysis remains in the model.

Task 2: Change the tangency between the two curved surfaces.

1. Edit the sketch associated with **Extrusion1**.

2. In the *Sketch* tab>Constrain panel, click . Select the two sketch entities shown on the left side of Figure 15–21 to make them tangent. Select the left edge first and the right second. The sketch updates as shown on the right side.

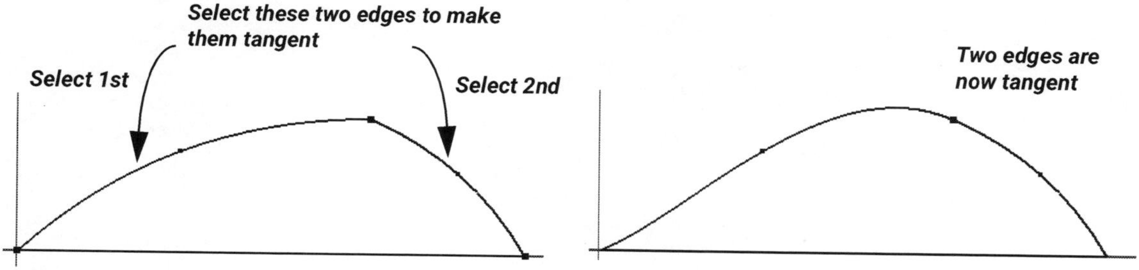

Figure 15–21

3. Finish the sketch.

4. In the Model browser, right-click on **Analysis:Zebra1 (Off)** and select **Analysis Visibility**. This toggles on the display of the stripes on the model, as shown in Figure 15–22. The stripes have updated to reflect the change in tangency between the two surfaces. They now line up with each other; however, they do not smoothly transition to the stripes on the adjacent face. There is an angle between the two.

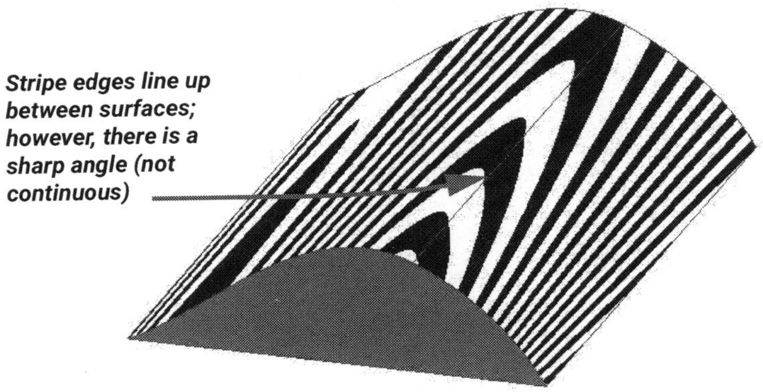

Figure 15–22

Task 3: Change the continuity between the two curved surfaces.

1. Edit the sketch associated with **Extrusion1**.

2. In the *Sketch* tab>Constrain panel, click . Select the two sketch entities shown on the left side of Figure 15–23 to make them G2 Continuous. Select the right edge first and the left second. The sketch updates as shown on the right side.

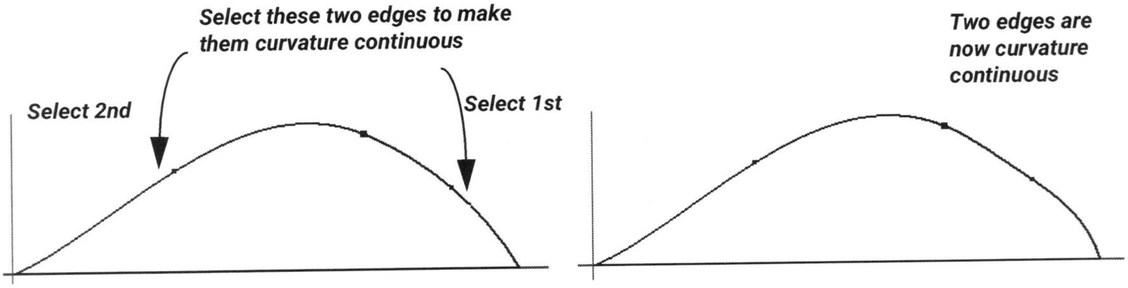

Figure 15–23

3. Finish the sketch. The stripes have updated to reflect the change in curvature continuity between the two surfaces, as shown in Figure 15–24. The stripes now line up with one another and smoothly transition to the stripes on the adjacent face. There is no angle between the two.

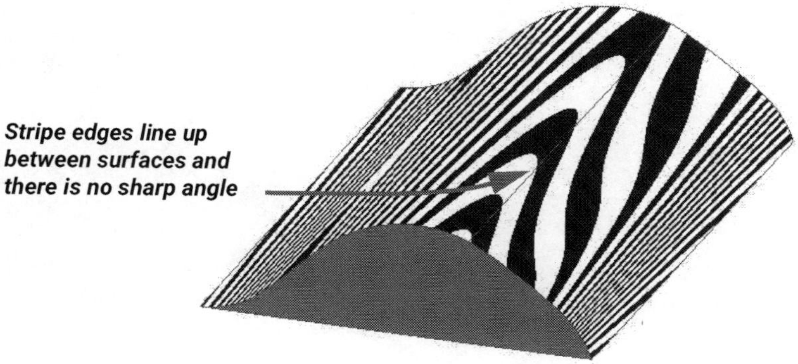

Figure 15–24

4. Save the model and close the window.

Task 4: Perform a Curvature analysis.

Perform a Curvature analysis to obtain a visual representation (in the form of a curvature comb) of the curvature on selected faces. In the next series of tasks, you will use the same model and similar steps to review non-continuous, tangent, and curvature continuity on surfaces.

1. Open **curvature.ipt**. The Zebra analysis has also been included in this model and is automatically toggled off when a model is initially opened.
2. In the *Inspect* tab>Analysis panel, click  (Curvature). The Curvature Analysis dialog box opens.
3. Keep the analysis name as **Curvature1**. Select the two curved faces on the model, maintain the default settings, and click **OK**. The curvature spines are too small to easily see the curvature change between the two surfaces.
4. In the *Analysis* folder, right-click on **Curvature1** and select **Edit**.
5. Adjust the sliders for each option, as shown in Figure 15–25.
   -  (Comb Density): Controls the spacing between the spines.
   -  (Comb Scale): Controls the scale or length of the spines.
   -  (Surface Density): Controls the density of the sample curves for interior faces.

6. Click **OK**. The model displays as shown on the right side of Figure 15–25.

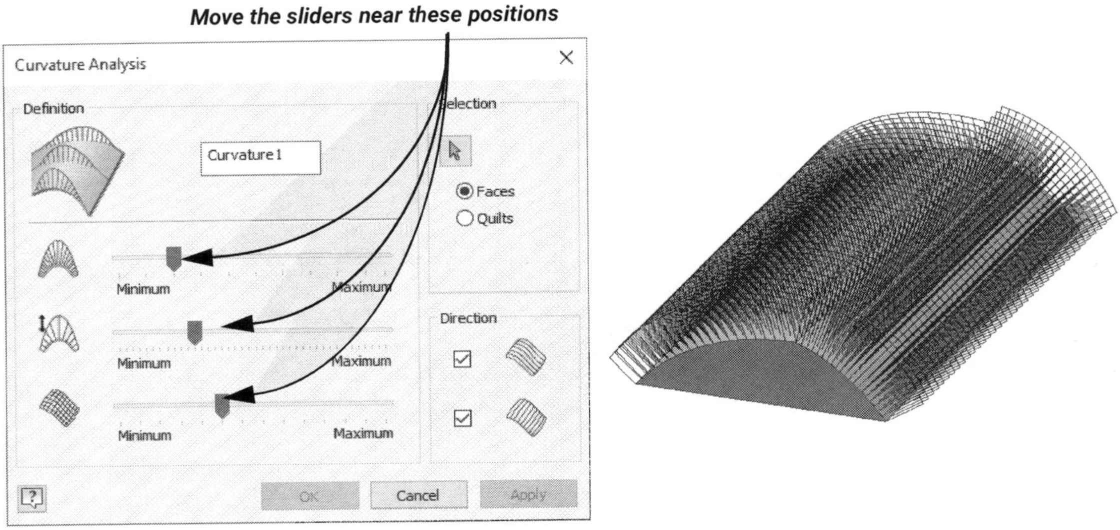

Figure 15–25

7. Orient the model to the FRONT view using the ViewCube. The model should display similar to that shown in Figure 15–26. Note that the curvature comb separates at the boundary between the two surfaces. This means that the two surfaces are discontinuous.

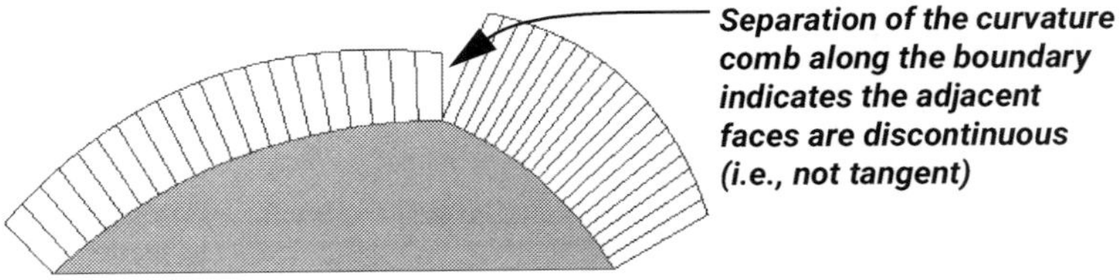

Figure 15–26

8. Using the sketching techniques previously discussed, apply tangency between the two surfaces. The Curvature analysis display updates, as shown in Figure 15–27. It might vary slightly based on the slider values that you set.

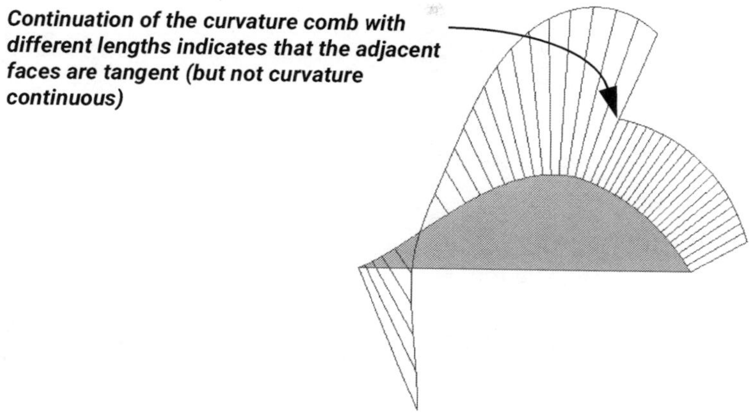

Figure 15–27

9. Using the sketching techniques previously discussed, apply curvature continuity between the two surfaces. Be sure to select the curves in the same order as was described earlier. The Curvature analysis display updates, as shown in Figure 15–28. It might vary slightly based on the slider values that you set.

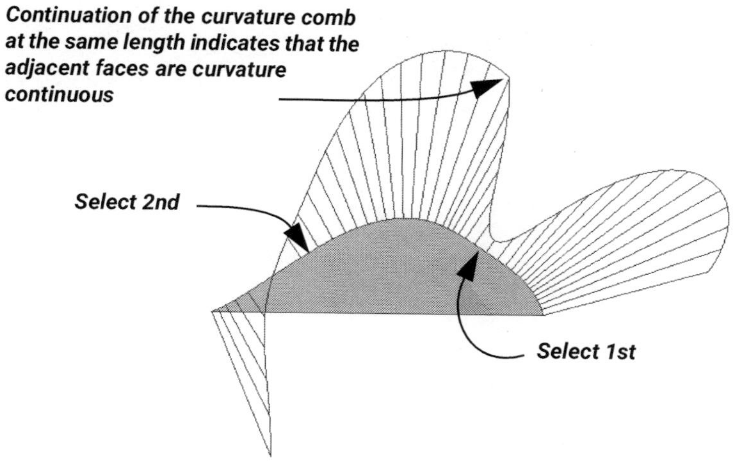

Figure 15–28

Task 5: Activate and edit an existing analysis.

1. Currently, the **Curvature1** analysis is active. In the Model browser, double-click on the **Zebra1** analysis to activate it. The Zebra analysis displays on the model.
2. In the Model browser, right-click on **Zebra1** and select **Edit**. The Zebra Analysis dialog box opens with the current settings.
3. Increase the Density slider to the maximum value. Click **OK** to apply the changes and close the dialog box. The Zebra analysis updates with more stripes.
4. Right-click on the *Analysis* folder and select **Analysis Visibility** to toggle off the display of all analyses. The model displays without any visible analysis results.
5. Save the model and close the window.

End of practice

Practice 15b
Draft Analysis

Practice Objective

- Conduct a Draft analysis that enables you to visually evaluate whether the applied draft values in a model are within a specified range.

In this practice, you will analyze the draft on a model. The results of the Draft analysis are shown in Figure 15–29, where two distinct draft angles are detected.

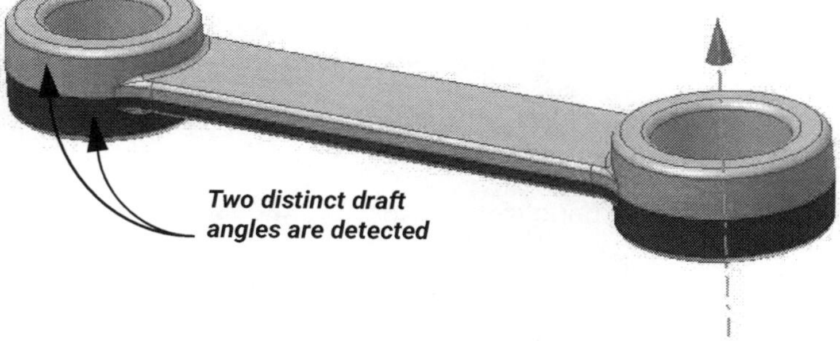

Figure 15–29

Task 1: Perform a Draft analysis.

1. Open **analyze_connecting_rod.ipt**. Orient the model as shown in Figure 15–30.

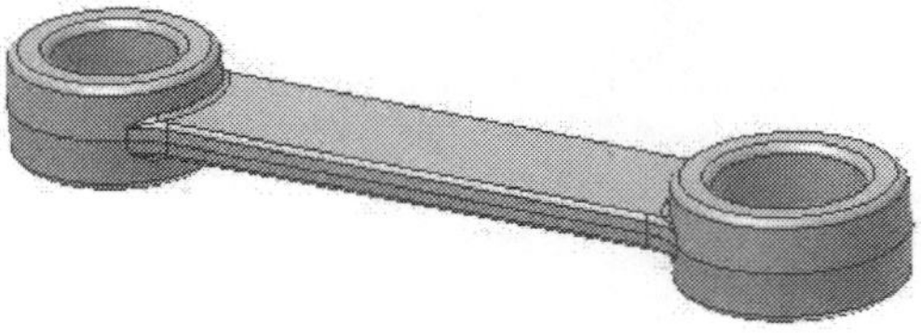

Figure 15–30

2. In the *Inspect* tab>Analysis panel, click (Draft). The Draft Analysis dialog box opens.
3. In the *Selection* area, clear the **All** option and verify that **Faces** is selected.

4. Select all 16 faces, including the opposite side's, as shown in Figure 15–31.

5. In the dialog box, in the *Pull* area, click and select the inside cylindrical surface of one of the holes, as shown in Figure 15–31.

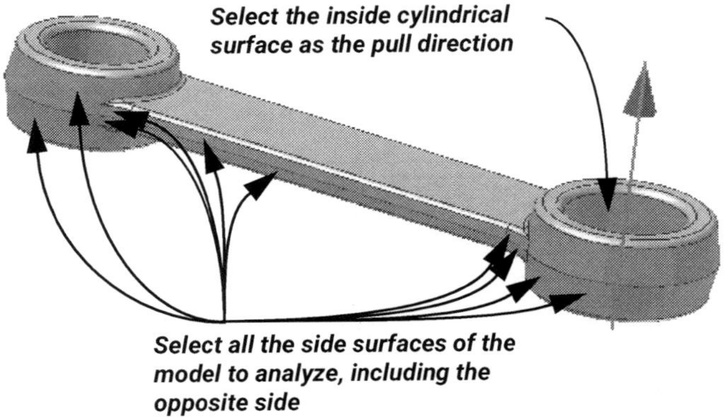

Figure 15–31

6. Specify the start and end draft angles as **-1** and **1** degrees respectively, as shown in Figure 15–32.

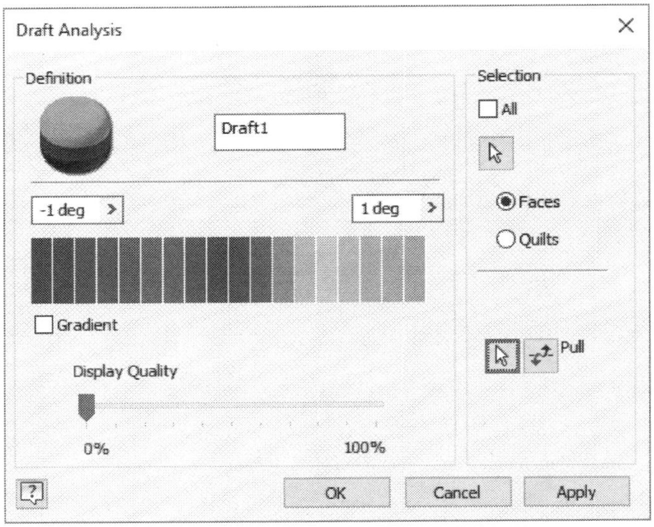

Figure 15–32

7. Click **Apply**.

8. The sides of the part turn two different colors, indicating that the draft angle is different on the top and bottom. It might be difficult to identify from that shown in Figure 15–33. Compare the color on the model to that in the dialog box; you should be able to tell that the current draft angle on the model is outside of the +/-1 range.

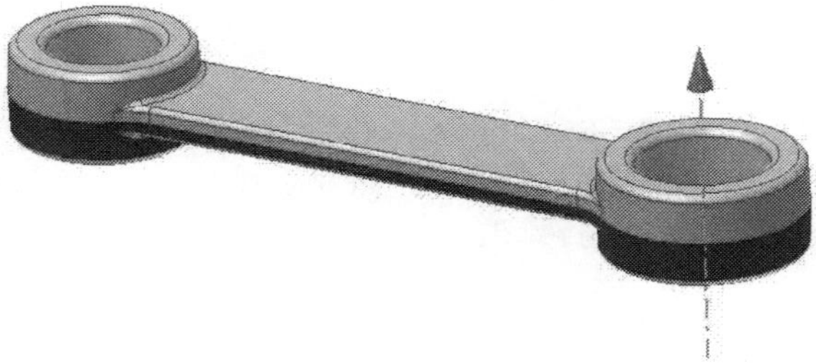

Figure 15–33

9. Click **Cancel**. In the next step you are required to change the range. You cannot reset the range without closing the analysis and editing it.
10. In the Model browser, expand the *Analysis* folder and double-click on **Draft1** to edit it.
11. Change the range to **+/-5** degrees and **Apply** the change. The colors on the model change and now indicate that the draft is within this range. If this is not accurate enough for you can continue to reduce the range or use other tools to measure or show the dimension on these surfaces.
12. Click **Cancel**.
13. Save the model and close the window.

End of practice

Practice 15c
Section Analysis

Practice Objectives

- Conduct a Cross Section analysis that displays the model sectioned through a single plane.
- Conduct a Cross Section analysis that displays the model sectioned through a series of planes and identifies areas of the model that conflict with maximum wall thickness criteria.

In this practice, you will analyze the sections through a model using a simple section analysis and an advanced section analysis. The results of the analyses are shown in Figure 15–34.

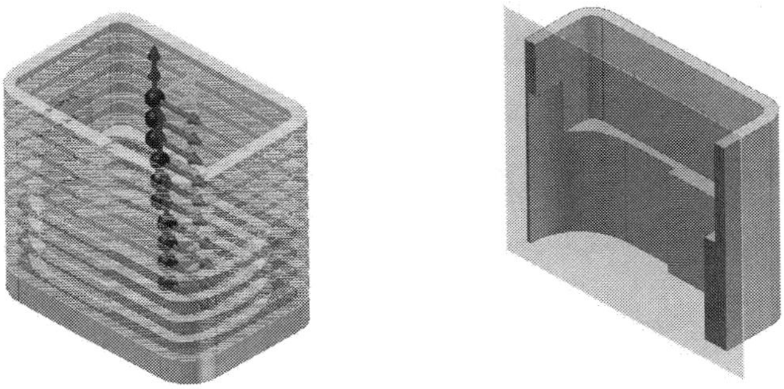

Figure 15–34

Task 1: Perform a simple Cross Section analysis.

A simple Cross Section analysis displays the model sectioned through a plane on the part.

1. Open **section_analysis.ipt**. The model displays as shown in Figure 15–35.

Figure 15–35

2. In the *Inspect* tab>Analysis panel, click (Section). The Cross Section Analysis dialog box opens.
3. Keep the default name of **CrossSection1**.
4. On the left side of the dialog box, verify that (Simple) is selected. This enables you to conduct a simple Cross Section analysis.
5. The XZ origin plane is already displayed. Select this plane.
6. Flip the direction of the cross-section. The arrow points in the direction where the material is to be removed.
7. Maintain the *Section Offset* value as **0 mm**.
8. Click **OK**. A cutaway view of the part based on the selected plane is displayed, as shown in Figure 15–36.

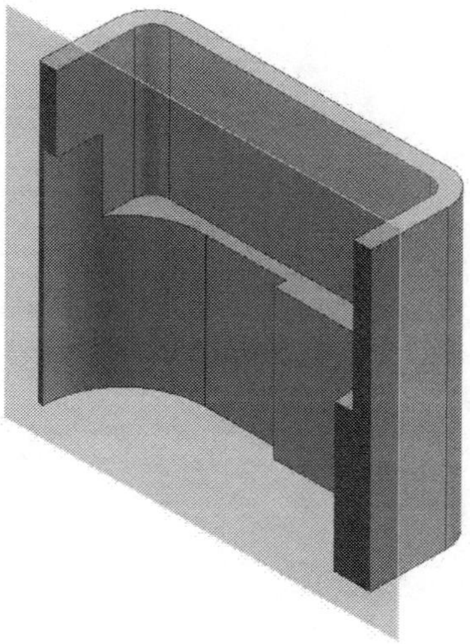

Figure 15–36

9. Clear the visibility of the XZ plane in the model.
10. In the Model browser, right-click on **Analysis:CrossSection1 (On)** and select **Analysis Visibility**. This toggles off the display of the active sectioned view of the model; however, the analysis remains in the model.

Task 2: Perform an advanced Cross Section analysis.

An advanced Cross Section analysis enables you to define multiple section planes by either selecting or creating them, and verify their maximum and minimum wall thicknesses.

1. In the *Inspect* tab>Analysis panel, click  (Section).
2. Keep the default name of **CrossSection2**.
3. On the left side of the dialog box, click  (Advanced). This enables you to conduct an advanced Cross Section analysis using the advanced options shown in Figure 15–37.

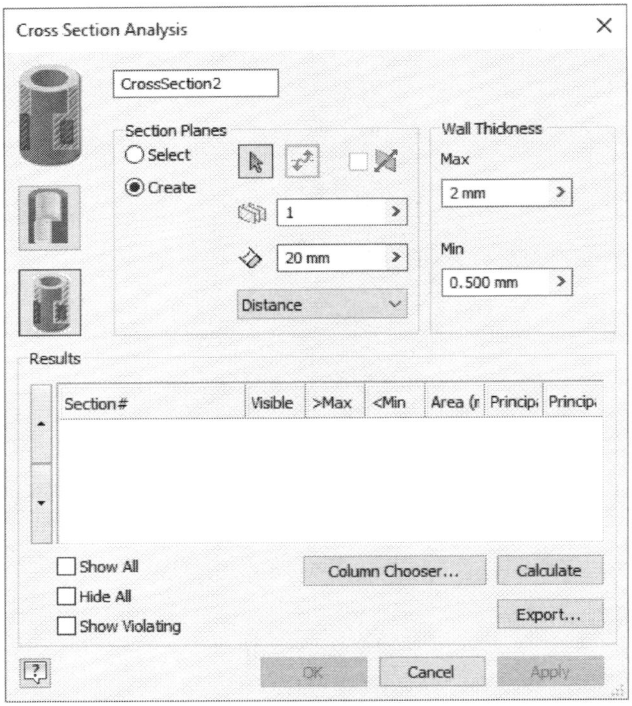

Figure 15–37

4. In this dialog box you can define whether to select an existing plane or create a new one. Keep **Create** selected and select the top plane, as shown in Figure 15–38.

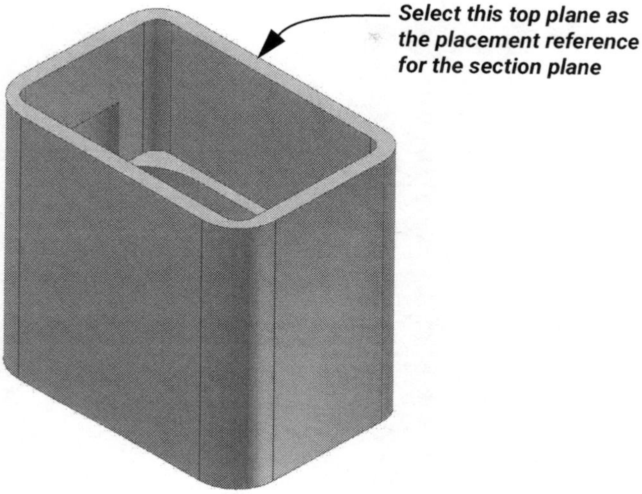

Figure 15–38

5. Click [icon] to flip the direction of the section planes downwards into the model.
6. Change the measurement type from *Distance* to **Spacing**, enter **10** for the number of planes, and **10 mm** for the spacing between the planes. Set the *Max Wall Thickness* to **10 mm** and the *Min Wall Thickness* to **4 mm**, as shown in Figure 15–39.

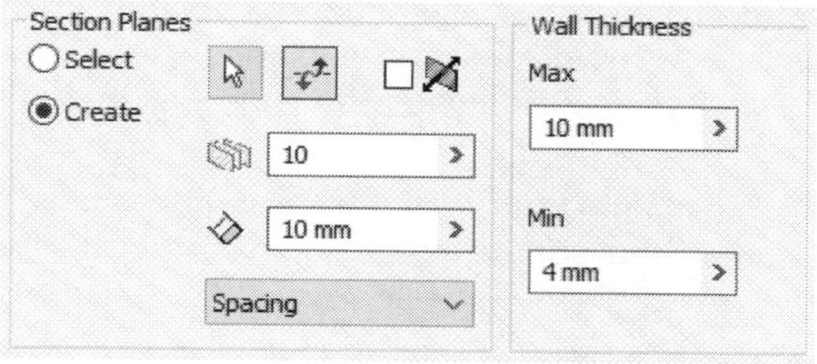

Figure 15–39

7. Click **Apply**. The model updates to display the cross-sections and the dialog box provides numerical data on the sections, as shown in Figure 15–40.

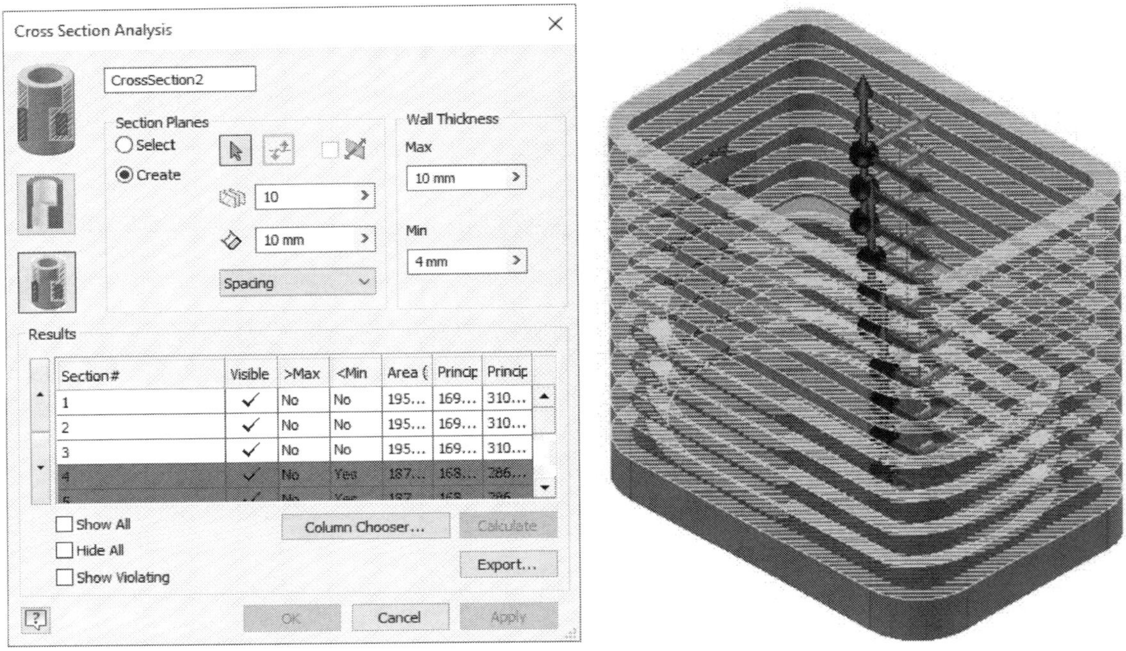

Figure 15–40

8. At the bottom of the dialog box, select **Show Violating**. This toggles off all sections that are within the min and max wall thickness restrictions. Note that seven sections remain. The blue highlighted areas on the model indicate where the wall thickness is smaller than required. The red highlighted areas indicate where the wall thickness is larger than required.

9. Review the list of sections at the bottom of the dialog box. The columns provide information on the section and whether or not it passes the wall thickness criteria that was specified.

10. Click **Cancel** to close the Cross Section Analysis dialog box. Leave the display of the Cross Section Analysis on so that as changes are made to the model, you can see the results in the analysis.

Task 3: Edit geometry.

1. Edit **Sketch3** and change the 27.204 dimension to **24.5**.
2. Finish the sketch and note that the blue highlighted (min wall thickness) violations are gone.
3. In the Model browser, in the *Analysis* folder, double-click on **CrossSection2** to open the Cross Section Analysis dialog box. Only four sections remain that violate the wall thickness restriction.

Based on this design, there is no combination of dimensions for **Sketch3** that will satisfy both restrictions on the wall thickness. The design requires that the minimum thickness be met; however, the max thickness can be larger.

4. In the Cross Section Analysis dialog box, modify the *Max Wall Thickness* to **20 mm**. Click **Apply**.
5. At the bottom of the dialog box, select **Show Violating**. Now, there are no longer any sections in conflict.
6. Click **Cancel** to close the Cross Section Analysis dialog box.
7. Save the model and close the window.

End of practice

Chapter Review Questions

1. Which of the following best describes the strips that are displayed when identifying tangent surfaces that are not curvature continuous in a Zebra analysis?
   a. Stripe edges that do not line up between surfaces indicate that the adjacent surfaces are tangent, but not curvature continuous.
   b. Stripe edges that line up between surfaces where there is a sharp angle are tangent, but not curvature continuous.
   c. Stripe edges that line up between surfaces where there is no sharp angle are tangent, but not curvature continuous.

2. Which of the following best describes the curvature comb that is displayed when identifying tangent surfaces that are also curvature continuous in a Curvature analysis?
   a. Separation of the curvature comb along the boundary indicates that adjacent faces are tangent and curvature continuous.
   b. Continuation of the curvature comb with different lengths indicates that adjacent faces are tangent and curvature continuous.
   c. Continuation of the curvature comb at the same length indicates that adjacent faces are tangent and curvature continuous.

3. Which Section analysis type enables you to analyze the min and max wall thickness for a single cross-section through the model?
   a. Simple Section Analysis
   b. Advanced Section Analysis

4. If the default comb spacing between splines is not sufficient to easily study curvature changes on a surface, which setting do you use to change it?
   a. 
   b. 
   c. 

5. A Draft analysis was completed on a model using an acceptable range of +/- 3 degrees. If the color on one surface is outside the color gradient in the Draft Analysis dialog box, the draft on the model is within the acceptable range.

   a. True

   b. False

6. Match the Analysis Type in the left column to its icon in the right column.

Analysis Type	Icon	Answer
a. Zebra		
b. Draft	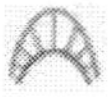	
c. Surface		
d. Section		
e. Curvature		

7. Which of the following statements is true regarding the Model browser shown in Figure 15–41?

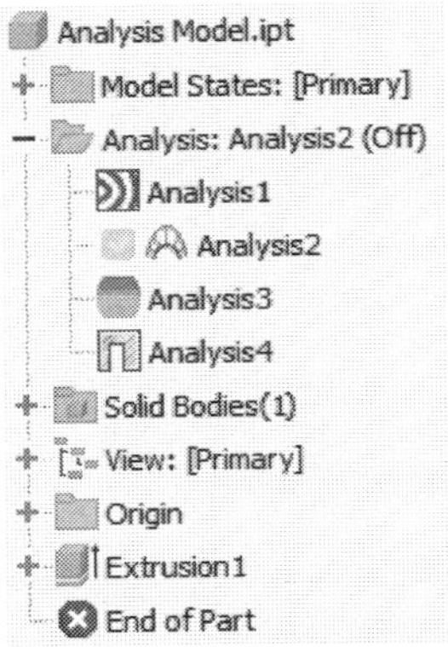

Figure 15–41

a. Analysis2 is the currently active analysis that is being displayed on the model.
b. There are four analysis types that are currently being displayed on the model.
c. Analysis4 is currently the active analysis, however, its visibility is not currently displayed on the model.
d. There is no analysis being displayed on the model.
e. None of the above.

Command Summary

Button	Command	Location
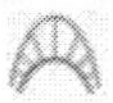	**Curvature Analysis**	• **Ribbon:** *Inspect* tab>Analysis panel
	**Draft Analysis**	• **Ribbon:** *Inspect* tab>Analysis panel
	**Section Analysis**	• **Ribbon:** *Inspect* tab>Analysis panel
	**Surface Analysis**	• **Ribbon:** *Inspect* tab>Analysis panel
	**Zebra Analysis**	• **Ribbon:** *Inspect* tab>Analysis panel

Appendix

A

Creating Emboss and Decal Features

Emboss and Decal features are specialty features that can be added to model geometry to add special details to the model. Emboss features enable you to create a raised or recessed area on a part that can be used to create a flat area or add text. Labels, bar codes, brand names, art works, logos, or stamps are added to a model using the Decal features.

Learning Objectives

- Create a raised or recessed area on a part using the Emboss feature.
- Add an image to represent information on the surface of a model.

A.1 Emboss Features

Emboss features create a raised or recessed area on a part. They are often used to supply a flat area for a label, add text that is molded into the part (as shown in Figure A–1), or provide clearance for another part. Emboss features can add or remove material from the part.

Figure A–1

Creating the Emboss Profile

The emboss profile is a sketch of the entities that will be embossed on the model. The entities can be either standard sketched entities or you can add text.

How To: Create a Sketch that Contains Text

1. In the Model panel, click (Start 2D Sketch) and select a sketching plane.
2. Click (Text) or (Geometry Text) in the Create panel to add text to the sketch and select a location to place the text. Figure A–2 shows the two text options and how they differ when adding text. To place Geometry Text, select a geometry entity (e.g., arc or circle) for the text to follow.

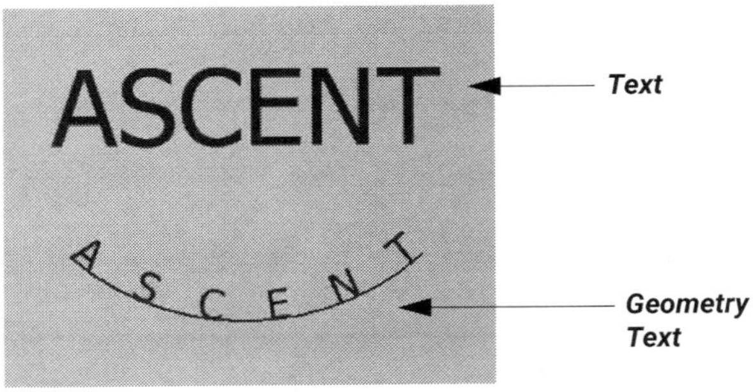

Figure A–2

3. The Format Text dialog box opens. Enter the text in the dialog box and adjust the text properties (e.g., color, font, justification, etc.) as required. Consider the use of Model and User Parameters to incorporate parametric parameter values from the model into the text.
    - Most settings in the Format Text dialog box (such as font, style, and justification) are similar to other Windows programs. To change the font or style of existing text, highlight the text to be changed in the dialog box and make changes as required. Changing the color, rotation, line spacing, or stretch of the text will change that property for the entire text object and not only the selected text.
4. Click **OK** to close the dialog box.
5. Add dimensions as required to locate the text and any geometry entities on the part.
6. Finish the sketch.

Hint: Converting Text to Geometry

While in the sketch, text that is added to a sketch can be converted to geometry by selecting the text, right-clicking on it, and selecting **Convert to Geometry**. Once converted to a selected text style, each entity acts independently and can be manipulated as required.

Creating the Emboss Feature

Once the emboss profile has been created in a sketch it can be used to create the emboss feature.

How To: Create a Emboss Feature

1. In the *3D Model* tab>Create panel, click (Emboss). The Emboss dialog box opens as shown in Figure A–3.

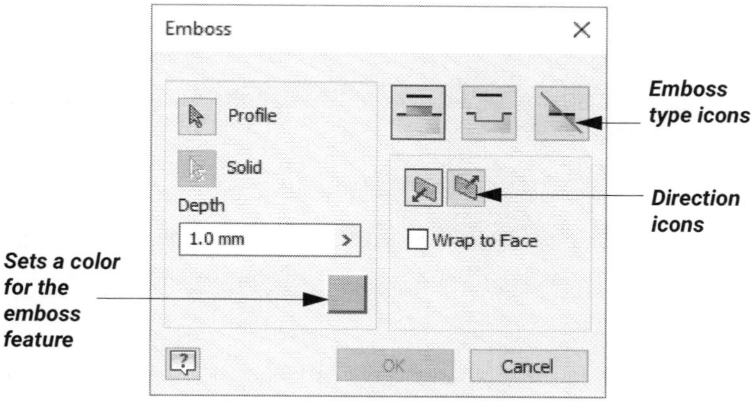

Figure A–3

2. Select the Emboss profile.

3. Select the type of emboss by selecting from the three available types. The resulting geometry for each type is shown in Figure A–4.

   - Click (Emboss from Face) to create the emboss to add material, so the feature is raised.
   - Click (Engrave from Face) to create the emboss to remove material, so the feature is recessed.
   - Click (Emboss/Engrave from Plane) to create the emboss to add and remove material, so parts of the feature are above and below the sketch plane.

Emboss from Face ***Engrave from Face*** ***Emboss/Engrave from Face***

Figure A–4

4. Enter a depth for the Emboss/Engrave feature and select the direction of the feature. The new surface is parallel to the surface of the part.
   - The Emboss Depth only displays when you click (Emboss from Face) or (Engrave from Face).
5. Enter a taper value to specify the angle of the feature.
   - The Taper Angle only displays when you click . Taper specifies the angle of the feature.
   - This setting enables inclusion of a draft angle when the part is manufactured. A positive angle looks toward the face of the part.

   Note: *When wrapped, text objects cannot be self-intersecting.*

6. (Optional) Select **Wrap to Face** to ensure that the feature follows the surface of the part.

   Click (Face) to select the destination face for wrapping.

   - The **Wrap to Face** option only displays when you click (Emboss from Face) or (Engrave from Face).
7. Once the Emboss feature is defined, click **OK** in the Emboss dialog box.

A.2 Decal Features

You might want to add labels, bar codes, brand names, art work, logos, or stamps to the part when it is manufactured. When modeling, you can place these items as decals. A Decal feature can be applied directly to the part, or be created as its own part and added to an assembly. A Decal feature is created from an image. An image can be a .BMP, .XLS, or .DOC file. An example of a part with Decal features is shown in Figure A–5.

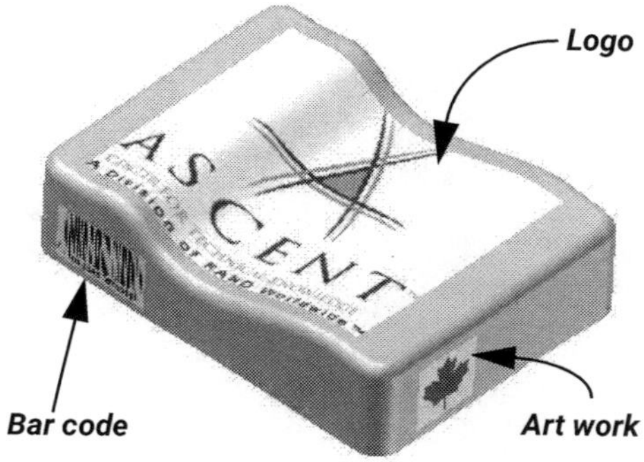

Figure A–5

Prior to creating a decal the image being used must exist in a sketch. To insert it, create a new sketch on a work plane/face and click (Insert Image) in the Insert panel to select the image.

- Once the image is inserted, constrain the image by adding dimensions and constraints to its edges.
- When importing an image, consider using **Link** on the Open dialog box to maintain a link to the source file.
- Once the image is placed in the sketch, you can right-click on it and select **Properties** to open the Image Properties dialog box, as shown in Figure A–6. These properties set transparency masking and color, rotation, or mirroring.

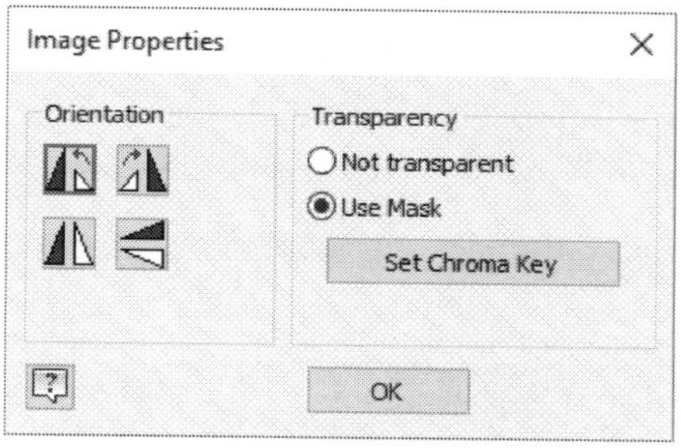

Figure A–6

How To: Create a Decal Feature

1. In the Create panel, click (Decal). The Properties panel opens, as shown in Figure A–7.

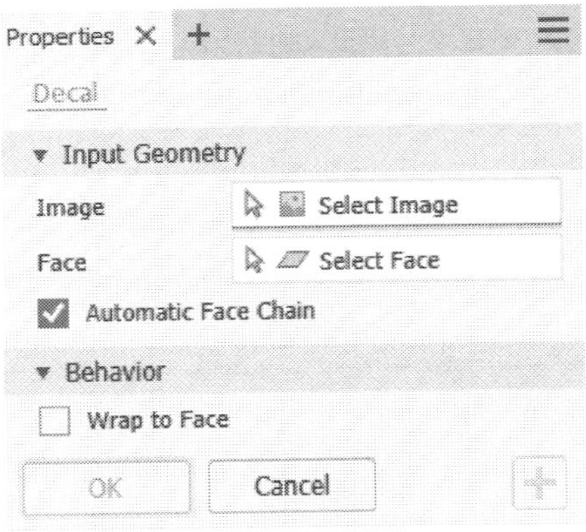

Figure A–7

2. Select **Decal** (default feature name) at the top of the Properties panel to assign a new name for the feature.
3. Ensure that the *Image* field is active and select the inserted image. If only one image exists in the model, this field is automatically populated for you.
4. Select in the *Face* field to activate it and select the face to which to apply the image.

   Note: *A decal cannot be applied across a seamed face. In such a case, the decal should be added to the assembly. However, the decal can be applied across tangent faces using* ***Automatic Face Chain****.*

5. Define how the decal will be applied to the selected face by selecting the following options, as required.
   - Select **Automatic Face Chain** to place the image over an edge or a fillet.
   - Select **Wrap to Face** to wrap the image to a curved face.
6. Once the decal feature is defined, click **OK**. Alternatively, right-click in the graphics window and select **OK [Enter]**. To continue creating additional decal features without closing the panel, click (Apply) and define the references as needed. Once all decals have been completed, click **OK**.

Hint: Decal Features in Drawings

Decal features are only visible on IDW and DWG drawing views when the view is in the Shaded state. A potential workaround is to add the imagery to the drawing as a Sketched Symbol instead of as a Decal in the part file.

Practice A1
Emboss and Decals

Practice Objectives

- Create raised areas of text on the surface of the model.
- Add an image on the surface of a model.

In this practice, you will create a sketch that contains text and use it to create an Emboss feature on the part shown in Figure A–8. You will also place images on the part and create decals from the images.

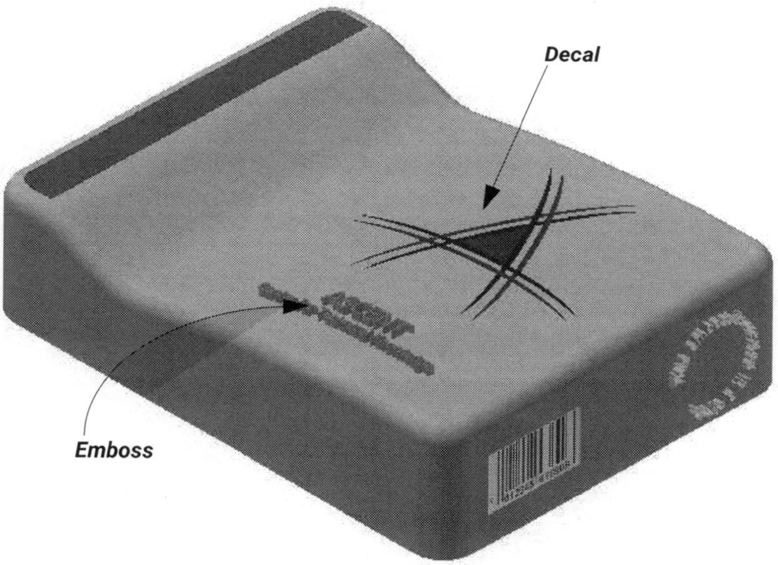

Figure A–8

Task 1: Create the text sketch for the emboss feature.

1. Open **emboss_decal.ipt**.
2. Create a sketch using the blue face as the sketching plane. The *Sketch* tab is the active tab.
3. In the Create panel, click A (Text) and select a point in the lower right area of the part. The Format Text dialog box opens.

4. Enter the text shown in Figure A–9.

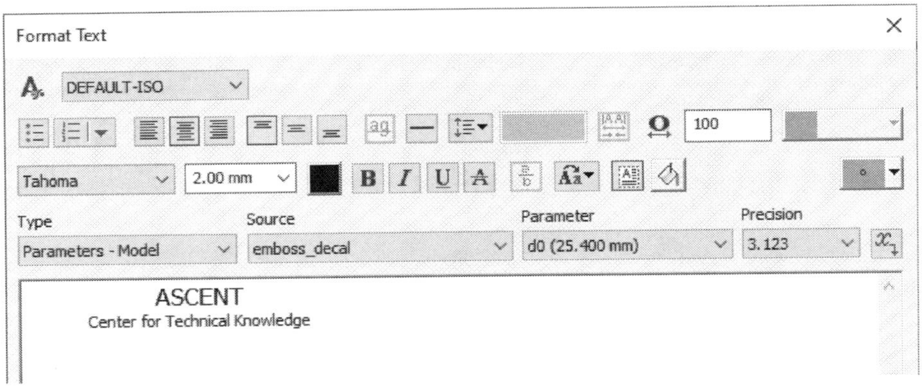

Figure A–9

5. Click **OK** to close the Format Text dialog box.
6. Dimension the text, as shown in Figure A–10.

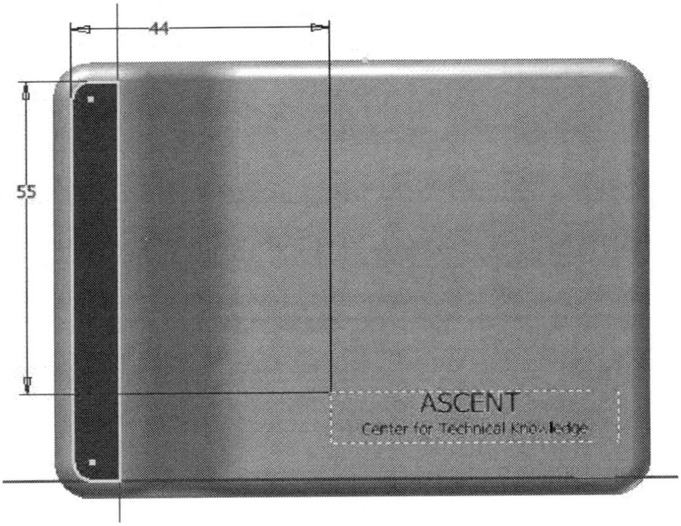

Figure A–10

7. Finish the sketch.

Task 2: Create the emboss feature.

1. In the *3D Model* tab>Create panel, click (Emboss) to open the Emboss dialog box.
2. Select the text as the emboss profile, and in the *Depth* field, change the emboss depth to **1.5** mm.

3. Change the color of the emboss to **Gold - Metal**. Click **OK**.

4. Accept the default  (Emboss from Face).

5. Select **Wrap to Face** and select the face shown in Figure A–11.

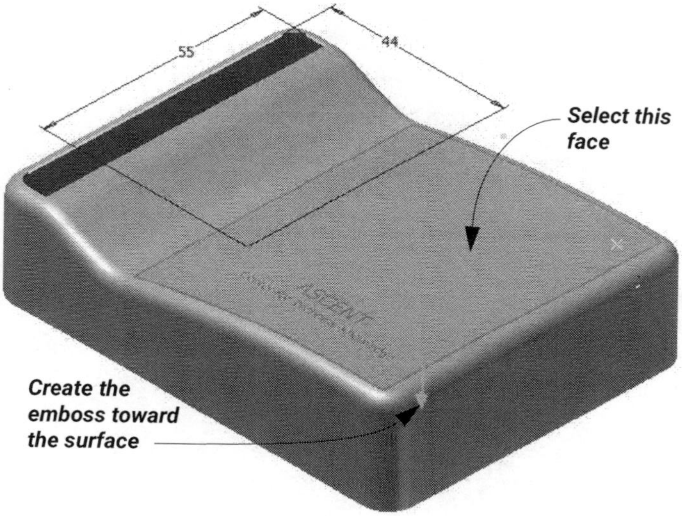

Figure A–11

6. Verify that the direction of the emboss is downward, toward the surface. If not, flip the direction.

7. Click **OK** to create the feature. The emboss displays as shown in Figure A–12. If the emboss is not visible, edit the feature and verify the direction is set in the down direction.

Figure A–12

Task 3: Insert the decal image.

1. Create a sketch using the blue face as the sketching plane. The *Sketch* tab is now the active tab.
2. In the Insert panel, click (Insert Image). Select and open **ASCENT.bmp**.
3. Place the logo image above the emboss feature, right-click and select **OK**.
4. Dimension the image, as shown in Figure A–13.
5. Select the image, right-click, and select **Properties**. The Image Properties dialog box opens.
6. Select **Use Mask**. This masks the background of the image to make it transparent, as shown in Figure A–13. Click **OK**.

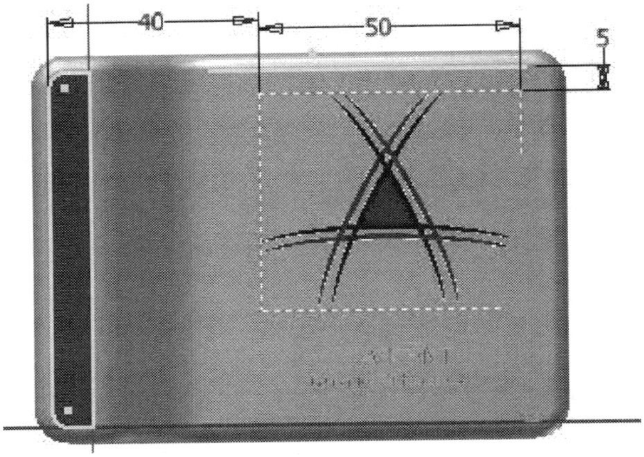

Figure A–13

7. Finish the sketch and toggle off the dimension visibility.

Task 4: Create the decal.

1. In the *3D Model* tab>Create panel, click (Decal). The Properties panel opens.
2. The logo image is pre-selected because it is the only visible sketch in the model. Ensure that the *Face* field is active and select the curved face.

3. Click **OK** to create the decal. The decal displays as shown in Figure A–14.

Figure A–14

Task 5: Add another decal and an emboss feature to the model.

1. Add the decal and emboss features shown in Figure A–15. Use the **Barcode.bmp** image for the decal.

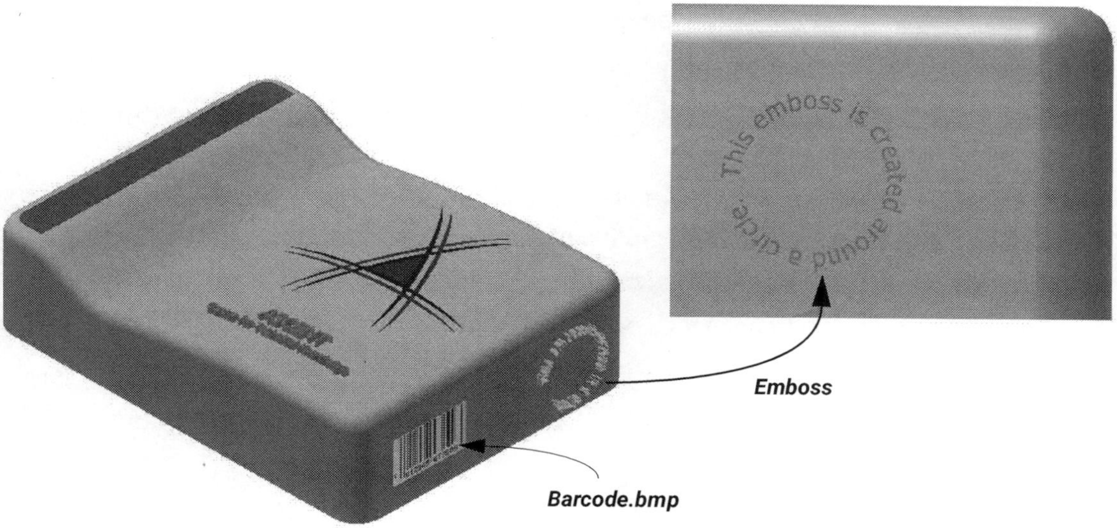

Figure A–15

2. Save the model and close the window.

End of practice

Chapter Review Questions

1. Which **Emboss** option enables you to add and remove material at the same time from a model?

    a.  (Emboss from Face)

    b.  (Engrave from Face)

    c.  (Emboss/Engrave from Plane)

2. Which **Emboss** options enable you to specify the depth to which the emboss geometry is created? (Select all that apply.)

    a.  (Emboss from Face)

    b. 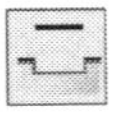 (Engrave from Face)

    c.  (Emboss/Engrave from Plane)

3. Which of the following best describe what an emboss feature can be used for in a model? (Select all that apply.)

    a. An emboss adds material to the part creating a raised area.

    b. An emboss removes material from the part creating a recessed area.

    c. An emboss is a 2D image placed on the part surface to add material to the part.

    d. An emboss is a 2D image placed on the part surface to remove material from the part.

4. Decal images can only be .BMP files.

    a. True

    b. False

5. How do you insert a decal image?
   a. During Decal creation, browse and open the image using options in the Decal Properties panel.
   b. The image must be inserted into a sketch and is referenced during Decal creation.

Command Summary

Button	Command	Location
	**Decal**	• **Ribbon:** *3D Model* tab>Create panel
	**Emboss**	• **Ribbon:** *3D Model* tab>Create panel

Appendix

B

Custom Sketched Symbols

Creating your own custom symbols provides more flexibility than using only the standard symbols that are provided with the Autodesk® Inventor® software. To use custom sketched symbols, you must learn how to create them, store them, and place them in a new drawing. Additionally, the use of AutoCAD® blocks in an Autodesk Inventor drawing file can provide additional symbols that have been created in the AutoCAD software.

Learning Objectives

- Create a custom sketched symbol using the standard sketching and text tools and save it for reuse.
- Manage the list of sketched symbols by creating and organizing symbols in folders.
- Edit a custom sketched symbol.
- Place a custom sketched symbol by defining its placement options and locating it relative to the defined insertion point.
- Modify the placement and definition of the sketched symbol to ensure that it communicates the required information.
- Insert an imported AutoCAD block into a new drawing.

B.1 Create Sketched Symbols

Several standard symbols (e.g., weld symbols or surface finish symbols) can be shown in drawings and allow for some customization, such as entering text in particular areas of the symbol. A custom sketched symbol enables full customization of the symbol and it consists of symbol geometry, text (if required), and its properties (e.g., placement type, instance height, attributes).

How To: Create a Sketched Symbol

1. Create or open a drawing file or drawing template for adding the sketched symbol.
2. In the *Manage* tab>Define panel, click (Symbol). The *Sketch* tab and sketching environment are activated. As an alternative, you can right-click on the **Sketch Symbols** node in the Model browser and select **Define New Symbol** to create a new symbol.
3. Use the standard sketching tools to create the symbol.
   - Text can be added to the symbol as required. The text can be static or variable. Variable text is text that is prompted for when the symbol is placed in a drawing.
   - To place text in a symbol, in the Create panel, click A (Text) and use the Format Text dialog box. If the text is to be variable, in the Type drop-down list, select **Prompted Entry**, as shown in Figure B–1.

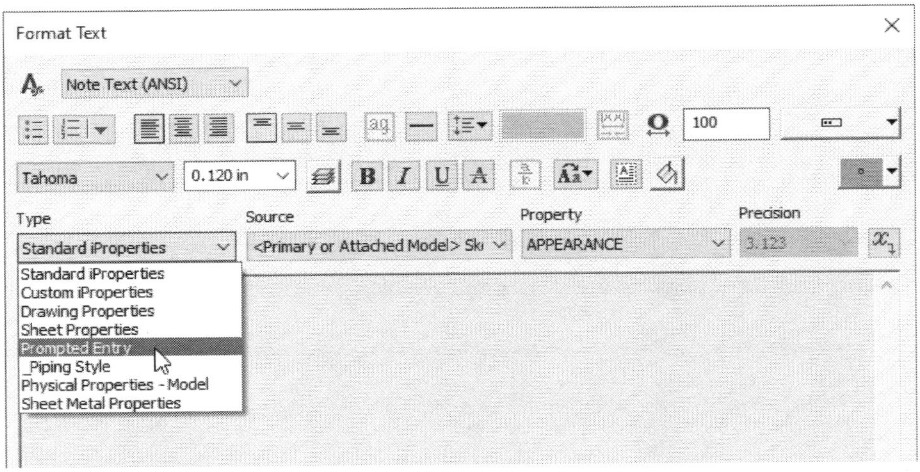

Figure B–1

4. (Optional) To define an insertion point, select a point on the sketched symbol and in the Format panel, click (Set Insertion Point Grip), as shown in Figure B–2.

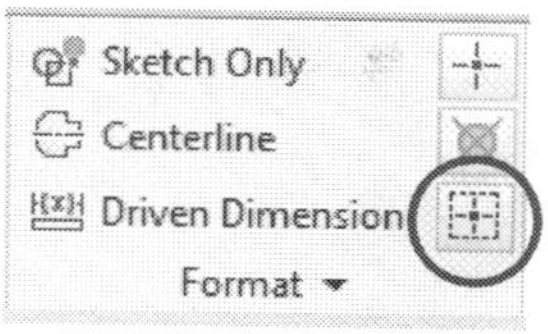

Figure B–2

The insertion point is the location on the sketched symbol that is used during placement.

- If a leader is added to the symbol, the insertion point is where the leader connects to the symbol.
- You can also use it to snap to other drawing entities as well as move, rotate, and resize symbols after they are placed.
- Only one insertion point can be defined.

Note: *If you redefine an insertion point for a sketched symbol, all of the symbols that already exist in the drawing update.*

5. (Optional) To assign a connection point, select a point on the sketched symbol and in the Format panel, click (Connection Point Grip). Connection points can be used to snap to other drawing entities or used as the attachment point for leaders.
   - For example, they can be used to snap to the drawing border, views, and tables.
   - In addition, they are used to move, rotate, and resize symbols after they are placed.
   - Unlike insertion points, you can assign as many connection points as required.

6. Once you have finished creating the symbol, in the Exit panel, click (Finish Sketch).
7. Enter a name for the symbol and click **Save**. The sketched symbol is added to the **Drawing Resources>Sketch Symbols** node in the Model browser and can be added to the drawing.

The list of symbols that are available in a drawing can become substantial. Consider the following tips to help you work with symbols:

- Subfolders can be created in the **Sketch Symbols** node by right-clicking on it and selecting **Create New Folder**, or selecting and right-clicking on the symbol and select **Add to New Folder,** as shown in Figure B–3. Once symbols are created, you can drag and drop them into folders to organize and group. Consider adding folders to your template file if you continually use the same symbol folder structure.

- For sketched symbols that have multiple prompted entries, you can reorder prompts so that they are prompted for in a required order. To reorder, right-click on the symbol and select **Reorder Prompted Entries**, as shown in Figure B–3. Change the order of prompts in a dialog box.

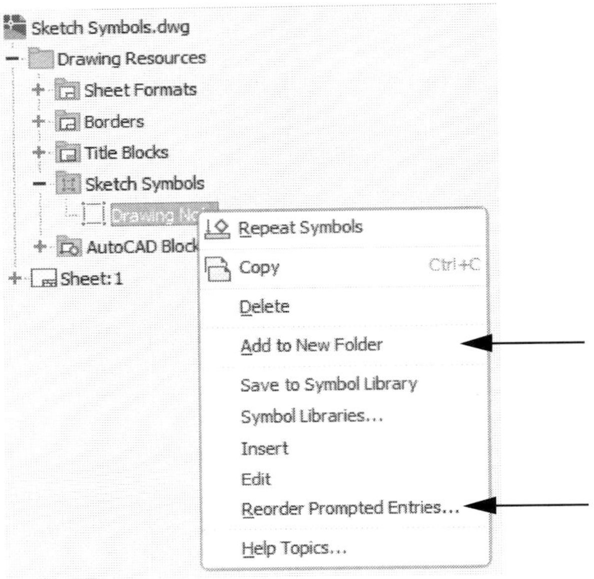

Figure B–3

Editing Sketched Symbols

Sketched symbols can be edited once they have been created. Right-click on the sketched symbol from the **Sketch Symbols** node in the *Drawing Resources* folder and select **Edit**. Make the required changes, and finish the sketch.

- If you edit a sketched symbol in a drawing, all placed instances of the symbol update in that drawing.
- If you edit a sketched symbol in a template file or library file, new drawings using that template or library file will contain the modified sketched symbol; however, any custom symbol used in a drawing based on the template or inserted from the library before the change will not reflect the change.

Saving Symbols

The drawing can be saved for use as a drawing template using the **Save Copy as Template** option in the **File** menu, or it can be saved to the symbol library. Using either method enables you to quickly access custom symbols for reuse.

Symbol Libraries

Once saved to the drawing, you can explicitly save a custom sketched symbol to a Symbol Library. The library is a drawing file that is used to provide easy access to symbols. Multiple libraries can be created. By saving the custom sketched symbol to a library, you do not need to store the symbols in templates, or copy and paste them between drawings.

How To: Save to the Symbol Library

1. In the Drawing Resources dialog box, in the **Sketch Symbols** node, right-click on the symbol and select **Save to Symbol Library**.
2. In the Save to Symbol Library dialog box, select an existing library from the list, or click  (Create a new Library) to create a new library in the list.
3. (Optional) Click  (Create a new folder) to create a new folder in the selected library to organize the symbols.
4. Click **Save**. The Symbol Library is stored in the *Design Data* directory on your system.

B.2 Place Sketched Symbols

Sketched symbols can be inserted either from the **Sketched Symbols** node in the *Drawing Resources* folder, or from a Sketched Symbols Library.

- Any symbols that have been created in the current drawing are saved to the **Drawing Resources>Sketch Symbols** node.
- Symbols can be copied between drawings. Once copied, they are placed in the **Drawing Resources>Sketch Symbols** node.
- By default, sketched symbols in the *Drawing Resources* folder contain the symbols that exist in the original drawing template. Any of these symbols can be inserted into the current drawing.
- Sketched symbols that have been explicitly saved to the Symbol Library can be inserted in the current drawing. Once inserted, they are added to the **Drawing Resources> Sketch Symbols** node.
- To copy sketched symbols from one drawing to another, right-click on the sketched symbol, select **Copy**, right-click on the *Drawing Resources* folder in the target drawing, and select **Paste**. You can also use the Drawing Resource Transfer Wizard, which is available as a tool outside of the Autodesk Inventor software.

How To: Place a Sketched Symbol

1. In the *Annotate* tab>Symbols panel, click (Insert Sketch Symbol). The Sketch Symbols dialog box opens, as shown in Figure B–4.
   - All of the symbols available in the drawing are listed in the **Local** node and any symbols located in the library are listed in the **Symbol Libraries** node.

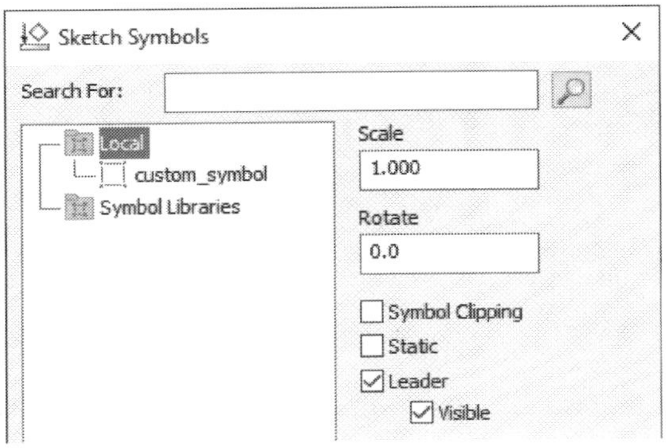

Figure B–4

   - Alternatively, you can right-click on the symbol in the *Drawing Resources* folder and select **Insert**. Using this method to add a symbol does not provide you with options for scaling, rotating, or other options that are provided in the Sketch Symbols dialog box.

2. Select a sketched symbol from the list of local or library symbols. Once selected a preview of the symbol appears in the Sketch Symbols dialog box.
    - Consider using the *Search For:* field to search for symbols.
3. Define the following options in the Sketch Symbols dialog box:
    - Specify a scale and rotation value.
    - Activate **Symbol Clipping** to trim dimension lines, leader lines, and extension lines behind symbols attached to drawing views.
    - Activate **Static** to prevent the symbol from being modified using the scale and rotation grip points.
    - Activate **Leader** to add a leader to the symbol. Activate or deactivate the **Visible** option to make the leader visible or invisible.
4. Click **OK** to begin placement of the sketched symbol.
5. Move the cursor to the required location and click to place it.
    - To associate the symbol with a view, select an entity on a view as the reference.

Note: *To stack sketched symbols that contain geometry, press and hold <Shift> and move the cursor over the bounding box of an existing sketched symbol until the constraint icon displays.*

6. Continue to place symbols by clicking in the drawing. Once finished, right-click in the graphics window and select **Cancel [ESC]**. The sketched symbol is placed in the drawing and is added to the **Sketch Symbols** node for the active sheet, as shown in Figure B–5.

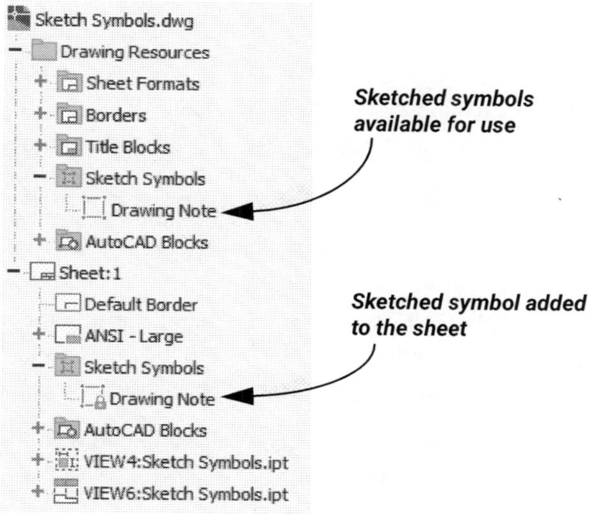

Figure B–5

Editing Placed Symbols

To access the symbol modification options, right-click on the sketched symbol in the **Sketch Symbols** node for the active sheet, as shown in Figure B–6.

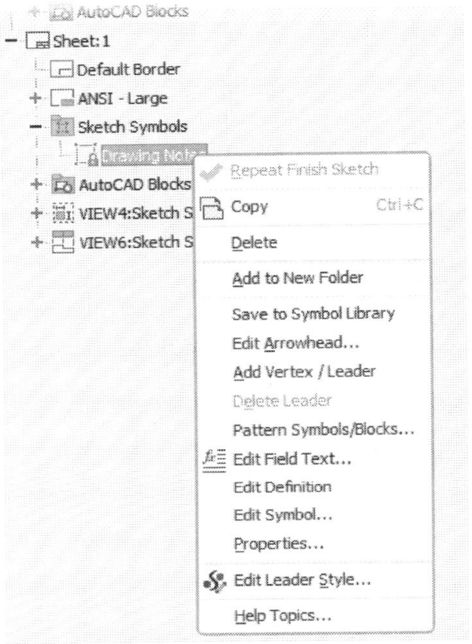

Figure B–6

The editing options include:

Option	Description
Save to Symbol Library	Enables you to save the symbol to a library for quick access without having to use a specific template or copy a symbol from another file.
Pattern Symbols/ Blocks	Enables you to pattern symbols, sketched symbols, or AutoCAD blocks. The pattern can be defined in one or two directions, similar to defining sketch or feature patterns.
Edit Arrowhead and Delete Leader	Enable you to manipulate existing symbol leaders. The **Add Vertex/Leader** can also be used to add leaders if placed without a leader.
Edit Field Text	Enables you to edit the values for prompted entries.
Edit Definition	Returns you to the sketch environment to edit the initial definition of the symbol.
Edit Symbol	Enables you to modify the options that were selected when the symbol was placed.

B.3 AutoCAD Blocks

AutoCAD templates that are converted for use in Autodesk Inventor software maintain the blocks that were created in the AutoCAD software. Although the functionality available for Autodesk Inventor symbols is reduced for AutoCAD blocks, having access is useful. Common uses for AutoCAD blocks in Autodesk Inventor drawings include simplified schematics, legacy blocks, and legacy notations. Figure B–7 shows a *Drawing Resources* folder with AutoCAD blocks available.

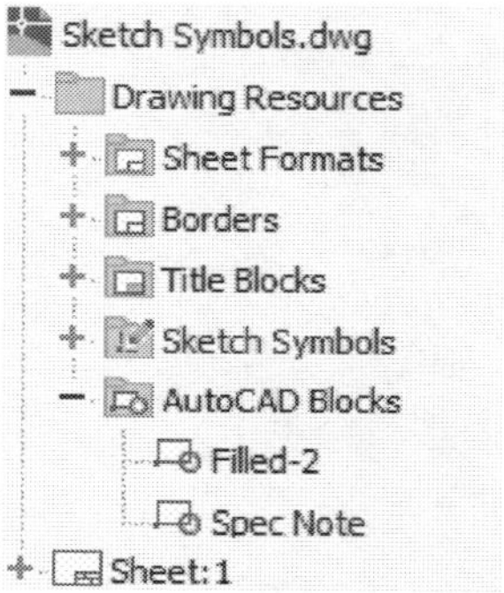

Figure B–7

Note: *Consider reviewing the DWG TrueConnect Help topics for further information on using AutoCAD files in the Autodesk Inventor software.*

Any AutoCAD blocks that have been converted into an Autodesk Inventor template include the original attributes. When the block is placed, the user is prompted for these values and the block can be scaled and rotated. Once inserted into a drawing, the block is a native object in the drawing. For example, you can reference the block with other entities. AutoCAD blocks cannot be edited in the Autodesk Inventor software and you cannot create them; however, you can scale and rotate them. To scale and rotate, select the block in the graphics window and use grips, as shown in Figure B–8.

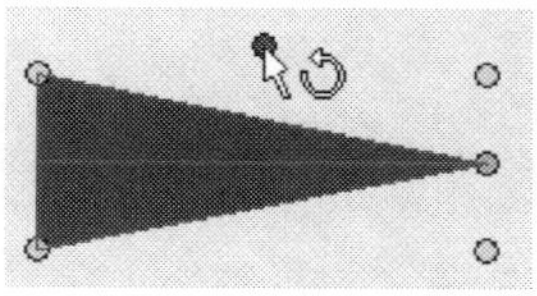

Figure B–8

Note: *If grip handles do not display when you select an AutoCAD Block, right-click, select* ***Edit AutoCAD Block****, and clear the* ***Static*** *option in the AutoCAD Blocks dialog box.*

- If changes must be made to the sketched content of the block, it is recommended to recreate it as a sketched symbol. If an AutoCAD block is required in an Autodesk Inventor drawing, consider opening the Autodesk Inventor .DWG file in AutoCAD and adding the block. When the .DWG is opened again, the block will be available.

- AutoCAD blocks can be imported directly from other .DWG files into an Autodesk Inventor .DWG file. To import, right-click on the **AutoCAD Block** node in the *Drawing Resources* folder and select **Import AutoCAD Block**, as shown in Figure B–9. In the Import Block dialog box, you can modify the scale and rotation values, and select the required block definition to be imported. Once imported, you can place the AutoCAD block in the drawing using the standard **Insert** command.

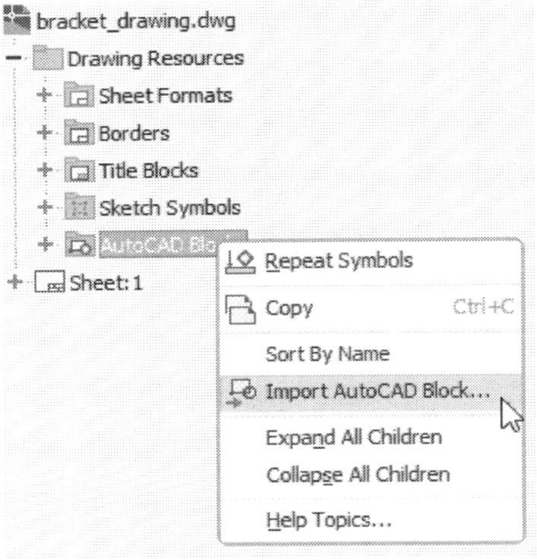

Figure B–9

- An inserted AutoCAD block can be patterned by right-clicking on the inserted block and selecting **Pattern Symbols/Block**. Using the Pattern Symbols/Blocks dialog box, as shown in Figure B–10, you can define a reference direction, number of instances, and spacing of the instances. The interface is similar to pattern sketches in the sketch environment. The Pattern Symbols/Blocks dialog box can also be used to pattern symbols in a drawing.

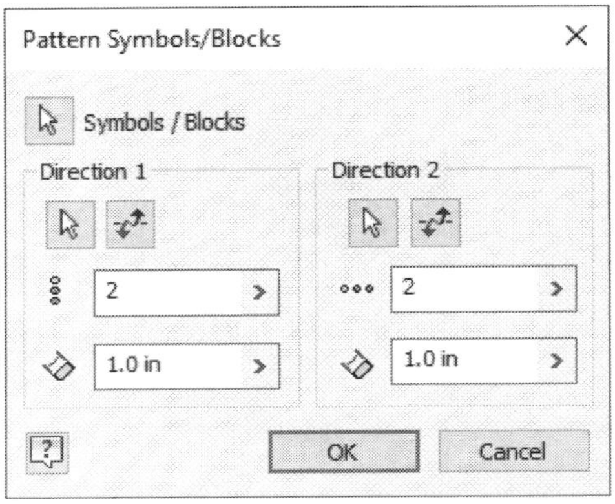

Figure B–10

Practice B1
Custom Sketched Symbols I

Practice Objectives

- Create a custom sketched symbol using standard sketching tools.
- Copy a custom sketched symbol to the Drawing Resources folder of a target drawing and display it on a sheet.
- Save a custom symbol to the Symbol Library, and place it in the drawing.

In this practice, you will create a custom sketch symbol for reuse in drawings. The custom sketch symbol is shown in Figure B–11.

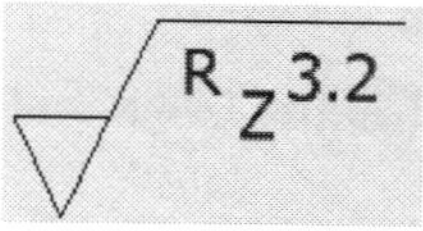

Figure B–11

Task 1: Create a new drawing and add a custom sketch symbol.

1. Create a new drawing using the **standard.dwg** drawing template.
2. In the *Manage* tab>Define panel, click (Symbol). As an alternative, you can right-click on the **Sketch Symbols** node in the *Drawing Resources* folder and select **Define New Symbol**. The *Sketch* tab and sketching environment are now activated.
3. Sketch and add the text shown in Figure B–12. To simulate a subscript for the *Z* value, position the text lower. The sketch will consist of two separate pieces of text. Consider adding the text first to ensure the correct scale for the sketched lines.

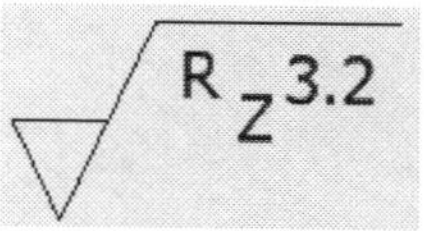

Figure B–12

4. The insertion point is defined when a symbol is created and used to locate it during placement. If a leader is used, it is where the leader connects to the symbol. Begin by selecting the bottom point of the triangular portion of the symbol. With the point selected on the symbol, in the Format panel, click  (Set Insertion Point Grip) as shown in Figure B–13. The insertion point grip is now set.

Figure B–13

5. Once finished creating the symbol, in the Exit panel, click  (Finish Sketch). The Sketched Symbol dialog box opens.
6. Enter **custom_symbol** as the name and click **Save**. The custom sketch symbol is created and added to the Model browser under the **Drawing Resources>Sketch Symbols** node, as shown in Figure B–14.

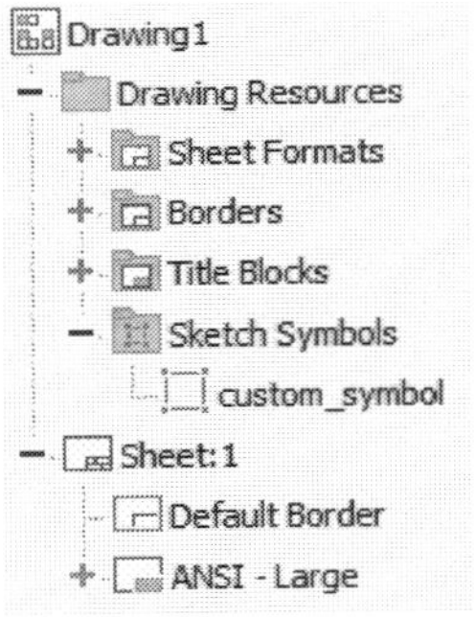

Figure B–14

7. Save the drawing as **custom_symbol_drawing**. The symbol has currently not been added to the drawing; however, it is accessible for use in the drawing.

Task 2: Copy the custom symbol to a drawing.

Custom sketch symbols must exist in the *Drawing Resources* folder for use in a drawing. If a symbol is created in a drawing template, it will be available for use in any drawing using that template. If the symbol is created in one drawing, you need to copy the custom sketch symbol into any other drawing in which you want to use the symbol.

1. Open **bracket_drawing.dwg**.
2. In the Model browser, expand the *Drawing Resource* folder. Note that there are no sketched symbols.
3. Switch back to the **custom_symbol_drawing.dwg** drawing.
4. Expand the **Drawing Resources>Sketch Symbols** node, if not already expanded.
5. Right-click on **custom_symbol** and select **Copy**.
6. Switch to the **bracket_drawing.dwg** window.
7. Right-click the *Drawing Resources* folder and select **Paste**. The custom symbol is copied to the **Sketch Symbols** node. Now the custom symbol can be used in this drawing.

Task 3: Add the custom symbol to the drawing.

1. In the *Annotate* tab>Symbols panel, click  (Insert Sketch Symbol). The Sketch Symbols dialog box opens, as shown in Figure B–15. The **custom_symbol** symbol is listed in the **Local** node because it now exists as a sketched symbol in the *Drawing Resources* folder for the active (local) drawing. Alternatively, you can right-click on the symbol in the *Drawing Resources* folder and select **Insert**. Using this method does not provide you with options for scaling, rotating, or other options that are provided in the Sketch Symbols dialog box.

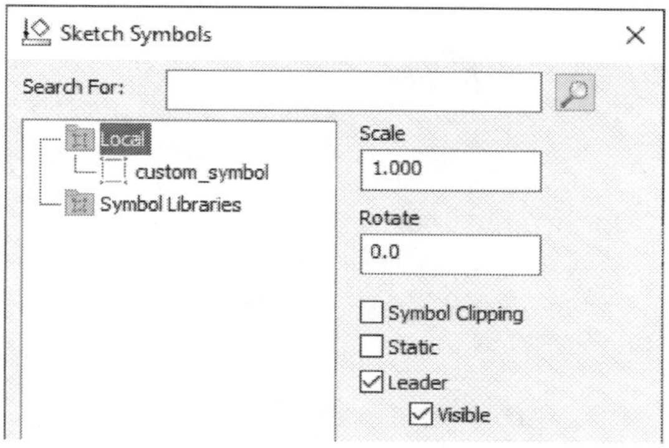

Figure B–15

Note: *You can activate* ***Leader*** *to add a leader to the custom sketch symbol. Place it as you would for a regular surface texture symbol with a leader.*

2. Select **custom_symbol** in the **Local** node.
3. Set the *Scale* to **0.5**.
4. Ensure that the **Leader** option is cleared and **Static** is selected.

5. Click **OK**. Click to place the symbol on the reference as shown in Figure B–16.

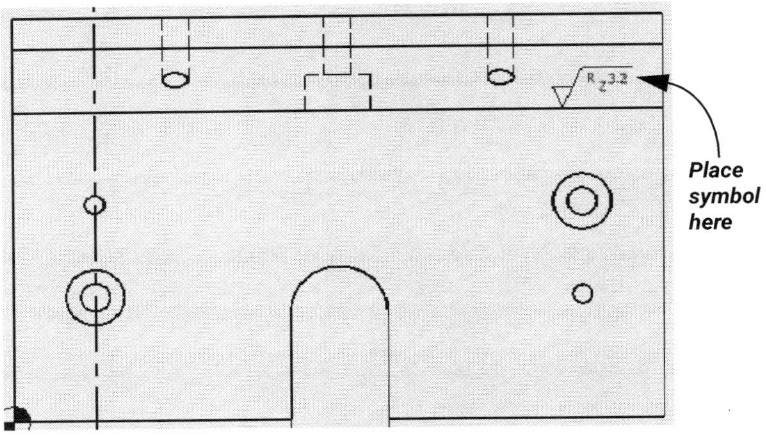

Figure B–16

6. Right-click and select **Cancel [Esc]** to discontinue placing additional symbols.
7. Depending on the size of your original custom sketch, you might need to edit the scale of the symbol to correctly place the sketch in the drawing. Right-click on **custom_symbol** in the Model browser for **Sheet:1** and select **Edit Symbol**. Modify the scale, if required and close the dialog box.

   Note: Using the ***Edit Symbol*** *command enables you to edit the rotation and scale of symbols that are added using the* ***Insert*** *command, which does not have those options available on placement.*

The **custom_symbol_drawing.dwg** file could be saved as a template for future use by simply saving it using the **Save>Save Copy as Template** option in the **File** menu. The next time you create a new drawing file, the new template will be available. Alternatively, you can save the symbol to a custom symbol library.

Task 4: Create a custom symbol and save it to the library.

1. Return to the **custom_symbol_drawing.dwg** file.
2. In the *Drawing Resources* folder, right-click on **custom_symbol** in the **Sketch Symbols** node, and select **Save to Symbol Library**. The Save to Symbol Library dialog box opens, similar to that shown in Figure B–17. It might vary if any libraries have already been created on your system.

   Note: The Save to Symbol Library dialog box always references the symbol library drawing files that have been created. This list is only empty the first time you access the command and create a library.

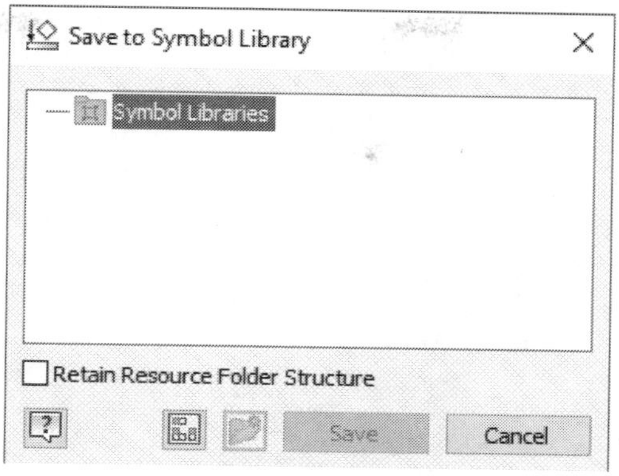

Figure B–17

3. In the Save to Symbol Library dialog box, click (Create a new Library) to create a new library in the list. Enter **My Library** as the name of the new library. If this library already exists, select it.

4. Click **Save**. The Symbol Library (**My Library.idw**) is stored in the *Design Data* directory on your system and now contains the new symbol.

   Note: *The symbol library is located in C:\Users\Public\Public Documents\Autodesk\Inventor <ver#>\Design Data\Symbol Library.*

5. Close the **custom_symbol_drawing.dwg** file without saving it.

Task 5: Add the custom symbol to the drawing.

1. Activate **bracket_drawing.dwg.**
2. Delete the previous copy of **custom_symbol** that was added to the drawing.
3. In the *Drawing Resources* folder, right-click on **custom_symbol** in the **Sketch Symbols** node and select **Delete**. This symbol is removed from the drawing. In the next task, you will add it back into the drawing from the library to simulate working with the symbol library.
4. In the *Annotate* tab>Symbols panel, click (Insert Sketch Symbol).

5. Expand the **My Library.idw** library, as shown in Figure B–18. Note that the new symbol is listed in the library. Also, there are no symbols in the current drawing, as shown by the empty **Local** node.

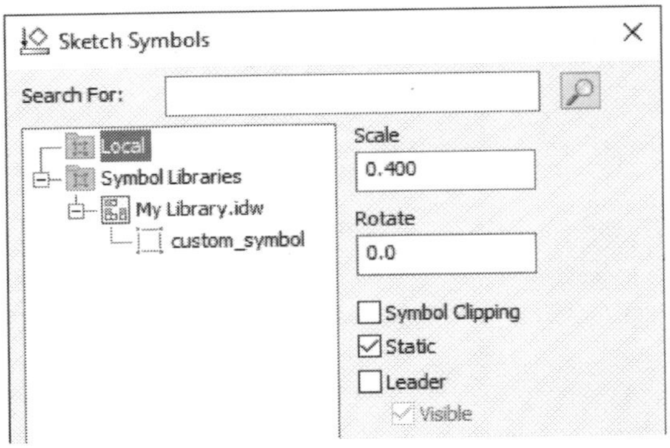

Figure B–18

6. Select **custom_symbol.** The symbol appears in the *Preview* area in the Sketch Symbols dialog box. Maintain all of the default settings and click **OK**.
7. Place the symbol in the drawing, similar to how it was previously placed. Right-click and select **Cancel [Esc]** to discontinue placing additional symbols.
8. Save the drawing and close all the files. Now that the symbol has been saved to the library it can be reused as required, without having to have it in a template file or copying and pasting between drawings.

End of practice

Practice B2
Custom Sketched Symbols II

Practice Objectives

- Insert an imported AutoCAD Block into a new drawing.
- Create a custom Sketched Symbol that consists of text and prompted entry.
- Insert a custom Sketched Symbol that requires user entry to populate the fields in the symbol.

In this practice, you will place an AutoCAD block in a drawing and create a custom sketch symbol. The custom sketch symbol will contain user prompts and pull information from the model properties. The custom symbol that will be created is shown in Figure B–19.

Rockwell Hardness	80
Heat Treatment	Yes
Paint Application	No
Material	Cast Iron

Figure B–19

Task 1: Create a new drawing and insert an AutoCAD block.

1. Open **Sketch Symbols.dwg**. Three views have been added to the drawing for you.
2. Expand the **Drawing Resources>AutoCAD Blocks** node, as shown in Figure B–20.

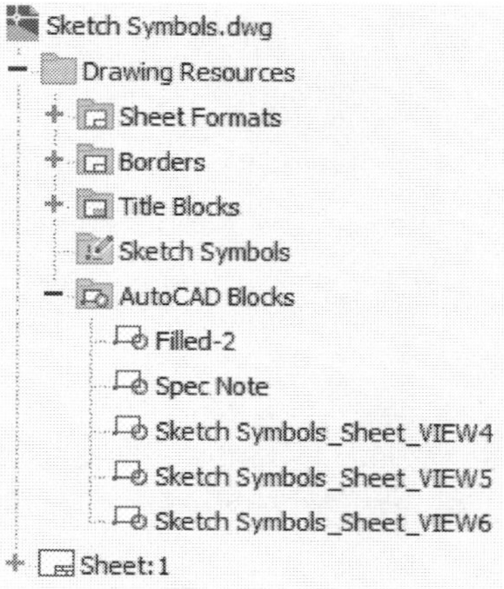

Figure B–20

These AutoCAD blocks had been imported into the drawing template that was used for this drawing. Because they are in the template, they are available for use in the Autodesk Inventor drawing. As views are created in the Autodesk Inventor drawing, these are added as AutoCAD blocks upon saving. Therefore, the parametric views are visible when opened in AutoCAD.

3. Right-click on **Spec Note** and select **Insert**.

   Note: *As opposed to sketched symbols, the only method you can use to add an AutoCAD block to a drawing is to right-click on the block and select* ***Insert****. There are no options on the Annotate panel to insert a block.*

4. Place the symbol anywhere on the drawing.
5. The Edit Attributes dialog box opens, requiring you to enter a value for the *Spec Number*. Enter **5**, as shown in Figure B–21, and click **OK**.

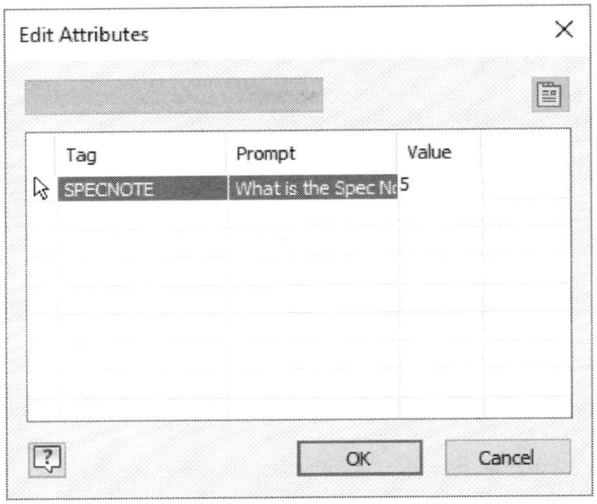

Figure B–21

6. Right-click and select **Done** to cancel symbol placement.
7. Right-click on the symbol and note that the symbol cannot use Leaders like an Autodesk Inventor Sketched Symbol can.

Task 2: Define a new symbol.

1. In the *Manage* tab>Define panel, click (Symbol). As an alternative, you can right-click on the **Drawing Resources> Sketch Symbols** node and select **Define New Symbol**. The *Sketch* tab is activated.
2. Using the **Text** command, add the text and prompted entries shown in Figure B–22.

   Note: *Consider toggling on the grid display (Tools tab> Application Options> Sketch tab) and enabling grid snap (right-click and select* ***Snap to Grid****) to help position the text.*

- The four entries shown on the left side (Rockwell Hardness, Heat Treatment, Paint Application, and Material) are text only.
- The top three entries on the right side (<Rockwell Hardness>, <Heat Treatment>, and <Paint Application>) use prompted entry. In the Type drop-down list, select **Prompted Entry** and edit the text field to display the prompts shown in Figure B–22.
- The bottom entry on the right side (<Material>) uses a parameter from the model to populate the field. In the Type drop-down list, select **Standard iProperties** and in the Property drop-down list, select **Material**. Ensure that you click to assign the parameter.

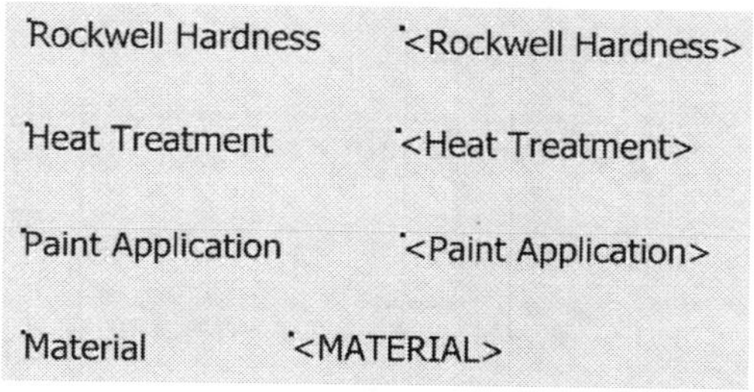

Figure B–22

Note: *To set up relationships between dimensions while in a sketch, select the dimension value that is to be driven to edit it, and then select the driving dimension. The driving dimension's parameter displays in the Edit Dimension dialog box. Press <Enter> to establish the relationship.*

3. Constrain the text entries using the Vertical and Horizontal constraint options, located in the Constraint panel. Add dimensions, as shown in Figure B–23. These dimensions will display in the sketch environment but not be visible in the final symbol.

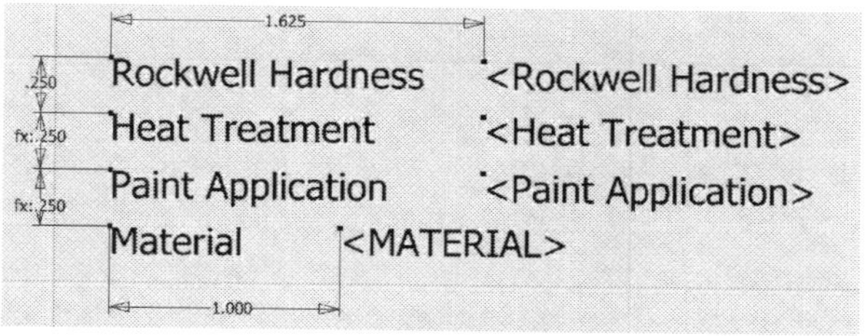

Figure B–23

4. Select the dot in the top left corner of the symbol. This dot is associated with the **Rockwell Hardness** text. In the Format panel, click (Set Insertion Point Grip). The insertion point grip is now set.

5. In the Exit panel, click (Finish).

6. Enter **Drawing Notes** as the name of the sketched symbol.
7. Expand the **Drawing Resources>Sketch Symbols** node. Right-click on the new symbol and select **Reorder Prompted Entries**. The Reorder Prompted Entries dialog box opens as shown in Figure B–24. The three prompted entries are displayed.

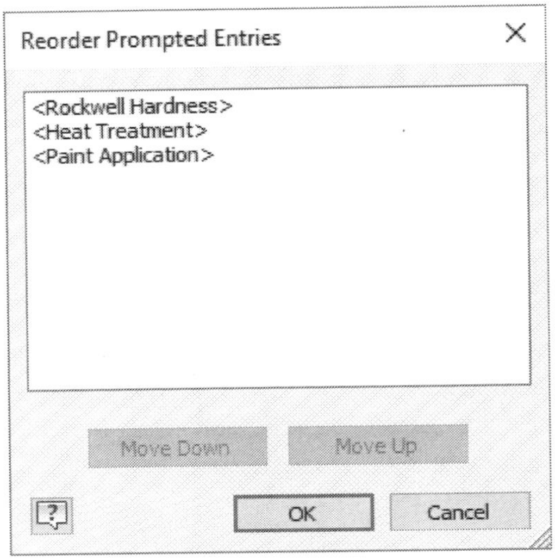

Figure B–24

- The **Reorder Prompted Entries** option enables you to reset the order in which entries are prompted for when the symbol is placed. In this case, with only three prompts, it is not that beneficial; however, if you are working with symbols that have a longer list of entries, it can be very helpful.

8. Click **OK** to close the dialog box without making any changes.

Task 3: Insert the symbol.

1. In the *Annotate* tab>Symbols panel, click 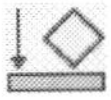 (Insert Sketched Symbol). As an alternative, you can right-click on the symbol in the *Drawing Resources* folder and select **Insert**.
2. Ensure that the **Drawing Notes** symbol is selected in the **Local** node in the Sketched Symbols dialog box. Clear the **Leader** option, if enabled, and click **OK**.
3. Click anywhere on the drawing to place the symbol.
4. The Drawing Notes Prompted Texts dialog box opens. You can enter the following values for the prompted entries, as shown in Figure B–25.
   - *Rockwell Hardness*: **80**
   - *Heat Treatment*: **Yes**
   - *Paint Application*: **No**

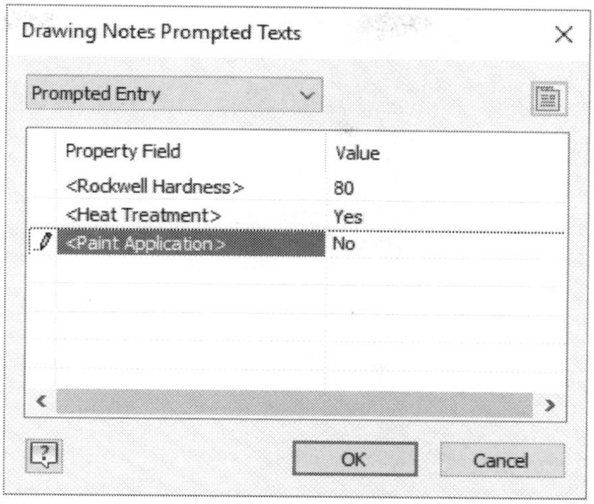

Figure B–25

5. Click **OK**. Right-click and select **Cancel [Esc]** to finish placement. The symbols display as shown in Figure B–26. Note how the material for the model automatically populates.

Rockwell Hardness	80
Heat Treatment	Yes
Paint Application	No
Material	Cast Iron

Figure B–26

6. Save the drawing and close the window. The Drawing Notes symbol was created in the drawing and is only stored locally. This could also be stored as a library drawing template or to the symbol library.

   Note: *With Inventor 2024,* ***Finish*** *features were added to the software. These assign parameters in a model that define an appearance, a material coating, a heat treatment, a surface texture, or detail on paint that will be applied. This parametric information can be used in drawing notes. This exercise used hardness, heat treatment, and paint application as prompted entry to teach that text can incorporated in this way; however, if your model has Finish features assigned, you could have incorporated their parameters similar to how the Material parameter was added.*

End of practice

Chapter Review Questions

1. Based on the Model browser shown in Figure B–27, how many sketched symbols have been placed in the drawing?

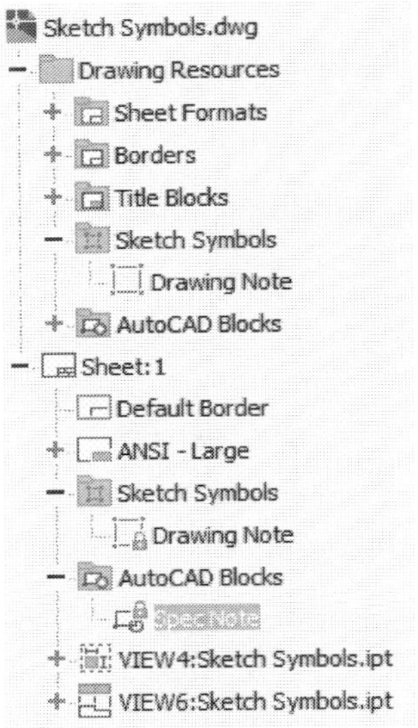

Figure B–27

a. 1
b. 2
c. 3
d. 5

2. Which of the following are true regarding insertion points? (Select all that apply.)
   a. The insertion point is the location on the sketched symbol that is used during placement.
   b. The insertion point defines the point where the leader attaches to the symbol.
   c. A single insertion point must be assigned in the sketched symbol in order to create it.
   d. If you redefine an insertion point for a sketched symbol, all symbols that already exist in the drawing update.

3. How many connection points can be assigned to a sketched symbol?
   a. 1
   b. 2
   c. Depends on the number of vertices in the sketch.
   d. Unlimited

4. AutoCAD blocks that exist in an Autodesk Inventor file can be scaled, rotated, and the entities can be edited once placed in an Autodesk Inventor drawing file.
   a. True
   b. False

Command Summary

Button	Command	Location
	**Connection Point Grip**	• **Ribbon:** *Sketch* tab>Format panel
	**Define New Symbol**	• **Ribbon:** *Annotate* tab>Symbols panel • **Context menu: In Model browser in** *Drawing Resources folder with* Sketch Symbols node selected
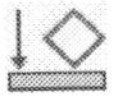	**Insert Sketch Symbol**	• **Ribbon:** *Annotate* tab>Symbols panel • **Context menu: In Model browser in** *Drawing Resources folder with* Sketch Symbols node selected
	**Set Insertion Point Grip**	• **Ribbon:** *Sketch* tab>Format panel
	**Text**	• **Ribbon:** *Sketch* tab>Create panel

Appendix

C

Drawing and Style Management

When working with drawing files, both administrators and users can benefit from knowing how to customize title blocks and borders. Additionally, knowledge of the Style Library Manager enables you to create new style libraries, compare style libraries, and transfer styles between existing style libraries to ensure that company standards are met.

Learning Objectives

- Delete the existing title blocks that are included with a default drawing template.
- Create a title block and border using sketch and text tools.
- Add a new title block to a drawing file and save the drawing as a template that can be used to create new drawings.
- Apply a style library to an Autodesk Inventor project file to ensure that all models created in the project use this library.
- Use the Style Library Manager to create new style libraries and copy styles between existing libraries.

C.1 Title Block and Border Customization

You can add a title block and border to a drawing using one of two methods:

- Use an existing title block and border.
- Create a new title block and border.

Use Existing Title Blocks and Borders

The drawing templates included in the software contain title blocks and borders. However, you or your CAD administrator may need to customize drawing templates to show your company's specific title blocks and borders.

How To: Apply a New, but Existing, Title Block and Border

1. Create or open the drawing with the title block and border that requires changing.
2. Access the required sheet in the drawing and expand the **Sheet** node in the Model browser.
3. In the Model browser, right-click on the title block name and select **Delete**, as shown in Figure C–1.

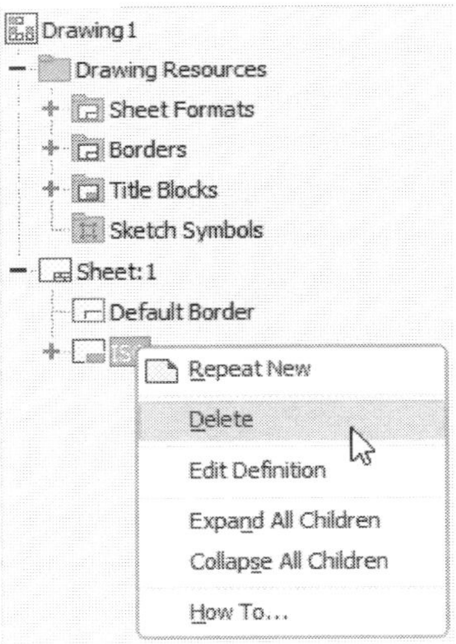

Figure C–1

4. In the Model browser, expand the *Drawing Resources* folder.
5. In the **Title Blocks** node, right-click on the required title block name and select **Insert**, as shown in Figure C–2.

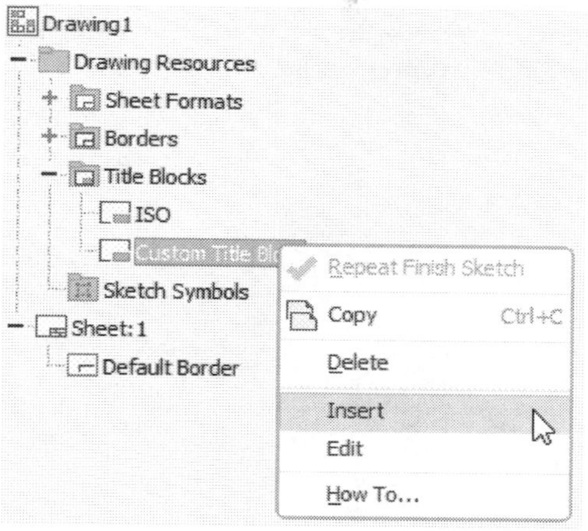

Figure C–2

6. If the title block requires entries, enter the values in the dialog box.
7. Repeat Steps 4 to 6 for the required border using Borders available in the **Borders** node.

Create a New Title Block and Border

In some cases, you might need to create a new title block.

How To: Create a New Title Block and Border

1. To create a new drawing template that includes a new title block and border, you can:
   - Open one of the existing templates from the *C:\Users\Public\Public Documents\Autodesk\Inventor 2024\Templates* directory.
   - Create a new drawing based on an existing template.
2. In the *Manage* tab>Define panel, click (Title Block) or (Border) to create a new title block or border, respectively. The current sheet becomes an active sketch.
3. Use the *Sketch* tab to draw the title block or border. Dimension the sketch, as required.

4. Add text to the title block or border by clicking (Text) in the Create panel.
   - Model and drawing properties can be added so that they automatically update in the title block. Use the Type drop-down list to select the type you want to add. Select the property and click to add the parameter to the field. The Type drop-down list options are shown in Figure C–3. Once a type is selected, the options in the Property drop-down list update.

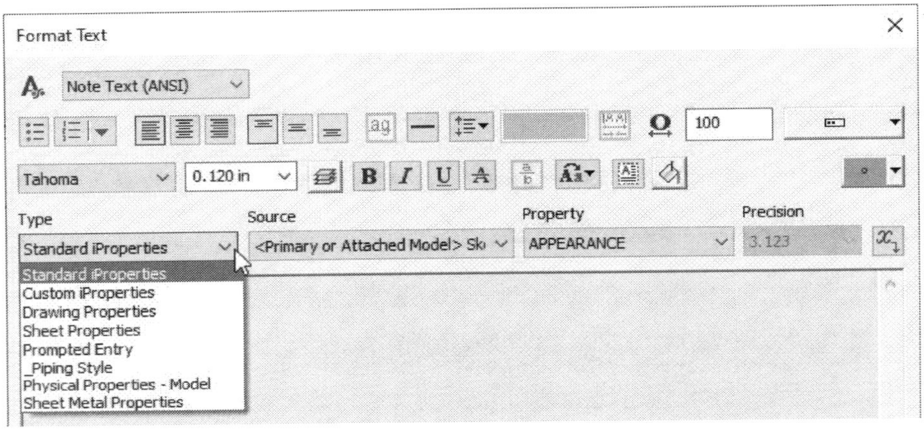

Figure C–3

Note: *The Prompted Entry property type displays a prompt for you to input information when the title block is added.*

5. Once you have completed the title block or border, click .
6. Enter a name for the title block or border and click **Save**. The new title block or border is added in the Model browser to the *Drawing Resources* folder, as shown in Figure C–4.

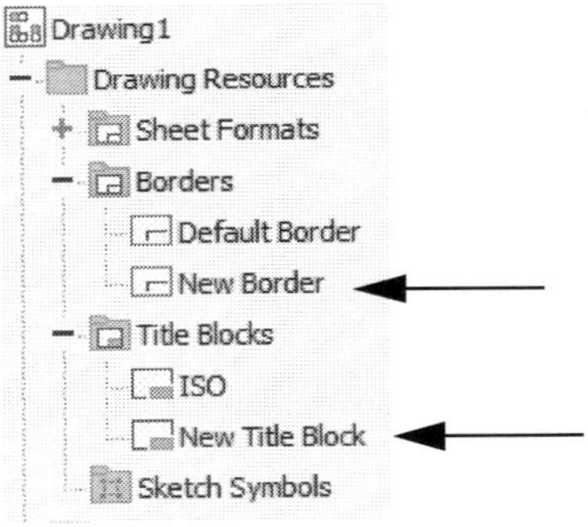

Figure C–4

To use the new title block and border as a template for future drawings, save the drawing in the *Templates* folder using **Save Copy As Template** in the **File** menu or save to a folder in the *Templates* folder.

C.2 Style Library Manager

Style

A style is a set of predefined properties, such as lighting, dimensions, and drawing standards. You can apply a style to an object, such as an annotation, edge, face, part, assembly, or drawing.

Style Library

A style library contains a set of styles, including lighting, dimensions, and drawing standards. Companies can use the style library to suit their unique needs.

To change the style library for a project, open the Projects dialog box and select the project to modify. Expand **Folder Options**, right-click on the *Design Data* folder, and select **Edit**, as shown in Figure C–5. Browse to the required style library.

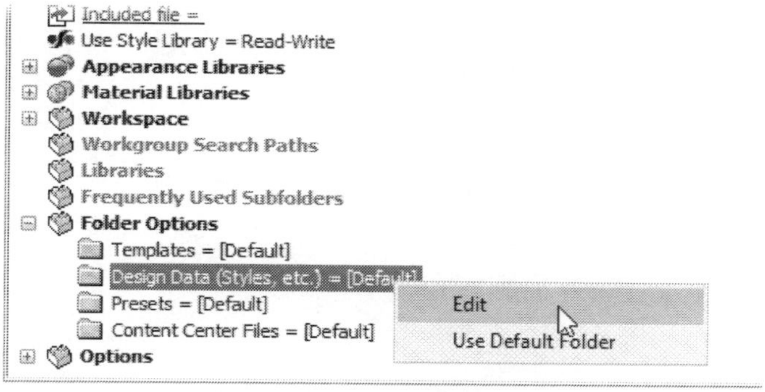

Figure C–5

*Note: Each project uses the default style library, unless otherwise specified. The default style library is set in the Application Options (Tools tab>**Application Options**>File tab> Design Data).*

Style Library Manager

The style library manager enables you to copy styles between style libraries and rename or delete styles.

How To: Edit a Style in the Style Library

1. Access the Style Library Manager by selecting **Start> Autodesk Inventor 2024>Style Library Manager 2024**. The dialog box opens, as shown in Figure C–6.

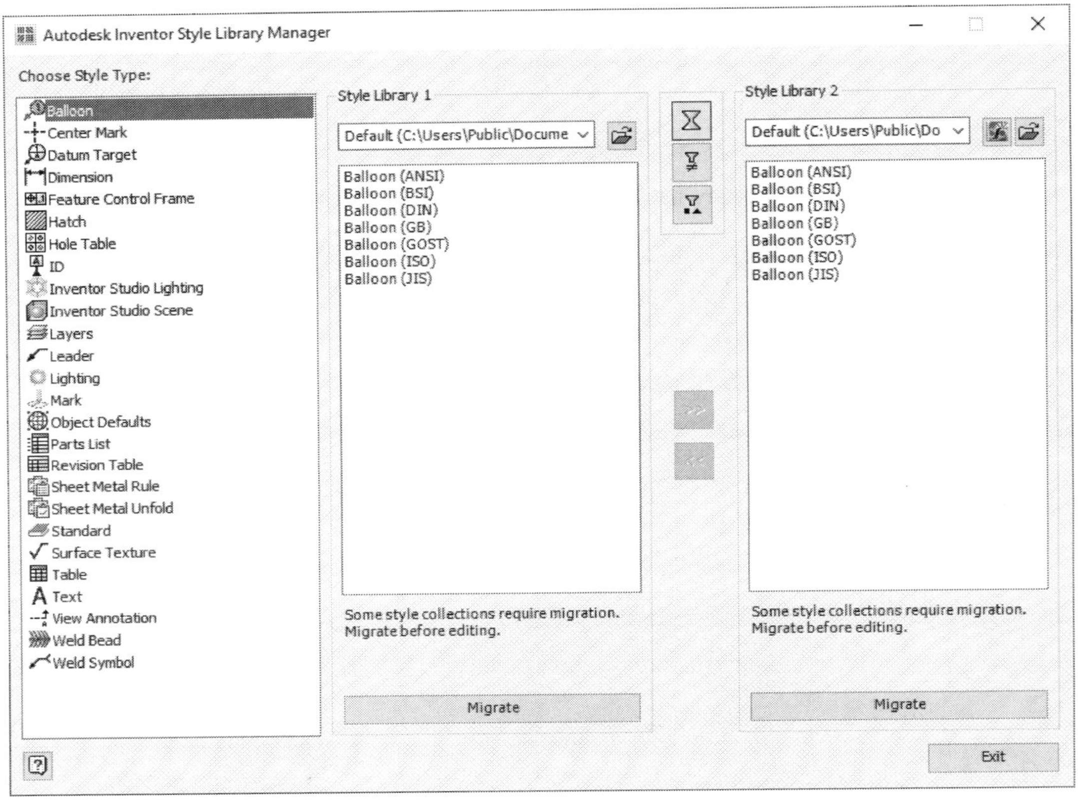

Figure C–6

2. Select the style type to edit from the list on the left side of the dialog box.
3. There are two areas on the right side: *Style Library 1* and *Style Library 2*. These two areas enable you to compare two different style libraries and transfer required styles from one style library to the other.

   To display a different style library, in *Style Library 1* or *Style Library 2,* expand the drop-down list and select from the list of projects that use style libraries. Alternatively, use the  icon to browse to and open a different style library.

4. Once you have selected the required style libraries, use the filter icons to help compare the two style libraries. The filter options are described as follows:

	Shows all styles in the style libraries.
	Shows styles that have the same name but different style definitions or properties.
	Shows styles that exist in one style library but not the other.

- A style name displayed in blue, with italic and bold font indicates that the style does not exist in the other style library.
- A style name displayed in black with regular font indicates that the two styles are the same.
- A style name displayed in red, with bold and underlined font indicates that although the names are the same, their definitions are different.

An example of each is shown in Figure C–7.

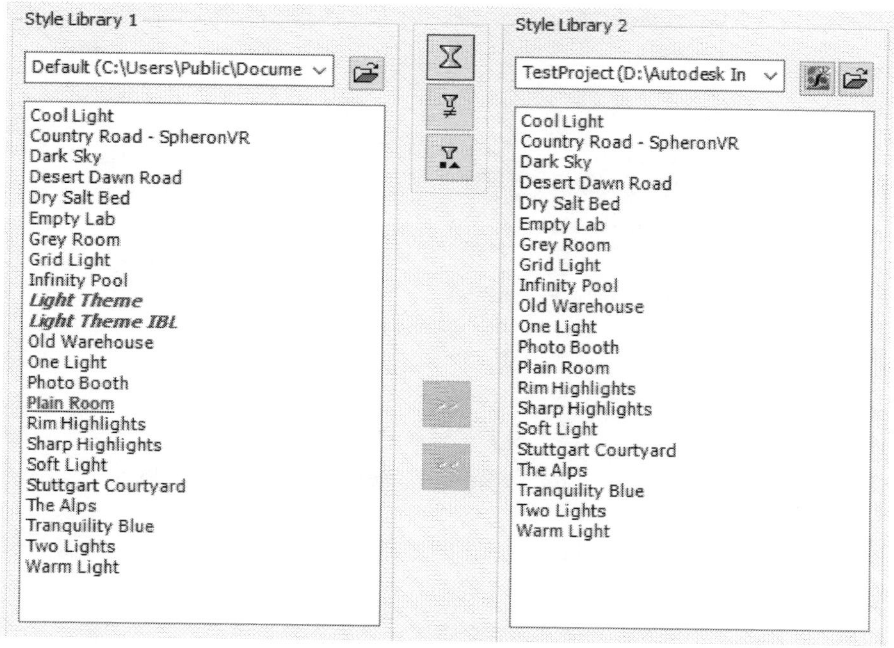

Figure C–7

Copy Styles Between Style Libraries

To copy a style from one style library to another, select the style and use the << or >> icons. Styles sometimes reference other styles, called substyles. A hole table, for example, references the text style as a substyle. When a style with a substyle is copied, the substyle is only copied if it does not already exist in the destination library. Changes made to a style library do not have any effect until the current session is closed and a new one is opened.

Rename or Delete Styles

To rename or delete a style, right-click it in the style library list and select **Rename Styles** or **Delete Styles**.

Create a New Style Library

How To: Create a New Style Library

1. Click (Create New Style Library) to open the Create New Style Library dialog box, as shown in Figure C–8.

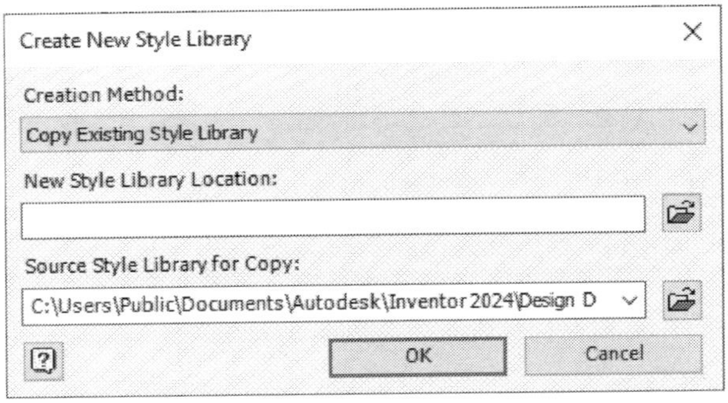

Figure C–8

2. In the Creation Method drop-down list, select **Copy Existing Style Library** or **Create Empty Style Library**.
3. Enter the full path directory, including the folder name, in the *New Style Library Location* field.
   - This directory specifies where the style library is stored.
   - The .XML files containing the different style types are saved into the folder specified in this field.
   - If you enter the name of a folder that does not exist, a folder with the specified name is automatically created.

4. If you selected **Copy Existing Style Library**, select the required library from the Source Style Library for Copy drop-down list or use the  icon to browse to the library.
5. Click **OK**.

Practice C1
Customizing the Title Block

Practice Objectives

- Sketch and dimension line entities that makeup the title block layout for a custom title block file.
- Add text to incorporate both static and parametric text into the title block.
- Delete existing title blocks that are included with a default drawing template.
- Add a new title block to a drawing file and save the drawing as a template that can be used to create new drawings.

In this practice, you will create a new title block, add it to a blank drawing, and make it available as a template.

Task 1: Delete the existing title block from a new drawing.

1. Create a new drawing using the **ISO.idw** template in the *Metric* tab.
2. Right-click on the title block called **ISO** and select **Delete**, as shown in Figure C–9.

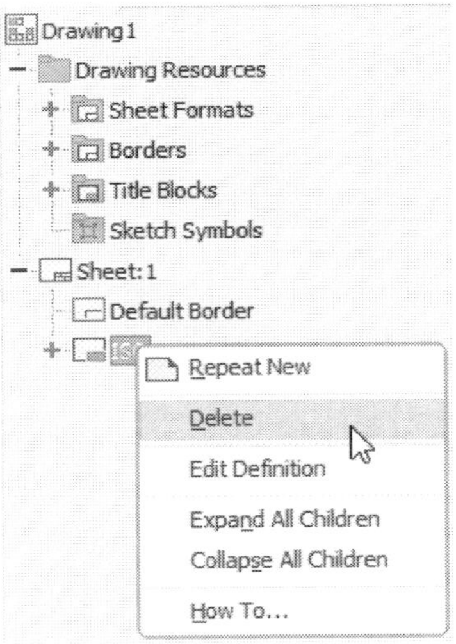

Figure C–9

Task 2: Create the title block borders.

1. In the *Manage* tab>Define panel, click (Title Block). The sketch environment is activated.

2. Using rectangles, lines, and general dimensions, create the title block shown in Figure C–10. Align the title block as close as possible to the border.

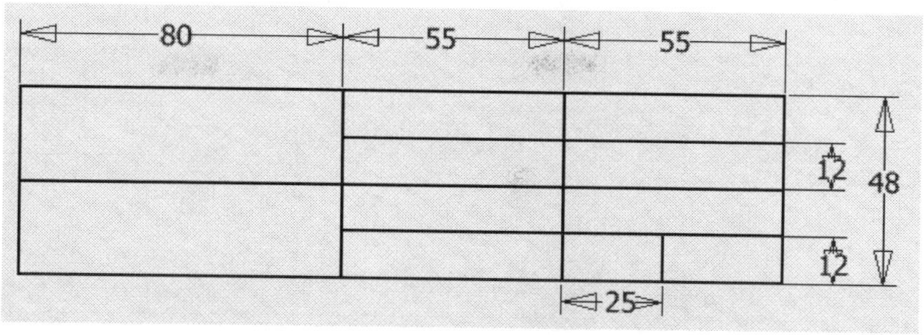

Figure C–10

Task 3: Add regular text.

1. In the Create panel, click **A** (Text) and add the text shown in Figure C–11. Use a size of **2.00 mm** for the text.

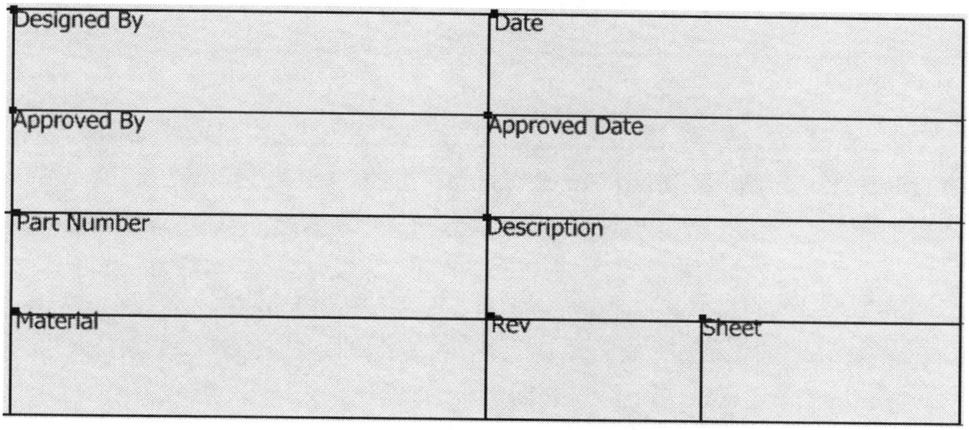

Figure C–11

Task 4: Add model and drawing properties.

1. In the Create panel, click **A** (Text) and click in the *Designed By* cell in the title block. The Format Text dialog box opens.
2. In the Type drop-down list, select **Standard iProperties**.
3. In the Property drop-down list, select **Designer**.

4. Click . The property is added to the text field, as shown in Figure C–12.

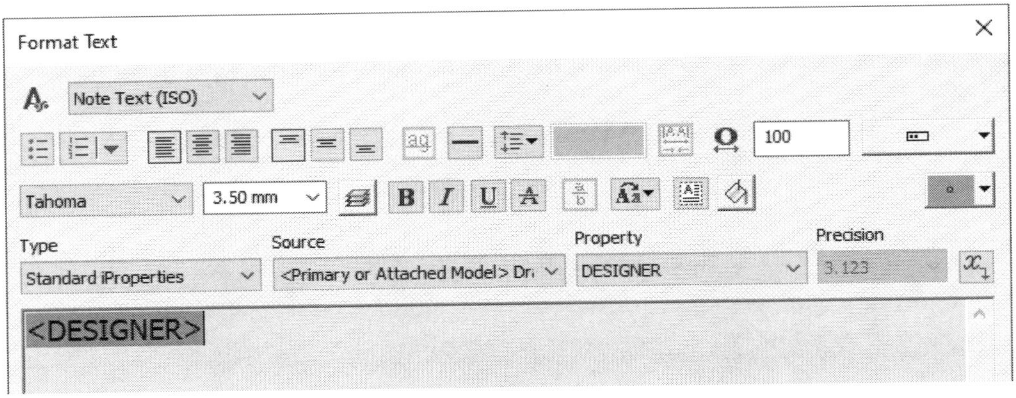

Figure C–12

5. Click **OK**. The property displays as shown in Figure C–13. Move the text, if required, by selecting the text and dragging it to the new location.

Figure C–13

6. Repeat the previous steps for the remaining properties shown in Figure C–14. All but the sheet properties are of the *Standard iProperties* type. Create the sheet property using a combination of the *Sheet Properties* and *Drawing Properties*.

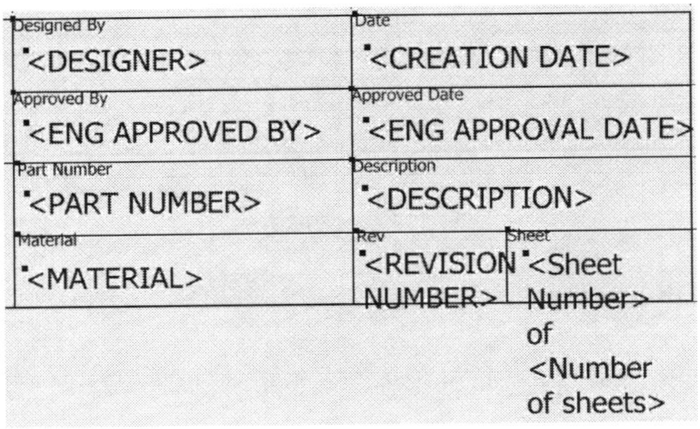

Figure C–14

Task 5: Save the title block.

1. In the exit panel, click (Finish Sketch) to exit the sketch.
2. Enter **Custom Title Block** as the name of the new title block and click **Save**. The newly created title block is stored in **Title Blocks** node in the *Drawing Resources* folder, as shown in Figure C–15.

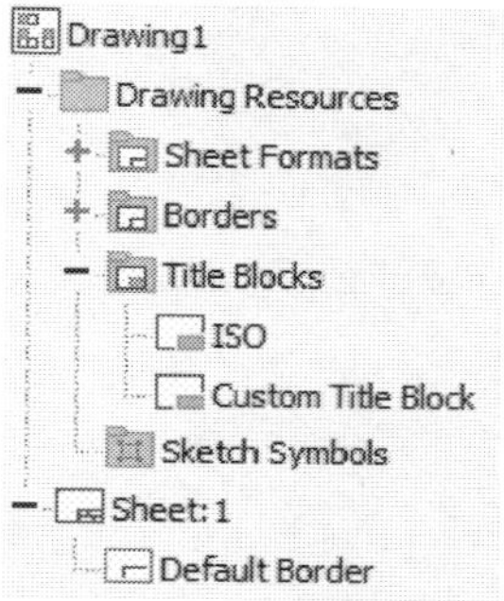

Figure C–15

Task 6: Insert the newly created title block into the drawing.

1. Right-click on **Custom Title Block** and select **Insert**, as shown in Figure C–16.

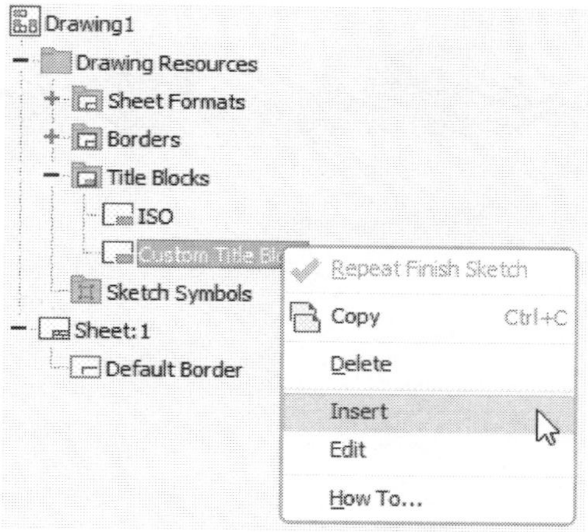

Figure C–16

2. The title block is added to the drawing and the Model browser, as shown in Figure C–17.

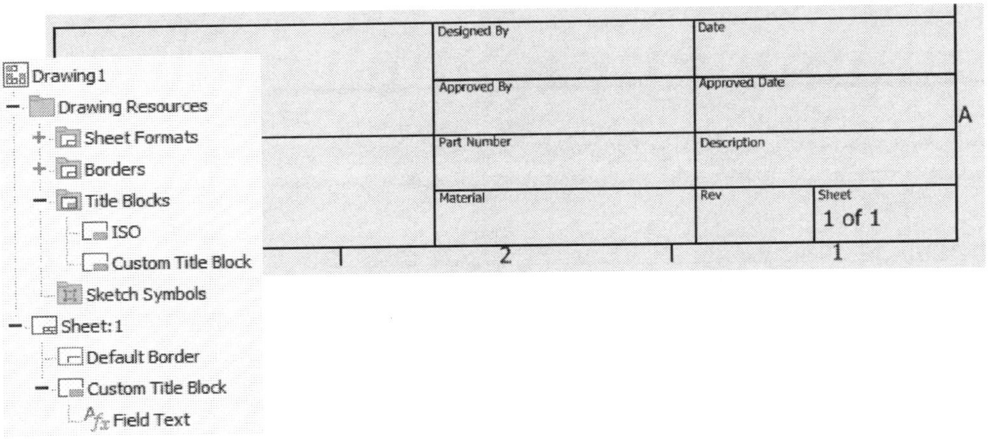

Figure C–17

Note that only the sheet properties have been automatically entered. The remainder of the properties were created using **Standard iProperties** from the Type drop-down list so that their values will be populated when a model is added to the drawing.

Task 7: Save the drawing as a template.

1. Save the drawing using **Save Copy As Template** to save the file as a template in the default *Templates* directory. The next time you access the New File dialog box, the new drawing template will be available for use.

End of practice

Practice C2
Managing Styles

Practice Objectives

- Use the Style Library Manager to copy styles between libraries.
- Associate libraries to new project files.

In this practice, you will use the Style Library Manager to manage styles that are associated to both style libraries and documents.

Task 1: Open the Style Library Manager.

1. From outside of the Autodesk Inventor software, select **Start>Autodesk Inventor 2024>Style Library Manager 2024**. The Style Library Manager opens, as shown in Figure C–18.

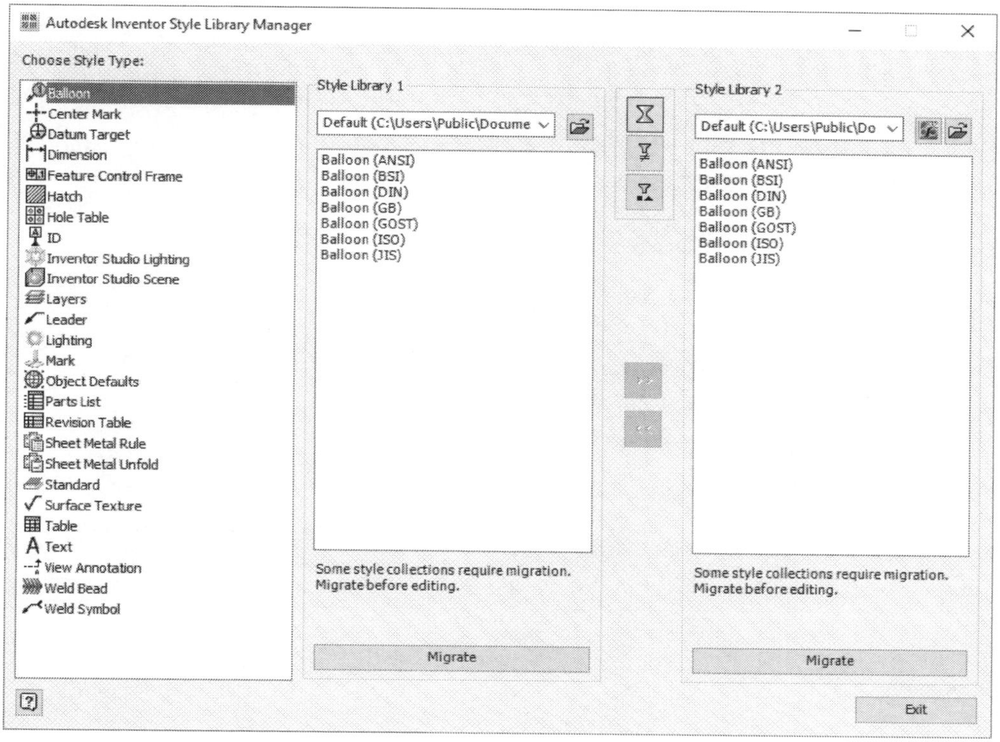

Figure C–18

Task 2: Create two new style libraries.

In this task, you create two new style libraries. *TestStyleLibrary* and *EmptyStyleLibrary* are used to demonstrate the Style Library Manager.

1. Click (Create New Style Library). The Create New Style Library dialog box opens, as shown in Figure C–19.

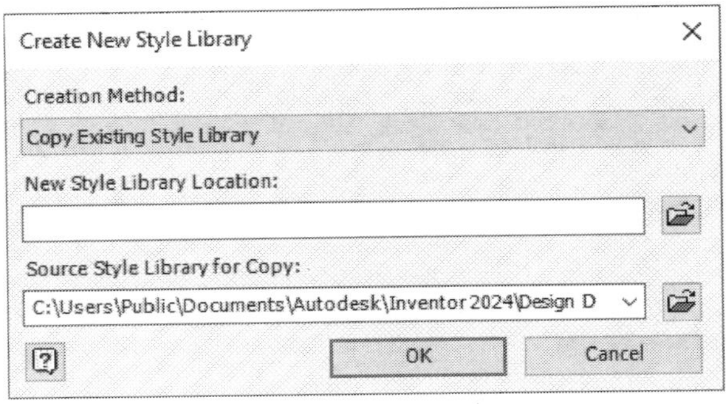

Figure C–19

2. In the *Creation Method* field, leave the default selected and next to the *New Style Library Location* field, click .
3. Browse to the practice files location for this course and create a new folder called **TestStyleLibrary**. Click **OK**.
4. In the *Source Style Library for Copy* field, leave the default selected, as shown in Figure C–20.

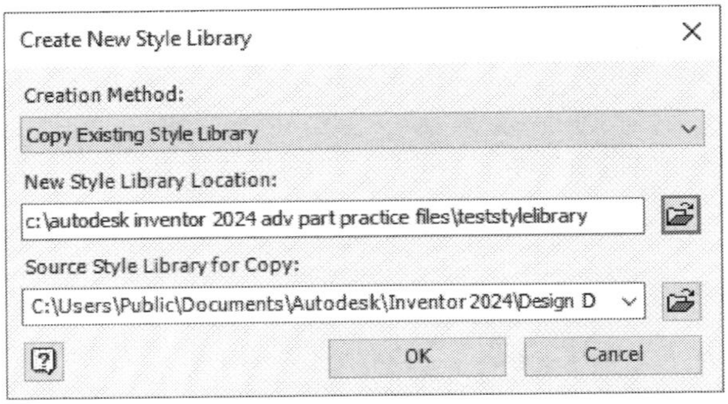

Figure C–20

5. Click **OK**.

6. Create a second style library using the **Create Empty Style Library** creation method and call it **EmptyStyleLibrary**, as shown in Figure C–21.

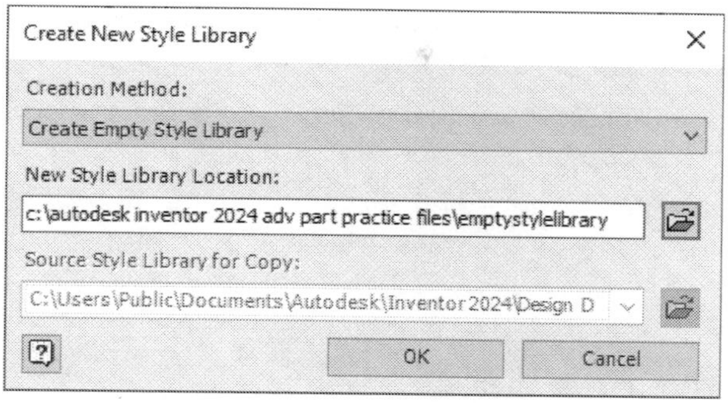

Figure C–21

Task 3: Compare TestStyleLibrary and EmptyStyleLibrary.

In this task, you use the Style Library Manager to determine which styles are common and uncommon between TestStyleLibrary and EmptyStyleLibrary.

1. Select **UserStyleLibrary (C:\.....\teststylelibrary)** from the drop-down list for *Style Library 1*.
2. Select **UserStyleLibrary (C:\.....\emptystylelibrary)** from the drop-down list for *Style Library 2*.
3. Select a few different style types from the *Choose Style Type* column, such as Dimension, and Text. Note that the test style library (Style Library 1) contains styles shown in blue lettering, whereas the empty style library (Style Library 2) does not contain any styles.
4. Any styles that exist in the selected style library are listed. If no styles are listed, then the selected style library contains no styles for the particular style type. In the case of the empty style library, there are no styles for any style type.

   The color of the styles that are listed indicate additional information. A blue color indicates that the particular style does not exist in the other style library that is being compared.
5. Select the *Inventor Studio Lighting* style type.
6. Select **Country Road - SpheronVR** from TestStyleLibrary and click 

to move the style to the empty style library. Note that **Country Road - SpheronVR** is now listed in both style libraries and displays black rather than blue. The style is in black because it now exists in both the style libraries being compared.

   If you are unable to transfer the style, you may need to migrate the style collection. Click **Migrate** at the bottom of the Style Library 1 area, if necessary. Confirm that you wish to migrate the library. Repeat step 6 to move the style to the empty style library.
7. Click **Exit** to close the style library manager.

Task 4: Create a project called TestProject.

1. In the Autodesk Inventor software, in the **File** menu, select **Manage>Projects**. The Projects dialog box opens. Note that all files must be closed to change a project.
2. Right-click in the upper panels where the projects are listed and select **New**. The Inventor project wizard dialog box opens.
3. Depending on whether Vault is installed, you might be prompted for what type of project you are creating. Select **New Single User Project**, if prompted. Click **Next**.
4. Define the new project, called **TestProject**, as shown in Figure C–22.

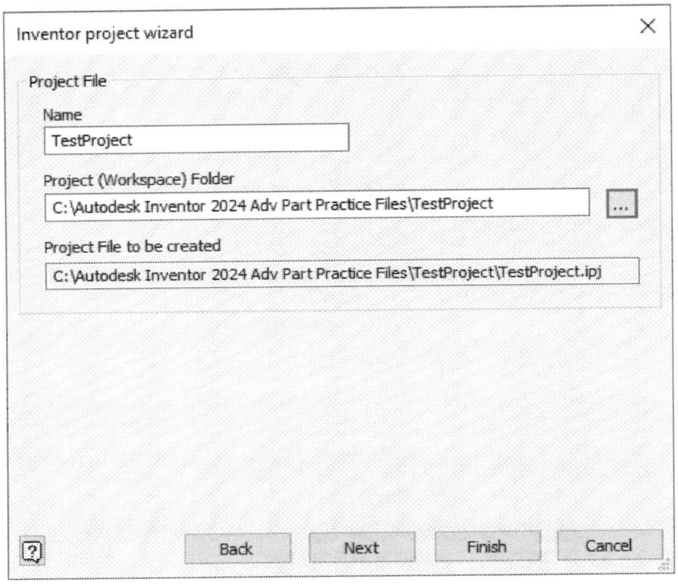

Figure C–22

5. Click **Finish** to create the project. The new project displays in the project list. If any files are open, the new project will not be set as the active project.

Task 5: Change the project options for the project.

In this task, you set TestProject to use TestStyleLibrary for its style library. The project will also be set so that the style library can be modified.

1. In the Projects dialog box with the list of projects showing, double-click on **TestProject** to activate it, if not already active. The checkmark should now display next to **TestProject**, indicating that it is the active project.

2. In the project options area for **TestProject**, right-click on **Use Style Library** and select **Read-Write**, as shown in Figure C–23, to enable you to make changes to the style library.

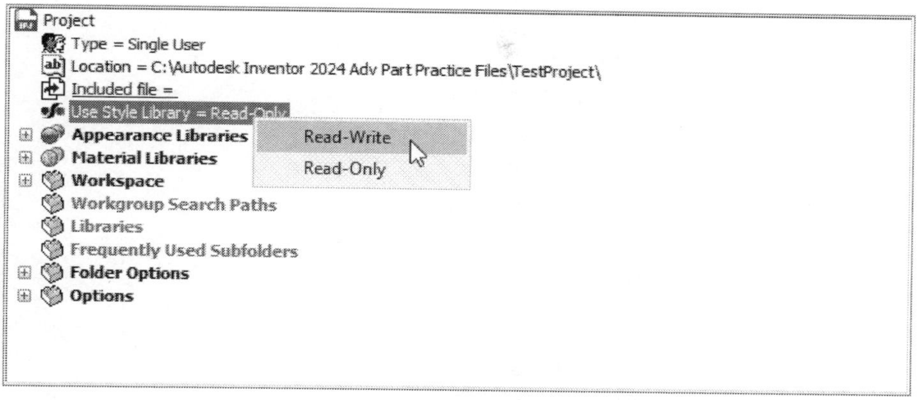

Figure C–23

3. Expand **Folder Options**, right-click on **Design Data**, and select **Edit**, as shown in Figure C–24.

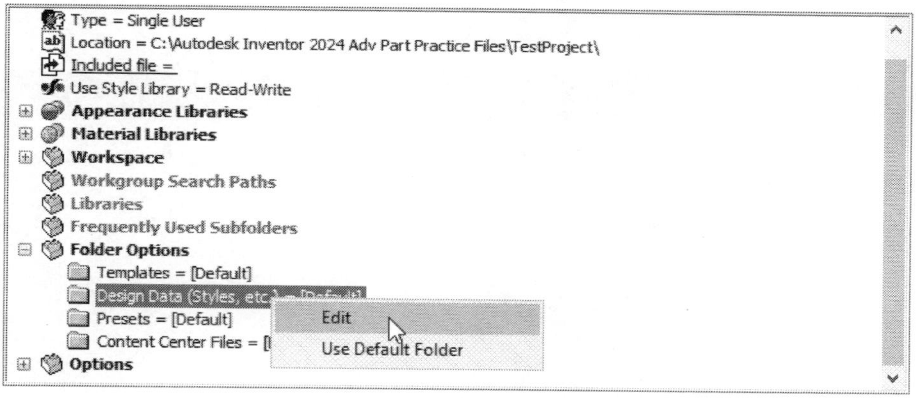

Figure C–24

4. Browse and select the *TestStyleLibrary* folder that you created earlier (*C:\.....\TestStyleLibrary*). The style library path displays, as shown in Figure C–25. Press <Enter>.

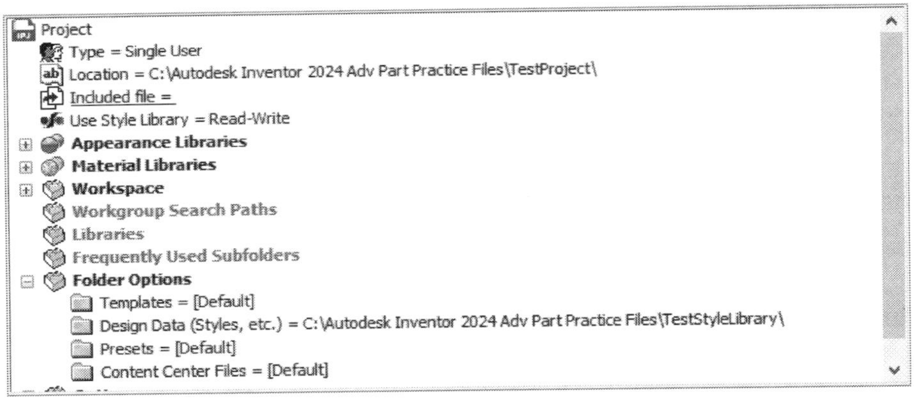

Figure C–25

5. Save the changes you made to the project by clicking **Save** in the Projects dialog box. The style library has now been assigned. Any models created in this project will use the assigned style library.

End of practice

Chapter Review Questions

1. To remove an existing title block and border that is currently being displayed in a drawing, expand the *Drawing Resources* folder in the Model browser, right-click on the title block in the *Title Block* node, and select **Delete**.
    a. True
    b. False

2. Which command enables you to save an existing drawing so that it and all of its Drawing Resources can be used to create a new drawing document?
    a. File menu>Manage>Projects
    b. File menu>Save>Save All
    c. File menu>Save As>Save Copy As
    d. File menu>Save As>Save Copy As Template

3. Which tool do you use to compare the styles that exist in two style libraries?
    a. Style Library Manager
    b. Styles Editor

4. If a specific style exists in Style Library 1 and is being compared to a style with the same name but different properties in Style Library 2, how does it display?
    a. Blue, with italic and bold font
    b. Black, with regular font
    c. Red, with bold and underlined font

5. If a particular style exists in one library (Style Library 1) and does not exist in the library that it is being compared to (Style Library 2), how does it display?
    a. Blue, with italic and bold font
    b. Black, with regular font
    c. Red, with bold and underlined font

6. If a new library is created using the **Copy Existing Style Library** option, how would the two libraries (new and the source) display when being compared?
    a. Blue, with italic and bold font
    b. Black, with regular font
    c. Red, with bold and underlined font

Command Summary

Button	Command	Location
	**Border (create)**	• **Ribbon:** *Manage* tab>Define panel
N/A	**Delete (title block)**	• **Context Menu:** In Model browser with current title block selected
N/A	**Insert (title block)**	• **Context Menu**: In Model browser with title block selected
N/A	**Save Copy as Template**	• **File menu: Save As**
N/A	**Style Library Manager**	• **Start>All Programs>Autodesk>Autodesk Inventor 2019>Tools>Style Library Manager 2019**
	**Text**	• **Ribbon:** *Sketch* tab>Create panel
	**Title Block (create)**	• **Ribbon:** *Manage* tab>Define panel

Appendix

D

Working with Imported Surfaces

The data that is imported from other CAD systems may have errors that prevents it from being created as a solid in Autodesk® Inventor®. Additionally, surfaces that are imported may need to be individually selected for modification to make a required design change. Situations like these require you to fix the problem areas or finish surface modeling. There are many options that can be used to help you identify and fix these errors.

Learning Objectives

- Set the import options to import surface data from other file format types.
- Transfer imported surface data into the Repair Environment to conduct a quality check for errors.
- Appropriately set the stitch tolerance value so that gaps in the imported geometry can be automatically stitched and identify the gaps that are not stitched.
- Use the Repair Environment commands to repair gaps or delete, extend, replace, trim, and break surfaces to successfully create a solid from the imported geometry.

D.1 Importing Surfaces

As previously discussed, the Import dialog box can be used to import many different CAD file formats. In addition to this, it also has the flexibility to only import surface data from a file. Once the surface data is imported, you can manipulate it using the standard surfacing tools to create required geometry or edit existing surface geometry. The workflow is similar, however you should consider the following:

- Ensure that the selected *Import Type* option captures your design intent, so that the model is either referenced or converted for use in Autodesk Inventor.
- In the *Object Filter* area, select the **Surface** option to provide you with the required surfaces.
- Consider using the *Select* tab to selectively include or exclude surfaces that are to be imported, if available. For example, when importing an .IGS file, you can select the specific surfaces to import, as shown in Figure D–1.

Figure D–1

How To: Include or Exclude Surfaces

1. Select the *Select* tab.
2. Select **Load Model** to add all of the model data to the dialog box and display a preview of the model in the graphics window.
3. Click the circular node associated with each surface to toggle its inclusion. By default, all surfaces are included (). When the  node is displayed, the surface is excluded. To toggle multiple surfaces, select them and use the appropriate Status symbol at the top of the Import dialog box.

D.2 Repairing Imported Surfaces

When you import surfaces, the data might have to be repaired and stitched together into a quilt (a group of surfaces), before the surfaces can be used. Alternatively, you simply might want to make design changes to the geometry. To accomplish this, you should use the Repair environment. In the Repair environment, you can analyze, repair, and stitch the surfaces. You can then return to the Part environment to repair any remaining problem areas, such as creating missing surfaces, and finally stitching the surfaces together. If the surfaces you stitch form a closed boundary, you can obtain a solid geometry.

Use the following general steps to repair imported surfaces:

1. Switch to the Repair environment.
2. Perform an error check.
3. Stitch surfaces together.
4. Repair imported surfaces.
5. Stitch surfaces together, as required.
6. Perform an error check.
7. Complete the repair.
8. Repair remaining problem areas, as required.
9. Stitch surfaces together, as required.

Step 1 - Switch to the Repair environment.

To access the Repair environment, right-click on the imported geometry node and select **Repair Bodies**. Alternatively, in the Surface panel, you can click  (Repair Bodies) and then select the body to be repaired.

The *Repair* tab displays as shown in Figure D–2.

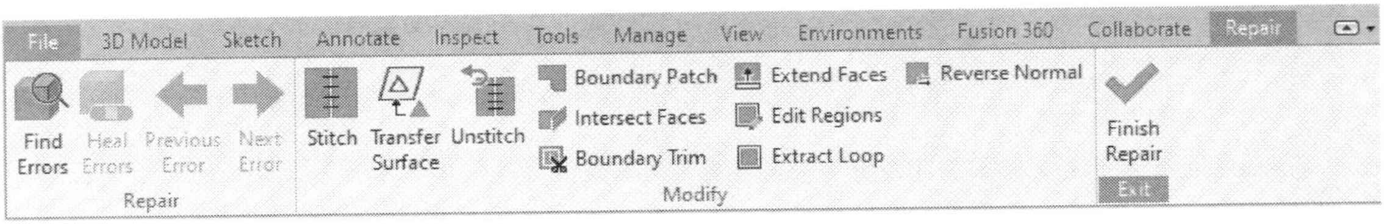

Figure D–2

Step 2 - Perform an error check.

Perform an error check to check for surface topology, geometry, and modeling uncertainty errors. In the Repair panel, click (Find Errors). Alternatively, you can right-click on the repair node or in the graphics window and select **Find Errors.** The Find Errors dialog box opens. Click **Select All** to select all the bodies in the imported geometry or manually select bodies. Click **OK** to run the check. The check analyzes the imported data and reports the errors, by type, in the Model browser. The error type is identified by the following symbols:

- The symbol identifies healthy geometry in the model.
- The symbol identifies geometry that needs further investigation.
- The symbol identifies geometry that contains errors and requires repairing.

> ***Note:*** *Refer to the Help documentation for a complete list and description of the possible error types that can be found. A glyph for each error can be displayed on the model. Right-click on the error folder and select* ***Error Glyph Visibility****.*

Similar errors are all grouped into folders. To locate an error in the model, in the Model browser select the error and the error symbol. Its associated entity is highlighted in the model and an error glyph is displayed. Additionally, you can use the (Previous Error) and (Next Error) options to progress through the list.

Heal Errors

The **Heal Errors** command can also be used in the Repair panel when errors exist. Click (Heal Errors), select the bodies that are required to be healed, and enter a healing tolerance value. With the required bodies selected, you can click (Analyze Selected Bodies) to analyze if the assigned tolerance will resolve the issues. Click **OK** to run the healing process. The bodies are analyzed and any problems are reported. Errors that can be healed are corrected in the model, otherwise continue to use the options in the Modify panel to correct the geometry.

Repairing Using the Mini-Toolbar

Not all errors can be resolved using the **Heal Errors** command. As each error is selected, a Repair mini-toolbar is displayed to help resolve the error. The resolution options that are available are dependent on the error. For example, you may be provided tools to delete faces, create patches or stitch the geometry. Click once the error is healed.

Step 3 - Stitch surfaces together.

Perform a stitch to close any insignificant gaps that might have resulted from the import. It also helps to locate the significant gaps and over-extended surfaces. Stitch creates a quilt of the stitched surfaces. It is better to initially use a smaller tolerance to avoid undesirable changes in the geometry and then increase the tolerance, as required. When a gap or overlap exists that is too large to stitch without affecting the integrity of the surfaces, use the other surface repair options available.

How To: Stitch the Surfaces

1. In the Modify panel, click (Stitch) or right-click in the graphics window and select **Stitch**.
2. In the *Select* area of the dialog box, define whether the entities to be stitched are to be selected as faces or bodies. The faces or bodies can be selected in the Model browser or directly on the model. To select all entities in the model, select and drag a bounding box around the model. The Stitch dialog box updates showing the number of faces selected.
3. Enter a value in the *Fill gaps smaller than* field. This maximum tolerance value identifies the maximum gap and overlap between two surfaces that will be stitched together. Surface edges that contain a gap or overlap less than the maximum tolerance are stitched.
4. To preview a list of edges that will not be stitched, click (Find remaining gaps and free edges). Edges that could not be stitched (due to them being further apart than the defined maximum tolerance) are highlighted in the model and listed in the Stitch dialog box. An example of a model that is stitched but still contains free edges is shown in Figure D–3.

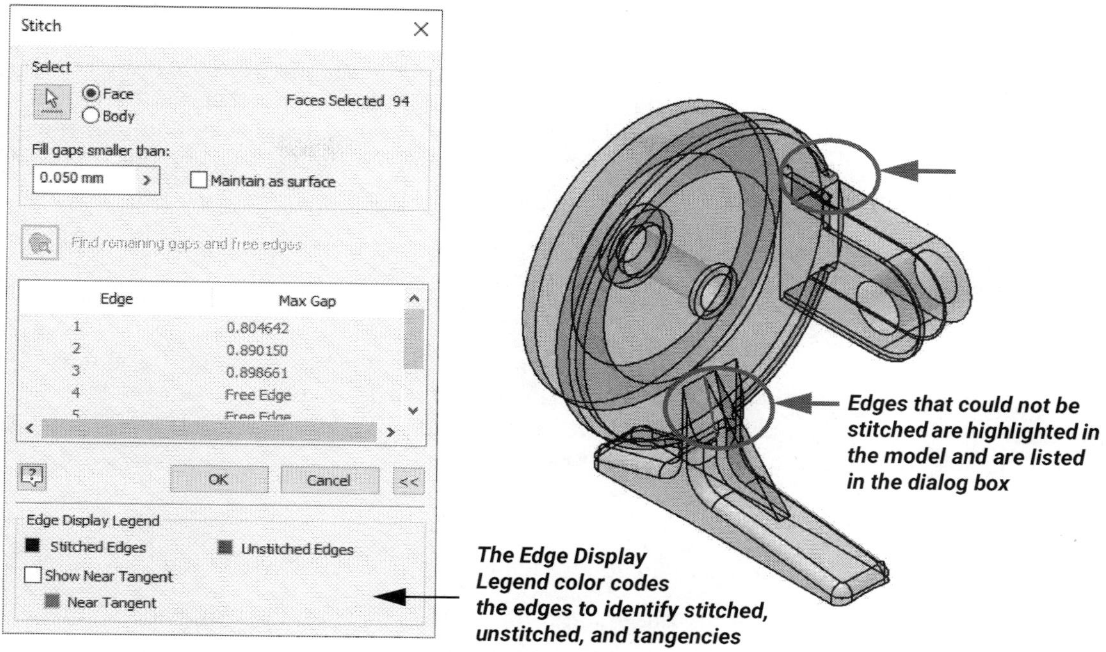

Figure D–3

5. To determine which edge in the model corresponds to which edge listed in the dialog box, select a row in the list. The corresponding edge highlights in the model. Some of the edge gaps and overlaps might be small so you might need to zoom in to see them.
6. Review the list of gaps or overlaps. If they are insignificant and can be repaired by adjusting the tolerance value without adversely affecting surrounding surfaces, change the tolerance and click **OK**. If not, maintain the original tolerance and click **OK**. Plan to use the tools on the Modify panel to fix the model.

Step 4 - Repair imported surfaces.

Use the following options in the Modify panel of the Repair environment or in the right-click on the marking or context menu to repair the imported surfaces.

Transfer Surface

The **Transfer Surface** command works in a similar way to the Stitch command. The only difference between the commands is that the Transfer Surface dialog box provides a field that enables you to select a destination body to move the selected face or body to or you can generate a new composite. To access the command, in the Modify panel, click  (Transfer Surface) or right-click in the graphics window and select **Transfer Surface**.

Add Surface

The **Add Surface** command is only available in the shortcut menu directly in the model or through the Model browser. The command can be used to add a new surface to an existing face or body. To add a surface, right-click on the surface to be added and select **Add Surface**. In the Stitch: Add dialog box, select the face/body to which the new surface will be added, enter the gap tolerance value, and click **OK**.

Unstitch

There are times when you need to select particular surfaces in a quilt. Unless the required surface is unstitched from the quilt, you cannot select it. To unstitch, click (Unstitch), select the surface(s) to exclude from the quilt, and click **Apply**. You can also access the **Unstitch** command by right-clicking in the graphics window. The unstitched surface(s) can then be selected separately from the rest of the quilt.

Extend Faces

Use Extend Faces to extend faces at an edge, as shown in Figure D–4. To extend a face, click (Extend Faces), select the edge reference(s) for the extend, enter the extension distance, and click **Apply**. The face is extended by the specified distance.

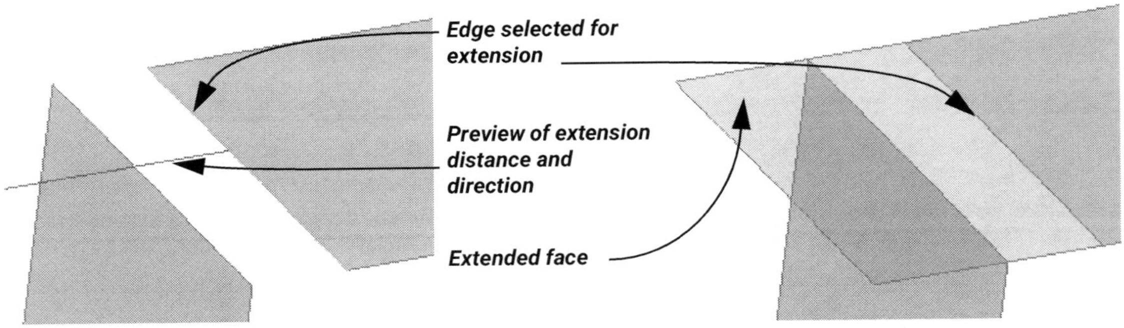

Figure D–4

__Note:__ To select a reference to which a surface can extend up to (instead of having to specify a distance), use __Extend Surface__ in the Part Features Panel.

Intersect Faces

Use Intersect Faces to trim or break faces that intersect one another, as shown in Figure D–5.

To trim faces, click (Intersect Faces), click (Trim), and select the portions of the faces to keep when selecting the faces for the trim. The portions of the faces you did not select are removed starting at the line of intersection. To break faces, click (Intersect Faces), click (Break), and select the faces for the break. The faces are broken in two at the line of intersection.

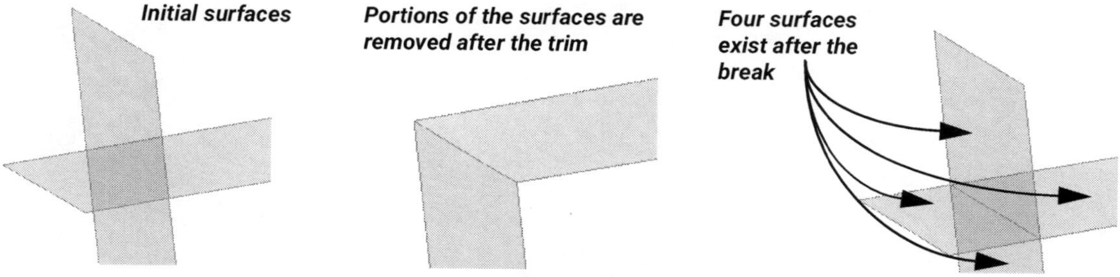

Figure D–5

Edit Regions

Edit Regions removes unnecessary regions and loops (e.g., a surface containing a hole that needs to be removed or a self-intersecting loop needs to be removed). To edit regions, click (Edit Regions), select a face to repair, select regions in the face to keep, and click **Done**. The regions you selected are retained and the regions and unnecessary loops are removed.

Extract Loop and Boundary Trim

During IGES or STEP surface data translation, faces can be trimmed unexpectedly. Use **Extract Loop** to untrim surfaces and then use **Boundary Trim** to trim the surfaces using the required boundary.

To extract loop, click (Extract Loop), select one or more loops from one surface, select **Delete Wires** to delete the original loop on the surface, and click **Apply**. Click **Done** if no additional extractions are required. An example of a loop that was extracted is shown in Figure D–6.

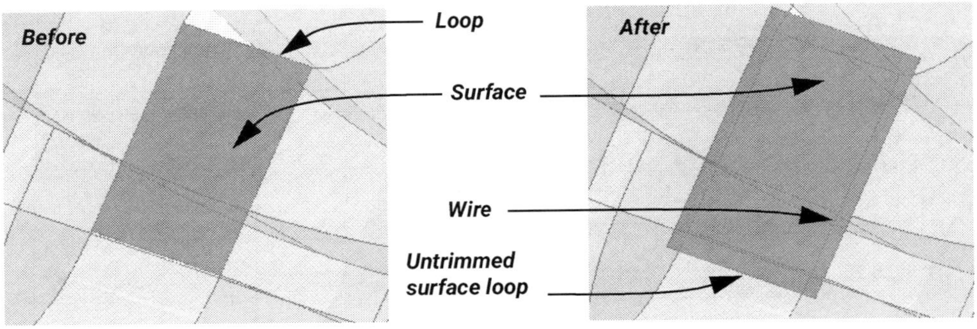

Figure D–6

To trim a boundary, click (Boundary Trim) and select edges that form a closed loop. Once the loop is closed, select the side of the face to keep or the loop to replace. An example is shown in Figure D–7.

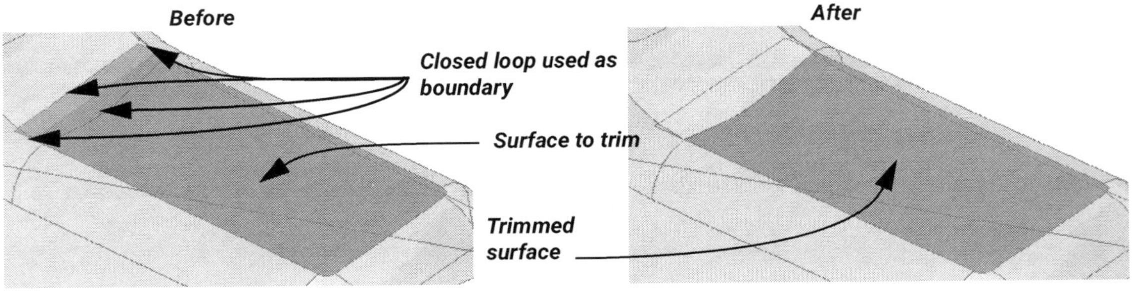

Figure D–7

Boundary Patch

Boundary Patch enables you to create a surface from closed boundary edges. To create a Boundary Patch, click (Boundary Patch), and select a closed 2D or 3D sketch, or select edges from existing objects to form a closed profile. Click **OK** to create the surface. A planar patch surface created from a closed 2D sketch is shown in Figure D–8.

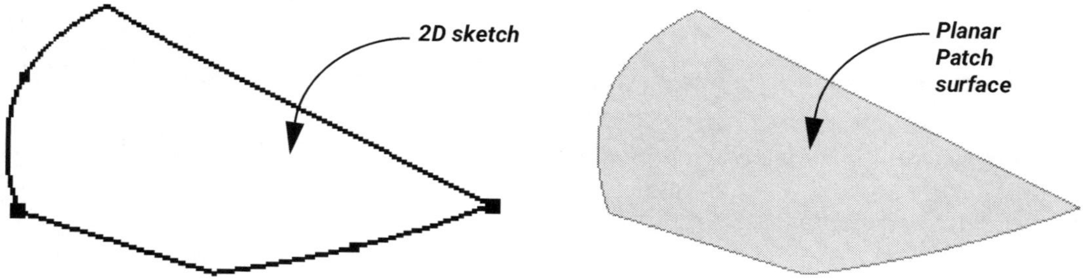

Figure D–8

> ***Note:*** *Boundary Patches can be created both in the repair and part environments.*

Reverse Normal

The **Reverse Normal** option enables you to toggle the direction of the surface normal for a face or a lump. Once you select a reference, the surface is highlighted in green and shows the default normal direction with an arrow. This is only available while in the Repair environment.

Step 5 - Stitch surfaces together, as required.

Stitch any additional surfaces you created together, as required. If the stitched surfaces form an enclosed boundary, it will be indicated in the Model browser as a Solid surface.

Step 6 - Perform an error check.

Perform an additional error check to verify the validity of the surfaces. If issues still remain, use any of the repair options to resolve the issues.

Step 7 - Complete the repair.

Once you have finished working in the Repair environment, you can right-click in the graphics window and select **Finish Repair** or in the Exit panel, click ✔ (Finish Repair).

Step 8 - Repair remaining problem areas, as required.

Once you have left the Repair environment you are placed in the Modeling environment. You can continue to interact with your model using the standard *3D Model* tab options (e.g., Patch, Trim, Extend) to further resolve any problem areas.

Step 9 - Stitch surfaces together, as required.

Stitch the additional surfaces that were created or modified, as required. If the stitched surfaces form a fully enclosed boundary (and assuming that no other solid bodies exist in the part) the quilt generates a solid base feature in the part.

Practice D1
Repairing Imported Data

Practice Objectives

- Set the import options to retrieve data from an .IGS file.
- Review the Translation Report that is generated when an .IGS file is imported.
- Transfer the imported .IGS data into the Repair environment and conduct a quality check for errors in the imported geometry.
- Appropriately set the stitch tolerance value so that gaps in the imported geometry can be automatically stitched.
- Use the Repair environment commands to repair gaps, delete and replace surfaces to successfully create a solid from the imported geometry.

In this practice, you will import an IGES file, analyze it, and repair the surfaces. Once you finish repairing the surfaces to obtain a fully enclosed surface, you will stitch it to obtain the solid model shown in Figure D–9.

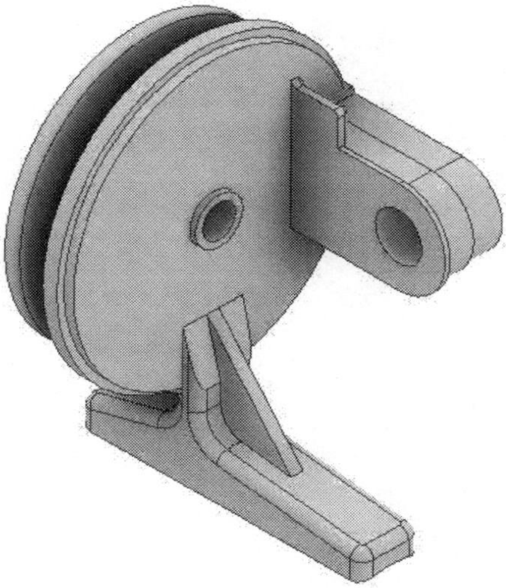

Figure D–9

Task 1: Import the IGES file.

1. Open **import_surf.igs**. The Import dialog box opens.
2. In the *Object Filters* area, select **Solids** and **Surfaces** and leave the other options in this area cleared, as shown in Figure D–10.

3. Maintain the default in the *Inventor Length Units* area to use the units from the source model.
4. In the *Part Options* area, select **Composite**, as shown in Figure D–10.
5. By default, the file will be created in the working directory. By enabling the **Save In Subfolder** option, a subfolder will be created for you. You can change the option in the drop-down list to **User Path** to use the browse button to change directories, if required. You can also add a prefix or suffix to the file name, as shown in Figure D–10. For this file, leave the *Name* field empty and the *Output Location* as default (Source Path saved in a subfolder).

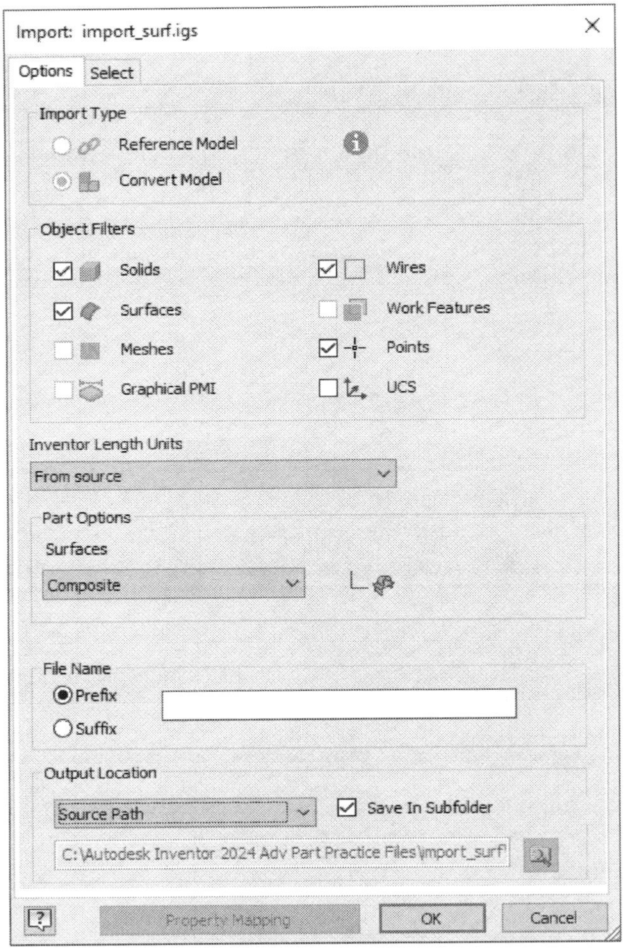

Figure D–10

6. Click **OK** to import the IGES file. The Model browser and model appear as shown in Figure D–11.

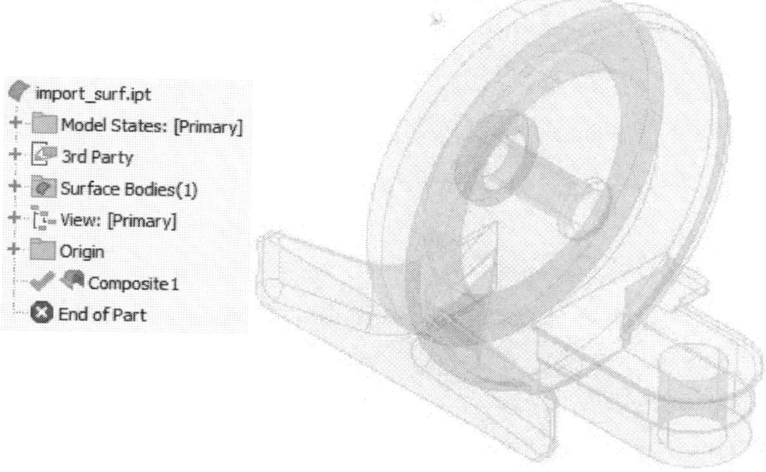

Figure D–11

7. Save the file and review Windows Explorer to see that a new folder called **import_surf** has been created in the practice files folder and that the file is stored in this folder.

Task 2: Examine the translation report.

Examine the translation report that is generated to review information such as the translation type, translation options used, component names, system from which the file was created, and success status.

1. In the Model browser, expand the **3rd Party** node and double-click on **import_surf.htm** to open and review the translation information.
2. Close the Autodesk Inventor Translation Report window.

Task 3: Examine the Model browser.

Examine the Model browser to determine what has been imported. This helps determine what is required with the model.

1. The import file contains a single composite surface. No solids have been imported (otherwise a feature named **Base1** would display in the Model browser).

Task 4: Perform a quality check to find errors in the imported geometry.

1. In the Model browser, right-click on **Composite1** and select **Repair Bodies**. The *Repair* tab displays.

2. In the Repair panel, click (Find Errors). The Find Errors dialog box opens. Click **Select All** to select all the Bodies in the imported geometry. Click **OK** to run the check. The bodies are analyzed and no problems are reported. If problems were reported they would be identified with symbols in the Model browser.

Task 5: Perform a preliminary stitch.

Perform a preliminary stitch to close up any insignificant gaps that might have resulted from the import and to help locate the significant gaps and over-extended surfaces. Use a small tolerance to avoid undesirable changes in the geometry.

1. In the Modify panel, click (Stitch). The Stitch dialog box opens.
2. Drag a bounding box around all of the geometry to select it. Ninety four (94) faces are selected.
3. Change the *Fill gaps smaller than* value to **0.05 mm**.

4. Click (Find remaining gaps and free edges). The Stitch dialog box and model display as shown in Figure D–12.
   - Edges that could not be stitched (due to them being further apart than the defined maximum tolerance of 0.05 mm) are highlighted in the model and are listed in the Stitch dialog box.
   - Edges that were less than 0.05 mm apart have been stitched together.
   - There are 5 remaining free edges. To determine which edge in the model corresponds to which edge listed in the dialog box, select a row in the list. The corresponding edge highlights in blue on the model. Some of the edges are small and so you need to zoom in to see them.

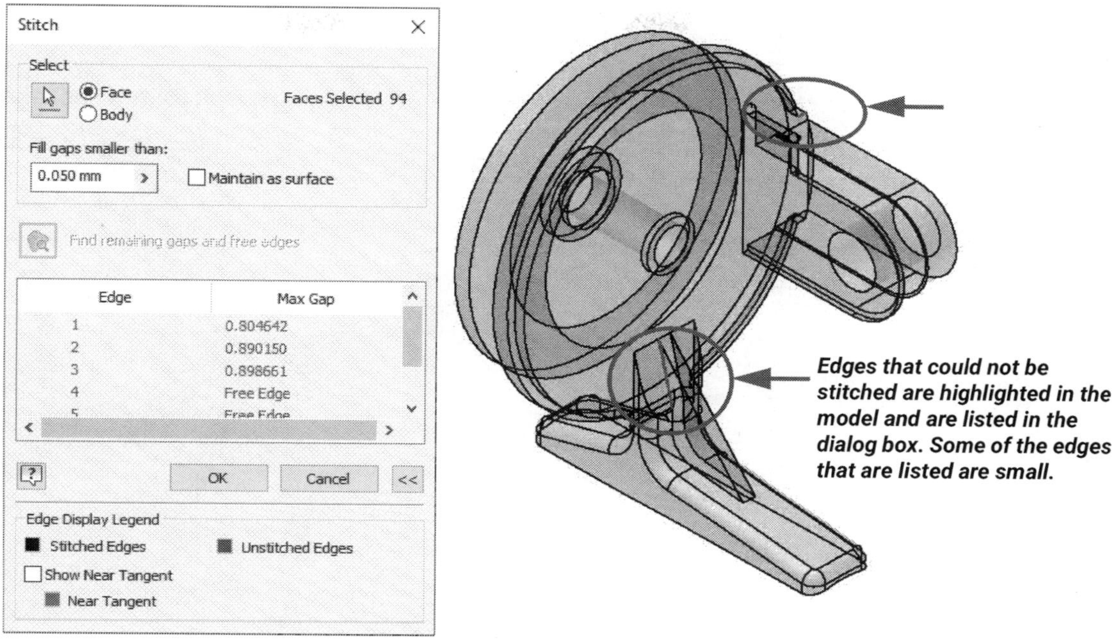

Figure D–12

5. While keeping the Stitch dialog box open, rotate and zoom in on the model to get a better look at the highlighted edges that need to be resolved before the model can become solid. Some surface edges extend further than required and some adjacent surfaces contain a gap between them. There are two areas on the model (which contain the problem edges) that need to be repaired.

6. Click **OK** to close the Stitch dialog box. Note in the Model browser, the imported surface body has been changed to a single quilt, as shown in Figure D–13, because the surfaces were stitched together. However, the gaps between surfaces still remain.

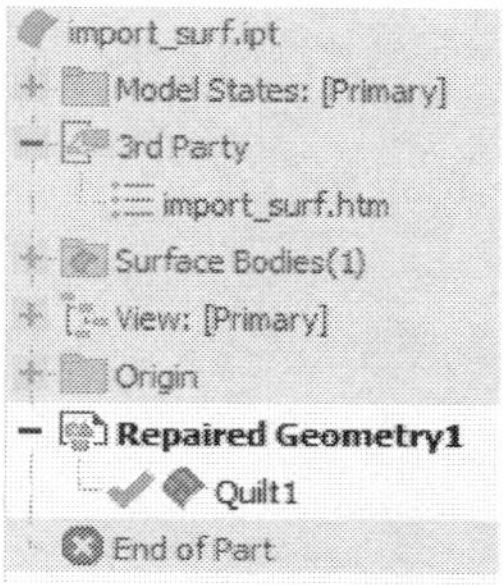

Figure D–13

Task 6: Use Extract Loop and then Boundary Trim.

In this task, you use **Extract Loop** to extend the edges and then **Boundary Trim** to trim back the surface to the required boundary.

1. Reorient the model and zoom as shown in Figure D–14.

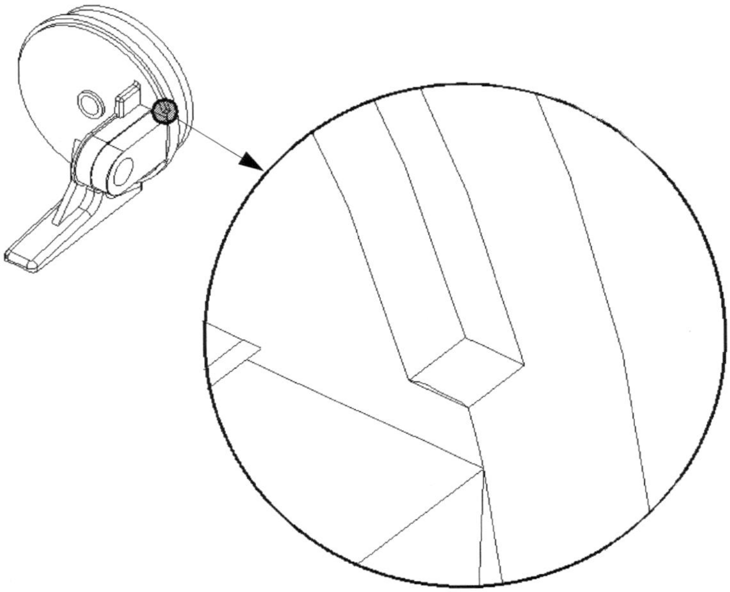

Figure D–14

2. Position the cursor over the surface shown in Figure D–15 in Shaded display mode to get a better idea of what needs to be repaired. Note that a gap exists.

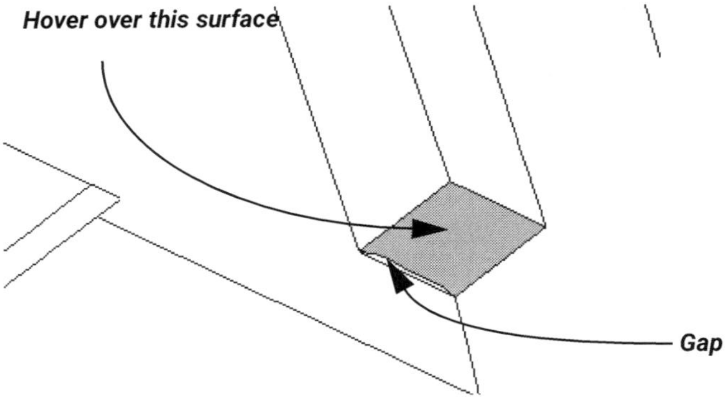

Figure D–15

3. In the Modify panel, click  (Extract Loop) to extend the surface.

4. Select the loop by selecting the surface shown in Figure D–16.

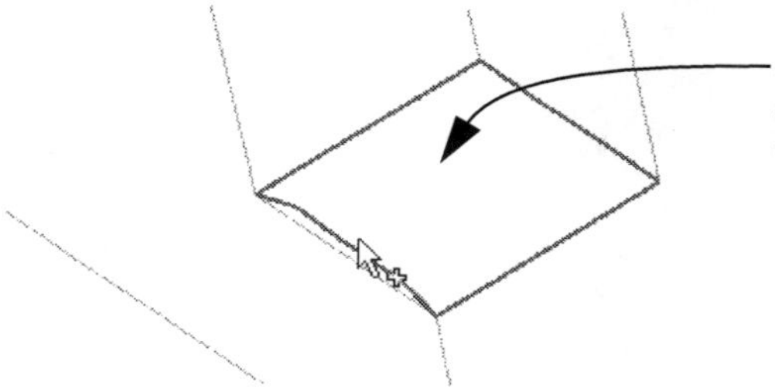

Figure D–16

5. Select **Delete Wires** to delete the original loop of the surface.
6. Click **Apply** and then click **Done**. The surface edges are extended, as shown in Figure D–17.

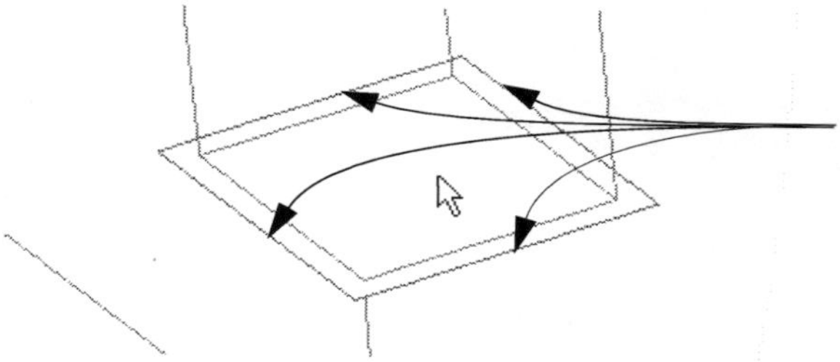

Figure D–17

7. In the Modify panel, click (Boundary Trim).
8. Select the edges shown in Figure D–18 as the cutting edges.

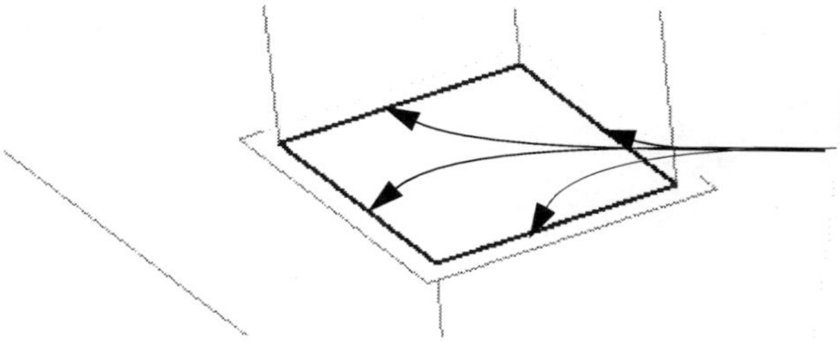

Figure D–18

Note: *If an incorrect surface is selected, hold <Ctrl> and select the surface to clear it.*

9. Click (Face or Loop) and select the loop to keep, as shown in Figure D–19. Verify that the required loop is selected and is displayed in green, otherwise the incorrect portion of the surface is trimmed.

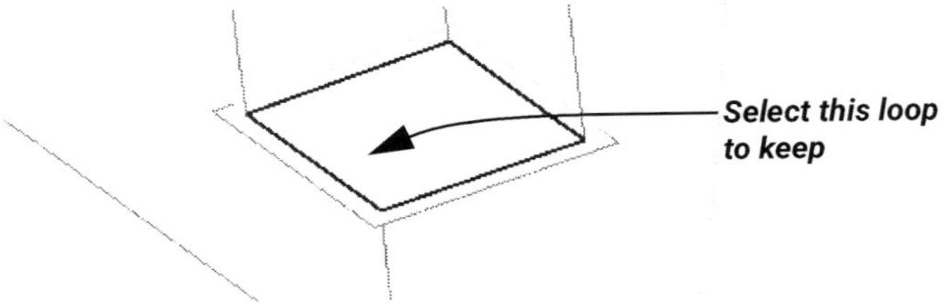

Figure D–19

10. Click **Apply** and then click **Done**. The surface is trimmed, as shown in Figure D–20.

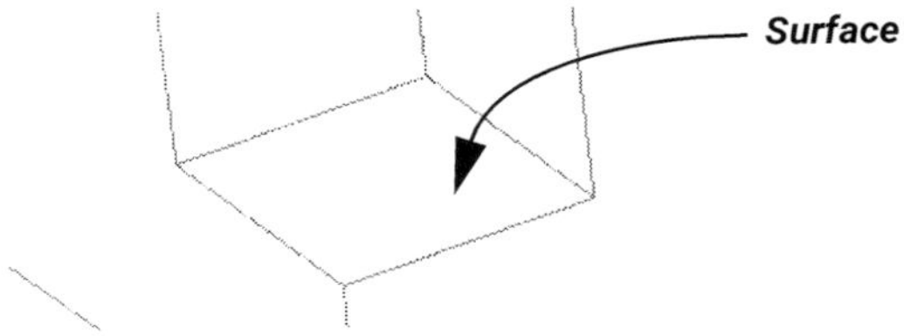

Figure D–20

Task 7: Use Extract Loop and Boundary Trim a second time.

1. Reorient the model and zoom, as shown in Figure D–21.

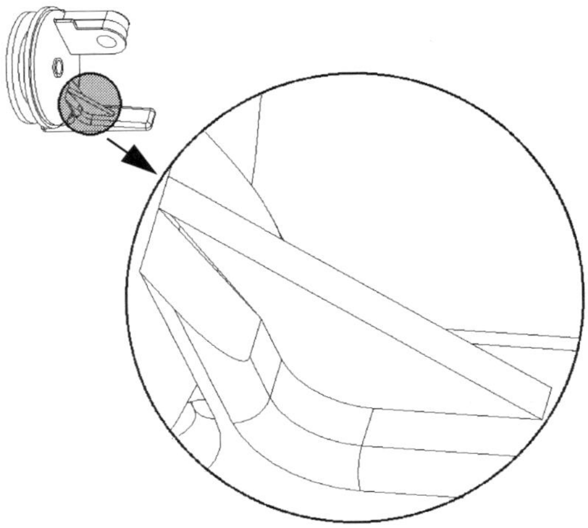

Figure D–21

2. Position the cursor over the surfaces shown in Figure D–22 to help visualize what needs to be repaired. Note the gap that exists between the surfaces.

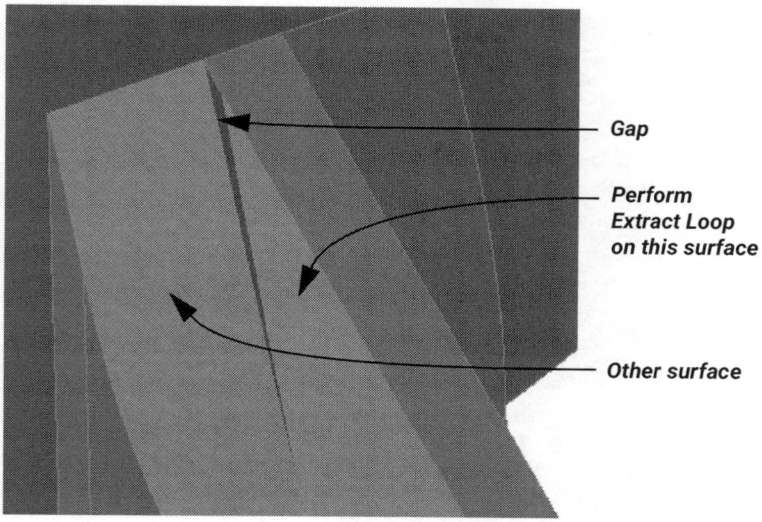

Figure D–22

3. With **Delete Wires** selected, use **Extract Loop** to obtain the surface shown in Figure D–23.

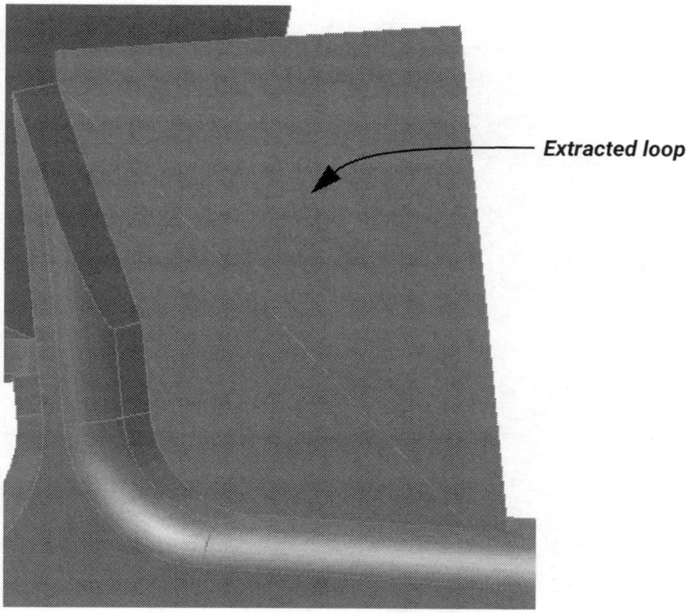

Figure D–23

4. Perform a Boundary Trim and select the edges shown in Figure D–24 as the cutting edges.

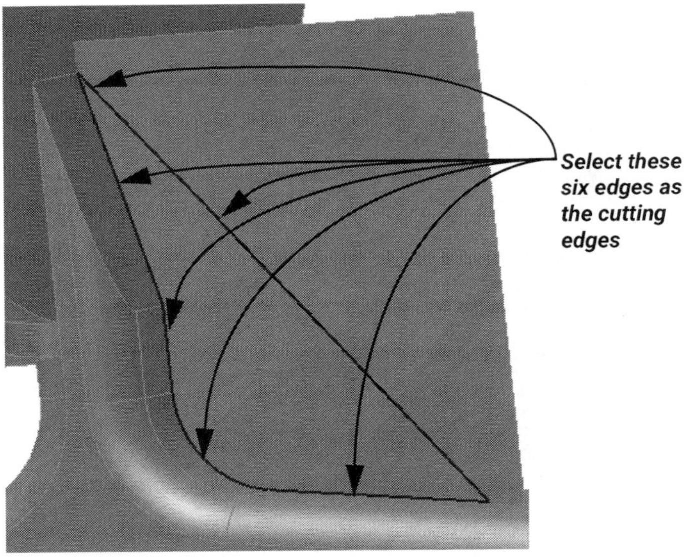

Figure D–24

5. Select the Face or Loop reference, within the area to be kept, so that the model is trimmed as shown in Figure D–25. Note that the gap no longer exists.

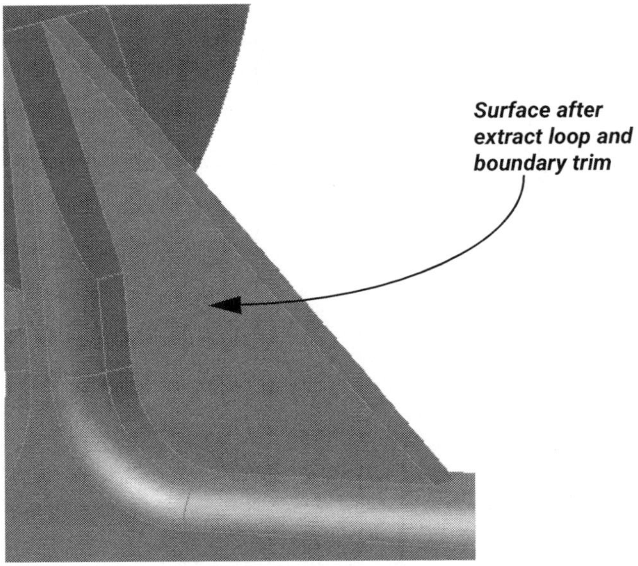

Figure D–25

Task 8: Stitch the surfaces.

1. In the Modify panel, click (Stitch).
2. In the *Select* area, select **Body**. Select the model. Now that the model is a Quilt, the **Face** option cannot be used to select the geometry.
3. Verify that the *Fill gaps smaller than:* value is set to **0.05 mm**.
4. Click (Find remaining gaps and free edges). No open edges remain in the model and it is automatically converted into a solid.
5. Click **OK**.

Task 9: Delete a surface from the stitched quilt.

The design intent of the model requires that the base be longer. In this task, you delete one of the faces that has been combined to create the current solid.

1. Reorient the model so that you can see the bottom surface of the model. Right-click on the bottom face and select **Delete**, as shown in Figure D–26.

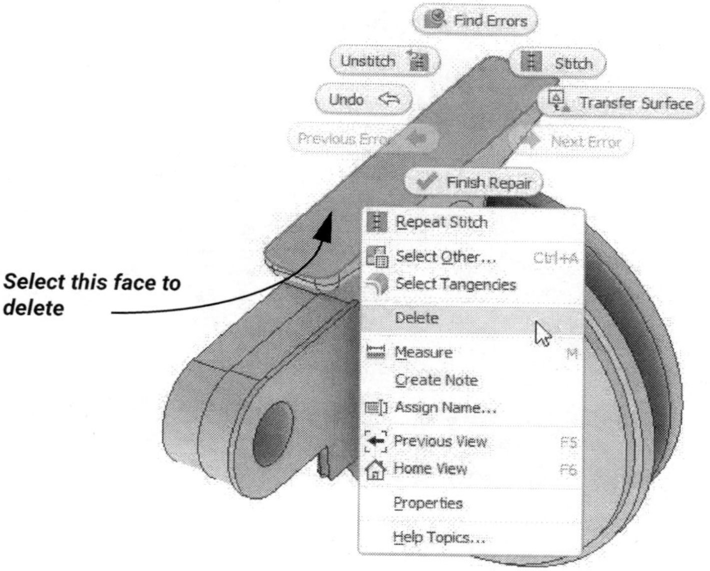

Figure D–26

Task 10: Create a new surface.

In this task, you will extend an existing surface and create a new surface to replace the one that was deleted.

1. Reorient the model so that you can see the bottom surface of the model.
2. In the Modify panel, click (Extend Faces).
3. Select the closed loop edge that represents the base of the model, as shown in Figure D–27.

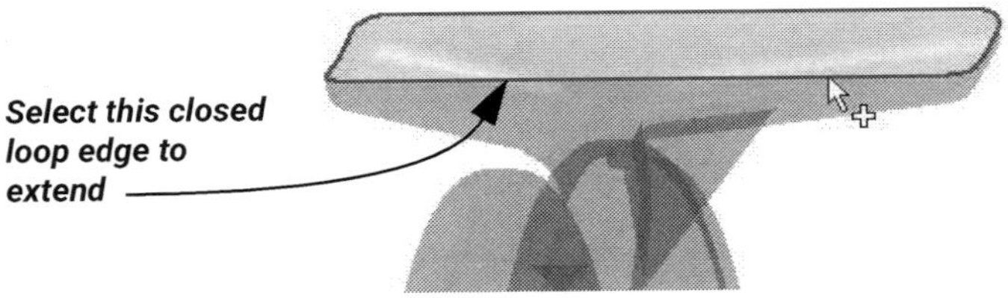

Figure D–27

4. Set the extend distance to **2 mm**. Click **Apply** and then click **Done**.
5. In the Modify panel, click (Boundary Patch).
6. Select the extended edge as the reference for the Boundary Patch, as shown in Figure D–28.

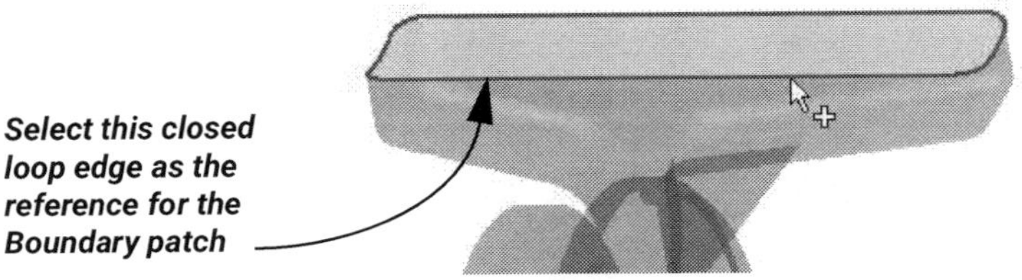

Figure D–28

7. Click **Apply** to create the new surface. Click **Done** to close the dialog box.

Task 11: Add the new surface to the stitched quilt.

In this task, you will add the newly created surface to the model.

1. In the Model browser, in the **Repaired Geometry** node, right-click on **Quilt3** and select **Add Surface**. The Stitch: Add dialog box opens. As an alternative, you can also right-click on the newly created bottom surface of the model and select **Add Surface**.
2. In the *Select* area, select **Body** and select the existing quilted surface body.
3. Change the *Fill gaps smaller than:* value to **0.05 mm**.

4. Click (Find remaining gaps and free edges). No open edges should be reported.
5. Click **OK**.

   Note: *As as alternative to modifying the bottom face in the Repair Environment, you could have also used the Direct Edit method in the 3D Model environment.*

6. In the Exit panel, click (Finish Repair) to exit the Repair environment. You are now placed in the standard part environment and can perform any regular operation on the solid model.

   The model becomes a solid with the addition of the cap surface, as shown in Figure D–29. The **Surface Bodies** node has now been changed to a **Solid Bodies** node, identifying that the model is now a solid.

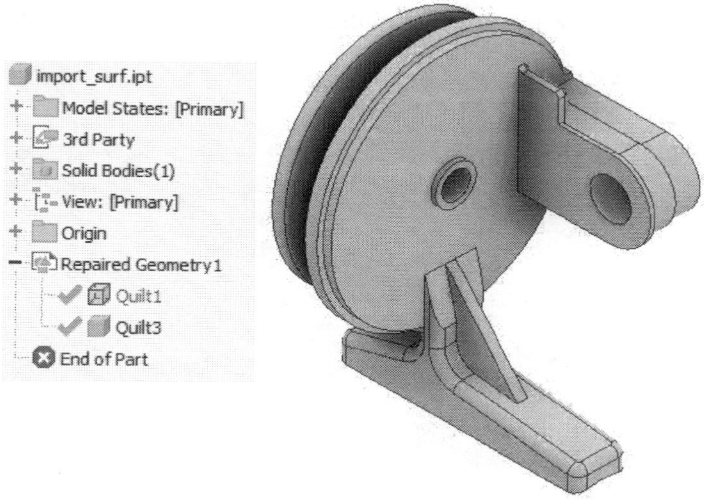

Figure D–29

7. Save and close the model.

End of practice

Practice D2
Manipulating Imported Surfaces

Practice Objectives

- Set the options to import data from a CATIA file.
- Appropriately set the stitch tolerance value so that gaps in the imported geometry can be automatically stitched to create a solid.
- Manipulate the resulting solid model using the surface Patch and Sculpt commands to add and remove solid geometry.

In this practice, you will work with a file that has been imported from CATIA V5. You will import the geometry and then modify and remove features. The final part is shown in Figure D–30.

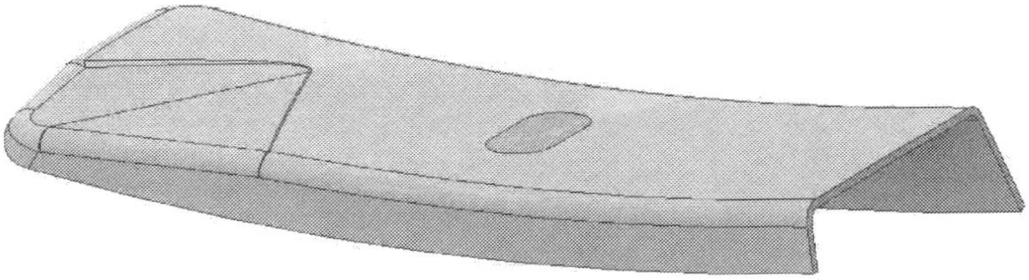

Figure D–30

Task 1: Open a CATIA file.

1. In the Quick Access Toolbar, click . Ensure that the Files of type drop-down list is set to display all files or CATIA V5 files. Select **Trim_Panel.CATPart**. Click **Open**. The Import dialog box opens.
2. In the *Import Type* area, select **Convert Model** to convert the model without keeping any associative links to the CATIA file.
3. In the *Object Filters* area, select **Solids** and **Surfaces**. Leave the other options in this area cleared.
4. Maintain the default in the *Inventor Length Units* area to use the units from the source model.
5. In the *Part Options* area, select **Composite**.
6. Maintain the defaults in the *File Name* area.
7. In the *Select* tab, click **Load Model**. The model preview displays, as shown in Figure D–31. Individual surfaces cannot be added or removed for this model. Surface manipulation for this CATIA part can be done in the Repair Environment.

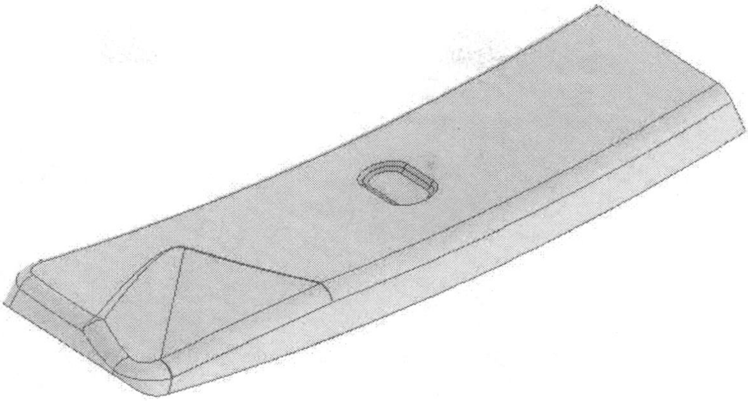

Figure D–31

8. Click **OK** to close the dialog box and import the geometry.

Task 2: Stitch the Trim_Panel.CATPart file.

In this task, you switch to the Repair environment and stitch together the imported surfaces.

1. In the Model browser, right-click on **Composite1** and select **Repair Bodies**. The *Repair* tab displays.
2. In the Modify panel, click (Stitch). The Stitch dialog box opens.
3. Drag a bounding box around all of the geometry to select all 29 faces.
4. In the *Fill gaps smaller than:* field, leave the default value.
5. Click (Find remaining gaps and free edges). No open edges are reported. Only free edges are located around the exterior of the model.
6. Click **OK** to close the Stitch dialog box.
7. In the Exit panel, click (Finish Repair) to exit the Repair environment. You are now placed in the standard part environment and can perform any regular operation on the model.

Task 3: Use the Thicken/Offset command to create a solid.

1. In the Modify panel, click (Thicken/Offset). The Properties panel displays.
2. Select to enable Quilt selection to easily select the stitched surface.
3. Select the stitched surface and enter a *Distance* of **4 mm**. Ensure that the geometry is added to the inside of the geometry.

4. Click **OK**. The model displays as shown in Figure D–32.

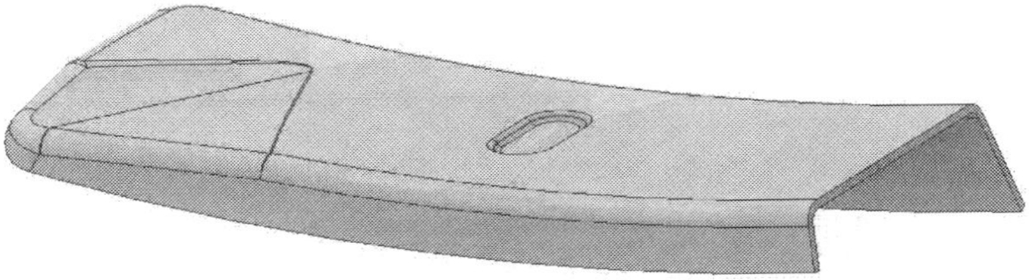

Figure D–32

Task 4: Modify surfaces to incorporate design intent.

In this task, you will create four boundary patch surfaces that will be used to modify the model.

1. Right-click on the **Repaired Geometry1** node in the Model browser and select **Repair Bodies**. Alternatively, double-click on the node.
2. Select the nine surfaces that make up the indented area shown in Figure D–33. Right-click and select **Delete** to remove them from the surface. Alternatively, press the Delete key.

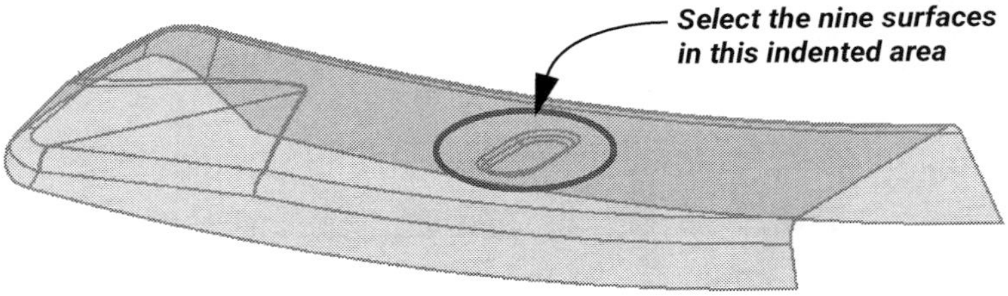

Figure D–33

3. In the Modify panel, click (Boundary Patch).
4. Select the loop of edges that remain once the surfaces have been deleted as the reference for the Boundary Patch.
5. Click **Apply** to create the new surface. Click **Done** to close the dialog box.
6. In the Model browser, in the repair node, right-click on **Quilt2** and select **Add Surface**. The Stitch: Add dialog box opens.
7. In the *Select* area, select **Body** and select the existing quilted surface body.
8. Change the *Fill gaps smaller than:* value to **0.05 mm**.
9. Click (Find remaining gaps and free edges). Eleven open edges should be reported. These are the outside edges of the surface.
10. Click **OK**.

11. In the Exit panel, click ✔ (Finish Repair) to exit the Repair environment.
12. The Thicken feature might fail due to the changes in the surface. If so, click **Accept**.

    Note: *Consider using the* ***Adjust*** *tool to manipulate the color of the new boundary patch so that it matches the rest of the model.*

13. Double-click on the **Thicken1** feature in the Model browser to edit it and select the reference surface again. The reference was lost when the modification was made. Click **OK**. The model displays as shown in Figure D–34.

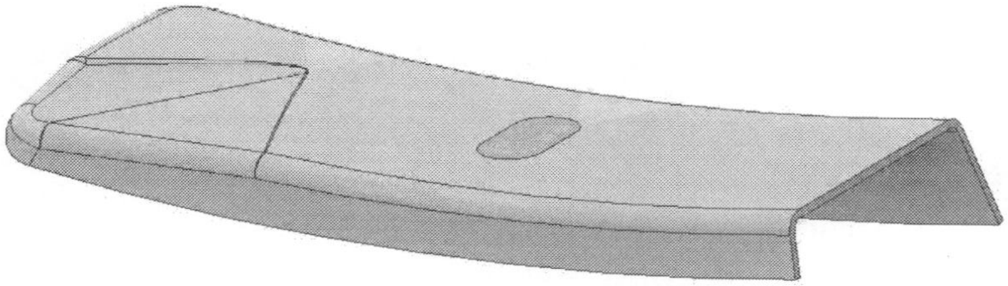

Figure D–34

14. Save the model.
15. (Optional) Consider clearing the appearance overrides as was discussed in Chapter 1.

End of practice

Chapter Review Questions

1. How can you bring imported data into the Repair environment, if it is not already imported into this environment?
   a. Right-click on the imported data and select Repair Bodies.
   b. Right-click on the imported data and select Copy to Repair.
   c. This cannot be done. It must be done during import.

2. In the Repair environment, which option can you use to close small gaps between surfaces?
   a. Extend Faces
   b. Intersect Faces
   c. Stitch
   d. Unstitch
   e. Boundary Trim

3. Which two commands function in the same way except that when one of the commands is executed, you specify a destination body?
   a. Stitch
   b. Transfer Surface
   c. Unstitch
   d. Boundary Patch
   e. Boundary Trim
   f. Extend Faces

4. In the Repair environment, which option can you use to create a new surface referencing a closed set of adjacent edges?
   a. Extend Faces
   b. Intersect Faces
   c. Boundary Trim
   d. Boundary Patch
   e. Extract Loop

5. Match the error types in the left column to its symbol that identifies their type in the right column.

Error Types	Icon	Answer
a. Geometry that contains errors		
b. Geometry needing further investigation		
c. Healthy geometry		

Command Summary

Button	Command	Location
N/A	**Add Surface**	• **Context menu:** In graphics window • **Context menu:** In Model browser with surface selected
	**Boundary Patch**	• **Ribbon:** *Repair* tab>Modify panel
	**Boundary Trim**	• **Ribbon:** *Repair* tab>Modify panel
	**Edit Regions**	• **Ribbon:** *Repair* tab>Modify panel
	**Extend Faces**	• **Ribbon:** *Repair* tab>Modify panel
	**Extract Loop**	• **Ribbon:** *Repair* tab>Modify panel
	**Find Errors**	• **Ribbon:** *Repair* tab>Repair panel • **Context menu:** In graphics window
	**Finish Repair**	• **Ribbon:** *Repair* tab>Exit panel • **Context menu:** In graphics window
	**Heal Errors**	• **Ribbon:** *Repair* tab>Repair panel
	**Intersect Faces**	• **Ribbon:** *Repair* tab>Modify panel
	**Next Error**	• **Ribbon:** *Repair* tab>Repair panel • **Context menu:** In graphics window
	**Previous Error**	• **Ribbon:** *Repair* tab>Repair panel • **Context menu:** In graphics window
	**Repair Bodies**	• **Ribbon:** *3D Model* tab>Surface panel • **Context menu:** In Model browser with repair node selected
	**Reverse Normal**	• **Ribbon:** *Repair* tab>Modify panel
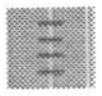	**Stitch**	• **Ribbon:** *Repair* tab>Modify panel • **Context menu:** In graphics window
	**Transfer Surface**	• **Ribbon:** *Repair* tab>Modify panel • **Context menu:** In graphics window
	**Unstitch**	• **Ribbon:** *Repair* tab>Modify panel • **Context menu:** In graphics window

Index

#

2D Sketch
- Spline **2-2**

3D Mesh **6-2**

3D Sketch
- 3D Transform **2-18**
- Arc **2-12**
- Bend **2-13**
- Constraining **2-18**
- Create **2-8**
- Curve on Face **2-16**
- Dimensioning **2-18**
- Edit **2-4, 2-9, 2-17**
- Equation Curve **2-13**
- Helical Curve **2-10**
- Include Geometry **2-16**
- Intersection Curve **2-14**
- Line **2-9**
- Mirror **2-17**
- Point **2-13**
- Points **2-17**
- Project Curve to Surface **2-14**
- Silhouette Curve **2-15**
- Spline **2-2, 2-12**

A

Analysis
- Cross Section **15-5**
- Curvature **15-3**
- Draft **15-2**
- Procedure (all types) **15-7**
- Surface **15-4**
- Zebra **15-2**

AnyCAD **13-2**

Appearance
- Adding to Document **1-14**
- Assign **1-17**
- Assign Appearances **1-2, 1-7, 1-10**
- Assigning **1-10, 1-17**
- Browser **1-12**
- Creating **1-14**
- Ground Plane **1-4**
- Lighting Styles **1-7**
- Orthographic View **1-6**
- Perspective View **1-6**
- Ray Tracing **1-3**
- Reflections **1-6**
- Shadows **1-5**
- Visual Style **1-2**

AutoCAD
- AutoCAD Blocks **B-10**
- Blocks in Inventor **B-9**
- DWG files in Inventor **14-1**

Autodesk ReCap **13-22**

B

Bend Part **2-20**

Bridge **12-22**

C

Clear Symmetry **12-28**

Coil **5-8**

Colors **1-10**

Constraints **1-2**

Copy Feature **10-10**

Copy Surface **8-7**

Crease Edges **12-18**

Cross Section Analysis **15-5**

Curvature Analysis **15-3**

D

Decal **A-5**

Delete
- Delete Face **8-6**
- Face **12-29, 13-20**
- Freeform **12-29**

Direct Edit **13-12**
- Delete **13-20**
- Move **13-12**
- Rotate **13-18**
- Scale **13-16**
- Size **13-15**

Draft Analysis **15-2**

Drawing
- Borders **C-2**
- Symbol
  - Create **B-2**
  - Place **B-6**
- Title Block **C-2**

DWG Files **14-1**

E

Edit Base Solid **13-8**
Edit Form **12-10**
Edit Freeform **12-9**
Emboss **A-2**
Equation Curve **2-13**
Export **13-6**
Extend Surface **8-3**
Extract iFeature **10-2**

F

Flatten **12-25**
Freeform
- Convert Geometry **12-7**
- Create Shapes **12-3, 12-6**
- Edit **12-10**
  - Bridge **12-22**
  - Clear Symmetry **12-28**
  - Crease Edges **12-18**
  - Delete **12-29**
  - Edit Form **12-10**
  - Edit Freeform **12-9**
  - Flatten **12-25**
  - Insert Edge **12-15**
  - Insert Point **12-24**
  - Match Edge **12-19**
  - Merge Edges **12-16**
  - Mirror **12-28**
  - Subdivide **12-21**
  - Symmetry **12-27**
  - Thicken **12-26**
  - Uncrease Edges **12-18**
  - Unweld Edges **12-18**
  - Weld Vertices **12-24**
- Introduction **12-2**

G

Generative Shape Design **6-1**
- Constraints **6-5**
- Loads **6-6**
- Material Assignment **6-4**
- Preserving Regions **6-8**
- Promote 3D Mesh **6-12**
- Run **6-11**
- Settings **6-7**
- Symmetry **6-10**
- Workflow **6-2**

Ground Plane **1-4**
Grounded work point **4-2**

H

Helical Curve
- Constant Helical Curve **2-10**
- Variable Helical Curve **2-10**

I

iFeature
- Create **10-2**
- Create from iPart **11-17**
- Edit iFeature Image **10-16**
- Edit Inserted **10-15**
- Edit Stored File **10-15**
- Insert **10-6**
- Keys **10-13**
- Placement Help **10-16**
- Table-driven **10-11**

Import Data
- AutoCAD Data **14-2, 14-9**
- Direct Edit
  - Delete **13-20**
  - Move **13-12**
  - Rotate **13-18**
  - Scale **13-16**
  - Size **13-15**
- Editing Base Solid
  - Delete Face **13-11**
  - Extend or Contract **13-10**
  - Offset **13-10**
- Import **13-2**
- Surfaces **D-2**

Insert Edge **12-15**
Insert iFeature **10-6**
Insert Point **12-24**
Intersection Curve **2-14**
iPart
- Adding Features **11-16**
- Create **11-2**
- Drawing Creation **11-18**
- Edit **11-16**
- Edit Factory Scope **11-16**
- Edit Member Scope **11-16**
- Generate Members **11-11**
- Keys **11-5**
- Placement **11-12**

J

Join **3-12**

K

Keys **11-5**

L

Level of Detail Representations
- Drawing Views **9-8**

Lighting Styles **1-7**
Loft
- Area Loft **5-2**

M

Match Edge **12-19**
Materials **1-10**
Merge Edges **12-16**
Mirror 3D Entities **2-17**
Mirror Freeform **12-28**
Model States **9-2**
  Create **9-2**
  Drawing Usage **9-8**
  Edit via Spreadsheet **9-4**
  Open **9-6**
Multi-Body Part Modeling
  Assigning Features **3-3**
  Combine Bodies **3-7**
  Display **3-8**
  Move Bodies **3-4**
  New Solid **3-3**
  Properties **3-9**
  Split Bodies **3-5**

O

Offset Surface **7-12**
Orthographic View **1-6**

P

Patch **7-5, D-11**
Perspective View **1-6**
Point Cloud Data **13-22**

R

Ray Tracing **1-3**
Reflections **1-6**
Repair Environment **D-4**
Repair Environment Tools
  Add Surface **D-8**
  Boundary Patch **D-11**
  Boundary Trim **D-10**
  Edit Regions **D-9**
  Error Check **D-5**
  Extend Faces **D-8**
  Extract Loop **D-10**
  Intersect Faces **D-9**
  Reverse Normal **D-11**
  Stitch **D-6**
  Transfer Surface **D-7**
  Unstitch **D-8**
Replace Face **8-5**
Ruled Surface **7-6**

S

Save Copy As **13-6**
Scale **13-16**
Sculpt **7-10**
Shadows **1-5**
Silhouette Curve **2-15**
Sketched Symbol
  Create **B-2**
  Place **B-6**
Spline **2-2**
Springs **5-8**
Stitch **7-8, D-6**
Styles
  Assigning to Projects **C-5**
  Copy **C-8**
  Delete **C-8**
  Lighting **1-7**
  New Library **C-8**
  Rename **C-8**
  Style Library Manger **C-5**
Subdivide **12-21**
Surface Analysis **15-4**
Surfaces
  Copy **8-7**
  Copy Object **8-7**
  Delete Face **8-6**
  Extend **8-3**
  Introduction **7-2, 7-3**
  Patch **7-5**
  Repair **D-4**
  Repair Environment Tools
    Add Surface **D-8**
    Boundary Patch **D-11**
    Boundary Trim **D-10**
    Edit Regions **D-9**
    Error Check **D-5**
    Extend Faces **D-8**
    Extract Loop **D-10**
    Intersect Faces **D-9**
    Reverse Normal **D-11**
    Stitch **D-6**
    Transfer Surface **D-7**
    Unstitch **D-8**
  Replace Face **8-5**
  Ruled **7-6**
  Sculpt **7-10**
  Stitch **7-8, D-6**
  Thickening/Offset **7-12**
  Trim **8-2**
Sweeps
  Guide **5-5**
  Path and Guide Surface **5-7**
Symbol
  Create **B-2**
  Place **B-6**
Symmetry **12-5, 12-27**

T
Table
    Factory members (iPart) **11-18**
Textures **1-10, 1-17**
Thicken **7-12**
Thicken Freeform **12-26**
Threads **5-8**
Title Block **C-2**
Trim Surface **8-2**

U
Uncrease Edges **12-18**
Unweld Edges **12-18**
Unwrap **2-23**
User Coordinate Systems **4-4**

V
Visual Style **1-2**

W
Weld Vertices **12-24**
Work Feature
    Grounded Work Points **4-2**
    User Coordinate Systems **4-4**

Z
Zebra Analysis **15-2**

Made in the USA
Monee, IL
08 November 2026

68144970R20372